THE ETERNAL PURPOSE

Living In Christ

WILLEM J. OUWENEEL

AN EVANGELICAL INTRODUCTION TO
REFORMATIONAL THEOLOGY
VOL III/1

PART III: REDEMPTION:
THE CHRIST-CENTERED HEART OF THEOLOGY

AN EVANGELICAL INTRODUCTION TO REFORMATIONAL THEOLOGY

Part I: Scripture: The Revealed Source For Theology
    I/1 *The Eternal Word:* God Speaking To Us
    I/2 *The Eternal Torah:* Living Under God

Part II: God: The Personal Source Behind Theology
    II/1 *The Eternal God:* God Revealing Himself To Us
    II/2 *The Eternal Christ:* God With Us
    II/3 *The Eternal Spirit:* God Living In Us

Part III: Redemption: The Christ-Centered Heart of Theology
    III/1 *The Eternal Purpose:* Living In Christ
    III/2 *Eternal Righteousness:* Living Before God
    III/3 *Eternal Salvation:* Christ Dying For Us
    III/4 *Eternal Life:* Christ Living In Us

Part IV: Consummation: The Lived Shape of Theology
    IV/1 *The Eternal People*: God in Relation To Israel
    IV/2 *The Eternal Covenant*: Living With God
    IV/3 *The Eternal Kingdom*: Living Under Christ

Part V: Method: The Comprehensive Foundation of Theology
    V/1 *Eternal Truth:* The Prolegomena to Theology

THE ETERNAL PURPOSE

Living in Christ

WILLEM J. OUWENEEL

The Eternal Purpose: Living In Christ

This English edition is a publication of Paideia Press (P.O. Box 500, Jordan Station, Ontario, Canada L0R 1S0). Copyright © 2024 by Paideia Press. All rights reserved. Except for brief quotations in critical publications or reviews, no part of this book may be reproduced in any manner without prior written permission from Paideia Press at the address above.

Unless otherwise indicated, Scripture quotations are from the ESV® Bible (The Holy Bible, English Standard Version®). Copyright © 2001 by Crossway, a publishing ministry of Good News Publishers. Used by permission. All rights reserved.

Scripture quotations or references marked as NKJV are taken from the New King James Version®. Copyright © 1982 by Thomas Nelson, Inc. Used by permission. All rights reserved.

Scripture quotations or references marked as NIV are taken from the Holy Bible, New International Version®, NIV®. Copyright © 1973, 1978, 1984, 2011 by Biblica, Inc.™ Used by permission of Zondervan. All rights reserved worldwide. www.zondervan.com. The "NIV" and "New International Version" are trademarks registered in the United States Patent and Trademark Office by Biblica, Inc.™

Book Design by: Michael Wagner

ISBN 978-1-998711-04-8

Cataloguing-in-Publication data:

Printed in the United States of America

*To me, though I am the very least of all the saints, this grace was given, to preach to the Gentiles the unsearchable riches of Christ, and to bring to light for everyone what is the plan of the mystery hidden for ages in God who created all things, so that through the church the manifold wisdom of God might now be made known to the rulers and authorities in the heavenly places. This was according to the **eternal purpose** that he has realized in Christ Jesus our Lord, in whom we have boldness and access with confidence through our faith in him.*
Ephesians 3:8-12

*Blessed be the God and Father of our Lord Jesus Christ, who has blessed us in Christ with every spiritual blessing in the heavenly places, even as he chose us in him **before the foundation of the world**, that we should be holy and blameless before him in love, having **predestined** us for adoption as sons through Jesus Christ, according to the **purpose** of his will, to the praise of his glorious grace, with which he has blessed us in the Beloved.*
Ephesians 1:3-6

*And we know that for those who love God all things work together for good, for those who are called according to his **purpose**. For those whom he **foreknew** he also **predestined** to be conformed to the image of his Son, in order that he might be the firstborn among many brothers.*
Romans 8:28-29

*... God, who saved us and called us with a holy calling, not because of our works but because of his own **purpose** and grace, which he gave us in Christ Jesus **before times eternal**, and which now has been manifested through the appearing of our Savior Christ Jesus, who abolished death and brought life and immortality to light through the gospel.*
2 Timothy 1:8-10 (note)

Table of Contents

Series Preface		i
Author's Preface		v
Abbreviations		ix
Chapter 1	Preliminary Orientation	1
Chapter 2	The Counsel of God	47
Chapter 3	The Approach of Decretalism	89
Chapter 4	The Approach of Open Theism	135
Chapter 5	The Approach of Viatorism	179
Chapter 6	God's Sovereignty, (Im)mutability, (Im)passibility, and (In)temporality	219
Chapter 7	God's Omniscience and Omnipotence	259
Chapter 8	The Meaning of Prayer	295
Chapter 9	The Problem of Suffering	339
Chapter 10	Introduction to Predestination	379
Chapter 11	Predestination in the New Testament	423
Chapter 12	The Battle Over Predestination	469
Chapter 13	The Universal Offer of Grace	519
Chapter 14	Predestination: Remaining Topics	559
Bibliography		601
Scripture Index		623
Subject Index		641

Table of Contents Expanded

Series Preface	i
Author's Preface	v
Abbreviations	ix
1 Preliminary Orientation	1
1.1 God's Counsel	2
1.1.1 Reformed versus Evangelical	2
1.1.2 "Counsel" and "Purpose"	4
1.2 Features of God's Purpose	6
1.2.1 General Features	6
1.2.2 Revealed Yet Unfathomable	9
1.2.3 God's Purpose Stands Firm	12
1.3 God's Ways	14
1.3.1 The Term "Way"	14
1.3.2 God's Counsel and God's Ways	15
1.3.3 Backgrounds	17
1.4 Examples	20
1.4.1 Old Testament	20
1.4.2 New Testament	21
1.4.3 Evaluation	24
1.5 Basic Questions	25
1.5.1 Creation and the Fall	25
1.5.2 Four Views	27
1.5.3 Redemption	29

	1.6	Battle	30
		1.6.1 Calvinists Against Open Theists	30
		1.6.2 Open Theists Against Calvinists	32
	1.7	Persiflages	..35
		1.7.1 In General	35
		1.7.2 Persiflages of Arminianism	37
		1.7.3 Persiflages of Decretalism	39
	1.8	The Doctrine of Grace	42
2	The Counsel of God		47
	2.1	Is God's Counsel Eternal?	48
		2.1.1 Eternal Decrees	48
		2.1.2 Non-Eternal Decrees	49
		2.1.3 Other Examples	52
	2.2	All Things Decreed by God from Eternity?	54
		2.2.1 Heyns, Bavinck, Schilder	54
		2.2.2 Velema and Venema	56
	2.3	Temporal Decrees	57
		2.3.1 Exodus 33	57
		2.3.2 Ezekiel 20	58
		2.3.3 Ezekiel 33	59
		2.3.4 God's Relenting	60
		2.3.5 Hastening God's Day	61
		2.3.6 Advice	62
	2.4	Is God's Counsel "in Christ"?	63
		2.4.1 Christocentrism	63
		2.4.2 Common Grace	65
		2.4.3 Supra- and Infralapsarianism	66

	2.5	God's Counsel and Sin: The Decretalist View	68
		2.5.1 The First View	68
		2.5.2 Reformed Discord	70
		2.5.3 Compatibilism	72
	2.6	Problems with Decretalism	74
		2.6.1 The Father's Will	74
		2.6.3 Calvin's Trap	76
		2.6.4 More Prudence	77
	2.7	The Open Theist Reply	79
		2.7.1 Is God Omniscient?	79
		2.7.2 Objections	80
	2.8	A Third Option?	82
		2.8.1 Foreknowledge and Predestination	82
		2.8.2 Three Types of God's Will	84
		2.8.3 Comments	86
3	The Approach of Decretalism		89
	3.1	Arguments for Decretalism	90
		3.1.1 Joseph	90
		3.1.2 Permitting Evil	91
		3.1.3 Four Options	93
		3.1.4 Comments	94
	3.2	Key Passages	96
		3.2.1 Psalms	96
		3.2.2 Proverbs	98
		3.2.3 Prophets	99
		3.2.4 New Testament	100
	3.3	All Things Decreed?	102
		3.3.1 Reformed Testimonies	102

	3.3.2 Calvin and Followers	103
	3.2.3 Extreme Consequences	105
3.4	Unwarranted Speculation	107
	3.4.1 Three Counter-Arguments	107
	3.4.2 1 Timothy 2:3–4	108
	3.4.3 Other Passages	110
	3.4.4 Comments	111
	3.4.5 Absurdity	114
3.5	Preliminary Summary	115
	3.5.1 Puppets	115
	3.5.2 Illogical Logic	117
	3.5.3 Deuteronomy 29:29	118
3.6	Other Ways	120
	3.6.1 No Biblical Proof	120
	3.6.2 Five Approaches	122
3.7	Errors on All Three Sides	123
	3.7.1 Decretalism Mistaken	123
	3.7.2 Arminianism Mistaken	124
	3.7.3 Open Theism Mistaken	126
3.8	Concepts and Ideas	127
	3.8.1 Basic Confusion	127
	3.8.2 Superrational Knowledge	129
	3.8.3 Ideas and Metaphors About God	130
	3.8.4 Examples	131
4	**The Approach of Open Theism**	**135**
4.1	Structure and Direction	136
	4.1.1 Is the Will Free?	136
	4.1.2 The Corrupted Will	137

	4.1.3 The Responsible Will	139
4.2	More on Open Theism	140
	4.2.1 A New View	140
	4.2.2 Earlier Representatives	142
	4.2.3 Protest	144
4.3	An Open Future?	146
	4.3.1 "Perhaps"	146
	4.3.2 "If"	147
	4.3.3 Investigation	149
	4.3.4 Further Examples and Comments	151
4.4.	Strange Predictions	153
	4.4.1 Implicitly Conditional Predictions	153
	4.4.2 Explicitly Conditional Predictions	155
	4.4.3 God Leaves the Choice to a Person	157
4.5	God's Responses	158
	4.5.1 Disappointment	158
	4.5.2 Regret	160
	4.5.3 Fury	162
4.6	Comments	164
	4.6.1 No Attack on God's Sovereignty	164
	4.6.2 The Grandmaster	166
	4.6.3 A Certain Ignorance After All?	168
	4.6.4 Middle knowledge	169
4.7	Wider Foreknowledge After All?	171
	4.7.1 Josiah and Cyrus	171
	4.7.2 Gentile Kings	173
	4.7.3 Judas	175
	4.7.4 Peter	177

5	The Approach of Viatorism	179
	5.1 Failed Logic	180
	5.1.1 Two Views Rejected	180
	5.1.2 Decretalism	181
	5.1.3 Open Theism	183
	5.2 The Logical Error	184
	5.2.1 Concept and Idea Again	184
	5.2.2 Similar Errors	185
	5.2.3 Examples	186
	5.3 A Third Way	188
	5.3.1 Two Extreme Viewpoints	188
	5.3.2 Examples of Healing	190
	5.4 Congruism	192
	5.4.1 Warfield	192
	5.4.2 The Initiative	193
	5.4.3 No Real Solution	194
	5.5 A Gap Narrowed	196
	5.5.1 Human Freedom	196
	5.5.2 The Battle Goes On	199
	5.5.3 A Parallel	200
	5.6 Viatorism and Prophecy	202
	5.6.1 Conditional Prophecies	202
	5.6.2 Unconditional Prophecies	204
	5.6.3 Summary	205
	5.7 Contents of God's Plans	207
	5.7.1 Beginnings	207
	5.7.2 Before and Since the World's Foundation	209
	5.7.3 Connections	211

		5.8 General Principles	212
		5.8.1 God's Counsel and Ways	212
		5.8.2 Christ the Center	214
		5.8.3 Comments	215
6	God's Sovereignty, (Im)mutability, (Im)passibility, and (In)temporality		219
	6.1	God's Sovereignty	220
		6.1.1 Introduction	220
		6.1.2 A Bit of History	221
		6.1.3 Concepts and Ideas Again	223
	6.2	Two Kinds of Will	224
		6.2.1 Decretive and Preceptive	224
		6.2.2 A Different Approach	225
		6.2.3 The Only Solution	227
	6.3	Sovereignty Viewed Differently	229
		6.3.1 "Unworthy" of God?	229
		6.3.2 God's Counsel and Ways	231
		6.3.3 Open Theism Again	232
	6.4	The Classical Idea of God	234
		6.4.1 The Hellenistic Idea of God	234
		6.4.2 God's Emotions	235
		6.4.3 The Bible versus Hellenism	237
	6.5	God's (Im)mutability	239
		6.5.1 Scholasticism and Its Opponents	239
		6.5.2 Breakthrough	241
		6.5.3 The Name YHWH	243
	6.6	Impassibility	244
		6.6.1 God's Emotions	244
		6.6.2 Criticism	246

	6.6.3 Anthropopathisms	249
6.7	Temporality	251
	6.7.1 God Beyond Time?	251
	6.7.2 "Entirely Human"	253
	6.7.3 Evaluation	254
	6.7.4 Again: God's Temporality	256
7 God's Omniscience and Omnipotence		259
7.1	God's Omniscience	260
	7.1.1 Is God Omniscient?	260
	7.1.2 Omniscience and Responsibility	263
	7.1.3 False Contradictions	265
7.2	God's Omnipotence	267
	7.2.1 The Almighty	267
	7.2.2 Proper Distinctions	269
	7.2.3 Recent Insights	270
7.3	Protestantism versus Humanism	272
	7.3.1 Erasmus and Luther	272
	7.3.2 Melanchton and Calvin	274
	7.3.3 Later Development	276
7.4	Modern Science	277
	7.4.1 Erasmus and Descartes	277
	7.4.2 Science and Decretalism	280
	7.4.3 Ancient versus Modern Philosophy	281
	7.4.4 The View of Time	282
7.5.	God's Omnipotence in Job	284
	7.5.1 God versus Job's Friends	284
	7.5.2 God's Answer to Job	285
	7.5.3 God's Counter-Questions	287

	7.6	Other Aspects of Job	289
		7.6.1 Behemoth and Leviathan	289
		7.6.2 Chaos in Job?	291
8	The Meaning of Prayer		295
	8.1	The Power of Prayer	296
		8.1.1 Does Praying Help?	296
		8.1.2 Why Then Pray?	297
		8.1.3 Conditions for Answered Prayers	300
		8.1.4 No Resignation But Perseverance	302
	8.2	Can Prayer Change God's Ways?	304
		8.2.1 Are Prayers Effective?	304
		8.2.2 God Persuaded by Prayer	306
		8.2.3 God Answers Prayer	309
	8.3	God's Change After a "Definitive" Statement	311
		8.3.1 Moses	311
		8.3.2 Jonah	314
	8.4	Other Examples	316
		8.4.1 Kings David, Solomon, Rehoboam	316
		8.4.2 King Hezekiah	318
		8.4.3 Not Granting One's Prayer	321
	8.5	God Loves to Act Upon Prayer	322
		8.5.1 "Pray, and You Will Receive"	322
		8.5.2 Other Examples	324
		8.5.3 Ezekiel 22	326
	8.6	Special Circumstances	328
		8.6.1 Worship: Old Testament	328
		8.6.2 Worship: New Testament	330
		8.6.3 "Stop Praying!"	331

	8.6.4 God Refuses to Listen	333
8.7	The Ministry of Healing	335
	8.7.1 The Role of Prayer	335
	8.7.2 The Underlying Conflict	337
9	**The Problem of Suffering**	**339**
9.1	The Decretalist's Answer to Suffering	340
	9.1.1 "It Is God's Will"	340
	9.1.2 Consolation of the Sick	341
	9.1.3 Who Is Responsible?	343
9.2	Omnipotence versus Love	344
	9.2.1 Four Options	344
	9.2.2 God Fights Evil	346
	9.2.3 Fighting *and* Permitting Evil	347
9.3	Divine Arbitrariness?	348
	9.3.1 "Who Can Resist His Will?"	348
	9.3.2 "Prepared for Destruction/Glory"	350
	9.3.3 Priest or Physician?	351
9.4	God or People?	353
	9.4.1 God's Part	353
	9.4.2 The Human Part	355
9.5	Suffering as a Facet of God's Ways	356
	9.5.1 A Means to a Goal?	356
	9.5.2 Testing the Best	358
	9.5.3 Christ in the Psalms	360
	9.5.4 The Three Tests	362
9.6	Again: the Book of Job	363
	9.6.1 The Meaning of Job	363
	9.6.2 Consolation	365

9.6.3 The Sufferer and His God	366
9.7 God and Satan	368
9.7.1 The Will of God	368
9.7.2 The Boy with the Unclean Spirit	369
9.7.3 Again: Resignation	371
9.8 The Role of Satan	373
9.8.1 Satan or God's Spirit?	373
9.8.2 The Superior Master	374
9.8.3 Sickening Spirits	375
10 Introduction to Predestination	379
10.1 Introductory Questions	380
10.1.1 Five Questions	380
10.1.2 Five Options	381
10.1.3 A Heated Debate	382
10.2 The Conflict	384
10.2.1 The Two Sides	384
10.2.2 The Proof Texts	386
10.2.3 The Response of Viatorism	388
10.3 Predestination and God's Counsel	389
10.3.1 Election	389
10.3.2 Responsibility	391
10.3.3 The Prodigal Son	392
10.4 Doxology	393
10.4.1 Doxological Context	393
10.4.2 Doxological Goal	395
10.5 Essential Aspects	396
10.5.1 Two Questions	396
10.5.2 Four More Questions	397

10.6	Three Theses	400
	10.6.1 First Thesis	400
	10.6.2 Second Thesis	401
	10.6.3 Third Thesis	402
10.7	Terminology	404
	10.7.1 Basics	404
	10.7.2 Choosing, Election	406
	10.7.3 Other Terms	409
10.8	Categories	410
	10.8.1 Chosen for the Earth and for Heaven	410
	10.8.2 Christ the Chosen One	412
	10.8.3 Temporary Election and Rejection	413
	10.8.4 Chosen Unbelievers	414
	10.8.5 A Special Category	415
	10.8.6 Eternal Election	416
10.9	The Book of Life	417
	10.9.1 The Old Testament	417
	10.9.2 Judaism	419
	10.9.3 The New Testament	421
11	Predestination in the New Testament	423
11.1	The Synoptic Gospels	424
	11.1.1 The "Elect"	424
	11.1.2 "Few Are Chosen"	425
	11.1.3 Who Are the Chosen?	426
11.2	John's Gospel	428
	11.2.1 Given by the Father	428
	11.2.2 Temporary Election	429

11.2.3 Election and Responsibility	430
11.3 Romans 8	433
11.3.1 Foreknowing and Foreordaining	433
11.3.2 Predestination and Sin	434
11.3.3 Destined for Righteousness and Glory	437
11.4 Other Passages in Romans	438
11.4.1 Twice "Prepared"	438
11.4.2 The Election of Grace	440
11.5 Ephesians 1	442
11.5.1 Elected for Heavenly Blessing	442
11.5.2 Comparison with Adam	443
11.5.3 Predestination Is for God	445
11.5.4 Purpose and Will	446
11.6 Other Aspects	447
11.6.1 "In Christ"	447
11.6.2 Ephesians 2:10	450
11.7 Thessalonians and Timothy	451
11.7.1 Knowing One's Election	451
11.7.2 Other Passages in 1 Thessalonians	454
11.7.3 2 Thessalonians 2:13	455
11.7.4 2 Timothy	457
11.8 The Book of Acts	458
11.8.1 The Divine Side	458
11.8.2 The Human Side	460
11.8.3 Other Passages	461
11.9 Other Letters	463
11.9.1 James	463
11.9.2 1 Peter 1:1-2	463

11.9.3 2 Peter 1:10	464
11.9.4 Summary	466
12 The Battle Over Predestination	**469**
12.1 Augustine	470
12.1.1 The Earlier and the Later Augustine	470
12.1.2 An Eternal Decree of Reprobation?	472
12.2 Creeds	473
12.2.1 The Belgic Confession	473
12.2.2 Righteousness and Mercy	474
12.2.3 An Insoluble Problem	475
12.3 TULIP	476
12.3.1 Total Depravity	476
12.3.2 Unconditional Election	478
12.3.3 Limited Atonement	479
12.3.4 Irresistible Grace	480
12.3.5 Perseverance of the Saints	481
12.3.6 Additional Comments	482
12.4 The Remonstrance	484
12.4.1 Introduction	484
12.4.2 The First Article	486
12.4.3 The Second Article	487
12.4.4 The Third Article	488
12.4.5 The Fourth Article	489
12.4.6 The Fifth Article	490
12.5 The Antithesis	491
12.5.1 The First Three Contrasts	491
12.5.2 The Last Four Contrasts	492
12.6 The Canons of Dordt	493

	12.6.1 Introduction	493
	12.6.2 Head I, Article 6	494
	12.6.3 Head I, Article 7	496
	12.6.4 Head I, Article 9	497
	12.6.5 Head I, Article 15	499
12.7	Antithetical	501
	12.7.1 The Fifth Objection	501
	12.7.2 The Eighth Objection	502
	12.7.3 In Retrospect	503
12.8	Further Developments	505
	12.8.1 Contra-Remonstrants	505
	12.8.2 Moderate Calvinism	506
	12.8.3 Gravamina	509
12.9	Hyper-Calvinism	511
	12.9.1 The Path of Subjectivism	511
	12.9.2 Deviation from the Canons of Dordt	513
	12.9.3 Harshness	514
13	The Universal Offer of Grace	519
13.1	Freedom	520
	13.1.1 In Brief: the Issue Again	520
	13.1.2 Human Choice	521
13.2	Christ Came for All	522
	13.2.1 Salvation Offered to All	522
	13.2.2 All and Many	524
	13.2.3 God's Will: Salvation for All	526
13.3	Evaluation	527
	13.3.1 Sufficient and Efficient	527
	13.3.2 "The World"	528

13.4	No Equal Opportunities	531
	13.4.1 The Reach of the Gospel	531
	13.4.2 Limited Atonement Again	532
13.5	God's Pressing Appeal	533
	13.5.1 God's Will—the Human Will	533
	13.5.2 Examples	535
	13.5.3 The Pleading God	536
13.6	God's Sincerity	538
	13.6.1 No Noncommittal Offer	538
	13.6.2 The Well-Meant Offer	539
13.7	The Command to Repent	541
	13.7.1 Compelled or Coerced?	541
	13.7.2 Examples	542
13.8	The Ability to Repent	544
	13.8.1 "Convert me"	544
	13.8.2 Balanced Emphases	546
	13.8.3 The "Order of Salvation"	547
13.9	Again: Structure and Direction	549
	13.9.1 The Image of God	549
	13.9.2 Greatness and Wretchedness	551
	13.9.3 The Role of the Human Will	553
	13.9.4 Contemporary Arminianism	555
14	**Predestination: Remaining Topics**	**559**
14.1	An Eternal Decree of Reprobation?	560
	14.1.1 Contradictory Statements	560
	14.1.2 Tension in the Canons of Dordt	561
	14.1.3 Eternal Reprobation in the Bible?	562
14.2	Relevant Bible Passages	564

- 14.2.1 The Wicked Made for the Day of Evil — 564
- 14.2.2 Rejected Before or After? — 566
- 14.2.3 Destined "Long Ago" — 568
- 14.3 Romans 9 Again — 570
  - 14.3.1 Mistaken Views — 570
  - 14.3.2 Two Nations — 571
  - 14.3.3 Pharaoh's Hardening — 572
  - 14.3.4 Two Kinds of Vessels — 573
- 14.4 Historical Aspects of the Reprobation Doctrine — 575
  - 14.4.1 Again John Calvin — 575
  - 14.4.2 John Wesley and Karl Barth — 577
- 14.5 Two Types of Decrees — 579
  - 14.5.1 Once More: The Canons of Dordt — 579
  - 14.5.2 Living with the Tension — 581
- 14.6 Infra- and Supralapsarianism — 583
  - 14.6.1 Description — 583
  - 14.6.2 Positions — 585
  - 14.6.3 Differences — 587
- 14.7 Evaluation — 589
  - 14.7.1 Three Theses — 589
  - 14.7.2 Twofold Opposition — 590
  - 14.7.3 "Calminianism" — 592
- 14.8 Election As Threat *and* Comfort — 594
  - 14.8.1 Imaginary Salvation — 594
  - 14.8.2 Election Within Election — 595
  - 14.8.3 The Extremes Meet — 596
  - 14.8.4 Conclusion — 598

Bibliography	601
Scripture Index	623
Subject Index	641

Series Preface

BY MEANS OF THIS PREFACE, the editor and publisher of this series wish to help the reader both understand and process the content of these volumes.

The capacities and erudition of Dr. Willem Ouweneel need no demonstration or defense from us. His voluminous work and prodigious writing stand as a testimony to his love for the Lord Jesus Christ, God's Word, and God's people.

But these volumes present ideas that will surprise some, anger others, and possibly confuse still others. Both the editor and publisher disagree with some of Dr. Ouweneel's assertions and conclusions, but this is not the place for offering our counter-arguments. That requires an altogether different venue. Nevertheless, discerning readers will legitimately wonder why this editor and publisher invested effort and resources in putting these volumes into print.

At least three reasons justify that investment. Each of them is very sensitive.

The first reason is: *self-examination*. Some of our readers may conclude that, in presenting his exegetical, doctrinal, and historical case, Dr. Ouweneel is "coloring outside the lines" of what they have come to believe. He challenges deeply and firmly held convictions and beliefs, like those associated with Israel, with the law of God, with election and reprobation, with infant baptism, with covenant theology, and with justification. At each point, his challenges call us readers to self-examination, regarding our love for Scripture, for the God of Scripture, and for the Truth revealed and incarnated personally in Jesus Christ. One of Ouweneel's challenges is for us believers in Jesus Christ who are Reformed and Presbyterian church members to recognize that there are millions, even billions, of Jesus-believers who disagree with us *and are nevertheless genuine Christians*. And they ought to be acknowledged as such.

The second reason is: *repentance*. Coming, as they do, from one who lives and teaches outside the orbit of many of our readers, Dr. Ouweneel's observations about the state of our (numerous) churches and of our (interminable) doctrinal squabbles ought to embarrass us Reformed and Presbyterian church members. Our incessant polemicizing, our cantankerous stridency, and our offenses against the unity of Christ's church seriously compromise the gospel's witness to the watching world. Brothers and sisters, we must repent of these, for the sake of the gospel, for the sake of the church's witness, and for the sake of our children.

The third reason is: *ecumenicity*. This reason may indeed strike you as strange, but one of the salutary outcomes of reading Dr. Ouweneel's arguments can be this: *not* that you surrender your commitments and convictions that are being challenged, but instead that you come to *respect* and *love* those Jesus-believers who don't share them with you. These Christians are those whose spiritual pilgrimage and gospel-guided history have not brought them to the same place on the road, but who nonetheless are walking the same road as we.

You may well be asking: How, then, is this different from advocating doctrinal relativism? If these distinctive features of Reformed confession and theology are biblical, then why is Dr. Ouweneel being given a microphone for proclaiming his criticisms and rejections of these distinctive emphases of Reformed teaching? The short answer is this: So that from this brother in Christ, this close cousin in the faith, this fellow pilgrim-soldier, we may learn how to lock arms with other Jesus-believers as we face unbelief in our day, even if we can't hold hands. So that we may learn what it means to be Jesus-believers *first*, Reformed or Presbyterian confessors *second*, and only then, *thirdly, theological advocates.*

So we leave you with this challenge: Why do you believe what you believe? What is your biblical warrant? Dr. Ouweneel presents fairly the various positions prevalent within Christianity. The reader will learn why others believe what they believe, and why they don't emphasize certain teachings in the same way that we do.

These books, then, are *not* for the faint of faith. But they *are* for those wanting to grow up and mature into the unity of faith in our Lord Jesus Christ (John 17: 20–23; Eph. 4:13).

Nelson D. Kloosterman, editor
John Hultink, publisher

Author's Preface

THIS BOOK IS A RE-WORKING and expansion of volume 4 of my *Evangelisch-Dogmatische Reeks* (*Evangelical Dogmatic Series*, published in Dutch by Medema, Heerenveen, consisting of twelve volumes in total).[1] My intention with this series was, and is, to offer an Evangelical analysis of various subjects that have traditionally played a great role in Reformational—especially Reformed—thinking: the law, the covenant, justification, predestination, and to a lesser extent, the kingdom.

By "Reformational" I mean all that refers to the sixteenth-century Protestant Reformation. "Reformed" refers to one specific brand of Reformational thinking, namely, Calvinist. Unless specified otherwise, the word "Reformed" also encompasses "Presbyterian," not as referring to a specific type of church government but to Calvinist thought of Scottish and English origins. "Reformed" in the narrower sense refers to Calvinist thought of German and especially Dutch origins.

In these volumes, "Evangelical" means little more than orthodox Protestant (in which "orthodox" refers to Protestants rooted in the Apostolic and Nicene Creeds, as well as in the sixteenth-century Reformation). I use the term Evangelical to indicate that I am neither a Lutheran, nor a Calvinist, and that I feel more at home with pre-scholastic Christianity. This

---

1. Ouweneel (2008b).

Christianity apparently did not yet feel constrained to develop what I call an "inferential theology": an elaborate thought system built upon inferences drawn from inferences drawn from still other inferences (inferentialism, or conclusivism). These matters have been explained in the second volume of this series.

I write this preface in Toledo (Spain, not Ohio!), an ancient capital of tremendous historical significance. To mention just one fact: from AD 400 till 702 no fewer than eighteen councils were held in Toledo, capital of the Visigothic kingdom of the time. Thirteen of these councils were held in the seventh century alone (*Siglo de Concilios*, "Century of Councils"). They were especially important for the development of ecclesiastical law. But what is most striking is how many negative measures were enacted against the Jews at these councils. The more "Christian" the country became, the greater became the hatred against the Jews, God's chosen people. All this hatred culminated in the Spanish Expulsion of the Jews in 1492 — one of the greatest catastrophes in Spanish, and in Western, history. Very few Jewish synagogues in Spain were spared; two of them are still here in Toledo (the other eight or more synagogues in this city were destroyed). Both of them became Catholic churches, but are now museums. The royal and spiritual leaders of Spain of that epoch explicitly called the (Roman Catholic) Church the new "chosen people." And thus, one "chosen people" expelled another "chosen people." How would the God of these two "chosen peoples" have felt at the time?

To make things even more complicated: the Muslims, who ruled in Toledo from AD 712 until 1085, were relatively tolerant toward both Jews and Christians. They viewed all true Muslims as well as all sincere Jews and Christians as "chosen people of God." While visiting ancient churches, synagogues, and mosques here, I muse a lot about the claims of these three religions, and about the concept of chosenness in general, that is, about being God's special people. Sometimes it is not easy to be chosen. I have heard Jews say that they prefer that God would "choose" another nation for a while, to lift the burden from their shoulders. And what about the church, the body of Christ, a company of people living in thousands of denominations? It too is a company of chosen people. What does this mean? How does Christian chosenness relate to that of Israel? Is being chosen the same as being saved? When was Israel chosen, and when were Christian believers chosen? For what purpose was each group chosen?

Are some Christians within the entire chosen Christian community specially chosen? I know that, at times, Calvinists in the Netherlands viewed themselves as such a chosen company ("God, [Reformed] Netherlands, and [the House of] Orange" was the slogan of some of them). The same was true for early Calvinists in France (the Huguenots), the Reformed Boers in South Africa, the staunch Calvinists in Ulster (Northern Ireland), and the early Presbyterians of New England.

This book is about God's eternal purpose, which includes God's eternal decrees, especially his eternal decree of election of true believers in Christ. Was Israel as a nation also elected from eternity? And if you are not chosen, then what are you? Is there such a thing as an eternal decree of reprobation? What does this mean? How does God's eternal purpose relate to human responsibility and human guilt?

As I reflect here in Toledo about all those church meetings held in this city, I think of that one and only Synod of Dordrecht ("Dordt"), far away from Toledo (a drive of 1,100 miles), a Synod that plays a great role throughout the present book. No wonder: a battle was fought at this Synod over the great issues of election and reprobation, a battle that produced, among other things, the Canons of Dordt. What a different city (but I dearly love them both)! I have wandered through both Toledo and Dordrecht. I know the place where the Synod of Dordt was held (unfortunately, these *Kloveniersdoelen* have been demolished), the *Grote Kerk* (Great Church, or Church of Our Lady), where the first and the last sessions of the Synod were held, as well as the *Augustijnenkerk* (Augustinians' Church), where chairman Johannes Bogerman read aloud to the public the brand new Canons of Dordt. Delegates to the Synod gathered in the neighboring *Hofcomplex* (Court Complex), which had earlier been the Augustinians' Convent.

What a different Synod than those synods in Toledo, a Synod of staunch Protestants, even in the middle of a war—against the Spanish! And what consequences this Synod has had, until this very day! Calvinists and Arminians are still fighting over the issues involved, not least in the Anglo-Saxon world. This book tries to find a safe route through this battlefield.

Bible quotations in this book are usually from the English Standard Version.

I thank Dr. Nelson D. Kloosterman again very warmly for his expert editorial work on the manuscript of this book. And I am again deeply thankful to my publisher, John Hultink, for his constant encouragement in this entire project.

Willem J. Ouweneel
Spring, 2016

Abbreviations

Bible Versions

AMP	Amplified Bible
AMPC	Amplified Bible, Classic Edition
ASV	American Standard Version
CEB	Common English Bible
CEV	Contemporary English Version
CJB	Complete Jewish Bible
DARBY	Darby Translation
DLNT	Disciples' Literal New Translation
DRA	Douay-Rheims 1899 American Edition
ERV	Easy-to-Read Version
ESV	English Standard Version
EXB	Expanded Bible
GNT	Good News Translation
GNV	1599 Geneva Bible
GW	God's Word Translation
HCSB	Holman Christian Standard Bible
ICB	International Children's Bible
ISV	International Standard Version
JUB	Jubilee Bible 2000
KJ21	21st Century King James Version

KJV	King James Version
LEB	Lexham English Bible
MEV	Modern English Version
MOUNCE	Mounce Reverse-Interlinear New Testament
MSG	The Message
NABRE	New American Bible (Revised Edition)
NASB	New American Standard Bible
NCV	New Century Version
NET	New English Translation
NIV	New International Version
NLV	New Life Version
NKJV	New King James Version
NOG	Names of God Bible
OJB	Orthodox Jewish Bible
RSV	Revised Standard Version
TLB	Living Bible
TLV	Tree of Life Version
VOICE	The Voice
WE	Worldwide English (New Testament)
WEB	World English Bible
YLT	Young's Literal Translation

Other Sources

BabT	Epstein, I., ed. 1961. *The Babylonian Talmud*. London: Soncino Press.
BT	Kelly, W., ed. 1856–1920. *Bible Treasury: A Monthly Review of Prophetic and Practical Subjects*. Available at https://bibletruthpublishers.com/bible-treasury/lpvl22465.
CNT	Commentaar op het Nieuwe Testament

Abbreviations

COT	Commentaar op het Oude Testament
CR	*Corpus Reformatorum*. 1st series and 2nd series. 87 vols. Brunswick: Schwetschke, 1834–1900.
CW	Darby, J. N. n.d. *The Collected Writings of J. N. Darby*. Kingston-on-Thames: Stow Hill Bible and Tract Depot.
EBC	The Expositor's Bible Commentary
EDR	Evangelische Dogmatische Reeks
EGT	Expositor's Greek Testament
KV	Korte Verklaring der Heilige Schrift
NICNT	*New International Commentary on the New Testament*
NICOT	*New International Commentary on the Old Testament*
NIDNTT	Brown, C., ed. 1992. *The New International Dictionary of New Testament Theology*. 4 vols. Carlisle: Paternoster.
NIGTC	New International Greek Testament Commentary
RCET	Dennison, J. T., Jr., ed. 2008–2014. *Reformed Confessions of the 16th and 17th Centuries in English Translation*. 4 vols. Grand Rapids, MI: Reformation Heritage Books.
RD	Bavinck, H. 2002–2008. *Reformed Dogmatics*. Edited by J. Bolt. Translated by J. Vriend. 4 vols. Grand Rapids, MI: Baker Academic.
ST	Chafer, L. S. 1983. *Systematic Theology*. 15th ed. 8 vols. Dallas, TX: Dallas Seminary Press.
TDNT	Kittel, G. et al., eds. 1964–1976. *Theological Dictionary of the New Testament*. Translated by G. W.

	Bromiley. 10 vols. Grand Rapids, MI: Eerdmans.
TNTC	Tyndale New Testament Commentaries

Chapter 1
Preliminary Orientation

Can you find out the deep things of God?
  Can you find out the limit of the Almighty?
It is higher than heaven – what can you do?
  Deeper than Sheol – what can you know?
Its measure is longer than the earth
  and broader than the sea.
If he passes through and imprisons
  and summons the court, who can turn him back?
                                          Job 11:7–10

Summary: God's purpose, or counsel, plays a great role in both the Old and the New Testaments. It involves God's eternal, sovereign, fixed, and unfathomable decree concerning his creation, and his people in particular. A central thesis of this book is that not all events that ever occur fall within this divine decree, and that we have to distinguish between God's unchangeable **counsel** and God's changeable **ways** through which he realizes his counsel. These ways are changeable because they are integrally related to choices that people make according to their responsibility and freedom of will. I call this view Viatorism. Central to the discussion is the place in God's counsel and ways of the Fall and of redemption. A view similar to Viatorism is Open Theism (a special form of Arminianism), but Viatorism differs essentially from Open Theism with regard to the foreknowledge of God. This chapter ends with an analysis of the battle between Calvinism and Open Theism, and the miserable persiflages (frivolous treatments) that both parties often give of each other.

1.1 God's Counsel
1.1.1 Reformed versus Evangelical

AFTER ALL THESE DECADES, I still remember my Reformed headmaster at primary school saying that all things that have ever happened, or are happening today, or will ever happen, have been decreed by God from eternity. The point was not only that God *knows* all things beforehand, but that, according to my teacher, he has *determined* all things beforehand. Even as a child, this gave me much to think about. How could one ever imagine that all things that occur have been decreed (decided, determined) by God from eternity? What room did this leave for a person's own will and responsibility? If everything that a person in every situation would choose and decide has been foreordained, how could there ever be such a thing as a freedom of choice?

Such a view did not correspond at all with my actual experience of reality. Am I free to choose tea or coffee in the morning, I wondered, or was this decreed by God from eternity? As people, we make decisions and choices every day, about which we have the inner certainty that we are making them in freedom (within the limits of our possibilities, of course). Only certain mentally disturbed people have the feeling that they are marionettes or robots.

These things are all the more pressing when it comes to eternal divine election. If a person chooses to believe in Christ and serve him, then it was God himself who from eternity decreed that this person at this instant would choose to accept the gospel. Thus, in fact, it was not a real choice at all; it was rather God who chose that *person*, and even the moment of his conversion. This is an act of pure grace. But what about the people who did *not* choose to accept Christ? This, too, had been decreed by God from eternity, my Reformed headmaster told us. These people had been "reprobated" by God from eternity. They did not choose to serve God, and in fact *could not* at all choose to do so. God kept his grace from them. Why did God do that? Why was one person elect, and another person was not? The answer to that question the headmaster did not know. In his view, nobody could know the answer; it was a mystery, which in some way had to do with what he called the sovereignty of God.

At that time, still being a lad, I turned to a wise Bible teacher who had a hyper-Calvinist background. By that time you could call him an "Evangelical," although at that time nobody in the Netherlands gave to that word the meaning that is given to it today. I asked him how *he* saw eternal election. He told me it was very simple: God knew all things beforehand. Therefore he also knew from eternity which people would believe in Christ, and which would not. The former group was destined by God for eternal glory, the latter group would ultimately end up in eternal perdition by its own fault.

At that moment this answer gave me some satisfaction. At any rate, it seemed better than the headmaster's reply, which seemed to ruin the human freedom altogether. Still, I was not entirely content. If God predestines a person for eternal blessedness on the basis of God's foreknowledge—that is, because he knew that that person would come to faith in Christ—then what was there for God to *destine*? Did God *actively* choose according to his own sovereign will, or did he *passively* choose on the basis of people's foreseen faith or unbelief?

In both cases, someone's choice seemed to vanish. It appeared to me that, in my headmaster's answer, nothing was left of human freedom. And it seemed to me that, in the Bible teacher's answer, nothing was left of divine choice. Years later, I addressed that same brother again. By that time I had learned that his view was called Arminianism, named after the Leyden professor Jacob Arminius (1560–1609). I asked him how it was possible that someone like him, who had been raised a hyper-Calvinist, could have ever turned from the Reformed to the Arminian standpoint. What had been his arguments for this step? The brother solemnly answered that, at the time, the Lord had made this clear to him.

This reply impressed me, but it also disappointed me. Reformed Christians had received their view from God, hadn't they, and Arminians, too? I would not like to underestimate the guidance of the Holy Spirit, but if both parties appealed to the Spirit, both could not be right. It would be theological *arguments* that ultimately had to decide the matter. Therefore, the present book neither claims nor denies that its view is the work of the Spirit—but it supplies only theological arguments. I will try to do that as extensively and thoroughly as the subject demands and deserves, and as I am able to do.

1.1.2 "Counsel" and "Purpose"

This book is not about election and predestination only; much more broadly, it deals with the purposes or plans of God in a general sense. A somewhat old-fashioned term (by today's standards) is the "counsel" of God, one part of which is God's (supposed) counsel regarding the eternal predestination of all people (see chapters 10–14). In practical parlance, a "counsel" (not to be confused with "council") is professional (legal, psychological, social, religious, etc.) advice; the one giving the counsel is a counselor or an adviser. This is different from the use of the word in our Bibles; therefore in more modern translations the word is often avoided. For instance, the word occurs twenty-three times in the New Testament KJV, but only eight times in the New Testament ESV, and then in the sense of "taking" or "holding counsel," that is, "deliberating."

In older Bible translations and in theology, the word "counsel" often has a very different meaning, which does relate to the process of deliberation, but especially to the outcome of deliberation: "plan, decision, decree." For instance, Job 5:13 (KJV) speaks of the "counsel of the froward," which in the ESV is the "schemes of the wily." Psalm 64:2 (KJV) speaks of the "secret counsel of the wicked," which in the ESV is the "secret plots of the wicked." The "counsel of the Lord" (Ps. 33:11; cf. 73:24; Prov. 19:21) is his "plan" (NIV, etc.) or "plans" (GNT, etc.) or "decisions" (ERV, NET). "Thy counsel" in the KJV (Acts 4:28) is "your plan" in the ESV. "The counsel of God" in the ASV (Acts 13:36) is the "purpose of God" in the ESV, and "God's plan" in the HCSB. "The counsel of God" in the KJV *and* the ESV (Acts 20:27) is the "plan of God" in the CEB, the CJB, etc., and "the purpose of God" in the DLNT, the GNT, etc.

The study of the plan of God, which is one of the most complex topics in systematic theology, can be described with the rare term *boulology*, "doctrine of the counsel," the theology of God's counsel.[1] The term is derived from Greek *boulē*, "counsel, plan." One could hardly think of a subject about which, on the one hand, Scripture speaks so circumspectly, and, on the other hand, where theological speculation has wreaked so much havoc. I speak of speculation if theory formation can no longer be directly accounted for on the basis of Scripture, and instead follows its own (supposedly) logical-rational pathway, ends in system coercion, inferentialism, and conclusivism, and thus begins to deviate from Scriptural parlance.

Another important term, which even occurs in the title of the present book, is "purpose." This is Greek *prothesis* (related to English *prosthesis*, but of a very different meaning), meaning "purpose, intent(ion), resolution, decision, aim, plan, will." It is used at various places for God's counsel (Rom. 8:28; 9:11; Eph. 1:11; 3:11; 2 Tim. 1:9). Sometimes, "purpose" is the translation of *boulē* (see above). In Ephesians 1:11, we have both terms: ". . . having been predestined according to the purpose (Gr. *prothesis*) of him who works all things according to the counsel (*boulē*) of his will" (cf. the ERV: "God had already planned for us to be his people, because that is what he wanted. And he is the one who makes everything agree with

---

1. On the Internet I found the term in the meaning intended here at, for instance, the Austin Bible Church (https://austinbiblechurch.com).

what he decides and wants").

A common Hebrew word for God's "counsel," "purpose," or "plan" is *'etsah*: "The counsel of the LORD . . ., the plans [*machshevot*, lit., thoughts] of his heart" (Ps. 33:11; cf. 106:13); "the words of God, . . . the counsel of the Most High" (107:11); "the counsel of the Holy One of Israel" (Isa. 5:19; cf. 28:29); "My counsel . . . my purpose [*hephets*, pleasure; cf. 44:28; 48:14; 53:10] . . . the man of his counsel" (46:10–11); "the purpose that the LORD of hosts has purposed" (19:17; cf. 14:26; Prov. 19:21); "the plan that the LORD has made" (Jer. 49:20; 50:45; "plans": Isa. 25:1); "the thoughts [*machshavot*] of the LORD . . . his plan" (Mic. 4:12).

Indeed, the Hebrew word for "thoughts" (*machshavot*) sometimes has the sense of "plans," for instance: "I know the thoughts that I think toward you, . . . thoughts of peace, and not of evil" (Jer. 29:11); in the ESV: "I know the plans I have for you, . . . plans for welfare and not for evil." Elsewhere, we find another relevant term: "The anger of the LORD will not turn back until he has executed and accomplished the intents (Heb. *m'zimmot*) of his heart" (23:20). The word *m'zimmah* sometimes refers to human (often evil) intentions, and sometimes to God's purposes or intentions (cf. 30:24; 51:11; Job 42:2). A third interesting Hebrew term is *sod*, which has the basic meaning of "secret," sometimes with the sense of "(secret) plan, purpose": "For the LORD God does nothing without revealing his secret [TLV, YLT: counsel; CJB, NIV, etc.: plan; ISV, MEV: purpose] to his servants the prophets" (Amos 3:7).

1.2 Features of God's Purpose
1.2.1 General Features

Let us now look at some Scriptural data concerning the purpose of God, about which most people holding various theological positions will presumably agree.

(a) *God's purpose is sovereign*. There *is* such a thing as God's "counsel" (Latin *consilium*), "decree" (*decretum*), "good pleasure" (*beneplacitum*, Eph. 1:5, 9 KJV; Gr. *eudokia*), "will" (*volun-*

tas; Gr. *thelēma*), or "purpose" (*propositum*, a literal rendering of Gr. *prothesis*).[2] Especially terms like "good pleasure" and "will" emphasize the fact that God's purpose is perfectly voluntary and perfectly sovereign: "Who has measured the Spirit of the LORD, or what man shows him his counsel? Whom did he consult, and who made him understand? Who taught him the path of justice, and taught him knowledge, and showed him the way of understanding?" (Isa. 40:13-14). Thus, Luke 2:14 speaks of "those with whom he is pleased."[3] Ephesians 1:9-10 speaks of "his purpose, which he set forth in Christ as a plan for the fullness of time, to unite all things in him, things in heaven and things on earth," and James 1:18 says, "Of his own will he brought us forth by the word of truth." This sovereign will also applies to the new creation: "All these are empowered by one and the same Spirit, who apportions to each one individually as he *wills* [Gr. *kathōs bouletai*]. . . . God arranged the members in the body, each one of them, as he *chose* [ethelēsen, wanted it]" (1 Cor. 12:11, 18). "God gives it a [resurrection] body as he has *chosen* [ethelēsen, has wanted]" (15:38).

(b) *God's purpose is entirely of himself.* By no coercion from outside has this counsel been brought about, nor by any coercion from inside, as if God *had to* make his eternal decisions on the basis of his being or else. Nonetheless, some—in my view by the coercion of their theological system—did speak of a certain "must" in God's purpose, for instance, why he "had to" make the decree of reprobation.[4] In my view, this definitely goes too far. If God calls people into existence, his love compels him to love them. But his love could not force him—at best, it could only induce him—to create people in

---

2. Western theologians still use a lot of Latin because for more than 1,600 years it was *the* language of theologians, both Roman Catholic and Protestant.
3. Greek: *anthrōpois eudokias*, lit.: "people of [God's] good pleasure"; KJV, etc. follow another reading: *en anthrōpois eudokia*, "among people [God's] good pleasure."
4. Hoeksema (1927, 16–17).

the first place.⁵ We will return to this point.

(c) *God's purpose concerns his creation.* The counsel of God applies to reality as created by him, and thus implies a certain duality (not dualism, i.e., an antithetical opposition!) of God and reality. In the pantheist view, in which the divine and the cosmic coincide, there is no room for the counsel of God. The same holds for the deist view, in which God is not concerned with his creation. The purpose of God as well as its realization within history presuppose divine providence and a situation in which the cosmos continually depends on its Creator.⁶

(d) *God's purpose involves his active dealings with creation.* The counsel of God does not involve the actions of others primarily—angels or people—so that this counsel itself would be passive, but involves God's own active dealings: "[H]e will complete what he appoints for me" (Job 23:14). "Our God is in the heavens; he does all that he pleases" (Ps. 115:3). "The works of his hands are faithful and just; all his precepts are trustworthy; they are established forever and ever, to be performed with faithfulness and uprightness" (111:7-8). "My counsel shall stand, and I will accomplish all my purpose" (Isa. 46:10). "The former things I declared of old; they went out from my mouth, and I announced them; then suddenly I did them, and they came to pass" (48:3). "In a time of favor [i.e., God's good pleasure] I have answered you" (49:8). "[I]t was the will of the LORD to crush him" (53:10).

In addition to verbs that mean "to complete," "to accomplish," etc., one verb is of special interest: "to form" (Heb. *y-ts-r*). God is the One who "forms" (designs) the future:⁷ "Your eyes saw my unformed substance; in your book were written, every one of them, the days that were formed [*y-ts-r*] for me, when as yet there was none of them" (Ps. 139:16; cf. Job 14:5). "[Y]ou [i.e., Israel] did not look to him [i.e., God] who did it, or see him who planned [*y-ts-r*] it long ago"

---

5. Erickson (1998, 378–79).
6. Heyns (1988, 77).
7. Erickson (1998, 373).

(Isa. 22:11b). "Have you not heard that I determined [lit., made] it long ago? I planned [*yts-r*] from days of old what now I bring to pass" (37:26). I am God, "calling a bird of prey from the east, the man of my counsel from a far country. I have spoken, and I will bring it to pass; I have purposed [*y-ts-r*], and I will do it" (46:11).

(e) *God's purpose serves his honor.* The aim of God's counsel is certainly the blessing of people, but it is first and foremost his own glorification: "For my own sake, for my own sake, I do it, for how should my name be profaned? My glory I will not give to another" (Isa. 48:11). "I acted for the sake of my name" (Ezek. 20:9). "For from him and through him *and to him* are all things. To him be glory forever" (Rom. 11:36). "[A]ll things were created through him [i.e., Christ] and *for him*" (Col. 1:16). God has "predestined us for adoption as sons through Jesus Christ, according to the purpose of his will, to the praise of his glorious grace, with which he has blessed us in the Beloved. . . . so that we . . . might be to the praise of his glory" (Eph. 1:5–6, 12, 14). "Worthy are you, our Lord and God, to receive glory and honor and power, for you created all things, and by your will they existed and were created" (Rev. 4:11).

1.2.2 Revealed Yet Unfathomable

God has revealed *himself*—in his being—to humanity, whereas at the same time his infinite being remains unfathomable and inscrutable for finite human beings.[8] It is the same with his counsel.

(a) *God reveals his purpose.* God's counsel begins to be revealed as soon as his work of creation begins. This purpose comes to light in this word by God: "Let us make man in our image, after our likeness," in which our human calling is established right from the start: "And let them have dominion over the fish of the sea and over the birds of the heavens and over the livestock and over all the earth and over every creep-

---
8. See Ouweneel (2007b, 293–96).

ing thing that creeps on the earth" (Gen. 1:26; cf. v. 28; 9:1). Each covenant that God makes with people, every prophecy that he pronounces through his servants the prophets, goes back to the decree of God, and in due time is revealed by him: "For the LORD God does nothing without revealing his secret to his servants the prophets" (Amos 3:7; see §1.1.2). Jesus told his disciples: "I have called you friends, for all that I have heard from my Father I have made known to you" (John 15:15). Paul said, "I did not shrink from declaring to you the whole counsel of God" (Acts 20:27), the counsel that he had first received from God himself (cf., e.g., 1 Cor. 11:23).

(b) *God's purpose is specific.* How accessible God's counsel is for people becomes manifest in the specificity of this revelation: he often communicates his purpose in detail. Moreover, the manifestation of his counsel refers to matters that, for people, are understandable to a certain extent. Thus, Scripture speaks of God's will in regard to creation (Rev. 4:11); of a "decree of the LORD" with respect to the Davidic kingship, especially to the Messiah (Ps. 2:7 NASB; cf. Acts 4:27-28); of a kingdom that is "assigned" to Jesus' followers (Luke 22:29); of David, who had "served the purpose of God" (Acts 13:36). Also the surrender of Christ into the hands of the Gentiles to be crucified took place "according to the definite plan and foreknowledge of God" (2:23). Believers are described as "those who are called according to his purpose" (Rom. 8:28; cf. 9:11, "God's purpose of election"). This can all be grasped to a certain extent by the believer who is illuminated by the Holy Spirit: ". . . that the God of our Lord Jesus Christ, the Father of glory, may give you the Spirit of wisdom and of revelation in the knowledge of him, having the eyes of your hearts enlightened, that you may know. . ." (Eph. 1:17-18).

(c) *God's purpose is unfathomable.* Compare the previous point: God's counsel is to a certain extent accessible, but at the deepest level it remains inscrutable: God "does great things and unsearchable, marvelous things without number" (Job 5:9; cf. 9:10). "Can you find out the deep things of

God? Can you find out the limit of the Almighty?" (11:7). "Have you listened in the council of God? And do you limit wisdom to yourself?" (15:8). "For as the heavens are higher than the earth, so are my ways higher than your ways and my thoughts [CEB, NET: plans] than your thoughts" (Isa. 55:9). "[H]e reveals deep and hidden things" (Dan. 2:22). "[H]e is wonderful in counsel and excellent in wisdom" (Isa. 28:29). "[W]ho among them has stood in the council of the LORD to see and to hear his word, or who has paid attention to his word and listened?" (Jer. 23:18; cf. v. 20, "the intents of his heart"). "O great and mighty God, whose name is the LORD of hosts, great in counsel and mighty in deed. . ." (32:18–19). "Call to me and I will answer you, and will tell you great and hidden things that you have not known" (33:3). And Jesus said, "It is not for you to know times or seasons that the Father has fixed by his own authority" (Acts 1:7).

God's counsel is so lofty that people cannot reach for it, let alone assist God in deciding it: "Who has measured the Spirit of the LORD, or what man shows him his counsel? Whom did he consult, and who made him understand? Who taught him the path of justice, and taught him knowledge, and showed him the way of understanding?" (Isa. 40:13–14). "Oh, the depth of the riches and wisdom and knowledge of God! How unsearchable are his judgments and how inscrutable his ways! 'For who has known the mind of the Lord, or who has been his counselor[9]?' 'Or who has given a gift to him that he might be repaid?'" (Rom. 11:33–35; cf. Isa. 40:13–14; Job 41:11).

There is another side, however. In Romans 11:34, Paul alludes to Isaiah 40:13 to underscore the loftiness of God's counsel. But in 1 Corinthians 2:16 he refers again to this passage, this time to emphasize how great is the privilege of the believer, who by the Holy Spirit is enabled and permitted to penetrate the deepest thoughts of God: "The natural person does not accept the things of the Spirit of God, for they are

---

9. Gr. *symboulos*, lit. "co-counselor," co-designer of God's counsel.

folly to him, and he is not able to understand them because they are spiritually [or, Spirit-ually!] discerned. The spiritual person judges all things, but is himself to be judged by no one. 'For who has understood the mind of the Lord so as to instruct him?' But we have the mind of Christ" (vv. 14-16).

1.2.3 God's Purpose Stands Firm

It is said in a very general sense: "The counsel of the LORD stands forever, the plans of his heart to all generations" (Ps. 33:11; cf. 106:13; 107:11); "the counsel of the LORD, that shall stand" (Prov. 19:21 KJV; cf. Isa. 5:19; Mic. 4:12; Heb. 6:17). "The LORD of hosts has sworn: 'As I have planned, so shall it be, and as I have purposed, so shall it stand. . . . This is the *purpose* that is *purposed* concerning the whole earth, and this is the hand that is stretched out over all the nations. For the LORD of hosts has *purposed*, and who will annul it?" (Isa. 14:24-27; cf. 19:12, 17; 23:9; Job 38:2; 42:3; Jer. 49:20; 50:45). "I am God, . . . declaring the end from the beginning and from ancient times things not yet done, saying, 'My counsel shall stand, and I will accomplish all my purpose'" (Isa. 46:9-10).

We have seen in §1.2.1 (point [b]) that there is no "must" *in* God's counsel; he is sovereign. God is not forced to pursue his purpose by any authority outside him. However, there *is* a "must" on the *human* side, which *goes back* to the immutable counsel of God. This means that, whatever God has decreed, *must* happen: "Did you not know that I *must* be in my Father's house?" (Luke 2:49). "I *must* preach the good news of the kingdom of God to the other towns as well; for I was sent for this purpose" (4:43). "The prophets said the Messiah *must* suffer these things before he begins his time of glory" (24:26 ERV). "[A]s Moses lifted up the serpent in the wilderness, so *must* the Son of Man be lifted up" (John 3:14). "[H]e *had to* pass through Samaria" (4:4). Jesus "whom heaven *must* receive until the time for restoring all the things" (Acts 3:21). "And when you hear of wars and rumors of wars, do not be alarmed. This *must* take place, but the end is not yet. . . . And the gospel *must* first be proclaimed to all nations" (Mark 13:7, 10). It is *people* who make wars or preach the gospel, but in these things God's counsel becomes manifest: what he has decreed, must occur.

Strikingly enough, we get the impression that in some situations God's counsel is in vain: "When all the people heard this, and the tax collectors too, they declared God just, having been baptized with the baptism of John, but the Pharisees and the lawyers rejected the purpose of God for themselves, not having been baptized by him" (Luke 7:29-30). The common people agreed with the counsel (purpose, plan) of God, which manifested itself in the ministry of John the Baptist, and which was intended for the entire nation, namely, that they repent and have themselves baptized. But the Pharisees and the Torah-scholars ("lawyers") did not do this, whereas they were the very ones who needed repentance.[10]

In this case, "purpose" or "counsel" is indeed a fixed decree of God, but one that does not apply beforehand to each member of the target group. It is a purpose that involves salvation, but on the condition of repentance and baptism, that is, on the basis of one's own responsibility. Notice here the *eis heautous*, "for themselves," which further qualifies the term "purpose":[11] God's redemptive purpose was also applicable to the spiritual leaders, but they rejected God's purpose. This is an important point, because it implies that God's purpose is not effectuated in all cases. Perhaps we have to think here of the distinction that earlier theologians made between God's "counsel/will of precept" and his "counsel/will of decree" (cf. further §§2.8.2, 3.4.2). What God demands of people is not always done; but what he has decreed *will* be done.[12]

---

10. Bruce (1979, 514).
11. *TDNT* 1:635n10. KJV, etc., read "against themselves" (cf. Greijdanus [1955, 186–87]), that is, "to their own destruction."
12. Cf. *TDNT* 4:1088.

1.3 God's Ways
1.3.1 The Term "Way"

Just as in the case of the term "purpose" or "counsel," the theological use of the term "way" (Hebrew *derekh*; Gr. *hodos*) deviates from normal, literal parlance—at least in the present book, and in the thinking of several other theologians. To be sure, the common use occurs in the Bible as well, as early as Genesis 3:24: God "drove the man out, he placed on the east side of the Garden of Eden cherubim and a flaming sword flashing back and forth to guard the way to the tree of life," NIV). The next time the term occurs in a figurative sense: "God saw the earth, and behold, it was corrupt, for all flesh had corrupted their way on the earth" (6:12).

When the text deals with God, the term "way" sometimes possesses more or less the literal (physical) meaning: "In the wilderness prepare the way of the LORD; make straight in the desert a highway for our God" (Isa. 40:3; cf. Luke 1:76). "His way is in whirlwind and storm, and the clouds are the dust of his feet" (Nah. 1:3). "Your way was through the sea, your path through the great waters; yet your footprints were unseen" (Ps. 77:19). More figurative is verse 13: "Your way, O God, is holy" (cf. Ps. 67:2; Ezek. 18:25, 29). Sometimes, God's "way" is his way of acting, but this phrase can also refer to a human's way of acting that is according to God's will (Gen. 18:19; Judg. 2:22; Ps. 86:11).

Concerning this latter point: in the Old Testament, the plural "ways" is often more or less synonymous with "commandments." To go in the "ways of the LORD" is to walk in his commandments; they are the ways "of the LORD," but it is human beings who walk in them (cf. Deut. 8:6; 10:12; etc.; Josh. 22:5; 2 Sam. 22:22; 1 Kings 2:3; 3:14; etc.; 2 Chron. 6:31; 17:6; Job 21:14; 34:27; Ps. 18:21; 25:4, 9; etc.; Isa. 2:3; 42:24; etc.; Hos. 14:9; Mic. 4:2; Zech. 3:7; Mal. 2:9). In other cases, the word refers instead to the ways in which the LORD himself walks throughout history. The connection between these two meanings is obvious: "The LORD is righteous in all his ways and kind in all his works" (Ps. 145:17). If God is righteous in his ways, he may expect that his image-bearers, human beings, are righteous in God's ways as well. In the negative form: "They are a people who go astray in their heart, and they have not known my ways" (95:10; cf. Heb. 3:10).

The second meaning—God's "ways" throughout redemptive history—is the one being discussed in the present book. Let me give a few examples. Moses asks, "[P]lease show me now your ways, that I may know you" (Exod. 33:13). God is "[t]he Rock, his work is perfect, for all his ways are justice" (Deut. 32:4). God "stilled the sea; by his understanding he shattered Rahab. By his wind [or, breath, or Spirit] the heavens were made fair; his hand pierced the fleeing serpent. Behold, these are but the outskirts of his ways" (Job 26:12–14). "All the kings of the earth . . . shall sing of the ways of the LORD, for great is the glory of the LORD" (Ps. 138:4–5). "For my thoughts are not your thoughts, neither are your ways my ways, ... For as the heavens are higher than the earth, so are my ways higher than your ways and my thoughts than your thoughts" (Isa. 55:8–9). "Great and amazing are your deeds, O Lord God the Almighty! Just and true are your ways, O King of the nations!" (Rev. 15:3; see also Ps. 103:7; 145:17; Prov. 8:22; Ezek. 18:25, 29).

1.3.2 God's Counsel and God's Ways

The biblical connection between the counsel of God and the ways of God constitutes one of the main subjects of this book. It is here that the paths of many Calvinists and many Evangelicals part. In this book, when I say "Calvinists," I usually mean hyper-Calvinists. To be sure, nobody calls himself a hyper-Calvinist (or ultra-Reformed); just as nobody says of himself that he is a legalist, or that he has no sense of humor. "Hyper-Calvinist" is a designation that others give to certain Calvinists. To state it simply: hyper-Calvinists emphasize God's sovereignty much more strongly and one-sidedly (at the expense of human responsibility) than Calvin did, and than the Canons of Dordt do, for instance. It is not easy, though, to define the precise boundary between Calvinism and hyper-Calvinism; at any rate, I will leave this matter unresolved for the moment (see further §10.4.1).

The two most characteristic claims of traditional, consistent Calvinism and hyper-Calvinism, as far as the counsel of God is concerned, are, in my view, the following:[13]

(a) Everything that ever happens has been decreed by God in his counsel; things occur not only because he allows them, but also because he has foreordained that they occur this way.

(b) In his eternal decree of election, God has predestined sovereignly (without any influence from outside, such as the foreseen faith or unbelief of people) a certain number of people for eternal salvation, and in his eternal decree of reprobation, God has predestined all the other people for eternal perdition.

I cannot agree with either conviction because I cannot find (a) and the second half of (b) in the Bible, nor are these claims at all logically necessary, as we will see. Because of my disagreement I suppose that I am not a Calvinist. Does this mean I am an Open Theist, to mention the movement that, today, is the strongest opponent of Calvinism, emphasizing an open future, open to God as well? The two most characteristic claims of Open Theism, as far as the counsel of God is concerned, are, in my view, the following:

(a) In his eternal decree of election, God has predestined to eternal salvation those people whom he saw beforehand would believe in him (this is typically Arminian).

(b) God does not know beforehand everything that happens, for this would destroy human freedom; he knows only those events that he himself will bring about as well as all *possible* events (on this point, Open Theism essentially deviates from both Calvinism and Arminianism).

---

13. References appear below.

With these two convictions I cannot agree, either, because I cannot find them in the Bible, nor are these claims at all logically necessary, as we will see. Because of my disagreement I guess I am not an Open Theist either.

So what am I? In a time when many conservative Protestant theologians believe that there is no middle way—you are either something of a Calvinist, or something of an Open Theist (with a number of varieties)—there seems to be little room for the kind of Evangelicals with whom I identify. In the course of this book, I hope to make clear what this room is: I choose what I would call a *Viatoric* approach. The Latin *viator* means "wayfarer, traveler," literally "he who goes a certain way (Lat. *via*)." *Viatorism* is an approach that leaves room not only for the eternal, immutable counsel of God (*contra* Arminianism and Open Theism), but also for temporal, variable ways of God that are co-determined by human actors, through which God's counsel is realized (*contra* Calvinism).

1.3.3 Backgrounds

Viatorism does not constitute an entirely new view. Similar ideas have been encountered in the writings of the fifth-century Calcidius, and in those of some nineteenth-century Methodist and other theologians.[14] In a broader sense, one can say that others would refer to the "ways" of God as I understand them with the term "providence." As to the relationship between counsel and providence, according to Arminius, the decree of the Father to send his Son to atone for our sins precedes the decree of election, so that the latter, strictly speaking, does not belong to God's predestination but to God's providence. The "natural" person *can* believe, and the "prevenient" grace of God (see §13.8.2) exerts a mild pressure on such a person. Whether the person indeed *will* believe is a matter of providence, not of predestination. There is a divine predestination in the broad sense, which is identical with God's providence, as well as a predestination in the narrower sense, referring to

---

14. Boyd (2000, 114–15).

God's election.

Thus, there is a certain agreement between the "providence of God" as Arminianism speaks of it, and the "ways of God" as Viatorism speaks of them. The great difference is that in Arminianism the counsel of God is essentially determined by the foreseen acts of people, whereas in Viatorism the counsel of God is primarily determined by the sovereignty of God. The great difference between both of these two, on the one hand, and Calvinism, on the other hand, is that (a) what Arminianism and Viatorism call the "providence" and the "ways of God," respectively, is viewed by Calvinism as part of God's counsel, and that (b) according to Calvinism, the counsel of God (which includes the ways of God) is viewed as entirely determined by the sovereignty of God, with total exclusion of the foreseen faith or unbelief of the people concerned. All of this will be explained and set forth in subsequent chapters.

Of great importance is the distinction that Arminius made with regard to reprobation: according to him, reprobation belongs exclusively to the domain of God's providence (in my terminology: God's ways), not to that of God's eternal counsel.[15] This is the same as saying that God does not reprobate a person *a priori*, according to his sovereign counsel, but *a posteriori*, on the basis of the guilt and unbelief of the persons involved. My concern right now involves not whether Arminius was right with this kind of distinction, but the distinction between predestination (from eternity) and providence (within time) as such, as, to some extent, parallel with the terms "counsel" and "ways of God," respectively.

When it comes to the ways of God in general, and election and reprobation in particular, I am personally less happy with the term "providence" because it seems too broad to me. God's work of preserving his creation, and God's "hand in history" in the broadest sense, are also assigned to his providence.[16] When I use the term (temporal) "ways," I prefer to

---
15. See Verboom (2005, 31, 33, 37–39, 45 n68).
16. Cf. Berkouwer (1952, especially chapters 3 and 6).

think more specifically of the acts of God within *redemptive history*, in a continual correlation with the (eternal) counsel of God. I am especially interested in the ways by which God realizes his eternal counsel in redemptive history. In this context, Lewis and Demarest speak of "strategies."[17]

In the *counsel* of God we are dealing with God's gracious, sovereign decrees, which consist of two different kinds.

(a) Decrees *from before* the foundation of the world, that is, decrees from all eternity in reference to what will be in all eternity (cf. John 17:24; Rom. 16:25; 1 Cor. 2:7; Eph. 1:4; 3:9–11; Col. 1:26; 2 Tim. 1:9; Titus 1:2; 1 Pet. 1:20).

(b) Decrees *at* or *after* the foundation of the world, that is, decrees in reference to, and limited to, redemptive history on earth (cf. Matt. 13:35; 25:34; Heb. 4:3; Rev. 13:8; 17:8).

In the *ways* of God we are dealing with God's response *within time* to events that possibly have been foreseen by him (I leave this undecided for the moment; see chapter 4), but which have not been foreordained by him, and are the result of the free—and often very wrong—decisions of people.

Of course, Viatoric studies of the relationship between the counsel and the ways of God are part of a theological paradigm—just like, by the way, Calvinism, Arminianism, and Open Theism are theological paradigms. In many cases with which we will deal, the Bible uses neither the term "counsel" or "purpose," nor the term "way(s)." A starting point of the Viatoric model is that everything that seems *a priori* to be immutably and fixed *a priori* with God involves his counsel, and everything that does *not* seem to be fixed *a priori*, but belongs to the various manners in which God's counsel can be realized, involves his ways. If we follow this description, then, according to Calvinism, *everything* that occurs belongs to God's counsel, and according to Process Theology (§§3.6.2, 6.5.2), *everything* that occurs, belongs to God's ways. Just like Arminianism and Open Theism, though in a different

---

17. Lewis and Demarest (1996, 312).

manner, Viatorism explores a middle road: some events have been foreordained in God's eternal counsel, while other events belong to his temporal ways. The difference between, on the one hand, Viatorism and on the other hand, Arminianism and Open Theism, is the much larger emphasis that Viatorism places on God's sovereignty and sovereign plans as well as his foreknowledge.

1.4 Examples
1.4.1 Old Testament

Some biblical examples may help us grasp the difference between the counsel of God and the ways of God. His *counsel* comes to light especially in promises and prophecies that indicate the final goal of God's ways. In the variety of, and the changes in, the manners in which this final goal is reached, God's *ways* become manifest. In the following examples, I cannot always prove through direct biblical evidence that the one aspect belongs to the counsel and the other to the ways of God, but I hope that the general significance of our approach will become clear.

(a) It belonged to the *counsel* of God that he gave Abraham a rich progeny through his son Isaac, to whom he entrusted his promises and blessings. It was part of the *ways* of God that, when Abraham followed a way of disobedience and unbelief to father Ishmael with Hagar, God gave blessings to this son as well (Gen. 17:20).

(b) It belonged to the *counsel* of God that Moses led the people of Israel out of Egypt. It was part of the *ways* of God that, when Moses resisted his calling and God became angry with him, God gave him his brother Aaron to accompany him (Exod. 4:10–15).

(c) It belonged to the *counsel* of God that Israel would enter the promised land in the sense that Israel's occupation of the land Canaan rested entirely and exclusively on God's gracious and sovereign decree. However, it was part of the *ways* of God that it would take Israel forty years to reach this destination. This was because the people were disobedient to God (cf. 1 Cor. 10:5). Therefore, he decided that the people would enter the land only after all those older than twenty years of age had died in the wilderness (Num. 14:28-35).

(d) It belonged to the *counsel* of God to place the house of David over Israel; not Saul but David was the man "after God's heart" (1 Sam. 13:14; Acts 13:22; cf. Ps. 18:50; 78:70-72; 89:3-4, 19-21; 132:11-12). It was part of the *ways* of God to follow a detour through Saul — Saul had been chosen by God but entirely according to the carnal desires of the people (1 Sam. 8:7-9) — and afterward to limit the authority of David's house temporarily to the two tribes (2 Sam. 2:4, 11; 5:1-5).

(e) It belongs very generally to the *counsel* of God that Israel will ultimately receive the fulfillment of all God's promises, and to this end Israel is repeatedly delivered from the hands of all its enemies. Thus, it had been decreed that, for instance, the plan of Haman, the "enemy of the Jews" (Esther 3:10; etc.) to destroy Israel would utterly fall to the ground. However, the *way* through which this would happen had *not* been determined beforehand. We see this very strikingly in Mordecai's appeal to Esther: "[I]f you keep silent at this time, relief and deliverance will rise for the Jews from another place, but you and your father's house will perish. And who knows whether you have not come to the kingdom for such a time as this?" (4:4). This means: Ask yourself, Esther, whether God has not placed you in this special position as main consort of king Ahasuerus in order to bring about redemption for his people. But know at the same time that God does not depend on you: if you are not prepared to act, he will find another way, for Israel will ultimately be redeemed. God's *counsel* stands; but the *way* in which he realizes his counsel depends partially on human choices.

1.4.2 New Testament

(a) It belonged to the *counsel* of God that Jesus would descend from Abraham, or more specifically, from the house of David.

It was part of the *ways* of God, in interaction with the (often evil) acts of human beings committed according to their own freedom and responsibility, that Jesus' ancestors (Matt. 1:1-17) would include women like Tamar and Rahab, who both prostituted themselves (Gen. 38:15, 21; Josh. 2:1), or Ruth the Moabitess (cf. Deut. 23:3-6), or Bathsheba, who entered into an adulterous relationship with David (2 Sam. 11:2-5). These sins were definitely *not* part of God's counsel. Yet, in spite of these sins, and even employing the results of these sins, God realized his purpose.

(b) It presumably belonged to the *counsel* — or only to the biblically recorded foreknowledge? — of God that one of Jesus' followers would betray him: "[N]ot one of them has been lost except the son of destruction, *that the Scripture might be fulfilled*" (John 17:12b). However, there is no biblical basis for the idea that Judas personally had been destined from eternity to this role, on the contrary: "Did I not *choose* you, the Twelve? And yet one of you is a devil" (6:70). Here we are dealing with a temporary election for a function on earth (see §§10.7.2, 10.8.1, and 10.8.4). As I see it, the fact that Judas would manifest himself as a devil by betraying Jesus, had not been decreed *a priori* regarding him personally, but was the consequence of his own false choices. Thus, it belonged to the *ways* of God that Judas Iscariot in the end became this traitor.[18] Here we have another example why the distinction between God's counsel and God's ways is so important: God's (eternal) *counsel* depends exclusively on himself, on his sovereign will and choices. But in God's (temporal) *ways* the freedom of will and the responsibility of human beings are implied. These can never obstruct or invalidate God's counsel; but they do often lead to situations in which God chooses a new way — sometimes even a very different one than he had announced beforehand — in order to reach his goal and to realize his purpose. We will discuss this extensively in subsequent chapters.

---

18. Cf. Boyd (2000, 37–39; cf. 45).

(c) It belonged to the "definite plan and foreknowledge of God" that Jesus was delivered up to be crucified (Acts 2:23). It was part of the *ways* of God that Caiaphas, Herod, and Pilate became the actual executors of this plan, in entire agreement with their own free choices. None of their evil acts was decreed by God, whether from eternity or in the course of time, for such a thought would destroy their responsibility, not to mention their very humanity. In my view, this is the deeper meaning of Jesus' prayer in Gethsemane: "My Father, if this cannot pass unless I drink it, your will be done" (Matt. 26:42; cf. Luke 22:42, "Father, if you are willing, remove this cup from me. Nevertheless, not my will, but yours, be done"). God's *counsel* stood, and was perfectly known to Jesus: "[T]he Son of Man came . . . to serve, and to give his life as a ransom for many" (Matt. 20:28). However, Jesus apparently could still ask whether there was another *way* through which God's purpose could be accomplished. If the counsel and the ways of God were identical, and all events had been determined beforehand, Jesus' question would be incomprehensible.[19]

(d) It belongs to the *counsel* of God that person X has been elected before the foundation of the world. It belongs to the *ways* of God in what manner X will come to salvation, because this partially depends on X's own choices and decisions. Theologians of an Arminian or Open Theistic orientation would express this in a much stronger manner (which, in my view, goes too far, as I will argue): it supposedly belongs to the *counsel* of God that in eternity there will be a church of the elect. It supposedly belongs to the *ways* of God, in interaction with people's own responsibility, to determine which persons will eventually belong to this church of the elect.

---

19. Grosheide (1954, 401) thinks less rationally (and, in my view, less accurately): "Here one should not say: Jesus did know after all that he had to die, and he had declared himself to be willing; the fact that Jesus' prayer to the Father is reported to us is so that we would see how deeply he suffers. . . . In advance, he accepts the decision of the Father, John 5:30; 6:38, which he approves, but he shudders before the route he will have to travel."

1.4.3 Evaluation

In all the cases mentioned we find the same pattern: God's *counsel* refers to decisions that he himself makes, not on the basis of foreseen human decisions but sovereignly, that is, entirely on the basis of his own free will. God's *ways* refer to the manner in which he realizes his counsel; these depend partially on human responsibilities and choices. God attains his *goal* in a sovereign and almighty way, but not through *ways* that have been entirely foreordained. His purpose stands firm, but not the routes through which he attains his goal. These depend partially on human decisions, and these decisions are often wrong (sinful).

I agree here with the view of Clark H. Pinnock, who argued that history has not been determined beforehand, and that God is free to turn in new directions whenever this is appropriate.[20] If it is possible that God "relents" (see §4.5.2), this indicates that God does not work according to a plan whose every detail is fixed, but with general goals that can be realized in various ways. God is faithful in the realization of these goals but flexible when it comes to the manner of realization. God does have his own plans, but he is open to the input of his creatures. What God wants to happen does not always happen, which is a consequence of human freedom. There are catastrophes and setbacks, and God can even undergo humiliation because love makes him vulnerable. In fact, God has made himself more vulnerable than we are because, though we can count on this steadfast love, he cannot count on ours.

Now we do have to realize that Pinnock is an adherent and one of the best-known representatives of Open Theism. We will be dealing extensively in subsequent chapters with this movement. But at this point I wish to declare that, on important points, I cannot go along with Open Theism because, in my view, (a) it limits God's foreknowledge unnecessarily, and (b) it leaves too little room for God's sovereignty. As to

---

20. Pinnock (2001, 43–45).

(a): the core question is this: Can God know beforehand certain choices that people can make in absolute freedom of will? Open Theism believes that this is impossible, because foreknowledge excludes real freedom. I think it *is* possible, and that the Bible gives examples of this.

In this book we are seeking a middle road between, on the one hand, Calvinism and, on the other hand, Arminianism and Open Theism. The key term that I have introduced for this purpose is the (temporal) *ways* of God, as clearly distinct from God's (eternal) *counsel*. In this manner, I oppose (hyper-)Calvinist decretalism, and side with Open Theism. By emphasizing God's foreknowledge—which is not the same as predestination—as well as God's sovereignty, I also oppose Open Theism. According to Viatorism, God travels certain "ways" (Latin *viae*) through history with people—junior partners whom he himself has sovereignly chosen. Together with humanity he reaches the goals that were foreordained in his counsel. God's absolutely sovereign counsel is fixed; nothing and nobody can change it. His ways are not fixed; they are unfolded by God and by the free choices that people make within the limitations of the freedom sovereignly allotted to them by God.

This view being presented here must not be confused with process theology, mentioned earlier, which views God and humanity as equal partners in this developmental process (see §§3.6.2, 6.5.2).

1.5 Basic Questions
1.5.1 Creation and the Fall

Just like any other theology that has dealt with this subject—Roman Catholic, Calvinist, Lutheran, Arminian, Open Theism, to name the most important ones—Viatoric theology is confronted with the profound question concerning the relationship between, on the one hand, the divine counsel (election, predestination) and on the other hand, human responsibility (freedom of will, free options, and choices). This question involves the tension between human religious dependency and human moral responsibility. This essentially philosophical question as such is not found in Scripture; the Bible does not deal with philosophical problems as such. However, the question is raised time and again by theoretical reflection. The theologian has the duty to try to reflect on this issue thoroughly, and at the same time he has to realize that he will never entirely solve it.[21]

The background of this matter involves first and foremost questions concerning the meaning and the goal of *creation*, and especially of *humanity*.[22] Why did God make the world? Is it nothing but the stage on which God executes his eternal counsel, through ways that themselves belong to this counsel, and thus are fixed from eternity as well? Are people nothing but "stocks and blocks" in this totality, without any inherently meaningful input on their part?[23] If everything that has ever happened, happens, and will happen, is fixed in God's counsel from all eternity, what room is there for personal responsibility and freedom, which the Creator has personally assigned to people according to his sovereign decree?

A special issue in this context is the place and significance of the *Fall into sin*.[24] One of the most difficult questions in this context is this: How does the Fall relate to the counsel of God? Everybody agrees that a holy and righteous God as such cannot want sin; on the contrary, he hates sin (cf., e.g., Hab. 1:13). But does the Fall not fit in some way or another into the counsel of God? If everything that ever occurs was eternally decreed by God, why not the Fall? But how can God have decreed something that so strongly goes against his nature? Did God, although hating sin, in some way still desire and decree the Fall, perhaps in order to reach a higher goal in this way? If God did *not* decree the Fall, how can we say that all that has

---

21. Hervormde Kerk (1962, 11).
22. Ouweneel (2008a, chapters 2–8).
23. The expression "stocks and blocks" occurs in the Canons of Dordt III/IV.16.
24. Ouweneel (2008a, chapters 9–14).

happened was from eternity decreed by God? Or should we say only that God has "allowed" the Fall? But what does this mean? If God allows something, he must in some way also desire it, because if he really did not want it he would not have allowed it, would he?

Or should we not speak at all in terms of "desiring" and "allowing"? Is it true, as others (Arminians, Open Theists) believe, that God has sovereignly decreed to assign people their own freedom of will, because he desires to receive from them not an enforced but only a voluntary love? In that case, must the Fall be accredited only and exclusively to humanity? May we say that God assumed the "risk" of the Fall, and when the Fall actually happened God was not baffled, but does reach his great goal after all — the ultimate perfect blissful communion between God and humanity — namely, through the way of redemption? But does redemption therefore belong, not to the counsel but only to the ways of God? And what about that term "risk"? Even if we consider the possibility that God did not *decree* the Fall, must we not assume that he *foreknew* it? No predestination, but certainly foreknowledge?

1.5.2 Four Views

The few questions just mentioned yield at least four different responses, which I enumerate here only briefly.

(a) (Hyper-)Calvinist *decretalism*:[25] God desired and decreed the Fall, just as he decreed *all* things that ever happen, yet without being responsible for humanity's sinning as such. – The predestination of people who had to be redeemed is founded exclusively upon the sovereign will of God.

(b) *Viatorism*: God neither desired nor decreed the Fall but knew that it would take place, without this foreknowledge affecting humanity's freedom. – The predestination of people who had to be redeemed is founded primarily upon the sovereign will of God.

---

25. Decretalists themselves have often fiercely denied that they are determinists; I think they are wrong (see chapter 3).

(c) *Arminianism*: God neither desired nor decreed the Fall but knew that it would take place, without this foreknowledge affecting humanity's freedom. – The predestination of people who had to be redeemed is founded primarily upon the foreseen faith of a part of humanity.

(d) *Open Theism*: God neither desired nor decreed the Fall, nor did he foreknow it with certainty, for if he had had foreknowledge of it, humanity would have had no real choice, and the Fall would have *had to* take place. – The predestination of people who had to be redeemed is founded primarily upon the foreseen faith of a part of humanity.

Even the strongest adherents of each of these views will have to admit that each has its own problems with respect to God's counsel concerning the Fall.

(a) Is it indeed possible to maintain the view that God both desired and decreed the Fall in such a way that he is not responsible for Adam and Eve's sin, or could be made accountable for it? Is it indeed possible to maintain a strong decretalism—"all that happens has been foreordained by God"—without making God the author of sin? In what way can this be reasonably accounted for?

(b) and (c) Is it indeed possible to maintain the view that God foreknew that the Fall would take place without in this way endangering humanity's freedom? If God, or anyone else, *knows* beforehand with certainty that an event will occur, it is no longer possible that anything other than that event will take place. In this way, how can we still guarantee the freedom of will of the persons concerned?

(d) Supposedly, if we wish to maintain humanity's freedom of will, God could not possibly foreknow the Fall; he only foreknew the *possibility* of the Fall. Is it indeed defensible to maintain such a view? How does it relate to the omniscience of God, the One who is "declaring the end from the beginning and from ancient times things not yet done" (Isa. 46:10)?

1.5.3 Redemption

Already at this point I must say that obtaining definitive answers to these and similar questions is doubtful. Viatoric theology assumes a sharp distinction between God's counsel and God's ways, but this does not mean that we will always be able to indicate the precise boundary between the two. For instance, take the question already mentioned: Does redemption belong to the counsel of God or to the ways of God? I see two main possibilities.

(a) If redemption belongs to God's *ways* only, how could such a view be reconciled with biblical statements such as this one about "the precious blood of Christ, like that of a lamb without blemish or spot . . . foreknown before the foundation of the world" (1 Pet. 1:19–20)? Is "foreknowledge" here not "predestination"? But then what about Ephesians 1:4, "[H]e chose us in him before the foundation of the world, that we should be holy and blameless before him"? Do not "holy and blameless" presuppose unholiness and blame to be redeemed from, and thus the Fall?

(b) If redemption belongs to the *counsel* of God, then many will argue that humanity's Fall into sin must somehow be part of God's counsel as well. If the healing was planned, then the disease was at least foreknown. But if foreknown, then (as many say) the Fall *had to* take place. How could one seriously defend this view without making God responsible for sin? Augustine has uttered the great saying that what happens against God's will (*contra voluntatem Dei*) does not necessarily have to happen apart from God's will (*praeter voluntatem Dei*).[26] Could we say that the Fall as such was against God's will, yet did not occur apart from God's will? It is questionable whether this is a satisfactory idea: if a thing does not happen apart from God's will, how can we avoid saying that God *wants* this thing to happen?

It seems virtually impossible to deny that God's plan of

---

26. Enchiridion 100.

redemption in Christ was part of God's *counsel*, for we read about the "definite plan and foreknowledge of God" that Jesus was delivered up to be crucified (Acts 2:23). Jesus' enemies did with him "whatever your [i.e., God's] hand and your plan had predestined to take place" (4:28). But if redemption, then the Fall too? Decretalism says that the Fall was *decreed* by God — which seems to conflict with his holiness. Open Theism says that God did not know the Fall beforehand, and even *could* not foreknow it without affecting human freedom of will — which seems to conflict with the fact that redemption was unmistakably a part of God's counsel, and not just part of his ways.

Viatorism undertakes the seemingly impossible task of finding a middle path: redemption is part of God's eternal counsel; this involves the eternal predestination of believers. However, the Fall belongs to the events that God did not foreordain (*contra* [hyper-]Calvinist decretalism) but did foreknow (*contra* Open Theism). It is even more complicated: ultimately, God will create a perfect world that would never have been possible without the Fall and redemption. God *decreed* this world from eternity, and the Fall was calculated into his decree. And yet, Viatorism maintains that God did not decree the Fall itself, and that it would affect his righteousness if we would say otherwise. In Viatorism, the tension is pervasive and persistent, which is one of the main subjects of this book. All the attempts (Calvinist, Open Theist) to alleviate the tension are worse than the tension itself. Viatorism wishes to *endure* the tension, to *live* with it.

1.6 Battle
1.6.1 Calvinists Against Open Theists
In my own country, the Netherlands, orthodox Protestant theology is still affirmed by a large majority of Reformed theologians (though in many different versions), and thus there is little theological discussion about the counsel and the ways of God. Once in a while, a dissident throws a few stones into

the pond,[27] but the energy of the ripples eventually dissipates. There are some Evangelical theologians with Arminian leanings in our part of the world, but they do not throw stones.

In North America the situation is very different. Here, for years a fight has been going on between Calvinists and Open Theists. Actually, one could speak of a battle between *three* parties. First, Calvinism is represented by people like Joel R. Beeke, John S. Piper, Robert C. Sproul, and James R. White. Opposed to them is Open Theism, represented by theologians like David Basinger, Gregory A. Boyd, Clark H. Pinnock, and John E. Sanders. The third party contains, for instance, the well-known Evangelical theologian Norman L. Geisler, who, starting from Thomism, tried to take a middle position, and therefore was attacked from both sides.

The war is conducted with powerful weapons. Thus, Sproul and Piper said that they viewed Open Theism as pagan, anti-Christian, and blasphemous. Sproul even said of Pinnock that he did not view him as a believer, and would have no fellowship with him.[28] Elsewhere Sproul said of Open Theism that it is an attack, not only on Calvinism, or even on classical Theism, but on Christianity itself.[29] Richard L. Mayhue said of Boyd's book, *God of the Possible*, that it deifies Man, and humanizes God, and asserted that Open Theists are closer to idolatry than they realize or want to admit.[30] Such grossly offensive parlance raises the suspicion of being needed to cover up the weaknesses of one's own position.

James R. White even claimed that Open Theism was specifically designed to undermine and deny the sovereignty of God.[31] This is simply an affront, a false judgment of motives (*contra* Matt. 7:1), and substantially incorrect. One does not have to agree with Open Theism in order to appreciate its

---

27. E.g., Woelderink (1951); Venema (1992).
28. Quoted in Pinnock (2001, 16).
29. Sproul (1997, 143).
30. Mayhue (2001, 203).
31. White (2000, 61).

sincere attempt to develop a more biblical view of God's sovereignty than is current in traditional Protestantism. C. Stephen Evans therefore wrote that the "open God" position is motivated by a desire to be faithful to the Bible, and that it agrees both with classical Christian orthodoxy and with Evangelical distinctives.[32]

Although Norman L. Geisler tried to assume a middle position, he nevertheless called Open Theism a dangerous trend within Evangelical circles, and a considerable deviation from the God of the Bible and traditional theology, with dangerous consequences for the historic faith.[33] Also notice the title of one of his publications: *Creating God in the Image of Man?* If Geisler believed he could in this way obtain a seat at the table of the traditionally Reformed, he was mistaken. Two years later he wrote a book in which he presented himself as a "moderate Calvinist." Such an expression was enough to irritate some staunch Calvinists: he was severely attacked by the same Reformed theologians who had also attacked Open Theism. White turned just as fiercely against Geisler, and ridiculed his "moderate Calvinism."[34] Geisler had earlier called himself a "Calminian" (a combination of Calvinist and Arminian), and now tried to obtain a seat at the Calvinist table, while still believing in some form of free will (see §14.7.3).

1.6.2 Open Theists Against Calvinists

If some Reformed theologians opposed Open Theists as well as Geisler, some Open Theists did the same with Calvinists. Thus, Clark H. Pinnock blamed Calvinists for defending the "glory" of God, a glory that—in Pinnock's representation—implied that God is the sovereign author of every rape and murder, that God closes the future for any meaningful creaturely contribution, and holds people responsible for acts to which he himself has predestined them, and which they

---

32. On the dustjacket of Boyd (2000).
33. Geisler (1997, 11–12).
34. White (2000, 15).

therefore could not have avoided doing.[35] This representation of (hyper-)Calvinism is way over the top. It is unfair to blame Calvinists for making God responsible for every rape and murder, whereas Calvinists themselves reject such a thought with indignation. If people claim that this idea is a logical consequence of (hyper-)Calvinism, they are simply confusing logical concepts with logical ideas.[36] You can draw all kinds of logical conclusions from concepts ("if this is snow, it must be white") but not from ideas (God is Father, but it does not follow from this that he is a male). Interestingly, such a disturbing confusion of concepts with ideas takes place on both the Reformed and the Open Theist sides. Ideas of one party are ridiculed by drawing absurd logical conclusions from them that are ardently rejected by that party.[37] In this way, both Sproul & Co. and Pinnock & Co. have thoroughly sullied the debate.

Take what Pinnock has said about John Piper. If the latter spoke of a "compatibilistic freedom," Pinnock asserted that Piper could do so only with bad intentions.[38] So Pinnock sinned against Matthew 7:1, just as, for instance, White did (see above). Pinnock blamed Piper for using the term "compatibilism" only to cover up the fact that he really is a decretalist, who basically does not believe in human freedom. This is simply an *ad hominem* argument, rooted in Pinnock's incapacity to imagine how a Calvinist believes he can speak of God's sovereignty as well as of a certain human freedom. One does not have to agree with the Reformed view, but it is offensive not to take the other seriously on this point by ascribing ignoble motives to him.

In a similar way, Pinnock accused Loraine Boettner[39] of *knowing* that Calvinism conflicts with human freedom and

---

35. Pinnock (2001, 16; cf. 46–47).
36. For an explanation of this distinction, see Ouweneel (2014b, chapter 6).
37. See extensively, Ouweneel (2008a, §§1.2–1.3).
38. Pinnock (2001, 115n6).
39. Pinnock refers to Boettner (1941, 15–22).

moral responsibility, that it makes God the author of sin, that it disincentivizes people from putting forth effort, that it accuses God of "respecting the person" and of unrighteous partiality, that it excludes a sincere offer of the gospel to the non-elect, and that it contradicts universalist Bible passages.[40] Of course, the reality is that Boettner does not "know" or believe this at all. He is simply acknowledging that Calvinists have often been accused of these things — which is something very different. Person A ridicules the views of B by drawing conclusions from them that B himself utterly rejects. B does the same with A. What profit is to be harvested from such a debate?

Poor "middle man" Geisler, who combated both (hyper-)Calvinists and Open Theists, was attacked by both, especially by Sproul and Pinnock, respectively. Whereas Calvinists make the "sovereignty" of God their key term, Geisler does this with the "immutability" of God (cf. §6.5). Pinnock sarcastically referred to him as "our own evangelical Thomist Geisler."[41] He blamed him for seeing the bad practical consequences of "extreme Calvinism" but not the bad consequences of his own (Pinnock's) views.

This is the general picture: it is always the consequences that the allegedly blind person A does not see but that his opponent B triumphantly brings to light. Fierce Calvinists fight Open Theism because of its terrible consequences, which Open Theists often do not accept at all, or do not accept as inevitable consequences. Open Theists do exactly the same with Calvinism. I repeat, in many respects this is because Calvinists and Open Theists usually make the very same mistake: they confuse concepts with ideas, and thus draw invalid conclusions from the other party's views, simply to oppose these views. They never do this with their own views, of course; this is left to the opponents. Let us look at some examples of such persiflages. Each party presents what it sees as a logical-

---

40. Pinnock (2001, 155–56n8).
41. Pinnock (2001, 78n48).

ly consistent paradigm, which subsequently is debunked by the other party—and rightly so. Both parties defend an impossible system; that is, neither party seems to realize that a *conceptually* consistent system with respect to the matter of God's counsel and ways *is impossible a priori*.

1.7 Persiflages
1.7.1 In General

In the previous sections I gave some examples of *ad hominem* arguments, of suspecting each other's motives, and the like. Let me now give some examples of the way the various parties give persiflages of each other's standpoints. It is shocking to see how fiercely the war between decretalists and anti-decretalists has been conducted, in both the past and the present. We need think only of Augustine versus Pelagius (early fifth century), Luther versus Erasmus (early sixteenth century), Gomarus versus Arminius (early seventeenth century), and present-day North American Calvinists versus Open Theists. Unfortunately, even today we see the nasty way in which both parties depict their opponents. Usually, such distortions follow this method: draw the most absurd "logical" consequences of the other party's views, ridicule these, or put the enemy in a bad light.

As I said, apparently *both* parties are unaware of the distinction between concepts and ideas.[42] Because of this misunderstanding, conclusions are drawn from the other party's position that are in fact fallacies because the other party's views are taken in a conceptual way, and not as ideas. The meanness of this error becomes evident when we learn that the other party, which has thoroughly investigated the underlying problems, does not draw these conclusions at all, but ardently rejects them.

A few examples: God's absolute sovereignty does *not* necessarily exclude human responsibility. God's eternal election

---

42. For an explanation of this distinction, see extensively, Ouweneel (2008a), §§1.2–1.3).

of a certain part of humanity does *not* necessarily imply the reprobation of the rest of humanity from all eternity. That God supposedly does not foreknow all future events does *not* necessarily imply a lack of sovereignty. God's sovereignly choosing human beings as his partners in history does *not* necessarily affect the absoluteness of his eternal counsel. Human freedom does *not* necessarily imply a lack of divine sovereignty.

These assertions do not necessarily entail a lack of logical insight on my part, or even a rejection of a rational approach. On the contrary, not distinguishing between concepts and ideas betrays a lack of logical insight. Person A says that God is Father. Person B says, See how unorthodox A is because he implicitly accuses God of being a male who has had intercourse with one or more women. Now who is the dummy here? Please note that this example cannot be dismissed by saying that God's Fatherhood is "only" a metaphor. It *is* indeed a metaphor, but (a) one that touches upon God's deepest being ("God is Father, Son, and Holy Spirit"), and (b) one that cannot be expressed in any other terms.

Moreover, "metaphor" is a term from the literary sciences, "idea" (or super-concept) is a term from the logical sciences (see §3.8.3). We can speak of God (and of his sovereignty, and of his eternal counsel, and also of human freedom and responsibility, for that matter) only in terms of ideas, not concepts. This means that I can logically analyze a human counsel (plan, purpose), but I cannot logically analyze God's counsel. This is so because I can conceptualize a human counsel but I cannot do this with God's counsel; I can form only an idea (a logical approximation) of it.

This is not mysticism, because the mystical is irrational; but ideas are not at all irrational. Theologians can speak in a very rational way about God's sovereignty, his eternal counsel, and human freedom and responsibility. If this were not the case, theology would be impossible. However, finally these matters all surpass the strictly rational; they are suprarational (which is very different from irrational).[43] If divine sovereignty and human freedom were concepts, they would exclude each other as A and non-A. However, they are ideas, about which we can speak rationally but from which we cannot draw any possible logical conclusion so as to exclude the one by the other.

In this way, we may begin to see that Calvinists can speak of God's absolute sovereignty without denying human responsibility, even though Open Theists argue that such a denial follows from the notion of an absolute divine sovereignty. Similarly, we may begin to see that Open Theists can speak of God not foreknowing all that is going to happen without denying his sovereignty, even though Calvinists argue that such a denial follows from the notion of a non-absolute divine foreknowledge. Both parties are mistaken.

Please note that I am not defending either position, nor seeking sympathy for either position. The only point I am making right now is that both parties are committing the same logical fallacies, and are treating the other party in a way they themselves would not like to be treated. "So whatever you wish that others would do to you, do also to them, for this is the Law and the Prophets" (Matt. 7:12).

1.7.2 Persiflages of Arminianism

In his battle against Arminianism, hyper-Calvinist G. H. Kersten depicted the views of his opponents as negatively as possible. Without any basis, he claimed that Arminians make God's will dependent on the human will, and make him adapt to people. Kersten called this a "false doctrine, denying God."[44] He spoke of the "pernicious spiritual seed" of Pelagians, Arminians, and others; he called Pelagians "coarse," suggesting that these are people who "despise" the truth, and to whom "the devil has given his poison," and he spoke

---

43. On this, see Ouweneel (2014a, passim).
44. Kersten (1980, 1:65, 68, 88, 110, 112–13).

of "the Pelagian error."⁴⁵ With William Perkins (c. 1600)⁴⁶ he called it wicked if someone asserts that God did indeed know the Fall beforehand but did not decree it. He also suggests that Arminians place "coincidences" in the decree of God, and "restrain" God. I could continue like this. Let me add only that Kersten tries to undergird his own views mainly with apodictic statements, not with biblical arguments.

Needless to say, Kersten's opponents would not accept his allegations at all. Kersten is combating only his *representation* of Arminianism, and his own supposedly logical conclusions from it, not Arminianism as such, certainly not in a way Arminians would recognize and acknowledge. Discussion can start in a profitable way only if A can recognize himself in the picture that B gives of his (A's) views, and *vice versa*. Otherwise both parties are tilting at windmills.

Calvinism accuses Open Theism of the following errors (which always involve Calvinism's own conclusions, not necessarily the Open Theist views themselves). Open Theists allegedly deny God's sovereignty, omnipotence, and omniscience, and thus they deny God himself.⁴⁷ In reality, Open Theists do not necessarily deny the God of the Bible, but they deny the *Calvinist view* of God's sovereignty, omnipotence, and omniscience. That is a very different matter. John G. Stackhouse therefore describes these Calvinists as "cultic" (this is equivalent to being sectarian) in their claim of infallibility as far as their own views are concerned, and their claim that they speak for all Evangelicals (i.e., conservative Protestants).⁴⁸ Open Theists emphasize that their position does not at all affect God's sovereignty and omnipotence because, in their view, it is God himself who has *sovereignly and omnipotently* decreed to allow humanity a certain freedom of will and some room for affecting world history. They also

---

45. Kersten (1980, 1:112, 120, 136, 142; 1980, 2:400).
46. See on his doctrine of predestination, Graafland (1987, 71–83).
47. One of the fiercest examples of such accusations is Ware (2000).
48. Stackhouse (2000, 49–50, 57).

emphasize that their view does not affect God's omniscience, for they state that God knows all that *can* be known, namely, all future events that he himself will bring about, and all *possible* events insofar as these are co-dependent on human freedom of will. Others do not have to agree with this, but it is wrong to say that Open Theists thus deny God's omniscience; they are denying only the Calvinist version of God's omniscience, which they consider to be a fallacy.

Another striking example of an unfounded conclusion is the allegation of the Reformed author Harry Buis. He claims that, if the predestination of certain people were based on the fact that God knew beforehand that these people would believe, this would imply that redemption is based on human merit, and no longer on God's grace.[49] This, too, is a persiflage. As far as I know, no Arminian or Open Theist has ever based salvation on human merit.

Obedience of faith is no reason for boasting. Why would the cry for help of a person in an emergency (cf. Matt. 8:25), and his seizing the saving rope, be meritorious? I am not saying that the Arminian claim that God's predestination is based on a foreknown faith is correct; what I am saying is that Buis uses a misplaced argument.

1.7.3 Persiflages of Decretalism

Open Theists, too, accuse their opponents of various things that are products of Open Theist logic, but which the opponents, according to *their* logic, do not accept at all. Here again, a false representation of the opponents' views is given. Thus, John Wesley in his famous sermon on *Free Grace*, in which he sharply attacked Calvinism, asserted that this doctrine makes all gospel preaching and all striving for holiness superfluous.[50] To this very day, many anti-Calvinist opponents seem to agree with this.[51] I've already mentioned Clark H.

---

49. Buis (1958, 16).
50. Quoted in Buis (1958, 93).
51. See, e.g., Maddox (1994, 57); Sanders (1998, 240, 249); Pinnock (2001, 168–

Pinnock's allegation that, if in God's counsel everything is fixed from eternity, God is ultimately responsible for each murder and every rape.[52] In line with this, Open Theists claim repeatedly that Calvinism ultimately makes God the author of sin, a conclusion that Calvinists have always strongly resisted.

The entire difficulty is this: a claim may seem to have certain logical consequences within the Open Theist frame of thought, which it does not necessarily have within the Calvinist frame of thought. Thus, it may be difficult for the Open Theist to understand the place of prayer, missions, and a holy life in the Calvinist view, but the Open Theist cannot say *a priori* that this place logically cannot exist.[53] For instance, Harry Buis argues that prayer and missions do have meaning within the Calvinist view because, as means to a goal, they have been predestined in the sovereign counsel of God.[54] Prayer is meaningful because you cannot alter God's thoughts through it, but both prayer and the answer to it were *a priori* part of God's counsel (cf. chapter 8). The same is true for missions as a means that God has predestined in his counsel for the salvation of the elect.[55] Here again, we emphasize that one does not have to agree with this viewpoint; but it goes too far to claim that the Calvinist denies, or according to one's own logic, *ought* to deny, the usefulness of prayer, missions, and sanctification.

In the same way, the Calvinist belief in God having foreordained all events does not out of logical necessity make God ultimately the author of sin. There is a fine but important distinction between "God decreed the Fall" and "God decreed to allow the Fall." In the first case, *he* introduced sin, in the second case he allowed *people* to introduce sin. In the first case,

---

75).
52. See note 35 above.
53. See note 44 above.
54. Buis (1958, 131–32, 135).
55. Van Niftrik (1961, 73); Demarest (1997, 139–41).

the author of sin is God, in the second case humanity. However, I readily admit that the two formulations cannot easily be distinguished. R. C. Sproul chose the second formulation, but at the same time used the strong term "predestination."[56] He says that, if God predestines all that occurs, it follows that God must also have predestined the introduction of sin into the world. This does not mean, he argues, that God forced it to happen, or that he forced evil upon his creation, but it does mean that God must have decreed to allow it to happen. God did not decree it to happen, but he decreed to allow it to happen!

I fear that here Sproul has become a victim of his own formulations, for one cannot have both: either God decreed all future events, or he decreed to allow certain events to happen, but then he did *not* decree all future events.

Another nasty persiflage of Calvinism is the following one, uttered by a president of an American Presbyterian Seminary.[57] He stated that he was not a Calvinist because he did not believe that God brings certain people kicking and screaming, against their will, into his kingdom (because of eternal election), whereas others, who would love to get in, are excluded from this kingdom (because of eternal reprobation). Two Pentecostal theologians gave the following distortion of Calvinism: the doctrine of election is sometimes presented in such an extreme way as if the elect will certainly be saved irrespective of their response to the gospel and their way of life, whereas those who have been selected to perish will certainly go to eternal perdition, irrespective of their possible attempts to come to God by faith in Christ.[58]

This is absurd. Duffield and Van Cleave might have come across some hyper-Calvinist extremists, but mainstream Calvinists will always say that, on the one hand, through his Spirit, God works a longing for Christ and salvation in a person's

---

56. Sproul (1986, 31).
57. Quoted in Sproul (1986, 122); Presbyterianism is rooted in Calvinism.
58. Duffield and Van Cleave (1987, 206).

heart, so that the latter enters the kingdom with joy. Those who do not exhibit a positive response to the gospel, or live an evil life, prove in this way only that they have never truly repented and come to faith. On the other hand, nobody is excluded from the kingdom of God; those who are outside are there because they themselves want it so, according to their corrupt will. Intelligent representatives of Calvinism will have no difficulty claiming that there has *never* been a person who sincerely longed to come to God through Christ, but did not manage because he had the bad luck of being reprobate.

One does not have to agree with the Calvinist view. For instance, one could believe on good grounds that God gives *all* people the grace to believe in him, but that not all accept this grace and do something with it. One might even consider hyper-Calvinism to be a very bad doctrine, for instance, because it *keeps* people effectively *away* from the gospel by warning them not to go to hell with a "stolen" Jesus. No matter what the case may be, nobody has the right to fight his opponent by first giving a distorted picture of the latter's views.

1.8   The Doctrine of Grace

The various views concerning the counsel and the ways of God in reference to salvation can be elegantly illustrated by means of the central notion of grace. The fact that grace plays a substantial role in Scripture, from Genesis 6:8 to Revelation 22:21, is undisputed. Seven times we hear in the Old Testament that the LORD is "merciful and gracious, slow to anger, and abounding in steadfast love and faithfulness" (Exod. 34:6; Neh. 9:17; Ps. 86:15; 103:8; 145:8; Joel 2:13; Jonah 4:2; also cf. Num. 14:18; 2 Chron. 30:9; Neh. 9:31). Paul says, "*by grace* you have been saved through faith. And this is not your own doing; it is the gift of God" (Eph. 2:8), and we "are justified by his grace as a gift, through the redemption that is in Christ Jesus" (Rom. 3:24; cf. 4:16; 5:1–2; Acts 15:11; Eph. 1:6–7; 2:7; etc.).

Now the issue involves the precise role that grace plays in

the gift of salvation. In a certain sense, we can say that every view of the counsel of God as well as God's salvation is related to one's view of God's grace.[59] Bruce Demarest enumerated six different approaches, five of which I describe here, in my own words.[60]

(1) *Grace expresses itself in the natural gifts of conscience, reason, and free will.* This means that all people, believing and unbelieving, already possess grace, as creatures of God, and in equal measure. Because of this grace, they have the natural capacity to do good and to come to God in spite of their natural sinfulness. In the Christian world, this is the view of Pelagians and liberals. The kernel of truth in this view is that the natural gifts of people are also gifts of God's grace, for all that a person receives from God without having merited it is grace (cf. Rom. 4:4).

The difficulty with this view is that it ignores the Fall. Since humanity's Fall into sin, the natural person is able to do only evil, and thus, for his salvation, he depends entirely on God's converting, saving, justifying, and sanctifying grace.

(2) *Grace supplements people's own striving for good.* This is the view of semi-Pelagians and Roman Catholics, and in fact also of orthodox Jews. It differs from the previous view by acknowledging that fallen people do need the special grace of God. But it sees this grace as working together with a person's own striving of faith (synergism). If a person begins with faith, God answers with grace, by which the person's spirit is enlightened and his faith increased.

The difficulty with this view is that it ignores the total depravity of humanity, and thus presupposes something good in people with which God's grace could cooperate.

(3) *Grace comes equally to all fallen people.* This is the view of Arminians, Wesleyans (Methodists), and most Evangelicals.

---

59. Regarding the biblical notion of grace see extensively, Demarest (1997, 70–96).
60. Demarest (1997, 50–69); of his six views, I omitted only that of Vatican II.

According to this view, Christ died for all people, and God in his grace wholeheartedly offers salvation to all people, without any distinction. The only reason why some do not receive salvation is that they themselves consciously reject it. In contrast with the previous two views, this view acknowledges the total depravity of humanity. Yet, it considers people to be able to accept God's grace.

In the latter point lies the difficulty of this view: if human nature is indeed totally corrupt, how can it do a good work, namely, accept God's salvation?

(4) *Grace is identical with Jesus Christ*. This is the view of Karl Barth and his followers. In this view, Christ at the cross has removed human hostility, so that people are now open for God and his grace. Here, election involves the covenant of grace that God has made with all humanity. Christ himself is the wonder of grace; according to Barth, he is the actual content of election and covenant. In contrast with the previous views, Barth rejects every form of synergism. Salvation is pure grace of God; there is nothing of people in it. It is also irresistible.

This latter point constitutes the difficulty of this position, since it views salvation in a universalist way; ultimately this leads to total universalism (in the end all people will be saved).

(5) *Grace expresses itself in two ways: as general grace for all people, and as special grace for the elect.* This is generally the view of Augustine, Luther, Calvin, and Calvinism. Here, too, as we will see extensively, humanity is viewed as totally depraved, and special (i.e., redemptive) grace as irresistible; all notions of synergism are rejected. The great difference with Barth is that, in opposition to his universalism, it defends particularism: only those who have been elected from eternity will share in redemptive grace, whereas the others have been reprobated from eternity.

The main difficulties with this view are that (a) in the end it does not seem to leave much room for human responsibility, and (b) Scripture does not teach a decree of reprobation from eternity.

The most important points that have been enumerated here will be dealt with extensively in the rest of this book.

Chapter 2
The Counsel of God

> *And we know that for those who love God*
> *all things work together for good,*
> *for those who are called according to his purpose.*
> *For those whom he foreknew*
> *he also predestined to be conformed to the image of his Son,*
> *in order that he might be the firstborn among many brothers.*
> *And those whom he predestined he also called,*
> *and those whom he called he also justified,*
> *and those whom he justified he also glorified.*
>
> Romans 8:28–30

Summary: *In agreement with the general thesis of this book, we first must see that there are both eternal and non-eternal decrees of God; the Bible gives us examples of both. I disagree here with several Reformed expositors and dogmaticians. God's temporal decrees are inseparable from his ways, and these are inseparable from human choices and decisions, as Scripture clearly shows. God can even "regret" his earlier ways, and believers can "hasten" the coming day of the Lord. Another question is whether all God's eternal decrees are "in Christ," or whether some of them have to do with God's general* *providence only; this is related to the theological problem of common grace. Perhaps the most difficult problem involves the relationship between God's eternal counsel and human sin. If everything is included in God's counsel, must we say that he also decreed the Fall? And if not, how do we distinguish God's counsel from human freedom and responsibility? Reformed authors do not agree among themselves; some have proposed the solution of compatibilism. The Open Theistic response is not satisfactory either because it denies to a certain extent God's foreknowledge of events. The challenge that comes to Viatorism is to maintain both God's sovereign predestination and his perfect foreknowledge, as well as human freedom of will.*

2.1 Is God's Counsel Eternal?
2.1.1 Eternal Decrees

IN CHAPTER 1, I MADE a number of introductory remarks about the counsel of God (*decretum Dei*) by way of a preliminary orientation. Let us now enter somewhat more deeply into the many questions surrounding this complicated subject, such as: Is God's counsel eternal? Has all that ever occurs been decreed by God from eternity? Is all of God's counsel "in Christ"? How does God's counsel relate to sin?

A first question that arises is whether all the things that in Scripture are assigned to the counsel of God involve *eternal* decrees of God. The answer to this question is of great importance for a further elaboration of our distinction between the eternal-transcendent counsel of God (present chapter) and the temporal-immanent-historical ways of God (chapter 4).

The following passages speak explicitly of the *eternal* counsel of God, including those in which the prefix "pre-" is used (Gr. *pro*, especially in *prohorizō*, "to predestine"; Latin *prae*, especially in *praedestinare*, "to predestine"). In general, *pro-* or *prae-* refers to the eternality of God's counsel; "pre" is then identical with "before the foundation of the world" (cf. John 17:24; Eph. 1:4; 1 Pet. 1:20; Rev. 13:8). For example: "[T]ruly in this city there were gathered together against your holy servant Jesus, . . . both Herod and Pontius Pilate, along with the

Gentiles and the peoples of Israel, to do whatever your hand and your plan had *predestined* to take place" (Acts 4:27–28; cf. 2:23). "For those whom he foreknew he also *predestined* to be conformed to the image of his Son, ... [T]hose whom he *predestined* he also called" (Rom. 8:29–30). Of the "vessels of mercy" it is said that God had "prepared" them "beforehand for glory" (9:23); "prepared beforehand" is one word: *proētoimasen* (cf. v. 11: ". . . in order that God's *purpose* [Gr. *prothesis*] of election might continue, not because of works but because of him who calls").

Paul says, "[W]e impart a secret and hidden wisdom of God, which God decreed before the ages [*prohōrisen pro tōn aiōnōn*] for our glory" (1 Cor. 2:7, *pro* appears twice). "[H]e chose [*exelexato*, elected] us in him before [*pro*] the foundation of the world, . . . he predestined [*prohorisas*] us for adoption as sons through Jesus Christ, according to the purpose [*eudokia*] of his will" (Eph. 1:4–5, again, *pro* appears twice). "In him we have obtained an inheritance, having been predestined [*prohoristhentes*] according to the purpose [*prothesis*] of him who works all things according to the counsel [*boulē*] of his will" (v. 11, again, *pro* appears twice; also cf. "purposed" [*proetheto*] in v. 9). "[T]hrough the church the manifold wisdom of God" is "made known . . . according to the *eternal purpose* [*prothesis tōn aiōnōn*] that he has realized in Christ Jesus our Lord" (Eph. 3:10–11). Paul speaks of God's "own *purpose* [*prothesis*] and grace, which he gave us in Christ Jesus *before the ages began* [lit., "before the times of the ages," JUB, YLT]" (2 Tim. 1:9), and of the "hope of eternal life, which God, who never lies, promised *before the ages began* [lit., "before the times of the ages," JUB]" (Titus 1:2). Acts 15:18 speaks of things "known from of old [*ap' aiōnos*, "from eternity," NKJV, WEB]."

2.1.2 Non-Eternal Decrees

Now the question arises whether *every* decree of God is necessarily an eternal decision, that is, a decision made from eternity. I believe this is not the case. A decree from eternity is necessarily a decree made before the foundation of the world (Gr. *pro kataboles kosmou*); I already mentioned "[H]e chose us in him before the foundation of the world" (Eph. 1:4). The Son was loved by the Father "before the foundation of the world" (John 17:14), the Lamb was "foreknown before the foundation of the world" (1 Pet. 1:20), and the names of the elect were "written before the foundation of the world in the book of life of the Lamb" (Rev. 13:8). In all these cases we are dealing with matters that were true, or decreed, from eternity, just as in the expressions *pro tōn aiōnōn* ("before the ages," i.e., "before all eternity," 1 Cor. 2:7), *pro pantos tou aiōnos* ("before all eternity," Jude 25), and *pro chronōn aiōniōn* ("before times of ages," 2 Tim. 1:9; Titus 1:2), and also *apo tōn aiōnōn* ("from the ages," i.e., "from all eternity," Eph. 3:9; Col. 1:26), *ap' aiōnos* ("from eternity," Acts 15:18), and *ek tou aiōnos* ("from eternity," John 9:32).

However, there are also decrees that explicitly date *from* the foundation of the world (Gr. *apo kataboles kosmou*), that is, they began with creation, and thus apparently were not part of God's eternal counsel. For instance, the kingdom of God was "prepared *from* the foundation of the world" (Matt. 25:34). This is essentially different from "prepared *before* the foundation of the world"; the former is in time, the latter is from eternity (see, e.g., Rom. 9:23, "prepared beforehand for glory"). In my view, the word "prepared" refers to the counsel of God—but apparently this counsel is not always an eternal counsel. The "prepared" of Matthew 25:34 is just as embedded in time as the matters mentioned elsewhere: "the blood of all the prophets, shed from the foundation of the world," that is, from the beginning of history (Luke 11:50); "his works were finished from the foundation of the world," that is, from the week of creation (Heb. 4:3); ". . . for then he [i.e., Christ] would have had to suffer repeatedly since [*apo*] the foundation of the world," that is, since the earliest days of the universe (9:26).

Not everyone accepts this exegetical distinction between

pro and *apo*, though. Thus, Friedrich Hauck asserts that *apo* (instead of *pro*!) *katabolēs kosmou* expresses the eternity of the divine plan of redemption, which was conceived before all ages and was fulfilled in the end time.[1] In his view, the phrase *pro katabolēs kosmou* expresses the pre-temporality of the divine action. In this way, the difference between *before* and *since* the world began is eliminated.

Hans-Helmut Esser did seem to make the distinction mentioned by saying that, when God's free activity is dated before this point in time, that is, the foundation of the world (*pro katabolēs kosmou*), the intention is to testify that God's providence is independent of the absolute beginning that he himself determined, and is independent of history[2] — apparently in contrast with *apo katabolēs kosmou*. William Vine distinguished the two expressions as well, and says that the *pro* expressions (apparently other than the *apo* expressions) look back to past eternity.[3] *Apo* refers to the beginning of time, *pro* to what was before time (as we know it).

William Kelly claimed that our election "*before* the foundation of the world" (Eph. 1:4) implies, in contrast with "*since* the foundation," an election independent of creation and history.[4] It is in connection with the latter that the blessed Gentiles will have their share in the earthly kingdom (Matt. 25:34). The *church's* share is rather with the Creator instead of with creation. Her having been elected *before* the world began also means that she is viewed apart from this world. The present creation may pass, but the church's position and blessings are connected with the Creator himself, who created all things. Apparently, Kelly meant that the kingdom of God, even though it will endure forever, is embedded in time and history, just like God's counsel concerning this kingdom. But the position of the church, as having been made one with the

---

1. *TDNT* 3:620.
2. *NIDNTT* 1:377; see also 378.
3. Vine (1952, 128).
4. Kelly (1896, 529).

glorified Christ, is outside time, with regard to both the eternal counsel regarding this position, and this position itself.

Because of the frequent identification of "from/since" and "before the foundation of the world," we understand how the ESV in Revelation 13:8 could make the mistake of rendering *apo* as "before" instead of "from/since": "[A]ll who dwell on earth will worship it [i.e., the beast], everyone whose name has not been written before [read: since] the foundation of the world in the book of life of the Lamb who was slain." The parallel in Revelation 17:8 has been rendered correctly. The passages are implicitly saying that the names of some *have* been written "in the book of life since the foundation of the world." Because of the "since," this seems to suggest that all those who come to faith are enrolled in this book. This presentation is different from, for instance, Ephesians 1:4, which refers to God's eternal body of people, dating from before the present world began, and lasting even after the present world will have ended. It is a nation that is part of time and history — how else could we speak of church history? — and at the same time is from before, and beyond, time and history.

2.1.3 Other Examples

There are other examples of divine decrees that are not eternal, and are perhaps less controversial. Think of the decree concerning the seven plentiful years and the seven years of famine in Egypt: "And the doubling of Pharaoh's dream means that the thing is fixed by God, and God will shortly bring it about" (Gen. 41:32). I see no reason whatsoever to think here of an eternal decree; the fourteen years are part of God's ways with Egypt (and Israel). This is also true regarding the decrees concerning temporary judgments on Israel and the nations: "Destruction is decreed, overflowing with righteousness. For the Lord GOD of hosts will make a full end, as decreed, in the midst of all the earth" (Isa. 10:22–23; cf. 14:24–27). "For this the earth shall mourn, and the heavens above be dark; for I have spoken; I have purposed; I have not relented, nor will I turn back" (Jer. 4:28; cf. 51:12). "And on the wing of abominations shall come one who makes desolate, until the decreed end is poured out on the desolator" (Dan. 9:27; cf. 11:36). "Gather together, yes, gather, O shameless nation, before the decree takes effect—before the day passes away like chaff—before there comes upon you the burning anger of the LORD, before there comes upon you the day of the anger of the LORD" (Zeph. 2:1-2).

Some other arrangements by God are not necessarily from eternity, either, such as what he decreed about Job: "What he [i.e., God] desires, that he does. For he will complete what he appoints for me, and many such things are in his mind" (Job 23:13-14). These appointed things were part of God's *ways* with Job. Why (other than from Calvinist prejudice) must we assume that they were decreed about him from all eternity? God foreknew from eternity that this was going to happen to Job. But this foreknowledge does not necessarily mean foreordination.

It is the same with the Father's good pleasure: "I praise You, Father, Lord of heaven and earth, because You have hidden these things from the wise and learned and revealed them to infants. Yes, Father, because this was Your good pleasure [one word: *eudokia*]" (Matt. 11:25-26 HCSB; ESV: ". . . for such was your gracious will [or, so it pleased you well]"). In Ephesians 1:5 ("according to the good pleasure of His will," NKJV) and 9 ("according to His good pleasure"), *eudokia* refers unequivocally to God's eternal decree. However, in Matthew 11:26 this is not necessarily the case; I suggest that here we are instead dealing with the "good pleasure" of God's *ways* with the wise and learned as well as infants.

Another example is Judas' election: "Did I not choose you, the Twelve? And yet one of you is a devil" (John 6:7), or Paul's predestination: "The God of our fathers appointed [Gr. *proecheirisato*] you to know his will, to see the Righteous One and to hear a voice from his mouth" (Acts 22:14). Why would all God's choosing of his servants (both those who turn out to be devils and the good servants) necessarily have to go back to God's eternal decrees? This is self-evident only to those who have decided *a priori* that everything that God decrees must necessarily have been decreed from eternity. One argument could be that God — in spite of Open Theism — *foreknows* everything that will ever occur, including the decrees that he himself would make within time and history in response to human deeds. But this does not necessarily mean that the decisions themselves were also made from eternity. God may *foreknow* all the ways that he will take with humanity, but this does not turn these temporal ways into eternal decrees.

Another example of God's temporal decisions are the many answers to prayers, especially those cases in which God seems to have changed his mind (see §§8.2-8.4 below). The very notion of God "changing his mind" is already a disruption of hyper-Calvinist decretalism, as we will see.

Again, in terms of God's choice of his servants, Peter said, "Brothers, you know that in the early days God made a choice among you, that by my mouth the Gentiles should hear the word of the gospel and believe" (Acts 15:7). "In the early days" is Gr. *aph' hēmerōn archaiōn*, "from the days of old" (MOUNCE; cf. DLNT, YLT). This is not necessarily "from eternity"; this phrase refers far more likely to the earliest days of Jesus' ministry.[5] In all these cases, only the decretalist prejudice concerning the eternity of God's counsel insists that whenever the terms "decree" or "purpose" occur, they refer to eternal decrees, whereas, in my view, the context often does not demand this at all.

2.2 All Things Decreed by God from Eternity?
2.2.1 Heyns, Bavinck, Schilder

The question whether every decree of God was established from eternity is connected with a very fundamental question that touches upon our entire discussion. It is the question

---

5. Boyd (2000, 167).

whether all that has happened, happens, and will happen has been—not only foreknown but—decreed by God. In other words, are *all* things that ever happen fixed from eternity in the counsel of God? Yes, said Augustine, and Calvin after him, and many others in their wake. The matter is of the greatest importance, both for all theological thinking and for the practice of faith. We therefore will come back to this point extensively, especially when we enter further into the significant distinction between the counsel and the ways of God (§2.6, and chapter 4).

At this point, however, we must state the problem. If God has decreed everything that ever occurs, not only the things he himself does but also all the things people do, how can we avoid making God *responsible* for all the things people do, not only good things but also many bad things? We will return repeatedly to this problem. At this point, we are concentrating on a corollary issue: Is it true that all that happens (a) has been decreed by God, (b) from all eternity?

As we will see, it is only on the basis of certain prejudices that many believe every decree of God must necessarily be an eternal decree (see further in §3.1). Thus, Reformed dogmatician Johan Heyns says, on the one hand, "World history runs according to a program already established, so that every form of arbitrariness or coincidence is totally excluded."[6] On the other hand, he adds, apparently to avoid the appearance of a full-blown decretalism: "In the course of time, God not only executes decrees that had been made already; he is also busy making plans and carrying them out." That is, Heyns' answer to (a) is Yes, and to (b) is No.

The great Reformed dogmatician Herman Bavinck acknowledged: "In the Old Testament these two realities [of election and reprobation] are not described as eternal decrees but face us on every page as facts in history."[7] In other words, it is we who infer from these facts the eternal decrees

---
6. Heyns (1988, 73–74).
7. Bavinck (*RD* 2:343).

of election and reprobation. Nevertheless, his answer to both (a) and (b) is Yes.

Reformed theologian Klaas Schilder spoke of God's plan "as it *imposes itself every moment in time upon the created things* ... *and thus occurs every moment,* ... *and is actual, in* and simultaneously *with* the facts of historical life."[8] That is, we *see* God's plans working in time, we *infer* their eternal origin. The inevitable question posed by Viatorism is: On what basis do we infer this?

2.2.2 Velema and Venema

In connection with the latter statement by Schilder, Willem Velema said, God's decree "is not a set of specifications that once established, awaits implementation.... Schilder points out correctly that God continues to decree his eternal purpose every moment and continuously."[9] Now this seems to me not precisely the same as what Heyns means to say. Just like the eternal generation of the Son is thought of as being *from* eternity, but also as going on eternally, Schilder and Velema apparently want to say that God's decrees are *from* eternity, and at the same time are made continually. However, Heyns emphasizes the fact that God, as part of his ways with the world, continually makes *new* plans. This is an interesting view; we will have to investigate how it fits into classical Calvinism. (Actually, we should keep saying: Augustinianism; but it is undoubtedly in Calvinism that Augustine's views live on most purely and powerfully.)

Reformed theologian Henk Venema went still further:

> I believe the counsel of God is no fore-programming, not the establishment of a fixed and rigid program, in which beforehand, that is, before the foundation of the world or before the creation of heaven and earth, it has been laid down how the entire human history and also the history of each nation, yes, even of

---

8. Schilder (1947, 3:134).
9. Van Genderen and Velema (2008, 195).

every person in particular, will take place in all its details. Rather, in his counsel God occupies himself with what occurs in the world, especially in the human world. He intervenes in this.[10]

Here, the idea of an eternal counsel — at least an eternal counsel that involves all things that ever happen — has in fact been abandoned. This is rather striking for a Reformed theologian. Venema does not think that a passage as explicit as Acts 2:23 (Jesus was "delivered by [i.e., because of, on the basis of] the determinate counsel and foreknowledge of God," KJV) necessarily refers to an eternal decree.[11] No wonder, since he sees *nowhere* any reference to an eternal decree, not even in passages such as Ephesians 1:4.[12] Venema is a veritable reactionary theologian: if classical Reformed dogmatics views *everything* within an eternal decree of God, Venema wishes to view *nothing* within it. In my view, both extreme views are mistaken.

2.3 Temporal Decrees
2.3.1 Exodus 33

An interesting example of a decree of God that he has clearly made within time is Exodus 33:5. After Israel's sin with the golden calf and Moses' pleading, God says here, "So now take off your ornaments, that I may know what to do with you." Here, the Lord announces a decree that he apparently has yet to make; this is because an entirely new situation has occurred. God's thought is not: I always knew what you all would do, and from eternity my reply to this was prepared — but: You have acted against my will, so now I have to deliberate with myself as to how I will respond to this.

Such a statement must be taken seriously. It cannot be dismissed with the argument (serving to rescue one's own theory) that God's reply is merely an anthropomorphism. Even if for some reason we would have to view God's words as anthropomorphic, they must have a meaning. If we conclude

---
10. Venema (1992, 89); Berkouwer (1960, 148–49).
11. Venema (1992, 90).
12. Venema (1992, chapter 14).

from these words that God still has to make up his mind, we are in line with the purport of his own declaration. If we maintain that God had already made up his mind from eternity, we let him say here the opposite of what he actually means. We will find more examples of this phenomenon: people making a Bible passage say the opposite of what it does say, just to rescue their theological paradigm.

Of course, we would go to the other extreme if we asserted that God was totally surprised by the situation, as if he had had no idea that a thing like this could ever have happened. As we will see, this will constantly be the challenge for us: to find the middle path between two extremes. On the one hand, we are dealing with a far-fetched decretalism, in which all things that happen — good and evil — have been planned by God himself from eternity. On the other hand, we face an alternative view in which God lacks foreknowledge and can be continually surprised by new twists of history. To some extent, finding this middle path is the central and comprehensive task of the present book.

2.3.2 Ezekiel 20

Another striking example of a decree embedded in time, made after God apparently had other thoughts in his mind, is Ezekiel 20:8-10:

> [T]hey rebelled against me and were not willing to listen to me. None of them cast away the detestable things their eyes feasted on, nor did they forsake the idols of Egypt. Then I said I would pour out my wrath upon them and spend my anger against them in the midst of the land of Egypt. But I acted for the sake of my name, that it should not be profaned in the sight of the nations among whom they lived, in whose sight I made myself known to them in bringing them out of the land of Egypt. So I led them out of the land of Egypt and brought them into the wilderness.

Notice what happens here. When Israel in Egypt had become

apostate, God first said he would destroy the nation. But for his name's sake he came to another decision, and in his grace led his people out of Egypt: "I seriously considered inflicting my anger on them in force right there in Egypt. Then I thought better of it. I acted out of who I was, not by how I felt" (MSG). Again, this cannot be dismissed simply by explaining this as anthropomorphic speaking. I do not see how one could avoid the conclusion that either God lied the first time (knowing all the time what he was going to do), or he changed his mind (even if this does not fit into decretalist thinking).

In the wilderness, history repeated itself: Israel again became rebellious, God *considered* destroying them, but he did not do this for his name's sake (vv. 13–14). In verses 21–22 we find for the third time such a situation. If we take the words of Ezekiel 20 at all seriously, it is impossible to assume that God knew from eternity what he would do with Israel, or that he *decreed* how this entire history would unfold. Later we will see more extensively that one cannot rescue one's own theological paradigm by appealing to anthropomorphisms, certainly not if one makes these anthropomorphisms mean the opposite of what they actually say.

2.3.3 Ezekiel 33

Another example, again in Ezekiel, is found in 33:13–15:

> Though I say to the righteous that he shall surely live [Heb. *chayah yihyeh*], yet if he trusts in his righteousness and does injustice, none of his righteous deeds shall be remembered, but in his injustice that he has done he shall die. Again, though I say to the wicked, "You shall surely die [*mot tamut*]," yet if he turns from his sin and does what is just and right, . . . he shall surely live; he shall not die.

How does this fit into a decretalist view? How can God say to the righteous, "You shall *surely* live," and to the wicked, "You shall *surely* die," if God reckons beforehand with the possibility that the righteous may backslide, and the wicked may repent? Did he not *know*, yes, did he not *decree* that this righteous person either would live, or would backslide, and that this wicked person either would perish, or would repent and live?

In connection with this, notice this remarkable word: "[I]f anyone takes away from the words of the book of this prophecy, God will take away his share in the tree of life and in the holy city, which are described in this book" (Rev. 22:19). What does "his share" mean here? Apparently, the Lord is speaking here of the same kind of "righteous ones" as in Ezekiel 33: as long as they behave righteously, they have their God-given share (inheritance) in the tree of life and the holy city. But if these (supposed) righteous ones become apostate, these lose this share. The first striking thing is that in *both* cases (staying righteous or backsliding) God had assigned to them a share in the tree and the city. The second striking thing is that keeping or losing this share apparently depends not so much on God's counsel here but rather on the (un)faithfulness of the person. Elsewhere I have investigated the matter of what consequences this may have for the (im)possibility of true believers becoming apostate.[13]

2.3.4 God's Relenting

Very remarkable is the biblical speaking about God's "relenting" (see more extensively §4.5.2 below). Henry Ellison has pointed out that this relenting occurs both when evil things and when good things have to be eliminated.[14] A beautiful example is Jeremiah 18:7–10:

> If at any time I declare concerning a nation or a kingdom, that I will pluck up and break down and destroy it, and if that nation, concerning which I have spoken, turns from its evil, I will *relent* of the disaster that I intended to do to it. And if at any time I declare concerning a nation or a kingdom that I will build and plant it, and if it does evil in my sight, not listening to my voice,

---

13. See extensively, Ouweneel (EDR 4, §§12.1–12.2).
14. Ellison (1985, 383–84).

then I will *relent* of the good that I had intended to do to it.

Here we encounter the same thought that we find in Ezekiel 33 and Revelation 22: the righteous person who becomes apostate will perish after all; the wicked person who repents will be saved after all. God relents regarding both the evil that he had announced for the wicked person who later repents, and the good that he had announced for the righteous person who later backslides. Notice that in both cases the future takes place in a way different from what God had first announced. Only because of decretalist prejudices can one assert, against the gist of this passage, that God knew, and even decreed, everything beforehand.

Again, notice what is happening here. On the one hand, some theologians know for sure that God has decreed everything that occurs from eternity, *although the Bible nowhere says so*. On the other hand, these same theologians tell us that God's relenting (regretting, changing his mind) is just an anthropomorphism, which we must not take literally, *although the Bible explicitly tells us that God often relents*, and does other things than he had originally announced. Things are claimed that are never claimed by the Bible, and things that the Bible does claim are argued away—and all this to rescue one's own theological system.

2.3.5 Hastening God's Day

Very striking is 2 Peter 3:12, ". . . waiting for and hastening [Gr. *speudontas*] the coming of the day of God." There is no doubt about it that the second verb means "to hasten." Thus, the verse apparently says that, through believers' faithfulness, the coming of the day of God can be accelerated.[15] Of course, this does not fit at all into the decretalist depiction of things, according to which the day of God has been fixed from eternity in the counsel of God. As a consequence, translators committed to a decretalist system refuse to translate what the

---

15. See *NIDNTT* 2:245–46.

text says: "earnestly desiring the coming of the day of God" (ASV; cf. ERV, ICB, JUB, WEB), "hasting unto the coming of the day of the Lord" (KJV; cf. DRA, GNV). Interestingly, NKJV corrects the KJV here. The NIV has ". . . look forward to the day of God and speed its coming." The GNT: "do our best to make it come soon" (cf. CEV, NLV, WE).

For this reason, one should not conclude from Mark 13:32 that the Father has decreed from eternity the day and the hour of Jesus' parousia.[16] Jesus does not say anything more than that the Father alone has the *authority* to determine that day and that hour, as is clear from Acts 1:7, "It is not for you to know times or seasons that the Father has fixed by his own authority." The Father can and may decide when the right moment has come, and this may be partially dependent on the faithfulness of believers, who can hasten the coming of that day. In the same vein, through their testimony they influence the time when the entire world will have been acquainted with the gospel (Matt. 24:14), and the "fullness of the Gentiles" will have come in (Rom. 11:25).

In this context, Psalm 31:15 is of interest: "My times are in your hand." Others have, "My future" (CEB, GW, etc.), or "My life" (CEV, ERV, etc.), or "You determine my destiny" (NET), or "I give the moments of my life over to You" (VOICE). Is it true that God influences a person's destiny? Of course it is. However, this does not necessarily mean that from eternity he has determined it entirely, or that a person's actions play no role at all, or that the "time" for every event in a person's life has been fixed beforehand.

2.3.6 Advice

In §§4.3–4.5 below, we will encounter many more examples of uncertainties that have been built into our future, not only on our side, but also on God's side. The fact that, at any rate, not every counsel of God can be eternal, follows, as I see it, from the fact that the term sometimes simply has the meaning

---

16. Boyd (2000, 72–73).

that it still has in everyday parlance, namely, "advice." The word seems to have this meaning, for instance, in the following texts: "You guide me with your counsel" (Ps. 73:24). "But they soon forgot his works; they did not wait for his counsel" (106:13); "they had rebelled against the words of God, and spurned the counsel of the Most High" (107:11).

With reference to human counsel, this meaning is clearer, of course: "... the more part gave counsel to sail thence also" (Acts 27:12 YLT; cf. v. 21). Similar cases we find in the counsel (advice) of Ahithophel and Hushai (2 Sam. 16:15–17:14), and the counsel of Rehoboam's older and younger counselors (1 Kings 12:6, 9, 13–14). Also see the corresponding verb "to counsel," for instance in Psalm 32:8, "I will instruct you and teach you in the way you should go; I will counsel you with my eye upon you." In this meaning of the word, such counsel is inseparable from God's ways, and these are inseparable from human choices and decisions. A person wishes to choose P, and God advises him to pursue P, or rather to choose Q. Or a person does not know what to choose, and God advises him to choose R. Such advice given within time has nothing to do with God's eternal counsel.

2.4   Is God's Counsel "in Christ"?
2.4.1   Christocentrism

We now come to another vital question: Is the entire counsel of God Christocentric, or are there parts of God's counsel, for instance, those referring to the first creation, which do not presuppose the person of Christ, or the work of Christ?

Karl Barth wrote that, when the Old and the New Testament speak of what older theology called the divine decree, they are speaking directly or indirectly of Jesus Christ.[17] In his view, the one reality of the counsel of God becomes visible in Christ. Nothing of what belongs to God's counsel could be viewed apart from Jesus Christ. Everything that God wills is enclosed in this person. According to Barth, the *entire* counsel

---
17. Barth (1936, II/1:521–22; cf. II/2:91–93).

of God, also when dealing with purely cosmological aspects, is thoroughly Christocentric.

Herman Bavinck had no difficulty acknowledging that, already at the first creation, Christ had "both soteriological and cosmological significance. He is not only the mediator of re-creation but also of creation."[18] Thus, in his view, the plan of salvation is already included in the plan of creation. As he said, "The foundations of creation and redemption are the same. The Logos who became flesh [John 1:14] is the same by whom all things were made [v. 3]. The first-born from the dead [Col. 1:18] is also the first-born of every creature [v. 15]."[19]

The latter corresponds with Paul's statement: "For all the promises of God find their Yes in him. That is why it is through him that we utter our Amen to God for his glory" (2 Cor. 1:20). I see no reason to limit this verse to soteriological promises only, and not include cosmological promises as well. To give an example: a decree that seems to be typically linked with God's general providence, but not with redemption, is God's promise after Noah's flood: "While the earth remains, seedtime and harvest, cold and heat, summer and winter, day and night, shall not cease" (Gen. 8:22). However, this promise cannot be viewed apart from the "pleasing aroma" of Noah's burnt offering (v. 21), which, as is the case with all offerings, pointed to the sacrifice of Christ.

This finding has implications for understanding all those passages that speak of God's universal providence, such as: "In past generations he [i.e., God] allowed all the nations to walk in their own ways. Yet he did not leave himself without witness, for he did good by giving you rains from heaven and fruitful seasons, satisfying your hearts with food and gladness" (Acts 14:16–17). Or: God

---

18. Bavinck (*RD* 2:423).
19. Bavinck (1953, 27).

made from one man every nation of mankind to live on all the face of the earth, having determined allotted periods and the boundaries of their dwelling place, that they should seek God, and perhaps feel their way toward him and find him. Yet he is actually not far from each one of us, for "In him we live and move and have our being"; as even some of your own poets have said, "For we are indeed his offspring" (Acts 17:26–28).

None of this can be viewed apart from Christ and his work of atonement, even if this does not mean that all human beings will ultimately be saved.

2.4.2 Common Grace

This entire discussion is directly linked with the question whether not only redeeming grace, but also common grace—God's providential care for his creation—is Christocentric, and even a result of *salvation* in Christ.

It is typical of hyper-Calvinist author Henry Kersten that he deliberately seeks to separate common grace from Christ's work of atonement. I presume that this is because he cannot accept the thought that the work of Christ could bestow any good on the reprobate, even if this included only temporal blessings.[20] He is afraid that such an idea could lead to the doctrine of universal atonement, that is, the theory that Christ bore the sins of all people.[21] However, such an inference is not at all required. *All* promises, *all* manifestations of common grace, are not only "in Christ," but to some extent could not be separated from his work of redemption without leading inevitably to universal atonement.

Jesus himself said concerning this that he had accomplished the work that the Father had given him to do. As a consequence, the Father had given him "authority over *all* flesh," which he used to give eternal life to those given to him by the Father (John 17:1–5). However, these believers encom-

---

20. Kersten (1980, 1:73–74).
21. See Ouweneel (EDR 5, §12.2).

pass not *all* people, only part of the human race. The Father has given all judgment to the Son, which he uses to bring, on the one hand, "those who have done good to the resurrection of life, and," on the other hand, "those who have done evil to the resurrection of judgment" (5:22-29). It is not only *in spite of* his work that Jesus condemns the wicked, but also *on the basis of* his work that he has the power to do so (cf. 2 Cor. 5:10; Rev. 22:12). The eternal Father has given all judgment to the eternal Son because this Son has become the "Son of Man" (without ceasing to be the Son of God) (cf. John 5:22, 27). It is as the Son of Man that he has accomplished the work of redemption (Matt. 20:28), and on the basis of this work he will execute judgment upon *all humanity*, whether in view of eternal life, or of eternal death. Since Jesus' finished work, no dealings of God with humanity can be viewed apart from Christ and his work.

I quoted Bavinck earlier: he who is the "firstborn from the dead" (Col. 1:18; cf. Rev. 1:5) is also the "firstborn of all creation" (Col. 1:15). "In" Christ, "through" him, and "for" him all things were created (v. 16). In the eternal purpose of God, it was decreed "to unite all things in him [i.e., Christ], things in heaven and things on earth" (Eph. 1:10). Not only do believers find their final destination "in Christ," but unbelievers do as well. Also the apostate belong to the people whom "the Master bought" (2 Pet. 2:1) — not for their salvation (it says "bought," not "saved") but in order to obtain through his work on the cross a right to exercise authority over *all* people. (See also §5.8.2 below.)

2.4.3 Supra- and Infralapsarianism

One of the questions that has played a role in Calvinist debates involves whether Adam's Fall was presupposed in divine election (infralapsarianism), or not (supralapsarianism). I will return to this debate later (§§14.6-14.7). No matter how one answers this question, we can say that the counsel of God involves the well-being of the world. Even the supralapsarian position acknowledges that this well-being is, right from the start, inconceivable without Christ. Therefore, Hebrews 1:2 says first that God "appointed" his Son "the heir of all things," and only after this that he "through" this same Son "created the world," and subsequently made "purification for sins" (vv. 2-3). The text first states that in God's counsel, Christ was heir of the world, before the text speaks of its creation and redemption.

I add a little excursus here: the text may even be taken as an indication that the world was created, not only *in* [through] the Son, but even *for* the Son: he became heir of a world that still had to be created. In the Talmud we find this little discussion: "Rab said, 'The world was created only on David's account.' [That he might sing hymns and psalms to God.] [Rabbi] Samuel said, 'On Moses' account.' [That he might receive the Torah.] Rabbi Johanan said, 'For the sake of the Messiah.'"[22] To which we may add that both David and Moses were types of the Messiah, David as the greatest king, Moses as the greatest prophet. The world was created so that people would praise God (for which David laid the basis), and so that people would live by God's Torah (for which Moses laid the basis). But both towering figures found their culmination in the Messiah. We cannot imagine any eternal decree of God apart from the Messiah: "[T]he Son of God, Jesus Christ, . . . was not Yes and No, but in him it is always Yes. For all the promises of God find their Yes in him. That is why it is through him that we utter our Amen to God for his glory" (2 Cor. 1:19-20).

To return to our discussion of infra- and supralapsarianism: both thought systems speculate about a logical order in God's eternal decree. Supralapsarians view the decree of election and the decree of reprobation as logically prior to the Fall. God first decreed election and reprobation, then decreed the creation, then the Fall, then the incarnation of Christ and his work of redemption. In such a view, it is logically possible to

---

22. *BabT*: Sanhedrin 98b; also see the footnotes in the Soncino edition.

imagine the decrees of election and reprobation before Christ enters the picture. This will not do: it is *in Christ* that believers have been chosen before the foundation of the world (Eph. 1:4). Whatever logical and chronological orders people may invent within the counsel of God, Christ was the center of it from the very beginning, that is, from all eternity.

Lewis Sperry Chafer quoted Revelation 13:8 as follows: "... the book of the life of the Lamb that was slain from the foundation of the world" (JUB; cf. KJV, NIV, etc.). His view was that, whenever the cosmos had its beginning, a redeeming Lamb—even in the form of a divine anticipation—was an important feature of the divine purpose.[23] It could even be said: apart from what the redeeming Lamb has accomplished, God would not have created any cosmos in the first place.

Chafer calls the vast universe "redemptocentric"; that is, from its very beginning it has God's salvation in Christ as its center. God created the cosmos because in his mind he had a redeeming Lamb before him. From the very start, the world was Christocentric, not only because it was created through Christ, but also because, already then, God viewed it as redeemed by Christ. God created the world "in Christ" with the purposed end goal before his eyes as realized "in Christ" as well.

2.5 God's Counsel and Sin: The Decretalist View
2.5.1 The First View

In chapter 1, we discussed whether God's counsel is eternal and involves all that ever happens, and also the relationship between God's eternal counsel and Adam's Fall into sin. If God's counsel involves all events of all time, then it involves also the Fall. This is an issue with many problems and complications, which we must now probe a little further.

An example of the decretalist view is found in the Westminster Shorter Catechism (answer 7): "The decrees of God are, his eternal purpose, according to the counsel of his will,

---
23. Chafer (*ST* 2:237).

whereby, for his own glory, he hath foreordained whatsoever comes to pass"—apparently including Adam's Fall, and all further sins committed by people.

According to Greg Boyd, on a very fundamental level there are indeed only two views conceivable with respect to the counsel of God.[24] The *first* view implies that God consciously and deliberately designed a world that would grieve and oppose him. The *second* view (see §2.7 below) implies that God does *not* want to be grieved and opposed, and prefers a world without sin, yet created a world of people who *could* grieve and oppose him.

The consequence of the *first* view is that God's plan for the world entailed rebellion, sin and all its awfulness, for these are the things that grieve him. According to this doctrine, all things that happen, including the grossest sins, somehow belong to God's counsel. Augustine did not wish to go any further than that God's decree with respect to the Fall was a permissive decree, but even then the Fall is part of God's counsel.[25] Calvin says that God "govern[s] heaven and earth by his providence, he so regulates all things, that nothing happens without his deliberation," that "not only heaven and earth and the inanimate creatures, but also the plans and intentions of men, are so governed by his providence that they are borne by it straight to their appointed end. . . [and that] nothing is more absurd than that anything should happen without God's ordaining it," and that "whatever happens in the universe is governed by God's incomprehensible plans."[26]

Of course, this is the strong and harsh language so common during the sixteenth century, from Luther and other Reformers, as well as from their opponents. Yet it is condemnable. Consider this statement: "[T]here cannot be a greater absurdity than to hold that anything is done without the ordination of God." Not the *permission* of God, no, God's

---
24. Boyd (2001, 54).
25. Berkhof (1996, 118–25).
26. Calvin, *Institutes* 1.16.3, 1.16.8, and 1.17.2.

ordination. Not even the most heinous crime can be viewed apart from God's ordination. No wonder that, since then, many theologians have instead claimed the opposite: it is absurd to hold such a view!

The term "permission" is safer to work with, but then the question arises whether any permission can ever be part of God's eternal counsel. Arminius has denied that "allowing" is an aspect of God's decree, for God's decree involves his will, and in fact God permits things that he actually does not want. Or rather, interestingly enough, the *permissio* is neither a willing nor a non-willing of God.[27] He does not want P, but allows P, which in fact means that he does want P. He wants it insofar as P, which in itself is an undesirable evil, can help in realizing a higher goal that otherwise, without P, would have been unattainable, or at least much more difficult to attain.

2.5.2 Reformed Discord

In line with Augustine, Calvin, and the Westminster Shorter Catechism, Herman Bavinck says,

> The counsel of God is to be understood as his eternal plan for all that exists or will happen in time. Scripture everywhere assumes that all that is and comes to pass is the realization of God's thought and will and has its model and foundation in God's eternal counsel . . . .[28]

It is interesting to see how the word "everywhere" is used here. I would certainly agree that Scripture everywhere supposes that nothing of what is and occurs stands apart from God's thought and will, but, as far as I can see, Scripture *nowhere* suggests all that is and occurs "finds its example and foundation in God's *eternal counsel*" — on the contrary.

Therefore, in its absoluteness and extension, Bavinck's view is, to my mind, disastrous, even though he says, "Among Christians, accordingly, there can be no disagreement over

---
27. Verboom (2005, 33).
28. Bavinck (*RD* 2:372).

the existence of a divine counsel."[29] He even says, "Now, Reformed theologians all agree that sin and its punishment are willed and determined by God"[30]—that is, including evil (even though he acknowledges, of course, that evil as such is against the will of God). And a bit later: "The fall, sin, and eternal punishment are included in the divine decree and in a sense willed by God, but then always only in a certain sense and not in the same manner as grace and blessedness"[31]—not because of sin as such, which to him is an abomination, but as a means to a goal.

However, even among the Reformed, opinions differ on the matter. Thus, Henk Venema said about "the doctrine that God in his eternal counsel has arranged and determined everything": "[T]hus it is not possible to keep God free from the responsibility for the origin and existence of sin, and for the presence of distress and misery in the world."[32] Reformed theologian Jan Hoek summarizes Calvin's paradoxical position this way: "Thus, humanity falls [into sin] while God's providence ordains it this way; but it falls by its own fault,"[33] and then continues in a somewhat cryptic way: "At this extremely difficult point, thinking within dogmatic development after Calvin has never come to a rest. Would we ever get any further than Paul's cry in Romans 11:33, 'Oh, the depth of the riches and wisdom and knowledge of God! How unsearchable are his judgments and how inscrutable his ways!'?" Later he says, "[I]nwardly, we keep having great difficulty with every connection between God and sin."[34]

Over against all this prudence, I am astonished by the following sentence in the document of the Dutch Reformed Church in the Netherlands on election: "[L]ooking at the cross

---

29. Ibid.
30. Bavinck (*RD* 2:387).
31. Bavinck (*RD* 2:389).
32. Venema (1992, 24).
33. Hoek (1988, 29).
34. Hoek (1988, 67).

of Christ, we strengthen ourselves in the belief that human guilt and hardening, too, have been included in God's eternal counsel."[35]

2.5.3 Compatibilism

The doctrine that all events have been decreed by God, including Adam's Fall, has sometimes been referred to as *compatibilism*. This view sees this doctrine as compatible with the notion of human moral responsibility.[36] Compatibilism is a term for a special form of decretalism, namely, that form which tries to account for human responsibility. It is nevertheless a form of decretalism because it maintains that all events have been determined (decreed, decided) by God beforehand. Henry Kersten rejected the term "determinism" because of the (supposed) compatibility mentioned.[37] But Henk Venema rightly wrote: God "does not teach us that people are entirely bound by the decree of God made over them, *and* that they, at the same time, are free to make their own decisions. Therefore, maintaining that God has decided and arranged everything beforehand, the eternal destiny of people and also all their deeds, their deliberating and speaking, in this way eliminates people's responsibility."[38] So compatibilism is decretalism, after all. Where the eternal God and his eternal decree "coincide," "we are in the middle of determinism, in which a large part of the church has indeed ended up," said Reformed theologian Jan Gerrit Woelderink.[39]

I refer to this decretalism as hyper-Calvinistic (or ultra-Reformed), and leave aside the issue of the extent to which this view in fact represents the true, authentic, original doctrine of Calvin, or a later, extreme variety of it. Rather, I conclude — with satisfaction — that many Calvinist theologians have tried to develop a milder, more balanced position, and yet view

---

35. Hervormde Kerk (1962, 19).
36. Ibid.
37. Kersten (1980, 1:117).
38. Venema (1992, 23); also see Berkouwer (1960, 10–12, 25–27).
39. Woelderink (1951, 20).

themselves as full Calvinists (also see chapters 10–14 below).

Some outspoken hyper-Calvinists were not ashamed to explicitly apply the term "decretalism" to their viewpoint.[40] It is therefore significant that Louis Berkhof felt compelled to write: "Reformed [i.e., Calvinist] theology stands practically alone in its emphasis on the doctrine of the decrees"[41] — especially in the stark form in which Berkhof himself defended it. With this remark, he did not intend to disclose a weakness of Reformed doctrine on this point, but rather to indicate how mistaken other theologies are. Inadvertently he does hint at this weakness by quoting the American Lutheran Charles Krauth, who believed that (hyper-)Calvinism is an attempt to escape first Pelagianism, and later Arminianism. In other words, (hyper-)Calvinism might be, to some extent, *reaction theology*, that is, a theology that, in combating one extreme view, runs the danger of falling into the opposite extreme view.

In addition, allow me to refer here to what Reformed theologian Gerrit Berkouwer had to say about real decretalism; this would be a view that supposedly would go much further than the idea that God himself has foreordained all that happens. Berkouwer saw as one important symptom of what he called "determinism" (what we are calling "decretalism") the teaching of election and reprobation as entirely parallel because of the single causality of double predestination. This, in his view, would go entirely against the Canons of Dordt (see further §10.7.1 below).[42] This may be so, but I see no reason to limit the term "decretalism" to the latter view. The term merely expresses the fact that certain people believe that *all* events have been determined by God. Such people are decretalists. The fact that they often emphasize that they do not wish to undermine human responsibility does not change this at all. If a person believes that God decreed the Fall he is a

---

40. Woelderink (1951, 20).
41. Berkhof (1996, 100).
42. Berkouwer (1960, 180).

decretalist, no matter how much he may emphasize the fact that Adam and Eve were fully responsible for it, and that it was their choice to fall into sin. (This leaves unanswered the question about how the first responsibility of the first humans can be *reconciled* with the notion that God from eternity had *decreed* that they would fall.)

2.6 Problems with Decretalism
2.6.1 The Father's Will

It is important to understand what decretalism really entails. The difficulty with decretalism is not the claim that God's counsel concerns everything, involves "all things" — for this seems self-evident to me as well.[43] I cannot imagine that anything could ever happen apart from God's will. However, the term "decretalism" entails far more. God is not only *involved* in all things that occur, but supposedly he has *decreed* all that occurs, in the active-causative meaning of the verb "to decree" (to determine, to decide). Here I quote Augustine again (cf. §1.5.3), who said that even what goes against God's will (*contra voluntatem Dei*) does not occur apart form his will (*praeter voluntatem Dei*).[44] But that is something else than saying that, for instance, God has actively *wanted* the Fall, and thus indirectly even *caused* it.

The connection between "decreeing" and "causing" is important here. People may argue: God decreed the Fall, but Satan (or Adam and Eve) caused the Fall. But if God decreed the Fall, then the Fall *must* happen, whatever Satan, Adam or Eve may have wished or done. If a king decrees a hanging, what is the point of saying that *he* decreed it, but the hangman *caused* the hanging? Who is responsible for the hanging: the king or the hangman? If language means anything, decreeing means (fore)ordaining, deciding, determining that a thing must, and will, occur. The person who decrees *is always responsible for what he decrees*, not the person who executes the decree.

---

43. Cf. ibid.
44. *Enchiridion* 100.

Once we surrender the claim that God has *decreed* everything, then he may be compared to an all-seeing king who does not decree everything that happens in his kingdom but who *is* involved in the sense that things happen with his allowing them. This implies that there may be things that he actually does not want—let alone that he would have *decreed* them—but yet, for some purpose, he allows them (for instance, to expose certain opponents). If he decrees an event, he is responsible for it. If he merely allows an event, he is not responsible for it. If God *decreed* the Fall, not only are Satan, Adam, and Eve responsible for it, but God is as well. However, if God merely *allowed* the Fall, then Satan, Adam, and Eve are responsible for it, but not God.

A practical illustration of the underlying problem consists of the translation of Matthew 10:29, which is a key verse for decretalism: "Are not two sparrows sold for a penny? And not one of them will fall to the ground apart from your Father." Some translations render the last phrase as "without your Father," or somewhat freely "without your Father knowing it" (ICB, ERV, etc.). But others render it: "without your Father's consent" (CJB, GNT, etc.) or "permission" (GW, ISV, etc.), or even "without your Father's will" (AMP, EXB note, NET, NKJV, RSV, WEB).[45] Without any basis, the will of God is introduced into the translation, in line with the Calvinist view: it is God who *causes* the sparrow to fall. So also the Heidelberg Catechism (Q&A 1): God "watches over me in such a way that not a hair can fall from my head without the *will* of my Father in heaven."

The parallel verse, Luke 21:6, discloses the real meaning: "Are not five sparrows sold for two pennies? And not one of them is forgotten before God."[46] God does not *cause* certain sparrows to fall, but he is concerned with falling sparrows. No sparrow falls to the ground without God falling with them, as it were, suffering with them (cf. Isa. 63:9, "In all their affliction

---

45. Cf. the negative comment by König (2006, 480–81).
46. Cf. Ouweneel (2004, 74–75).

he [i.e., God] was afflicted"). Also the context in Matthew 10 points in this direction: the disciples had to go and preach, without worrying about their adversaries, because the Father himself would take care of his children. The entire passage is a beautiful illustration of Augustine's statement just quoted: God does not *want* sparrows to fall — or his children to be hurt — but if that happens, it does not happen apart from him either. He is always involved in some mysterious way.

2.6.3 Calvin's Trap

From his radical decretalist standpoint, Calvin wrote:

> ... And it ought not to seem absurd for me to say that God not only foresaw the fall of the first man, and in him the ruin of his descendants, but also meted it out in accordance with his own decision. For as it pertains to his wisdom to foreknow everything that is to happen, so it pertains to his might to rule and control everything by his hand.[47]

Notice how weak this argument is. God has the power to rule all events, so he must also have decreed all events! A textbook *non sequitur*. P has the power to do X, so P will do X. This argument is invalid.

Elsewhere Calvin even says that people were created weak and liable to fall,[48] so that apparently they *had to* fall. Does this fit with the Bible's statement that all that God had created was "very good" (Gen. 1:31)?[49] But even more importantly, does this not make God *(co)responsible* for the Fall? Greg Boyd says that, if a person unleashes a mad dog that he knows will bite someone, he is responsible for its behavior.[50] Similarly, if God lets out into the world people he knows will sin, is he not (co-)responsible for such behavior? Why — one might add — create such people in the first place? If it is worse to be in hell than never to have been born (cf. Matt. 26:24),

---

47. Calvin, *Institutes* 3.23.7.
48. Calvin (1989, 273).
49. Hughes (1989, 166).
50. Ibid.

would not a perfectly loving God refrain from creating people he knew with certainty would end up there? If God really does not wish that any should perish (2 Pet. 3:9), why then create people he knows *will* perish? Yes, I add, people whom decretalists assert God had *decreed* to perish?

Indeed, in the broadest sense of the word one will have to say that God is to a certain extent responsible for what happens in his creation because he created it with all the risks of failure involved, and all the suffering that has resulted from those failures. For it is obvious that this suffering would not have occurred if he had not created the world, or had created it differently.[51] However, decretalists go much further than this: they believe that God created people who *had to* fall, yes, people he had decreed *would* fall, and thus be forever lost. Neither biblical thought nor common sense is able to understand how God is honored by this. Therefore, in my view, we may not say that he created people who *had to* choose evil, but we may state that God created people who *were able to* choose evil. With this formulation, we more clearly understand, first, that God is not directly responsible for people's evil deeds, and second, that he is tirelessly trying to keep people from evil deeds.

2.6.4 More Prudence

Decretalism's usual reply to the objections just mentioned is, among other things, that God glorifies himself also in the judgment of the wicked. This is true when it is a matter of the wicked people whom God wanted to save but who reject all God's tokens of love, and whom, therefore, he ultimately *must* judge. But in what way is God honored if he predestines people *a priori* to eternal perdition, on the basis *not* of foreseen unbelief but of his own sovereign will, and if he allows these people to be born in order to subsequently cast them into hell forever? I cannot see anything dishonorable in a God who creates people who *were able to* fall, who by their own choice

---

51. Ibid.

do fall and are lost, but who did not *have to* be lost if only they had accepted God's salvation, and had entrusted themselves to God's preserving care. But what is honorable about a God who creates people who, because of his eternal decree, *must* fall, and thus be lost? This is not the God of the Bible but rather the God of the Platonist and the Stoic.

We do find other, less rigorous statements in Calvin, though. Thus, in The Second Helvetic Confession (chapter 8), we read,

> Other questions, as, whether God would have Adam fall, or whether He forced him to fall, or why He did not hinder his fall, and such like, we count among curious questions (unless perchance the forwardness of heretics or of men otherwise importunate compels us to open these points also out of the Word of God, as the godly doctors of the church have often done), knowing that the Lord did forbid that man should eat of the forbidden fruit and punished his transgression; and also that the things done are not evil in respect of the providence, will, and power of God, but in respect of Satan and our will resisting the will of God.[52]

Yet, Philip Hughes rightly asks whether Calvin's driving and forceful logic did not carry him to an overdogmatic and overrational view by postulating the inevitability of humanity's Fall and the reprobation of many people because of a divine decree made before creation.[53] In spite of all subtle solutions, Calvin's, and before him Augustine's, logic goes astray with the claim that something that in itself is *against* God's will, namely, the Fall, occurred *according to* God's will. God *hates* sin—and yet he supposedly *decreed* that it would enter his creation?

Here we may praise the thoughtful prudence of Reformed theologian Willem Velema with respect to the connection between God's counsel and the Fall: "This is a very difficult

---

52. Dennison (*RCET* 2:822).
53. Hughes (1989, 155).

question, and it is important to discuss it with great prudence, especially since there are no explicit Scripture passages to which we can point. If our knowledge is imperfect, it is definitely so in this regard!"[54] Likewise, Lewis Sperry Chafer also says in connection with the counsel of God, "The theologian is not to be discredited but rather commended who, when confronted with the secret things of God, is able to say, *I do not know.*"[55] I would add, though, that a theologian should be very hesitant about retreating to an *asylum ignorantiae* ("asylum of ignorance"). It is his very duty and task to analyze (supposed) mysteries as thoroughly as possible, and to disclose their core as clearly as possible. But indeed, we must admit that this is not always successful, or entirely successful.

2.7 The Open Theist Reply
2.7.1 Is God Omniscient?

The *second* view (see §2.5.1 for the first view) entails the opinion that God does not wish to be grieved and opposed, and prefers a world without sin, but nevertheless created a world in which sin, and thus also the grief to which it leads, were—not a *necessity*, yet—a *possibility*. God could not exclude this possibility if he desired a world that contained the possibility of voluntary love. Therefore, God took a calculated risk when he created the world without—says this view—being able to know beforehand whether this risk would become reality.[56]

The latter assertion shocked the traditional theologian to the core. Is it conceivable that there are things happening that God does not foreknow, and even *cannot* foreknow? Of course, say the adherents of this view, for if God had *known* that humanity would fall, that fall would not have been a risk. Moreover, if God had known *that* it would happen, humanity would have had no really free choice: the Fall would then have

---

54. Van Genderen and Velema (2008, 196).
55. Chafer (*ST* 1:227; cf. 233: "[W]ho among men is too proud to exclaim, *There are some things which I do not understand*"?).
56. See extensively, Boyd (2001, chapter 3).

been inevitable. This is because, if God knows for sure that something is going to happen—in this case, Adam's Fall—humanity cannot choose whether it will act for or against God. Surely knowing something beforehand, in the manner traditional theology posits this in relation to God's omniscience, actually means the same as saying that that event is certain beforehand. But, in that case, how could humanity be made responsible for the Fall? So say the adherents of this view.

This view is called Open Theism. Linguistically this is an unfortunate term, for at issue is not that theism (belief in God) is open, but that, for God, the future is partially open, that is, undetermined and unknown. Open Theism claims that God is certainly omniscient, but not in the sense that he knows beforehand all future events. Rather, God knows beforehand all events that *he himself causes* as well as all *possible* events. Thus, it is asserted, God perfectly knows all choices that will be *available* to people under certain circumstances, and also perfectly knows what are the most *likely* choices that people will make. But he supposedly does not, and cannot, know *what* concrete choices people will make. In this sense, for him, too, the future is open.[57]

2.7.2 Objections

It is understandable that this view has elicited many critical replies. Does it not imply a drastic restriction of God's omniscience, but also of his sovereignty, since choices made by people apparently are not part of God's counsel? And also: if God desired a world in which people *voluntarily* love him, why would he not have been able to create a world in which people indeed love him this way, yet do not fall into sin? Does it comport with what we understand from the Bible about God's omnipotence that he would have created a risk-filled

---

57. See especially Pinnock et al. (1994); Sanders (1998); Boyd (1997, 2000, 2001); Pinnock (2001); fierce opponents (partly, however, because of a decretalist paradigm): Ware (2000); Schreiner and Ware (2000); Frame (2001); Geisler and House (2001); Wilson (2001); Erickson (2003); more generally: Basinger (1986); Beilby and Eddy (2001).

world in which the possibility of sin was created without God wanting or foreseeing this sin? Or do we misunderstand God's omnipotence? And does Open Theism comport with what we understand from the Bible about God's omniscience with its claim that he created a risk-filled world without knowing what was going to happen? Or do we misunderstand God's omniscience? Conversely, if he did know what was going to happen, *and* hated sin, why did he create the kind of world that would succumb to the power of sin?

It is questionable whether the Bible gives us clear-cut answers to these and many similar questions. Perhaps one would need to be God to be able to answer them, as well as to understand the answers given. But at least they should be mentioned, because, as I see it, they make clear that a rejection of decretalism does not automatically lead to the acceptance of Open Theism (and *vice versa*).

Consistent decretalism puts all the emphasis on the *sovereignty of God*. It does pay lip service to mouth human responsibility, but actually not much of this can survive because, in the end, people cannot do anything other than what God has decided for them. People are here without any will of themselves, both at the Fall and at conversion. They could not help falling, for this had been decided about them from eternity, and they cannot help being saved or not being saved, for this too had been decreed about them from eternity.

Open Theism puts all the emphasis on *human responsibility*. It does pay lip service to God's sovereignty and omniscience—taken in a certain restricted sense—but at the same time, God supposedly created a world in which people of their own free will can undermine God's sovereignty by doing things that he decidedly does not want, things that grieve him. Here, it seems instead that God must passively watch what people he made to be so independent are going to undertake.

Each view is the other's absolute opposite, and in my view,

both suffer from the same error in a logic driven to excess. In a sense, both could be called "cheap" in that they try to solve the theological problems involved by putting all the emphasis either on God's sovereignty or on human responsibility, without trying to take the path, by far more difficult, of searching for a balance between the two.

2.8 A Third Option?
2.8.1 Foreknowledge and Predestination

The question that arises now is whether there is a third option, one that does full justice, on the one hand, to the sovereignty and foreknowledge of God (*contra* Open Theism), and on the other hand, to human responsibility and freedom of will (*contra* decretalism), no matter how much these two poles seem to repel each other. This may sound like a cheap compromise, but cheap it can hardly be, because of the various paradoxes that this model (which I called *Viatorism*) entails. Let me give a few examples.

The *first* point dealt with in Viatorism involves a question that does not exist for decretalism: Is the claim really true that God *knows beforehand all things* that ever happen? There can be no doubt that many passages in Scripture suggest otherwise (see §§4.3–4.5 below). But even if this were certain, is it equally certain that God has also *decreed* all things that ever happen? Knowing and decreeing are not the same, of course. In other words, God certainly has foreknowledge; but does this foreknowledge necessarily comprise *all* things that ever happen, without exception? If so, could there be things about which God has foreknowledge but which he himself did not actively foreordain? In other words, does God's foreknowledge (*praescientia*) always entail foreordaining (*praeordinatio*) or predestination (*praedestinatio*; notice the threefold *prae-*)? Yes, says Calvin, as we saw. But he gave us no compelling reasons *why* this must be so.

Paul seems to make a clear distinction between the two: "For those whom he foreknew [Gr. *proegnō*] he also predestined [*prohōrisen*]" (Rom. 8:29). What God predestines he obviously also foreknows. But is it equally certain that what he foreknows he also decided? Is it unthinkable *a priori* that things God knows will happen one day are things he has decreed? Some would say (by way of evasion): God has decreed that these things are going to be allowed by him. This might be so (although I am not aware of biblical evidence for this assertion). Yet, it does not help us very much, because there is a fundamental difference between what God *orders* to happen and what he *allows* to happen. If God decrees event P, he *wants* it to happen and will in due time actively *make* it happen. But if God allows event P (or decrees to allow P), he may not even *want* it to happen, he certainly is not the One who *makes* it happen; having *allowed* P to happen (due to other agents), he will not prevent P from happening.

If we apply this, for instance, to the Fall, we get the following possible views (see further in chapter 3).

(a) *Calvinism:* From eternity, God *decreed* the Fall. That is, he decided that one day (also determined by him) it would occur. He not only *foreknew* this, he *decided* this. If this is true, there can be no reason why we could not also say: God *made it happen*. Other agents may have pushed the buttons, but it was God who had decreed that, at a given moment, they would do this.

(b) *Viatorism:* God foreknew the Fall, but he did *not* decree it. When it happened, he allowed it, and he knew from eternity that he was going to allow it. But in no way must we introduce the term "decree" here, because it will inevitably make God (co)responsible for the Fall. What God decrees, must happen; whether he personally executes his own decree, or others do this, makes no difference. For everything that happens according to God's decrees, he is fully responsible. Satan, Adam, and Eve were responsible for the Fall — but the One who decided that the Fall *must* happen was responsible too. As soon as we abandon the term "decree" in connection with the Fall, Satan, Adam, and Eve remain responsible for the Fall, but not God. He knew that it was going to happen, but he had chosen to create intelligent people with freedom. He was responsible for creating such beings, but not for the wrong choices they would potentially make. He foreknew that humanity would indeed make such wrong choices, but he was not responsible for them.

(c) *Moderate Calvinism:* People who wish to maintain the notion of God having decreed all things from eternity, may find an escape in claiming that God did not literally decree the Fall, but decreed that, in due time, he would *allow* the Fall (cf. §1.7.3). I know that some Calvinists have proposed this solution,[58] but let us clearly establish the fact that, strictly speaking, this is *not* the Augustinian-Calvinist position. Either this middle position is nothing but a concealed variety of (b), or it is a softened variety of (a). I repeat what I said under (b): introducing the term "decree" at all is risky, because it inevitably seems to lead to the conclusion that God must be held (co)responsible for the Fall.

2.8.2 Three Types of God's Will

Let us now probe a little further the distinction between God's *permission* (namely, of things that he, because of their nature, actually does not want) and his *will* (concerning the things that he, because of their nature, actually desires). The problem is that the mere possibility of such a distinction is not obvious *a priori*: if God permits (allows) something, we would think that he must actually want this thing because, if he really did not want it, he would not have allowed it. To go one step further: if God indeed wants a certain thing, what else is this than that he decrees it?

A preliminary answer could be that, following an old tradition and *contra* Open Theism, we might distinguish between three types of God's will.[59]

---

58. Sproul (1986, 31).
59. Cf. Berkouwer (1960, 115–18).

(a) The decretive or irresistible will of God, that is, the will of his immutable counsel (*voluntas decernens* or *beneplaciti* or *arcana*). This is the will of God's good pleasure, which will be realized in due time under all circumstances, despite what his opponents do.

(b) The permissive will of God (*voluntas permittens*), which concerns things that in themselves God, according to his being, does not want, but which he allows in order through this means to reach a higher goal. In a sense one could say that this involves things that God simultaneously *wants* (for his purpose) and *does not want* (because of their evil nature).

(c) The preceptive or desiring or resistible will of God (*voluntas signi* or *praecipiens* or *revelata*), which actually has more the nature of a norm, a command, a prescription, which can be transgressed by people, such as the Ten Commandments, or God's desire or command that all people should repent.[60]

Sometimes, God allows things — this is his *permissive* will — that he, because of their nature, actually does not want — this is his *desiring* will — in order to be able, through a detour, to reach the goals of his desiring will. Thus, God *desires* salvation for humanity, but sometimes *permits* sin, in order to be able to realize salvation in a way that otherwise would not have been possible.

Reformed theologian Gerrit Berkouwer has said that we are confronted with the striking fact that, in all reflection upon God and sin, "a wholesome reluctance" arises when the *causality* of sin is discussed.[61] In other words, we hesitate to say that God is the cause of sin. However, as soon as we reject the idea that God is the cause of sin (*Deus non causa peccati*), we begin to speak with assurance and astonished reverence about the *finality* of God's dealings, about the *goal*, about his government, about his *superior power* over sin. That is to say, more important than the issue of where sin comes from is the

---

60. Cf. Bavinck (*RD* 2:242–45); Berkouwer (1971, 56).
61. Berkouwer (1971, 59).

issue of whether sin can play such a role in God's plans that in the end a goal is reached that, as far as we can see, without sin would not have been possible.

2.8.3 Comments

What God's desiring will would emphatically reject, God's permissive will may allow, if in this way, through his decretive will, a goal can be reached that perfectly meets God's desiring will — even better than in any other way. For instance, God did not desire the inherently terrible sin of Joseph's brothers, who took him captive and sold him (God's desiring will). Yet he allowed it (God's permissive will) in order to bring about salvation for these same brothers (God's decretive will): "[D]o not be distressed or angry with yourselves because you sold me here, for God sent me before you to preserve life" (Gen. 45:5); "[Y]ou meant evil against me, but God meant it for good, to bring it about that many people should be kept alive, as they are today" (50:20).[62]

Conversely, God "desires all people to be saved and to come to the knowledge of the truth" (1 Tim. 2:4). "The Lord is not slow to fulfill his promise as some count slowness, but is patient toward you, not wishing that any should perish, but that all should reach repentance" (2 Pet. 3:9) (God's desiring will). Yet, he allows them to reject him (God's permissive will). Perhaps we may say that he does so out of respect for the freedom and responsibility that he himself, according to his decretive will, has granted humanity.

In a remarkable way, Johan A. Heyns has tried to formulate a possible harmony between the desiring and the permissive will of God.[63] He spoke of God's "space creating" decision, which is stronger than "God has permitted this," but less strong than "God has decreed this." Heyns was seeking to maintain the thesis that everything lies within God's decree while avoiding any form of decretalism: "Being *against* the

---

62 Cf. Erickson (1998, 387–88).
63. Heyns (1988, 75).

will of God does not mean *outside* his counsel, and being *in* his counsel does not necessarily mean in *agreement* with his will."[64] The critical question at this point is why we need to speak of God's counsel here. Is it not more in line with the Bible to replace Heyns' distinction with the distinction between the *counsel* of God and the *ways* through which he realizes his counsel, which have *not* been foreordained? "He made known his ways to Moses, his acts to the people of Israel" (Ps. 103:7). "The LORD is righteous in all his ways and kind in all his works" (145:17). "[M]y thoughts are not your thoughts, neither are your ways my ways. . . . For as the heavens are higher than the earth, so are my ways higher than your ways and my thoughts than your thoughts" (Isa. 55:8-9).

Heyns' postulate of "space creating" decisions is part of four types of divine decisions that he wishes to distinguish: *causing* decisions (*veroorsakende*, regarding matters whose essence God himself has determined, such as the well-being of his creatures), *space creating* decisions (*ruimteskeppende*, see above), *employing* decisions (*indiensnemende*, in which he "employs" the sins of angels and people as instruments for the realization of his own goals; cf. §3.1.2), and *predestinating* decisions (*predestinerende*, which involve the eternal destiny of people; see chapters 10-14).[65] All of these will be dealt with more extensively in the following chapters.

---

64. Ibid., 75–76; cf. 77 point 2; cf. Augustine in note 44 above.
65. Heyns (1988, 75–77, 152–55, 164–65).

Chapter 3
The Approach of Decretalism

> *The* LORD *brings the counsel of the nations to nothing;*
>   *he frustrates the plans of the peoples.*
> *The counsel of the* LORD *stands forever,*
>   *the plans of his heart to all generations.*
> *Blessed is the nation whose God is the* LORD,
>   *the people whom he has chosen as his heritage!*
>
> Psalm 33:10–12

Summary: *This chapter investigates the supposedly biblical arguments supplied by decretalism from both the Old and the New Testaments. It is argued that none of these arguments really demonstrates that all things that occur have been foreordained by God. Of special importance is the relationship between God's counsel and human sin, and concomitantly the relationship between God's decreeing and his permitting human deeds. The way Reformed theology has dealt with decretalist arguments is examined, as is the way that the most extreme standpoints gravely endanger human freedom and responsibility. It is also argued that opposing viewpoints, such as classical Arminianism and Open Theism, have their own problems, and cannot resolve the underlying problems, either.*

3.1 Arguments for Decretalism
3.1.1 Joseph

WHAT ARGUMENTS DO PEOPLE ADDUCE for decretalism on the basis of Scripture?[1] These arguments involve, first, whether *some* matters in human history God not only *foreknew* but also actively *decreed*. Such matters undoubtedly exist. Therefore, decretalism must be partially correct. However, the crucial question is whether these arguments also prove that God actively determined beforehand *all* things that ever occur, that is, whether *all* things have been foreordained in God's counsel.

At the outset, I would declare that, in my view, the Bible does not teach such an absolute decretalism. This does not mean, though, that Open Theism is automatically correct, because this view goes a step further: it claims that God does not even *know* certain things beforehand. This will be discussed in later chapters. At this point we will consider the decretalists' argument that *some* events have been *foreordained* by God. I begin with some examples that strikingly suggest that God seems to have foreordained certain *evil* things.

Decretalists often point to Genesis 45:5, where Joseph tells his brothers: "[D]o not be distressed or angry with yourselves because you sold me here, for God sent me before you to preserve life," and 50:20, "[Y]ou meant evil against me, but God meant it for good, to bring it about that many people should be kept alive, as they are today."

On the basis of these texts, decretalists claim that God apparently decrees evil actions in order to attain good ends. Now the text does indeed say that God can use evil actions, too, in order to realize his goals. However, we must carefully read here. Joseph says that *God* sent him to Egypt, and *God* made something good out of the evil his brothers had concocted—but Joseph does *not* say that it was God who had

---

1. Cf. Boyd (2001, App. 5), who gives many examples, but with whose Open Theist approach I cannot always agree. See more extensively, Lindström (1983); Schreiner and Ware (2000).

enticed his brothers to sell Joseph to Egypt. As James 1:13 says, "Let no one say when he is tempted, 'I am being tempted by God,' for God cannot be tempted with evil, and he himself tempts no one."

To be sure, I am unaware of any decretalists who assert that God had *urged* the brothers to do evil. But what is the essential difference between a God who *decrees* that someone will do an evil thing—after which that person *cannot* do anything else than that evil thing—and a God who *urges* someone to do that evil? Is not such a distinction a mere sophism? Decretalists lean on the Canons of Dordt, which condemns "insolent sophists,"[2] without decretalists themselves being aware of how many sophisms are embedded within their own arguments.

Reading accurately, we discover that Genesis does not say that God had either decreed that the brothers would sell Joseph or urged them to do so. God had decided to send Joseph to Egypt, and he made use of the brothers' evil action of selling Joseph to Egypt. These are two very different things. Here again, the distinction between God's counsel and God's ways is useful: it was part of God's *counsel*—though not necessarily God's *eternal* counsel—that Joseph would go to Egypt, but it was part of God's *ways* that the brothers brought this about by selling Joseph into slavery. God made use of the brothers' action, but the text does not say that *he* had decreed *their* action; the brothers acted on their own initiative, according to their own freedom and responsibility.

3.1.2 Permitting Evil

Decretalists appeal to a second proof text, Exodus 21:12-13: "Whoever strikes a man so that he dies shall be put to death. But if he did not lie in wait for him, but God let him fall into his hand, then I will appoint for you a place to which he may flee." But this passage does not tell us very much with respect to decretalism. It does not prove that fatal events are

---

2. See Canons of Dordt, Conclusion, in Dennison (*RCET* 4:152).

sometimes deliberate deeds of God, or that they have been decreed by him, for the text does not necessarily say anything more than that God sometimes allows such terrible events.

However, God sometimes does actively perform certain acts that, taken by themselves, are evil, such as diseases.[3] In Scripture we read the following: "Who has made man's mouth? Who makes him mute, or deaf, or seeing, or blind? Is it not I, the LORD?" (Exod. 4:11); and ". . . the diseases . . . that I put on the Egyptians" (15:26). We read of the LORD's servant: God "made him sick" (Isa. 53:10 note), and of unfaithful Israel: "I will visit you with panic, with wasting disease and fever that consume the eyes and make the heart ache" (Lev. 26:16). "The LORD will strike you with wasting disease and with fever, inflammation and fiery heat . . . then the LORD will bring on you and your offspring extraordinary afflictions, afflictions severe and lasting, and sicknesses grievous and lasting. And he will bring upon you again all the diseases of Egypt, of which you were afraid, and they shall cling to you. Every sickness also and every affliction that is not recorded in the book of this law, the LORD will bring upon you, until you are destroyed" (Deut. 28:22, 59–61). "[T]he LORD struck him [i.e., king Jehoram] in his bowels with an incurable disease. In the course of time, at the end of two years, his bowels came out because of the disease, and he died in great agony" (2 Chron. 21:18–19). "Immediately an angel of the Lord struck him [i.e., king Herod Agrippa] down, because he did not give God the glory, and he was eaten by worms and breathed his last" (Acts 12:23).

Sometimes even the word "evil" is used: the LORD said, "I form light and create darkness, I make well-being [Heb. *shalom*, "peace," here: Judah's deliverance from Babylon] and create calamity [Heb. *ra*, "evil," here: the judgment upon Babylon], I am the LORD, who does all these things" (Isa. 45:7). This is a remarkably strong expression: God is *borē ra*, "creat-

---

3. Cf. Ouweneel (2004, 88–91).

ing evil." Amos says something similar, "[S]hall there be evil [*ra'ah*] in a city, and the Lord hath not done it?" (3:6b KJV).

The following is even more remarkable: "I [i.e., God] gave them [i.e., Israel] statutes that were not good [*huqim lo tobhim*] and rules by which they could not have life" (Ezek. 20:25). A moment ago, we read in Isaiah and Amos about the Lord doing, or creating, evil, and in this text we hear about the Lord actively giving to his people things that were "not good."

All these examples seem to lead to this unavoidable conclusion: God hates evil, and loves the good, but sometimes he allows evil, or — more actively — even sends things that are "not good." I suppose most theologians would agree that God does so in order to prevent a greater evil, or to lead his people back to the good. Thus, nobody should say that God ever wants sickness or catastrophes as such, for sicknesses and catastrophes are powers hostile to the Creator, which he abhors. Yet it is true that God sometimes allows such things in order to chastise, or instruct, or train, his children (cf. Job 2:4–10), or to reach a good that otherwise would not have been possible.

3.1.3 Four Options

It may be useful to introduce here the distinctions made by Millard Erickson,[4] which I will develop in my own way. In his view, God has four options with respect to sin:

(a) God *prevents* sin; for instance, see Genesis 20:6, where God says to king Abimelech: "I know that you have done this [i.e., taking Sarah] in the integrity of your heart, and it was I who kept you from sinning against me. Therefore I did not let you touch her [i.e., Sarah]." David prayed, "Keep back your servant also from presumptuous sins; let them not have dominion over me! Then I shall be blameless, and innocent of great transgression" (Ps. 19:14).

(b) God *allows* (*permits*) sin; for instance, see 2 Chronicles 32:31, "God left him [i.e., king Hezekiah] to himself, in order

---

4. Erickson (1998, 424–26).

to test him and to know all that was in his heart." God said, "I gave them [i.e., Israel] over to their stubborn hearts, to follow their own counsels" (Ps. 81:12; cf. Matt. 19:8; Acts 14:16). "Therefore God gave them [i.e., the pagans] up in the lusts of their hearts to impurity" (Rom. 1:24; cf. vv. 26, 28).

(c) God *employs* sin for his own purposes; for instance, see Genesis 39:2 (where the "sin" involved is the unrighteous captivity of Joseph): "The LORD was with Joseph, and he became a successful man" (also see, e.g., 37:21–22; 45:5, 8; 50:20). Peter said to the people, "[T]his Jesus, delivered up according to the definite plan and foreknowledge of God, you crucified and killed by the hands of lawless men" (Acts 2:23; cf. v. 36). Paul said about Israel, "[I]f their rejection means the reconciliation of the world, what will their acceptance mean but life from the dead?" (Rom. 11:15; cf. vv. 25–26).

(d) God *restricts* sin; for instance, see Job 1:12, where the Lord says to Satan, "Behold, all that he has is in your hand. Only against him do not stretch out your hand" (cf. 2:6). "If it had not been the LORD who was on our side—. . . when people rose up against us, then they would have swallowed us up alive, when their anger was kindled against us" (Ps. 124:1–3). "No temptation has overtaken you that is not common to man. God is faithful, and he will not let you be tempted beyond your ability, but with the temptation he will also provide the way of escape, that you may be able to endure it" (1 Cor. 10:13).[5]

3.1.4 Comments

As far as point (b) is concerned, decretalists rightly believe that the allowing (or permitting) should not be taken here in too passive a sense. I repeat: if God allows something, to some extent he must want it, for if he really did not want it, he would have prevented it. There is a strong tension here, which is inherent to the entire complicated subject of divine providence. Look again at the examples of disease in the

---

5. Cf. Heyns (1988, 153).

The Approach of Decretalism

Bible: God does *not* want illness, for it is an enemy, and he hates his enemies—and sometimes God *does* want illness, using it as an instrument in his service, in order to attain a higher goal than would have been possible without that illness. However, the aforementioned passages do *not* prove that *all* evil in the world falls under some decree of God, nor that such evil would have been decreed from eternity. Because of their dogma, people who claim otherwise want to prove much more than they can account for.

Decretalists quote passages in which people who are already wicked are used by God in evil actions, or in which we are dealing with some hardening of the heart. Think, for instance, of Shimei (2 Sam. 16:10), Ahithophel (17:14), Pilate and Herod (Acts 4:27-28), or in the second case, of the enemies of Israel (Ps. 105:24-25), of Israel itself (Prov. 16:4; Isa. 6:10), of the pagan world (Rom. 1:24), or of the (nominally) Christian world (2 Thess. 2:11-12). God "hardens whomever he wills" (Rom. 9:18b). However, in all these cases God employs or hardens people *after* these people had already manifested their identity in their wickedness. None of these cases provide a shred of evidence that people have been predestined to evil by a decree of God, much less an *eternal* decree. We will return to this matter when we speak of the doctrine of predestination, and especially the supposed decree of reprobation (see chapters 10-14, especially §§14.1-14.5).

In other cases, God allows evil, or even actively employs it (see Erickson's point [c]), but in such a way that Satan is the executor of this evil. This occurs in such a manner that Satan's own responsibility, and that of the people he uses, is fully maintained. A striking example of this is 2 Samuel 24:1, "[T]he anger of the Lord was kindled against Israel, and he incited David against them, saying, 'Go, number Israel and Judah'"—whereas the parallel passage says, "Then Satan stood against Israel and incited David to number Israel" (1 Chron. 21:1). Here, apparently Satan's dealings are subordinate to, and embedded in, God's dealings.[6]

We find this same tension in Job 1 and 2, where Job is the executor and God the permitter, so to speak. If one were to ask who robbed Job of his herds, three answers are possible, and in a sense they all three are correct: (a) it was God who had challenged Satan, and gave him permission to act against Job (1:8–12; 2:3–6); (b) it was Satan who was the executor of the calamities that fell upon Job; (c) it was the Sabeans who were the instruments in Satan's hands to carry out his plans (1:15).

3.2 Key Passages
3.2.1 Psalms

Apart from a number of passages linked with predestination (discussed below, in chapters 10–14), the most powerful arguments for decretalism seem to be derived from the following passages, a few from the Psalms, a few from Proverbs, a few from the Prophets, and a few from the New Testament:

Let us begin with this verse: "Whatever the LORD pleases, he does, in heaven and on earth, in the seas and all deeps" (Ps. 135:6). This verse clearly says that God does what he wants. But is this really an argument for decretalism? The fact that God does what he wants implies that no external power can coerce him to do anything he does not want, and that God does not do what he does not want to do. However, this is not the same as saying that everything *people* do is necessarily part of God's counsel. People often clearly act *against* God's will (Isa. 63:10; Luke 7:30; 13:34; Acts 7:51; Eph. 4:30; Heb. 3:8, 15; 4:7). The conclusion seems invalid that God's will entails that people sometimes act against his will. God does whatever pleases *him* — but people sometimes do things that may please themselves but not God, apparently without God preventing them from doing so.

Of course, I am not saying that God would not be *able* to prevent them. Nor am I denying that all those evil human

---
6. See Goslinga (1962, 453–55).

deeds could somehow be integrated into God's ways with humanity. I am only saying that the text offers no support for the view that all that happens, including evil deeds, has been included in an eternal decree of God.

Or take this verse: "[I]n your book were written, every one of them, the days that were formed for me, when as yet there was none of them" (Ps. 139:16). Does this mean that a person's entire life, moment by moment, has been recorded beforehand in God's book?[7] The CEV indeed translates: "Even before I was born, you had written in your book everything I would do." However, translations of this verse differ widely; compare: "[I]n thy book all my members were written, which in continuance were fashioned, when as yet there was none of them" (KJV; cf. BRG, ERV, JUB), with: "The days scheduled for my formation were inscribed, even though not one of them had come yet" (ISV), or with: "Thine eyes saw my imperfect substance, and all was written in thy Book; but when those days were formed, no man [was] there" (WYC).

The text does not necessarily suggest that the length of a person's life has been foreordained (despite the rendering by The Voice). On the contrary, Eliphaz says of the wicked, "Before his days be full he shall perish" (Job 15:32 DRA; cf. ERV, JUB; again, the translation is quite uncertain). The psalmist says, "He has broken my strength in midcourse; he has shortened my days. 'O my God,' I say, 'take me not away in the midst of my days'" (Ps. 102:23–24). Fifteen years were added to Hezekiah's life (Isa. 38:5). Therefore, the "book" mentioned in Psalm 139:16 is speaking at most about God's intentions, not about an immutable decree of God.

As an aside, note that if the phrase "book of life" refers to the book in which the living are recorded, then being blotted out of this book seems to involve a shortening of a person's normal duration of life (Exod. 32:32–33; Ps. 69:28; Rev. 3:5; see further §10.9 below).

---

7. So, e.g., De Groot (1952, 25).

3.2.2 Proverbs

"The heart of man plans his way, but the LORD establishes his steps [ICB, NCV: decides what he will do]" (Prov. 16:9). Here again, the translation is uncertain; compare, for instance, the MSG: "We plan the way we want to live, but only God makes us able to live it." The verse might give the impression that all of a person's thoughts and deeds have been determined by God, but in fact it seems to show the contrast between what people want and do, and what the LORD wants and does. The text does not say that every thought of a person has been established by God, nor that every thought has been foreordained in an eternal decree. Here a person's plans stand in *contrast* to God's plans. The verse shows that, whatever a person may plan and undertake, God achieves his own purposes with that person.

Something similar is stated in Proverbs 19:21, "Many are the plans in the mind of a man, but it is the purpose of the LORD that will stand [ERV: what the LORD says is what will happen]." Here we find the same contrast between a person's plans and God's plans, and the statement that in the end, God's plans will prevail. We should understand similar sayings in this light: "A man's steps are from the LORD" (20:24; cf. Jer. 10:23). "The king's heart is a stream of water in the hand of the LORD; he turns it wherever he will" (21:1).

The various passages indicate that, no matter how a person, in his own freedom and responsibility, may deliberate and decide, in the end his path can go only between the boundaries set by God's purposes. In Zechariah 6:1 the four chariots may seem to move freely, and to a certain extent they do, but in the end their routes are determined and restricted by mountains of bronze on both sides.[8] Again we think here of Augustine's statement (cf. §1.5.3 above): even what occurs against God's will does not occur apart from his will. God's plan does not compel people to act in certain ways, but

---

8. Cf. Henry (n.d., ad loc.): "the mountains of brass [are] the immoveable counsels and decrees of God; . . . ."

provides that they will act *freely* within the limitations of God's ways.[9]

3.2.3 Prophets

The book of Isaiah is of special interest for our subject: "I am the LORD, and there is no other. I form light and create darkness, I make well-being and create calamity, I am the LORD, who does all these things" (45:6-7). "I am God, and there is none like me, declaring the end from the beginning and from ancient times things not yet done, saying, 'My counsel shall stand, and I will accomplish all my purpose,' calling a bird of prey from the east, the man of my counsel from a far country. I have spoken, and I will bring it to pass; I have purposed, and I will do it" (46:9-11). "The former things I declared of old; they went out from my mouth, and I announced them; then suddenly I did them, and they came to pass" (48:3).

Such passages may never be abused to make them say that God could ever be, or has ever been, the instigator of evil.[10] God hates evil (Hab. 1:13), and can never be made the Author of sin.[11] Given the context of these passages, the "calamity" in 45:7, the "end" in 46:10, and the "former things" in 48:3 are specific past divine judgments upon Israel or future divine judgments upon Babylon and other nations.[12] It is the same with Amos 3:6b, "Does disaster come to a city, unless the LORD has done it?," where again the reference is to divine judgment. Or in the words of Jeremiah: "Who has spoken and it came to pass, unless the LORD has commanded it? Is it not from the mouth of the Most High that good and bad come?" (Lam. 3:37-38). Again, the reference is to God's blessings and God's judgments, as verse 39 makes clear: "Why should a living man complain, a man, about the punishment of his sins?"

Apart from the specific meaning of "evil" or "bad" in such

---

9. Cf. Erickson (1998, 380).
10. See extensively, Venema (1992, chapter 11).
11. So rightly the Belgic Confession, Art. 13.
12. Pinnock (2001, 55).

passages, we must also emphasize that they never say that *all* calamities, or more generally *all* events that ever occur, have been brought about by God. And as to God's judgments upon sin, they indicate that sin is not part of his eternal counsel but, on the contrary, that he combats sin with all his power. Where evil in any form does find a place in the ways of God, it is in order through them to reach a goal that otherwise could not have been reached.

3.2.4 New Testament

"[F]rom him and through him and to him are all things" (Rom. 11:36). "[A]ll things are from God" (2 Cor. 5:18 AMPC). How could one conclude from such short phrases that all things that have ever happened, good or evil, belong to an eternal counsel of God? This is what decretalists must prove, but what the verses do not say. Romans 11:36 is speaking about the great restoration of Israel as well as the blessings for the nations, which go back to God's counsel. But this does not mean that every *way* that has led to this realization would belong to this counsel as well.

In this passage, the expression "all things" refers not to the whole of God's counsel, but to God's counsel as well as God's ways by which he has realized his counsel. Israel's glorious future belongs to God's counsel—but their sins, which often opposed God's plan, as well as the ways of God to nevertheless reach his goal, did *not* belong to his counsel. Those sins belong to Israel's own freedom and responsibility, even if they are included in God's ways.

God reaches his goal not so much *by means of* these sins, but rather *in spite of* these sins. He realizes his immutable eternal *counsel* through variable temporal *ways*, which are often co-determined by human sins. Those who wish to absolutize a phrase like "All things are from God" apart from the context, will ultimately be unable to avoid assigning to God sin as well.[13] However, sin is not a "substance," a "thing," which

---

13. Berkouwer (1971, 16–17).

might be counted among all *things* that God has created. As Gerrit Berkouwer says, the church confesses that "God is the Creator and Origin of all things, but we do not allow that he is *therefore* the Author of our sin."[14] Earlier, Herman Bavinck had written that sin "has to be understood and described neither as an existing thing nor as being in things that exist but rather as a defect, a deprivation, an absence of the good, or as weakness, imbalance, just as blindness is a deprivation of sight."[15]

Let us finally look at this partial statement by Paul: "... him who works all things according to the counsel of his will" (Eph. 1:11). Again, the central issue involves the scope of this expression "all things" (Gr. *ta panta*). Is Paul here making a general statement about the scope of God's counsel, or is he referring to the things that he dealt with in the preceding verses? We have to be careful with the interpretation of such expressions; for instance, *ta panta* ("all [created] things") in verse 10 ("things in heaven and things on earth") are clearly something else than in verse 11, which speaks of the things that God "works."

Another consideration is this: some will say that "all that occurs" (if we assume that this is the meaning of *ta panta* here) somehow belongs to God's counsel, that is, cannot be viewed apart from God's will. Whether this is correct or not, it is not the same as saying that God himself, in an active-causative way, has *decreed* all that occurs. I am prepared to go as far as to say that even the greatest evil in this world fulfills a role in God's *ways* as these are subject to him who, in the end, perfectly realizes his *counsel*.[16] But I am not prepared to say that evil, in whatever form, could ever belong to God's

---

14. Berkouwer (1971, 260; italics in the original Dutch, but omitted from the English translaiton).
15. Bavinck (*RD* 3:136); on this notion of sin as *privatio*, see Ouweneel (EDR 3, §13.1.2).
16. Chafer (*ST* 2:229–30); cf. on this verse also Venema (1992, 95–96); Boyd (2001, 414–15).

eternal *counsel* as such.

3.3 All Things Decreed?
3.3.1 Reformed Testimonies

Reformed author Henry Kersten deals with a number of the passages mentioned in §3.2, and concludes that "God has decreed from eternity perfectly independently all things that He does and sovereignly permits, excluding all that He has willed should not happen."[17] However, when we study these passages carefully, we soon discover that they neither always necessarily involve the *eternal* counsel of God, nor do they say that God himself has actively decreed *all* things that happen. Apparently, we are dealing here with a prejudice of Kersten, which he has projected upon the passages mentioned. Such a procedure is a feature of all defective scholarship: projecting biased opinions on the facts, and thus, like a ventriloquist, making them say other things than they actually do say. In theology this entails forcing the Scriptural data into the mold of our human dogmas.

Nonetheless, the doctrine that all things that occur, including the Fall, have been decreed by God, has had many adherents. We call this a form of *monism*: overemphasizing one principle (God's sovereignty) at the expense of another (human freedom).[18] A clear example of such a monist approach is Johannes Maccovius (1588–1644), who taught that God has ordained humanity to sin; Maccovius had been reprimanded for this by the Synod of Dordt (1618–1619), but many (hyper-)Calvinists after him have said similar things. I can understand why; if God decrees a thing, this is like a command: things *must* happen this or that way. If God decrees the Fall, this is like commanding the Fall.

Samuel Maresius wrote, "This permission [of the Fall] is not empty and powerless, but real, decretive, ordaining . . . . God [has] decreed certain evil, otherwise solemnly hated and

---

17. Kersten (1980, 1:107).
18. See Ouweneel (EDR 3, §12.4.1).

abhorred and forbidden by him."[19] Because supposedly there is nothing passive in God, sin cannot have been a thing passively permitted, says Maresius. God *wanted* to permit sin, and thus wanted the Fall. William Perkins wrote that, to say that God knew the Fall of Adam beforehand but did not ordain it through an eternal decree is "entirely wicked," for even the smallest things in nature do not occur without God's decree and will.[20] In my view, the latter point is precisely what must first be proved.

Notice what all these authors supposedly know about God: what God decrees, this he commands; there is nothing passive in God; it is wicked to believe that anything could happen that was not foreordained (not only foreknown!) by God. Calvin had called it "absurd" (§2.5.1). The term "wicked" is an attack on our moral integrity, and the term "absurd" is an attack on our intellectual capacity. Let us look briefly at Calvin once more.

3.3.2 Calvin and Followers

The Synod of Dordt may have reprimanded Maccovius, and other Calvinists may have called Maresius and Perkins extreme. However, it is a fact that John Calvin preceded them with his strong statements. For instance, he said,

> It seems absurd to them for man, who will soon be punished for his blindness, to be blinded by God's will and command. Therefore they escape by the shift that this is done only with God's permission, not also by his will; but he, openly declaring that he is the doer, repudiates that evasion. However, that men can accomplish nothing except by God's secret command, that they cannot by deliberating accomplish anything except what he has already decreed with himself and determines by his secret

---

19. Quoted by Kersten in the Dutch original (1:285n1), but omitted from the published English translation; see extensively, Kersten (1980, 1:212–18). Cf. Arminius about Perkins; Verboom (2005, 29–36).
20. Quoted in Kersten (1980, 1:213).

direction, is proved by innumerable and clear testimonies.[21]

Elsewhere Calvin said, "For the first man fell because the Lord had indeed judged it to be expedient; why he so judged is hidden from us. . . . Accordingly, man falls according as God's providence ordains, but he falls by his own fault."[22] In his treatise on predestination he said that, according to the foreknowledge and will of God, Adam could do nothing else but fall. Calvin's solemn confession was that all that happened to Adam had thus been decreed by God.[23] Why could and should we not say today that *this* is absurd? Instead of saying that "we know not" why God made the first people fall, we may wonder if he *did* at all.

Nonetheless, entirely in line with Calvin, the Westminster Confession of Faith says in chapter III:

> I. God from all eternity, did, by the most wise and holy counsel of His own will, freely, and unchangeably ordain whatsoever comes to pass (Eph. 1:11; Rom. 11:33; Heb. 6:17; Rom. 9:15, 18); yet so, as thereby neither is God the author of sin (James 1:13, 17; 1 John 1:5), nor is violence offered to the will of the creatures; nor is the liberty or contingency of second causes taken away, but rather established (Acts 2:23; Matt. 17:12; Acts 4:27-28; John 19:11; Prov. 16:33).
>
> II. Although God knows whatsoever may or can come to pass upon all supposed conditions (Acts 15:18; 1 Sam. 23:11-12; Matt. 11:21, 23), yet hath He not decreed anything because He foresaw it as future, or as that which would come to pass upon such conditions (Rom. 9:11, 13, 16, 18).
>
> III. By the decree of God, for the manifestation of His glory, some men and angels (1 Tim. 5:21; Matt. 25:41) are predestinated unto everlasting life; and others foreordained to everlasting

---

21. Calvin, *Institutes* 1.18.1; see Berkhof (1986, 192–94) on this and similar views.
22. Calvin, *Institutes* 3.23.8.
23. Calvin (1989, 90–93, 127, 267); see Hughes (1989, 160).

death (Rom. 9:22-23; Eph. 1:5-6; Prov. 16:4).[24]

Henry Kersten concludes: "Man fell, then, according to God's decree, as also the fall of the angels was in His decree. God did not passively allow sin, and although according to all His perfections He hates sin, nevertheless, He willed it in order to glorify Himself in righteousness and mercy.... Thus God knew that man would fall *because He had decreed that man would fall*."[25] Kersten adds that this decree does not at all compromise human responsibility, and also that God's decree does not make him the Author of sin.[26] He thus chooses the view that, on the one hand, God not only passively allowed the Fall but ordained it, and on the other hand, that the Fall is not God's fault but only humanity's fault. Here we encounter the same paradox signaled earlier: how can a rational being actively ordain a certain event, whose realization falls under his authority, *without* being responsible for this event?

We feel this tension also with Reformed author Aart Moerkerken: "The fact that Adam and Eve in Paradise would tear away from God was not unknown to God. He not only knew this, he also decreed it, yes, he wanted it. He has not brought about sin—to think so would be blasphemous—but he did want the Fall in the will of his decree. It did not happen apart from his divine will. And why did he want it? Here we can only say, The hand on the mouth! We are not allowed to ask here any further."[27] True, we should not ask any further. But we do ask Moerkerken: Should he not have put his hand on his mouth (cf. Job 40:4) at an earlier point? What biblical ground does he have for the claim that God *wanted* and *decreed* the Fall? The honest answer is: None.

3.2.3 Extreme Consequences

At this point in our argument, some may reply that, in a case

---

24. Dennison (*RCET* 4:238).
25. Kersten (1980, 1:213).
26. Kersten (1980, 1:215); cf. Dijk (1924, 385–87); Berkhof (1996, 220).
27. Moerkerken (2004, 131–32).

like the Fall, God does decree that something *shall* happen but he himself does not *make* it happen. In this way, the responsibility would then belong partially, or even entirely, to humanity. But no, American Calvinist theologian and philosopher Gordon Clark said unreservedly that his view certainly made God the cause of sin; he called God the only ultimate cause of all things.[28] Notice the word "ultimate" here: God is not the immediate cause of sin, for then, according to Clark, God would be the Author of sin; no, God is the ultimate cause of sin. This means: it is not God who sins but people sin. However, they sin because God has actively decreed that this would happen, so that it *could* not but happen.[29]

Reformed dogmatician Louis Berkhof has formulated more or less the same thought in the following way: "By His decree God rendered the sinful actions of man infallibly certain without deciding to effectuate them by acting immediately upon and in the finite will."[30] He finds the notion of permission too passive, though, for this would imply that those sinful deeds would not belong to the decree of God after all. Philip Hughes rightly comments that, if God is the ultimate cause of humanity's Fall, then he is a cause after all, no matter how strongly it is argued that it was not God but Adam who committed the sin and was guilty of the Fall as its immediate cause.[31] In other words, if God is somehow a cause of the Fall, whether an immediate or an ultimate cause, how can we avoid the conclusion that God is an Author of sin after all, whether in the immediate or in the ultimate sense?

This same thin line between decree and permission comes to light in a striking way in the argument of hyper-Calvinist R. C. Sproul.[32] First, he calls all those who deny that God has

---

28. Clark (1961, 237–38).
29. See Clark (1961, 239–40) for a further explanation of the view that decreeing sin is not itself a sin (as many might easily assume).
30. Berkhof (1996, 105; cf. 107–108).
31. Hughes (1989, 160).
32. Sproul (1986, 25–26).

foreordained all events "atheists." All the millions of non-Calvinist Christians as well as all moderate Calvinists will have to live under this accusation (which is unsurprising after Calvin's term "absurd" and Perkins' term "wicked"). Subsequently, Sproul argues that God's sovereignty necessarily implies that he has foreordained all things. This would follow from the fact that all things must happen with his permission.

Now, I do agree with the latter sentence, and I would think that decreeing and permitting must be very different things. But not for Sproul, who argues that, if God permits something, then he must decree to allow it. If he decrees to allow it, he is somehow foreordaining it. Using this kind of hasty conclusivism, Sproul's entire book is filled with careless logic and insults, like the term "atheist." Over against this, I would like to make two simple assertions. First, there is no compelling reason whatsoever (except Sproul's logic) why God's sovereignty necessarily implies that he has foreordained all things. Second, there is no compelling reason whatsoever why it should follow from God allowing a thing that he thus "in a certain sense" has *preordained* this thing. Such logic is found with Gerardus Oorthuys as well, who argues that in God's providence foreseeing and foreordaining are the same thing[33] — this despite the fact that Romans 8:29 clearly distinguishes the two.

3.4 Unwarranted Speculation
3.4.1 Three Counter-Arguments

As I see it, the doctrine that everything that happens has been not only permitted but also decreed by God, is unacceptable for at least three reasons.

(a) It is inferred from speculations about the sovereignty and omnipotence of God (cf. §§6.1–6.3 and 7.2–7.4 below); such speculations are a consequence of the all too common confusion of concepts and ideas, as we will see (§3.8). That is, the claim that everything that happens has been foreordained

---
33. Oorthuys (1931, 76).

by God does *not* necessarily follow from God's sovereignty as the Bible speaks of it.

(b) Whether the adherents intend this or not, the doctrine that everything that happens has been decreed by God affects the righteousness and holiness of God by making him, no matter in what distant or ultimate a way, responsible for the origin of sin. In a subtle way, a fundamental distinction is made between *decreeing* sin (without committing it, but such that the Fall must inevitably happen) and personally *committing* sin. If God decreed that Adam and Eve must fall, and made all the circumstances such that Adam and Eve could do nothing else than fall, then God indeed did not commit their sin but he certainly was the ultimate Author of it.

(c) As we will see, the consistent Calvinist view is in many respects in direct conflict with Scripture. All evil things happen under the providential permission of God, and he always has good reason to permit them, namely, to attain through the detour of evil a goal that otherwise could not have been attained. However, this is not the same as saying that all evil things have been *foreordained* by God. On the contrary, there are many things that God explicitly does *not* want, and which yet happen. Jesus said to Jerusalem, "How often would [Gr. *ēthelēsa*] I have gathered your children together as a hen gathers her brood under her wings, and you were not willing [*ēthelēsate*]!" (Luke 13:34b). That is, *I* wanted, but you did *not* want. Only dogmatic prejudice leads one to read here: I wanted your salvation, but at the same time I wanted that *you* would *not* want it, and I even foreordained that you would not want it. If that were so, how could Jesus have been genuinely grieved about Jerusalem's unwillingness (see §§3.4.4-3.4.5 below)?

3.4.2   1 Timothy 2:3-4

Let us look at another example. Paul speaks of "God our Savior, who desires [Gr. *thelei*, "wants"] all people to be saved and to come to the knowledge of the truth" (1 Tim. 2:3-5;

cf. 4:10). God wants all people to be saved, but *they* do not all want this, and thus many of them are not saved. The outcome of all gospel preaching depends not only on God's will but also the person's will.

Some theologians wish to explain such passages by means of distinctions that in themselves are useful (see §2.8.2), such as between the decretive or irresistible will of God, that is, the will of his immutable counsel (*voluntas decernens* or *beneplaciti* or *arcana*), and the preceptive or desiring or resistible will of God (*voluntas signi* or *praecipiens* or *revelata*).[34] But who determines, and on what authority, which "will" is meant in 1 Timothy 2:4? Some even assert that the verse refers only to *elect* persons.[35] Because the article is lacking (*pantas anthropous*), Cornelis Bouma reads "all sorts of people" (of all classes), with an appeal to verse 1 ("thanksgivings for all people").[36] This is strange, for in verse 1 "all people" (again without the article) means "all without any exception." So why not also in verse 4?

Therefore, Reformed theologian Herman Ridderbos takes the term here in a generic sense: "all that is called human," without any limitation.[37] God wants all people to be saved, without any exception. This is why he sincerely offers salvation to *all* people; as Jesus said, "I, when I am lifted up from the earth, will draw all people to myself" (John 12:32). Jesus' redemptive work "leads to justification and life for all men" (Rom. 5:18). We read about ". . . God, who is the Savior of all people" (1 Tim. 4:10). "[T]he grace of God has appeared, bringing salvation for all people" (Titus 2:11; see extensively chapter 13 regarding this universal offer of grace).

The fact that nevertheless not all people are saved is because the reality of human responsibility is implicitly

---

34. So Kersten; cf. Clark (1961): *decretive will* and *preceptive will*.
35. So originally Augustine (*De correptione et gratia* 44); also see Kersten (1980, 1:65–66).
36. Bouma (1937, 57).
37. Ridderbos (1967, 73).

included in 1 Timothy 2, with regard to both the intercessors (vv. 1–2) and the people whom God wants to be saved. Newport White points out that Paul does not say, *thelei sōsai* ("[God] wants to save," referring to divine activity) but *thelei sōthēnai* ("[God] wants [them] to be saved," referring to divine passivity). Thus, this salvation is made to depend here not exclusively on God's actions (redemption) but on human actions (repentance, conversion) as well.[38]

Now what do hyper-Calvinists say to this claim that from eternity God partially wanted to save all people, but God also partially wanted to reprobate a large part of humanity (not because of foreseen unbelief, but because of his own sovereign will)? How does this work?

3.4.3 Other Passages

Peter says, "The Lord is . . . longsuffering toward us, not willing [Gr. *boulomenos*] that any should perish but that all should come to repentance" (2 Pet. 3:9 NKJV). Notice the verb here, which is related to *boulē*, "counsel"; as the YLT puts it: ". . . not counseling any to be lost" (CJB: ". . . it is not his purpose that anyone should be destroyed"). Here it is said explicitly that it is *not* God's counsel or purpose that anyone should perish — although in God's ways many *will* nevertheless perish because they keep turning their backs on him. (Hyper-)Calvinists claim the opposite of what Scripture says here: it *is* God's own counsel or purpose that many *will* perish. They clam what Scripture does not say, and they argue away what Scripture does say.

As a way out, the (Reformed) Annotations in the Dutch States Translation (Statenvertaling, 1637) claims that this verse refers exclusively to believers.[39] Also Reformed theologian Seakle Greijdanus, without any apparent reluctance, understands *pantas* to refer here to "all the elect,"[40] whereas

---
38. White (1979, 104).
39. Cf. Kersten (1980, 1:81).
40. Greijdanus (1931, 145).

the text says nothing of the kind. This is another striking example of how dogmatics can govern the exegesis of Scripture. Similarly, when John 3:16 says that God has loved the world, hyper-Calvinist Henry Kersten asserts without any ground in the text that this concerns here the "world of the elect"—an apparent effort to rescue his dogma. Such a dogma, supported by distorting or weakening explicit and unequivocal statements of Scripture, condemns itself.

This time, fortunately, the Annotators of the Dutch States Translation do not fall into this trap; their comment on "world" in John 3:16 reads: "That is, not onely the Jews, but also the Gentiles, scattered throughout the whole world." God offers salvation to all Jews and all Gentiles (see chapter 13 below).

In §3.4.1 above, I quoted Luke 13:34b (CEB), "How often I have wanted [Gr. *ēthelēsa*] to gather your people just as a hen gathers her chicks under her wings. But you didn't want [*ēthelēsate*] that" (cf. Matt. 23:37). Again, interpreters speak here of the preceptive or desiring or resistible will of God (here: the Son of God), that is, the desire of God that can be opposed by people, in contrast to the decretive or irresistible will of God, which cannot be opposed, and thus will inevitably be carried out. For theoretical thought, this is a useful distinction, as long as we keep in mind that dogmatics *imposes* such a distinction on the text; the text itself is not working with this distinction.[41] The human intellect creatively has formulated the distinction between a hidden will (the will of God's counsel) and a revealed will (the will of God's command), both of which apparently can be *squarely opposed to each other*.

3.4.4 Comments

I can live with the distinction between God's resistible and God's irresistible will, but not with the way the decretalist understands it: God's will of command says: "You shall not kill," but God's will of counsel may entail that X will kill Y

---

41. Berkouwer (1960, 238–39).

(or even, X *must* kill Y). God's will of command says: "Repent and turn back," but God's will of counsel may entail that the person has been reprobated from eternity, and therefore will never be *able* to repent. Reformed theologian Gerrit Berkouwer rightly said, "One wonders whether the gospel is not overshadowed here by theology, and whether such passages can really be understood only in the light of a distinction which does nothing but undermine the power of these very passages."[42]

Indeed, the view that I just mentioned supposes that there may be two contrasting wills in God. Again, I can live with the distinction between God saying: "You shall not sin," and God nonetheless temporarily allowing sin in order to reach a higher goal. But if we substitute "decreeing" for "allowing," I can no longer live with it. Allowing is passive, decreeing is active. Allowing the Fall means: I do not want it, but I let it happen. Decreeing the Fall means: I do want it, and I make sure it will happen. Allowing does not make God responsible, decreeing does make him responsible, no matter what hyper-Calvinists may say. Think again of the example given earlier in §2.6.3: if a person unleashes a mad dog that he is sure will bite someone, he is responsible for the dog's behavior.

What makes this entire view even less acceptable is that it supposes a behavior in God that borders on hypocrisy. Take Luke 19:41-42, which says, "[W]hen he [i.e., Jesus] drew near and saw the city, he wept over it, saying, 'Would that you, even you, had known on this day the things that make for peace! But now they are hidden from your eyes.'" Jesus *wept* over Jerusalem because its inhabitants had not seized their opportunity for repentance and salvation, which he *desired* so strongly for the city. However, decretalism says that this was only the *revealed* (preceptive, desiring, resistible) will of God (the Son)—whereas the *hidden* (decretive, irresistible) will of the Lord was not to save (the majority of) the city's inhabi-

---

42. Ibid.

tants at all! According to the decree of reprobation he wanted to save only a handful of elect from the city.

But then why the *weeping*? Why would God weep over people who are not even *able* to receive salvation because that same God has decreed to reprobate them forever? He says, "I spread out my hands all the day to a rebellious people, who walk in a way that is not good, following their own devices" (Isa. 65:2), and Paul says, "[W]e are ambassadors for Christ, God making his appeal through us. We implore you on behalf of Christ, be reconciled to God" (2 Cor. 5:20). Spreading out the hands, or appealing and imploring, have strongly emotional overtones. On a Viatoric standpoint these are perfectly understandable (cf. §13.5). However, decretalism must try to reconcile such emotions with its view that the majority of Israel, or the majority of the Gentiles, *cannot* repent and come to the Lord because that same God had already reprobated these majorities from all eternity.

Decretalism cannot avoid minimizing God's sadness about the things that happen against his will.[43] "The LORD saw that the wickedness of man was great in the earth, and that every intention of the thoughts of his heart was only evil continually. And the LORD *regretted* that he had made man on the earth, and it *grieved* him to his heart" (Gen. 6:5-6; cf. §§5.4.3 and 6.6). The Israelites "rebelled and *grieved* his Holy Spirit; *therefore* he turned to be their enemy, and himself fought against them" (Isa. 63:10; cf. Eph. 4:30). Notice the "therefore": God became an enemy to Israel not because he had decreed to do so from eternity but because they had rebelled and grieved his heart. How can God be genuinely grieved if people do exactly what he in his eternal counsel has decreed about them? If God passively foresaw (foreknew) their sins, we can understand his grieving; but if he actively foreordained these sins, such grieving becomes absurd.

---

43. Cf. extensively, Carson (1981).

3.4.5 Absurdity

To put it even more strongly: can Henry Kersten and other hyper-Calvinists maintain that they are not diminishing human responsibility in any manner? But how can people be guilty before God if they do only what God has *decreed*, that is, carry out God's *will*? It is not only that God *knew* (and regretted) that Adam would fall; no, he himself had *decided* this. That is the crux. God *decided* that the first humans would fall, and then was grieved when it happened, and punished them because they fell. This is what I find hard to believe. How can God ever complain that Israel is a "stiff-necked" or "stubborn" or "obstinate" people (Exod. 33:3, 5; Deut. 9:13; 10:16; 31:27; Isa. 48:4; Jer. 7:26) if each sin of that nation was in fact decreed (decided, determined, foreordained) by God himself?

Now at this point hyper-Calvinists may use my own weapons against me. They might argue that we should use terms like "decree," "regret," and "responsibility" not as concepts but as ideas (see §§3.8, 5.2.1, 6.1.3). If we do this, so they might argue, we can very well believe that God both decrees a thing *and* regrets it when it occurs; or decrees certain human deeds, yet assigns all responsibility to humanity. That is fine—but this works only if we can find independent biblical proof *that* God has decreed from eternity all things that will ever happen. So far, I have not seen such evidence. I have heard words like "absurd," "wicked," and "atheist" to describe those who believe otherwise, but this seems to be the weak response of someone who has little ground to stand upon except his scholastic conclusivism. And thankfully, barking dogs seldom bite.

This is the constantly unproven *and* improbable claim of (hyper-)Calvinism: everything that ever happens was not only passively foreknown by God, but actively foreordained by God. The sovereign and almighty God *decreed* the Fall, yet he cannot be called the Author of sin because it was not he who fell, but Adam and Eve. We are not even allowed to say that God *made* them fall; it was their own responsibility that they fell. At the same time, we are supposed to believe that God decided (decreed, foreordained, determined) that the first people, according to their own responsibility, would fall. They *chose* to fall, and that was their own fault. At the same time, they had no choice at all because it was God who had sovereignly and omnipotently *chosen* that they would fall. Adam and Eve had a choice—and they had no choice.

Now *this* is what I call absurd. I repeat, this absurdity is the consequence of an argument that goes astray already at its starting point: *the claim is not taught by Scripture, nor is its truth logically necessary, that everything that ever happens must have been decreed by God.* I will have ample opportunity in the rest of this book to provide support for this claim.

3.5 Preliminary Summary
3.5.1 Puppets

Let us try to draw a preliminary conclusion at this point. (Hyper-)Calvinist decretalism is an overly consistent system of thought, which is not very attractive for various theological reasons.

First, it is nowhere explicitly taught in Scripture. That is, there is no passage, or combination of passages, that teaches that *everything* that has happened, happens, or will happen, has been *decreed* (decided, foreordained, determined) by God from all eternity. Please note the three conditions: (a) everything (not just some things), (b) decreed (not just permitted or foreseen), (c) from eternity (not partially in time). (Hyper)Calvinism must satisfy all three conditions by means of biblical argument, which it has never managed to do. It is based on human logical conclusions only, drawn from an extreme and untenable view of God's sovereignty and omnipotence (see chapters 6 and 7). It was the wisdom of Augustine to say that nothing that happens occurs *praeter voluntatem Dei*, "apart from Gods will." That is, even the things that God permits cannot be separated from God's will, for if he really would not want a thing, he would not permit it. Yet, the distinction between decreeing and permitting is essential and must be carefully maintained if we do not want to land in absurdities.

Second, the Bible throughout teaches us that, instead of decreeing sin, God wholeheartedly hates sin, undertakes everything possible to oppose and avoid it, and is deeply grieved when it nevertheless occurs. "You who are of purer eyes than to see evil and cannot look at wrong" (Hab. 1:13). "How often they rebelled against him in the wilderness and grieved him in the desert!" (Ps. 78:40). We can very well imagine God *permitting* a certain amount of evil if, in this way, he can attain a lofty goal that otherwise would have been impossible to attain. But it is in conflict with God's revealed character to *decree* sin while at the same time possessing the power to avoid and combat sin.

Third, if this doctrine were right, the totality of world history, that is, all human behavior, would have been foreordained in God's eternal counsel. This would be the end of the notion of human freedom and responsibility, for how can a puppet be responsible to the one pulling the strings? However, the situation is very different if people possess genuine responsibility, and can make genuinely free choices. God can prevent wrong choices, and sometimes he does. But often he permits them — in order to achieve his own purposes — and passively looks on while people are doing their thing: "For thus the LORD said to me: 'I will quietly look from my dwelling like clear heat in sunshine, like a cloud of dew in the heat of harvest'" (Isa. 18:4). God says he will calmly watch and not interfere, while his enemies seem to prosper. The "clear heat in sunshine" and the "cloud of dew" ripen their "harvest," but "before the harvest, when the blossom is over, and the flower becomes a ripening grape, he cuts off the shoots with pruning hooks, and the spreading branches he lops off and clears away" (cf. v. 5). Instead of having decreed everything that occurs, God is often simply looking on at the strange actions of people, until the time is ripe for him to intervene.

3.5.2 Illogical Logic

One sometimes wonders whether (hyper-)Calvinists are fully aware of the force of the verb "to decree." Apparently some are not, those who suggest that "to permit" necessarily entails "to decree." Others, wishing to fully maintain human responsibility, seem able to do so only by weakening the notion of "decreeing" — for how can God decree that a thing *must* happen without being responsible for *that* it happens? Different than Open Theists, I can accept human responsibility even if God *foreknows* what people will do. But I cannot see how human responsibility can be maintained if God *decrees* that certain human actions *must* happen.

Decretalists follow a kind of Procrustean logic based on what they believe Scripture teaches about God's sovereignty (or as some put it: God's "absolute sovereignty") — although this very term seldom appears in Scripture. It appears in only a few translations, where other translations have different terms.[44] In other words, there is no need to translate any Hebrew or Greek word as "sovereign" or "sovereignty." Decretalists therefore must suffice with logical inferences from Scripture.

Fortunately, decretalists cannot maintain their Procrustean logic, because such a logic functions like a boomerang. Take their claim that God has decreed the Fall, such that it was an immutable fact that the first people *had to* fall. If anti-decretalists would apply the same kind of Procrustean logic, then the very first ironclad conclusion is that God is definitely the *primary* Author (origin and instigator) of sin (and Adam at most the secondary author). The reason is simple: if the sovereign God decides that a thing *must* occur, he is definitely

---

44. Some examples in various translations: Acts 4:24 and Rev. 6:10 (ESV) has "Sovereign Lord" (in Greek one word, *despotēs*) and 1 Tim. 6:15 (ESV) has "Sovereign" (*dynastēs*). The NIV has "Sovereign Lord" as a rendering for *Adonai YHWH* (Gen. 15:2; etc.). The NASB has "sovereignty" (e.g., Ps. 103:19) where others read "kingdom." The CJB has "sovereign choice" (Rom. 9:11; ESV: "election").

responsible for this thing occurring. If I give a razor to a little child, I am responsible for this child badly cutting himself. I cannot excuse myself by saying that *I* did not cut the child but that the child himself did so. Speaking of absurdities: *this* would be absurd.

The second ironclad conclusion—if we continue employing the decretalists' method—is the following: if all sin and suffering were decreed by God from eternity, there can be no room for genuine human responsibility or guilt, just as the little child cannot be responsible for cutting himself. Thus, neither did humanity require any atonement. *I* myself do not accept these conclusions, neither do the decretalists whom I know, but this is because they are not consistent in employing their own logical method. The degree of their consistency about God's sovereignty is matched by the degree of their inconsistency about the logical consequences of their view.

3.5.3 Deuteronomy 29:29

If one points out to decretalists the inconsistency of their logic, they might defend themselves by claiming that their paradoxes are divine mysteries that we must believingly accept. This is an understandable claim; anti-decretalists have their own paradoxes, because these arise with the complex subject as such. Yet, the argument must not be used as an escape. This technique is used, for instance, by Klaas Dijk, who appeals to Deuteronomy 29:29, "The secret things belong to the LORD our God, but the things that are revealed belong to us and to our children forever."[45] As Gerrit Berkouwer has pointed out, many have appealed to this verse, whether relevant or not.[46] He refers to John Calvin, who argued that this verse (in Berkouwer's words) "may never lead us to be silent about election, but rather must teach us to distinguish where the

---

45. Dijk (1924, 370).
46. Berkouwer (1960, 12–13); on this, see Berkouwer's own discussion, 107, and generally, chapter 4.

boundary of God's Word lies."⁴⁷

One may wonder, though, whether this verse has anything at all to do with the hidden counsel of God. Matthew Henry says about this verse: "We are forbidden curiously to inquire into the secret counsels of God, and to determine concerning them."⁴⁸ In connection with this verse, John Gill mentioned a number of such secret counsels:

> [N]ot only some of his perfections, as eternity, immensity, &c. are beyond our comprehension; but the mode of subsistence of the three divine Persons in the Godhead, the paternity of the one, the generation of the other, and the procession of the Spirit from them both; the union of the two natures, divine and human, in the person of Christ; the thoughts, purposes, and decrees of God within himself, until brought into execution; and so there are many things relating to his creatures, as the particular persons predestinated unto eternal life, what becomes of such who die in infancy, what will befall us in life, when we shall die, where and in what manner, and also the day and hour of the last judgment.⁴⁹

The Targum Jonathan and several of the rabbis have given a very different interpretation. They understand the "secret things" to refer to hidden *sins*, which God will judge (since open and obvious sins are judged by earthly tribunals). I feel more at home, though, with the common Christian interpretation, with a little adaptation: the "revealed things" are found in the Torah. Keeping the Torah is God's revealed path of blessing. This is God's *known grace*. The "secret things" are the hidden counsel *and ways* of God; more specifically, the "secret things" may refer to what God will do when the revealed things will have been carried out, namely, apostasy followed by punishment. *After* a time of punishment God will bring about full restoration, and this is described directly

---

47. Calvin, *Institutes* 3.21.4–5; cf. Berkouwer (1960, 15).
48. Henry (n.d., ad loc.).
49. Gill (1746, ad loc.).

after Deuteronomy 29:29, namely, in 30:1–10. This is God's *hidden grace*. The "secret things" are the sources of grace that God dispenses after Israel has totally failed under the Torah. They are "hidden," yet revealed immediately afterward in 30:1–10.[50]

Regardless of the validity of this view, decretalists cannot retreat behind Deuteronomy 29:29 when others identify the inconsistencies in their logic. That would be too superficial (cf. earlier comments in §2.6.4 about the *asylum ignorantiae*, "asylum of ignorance"). If they do so, what arguments can they adduce against those who use this passage as a guardrail against precisely that Procrustean logic of the decretalist? Such people simply but earnestly explain that Scripture nowhere teaches that God has *decreed* (decided, determined, foreordained) everything that has ever happened and will ever happen.

Decretalists do not succeed by constantly appealing to God's sovereignty (as they understand it), as though such an appeal brushes all counter-arguments off the table. On the contrary, anti-decretalists offer a powerful two-point rebuttal. (a) Just as decretalists appeal to God's sovereignty, anti-decretalists appeal to God's righteousness and holiness, which makes the idea that God would ever *decree* sin—in whatever sense—simply inconceivable. And (b), the anti-decretalist understanding of God's sovereignty includes the possibility that God *sovereignly* calls people to become his "junior partners"— not with respect to his counsel, but certainly with respect to his *ways* with the world and with humanity. This latter point will be unfolded in subsequent chapters.

3.6 Other Ways
3.6.1 No Biblical Proof

I cannot help but conclude that the doctrine that all events have been decreed by God from eternity does not follow from Scripture. The decretalist must prove that *anything* that

---
50. Mackintosh (n.d., 369); Kelly (1970, 512).

happens was not only foreknown, but foreordained by God, and that this was done *from eternity*. Neither claim can be proven, whether directly or indirectly. I have adduced arguments why I deem this doctrine highly *unlikely*. So I am not persuaded when, in support of the claim that "what will happen in the future is certain beforehand," Johan A. Heyns refers to a long series of Bible passages, none of which supports this assertion whatsoever.[51] The same is true when Louis Berkhof claims that God has foreordained all the wicked acts of people,[52] but whose biblical proof texts do not show this at all. Consider the two most conspicuous examples.

(a) *Proverbs 16:4* ("The LORD has made everything for its purpose, even the wicked for the day of trouble") says neither that the wicked was *foreordained* to be wicked, nor that this happened in eternity past. It says only that those who manifest themselves as wicked will eventually fall under God's judgment (cf. the ERV: "The LORD has a plan for everything. In his plan, the wicked will be destroyed"; the EXB: "The LORD makes everything go as he pleases. He has even prepared a day of disaster for evil people") (see further §§11.7.2 and 14.2.1).

(b) Neither *Acts 2:23* ("[T]his Jesus, delivered up according to the definite plan and foreknowledge of God, you crucified and killed by the hands of lawless men") nor *4:27-28* ("[T]ruly in this city there were gathered together against your holy servant Jesus, whom you anointed, both Herod and Pontius Pilate, along with the Gentiles and the peoples of Israel, to do whatever your hand and your plan had predestined to take place") prove that *all* wicked deeds of people have been decreed by God, nor that Herod and Pilate were personally foreordained to deliver Jesus, much less that they were foreordained to their actions *from eternity*. It was God's counsel from eternity that Jesus would die, but the texts do not necessarily say anything more than this: according to the *ways* of

---

51. Heyns (1988, 73).
52. Berkhof (1996, 105).

God, Herod and Pilate, in terms of their own responsibility and freedom, were available to carry out this counsel of God.

3.6.2 Five Approaches

I consider all the arguments supplied so far to have refuted decretalism in principle. Fortunately, it is not the only explanation of God's counsel and of the relationship between divine and human actions. We may distinguish at least five monotheist approaches (I thus omit poly- and pantheism and similar forms of theism).[53]

(a) *Decretalism*. This is the view that the *entire* future is foreknown to God in detail, simply because he himself has *foreordained* that future in detail. In general, this view is hyper-Calvinistic, but in essence it is a feature of *all* consistent Calvinism since John Calvin himself. As I said, some decretalists consider the following alternatives as "absurd" (Calvin), "wicked" (Perkins), or "atheist" (Sproul).

(b) *Arminianism*. No matter how many theologians may have underscored the significant contrasts between Calvinism and Arminianism, in fact these views agree on one important point: both views emphasize that the *entire* future is foreknown to God in detail. The difference is that, according to Arminianism, this is not because he himself has (actively) *foreordained* that future in detail, though he does (passively) *foresee* it in detail.

(c) *Process Theology*. As part of liberal Christianity, this view teaches that God neither foresees nor foreordains the (distant) future, due to limitations that belong to God's very being. The role of people has become so large in this view that God and humanity move forward as virtually equal partners, and respond to each other without either of them being able to foreordain or foresee the future consequences of these

---

53. Lewis and Demarest (1996, 294–99) distinguish: (a) Pelagian and liberal traditions, (b) semi-Pelagian and Arminian perspectives, (c) supralapsarian hypotheses, (d) Barthian neo-orthodoxy, and (e) the infralapsarianism of some church fathers, Medieval authorities, Reformers, and many Evangelicals.

perpetual interactions.[54]

(d) *Open Theism*. Here, the future is partially decreed (and thus also foreseen) by God, but partially determined by the free choices of people. As to the latter point: according to this view, God foresees all *possible* and also the *most likely* choices of people, but he does not, and cannot, foresee their *actual* choices. The reason is that, if God could foresee them, there could actually be no genuine human freedom.

(e) *Viatorism* (see chapters 1 and 5). This view seeks to harmonize the previous approaches. It does so by leaving room for genuine predestination unto salvation, while at the same time maintaining that *not* all things that ever occur were decreed by God from eternity (*contra* decretalism), and that at least in certain cases, God does foreknow the choices of people *and* that such choices are nevertheless genuinely free (i.e., non-foreordained) (*contra* Open Theism).

3.7 Errors on All Three Sides
3.7.1 Decretalism Mistaken

The Viatoric approach that I am defending in this book pays attention to the positive elements in approaches (a), (b), and (d). (I am omitting Process Theology because, as I see it, it cannot be viewed as belonging to orthodox theology.) Decretalism seems to be right insofar as it maintains that the future is known to God and sovereignly decreed by God, at least to a limited extent. Arminianism seems to be right insofar as God sometimes bases his decrees and actions on—foreseen or occurring—choices of people. Open Theism seems to be right insofar as God has *not* from eternity decreed the *entire* future, and Scripture gives the impression that he does not always foreknow certain situations, as we will see.

In addition to these considerations, it is important to note where these three approaches are mistaken.

First, decretalism is partially mistaken, since God did *not*

---
54. For the important differences between Process Theology and Open Theism, see Boyd (2001, 270–78) and Pinnock (2001, 140–50).

foreordain all events; for instance, God did not decree from eternity concerning *every* evildoer that evildoer P would commit evil Q at time R. God seems not to *know* all future events — we will find this in many Bible passages (see chapter 4 below) — and this is a good thing. As Boyd says, it demands a greater God to govern a world that is populated with freely acting beings than to govern a world of foreprogrammed automatons.[55] Elsewhere he says that, from a world of robots, God would receive everything he wants except the one thing that he *really* wants, namely, persons who in freedom *choose* to share in his triune love. Love must be chosen, and this means that love is inherently risky.[56] In order to share in God's eternal triune love, which *he* possesses by nature, *we* must choose it.[57]

C. S. Lewis has asked the same question: Why did God give us a free will?[58] It is because free will, even though it makes evil possible, is the only thing that makes possible meaningful love, or goodness, or joy. A world of automatons, of robots, of machines, would hardly be worth creating. The happiness to which God destines his higher creatures is the happiness of being voluntarily united with him and with each other in an ecstasy of love and rapture, compared to which the greatest rapture of love between man and woman on earth is only a mild approximation. And to achieve that purpose, people must be free. God wishes to be loved only by people who do so voluntarily, of their own choice, and I would add: not only before, but also after the Fall. God cannot possibly wish to be loved by people who have been foreordained to do so and who are not able to do anything else than to love God.

3.7.2 Arminianism Mistaken

Arminianism is wrong insofar as it does not leave room for

---

55. Boyd (2000, 31).
56. Ibid., 134.
57. Ibid., 137.
58. Lewis (2012, 64–65).

genuine predestination, that is, foreordaining based (and dependent) not on God's foreknowledge of what people will choose, but on his own sovereign choices alone. For instance, I cannot agree with Henry Thiessen, who says that election is a sovereign act of a gracious God, namely, that he, in Jesus Christ, chose all people whom he foreknew would accept him.[59] It may give some people a good feeling that God chose them before the foundation of the world because of what he saw *they* would do—I would almost say: what they would achieve. However, that gives people too much credit. It gives me personally a better feeling to know that all that I have done (repenting, converting, believing, serving, loving God) arises from nothing but the pure grace of God, and thus also from my eternal election.

Paul says, "[B]y grace you have been saved through faith. And this is not your own doing; it is the gift of God" (Eph. 2:8). Not my choice for God was first, but his eternal choice for me, on the basis not of my foreseen achievements but of his gracious intervention. Not only does knowing this give me a better feeling—I am convinced that it is more Scriptural, too (see chapters 10-14 below). A person is justified by (Gr. *dia*, "through, by means of") faith, but the true and only source of this justification, including the instrument of faith, is the *grace* of God (Rom. 3:22-25).

Greg Boyd chose another way of solving the problem by denying individual election. According to him, God predestined the church, but left it to people's own decisions who were going to be a part of this church.[60] This is not the way I think the New Testament describes election. Take Paul, for example, who says that, at the present time, there is a remnant of Israel "chosen by grace" (Rom. 11:5, more literally: "according to the election of grace"). The context suggests that, unless God had intervened by grace, no "Israel of God" (cf. Gal. 6:16) would have been left at all. But God, in his grace, secured for

---

59. Thiessen (1961, 344).
60. Boyd (2000, 46–48).

himself a remnant so that his grace had some surviving objects. The very existence of a remnant suggests that this was God's gracious initiative, rather than an election based on foreseen faith.

3.7.3 Open Theism Mistaken

Similar to Arminianism, Open Theism is mistaken in that it leaves too little room for genuine predestination based entirely on God's sovereign choice, not on foreseen human faith. Basically, its logical error is similar to that of decretalism, though in the opposite way. That is, it deals with divine notions as if they can be conceptualized, so that all kinds of logical inferences can be drawn from them.

There are numerous examples. If we are presented with a circle whose diameter is 1, we can with absolute certainty draw the conclusion that its circumference must be approximately 3.14159. If Liz is a biological mother, we can with absolute certainty draw the conclusion that she is a woman. If Bob is a painter, we can with absolute certainty draw the conclusion that he is not blind. However, sovereignty, predestination, foreknowledge, freedom, and responsibility are not concepts from which we can draw similar logically necessary conclusions. They are ideas, approximations of deep spiritual truths, from which we may draw only those conclusions that are made explicit by Scripture itself. Decretalism, Arminianism, and Open Theism are fighting each other by making precisely the same logical mistake. They draw unwarranted conclusions to support their own thinking, or they draw unwarranted conclusions from their opponents' thinking in order to ridicule the latter.

Thus, decretalism believes that it can draw various inferences from the concept of God's sovereignty. Because God is sovereign, it supposedly follows that he must have foreordained all things. But this does *not* follow.

Arminianism believes that it can draw various inferences from the concepts of human freedom and responsibility.

Because people are free, it supposedly follows that God cannot have predestined them (in the sense of sovereignly choosing people). But this does *not* follow.

Open Theism believes that it can draw its own inferences from the concepts of human freedom and responsibility. Because people are free, it supposedly follows that God cannot have foreknown all their deeds, for if he had foreknown them, these acts would have been certain beforehand, so that people could no longer choose in freedom. But this does *not* follow.

As long as theologians keep confusing concepts and ideas, they will keep making the same mistakes, and will continue fighting each other with these mistakes. This is a tragedy, as we will see in the next section.

3.8 Concepts and Ideas[61]
3.8.1 Basic Confusion

The Westminster Confession of Faith (1.6) says, "The whole counsel of God concerning all things necessary for His own glory, man's salvation, faith and life, is either expressly set down in Scripture, or by good and necessary consequence may be deduced from Scripture: . . . ."[62] This last phrase is perfectly correct as long as we are dealing with concepts, not ideas. If a person is called a shepherd, we may conclude that he has a herd of sheep. If Jesus calls himself a Shepherd, we may *not* conclude that he has a herd of sheep. If people would say, but "shepherd" is obviously a metaphor here, we must reply: how can we be so sure that divine "election," "predestination," etc., are not metaphors as well, approximating divine realities that surpass our conceptual knowledge?

Only what belongs to our immanent reality, what in principle can be conceived in a logical-analytical way, can be expressed in a concept. Each concept refers to a matter that can

---
61. One of the best introductions to the subject is still Strauss (1973); see also Strauss (2009, passim), Troost (2012, 281–82 and passim), and Ouweneel (2014a and 2014b).
62. Dennison (*RCET* 4:235).

be defined, that is, expressed in an encompassing definition. However, if human thought focuses on transcendent reality, it must realize that it can only form ideas of that reality. Knowledge in the form of ideas is true knowledge, even rational knowledge—there is nothing mystical about ideas—but this knowledge surpasses conceptual knowledge. Because we can speak of the divine world only in the form of ideas, we soon encounter various paradoxes. These would be genuine (and unacceptable) contradictions only if the underlying matters would be conceptualized, which would be a serious mistake.

Paradoxes are *apparent* contradictions. Scripture is full of them: it reveals both God's unity and his plurality, both his omnipresence and his being occasionally "far off," both his transcendence and his immanence, both his immutability and his "changing his mind," both his peace and his unrest, both his retribution and his mercy, both his love and his hatred, both his predestination and his respect for human freedom, both his eternal counsel and human responsibility, both his foreknowledge and his not-always-knowing-beforehand. It is only theologians who create contradictions between such notions by viewing them in a conceptual way. Two conceptual systems conflict with each other if a feature of one system can be predicated as A, and a feature of the other as non-A. However, two systems of *ideas* cannot conflict with each other in this way, because whether the one or another feature can be predicated as A or non-A either surpasses our knowledge, or is known only when revealed.

If this state of affairs is not properly grasped, this may lead—and often *has* led—to theologians asserting that Scripture says A but actually means non-A because A cannot be true within the conceptual framework they have assembled. God relents, but of course he cannot actually relent. (One could even quote 1 Sam. 15:29 for this.) God changes his mind, but of course he cannot actually change his mind. God descends to earth to find out, but he actually knows already. God pleads with sinners to repent, but many of them are actually already reprobate according to his eternal counsel. God knows what certain people will do, but he actually cannot know, otherwise people would no longer be free. God sovereignly predestines, but he actually does so on the basis of foreseen faith.

3.8.2 Suprarational Knowledge

Please notice what is happening here. In all these (decretalist, Arminian, or Open Theist) cases it is not Scripture that actually means the opposite of what it says, but it is the theologians' conceptual framework that is mistaken. Were they to abandon their framework and approximate divine truths as *ideas, not* all of whose features can be predicated, we could maintain all the divine attributes without any supposed *conceptual* contradictions. It is hubris—though often unintended and unrecognized—to claim that we would be able to treat biblical truths as conceptual systems, every feature of which could be predicated. Again, this claim does not imply mysticism; it merely indicates the limitations of logical thought. Ideas are rational, but they refer to—not *ir*rational but—*suprational matters.

Every theology contains logical objects about which no theoretical concepts can be formed. Examples of such logical objects are: (a) (the being of) God (even apart from the question of the Trinity);[63] (b) the unity of the divine and the human natures in the one person of Christ;[64] (c) the transcendent-religious meaning of (immanent-historical) Scripture as the eternal Word of God;[65] (d) the transcendent human heart and all its immanent utterances and movements, and the religious relationship between this heart and God (or the idols);[66] (e) the transcendent fullness and unity of the (immanent-historical) church;[67] (f) the relationship between divine

---

63. See Ouweneel (EDR 2, chapter 2).
64. See Ouweneel (EDR 2, chapters 8–9).
65. See Ouweneel (EDR 11,187–91 and passim).
66. See Ouweneel (EDR 3, chapters 5–8).
67. See Ouweneel (EDR 7, chapters 2–4).

sovereignty and human responsibility; (g) the relationship between divine foreknowledge and human freedom.

About such *transcendent* matters we can speak only in terms derived from our *immanent* reality, simply because we know no other terms. In such cases, these terms do not refer to concepts but to superconcepts or ideas, in the sense that they refer to matters of which we can rationally speak but which at the same time surpass the boundaries of strict conceptualization, and even surpass immanent reality. If we want to speak of God in a scholarly way—and this is what theology is all about—we can do so only with creaturely terms (except the term "God" itself), which involve ideas, not concepts, namely, ideas referring to (a) his attributes (holiness, mercy, sovereignty, etc.), (b) his actions (his descending from heaven, his judgment, his redemption, etc.), and (c) his being.[68]

3.8.3 Ideas and Metaphors About God

There is a tendency within theology to refer to what I and others have called "ideas" as "metaphors."[69] I believe this is a mistake (see §1.7.1). The term "idea" is of a strictly logical nature, whereas the term "metaphor" is of a strictly linguistic nature. In other words, just like concepts, ideas belong to the domain of logic, metaphors to the domain of linguistics and the science of literature. Metaphors always have something arbitrary about them; they can easily be replaced by other metaphors. They are characterized by the fluidity and flexibility that is proper to any language. But ideas, being of a logical nature, do not, or rarely, have this feature.

For example, when Jesus speaks of "my Father's house" (John 14:2), this is the place where the Father dwells, and it is hardly possible to replace the terms "house" and "dwelling" by other terms that, through very different metaphors,

---

68. Cf. Pailin (1986, chapter 7); Brümmer (1988, chapter 2); Peterson et al. (1991, chapter 8).
69. Cf., e.g., the studies by Jüngel (1983, 2003); McFague (1983, 1987); Van Herck (1999); Muis (2010).

express the same thing. But when we say that the Word of God is like a fire or a hammer (Jer. 23:29), like seed or milk (1 Pet. 1:23; 2:2), like a sword (Eph. 6:17; Heb. 4:12), or like bread (Matt. 4:4), these are describing features that could just as well be described by rather different metaphors.

However, I do not wish to stress the distinction between ideas and metaphors too much, because my argument does not require this. It is far more important to properly understand the distinction between concepts and ideas, because it plays a key role in the present book. Rational knowledge is not limited to conceptual knowledge, as rationalism (also within theology!) has often implicitly taught, but contains also knowledge in the form of ideas. Our suprarational knowledge of God and his Word can be made explicit in beliefs that are rational, but not conceptual.

If this is not grasped, people necessarily seek escape in one of two ways, as theological practice demonstrates. Either they claim that knowledge of the transcendent, including knowledge of God, is not rational but irrational, and they thereby land in mysticism and bigotry. Or people claim that knowledge of the transcendent is possible if, and because, the transcendent falls under the rational order that applies to the cosmos. This would mean that, for instance, the transcendent God would be subject to the logical laws that he himself as Creator has instituted, not for himself but for his creation. And thus, people draw supposedly logical conclusions from God's sovereignty, or his foreknowledge, that may seem logically correct (which they are not) but are biblically unwarranted.

3.8.4 Examples

Cornelius Van Til is a striking example of this type of reasoning.[70] He speaks continually of our "conception" of God, and tells us that our knowledge must be "analogous," that is, based on the knowledge that God has of himself and of the

---

70. Van Til (1969, 200–209; cf. 1955, 52-63).

world.⁷¹ He claims that people cannot without detriment to themselves know a fact without knowing God's interpretation of that fact. Human knowledge of a fact, Van Til says, is therefore a re-interpretation of God's interpretation, and this is what is meant when we say that human knowledge is analogous to God's knowledge. Some of my counter-questions would be: (a) Why re-interpret what God has already interpreted? (b) What do we *know* about God's knowledge? With what standards of measurement do we identify his knowledge without subjecting his knowledge to the rational order that applies to *our* knowledge? (c) Why can we not simply be satisfied with what God has revealed in order that *we* would know it, apart from the question what knowledge *God* possesses of things?

Another consequence of the wrong way of thinking just described was that people began making a distinction between God's (supposed) *attributa incommunicabilia* or *absoluta* ("incommunicable" or "absolute" attributes, proper to God, not communicated to people and independent of creation) and his *attributa communicabilia* or *relativa* ("communicable" or "relative" attributes, communicated by God to people, that is, relating to his creation).⁷² One effect of this distinction was that a negative theology was designed, which enumerated only what God was *not*. Another effect was the view that we know God only in terms of the created relationships in which he has chosen to reveal himself. This means that God has revealed only his relationships, not his *being*, that is, not *himself*. In this case, we would not at all possess a revelation *of God* — an idea that would affect the very foundations of Christianity. In this case, Christians would not know *God*, but only the form in which he wished to present himself to them.

We need no longer take refuge in such unsafe asylums once we begin to recognize that there is *rational* knowledge in the form of *ideas*, that is, knowledge that surpasses the bound-

---

71. Van Til (1969, 200).
72. Cf. Bavinck (*RD* 2:§§29–30); Strauss (1983, 53–54; 2009, 202–203; 2010).

aries of conceptualization. In this case, it is no longer a problem to say that God used creational terms to truly reveal his *being*, that is, *himself*.

Of course, this does not mean that God is entirely *enclosed* within our rational knowledge. On the contrary, any knowledge of the transcendent ultimately surpasses all rational knowledge. For instance, knowledge of God in the truest sense is itself *transcendent* (suprarational) knowledge in the sense that it is the existential possession of the suprarational heart. However, this suprarational heart is not *ir*rational, as mysticism has always insisted. Rational knowledge of God in the form of ideas nourishes and enriches the suprarational knowledge of the heart. Although there is no rational-*conceptual* knowledge of the transcendent, there is definitely rational-*idea-like* knowledge of it, such as we find in theology. This knowledge does not enclose the transcendent, but it does approximate it. Moreover, there is *supra*rational knowledge of the transcendent in the sense of knowledge in its full, transcendent, existential meaning.

Chapter 4
The Approach of Open Theism

O Jerusalem, Jerusalem,
  the city that kills the prophets
  and stones those who are sent to it!
How often would I have gathered your
  children together
  as a hen gathers her brood under her wings,
  and you were not willing!
                                    Luke 13:34

Summary: *In the discussion about so-called free will, we must carefully distinguish between structure and direction (or the anthropological and the ethical aspects). This point plays a role in evaluating Open Theism, a theory claiming that the future is (partially) open, even to God. Many biblical passages are investigated that are adduced as arguments for Open Theism (God's conditional remarks, his "trying to find out," his disappointments and regrets, etc.). The basic underlying problem is the foreknowledge of God (like foreordination in decretalism), and thus God's omniscience. Other biblical arguments are adduced that suggest that God does know the entire future in advance. The deepest underlying problem involves God's sovereignty: does Open Theism attack this notion by suggesting that God's deeds are partially dependent on what choices (unknown in advance) people will make? Or has God sovereignly decided to accept people as his "junior partners"?*

4.1 Structure and Direction
4.1.1 Is the Will Free?

VIATORISM PUTS GREAT EMPHASIS ON the distinction between structure and direction, which is important also for evaluating the battle between decretalism (hyper-Calvinism), on the one hand, and Arminianism plus Open Theism, on the other. I have dealt more extensively with this important subject elsewhere.[1] *Structure* has to do with the various law-structures that the Creator has placed within cosmic reality. The pre-given law-based "blueprint" is what makes each thing a concrete *thing* according to God's ordinances.

If we call the creational structures "horizontal," we may call the *direction* "vertical" because it involves the orientation of people and their societal relationships either toward God as Creator and Lawgiver, to serve and honor him, or, since the Fall, away from God in apostasy. Herman Dooyeweerd states it this way: "Not the creational ordinances have been changed by sin, but the *direction of the human heart*, which has turned away from its Creator. Undoubtedly, this *radical* Fall affects the way in which people will *unlock* the powers that are *enclosed* by God within his creation."[2]

There has been much discussion about whether, after the Fall, the human will is still free.[3] Think of the debate on free will (*librium arbitrium*) between Pelagius and Augustine (fifth century), after this between Desiderius Erasmus and Martin Luther (sixteenth century), and still later between Jacob Arminius and Francis Gomarus (seventeenth century). The more that divine predestination and total dependency on God's sovereign grace are emphasized, the more endangered is the notion of free will. And the more that free will is emphasized, the more endangered are predestination and total dependency on God's sovereign grace.

In my view, this discussion is mainly or entirely based

---

1. Ouweneel (EDR 3, §14.2; 2014a, chapter 4).
2. Dooyeweerd (1963, 58).
3. See more extensively, Ouweneel (EDR 3, §14.4.3).

upon a failure to distinguish between structure and direction. Consequently, the debate gets reduced to a matter of quantity: How much room remains for divine sovereignty, and how much for human responsibility—as if both are on the same plane, and as if the entire issue is reducible to percentages on both sides.

4.1.2 The Corrupted Will

The situation becomes very different when we introduce the distinction between structure and direction. On the one hand, we may view human responsibility horizontally, as an aspect of the creational structure of people, which has not been affected by the Fall. Sin and the devil cannot affect God's own law, which he has instituted for creation. People are responsible beings, which means they can account for the choices they make, both before and after the Fall. On the other hand, we may view human responsibility vertically, as an aspect of the apostatic (idol-oriented) *or* anastatic (God-oriented) directedness of the human heart. Arminians say that people can definitely make choices toward God and for God. They are right if they are here referring to the creational (anthropological) structure of people; they are wrong if the apostate orientation of the natural human heart is in view. Calvinists say that people by themselves *cannot* make choices toward God and for God. They are right if they are here referring to the apostate orientation of the natural human heart; they are wrong if the creational (anthropological) structure of people is in view.

Seen from the creational structure of people it is obvious that, also after the Fall, people continually make choices of their own free will (for instance, to write books against decretalists or Open Theists). The fact that people can still be held responsible is because they can still make choices in freedom; if those choices were not free, they would not need to be accounted for. Scripture explicitly says, "[C]hoose life" (Deut. 30:19-20); "choose whom you will serve" (Josh. 24:15); and speaks of "the way that [a person] should choose" (Ps. 25:12).

Just as, also after the Fall, people can still think logically and still possess authentic emotions, so too they can still deliberate and make choices. They do so every day, every hour.

However, their thoughts, feelings, deliberations, and choices proceed from their hearts (Mark 7:21-23), and by definition, since the Fall these thoughts and choices are still thoroughly sinful in unconverted people (Rom. 1:21; 2 Cor. 4:4; Eph. 4:17-18). In terms of their creational structure, their will is still free; otherwise they would not be able to make any choices at all. However, unregenerate people are *not* free to think sinless thoughts and make sinless choices. That is, in regard to their moral-religious orientation, their will is *not* free (cf. Gen. 8:21; Titus 3:3; Rom. 8:7; 1 Cor. 2:14). In this conclusion, as I see it, the entire debate about the free human will has been summarized in three sentences.

In the sense that the *direction* of the natural human heart is corrupt, people have no free will and are entirely dependent on God's grace. In the sense that the *structure* of their will has not been affected, unregenerate people remain entirely responsible for the morally wrong choices they make. When it comes to the *direction* of their hearts, people are totally corrupt, that is, full of egoism, full of immorality, full of arrogance and selfishness, full of wickedness, full of foolishness. When it comes to the *structure* of their being, we still admire in people the image of God,[4] their beauty, their intellectual and artistic giftedness, their humanity, and sometimes even altruism, their occasional high morals (cf. Rom. 2:14-15). However, as a consequence of the perverted orientation of their hearts, even "all our *righteous* deeds are like a polluted garment" (Isa. 64:6).

At the deepest level, all choices of unregenerate people are *apostate* choices because their choices are made independently of God: "[W]hatever does not proceed from faith is sin" (Rom. 14:23; cf. 1 Cor. 10:23; Col. 3:17). "[W]hoever knows the right

---

4. Ouweneel (EDR 3, §5.1.2).

thing to do and fails to do it, for him it is sin" (James 4:17) — how much more is this true of those who do not even *know* the right thing to do. Not only are all choices of unregenerate people *apostate* choices, but unredeemed people *cannot* make any other choices than those in apostasy toward God. This is the meaning of "not being able" that we find, for instance, in 1 Corinthians 2: "The natural person does not accept the things of the Spirit of God, for they are folly to him, and *he is not able* to understand them because they are spiritually discerned" (v. 14; also cf. Eph. 2:3; 1 Pet. 4:2-3).

4.1.3 The Responsible Will

If the will of unregenerate people is corrupt because of sin, this in no way diminishes their responsibility before God. On the contrary, we hear repeatedly in Scripture how an appeal to this will is made, and hyper-Calvinists have to take this fully seriously in their theories. Moses said, "You did not *want* to go into the land, and you refused to obey the Lord your God" (Deut. 1:26 CEV), and: "[Y]ou *would* not obey the voice of the Lord your God" (8:20). Isaiah said, "[T]hus said the Lord God, the Holy One of Israel, 'In returning and rest you shall be saved; in quietness and in trust shall be your strength.' But you were *unwilling*" (Isa. 30:15). "O Jerusalem, Jerusalem, the city that kills the prophets and stones those who are sent to it! How often would I have gathered your children together as a hen gathers her brood under her wings, and you were not *willing*" (Luke 13:34).

This human will(ingness) plays a great role in repentance and conversion: "If anyone's *will* is to do God's will, he will know whether the teaching is from God" (John 7:17). "The one who *wants*, let him take the water of life freely" (Rev. 22:17b LEB). Conversion is a matter of human responsibility and of obedience to the command of God: he "commands all people everywhere to repent" (Acts 17:30). This is why the Bible speaks of the "obedience of faith" (Rom. 1:5; cf. 6:17; 15:18); people have to "obey the gospel" (10:16; 2 Thess. 1:8;

1 Pet. 4:17), or "the truth" (Rom. 2:8; 1 Pet. 1:22; cf. v. 2), or "the word" (1 Pet. 2:8; 3:1; also see John 3:36; Eph. 2:2; Titus 3:3).

However, what Arminians in turn must take with full seriousness is the fact that the human will, though horizontally (structurally) free, is vertically (directionally) *unfree*. In the latter respect, people are totally dependent on divine grace: "For by grace you have been saved through faith. And this is not your own doing; it is the gift of God" (Eph. 2:8; cf. v. 5). We are "saved through the grace of the Lord Jesus" (Acts 15:11). We are "justified by his grace as a gift, through the redemption that is in Christ Jesus" (Rom. 3:24; cf. Titus 3:7). "In him [i.e., Christ] we have redemption through his blood, the forgiveness of our trespasses, according to the riches of his [i.e., God's] grace" (Eph. 1:7). God "saved us and called us to a holy calling, not because of our works but because of his own purpose and grace, which he gave us in Christ Jesus before the ages began" (2 Tim. 1:9).

Just as hyper-Calvinists might have to leave more room for the horizontal human responsibility and free will, Arminians and Open Theists might have to take more seriously vertical human apostasy, inability, and absolute dependence on divine grace. By emphasizing the distinction between structure and direction, Viatorism has mapped out what is right and wrong on both sides of the debate about human free will.

4.2 More on Open Theism
4.2.1 A New View

For a few decades now, a new movement, known as Open Theism, has been growing within Evangelicalism (see §2.7). This rather opaque term implies that the movement's adherents believe that the future is partially or entirely open, not only for people but also for God. In other words, God cannot possibly know all the things that *free* creatures are going to do, because if God knew them already, the future would be fixed and certain, and people would not possess any genuine freedom at all.

The traditional view involves God's absolute omniscience, implying that because of his infinite foreknowledge, God knows the entire history of the world from the beginning. A few well-known verses thought to support this view include the following: a prophet "cried against the altar by the word of the LORD and said, 'O altar, altar, thus says the LORD: "Behold, a son shall be born to the house of David, Josiah by name, and he shall sacrifice on you the priests of the high places who make offerings on you, and human bones shall be burned on you"'" (1 Kings 13:2). Supposedly long before king Cyrus, God knew his name: he "says of Cyrus, 'He is my shepherd, and he shall fulfill all my purpose'" (Isa. 44:28). God is "declaring the end from the beginning and from ancient times things not yet done, saying, 'My counsel shall stand, and I will accomplish all my purpose'" (46:10). And David said, "Even before a word is on my tongue, behold, O LORD, you know it altogether.... Your eyes saw my unformed substance; in your book were written, every one of them, the days that were formed for me, when as yet there was none of them" (Ps. 139:4, 16).

The strictest form of this view argues that God not only *foreknows* all that happens, but also has *foreordained* it to happen this way: what he foreknew he also predestined. Foreknowledge and predestination coincide here, in spite of the distinction made in Romans 8:29 ("those whom he foreknew, he also predestined"). This seems to be consistent: if all history can be foreknown, then it seems logical that history can unfold in only one manner, namely, the one foreknown by God. However, this position puts an end to the free, responsible choices of people: they can choose only what God foreknew they would choose. Or even stronger: human beings can choose only what God had *foreordained* they would choose (see the previous chapter on decretalism). A less strict view maintains that God foreknows the entire history of the world, even that all that happens somehow falls under God's decree, but that this should not be played off against human freedom and responsibility.

Open Theists (if we may use this awful term) have broken with both the stricter and the milder view. They believe that by virtue of his *high* view of the people he created, God has invited them in his love to shape the future together with him. According to this view, he did not and does not foreknow the entire future, nor did he decree it, but his sovereign desire is to leave the future open (partially or entirely) to the free choices of his creatures. History is thus the result of what both God and his creatures decide to do. As German Reformed theologian Otto Weber expressed it: "[T]he Christian doctrine of providence includes the creature's own activity, and acknowledges the reality of evil in the realm of creation"[5] — which he later significantly relativizes, by the way.

In connection with this, Open Theism believes that God can know things only as they occur. If God would foreknow all future events, the future would be entirely fixed and rigid. No future decisions need to be made, or these would necessarily be foreknown, and thus foreordained decisions. One necessary and consistent implication of this view is that human freedom is an illusion.

4.2.2 Earlier Representatives

Although the Dutch dogmatician Hendrikus Berkhof labored within the Calvinist rather than the Arminian (and Open Theist) tradition, we do find similar thoughts in his work: "By means of the freedom with which God endows [people] and the love to which he calls [them], God begins a journey with [them] and involves [them] in a hazardous adventure. In the doctrine of God we observed already that thereby God also involves himself in an adventure. For by creating somewhere in the cosmos a free being, God limits his freedom to make room for daughters and sons as partners and counterplay-

---

5. Weber (1981, 1:507).

ers."[6]

Although we must constantly protect the distinction and distance between God as Creator and people as creatures, we notice that the Bible does encourage the notion of people as "junior partners" of God. Think, for instance, of the expression "we are God's fellow workers" in 1 Corinthians 3:9, and the notion of being God's "helpers": "'Curse Meroz,' says the angel of the LORD, 'curse its inhabitants thoroughly, because they did not come to the help of the LORD, to the help of the LORD against the mighty'" (Judg. 5:23). We have to savor this extraordinary expression: "They did not come to help the LORD fight. They did not help the LORD against his powerful enemies" (ERV). This may sound very strange to many ears. Hence people tend to argue away the force of the passage: "to the help of the LORD's case or the LORD's people"[7] (cf. the MSG: "rally to God's side with valiant fighters"; NET: "to help in the LORD's battle").

To many, and especially to decretalists, it makes no sense at all to imagine people as God's "junior partners," or even "helpers." The thought horrifies them. They say that such an idea diminishes God's omnipotence (cf. §7.2). However, this would be the case only if God were forced into this state of affairs, a compulsion that, of course, is absolutely untenable. In his omnipotence, God himself has *sovereignly decided* to appoint people as his junior partners, and thus, to some extent, to make himself dependent on them. Therefore, Greg Boyd rightly says that God could have created a world in which he did not need any prayers or any creaturely free decision to carry out his will. If God *needs* something, this is because he himself has *sovereignly chosen* to need this thing.[8]

According to Open Theists, this implies that God cannot foreknow the free decisions of people. They do not doubt God's omniscience concerning the present and the past, but

---

6. Berkhof (1986, 189).
7. E.g., Goslinga (1987, 315–16).
8. Boyd (2001, 232).

with this restriction: God knows all things, but then only the things that really *can* be known. Since, however, the future is not yet reality but will be determined in part by people with a free will and free options, then according to Open Theism God cannot foreknow which of the possible options will be realized by people. If God *were to* foreknow that, then those choices would be determined beforehand, removing any possibility of genuine choice. Therefore, in this view, omniscience implies complete foreknowledge, not of all future events, but only of all *possible* future events.

Reformed theologian Henk Venema adheres to a similar view. He says that God neither effectuated nor desired the Fall of the first people. God did not even expect it, for this would have implied that there was something in God's creation that was not altogether good.[9] This means that, according to Venema, some things cannot be foreknown by God. "God did not even expect it" goes a step further: God did not realize the likelihood *that* the Fall would occur. By the way, Open Theists would not agree with this; in this respect, Venema is going too far, even for *their* tastes.

4.2.3 Protest

Open Theism has elicited irritation among all traditional theologians who have a high view of God's omniscience: God knows everything, not only all that has happened, and is happening at this moment, but also everything that *will* happen. Such theologians quote verses like these: "My times are in your hand" (Ps. 31:16). "[T]he righteous and the wise and their deeds are in the hand of God. Whether it is love or hate, man does not know; both are before him" (Eccl. 9:1). The latter verse's two parts suggests that God does know all things that are before him (and before people). The Lord clearly says that God declares "the end from the beginning and from ancient times things not yet done, saying, 'My counsel shall

---

9. Venema (1992, 170); cf. already Venema (1965); see especially Venema (1992, chapter 10).

stand, and I will accomplish all my purpose'" (Isa. 46:10). God knows beforehand every word a person will say: "Even before a word is on my tongue, behold, O LORD, you know it altogether" (Ps. 139:4).

In addition, we have to realize that not everyone agrees that foreknowledge of free human actions entails that those actions are not really *free*. They are convinced, as I am, that human actions can be both free and foreknown by God.[10] Precisely *how* these two features are compatible must be left aside here, because that discussion would lead us down too many philosophical sideroads. For our purposes, we suffice by noting that the claim that foreknowledge and freedom are mutually exclusive is rooted in the aforementioned confusion of concepts and ideas.

Interestingly, the great Rabbi Akiba said about 1,900 years ago: "Everything is foreseen [by God], but the right [of choice] [i.e., free will] is granted." In other words, God's absolute foreknowledge does not exclude human freedom.[11]

Open Theists not only assert that divine foreknowledge and human freedom of action are mutually exclusive. But they take another large step by pointing to many Bible passages that strongly suggest that God does *not* always know what is happening or what is going to happen. Apparently, Open Theists employ not only philosophical but also theological arguments. One may have a very high view of God's omniscience, but Scripture seems surprisingly clear about the openness of the future. Because this point is quite important for my purpose, I will be producing a somewhat exhausting number of relevant examples. At this point, I want to strongly emphasize the fact that each of the passages cited below constitutes an argument *against* the doctrine that everything has been *foreordained* by God. If it is true that God apparently does not foreknow certain things, it is impossible to maintain that

---

10. Cf. Boyd (2000, 120).
11. *BabT*: Aboth III.15 (with the footnotes in the Soncino edition).

he would have decreed beforehand that they would happen.[12]

4.3 An Open Future?
4.3.1 "Perhaps"

In a remarkable number of cases, God himself suggests that he does not know the future, for instance, by using the word "perhaps" or words with a similar meaning:[13] "God did not lead them [by] way of the land of the Philistines, although that [was] near; for God said, *'Lest perhaps* the people change their minds when they see war, and return to Egypt'" (Exod. 13:17 NKJV). God saw the *possibility*, but suggested he did not possess the *certainty* that Israel would wish to return to Egypt. He took precautions that seem to have been superfluous if he had foreknown exactly what Israel would do. The entire idea of God taking precautions seems to be in utter conflict with the traditional idea of God's omniscience.

Similarly, the Lord said to Jeremiah, "[S]peak to all the cities of Judah . . . all the words that I command you to speak to them; do not hold back a word. It *may be* they will listen, and every one turn from his evil way, that I may relent of the disaster that I intend to do to them because of their evil deeds" (26:2–3). "It *may be* that the house of Judah will hear all the disaster that I intend to do to them, so that every one may turn from his evil way, and that I may forgive their iniquity and their sin" (36:3). What else can this mean than that God was not certain whether Israel would repent?

Similarly the Lord said to Ezekiel, "As for you, son of man, prepare for yourself an exile's baggage, and go into exile by day in their sight. . . . *Perhaps* they will understand, though they are a rebellious house" (12:3). In other words, God did not yet know this.

Now before anyone exclaims that these are simply examples of anthropomorphisms, please be patient. I will return below to this matter of (possible) anthropomorphisms.

---
12. See extensively, Boyd (2000, 55–87, 157–69; 2001, 100–109).
13. Cf. Pinnock (2001, 47–48).

4.3.2 "If"

The future seems equally open when God says "if" to Moses: "*If* they will not believe you, . . . or listen to the first sign, they may believe the latter sign. *If* they will not believe even these two signs or listen to your voice, you shall take some water from the Nile and pour it on the dry ground, and the water that you shall take from the Nile will become blood on the dry ground" (Exod. 4:8-9). The second sign is only needed if the first sign is not believed, and the third sign is only needed if the second sign is not believed. But the question *whether* the first or the second sign is believed, is left open by God. The text suggests that he does not know — for if he had foreknown that the first or second sign would be believed, it would not have been necessary to supply Moses with a second and a third sign, respectively.

In other cases, eagerly mentioned by Open Theists, it seems less clear that God does not foreknow the future: "[I]*f* you will not listen to me and will not do all these commandments, *if* you spurn my statutes, and *if* your soul abhors my rules, so that you will not do all my commandments, but break my covenant, then I will" bring judgment upon you (Lev. 26:14-16; cf. vv. 18, 21). To king Solomon God said, "And as for you, *if* you will walk before me, as David your father walked, . . . then I will establish your royal throne over Israel forever. . . . But *if* you turn aside from following me, you or your children, . . . then I will cut off Israel from the land that I have given them" (1 Kings 9:4-7). To Israel God said, "[I]*f* you truly amend your ways and your deeds, *if* you truly execute justice one with another, *if* you do not oppress the sojourner, the fatherless, or the widow, or shed innocent blood in this place, and *if* you do not go after other gods to your own harm, then I will let you dwell in this place, in the land that I gave of old to your fathers forever" (Jer. 7:5-7). "[I]*f* you will indeed obey this word, then there shall enter the gates of this house kings who sit on the throne of David, ... But *if* you will not obey these words, I swear by myself... that this house shall become a desolation" (22:4–5).

To king Zedekiah God said, "*If* you will surrender to the officials of the king of Babylon, then your life shall be spared, and this city shall not be burned with fire, and you and your house shall live. But *if* you do not surrender to the officials of the king of Babylon, then this city shall be given into the hand of the Chaldeans, and they shall burn it with fire, and you shall not escape from their hand. . . . Obey now the voice of the LORD in what I say to you, and it shall be well with you, and your life shall be spared. But *if* you refuse to surrender," your end will be terrible (38:17–21).

In all these cases it is quite possible that God is simply presenting to certain persons, or to the people as a whole, certain options between which they may choose. He also describes what will be the consequences if option P or option Q is followed. Such presentations do *not* prove that God does not foreknow what the persons involved would actually choose. God may say to someone: If you fall into the water, you will get wet; and if you fall into the fire, you will get burned. This does not mean that God does not foreknow whether the person will indeed fall into the water or into the fire.

It is true, however, that such statements make sense only if the future offers various genuine options: if a person chooses P, then X will follow; but if he chooses Q, then Y will follow. Apparently, whether X or Y occurs has not been foreordained by God (*contra* decretalism) — although it may be fore*known* by him (*contra* Open Theism) — but depends on the person's choice. If, as decretalism claims, God had *decreed* beforehand what choices people will make, it would be totally inconceivable why, with such seriousness, God places people before a certain choice.

By the way, these observations also serve to clarify the difference between God's counsel and God's ways: God will realize his *counsel* in any case — if it is not by *way* X, then by *way* Y. Various ways can lead to the realization of the one counsel of God. This counsel has been determined exclusively and entirely by the sovereign God. The way whereby the counsel is realized depends on God but also on the good or bad choices that people make. God may earnestly plead with people to make good choices, but he created them as free beings that can make good, but also bad choices. But whatever they may choose, God always attains his own goals.

4.3.3 Investigation

On other occasions, God undertakes certain things in order to find out something about a particular situation: "Now out of the ground the LORD God had formed every beast of the field and every bird of the heavens and brought them to the man *to see* what he would call them" (Gen. 2:19). "And the LORD came down *to see* the city and the tower, which the children of man had built" (11:5). "I will go down *to see* whether they have done altogether according to the outcry that has come to me. And if not, *I will know*" (18:21). God investigates a matter to find out whether it is R, S, or T—and the text strongly suggests that he does so because he does not yet know.

"And you shall remember the whole way that the LORD your God has led you these forty years in the wilderness, that he might humble you, *testing* you *to know* what was in your heart, whether you would keep his commandments or not" (Deut. 8:2). "For the LORD your God is *testing* you, *to know* whether you love the LORD your God with all your heart and with all your soul" (13:3). "I will no longer drive out before them any of the nations that Joshua left when he died, in order *to test* Israel by them, whether they will take care to walk in the way of the LORD as their fathers did, or not" (Judg. 2:22). "They [i.e., the Canaanites] were for the *testing* of Israel, *to know* whether Israel would obey the commandments of the Lord, which he commanded their fathers by the hand of Moses" (3:4). "And so in the matter of the envoys of the princes of Babylon, who had been sent to him to inquire about the sign that had been done in the land, God left him [i.e., Hezekiah] to himself, in order *to test* him and *to know* all that was in his heart" (2 Chron. 32:31).

Also see other passages in which people are "tested": "After these things God *tested* Abraham" (Gen. 22:1). "Behold, I am about to rain bread from heaven for you, and the people shall go out and gather a day's portion every day, that I may *test* them, whether they will walk in my law or not" (Exod. 16:4). If we take these passages seriously, they mean that God sometimes undertakes steps to find out things that apparently he does not yet know. As a consequence, God sometimes, *after* he has carried out such an investigation, says he has learned something: "Do not lay your hand on the boy or do anything to him, for *now I know* that you fear God, seeing you have not withheld your son, your only son, from me" (Gen. 22:12). Compare the entirely analogous *human* "now I know" at other places (Exod. 18:11; Judg. 17:13; 2 Kings 5:15; Ps. 20:6). Both God and people may say after thorough examination of a case: "Now I know . . . ."

In some cases, expositors have suggested that the testing might occur not to enlighten God himself but to show other people what is in the hearts of those tested. Perhaps God tested Abraham (Gen. 22:1) in order that *we* all would see what was in the latter's heart.[14] However, this possibility is weakened by the cases in which God explicitly said that *he* wanted to know for himself the result of a certain test.

On his part, a person may appeal to God in order that he (God) will learn something: "*Search* me, O God, and *know* my heart! *Try* me and *know* my thoughts! And *see if* there be any grievous way in me, and lead me in the way everlasting!" (Ps. 139:23–24). "Know my heart/thoughts" clearly means: search me in order to find out what is in my heart and thoughts. This is the same David who began this same psalm as follows:

O LORD, you have searched me and known me! You know when

---

14. Thus, e.g., John Gill (1746, ad loc.).

I sit down and when I rise up; you discern my thoughts from afar. You search out my path and my lying down and are acquainted with all my ways. Even before a word is on my tongue, behold, O LORD, you know it altogether (vv. 1-4).

It sounds as if the prayer of verses 23-24 precedes the result as described in verses 1-4!

4.3.4 Further Examples and Comments

Perhaps, this apparent uncertainty with regard to the future can also be observed in various questions asked by God: "*How long* will you refuse to keep my commandments and my laws?" (Exod. 16:28). "*How long* will this people despise me? And *how long* will they not believe in me, in spite of all the signs that I have done among them? . . . *How long* shall this wicked congregation grumble against me?" (Num. 14:11, 27). "*How long* shall your wicked thoughts lodge within you?" (Jer. 4:14). "Woe to you, O Jerusalem! *How long* will it be before you are made clean?" (13:27). "I have spurned your calf, O Samaria. My anger burns against them. *How long* will they be incapable of innocence?" (Hos. 8:5). In each of these cases, God speaks as if he himself does not know the answer to this "how long?" However, in this case it is quite possible that these questions are only rhetorical exclamations. They do not necessarily suggest that God does not know the answers to them.

A similar type of question whose answer God does not seem to know is the "who" question: "*Who* will entice Ahab, that he may go up and fall at Ramoth-gilead?" (1 Kings 22:20). "*Whom* shall I send, and *who* will go for us?" (Isa. 6:8). However, these questions may not mean anything more than that God is testing his audience, and it is uncertain whether he knows the test's outcome. For instance, in Isaiah 6 God's question is asked in the young prophet's hearing, for the purpose of challenging him to offer himself.

Indeed, these examples are less convincing. Yet, enough

examples suggest that, even to God, the future in many respects is uncertain, or open. To rescue one's dogma, it is always possible to assert that an "as it were" or a "so to speak" is meant. But there must be some basis in the text for such an assertion. Nor is there any basis for suggesting that God could not have expressed himself otherwise to reach our human understanding. Why say "perhaps" or "maybe," instead of stating directly what was going to happen? Why speak of "testing," why say "that I may know," if God already knew from eternity? Why not simply tell his people what he already knew? Why should we brush all these examples off the table only to rescue *our* ideas about God's omniscience?

With this, I am not denying that there are many metaphors and anthropomorphisms in the Bible, or that God could say things "as it were" or "so to speak." What I mean is that we have to be consistent. We cannot accept God's *certain* statements about the future as being literal, and his *uncertain* statements about the future as being figurative, simply because this fits our preconceived ideas. If God says "maybe" or "if," he apparently *means* it, for instead of this he could easily have made apodictic statements about the future. Instead of saying "perhaps the people will repent," God could rather have said, "the people will *not* repent," and announce corresponding measures.[15]

Sometimes, God does say, for instance, "Pharaoh will not listen to you" (Exod. 7:4). God told Jeremiah, "So you shall speak all these words to them [i.e., Israel], but they will not listen to you. You shall call to them, but they will not answer you" (Jer. 7:27). I take this just as seriously and literally as the cases in which God says, "perhaps," or "maybe," or "if." Let us face it: predictive phrases like "they *will* (not) listen" are problematic for Open Theists; presumptive phrases like "perhaps they will (not) listen" are problematic for decretalists.

Terence E. Fretheim has written that the Old Testament

---

15. König (2006, 321–22).

speaks of a God who takes part in our human history as past, present, and future, and does so in such a way that we can even speak of a history of God.[16] God has bound himself in relationship to the world in such a way that we together, God and people, move through time and space. Although he is the uncreated member of this community, he too can exclaim, "How long?" (Jer. 4:14; 13:27; Hos. 5:8).[17]

In a remarkable way, this (seeming?) uncertainty is also observed in a verse like this one: "What shall I do with you, O Ephraim? What shall I do with you, O Judah? Your love is like a morning cloud, like the dew that goes early away" (Hos. 6:4). This sounds as if God himself no longer knows what to do with his blacksliding people, just like the desperation of a human father dealing with an unruly child.

4.4. Strange Predictions
4.4.1 Implicitly Conditional Predictions

Interestingly, God sometimes makes predictions that sound rather absolute, and yet have not been fulfilled. Thus, we read,

> Then David said, "O LORD, the God of Israel, your servant has surely heard that Saul seeks to come to Keilah, to destroy the city on my account. Will the men of Keilah surrender me into his hand? Will Saul come down, as your servant has heard?" . . . And the LORD said, "He will come down." Then David said, "Will the men of Keilah surrender me and my men into the hand of Saul?" And the LORD said, "They will surrender you" (1 Sam. 23:10–12).

None of these predictions was fulfilled, however, because David and his men left Keilah right away. The predictions turned out to be conditional, although the LORD had not said at all, "*If you stay in Keilah*, Saul will come down, and the citizens of Keilah will surrender you into Saul's hand." God speaks in such an absolute way that, under different circumstances, we

---
16. Cf. the title of Armstrong (2004).
17. Fretheim (1984, 44).

would certainly think of an unconditional prophecy. However, in this case, God is not describing the real future but only a *possible* future, which, at the moment David leaves Keilah, is *no* longer possible.

Naturally, we wonder in how many more cases God's predictions are actually conditional without us being able to discover that in the text. When Jonah told the Ninevites: "Yet forty days, and Nineveh shall be overthrown!" (Jonah 3:4), this was at God's instigation (see v. 2). Apparently, Jonah himself was unaware that this absolute sounding prediction was actually conditional (cf. 4:1): when the people of Nineveh repented, the judgment did not become reality. Isaiah's message to Hezekiah, "Set your house in order, for you shall die, you shall not recover" (Isa. 38:1), afterwards turned out to be conditional as well: when Hezekiah earnestly prayed to the Lord, fifteen years were added to his age (v. 5).

It is begging the question[18] when people claim that God foreknew that David would leave Keilah, or that Nineveh would repent, or that Hezekiah would beseech him. However, I hasten to add that these examples do not at all prove that God did *not* foreknow what David, the Ninevites, or Hezekiah would do. They unmistakably point to a certain openness of the future (*contra* the decretalists), but *these* examples do not necessarily prove that God does not know that future (*contra* the Open Theists).

If the decretalists were right, God would have consciously spoken untruth: he predicted something he foreknew would not occur. As I see it, God did speak the truth, though in each case with a silent condition: Keilah *will* surrender you to Saul (unless you leave right away), Nineveh *will* be overthrown (unless it repents), Hezekiah *will* die (unless he beseeches the Lord to let him live). Decretalists cannot claim that God foreknew that the "unless" would become true — but Open Theists cannot claim that God did *not* foreknow this. In both cases

---

18. As Calvin does, for example, in the case of Jonah (*Comm. Jonah*); Hughes (1989, 176–77).

the claimants would be saying more than they could account for. In my view, conditional predictions do not allow any conclusions for or against decretalism or Open Theism.

4.4.2 Explicitly Conditional Predictions

Some predictions, which bear the other features identified in the previous section, are explicitly conditional. Thus Jeremiah says to king Zedekiah,

> Thus says the LORD, the God of hosts, the God of Israel: "*If* you will surrender to the officials of the king of Babylon, then your life shall be spared, and this city shall not be burned with fire, and you and your house shall live. But *if* you do not surrender to the officials of the king of Babylon, then this city shall be given into the hand of the Chaldeans, and they shall burn it with fire, and you shall not escape from their hand" (Jer. 38:17-18).

God knows for *sure* what will happen if Zedekiah surrenders, and he also knows for *sure* what will happen if Zedekiah does *not* surrender. But *whether* Zedekiah will surrender or not is apparently an open question. However, the text does not allow any conclusion about whether this is an open question for God too.

The same is true in Jeremiah 23:22: "[I]*f* they [i.e., the false prophets] had stood in my council, then they would have proclaimed my words to my people, and they would have turned them from their evil way, and from the evil of their deeds." Similarly, Jesus tells us what *surely* would have happened if the miracles he had done in Galilee would have occurred in Tyre, Sidon, or Sodom:

> Woe to you, Chorazin! Woe to you, Bethsaida! For *if* the mighty works done in you had been done in Tyre and Sidon, they would have repented long ago in sackcloth and ashes. . . . And you, Capernaum, will you be exalted to heaven? You will be brought down to Hades. For *if* the mighty works done in you had been done in Sodom, it would have remained until this day (Matt. 11:21-23).

The apostle Paul writes about God's wisdom: "None of the rulers of this age understood this, for *if* they had, they would not have crucified the Lord of glory" (1 Cor. 2:8). In all these cases, the text speaks of certainties that become (or would have become) reality if certain conditions are (or would have been) fulfilled. This form of knowledge is called *middle knowledge* (Latin *scientia media*); since Luis de Molina (d. 1600), this notion is identified as Molinism (see §4.6.4).[19] Middle knowledge involves certain knowledge of the future if particular conditions have been fulfilled. It is *certain* knowledge, but whether the necessary conditions will be met is *not* certain, at least not to people. Again, whether this is uncertain to God as well is not answered by the text.

An interesting example is what the prophet Agabus said to the apostle Paul: "Thus says the Holy Spirit, 'This is how the Jews at Jerusalem will bind the man who owns this belt and deliver him into the hands of the Gentiles.'" The text continues: "When we heard this, we and the people there urged him not to go up to Jerusalem" (Acts 21:11-12). This is a form of middle knowledge. What Agabus apparently means is this: *if* Paul goes to Jerusalem, this and that will *certainly* happen to him. But *whether* Paul goes to Jerusalem is up to him. Apparently, Agabus' prophecy was taken this way by his companions and the local Christians: not as an immutable divine counsel, for they respected the freedom that Paul had *not* to go to Jerusalem, and thus to falsify the prediction. Apparently, they did not view Paul's freedom to be in conflict with "the will of the Lord" (v. 14).

By the way, Paul decided to go after all, and yet the precise details of the prophecy were not fulfilled, for it was not the *Jews* who bound Paul to deliver him to the Gentiles, but it was the *Romans* who rescued him from the hands of the Jews (21:27-33). If the Holy Spirit had really spoken through Agabus, why were the precise details of the prophecy not ful-

---

19. See extensively, Flint (1998); MacGregor (2015).

filled? I see only two possible answers: either Agabus did not infallibly prophesy precise details,[20] or in God's foreknowledge the future has not been determined in all its details.[21]

4.4.3 God Leaves the Choice to a Person

In 2 Samuel 24:12-13 (cf. 1 Chron. 21:7-13), God presents David with a real choice by sending the prophet Gad to him:

> Go and say to David, "Thus says the LORD, 'Three things I offer you. Choose one of them, that I may do it to you.'" So Gad came to David and told him, and said to him, "Shall three years of famine come to you in your land? Or will you flee three months before your foes while they pursue you? Or shall there be three days' pestilence in your land? Now consider, and decide what answer I shall return to him who sent me."

Here God is presenting a person with genuine alternatives. This may appear to support Open Theism, because it seems the future is open here. However, decretalists could retort that God not only foreknew what David would choose, but even decreed it. Open Theists may respond by wondering why, if this were true, God presented David with these alternatives in the first place. To test David's motives? But even these motives had been foreordained, if decretalists are right.

None of the three options was necessarily better or worse than any other, and David could freely choose between them. God adapted the future to the choice David would make. Open Theists argue that the choice would not have had any significance if God had *foreordained* David's choice, and had also decreed the consequences of the choice. This would be distorting the clear purport of the text. Apparently, the future is partially open since, at this point, it depended on the choice David would make. All freedom and responsibility are eliminated if we must believe that human choices are foreordained

---

20. Luke's record of what Agabus said was infallibly inspired, but that does not make Agabus himself infallible; see Ouweneel (EDR 11, chapters 7–8).
21. Boyd (2000, 167–69); Pinnock (2001, 50–51) gives another example: the destruction of Tyre (Ezek. 26:1–21; cf. 29:17–20).

by God. Again I ask, why not tell David immediately what God would do? Why (falsely) *suggest* to him that he had genuine options?

On the other hand, Open Theism does not hit the target here either. That is, I think Greg Boyd goes too far in asserting that, if God foreknew what David would choose, the aim of the offer would be inexplicable.[22] Such a conclusion is not necessary at all. Boyd should have said that, if God had *foreordained* what David would choose, the aim of the offer would be inexplicable. However, there is no reason why God could not present a person with a genuinely free choice, while he (God) foreknew what that person would choose. This is an important point, to which we must return.

4.5 God's Responses
4.5.1 Disappointment

The idea that the future is partially open, *also for God,* seems to follow in quite a compelling way from the emotional manner in which God responds to unwanted and undesired events that occur. Here again, I mention some examples that, in my view, are quite remarkable and convincing.

Several times, God states that he *expected* P to happen but was disappointed to find out that Q occurred. Thus we read of his "vineyard" Israel: "He *expected* [it] to bring forth [good] grapes, but it brought forth wild grapes.... What more could have been done to My vineyard That I have not done in it? Why then, when I *expected* [it] to bring forth [good] grapes, did it bring forth wild grapes?" (Isa. 5:2, 4 NKJV). And elsewhere: "I *thought*, 'After she [i.e., Israel] has done all this she will return to me,' but she did not return" (Jer. 3:7). "I *thought* you would call me, 'My Father,' and would not turn from following me. Surely, as a treacherous wife leaves her husband, so have you been treacherous to me, O house of Israel" (vv. 19–20).

David Pawson asks whether God knows exactly what

---
22. Boyd (2000, 161).

direction every person will go. To him this is doubtful for, if this were the case, God can never be really disappointed, for disappointment is the result of an unexpected (and unpleasant) response.[23] A striking example that Pawson quotes is Zephaniah 3:7, where the Lord had said, "*Surely* you will fear me; you will accept correction. Then your dwelling would not be cut off according to all that I have appointed against you." *But* "all the more they were eager to make all their deeds corrupt."

If God knows everything beforehand, how could anything occur other than what he had expected? Of course, God knew that backsliding *could* occur; but it seemed more obvious that Israel would remain faithful to him. Therefore he speaks as if he did not really expect that they would turn their backs on him. In a decretalist view, such passages do not make any sense at all. It does not help to appeal to anthropomorphisms or "God pretends" arguments because the text provides no basis for this. Moreover, even were one to stress that disappointment is a purely human emotion, and that God's disappointment is just an anthropomorphism, this does not change the fact that God himself says that something happened other than what he had expected.

Decretalists have no other option than to make the text say something other than it really says. They do so, not on the basis of the text, but because their dogma is unassailable, especially their Hellenist view of the immutability of God (§6.5). Even anthropomorphisms and metaphors have to be taken seriously; we cannot make them say the opposite of what they do say.[24] The LORD calls the sacrificing of children something "which I did not command or decree, *nor did it come into my mind*" (Jer. 19:5; ERV, ICB: ". . . I never even thought of such a thing"; cf. 7:31; 32:35). Saying that Israel's apostasy did not cross God's mind is precisely the opposite of saying that it had been in God's mind from eternity. To say nothing of the

---
23. Pawson (2005, 186).
24. Boyd (2000, 118–19); Pinnock (2001, 61).

horrible idea that God *decreed* this apostasy from eternity.

It is remarkable that, in the parable of the tenants, Jesus makes the master of the house say, when sending his son to the unrighteous tenants: "They will respect my son" (Matt. 21:37; Mark 12:6). It is rather disingenuous to dismiss this as "just" parabolic language. In the interpretation of the parable, it does suggest a real expectation on God's part, which did not come true.[25] Of course, we know perfectly well that the rejection of Jesus took place "according to the definite plan and foreknowledge of God" (Acts 2:23). But this seems to be just as true as God's lament that he expected faithfulness from Israel and got backsliding instead. Such biblical statements should not be played off against each other.

4.5.2 Regret

There are other cases in which God regrets—or relents concerning—things that he himself has done, such as the creation of humanity (Gen. 6:6), the appointment of Saul as king over Israel (1 Sam. 15:11, 35), the announcement of judgment upon Israel after its sin with the golden calf (Exod. 32:14), the same after David's counting the people (2 Sam. 24:16), the same in Amos' vision (Am. 7:1-6), and the same over Nineveh (Jonah 3:10; 4:2). In all these cases, it seems that God's plans with this world are possibilities that he would be pleased to realize, but certain factors stand in the way of this realization. It seems that God can foresee these factors as possibilities, but not as fixed outcomes.

God's regret when events occur differently from what he had intended contains genuine *grief*. He would have loved to see P occur, but alas! it was Q that happened. If God foreknew with certainty that it would be Q, why the disappointment when Q occurs? Why the intense grief in some cases? If I know for sure that I have failed my exam, I can no longer be disappointed. Only when I still have hope can I be disappointed.

---

25. See extensively, Venema (1992, 91–95).

The Bible mentions many examples of regret, disappointment, grief, and related emotions in God: "[T]he LORD regretted that he had made man on the earth, and it *grieved* him to his heart" (Gen. 6:6). "You shall not walk in the customs of the nation which I am casting out before you; for they did all these things, and therefore I was wearied [and] *grieved* by them" (Lev. 20:23 AMPC). "And they put away the strange gods from among them and served the LORD; and His soul was *grieved* for the misery of Israel" (Judg. 10:16 KJV). "How often they rebelled against him in the wilderness and *grieved* him in the desert!" (Ps. 78:40). "For forty years I was *grieved* with [that] generation" (95:10). "But they rebelled and *grieved* his Holy Spirit; therefore he turned to be their enemy, and himself fought against them" (Isa. 63:10). "[T]hey pour out drink offerings to other gods, to provoke me to *anger*" (Jer. 7:18). "[D]o not *grieve* the Holy Spirit of God, by whom you were sealed for the day of redemption" (Eph. 4:30).

Of course, this does not mean that new, unexpected circumstances would ever give God an unpleasant surprise, and would embarrass him as if he would not know what to do. In his ways with the world, he can always adapt his plans to the new developments. But always there are responsible people involved in such situations. *How* God will act is co-determined by the choices of these people. Thus, in Genesis 18 it appears still uncertain whether God will destroy Sodom: at Abraham's request, this will depend on the number of the righteous that God will find there.[26] At the moment he spoke with Abraham he suggested that he did not yet know this number. Verse 21 tells us emphatically that God *goes down* to find out how bad the situation of Sodom is.

Of course, we must argue here in a prudent way. On the one hand, it is cheap and contrary to other Bible passages to dismiss this regretting or relenting as anthropomorphic, or as "only a way of speaking." On the other hand, Scripture makes

---

26. Pinnock (2001, 102).

clear that this regret should not be understood in too human a way. The same chapter, 1 Samuel 15, which tells us twice that God regretted that he had made Saul king over Israel (vv. 11, 35), also says, "[A]lso the Glory of Israel will not lie or have regret, for he is not a man, that he should have regret" (v. 29; in all three cases it is the same verb *nhm*). God's regretting is different from human regretting, for the latter always entails lament, remorse, even repentance. However, God's regretting certainly involves matters that he had not intended (decreed!), which nonetheless occurred.[27]

Sometimes we do not find the words "regretting" or "relenting" where the idea as such is clearly present. Because of Ephraim's terrible sins God cannot do anything but deliver them to judgment; but: "How can I give you up, O Ephraim? How can I hand you over, O Israel? How can I make you like Admah? How can I treat you like Zeboiim? My heart recoils within me; my compassion grows warm and tender. I will not execute my burning anger; I will not again destroy Ephraim" (Hos. 11:8-9). Here, we see the Lord being torn up, as it were, by contrary emotions: anger and mercy. This is a picture very different from a kind of Stoic God, who knows, and even has decreed, from eternity what he will do with Ephraim. Surely it is a human way of speaking; but remember, we *have* no other way of speaking about God. We see here an inner battle within God, described in human terms but nonetheless truthful. We are spectators of this battle, and we may learn the outcome of it: ultimately God's mercy prevails over his fury.

4.5.3 Fury

Reformed theologian Henk Venema asked, "Why would God actually become angry and furious, although the Bible mentions this frequently enough? Is it not true that everything must go according to God's will and plan? Does this not actually amount to saying that God is fighting against himself,

---

27. Boyd (2000, 79).

and is angry with what he has caused himself?"[28] Indeed, hyper-Calvinism implies that God is a Stoic God, who does not experience emotions because he himself is elevated beyond all human emotions (cf. §6.6), and because everything occurs exactly the way he has from eternity foreseen, foreknown, and even foreordained. There can be no room for genuine disappointment, regret, or anger — only for *disguised* disappointment, regret, and anger.

However, in reality we read often that God's anger or fury is kindled when things do not go the way he wants. We should not theorize this anger away as a kind of "judicial anger," as if we can remove the emotional aspect from it. This is not how the Bible speaks, for it says: "He let loose on them his burning anger, wrath, indignation, and distress" (Ps. 78:49). Does this sound coldly judicial and matter-of-fact? And what about this: "I myself will fight against you with outstretched hand and strong arm, in anger and in fury and in great wrath" (Jer. 21:5)? Or this: "The LORD gave full vent to his wrath; he poured out his hot anger" (Lam. 4:11). Or this: "I am exceedingly angry with the nations that are at ease; for while I was angry but a little, they furthered the disaster" (Zech. 1:15; cf. vv. 2, 12; Num. 11:1; Deut. 1:34; 4:21; 9:19; 2 Kings 22:13, 17; 2 Chron. 6:36; 28:9; 34:21, 25; Ps. 95:10–11 [cf. Heb. 3:7–10]; Isa. 12:1; 47:6; 54:9; 57:16–17; 64:5, 9).

It is interesting to see the example of Assyria in relation to the wrath of God. In God's hand, Assyria is the "rod of my anger; the staff of their hands is my fury" (Isa. 10:5). However, Assyria is not a weak-willed instrument; on the contrary, it performs its task in its own way, and thus Assyria itself kindles God's indignation (vv. 7–19). What Assyria did was not what God had commanded it to do. Thus, this was definitely not the result of a decree of God; its behavior proceeded from its own sinful and corrupt heart. Apparently, it is possible that people, according to the freedom and responsibility that

---

28. Venema (1992, 23).

God himself has granted them, do things contrary to the will and the counsel of God.

Sometimes, things go in a way different from what God wants *without* this affecting his sovereignty, simply because in the end the outcome is what he had foreordained. As Venema put it, within the biblical perspective God's sovereignty does not depend on his decreeing beforehand all that occurs.[29] That is, his sovereignty is not necessarily affected when something occurs that God has not actively willed and decreed beforehand, *as long as at least three conditions are fulfilled:*

(a) God himself has sovereignly decided to grant humanity its own responsibility and freedom.

(b) God himself oversees all events so that no human can undertake anything apart from the permissive will of God.

(c) God guarantees that the final outcome of history is what he has decreed; no human deed can ever prevent this.

This is an important matter, which we will deal with later in this book (see §§4.6 and 6.1–6.4).

4.6 Comments
4.6.1 No Attack on God's Sovereignty

For a proper understanding, we must now make some comments with respect to all the biblical examples given. First, none of these examples means that God could be embarrassed by the circumstances, or that he would have erred, or that he would not be able to foresee *possible* events, or that he sometimes would have no counter-measures available. Those who believe such things really endanger God's sovereignty. By definition, none of the biblical examples given detracts at all from God's sovereignty (if properly understood).

On the contrary, in a sense they glorify his sovereignty since apparently God himself has *sovereignly* chosen to grant people their own freedom and responsibility. In this way, he *sovereignly* left the future open to a certain extent, and *sover-*

---
29. Ibid., 90.

eignly made it dependent on free human choices, even if these are corrupt choices.[30] God's sovereignty is also apparent from the fact that he surely and certainly realizes his counsels, whatever people may choose to do — though not always along the route that God had announced. We remember: God's *counsel* is fixed, but the *ways* by which he realizes his counsel are open.

In this entire debate, this is one of the essential questions: Which God is wiser, loftier, more sovereign, a God who foreknows all future events, like someone who knows the bus schedule by heart, *or* a God who voluntarily faces a partially open future, foreknowing *all* possible events and *all* possible consequences of them, as well as the *most likely* events and consequences, as well as *all* conceivable responses to them?[31] For the moment, it is unimportant whether the former or the latter picture of God is more biblical. I am just trying to expose our preconceived ideas. Do we restrict God's power in the second picture? Or do we restrict God more if we deny him all possibility of surprise, discovery, relief, disappointment, and genuine interaction with people, with all the risks that are part of it?

Does not traditional theology identify sovereignty too strongly with control, mastery, as, for instance, Robert K. McGregor Wright does to a great extent?[32] In opposition to this, David Pawson says that a God who has *complete* control is a God who issues his commands apart from any factor or influence outside himself. Such a God would be a despot, who manipulates people according to his own plans, without taking into account their own desires — which he himself created in them! In such a view, God is the only person in the universe who has a free will. In his dealings with people, he is not

---

30. Hughes (1989, 160).
31. Sanders (1998, 208); Boyd (2000, 126–27, 145, 148–49); Pinnock (2001, 31–33, 53–55, 81).
32. Wright (1996).

much better than a mass-hypnotist.[33] This is harsh language, but indeed, such a view reduces people to machines, robots, puppets. It is a denial of the true *humanity* of human beings, a humanity created by God himself.

We do not need to figure out how much control God's sovereignty necessarily implies. On the contrary, God is also "sovereign over his sovereignty," says Pinnock;[34] that is, he himself determines how his sovereignty is defined *in concreto*. Is not God equally sovereign if he *sovereignly* chooses to cede some of his control, as it were, by entrusting it to people whom he has equipped with responsibility and freedom of will? Only a perfectly sovereign God can decide in freedom to make himself vulnerable toward his own creatures, and, together with them, step into a risky future. David Pawson says that, to a certain extent, God has temporarily submitted himself and his creation to the will of his creatures. This may be offensive to people who wish to honor a God who would never be willing to humiliate himself in such a way.[35] To me, God submitting himself to the will of people definitely goes too far. However, the essence remains: the notion of a God taking the risk of working together with his creatures as "junior partners" honors his sovereignty more than the notion of a God who merely pushes the buttons of a huge automaton (or rather, who has programmed this automaton in eternity past).

4.6.2 The Grandmaster

To explain the things we have been discussing here, Greg Boyd used a remarkable analogy, which I will develop a bit further.[36] He compared God to a chess grandmaster, who deigns to play against a weak player. This grandmaster makes himself vulnerable by choosing to have to respond

---

33. Pawson (2005, 187).
34. Pinnock (2001, 92).
35. Pawson (2005, 188).
36. Boyd (2000, 127–28; 2001, 112–13); cf. Pinnock (2001, 52, 139).

to the awkward, silly moves of this opponent, which are an affront to the grandmaster's genial capacities. As one who oversees the entire chessboard, the grandmaster can envision *all* possible combinations, and also his opponent's most *probable* moves. However, especially because he plays against a weak player — or perhaps a player who tries to confuse him — he can never exactly predict what move the other player will make. Time and again, therefore, he will have to adapt his own moves to those of his stupid opponent, causing occasional disappointment and irritation.

One thing is sure, though: our grandmaster's superiority is so immense that he will win the victory, whatever the moves and schemes of his opponent. In no way can the weak player ever win. The grandmaster cannot predict the course of the match, because his opponent plays in such a foolish way. But the final result is certain.

The grandmaster does not prove his grandeur by determining the moves of his opponent, as decretalism would have it with regard to God's will. In other words, the grandmaster is not replaying a match that has been played before, with all the moves already written down on paper. No, he plays a real match, as Arminianism and Open Theism properly require.

The grandmaster wins by anticipating every possible move, and by responding adequately and sovereignly to his opponent's moves. His ultimate victory is just as certain as God's counsel. However, the ways by which he reaches this victory are uncertain because they partially depend on his opponent's moves. Similarly, the ways by which God realizes his counsel are uncertain because he has made himself partially dependent on his "opponents."

What Boyd does not mention, however, is the possible *difference* between such a chess match and the ways of God. Even the greatest grandmaster can never foreknow with certainty the moves of his opponent. However, it is quite conceivable that God does foreknow all his creatures' moves without in the least affecting their own freedom. In my view, something is possible that Open Theism claims is impossible. It is this: God has not *foreordained* his opponents' moves but he does *foreknow* them all. Correspondingly, he also knows all his own moves beforehand. Yet, the match is truly open because the human opponents are perfectly free to make the moves they want. God has perfect foreknowledge, as Calvinists have always said. People have perfect freedom, as Arminians and Open Theists have always said.

In summary, Calvinism confesses in all cases both God's foreknowledge and God's foreordination. Open Theism denies in many cases both God's foreknowledge and God's foreordination. Viatorism confesses in many cases God's foreknowledge, but denies in many cases God's foreordination.

4.6.3 A Certain Ignorance After All?

It is certainly conceivable that in a few of the cases discussed in §4.3 we are dealing with rhetorical questions, or with "asking for the obvious," or with pretended uncertainty. However, it hardly seems conceivable to assume this for *all* the cases mentioned. We cannot dismiss these examples as anthropomorphisms, understanding the text to mean the opposite of what it says. As we have seen, such an approach is arbitrary;[37] statements of and about God that do not fit with our dogmas are sent away as anthropomorphisms, whereas statements that do fit with our dogmas are welcomed literally. That does not work. Our dogmas should not determine our exegesis, but careful exegesis must support our dogmas. Therefore, one should indicate *a priori* methodologically why some expressions may and others may not be taken literally. If the Bible indicates that God sometimes speaks in terms of fixed events, but in other cases of possible events, this must be taken seriously in both cases.

On the basis of the examples discussed, it seems clear that God does not foreknow *some* events. In this respect, Open

---

37. Boyd (2000, 14); also Erickson (1998, 380–81) makes this mistake.

Theism seems to have a strong case. It is fascinating that a decretalist *pur sang* like Louis Berkhof has argued that, if human actions are really perfectly free, and thus unpredictable—for instance, because they are completely capricious—they can be known only as mere possibilities. However, to *him*, as a decretalist, this means that even the most capricious human actions are necessarily included in God's decree, and in this way can be foreknown.[38]

What Berkhof could hardly surmise is that, if decretalism must be rejected on other grounds, then automatically the other option mentioned by him remains: real foreknowledge is possible for God only in the form of mere possibilities, and this is exactly what Open Theism asserts.

Open Theism is not the first theory that has investigated divine (fore)knowledge and its relationship to human responsibility and freedom. First, there was Pelagianism, which later formed the core of Arminianism. To be precise: Arminius rejected Pelagianism on an important point; his view was really semi-Pelagian, as it is called: people come to God by an act of their own free will, but this is impossible without the gracious work of God's Spirit. Nonetheless, both Pelagianism and Arminianism place the full emphasis on human freedom and responsibility.

Building upon Augustine, Thomas Aquinas sought to determine the relationship between divine grace and foreknowledge, on the one hand, and human responsibility and freedom of will, on the other hand. He placed the emphasis more on the former pole, though not as strongly as Calvinism did and does. Between Pelagianism and Thomism, we find semi-Pelagian Molinism, named after the Spanish Jesuit Luis de Molina (d. 1600) (see the next section).

4.6.4 Middle Knowledge

As mentioned earlier, Molina distinguished a form of divine knowledge that he called *middle knowledge* (Latin *scientia*

---

38. Berkhof (1996, 107).

media). Molinists view middle knowledge as an intermediate form between, on the one hand, God's necessary knowledge, namely, knowledge of necessary truths (e.g., all circles are round, or all rain is wet), and on the other hand, God's free knowledge, namely, knowledge of contingent truths. These are those truths that God decides to realize, such as: David will become king of Israel. Such a decree is contingent because God could just as well have decided to make another Israelite king over Israel. However, it is not middle knowledge because it involves a matter that is entirely determined by God's will. Middle knowledge involves matters that are both contingent and not dependent on God's will.[39]

The difference with common foreknowledge is that it is unconditional: in this case, God certainly knows what is going to occur *for* he himself has decreed it, or he knows for sure that people are going to do this or that. However, middle knowledge is conditional: God knows that something will certainly occur *if* a person, or persons, according to his/her/their own free choice, will do this or that. However, *whether* he/she/they will do this, is, according to this view, not necessarily known to God. God's middle knowledge implies that God knows all possibilities as well as all their consequences, but does not necessarily know in all cases what possibilities will be realized by people according to the choices of their own free will. However, God does have unlimited possibilities to create situations such that he foreknows exactly how people will act in them. Therefore, because of this middle knowledge, God was able to create the best possible world.

Molinism is speculative, but can nonetheless serve to shed more light on certain theological problems, such as the relationship between God's sovereignty and providence, on the one hand, and human responsibility and freedom of will, on the other. *In concreto* this means that Molinism offers a middle way between, on the one hand, (hyper-)Calvinism (decretal-

---
39. See extensively, Boyd (2001, 124–28); Open Theism is described as neo-Molinism here.

ism), and on the other hand, Pelagianism as well as semi-Pelagian Arminianism (of which Open Theism is a variety).[40]

4.7 Wider Foreknowledge After All?
4.7.1 Josiah and Cyrus

In contrast to the Bible passages mentioned in §4.3, many other passages reveal God accurately predicting what will occur; in other words, precisely anticipating the free choices of people. Of course, Open Theists know this just as well; but they believe that such predictions refer exclusively to actions that God *himself* will take, through people or not. Indeed, God has made many true predictions about things that he *himself* has brought about; we call these "prophecies." It is superfluous to give an enumeration of them because decretalists and Open Theists do not disagree about whether genuine prophecies exist, that is, statements predicting certain events long before they occur.[41]

There are examples in which God predicts the behavior of specific people, but these involve cases in which these people are steered by God himself. Thus, in 1 Kings 13:2 a prophet predicts: "Behold, a son shall be born to the house of David, Josiah by name, and he shall sacrifice on you [i.e., the altar] the priests of the high places who make offerings on you, and human bones shall be burned on you" (see the fulfillment in 2 Kings 23:15–16). Here again, according to Open Theists, this could be prophesied because God himself would move king Josiah to do this.[42] Yet, we sense that they are inserting something into the text: the prophet *predicts* an action by Josiah, whereas the latter would definitely act freely and on his own responsibility (just as his parents were free in bringing forth this son, and in giving him his name, although God had

---

40. See Plantinga (1974); Hasker (1989); Craig (1987; 1991); Flint (1998); MacGregor (2015); you can find a general introduction to various viewpoints in Beilby and Eddy (2001).
41. See, e.g., Ouweneel (EDR 2, chapter 5; EDR 10, chapters 4–9).
42. Boyd (2000, 26; 2001, 121n7; is it telling that the matter is subordinated to a footnote?).

predicted this name).

If *decretalism* were consistent, it should not deny that God does not seem to foreknow certain events (§4.3). But if *Open Theism* were consistent, it should not deny the possibility that God can definitely foreknow actions that people will perform in perfect freedom. In other words, Open Theism should distinguish between *free* human actions that God cannot foresee, and *unfree* (or, less free) human actions (namely, brought about by God) that God does foresee as well as foreordain as well as foretell. In contrast to this, they should acknowledge that God sometimes clearly foreknows the *free* choices of certain people.

It is fair to say that some Open Theists indeed seem to do this. Take the example of the Persian king Cyrus, which is even stronger than that of king Josiah. God "says of Cyrus,[43] 'He is my shepherd, and he shall fulfill all my purpose'; .... Thus says the LORD to his anointed, to Cyrus, whose right hand I have grasped, to subdue nations before him .... I have stirred him up in righteousness, and I will make all his ways level; he shall build my city and set my exiles free'" (Isa. 44:28; 45:1, 13). Here we are clearly dealing with events that God not only predicts (including the name of the king involved) but which he has *decreed* (cf. Acts 2:23; 4:28). Yet, no one wishes to deny pagan king Cyrus' own responsibility and freedom. The same can be said about the rather precise predictions concerning the future of Israel, the four world empires in Daniel 2, 7, 8, and 11,[44] the life, death, and resurrection of the Messiah, and the end time.[45]

Greg Boyd admits that, in these cases, it seems that the

---

43. If the Deutero-Isaiah hypothesis is correct, this is no prophecy at all; see, e.g., Harrison (1969, 764–95); Grogan (1986, 6–11); Oswalt (1986, 17–28). Harrison (1969, 794) wishes to maintain the unity of the book but views Isa. 44:28 and 45:1 as post-exilic glosses.
44. At least if we accept the view that Daniel was written before the predicted events; see, e.g., Aalders (1962, 13–29); McDowell (1979); Archer (1985, 4–6).
45. Boyd (2000, 27–29, 33–34).

Lord decreed that he would exert the influence needed to perform these tasks through these persons. Thus, to this extent, the freedom of the will of these persons was restricted beforehand. However, says Boyd, these passages do not assert that everything concerning Josiah and Cyrus had been foreordained.[46] Of course, the latter is correct. Nevertheless, such passages do show that some human actions involve human responsibility and freedom of will, and yet have been foreknown, and even foreordained by God, and brought about by him through the people involved.

It does not follow, as decretalists claim, that *all* human deeds have been decreed by God. But, in my opinion, neither does it follow, as Open Theists claim, that we cannot have both at the same time: human actions that are both foreknown by God *and* entirely free. Only the embarrassing limits of his dogmatic paradigm bring Boyd to the assertion that God could foreknow the actions of Josiah and Cyrus only by restricting their freedom. Instead, I maintain that the prophecies show that *some* human deeds were foreseen, foreknown, and foreordained by God, and in due time brought about by God. There is no reason at all — except in the Open Theist dogma — to assume that such human actions would be less free than others, or not free at all.

4.7.2 Gentile Kings

A similar example is found in Exodus 4:21. Here, God predicts that Pharaoh would not voluntarily let the people of Israel leave his country. This prediction seems to be easy because the LORD adds that Pharaoh would refuse because he (the LORD) himself would harden Pharaoh's heart. And this is what happened (9:12; 10:20, 27; 11:10; 14:4, 8, 17). However, we must take into account here that Pharaoh himself hardened his own heart first (Exod. 7:13, 22; 8:19; 9:35),[47] and that only afterward the hardening by God occurred as a

---

46. Boyd (2001, 121n7).
47. Cf. Venema (1992, 98–99).

judgment. This is a universal rule in Scripture: hardening is always based upon the sinful behavior of people themselves, not on an *a priori* decree by God (see, e.g., Rom. 11:7, 25; 2 Cor. 3:14; cf. Rom. 1:26; 2 Thess. 2:11–12).

Thus, in the case of Pharaoh, too, the prediction cannot be separated from his own responsibility and freedom. Actually, this point is wholeheartedly granted by Open Theists, and is solved by them in the way that I will describe in §5.1. By the way, Herman Bavinck also says concerning, for instance, Pharaoh: "Certainly in all these works of God [in judgment within history] one must not overlook people's own sinfulness."[48] There is an interaction between God's working and human freedom (often an abused freedom).

In other cases, it is even clearer that God makes predictions concerning the free actions of people. God predicts that all Israel would fall into idolatry, and that therefore, in due time, he would bring judgment on the nation (Deut. 31:16–17). Daniel predicts the fall of Nebuchadnezzar without any hint that the king's sin would be anything other than his own free choice (Dan. 4). This is also true of the Antichrist, about whom we find precise predictions (e.g., 2 Thess. 2:3–10; 1 John 2:18, 22; Rev. 13), whereas I suppose nobody would care to assert that this in any way diminishes this person's own responsibility and freedom of will.

Open Theism's reply to this is that, given the nature of Israel, Nebuchadnezzar, and the Antichrist, God does not expect anything other than that they will act the way he predicts. But that is not sufficient: either God foreknows exactly what these people will do, and bases on this his certain pronouncements, or he does not foreknow it but can only presume it. However, in this case Open Theists should be prepared to admit that, if God's predictions are just calculated guesses, these predictions might sometimes be mistaken. If he really does not foreknow how people will act under certain circumstanc-

---

48. Bavinck (*RD* 2:393).

es, and yet always perfectly *guesses* what they will do, how then does this differ fundamentally from foreknowledge? If foreknowledge of free human actions is impossible, then it is also impossible that God would always correctly predict. The reason is that people often act in a very unpredictable way, according to their nature. A God who does not know, but can guess, will inevitably sometimes guess wrong.

In summary, in the cases of Israel, Nebuchadnezzar, and the Antichrist, are we really dealing only with a certain expectation of God, or with real *predictions*? I am convinced it is the latter. *God can predict perfectly free human actions.* To be sure, "[t]he king's heart is a stream of water in the hand of the LORD; he turns it wherever he will" (Prov. 21:1). But let us never abuse this as a tool to argue away the king's own responsibility and freedom.

4.7.3 Judas

A similar example is found in the judgment on Judas, predicted by Jesus: "'Did I not choose you, the Twelve? And yet one of you is a devil.' He spoke of Judas the son of Simon Iscariot, for he, one of the Twelve, was going to betray him" (John 6:70–71). "[H]e knew who was to betray him" (13:11). "Then after he [i.e., Judas] had taken the morsel, Satan entered into him. Jesus said to him, 'What you are going to do, do quickly'" (v. 27). Jesus says to the Father, "While I was with them, I kept them in your name, which you have given me. I have guarded them, and not one of them has been lost except the son of destruction, that the Scripture might be fulfilled" (17:12).

In no sense could Judas be excused for having betrayed the Master, whereas God, who knows the human heart, perfectly foresaw that he would act this way. There is a foreseeing that means "foreseeing what may reasonably be expected to occur." However, in Judas' case it was apparently a "foreseeing what certainly will occur," which is the same as foreknowledge, without at all diminishing the freedom and responsibility of Judas.

Yet, the situation is not as simple here, because Jesus said, "[T]he Son of Man goes as it has been determined, but woe to that man by whom he is betrayed!" (Luke 22:22). In other words, it seems that it had been decreed that Jesus would be delivered into the hands of his enemies, but not necessarily *through whom* this would occur. Woe, therefore, to the one who would make himself available to this purpose. God had decreed that *someone* would betray Jesus. And during Judas' life Jesus predicted that *Judas* would be the one (cf. John 6:70 and 13:27).

Here I have a question for both the Open Theists and the decretalists. To the former: How do you explain that God supposedly did not, and *could* not, foreknow what Judas would do, yet accurately predicted Judas' behavior? To the decretalists: Should we not here introduce the essential difference between foretelling and foreordaining? Judas did not betray Jesus because God had *decreed* that he had to do this; the Bible does not say so. Scripture only *predicted* that Judas would do this,[49] without at all diminishing his personal freedom and responsibility. On the contrary, a woe is proclaimed over him.

In addition, Jesus' prediction about what Jews and Gentiles would do to him (Matt. 17:22-23; 20:17-19; cf. John 18:4: "Jesus, knowing all that would happen to him . . .") should not be understood as diminishing his opponents' personal freedom and responsibility. However, here the matter is complicated for other reasons. First, *as a Man* Jesus himself did not (fore)know everything; see, for instance, Mark 13:32, "[C]oncerning that day or that hour, no one knows, not even . . . the Son."[50] Second, Peter later told the Jews: "Jesus, delivered up according to the definite plan and foreknowledge of God, you crucified and killed by the hands of lawless men" (Acts 2:23; cf. 4:27-28). However, the fact that God had *decreed*

---

49. See Ps. 41:9, "Even my close friend in whom I trusted, who ate my bread, has lifted his heel against me" (cf. John 13:18).
50. Ouweneel (EDR 2, §9.1.3).

that Jesus would be delivered does not necessarily imply that God had also decreed *through whom* Jesus would be delivered. At any rate, God's decree did not diminish his torturers' personal freedom and responsibility.

For our present subject, the most important point is this: apparently, it is possible that people make certain decisions, or do certain things, in their personal freedom and responsibility, according to their personal choice, while God has nonetheless foreseen and foretold these things, and *sometimes* even foreordained them. This is something other than having determined beforehand the *entire* history, *everything* that has ever occurred or will occur (*contra* decretalists). But it is also something other than the idea that truly free human choices could not be foreknown by God (*contra* Open Theism). Decretalists have read many of their own ideas into Scripture (eisegesis). But is it not eisegesis also to derive from Scripture the idea that God can predict free human choices only because he knows human nature? This is not predicting but, as I said, calculated guessing. Not predicting but presuming.

4.7.4 Peter

A clear example of Jesus' not guessing about but really *predicting* future events, without affecting the freedom and responsibility of the people involved, is what he said about the apostle Peter. He predicted that Peter would deny him three times before the rooster would crow twice (Mark 14:30). This case is even more fascinating than the previous one, because it involves a believer whose heart could not possibly have been hardened, or something similar. Open Theism is right in stating that, given Peter's character and the outward circumstances, this denial could be expected (guessed) with certainty.[51] But this does not explain how Jesus could predict that Peter would deny him exactly three times, and could relate this to a rooster crowing two times.

In none of the Open Theist publications that I have

---

51. Boyd (2000, 35–37; 2001, 130–33).

consulted is this problem analyzed adequately. Greg Boyd does assert that precise predictions of God in which free human actions are implied place "strict parameters" around the freedom of the persons involved.[52] But this statement is far too weak. In some cases, the prediction is very precise and detailed. Examples are the *names* of future persons (Josiah, Cyrus), the *location* of certain events (Christ's birthplace, a consequence of Augustus' command to a census), and the *time* of such events (Christ's death through Pilate exactly sixty-nine "weeks" after the command to rebuild Jerusalem, Dan. 9:25-27; or Peter's threefold denial before the rooster's second crowing). Such examples imply that, at the moment of the predicted events, the persons involved (Josiah, Cyrus, Augustus, Pilate, Peter, etc.) were *not* really free (as Open Theists might argue), or they *were* free, but then, apparently, God can definitely foreknow and foretell certain free human decisions (*contra* Open Theism). Trying some harmonization will not solve the problem: the people involved were just a *little* free, and God foreknows the events only a *little*. How is Scripture thought to support such a compromise?

In my view, the examples mentioned—and others could be added—constitute an essential problem for Open Theism. They clearly show that God possesses genuine foreknowledge of—and is not simply making calculated guesses about—events in which the people involved fully retain their responsibility and freedom. Therefore, the claim that God cannot foreknow with certainty events that fall under the full control of responsible individuals' personal free choices is, generally speaking, mistaken. If, in the previous chapter, we came to the conclusion that (hyper-)Calvinism is basically mistaken, here we come to the conclusion that Open Theism is basically mistaken. In the next chapter I will suggest a way out of this complex situation.

---

52. Boyd (2000, 34, 43).

Chapter 5
The Approach of Viatorism

*The LORD works righteousness
and justice for all who are oppressed.
He made known his ways to Moses,
his acts to the people of Israel.*
                                            Psalm 103:6-7

*Great and amazing are your deeds,
  O Lord God the Almighty!
Just and true are your ways,
  O King of the nations!
Who will not fear, O Lord,
  and glorify your name?
For you alone are holy.
All nations will come and worship you,
  for your righteous acts have been revealed.*
                                            Revelation 15:3-4

Summary: *In previous chapters, I have shown how, in my view, both decretalism and Open Theism have failed: the former because it diminishes human responsibility and freedom, the latter because it diminishes divine foreknowledge. The two movements suffer from the same problem: the confusion of logical concepts and logical ideas, as I try to argue extensively. Some alternative models, such as congruism and Molinism, do not help us very much either; the paradox remains, but a way is shown to approximate its solution. In the* *last part of the chapter, three basic elements in God's counsel are identified: the covenant, the kingdom, and the church, as well as the distinction between God's eternal and his temporal counsel, the distinction between God's counsel and his ways, and the Christocentric character of both God's counsel and his ways.*

5.1 Failed Logic
5.1.1 Two Views Rejected

OPEN THEISM CANNOT BE MAINTAINED in its strict form as described in the previous chapter. As far as I can see, only two options remain. *Either* — to take again the examples mentioned in §4.7.4 — God had foreordained Peter's behavior, in which case this behavior was not free, and whatever decretalism may claim to the contrary, Peter cannot be made responsible for it. *Or* God certainly foreknows such behavior (*contra* Open Theism), without having decreed it (*contra* decretalism), and without this affecting people's own freedom and responsibility.[1] With the latter view, Viatorism maintains a position that attempts to correct the errors of both decretalism and Open Theism.

At the same time, however, Viatorism seeks to learn from both standpoints. From Open Theism it learns, *contra* decretalism, that there are unmistakable appearances of God's ignorance concerning the future, as mentioned in §§4.3-4.5. From decretalism it learns, *contra* Open Theism, that God does foreknow human behavior in many cases, without this affecting human responsibility and freedom. It *rejects* decretalism's idea that everything that occurs — including all human behavior — has been foreordained by God. It *rejects* Open Theism's idea that divine foreknowledge by definition nullifies human responsibility and freedom. Neither of these erroneous ideas can be based on biblical evidence; they are simply the products of a run-away logic.

We will have to accept *both* (a) that God sometimes exhibits uncertainty concerning the future (*contra* decretalism),

---
1. This view has been defended extensively by Craig (1987).

and (b) that in other cases God foretells the future accurately, also where this touches upon the free choices of responsible people, without this taking anything away from these people's own responsibility and freedom (*contra* Open Theism). In other words: *not* all human behavior has been *foreordained* by God, *not* all human deeds are even *foreknown* by God, but where such deeds are foreknown by God, they do not affect the freedom of human choices.

5.1.2 Decretalism

Again we reached the conclusion that both decretalism and Open Theism are rooted more in the Procrustean logic of an adopted standpoint than in the biblical data. In *decretalism* it is this false argument: God's absolute sovereignty can be maintained only if we assume that everything that ever occurs falls under God's decree. This is maintained, even if this threatens God's righteousness and holiness (e.g., "God has foreordained the Fall"). Please note: the decretalist viewpoint does *not* rest on concrete biblical evidence but exclusively on what *people* think to be the necessary consequences of God's sovereignty.

This view concerning God's sovereignty exhibits almost fatalistic, and thus explicitly pagan, characteristics. Toward such a deity only an obtuse resignation is appropriate, more or less as Eli put the matter: "It is the LORD. Let him do what seems good to him" (1 Sam. 3:18) — in which we should not forget that this is said by a man, Eli, who, through his own failures, had called down God's judgment upon himself, a judgment that went back, not to a rigid decree of God, but to his own wrong choices and abused responsibility.

This threatening inclination to a certain fatalism[2] has also been heard in the Heidelberg Catechism (Lord's Day 10, Answer 27):

---

2. See extensively, Ouweneel (2004, §3.3; 2016a).

> ... [God] so governs them [heaven and earth] that herbs and grass, rain and drought, fruitful and barren years, meat and drink (Jer. 5:24), health and sickness (John 9:3), riches and poverty (Prov. 22:2), indeed, all things come not by chance, but by His fatherly hand.

And also Answer 28:

> That we may be patient in adversity (Rom. 5:3; James 1:3; Job 1:21), thankful in prosperity (Deut. 8:10; 1 Thess. 5:18), and for what is future have good confidence in our faithful God and Father, that no creature shall separate us from His love (Rom. 8:35, 38-39), since all creatures are so in His hand, that without His will they cannot so much as move (Job 1:12; Acts 17:25-28; Prov. 21:1).[3]

In fact, the accusation of fatalism is exaggerated here; this answer would be fatalistic only if it had said that God has *foreordained* drought, barren years, sickness and poverty for believers (as the writers of the Catechism probably believed themselves, for that matter). It makes a lot of theological difference if we only assume that God, under certain circumstances, may *allow* (*permit*) drought, barren years, sickness and poverty for believers, in order to reach a higher goal, which otherwise would not, or would hardly, be possible.

Among Old Testament believers, such acquiescence as the answer seems to suggest was generally unknown. They did not let God's deeds lead them to resignation because of an extreme view of God's sovereignty, but they invariably *argued* with God because of the firm conviction that he listened to them, and that they could influence his dealings by their entreaties.[4] This is what Abraham did (Gen. 18:16-33), and he managed to move God to withhold destruction from Sodom and Gomorrah if ten righteous people were found there. This is what king Hezekiah did (Isa. 38:1-8), and he managed to

---

3. Dennison (*RCET* 4:776).
4. See extensively, Laytner (2005); book title: *Arguing with God: A Jewish tradition.*

move God to add fifteen years to his life. This is what Moses did (Exod. 33–34), and he managed to move God to turn away the judgment that he had announced over Israel. This is what Job did, and the LORD restored his fortunes (Job 42). Those who argue with God, dispute with him, entreat him, could never have been consistent decretalists. We will return to this important matter in chapter 8.

5.1.3 Open Theism

In Open Theism we find this fallacious argument: human responsibility and freedom of will can be maintained only if we assume that God does not foreknow the free choices of people. The supposed reason is that, if he were to foreknow them, these choices would no longer be free: if God knows for sure that what is going to be freely chosen will occur, then there is no other possibility than that what is going to be freely chosen will be chosen. But then these choices are no longer free. God foreknows that a person will choose P; so what else could this person choose? In due time he makes his choice between P and Q, but what else can he choose than P? What God *knows* a person will choose, is therefore fixed and rigid beforehand; there can be no free choice.

Here again, this viewpoint does not rest on concrete biblical evidence but exclusively on what people *think* that the consequences of God's absolute foreknowledge must necessarily be. In this case, the theologians concerned believe that such a foreknowledge would lead to decretalism, and therefore should be rejected. Apparently, these theologians are incapable of facing the possibility that divine foreknowledge and human responsibility could coexist. Moreover, we have seen that the biblical evidence clearly suggests that there *are* human actions that were perfectly foreknown by God, and that nonetheless were taken in complete human freedom. Thus, Open Theism has neither the biblical evidence, nor human logic on its side — if indeed terms such as "foreknowledge" and "freedom" are used as ideas, not as concepts (see the next section).

We must conclude that the logic of both decretalism and Open Theism has failed. As such, I believe both paradigms must be fundamentally rejected. Let us see whether another one is available to us.

5.2 The Logical Error
5.2.1 Concept and Idea Again

In both "-isms," the views involved fall prey to their own conceptual logic. As explained before, the logical flaw committed here is the age-old confusion between concept and idea (see §3.8).[5] Terms like (divine) "sovereignty" and "foreknowledge" are treated as if they are *concepts*, from which certain logical conclusions can be drawn, which might then possibly lead to certain contradictions. In reality, we can speak of God's sovereignty and foreknowledge only as *ideas*, not concepts. That is, from the entire array of features that belong to *concepts* like "power" or "knowledge" only a limited number are also applicable to the corresponding *ideas* of "power" and "knowledge." The precise identity of these features can be derived from Scriptural evidence *only*, not from conceptual logic.

Take the age-old question whether God's omnipotence allows him to create a stone so heavy that he could not lift it himself. Whether one answers in the affirmative or in the negative, in both cases God's omnipotence seems to be affected (either "he cannot create such a stone," or "he cannot lift that stone"). This is because the term "omnipotence" is taken here as a concept.[6] "Omni-potence," God's being "al-mighty," does not mean that God has the "might" ("potency") to do "all" (*omnis*), for there are clearly things that he cannot do. For instance, he cannot deny himself (2 Tim. 2:13), and he cannot lie (Titus 1:2 NKJV); in summary, he cannot act against his own nature, at no moment can he ever stop being God. In the *idea*

---

5. See Ouweneel (EDR 3, §§1.2–1.3; 2014b, chapter 6).
6. Cf. Kalsbeek (1975, 72–75).

of omnipotence such "cannots" are no problem at all, but in the *concept* of omnipotence they are: if God cannot do P or Q, he cannot do *all* things, and therefore he is not *al*mighty (*om*nipotent).

We see that some conceptual logical deduction can never tell us what God's sovereignty or foreknowledge entails. That is, from the *concepts* of sovereignty and foreknowledge we may indeed draw certain conclusions that we, however, cannot necessarily draw from the *ideas* of sovereignty and foreknowledge. Whether certain conclusions are correct or not must follow directly from the biblical evidence. *In concreto*, the notion that God has foreordained *all* things that ever occur must be based on direct biblical evidence, and cannot be deduced from some concept of sovereignty (*contra* decretalism). And the notion that human choices foreknown by God cannot be free must follow from direct biblical evidence, and cannot be deduced from some concept of foreknowledge (*contra* Open Theism). On the contrary, direct biblical evidence shows that *not* all that happens has been decreed by God (*contra* decretalism), and that human deeds may be free in spite of being foreknown by God (*contra* Open Theism).

Not conceptual logic, but biblical evidence teaches us what sovereignty and foreknowledge do and do not involve. Thus, from the *ideas* of sovereignty and foreknowledge we may conclude that they exclude human responsibility and freedom of will only if this conclusion is supported by Scripture itself, *which is not the case at all*. On the contrary, absolute power of people over people may imply the latter's lack of freedom, but the *ideas* of sovereignty and foreknowledge as applied to God do not detract at all from human responsibility and freedom of will, no matter how paradoxical this may sound.

5.2.2 Similar Errors

Let us look at this fundamental question a little more closely. Decretalism and Open Theism commit the same logical flaw. Decretalism uses the term "sovereignty" in a *conceptual* way, and therefore infers that this term excludes human freedom.[7] This is an invalid conclusion. In the light of Scripture, it turns out that the *idea* of divine sovereignty does not exclude human freedom at all. This is because all the characteristics that may be predicated in the case of the *concept* of sovereignty cannot be predicated in the case of the *idea* of sovereignty.

Here is a simple example: from the *concept* of father we may safely conclude that we are dealing with a male who has fathered one or more children with one or more females; but from the *idea* of Father, as in the case of God, it may *not* be concluded that he is a male and has intercourse with females. Similarly, in the case of the *concept* of absolute human power over other people, such power excludes the latter's freedom. However, from the *idea* of absolute power, as in the case of God, human freedom is *not* excluded. As long as decretalists keep confusing concepts and ideas, they will not achieve clarity on this matter.

In an entirely analogous way, Open Theism commits its own logical error. It uses the term "foreknowledge" in a *conceptual* way, and therefore concludes that this term excludes human freedom. Since Open Theists wish to maintain human freedom, their conclusion is that not much can be left of God's foreknowledge. This too is an invalid conclusion. In the light of Scripture, we see that the *idea* of divine foreknowledge does not exclude human freedom at all. This is because all the characteristics that may be predicated of the *concept* of foreknowledge cannot be predicated of the *idea* of foreknowledge. As long as Open Theists keep confusing concepts and ideas, they will not achieve clarity on this matter.

5.2.3 Examples

We cannot speak of God and his decrees and deeds in a conceptual way, but only by way of ideas: we can only form

---

[7] It is remarkable that decretalists do accept the term "responsibility" with respect to the sinner but not the phrase "free will." Cf. Kersten (1980, 1:116–17). See more extensively, §9.2 below.

approximations and representations of them. This does not necessarily mean "vague" (although, see 1 Cor. 13:9, 12, "For we know in part.... For now we see in a mirror dimly"). But it does mean that conclusions from certain ideas are valid only insofar as these are supported by explicit biblical evidence. For decretalism, this means that divine sovereignty and human freedom do not exclude each other at all. For Arminianism, this means that divine predestination (rooted not in God's foreknowledge [alone] but primarily in his own sovereign decisions) and human freedom do not exclude each other at all. For Open Theism, this means that divine foreknowledge and human freedom do not exclude each other at all.

Arminians believe that human freedom excludes an eternal, one-sided fore*ordination* (not dependent on foreseen [un]belief but on God's own choice only). Open Theists go a step further: they believe that human freedom excludes even eternal fore*knowledge*. In §3.1.1, I quoted the Canons of Dordt, which condemn "insolent sophists,"[8] thinking of Arminians (and today its authors would no doubt include the Open Theists as well). However, (hyper-)Calvinists believing the opposite, namely, that God's eternal predestination excludes human freedom are, according to exactly the same reasoning, "insolent sophists" as well. Divine foreknowledge/-ordination and human freedom exclude each other in the conceptual sense, and therefore (hyper-)Calvinists overemphasize the former at the expense of the latter, and Arminians (Open Theists included) overemphasize the latter at the expense of the former. Who is to say who are the most "insolent sophists"? All groups concerned have committed basically the same logical error.

Berkouwer gives an excellent summary of the matter:

> It has often happened, for instance, that from the doctrine of divine sovereignty the conclusion was drawn that [*therefore*] man could not be held fully responsible for his deeds, while from the

---

8. See Canons of Dordt, Conclusion, in Dennison (*RCET* 4:152).

acceptance of man's responsibility as Scripture presents it the conclusion was drawn that [*therefore*] there could be no mention of an absolute sovereignty and of a truly *apriori* and [*independent*] sovereign divine election. It was believed that only logical consequences had been drawn, while actually the correct insight had been abandoned from the very beginning because divine sovereignty and human responsibility had been seen as factors that limited one another on one and the same level, and this view meant a deviation from the message of Scripture.[9]

Free choices by people can affect God's sovereignty as well as God's foreknowledge just as little as the heaviest stone can affect God's omnipotence. God is sovereign, also in the freedom that he himself has *sovereignly* granted to people. God foreknows human actions without this foreknowledge affecting their freedom.

5.3 A Third Way
5.3.1 Two Extreme Viewpoints

In §1.7, I gave some examples of the way (hyper-)Calvinists and Arminians each made a persiflage of their opponents. Such behavior is always wrong. Yet I can understand some of the criticisms. Thus, Open Theism may indeed be blamed for not accepting that God can have foreknowledge of future human choices without endangering human freedom of will *because the Bible teaches otherwise*. And (hyper-)Calvinism may indeed be blamed for not, or hardly, leaving any room for genuine (non-determined) human responsibility and freedom of will *because the Bible teaches otherwise*. Here, there is room for the approach of Viatorism (§1.3.2), which has room for both divine foreknowledge that does not affect human freedom (*contra* Open Theism), and for (non-decreed) human freedom of will that does not affect divine sovereignty (*contra* decretalism).

As a theological argument it is perhaps not very strong,

---
9. Berkouwer (1960, 21; italics and words within brackets were in the Dutch original, but were omitted from the published English translation).

but I would still like to mention the following existential argument. In fact, Christians could hardly *live* with the idea that God does not foreknow all things. According to the Bible, God seems to know less of the future than decretalists suggest, yet more than Open Theists suggest (chapter 4). This corresponds to our intuitive experience: "O LORD, you have searched me and known me! You know when I sit down and when I rise up; you discern my thoughts from afar. You search out my path and my lying down and are acquainted with all my ways. Even before a word is on my tongue, behold, O LORD, you know it altogether" (Ps. 139:1-4). How can this be reconciled with Open Theism in a convincing way? Whether I sit down or stand up, whatever I think, where and when I go or lie down, the words I am going to utter—are these not all things that, according to Open Theism, belong to the free choices of people, and are not decreed by God as if we were puppets? How does Open Theism explain that God nevertheless has foreknowledge of them? But more importantly, how could we ever *live* with the thought that it would be otherwise? Our Christian intuition, although it should not be overestimated, contradicts this.

However, a similar argument could be adduced against decretalism: can we really *live* with the idea that everything we say and do has been foreordained by God? Did God really bother in eternity past with what we would wear today, or what we would eat? Does not every Christian pray from the conviction that prayer helps, that is, can really accomplish something in the spiritual world (see chapter 8)? Do not all Christians act in practice as if they certainly can choose P or Q in freedom, and as if they are responsible for choosing either P or Q?[10] Do Christians not preach the gospel as if it is (at least partially) dependent on *their* commitment whether people will come to faith?

Notice the phrase "in such a way" (Gr. *houtōs hōste*) in

---

10. Cf. Pinnock (2001, 160–61).

this verse: "[A]t Iconium they [i.e., the apostles] entered together into the Jewish synagogue and spoke in such a way that a great number of both Jews and Greeks believed" (Acts 14:1), that is, with such persuasion and convincing power (although it is equally true what Luke wrote a few verses earlier: "[A]s many as were appointed to eternal life believed," 13:48). As Paul says, "[K]nowing the fear of the Lord, we persuade others" (2 Cor. 5:11a; cf. v. 20, ". . . God making his *appeal* through us. We *implore* you on behalf of Christ, be reconciled to God"). Can we live in any other way than in the certainty that our choices and those of others really matter *because they are free*? "[C]hoose this day whom you will serve" (Josh. 24:15) — this suggests genuine freedom, not foreordained "choices." In summary, in the practical, daily life of faith, could we really *live* with either Open Theism or decretalism?

5.3.2 Examples of Healing

Let me mention an example from the ministry of healing that illustrates both viewpoints rather well. Recently I heard a hyper-Calvinist claim — entirely from the viewpoint of God's sovereignty — that the sick person cannot turn to Jesus just like that; Jesus himself must turn to *that person*. All the initiative is on God's side; for people there is nothing to choose. What a selective way of reading the Bible! I find very different things in Scripture. The leper (Matt. 8:2-3), Jairus (9:18-19), the woman with the issue of blood (vv. 20-22), several blind persons (20:30-34) — all these are examples of people who came to Jesus *at their own initiative*. They received divine healing, although — no, *because* — they had come to Jesus, not Jesus to them. Therefore Jesus sometimes said, "*Your faith* has saved [or, healed] you," not I have, or God has, healed you (although the healing cannot be separated from the power of God) (Matt. 9:22; Mark 5:34; 10:52; Luke 8:48; 17:19; 18:42; cf. Luke 7:50; Acts 3:16).

Conversely, Clark Pinnock asserted — entirely from the viewpoint of human responsibility — that Jesus healed the sick if and when, and only if and when, they entreated him.[11] Again, what a selective way of reading the Bible! This time in a way opposite from the previous one. Here again the biblical facts are different. Of the man with the withered hand (Luke 6:6-10), the man who had been sick for thirty-eight years (John 5:1-9), and the paralytic at the Beautiful Gate (Acts 3:1-8) it is not said that they turned to Jesus or the apostles to receive healing. It was Jesus or the apostles who took the initiative; yet these people were healed.

Another interesting example of how the various paradigms work is the various ways in which Ephesians 2:10 is read: "[W]e are his workmanship, created in Christ Jesus for good works, which God prepared beforehand, that we should walk in them." It is easy to see how both decretalists and Open Theists use such a verse to their own advantage. Thus, Reformed theologian Seakle Greijdanus states, "In his eternal counsel [God] has not only appointed that [the good works involved] would be done by us, but, with a view to this and in connection with this, has also determined what ordained outcomes he actually realizes by his providential rule."[12] A more decretalist approach is hardly conceivable. But just as easily Open Theist Clark Pinnock quotes the verse to support his viewpoint by saying that we are responsible for combating the evils in the world, which are not according to the will of God. The decisions are ours to take or not to take. God has planned that good works are done, and it is up to us to do them (Eph. 2:10). We carry primary responsibility for what is and is not done.[13] That is Pinnock's view; a more Arminian approach is hardly conceivable.

It *must* be possible to find a middle way that both avoids these extremes and can be accounted for biblical-theologically, and also fits with our Christian intuition, fed by God's Word and Spirit. I believe Viatorism offers such a way.

---

11. Ibid., 163.
12. Greijdanus (1925, 54).
13. Pinnock (2001, 169).

5.4 Congruism
5.4.1 Warfield

Back in chapter 2, I briefly mentioned Viatorism as a position between two extremes. The first is (hyper-)Calvinism, which puts all the emphasis on the sovereign counsel of God, and with the mouth confesses human responsibility but actually leaves little room for it. The other is Arminianism, including Open Theism, which puts all the emphasis on human responsibility, and with the mouth confesses the sovereign counsel of God but actually leaves little room for it. Mediating views like Viatorism try to do justice to both the sovereign counsel of God and human responsibility. I have to admit that at the deepest level it will never be able to succeed. This is because Scripture does not exhaustively describe the *idea* of sovereign predestination and the *idea* of human freedom, and therefore we cannot derive from the biblical data a conclusive model, even were such a thing at all possible in theology.

One could say that we are dealing here with a mystery, but theologians should not claim that too quickly (see §3.5.2 on Deut. 29:29). They must be very reticent in fleeing into an *asylum ignorantiae*. Millard Erikson rightly said that we must go as far as we can with our human reasoning before we call something a mystery.[14] But Gerrit Berkouwer asks with equal legitimacy, "How can we speak of election [as a crucial element in God's counsel; WJO] without violating this divine mystery?"[15]

Benjamin Warfield belonged among those who have tried to design a mediating view. He described it as the most diluted form of Calvinism.[16] Some would not call it Calvinism at all, but of course, that is a matter of definition and of little importance. With this view we enter the subject of predestination (see chapters 10–14), but it is applicable to the entire problem of human freedom versus God's sovereign counsel.

---

14. Erickson (1998, 385n12).
15. Berkouwer (1960, 6).
16. Warfield (1942, especially 90–91); cf. Erickson (1998, 385–86).

Warfield called his view *congruism* because, in his view, the will of God and the will of repenting people are congruent (fitting together, harmonizing). This view is not classical Calvinism: it does not claim that God causes to be born again and come to faith those whom he has elected. Nor is this view Arminian: it does not claim that people take the initiative, and that God has only foreseen who would believe in him. Rather, the initiative proceeds from God; this is why Warfield still wants to describe his as a Calvinist view. This initiative involves the idea that God works in an alluring, persuasive way, so that people freely decide to believe in him, and *then* God causes them to be born again.

5.4.2 The Initiative

The term "initiative" must be further qualified here. In Calvinism, God's initiative not only implies the offer of salvation to the not-yet-reborn person (*vocatio externa*, "external call"), but also the regenerating work of God's Spirit within the person (*vocatio interna*, "internal call"). Congruism, however, refers only to the external call, which intends to create room for a voluntary human response. At the same time, this external call is so strong that the person involved cannot escape it. There is here a genuine interaction between God's call and the human response. Here the initiative is neither exclusively God's (Calvinism), nor exclusively human (Arminianism), but partially God's, partially the human person's, who freely, under pressure but not by force, decides to respond to God's persuasive voice.

It is important that, in this view, God retains the *first* initiative. Whether one prefers a predestinational or a redemptive-historical interpretation of Romans 9:10–23 (see §14.1.3), in either case Paul is strongly emphasizing this exclusive initiative by God: "... though they [i.e., the children] were not yet born and had done nothing either good or bad—in order that God's purpose of election might continue, not because of works but because of him who calls ..." (v. 11; cf. John 15:16,

"You did not choose me, but I chose you").

At the same time, the initiative of the repenting person should not be underestimated. Romans 9:13 is crucial here: "... As it is written, 'Jacob I loved, but Esau I hated.'" The connection that Paul makes between verses 11 and 13 appears to support the absolute sovereignty of God (in the sense of decretalism): God chose Jacob *because* he loved him, and he rejected Esau *because* he hated him. But we can also read this very differently.[17] Paul's quotation does not come from Genesis but from Malachi 1:3, which was written some 1,400 years *after* Jacob and Esau lived (see further §14.3). In other words, God testifies here to his love and hatred *after* the love-arousing life of Jacob (and Israel) and the hatred-arousing life of Esau (and Edom). On the basis of Romans 9:13, we could just as legitimately argue (in the sense of Arminianism, including Open Theism) that God chose Jacob because he foresaw that with all his shortcomings, Jacob would be a godly man, who aroused God's love, and that the wicked Esau would arouse his hatred.

Reformed theologian Henk Venema said, "For God's love, there are no motives in people, but for his hatred there are."[18] Here, he made an important distinction between God's relationship with the Jacobs and with the Esaus in the world: God loves the Jacobs exclusively because of the love that he, God, finds in himself, and God hates the Esaus exclusively because of the hatred that the Esaus themselves arouse.

5.4.3 No Real Solution

As far as the Jacobs are concerned, the difficulty remains: did God choose Jacob because he would be a love-arousing man (Arminianism), or did Jacob become a love-arousing man because God had elected him (Calvinism)? In other words, to put it the Arminian way: was Jacob elected because of his

---

17. See, e.g., Kelly (*BT* 9:218); Grant (1901, 259–60), and other references in §14.3.
18. Venema (1992, 111; cf. 104–105, 107–113).

foreseen faith, or to put it the Calvinist way, was he elected through a totally one-sided, sovereign decree of God? This is a central problem in Scripture. Of Noah we read, "Noah found favor in the eyes of the LORD. . . . Noah was a righteous man, blameless in his generation. Noah walked with God" (Gen. 6:8-9). The question arises: Did Noah find favor in God's eyes because he was a righteous and blameless man (Arminianism), *or* was he a righteous and blameless man because he had found favor in God's eyes (Calvinism)? Or is it both? Or is it neither? Or is this a false dilemma?

One difficulty in the discussion around this foreseen faith—that is, around a conditional predestination—is that the opponents of this idea sometimes suggest that, in this way, a certain quality or merit in people still constitutes a ground for election. However, there is no reason at all for such a reproach. Faith is not at all meritorious but is merely the surrender of a person in his distress to the graciously saving God. It is nothing but seizing a life preserver, which can hardly be viewed as meritorious. Moreover, even faith is a gift of God (if we may thus read Eph. 2:8), so that again everything begins and ends with God.

So we are not dealing here with some kind of synergism, as if God and people cooperate in election on equal footing. However, neither are we dealing here with some kind of "causal decretalism," in which, in effect, there is no longer any room for human responsibility. As Reformed theologian Gerrit Berkouwer says, people ended up "in determinism or—in reaction—in synergism. In the case of synergism, man claims autonomy for himself in defense against the pressure of determinism [and fatalism]." In some way, faith, as a real, responsible human decision, is involved in the room created by God himself,[19] *without* violating God's sovereignty and grace.[20] As Reformed theologian Johan Heyns says, faith

---

19. Berkouwer (1960, 25; the words within brackets were in the Dutch original, but omitted from the published English translation).
20. Heyns (1988, 84).

"does not for even one moment make God's election dependent on the human response, but it cannot be separated from it either."[21] We need to discuss this important statement later in chapters 10-14.

5.5 A Gap Narrowed
5.5.1 Human Freedom

Millard Erickson believed he could resolve the problem of the relationship between the divine counsel and human responsibility by making a distinction between certainty and necessity.[22] If God decrees that something *will* happen, this future event is *certain*; if God decrees something *must* happen, this future event is *necessary*. This view maintains that everything that occurs is included within God's decree. However, Erickson sees an essential distinction between things God decrees that *will* happen and things he decrees that *must* happen. This distinction comes to light in corresponding human behavior: in the former case, a person *will* not act in any other way than decreed by God; in the latter case, he *cannot* act in any other way than decreed by God. The core matter is this: human responsibility and freedom are maintained in the former case, Erickson believes, but not in the latter case.

The importance of Erickson's view is that he relativizes the very notion of human freedom.[23] A person is free to *do* what he wants (what pleases him), but he is *not* free with regard to what it is that he *wants* and does not want (what does or does not please him). Our decisions—in my words—are determined by many factors: our innate and (especially through education) acquired constitution, the micro- and macro-situation of the moment, our acquired skills, our innate and acquired tastes and preferences. This means that a person may choose what he wants, but he cannot *want* everything he wants. In popular terms: I cannot freely decide to

---

21. Ibid., 87.
22. Erickson (1998, 383-85).
23. See Ouweneel (EDR 3, §14.2.1), with regard to the doctrine of sin.

love pop music or buttermilk, for this goes against my nature. As Greg Boyd says after discussing the restricted freedom of Josiah and Cyrus (cf. §4.7.1), restricting a person's freedom in one respect does not undermine his general freedom any more than does every other restriction imposed on people, such as their physical, emotional, intellectual nature, and the circumstances of their time, location, and birth.[24]

Indeed, both our genes and our parents and other educators, yes, many of our life circumstances have been determined totally apart from our own will and choices, namely, under the providence of God. Every day we make free choices: what we will wear, and where we will go. But at the same time this freedom is heavily restricted by the kind of persons that we inevitably are genetically, and by the circumstances in which we happen to live. In the same way, we can imagine that we choose freely for or against God, but that this choice at the same time is strongly determined by our nature and circumstances—and these have both been determined by God's providence. We may conclude that the gap between God's sovereign counsel and human responsibility is not at all as wide as many people think.

Already Gottfried Leibnitz, in his *Theodicy*, argued that God foreknows all possible situations.[25] He chooses which one(s) of them he will realize. By carefully selecting certain individuals whom he calls into existence, namely, those individuals who will respond to certain stimuli precisely the way he wants them to, and by creating these stimuli at the proper location and time, he ensures the *free* decisions and deeds of those individuals—"free," yet "ensured."

On the one hand, God's decisions are perfectly free, that is, not determined by any factors outside him (e.g., a foreseen faith). On the other hand, the decisions of people are free as well, even though people can decide freely only within the narrow boundaries imposed upon them by God in his

---
24. Boyd (2001, 121n7; see extensively, his chapter 6).
25 Leibniz (1890).

providence.

Now we arrive at a point that is vitally important for Viatorism. The term "providence" suggests that not only God's eternal *decree* is important but also the *ways* that he takes with each human being within time. In such an approach, every appearance of deism is avoided, by emphasizing that at every moment God is actively working within this world.[26] It is precisely in decretalism that such deist overtones are clearly present, as if from eternity God would have determined the entire course of world history. People would thus be born into an entirely determined world; the main difference with classic deism is that what is called natural laws in the latter is called God's counsel in decretalism.

Here we see the significance of our distinction between God's counsel and God's ways: in addition to God's *eternal* counsel we are dealing with his ways *through time and history*. These ways have not been foreordained in his eternal counsel. On the contrary, they depend on God's providence but also on the (often wrong) human choices and decisions (which themselves are strongly influenced by God's providence), to which God must respond.

If we describe human freedom in a relativizing way, as we just did, we can ask the question: Would a person in a given situation have been able to choose differently from what he actually did? The answer is: In principle, yes, and in this way human responsibility and freedom are protected. But the counter-question is: Would this person really do that? This time the answer is No, and thus the sovereign decree of God is protected.[27] Consider a person who is drowning and to whom a life preserver is thrown: he is totally free to grab the life preserver, since nobody is forcing him to do so; but the circumstances are such that virtually every rational person will do it.

---

26. Erickson (1998, 385–86).
27. Ibid., 386.

5.5.2 The Battle Goes On

Is the solution really that simple? Of course not. Arminians might object that people are *really* free if the second question just mentioned can be answered in the affirmative as well. (Hyper)Calvinist decretalists, on the contrary, might object that God's sovereignty is *really* protected if also the first question can be answered in the negative. Thus, such a "solution" does not put the debate to rest. Yet, on the one hand, perhaps we may learn from it that Arminians have too high an idea of human freedom in general; I would almost say, a pre-modern view, dating from the time when we knew nothing about the enormous influence of our genes, of the unconscious, and of environmental influences during our early youth, etc. People could still allow themselves to believe in their own absolute freedom; compare, for instance, the very different way René Descartes spoke of human freedom in the seventeenth century, and Sigmund Freud in the twentieth century. We are no longer so convinced of the freedom of the human mind.

On the other hand, perhaps we may learn from the proposed "solution" that hyper-Calvinists have too high an idea—an unnecessary and non-biblical idea—of divine sovereignty, as if this can be guaranteed only by actually turning people into puppets (even if hyper-Calvinists would never admit the latter). Hyper-Calvinism is a typically pre-modern view as well, dating from the time when people could still do very little to resist the mighty powers of nature, and felt totally dependent on God. To use a simple example: in the Netherlands the most godly people lived near the sea, in towns from which many fishermen perished at sea, or which were often flooded by the sea or the large rivers. In such areas, people felt very much dependent on the Supreme Being, who often seemed to act in a capricious and cruel way. They could undertake nothing against his overwhelming power; God could do as he pleased, without accounting for what he did, and why he did it. By the way, the more people in such regions learned to defend themselves against the sea and the rivers, the more their faith in the all-powerful Supreme Being dwindled.

How do (post-)modern people live with pre-modern Arminianism and pre-modern Calvinistic decretalism? We are not puppets; within the boundaries mentioned, we can make free choices, and we do so every day. On this simple statement alone, the claim that people have no free will breaks down.[28] Decretalists who have *chosen* this strange doctrine, have done so by their own free will without realizing it. However, it is equally true that our freedom is tremendously restricted by our genes, education, and circumstances, which under God's providence are what they are, so that we can imagine very well that we *freely* choose what God has providentially arranged for us. In summary: we are free, for we can choose between various options; but at the same time, God is and remains sovereign, for he arranges circumstances such that our decisions and deeds are *a priori* virtually certain—as virtually certain as the fact that the rational drowning person will grab the life preserver.

5.5.3 A Parallel

There is a parallel between this view and Open Theism in the sense that neither assumes absolute foreknowledge in God with respect to all future events, but only foreknowledge of all *possible* events. As we have seen, according to Open Theism, the Arminian idea of God's foreknowledge—God foreknows who will believe in him, and who will not—yields the difficulty that, if God knows that person P will do Q, it is certain that P will do Q. If Q were not certain, God could not foreknow Q with certainty. However, if Q *is* certain beforehand, so that nothing but Q can happen, how can classical Arminians themselves maintain P's freedom? Open Theism's conclusion is that whether God foreknows Q passively (Arminianism) or decrees Q actively (Calvinism) in effect makes no difference to people: they cannot do anything other than P,

---

28. See Ouweneel (EDR 3, §14.2).

and thus they are not free.

Erickson's alternative is that God has foreknowledge of possibilities. God foresees what possible persons will do if they are placed in a certain situation with all the influences that will be present at that point in time and space. On the basis of this, he chooses which of the possible individuals will become realities, and what circumstances and influences will be present.[29] God foreknows what these people will freely do, for he himself has determined the circumstances such that they *will* do so. Please notice: not *must* do, as if they are puppets, but *freely will* do, given their nature, life history, and circumstances as arranged by God—and, we may add, given the opportunities that God grants them due to the gospel preaching as arranged by him. To use our simple example again: the drowning person *freely* grabs the life preserver, yet we foreknew with virtual certainty that he would do this.

The congruent view of Benjamin Warfield, supplemented with notions of Millard Erickson, is definitely Calvinist because the initiative is still with God, while at the same time human freedom and responsibility remain optimally protected. The most important non-Calvinist feature of this view is that, like Open Theism, it surrenders the idea of God's absolute foreknowledge and predestination of all future events. In this manner, already before the rise of Open Theism, Warfield identified a way that narrowed the gap between divine sovereignty and human responsibility.

Yet, I venture to doubt whether this view really constitutes an answer to my objection mentioned before, namely, that some events in the Bible are definitely predicted in a very accurate and detailed manner. Unmistakably, these predictions seem to go further than that God knows only all future *possibilities*. Indeed, the essential difference remains between foreknowing that a future event is certain, and foreknowing that such an event is extremely likely, no matter how small

---

29. Erickson (1998, 360).

the gap between the two may have become since Warfield, Erickson, and so many others.

This means that, in the end, each of the proposed explanations fails. It would take us too far afield to further compare and analyze Calvinism, hyper-Calvinism, Thomism, Molinism, Congruism, Arminianism, Open Theism, etc. It is already very beneficial to have established that the discussion of the last half-century has brought to light that in one respect both Calvinists and Arminians, each in their many varieties (including Open Theists), will have to rethink their positions. This concerns the matter of God's foreknowledge with regard to the future: does God foreknow what he himself has foreordained (namely, *all* future events) (Calvinism)? Or does God foreordain what he foreknows will happen (e.g., foreseen [un]belief) (classic Arminianism)? Or does God foreknow only what he has ordained, but does he not foreknow the many things he has *not* foreordained (Open Theism)?

In a sense, the debate on this matter seems only to have begun—it remains to be seen whether it will produce useful and concrete answers. But we cannot ignore it. In the previous sections, I have simply tried to sketch the contours of this battle.

5.6 Viatorism and Prophecy
5.6.1 Conditional Prophecies

One of the important aspects of prophecy is that, in and through it, God predicts the future. The common goal of prophecy is "forthtelling" (cf. 1 Cor. 14:3, edification, exhortation, consolation) but often this contains foretelling. This may be conditional foretelling: if you remain faithful to the Lord, you will receive his blessings; but if you are unfaithful to him, and you persevere in this attitude, he will come with his judgment. After some time, this conditional prophecy may pass into an unconditional prophecy. For instance, you have remained faithful to the Lord, so you will receive his blessings. Or, you have for such a long time persevered in your unfaithfulness, your wickedness and transgressions, that God's judgment has become inevitable.

Now Viatorism must face this question: Does (unconditional) prophecy refer to God's *counsel* or to God's *ways*? For decretalism this is no issue: *all* prophecies are directly linked to God's counsel since they refer to the realization of it. For Open Theism this is no issue, either: the future is largely open; only a limited part of prophecy involves unconditional predictions flowing from God's counsel (see §4.7.1).

For Viatorism, *conditional* prophecies are obvious examples of God's *ways* with people: he predicts that if they do A, he will do P; he predicts that if they do B, he will do Q. What God will do depends on his own sovereign choices, but they also depend on the free choices of responsible people. This is characteristic of God's *ways*: there is a continuous interaction between human choices and God's choices. Yet, the final goal is certain: whatever routes both God and people may be following, in the end all these routes cooperate in realizing the goals that God had determined in his counsel.

Here are two simple examples from the Bible. God told Cain, "If you do well, will you not be accepted? And if you do not do well, sin is crouching at the door. Its desire is for you, but you must rule over it" (Gen. 4:7). God placed two options before Cain, and said as it were: if you do well, I will bless you; if you do you wrong, I will judge you. Cain did wrong, and God punished him for it. Promising blessing after doing the right thing always has the character of a conditional prophecy. Peter said, "Repent!" (Acts 2:38; 3:19; 8:22) That is, if you repent and believe, you will be saved; if you do not repent, you will perish. On the Day of Pentecost, about three thousand did repent and believe (2:41); the other people who heard him preach did not repent, and if they persevered in this attitude, they ultimately perished.

Please note that some prophecies did not sound conditional but in fact turned out to be so. God said to the priest

Eli, "'I promised that your house and the house of your father should go in and out before me forever,' but now the LORD declares: 'Far be it from me, for those who honor me I will honor, and those who despise me shall be lightly esteemed'" (1 Sam. 2:30). That is, God's initial promise was apparently conditional: "I promised that your house and the house of your father should go in and out before me forever, *if you remain faithful to me.*" Jonah's prophecy, "Yet forty days, and Nineveh shall be overthrown!" (Jonah 2:4) apparently meant: "Yet forty days, and Nineveh shall be overthrown *unless you repent!*"[30]

5.6.2 Unconditional Prophecies

But what about God's *unconditional* prophecies? Many such prophecies undoubtedly have everything to do with the *counsel* of God. All prophecies concerning the coming of the Messiah and the establishment of his kingdom of peace and righteousness in this world are rooted in God's counsel. However, Viatorism claims that there are several ways by which this counsel can be realized, depending on the free choices of people. The point here is that some of these ways are also the object of God's *unconditional* prophecies. In my view, it is perfectly certain that the sinful ways of humanity can never be the object of God's *counsel*; in no way can he ever be said to have foreordained sin. But if God foreknows the sinful ways that people will go, we can also understand how these ways can be the object of God's unconditional prophecies.

Good examples are Leviticus 26 and Deuteronomy 28–29. Here, Israel is confronted with blessings and curses: if they serve God, he will bless them; if they become unfaithful to him, he will curse them. This sounds like purely conditional prophecies. However, if we read these chapters carefully, we discover a tone suggesting that God expects his people to become *un*faithful rather than to remain faithful. And when we read Deuteronomy 30:1–10, we see that unfaithfulness and

---

30. See A. Devine, *Catholic Encyclopedia* (1913): https://en.wikisource.org/wiki/Catholic_Encyclopedia_(1913)/Prophecy.

curse are assumed; this passage contains a prophecy concerning Israel's restoration *after* unfaithfulness and curse. Thus, on the one hand the chapters appeal to human responsibility but at the same time predict that the people will become unfaithful and must expect the curse—but also restoration because God will ultimately fulfill his counsel. Human sins are never part of God's counsel—they are part of the ways of humanity, and in his own ways God responds to them. However, apparently both these future sinful human ways and God's future responses to them *can be part of unconditional prophecy.*

Another example is Exodus 3:19, where God predicts that the Egyptian Pharaoh would not allow the people of Israel to leave Egypt, not even under pressure. Such a prediction means neither that Pharaoh's stubbornness was part of God's counsel, nor that God provoked Pharaoh to commit these sins. Predicting someone's behavior is essentially different from provoking this behavior. Pharaoh was fully responsible for his stiff-necked attitude—God only predicted that he would *have* this attitude. And he added what he himself would do: he would lead Israel out of Egypt, in a miraculous way, in spite of all Pharaoh's counter-actions (v. 20). In no way is God's counsel involved here, except for the fact that God would ultimately reach his goal. We have here before us the ways of people and the responsive ways of God—yet both types of ways were accurately foretold by God.

We cannot contradict these facts by pointing out that God himself hardened Pharaoh's heart so that the latter no longer had a choice. If we argue thusly, we forget that Pharaoh had first hardened *himself* (Exod. 7:13-14; 8:15, 19, 32; 9:7, 34-35) before we read that the LORD hardened his heart (9:12; 10:1, 20, 27; 11:10; 14:4, 8 [cf. v. 17]; though it was predicted already in 4:21; 7:3).

5.6.3 Summary

In summary, *conditional* prophecies always involve God's *ways* because the fulfillment of their conditions depends on people, and this outcome influences the manner in which God will respond to their behavior. *Unconditional* prophecies may involve either God's *counsel* or God's *ways* because God is able—naturally—to predict not only the realization of his own counsel but also many of the idle ways of humanity as well as his own responses to them.

Obviously, God can fore*tell* what he fore*knows*—but very often what he fore*knows* is not identical with what he fore*ordains*. If he foretells what he himself has foreordained, God's counsel is involved. If he foretells what he himself has *not* foreordained but only fore*knows*, this involves matters he has left to human responsibility as well as the way he responds to them.

According to Open Theism, God basically *cannot* foreknow the matters he has left to human responsibility. According to hyper-Calvinism, also the matters that God has left to human responsibility are part of his eternal counsel. Viatorism rejects both positions. It maintains, on the one hand, that God foreknows (some of) the evil ways of humanity—and even predicts them—and on the other hand, that such evil ways can never have been part of God's counsel.

Thomas Aquinas distinguished between three kinds of prophecy, which exhibit clear correspondence with the summary just given.[31] The first category, called "prophecy of denunciation," in effect corresponds with what I have called conditional prophecy. The second category is "prophecy of foreknowledge": this involves the unconditional prediction of events that depend on free human choices, not on divine decree. The third category is "prophecy of predestination": this involves the unconditional prediction of events that depend on God's sovereign decree alone.

---

31. Aquinas, *Summa Theologiae* 2-2.174.1 (quoted in https://en.wikisource.org/wiki/Catholic_Encyclopedia_(1913)/Prophecy).

5.7 Contents of God's Plans
5.7.1 Beginnings

This book is dealing especially with the counsel and the ways of God in their general as well as their individual character. Elsewhere I have discussed God's counsel regarding the world in general.[32] More specifically, God's counsel can be summarized under three headings: (1) God's *covenant*, (2) God's *kingdom*, and (3) God's *church*. These three divine projects date from eternity past, and refer to all of eternity future (neither of which projects can, in my view, be proven to apply to the people of Israel as such). There is direct biblical evidence for the fact that the project of the church dates from eternity past (Eph. 3:9-10), but such evidence does not exist for the covenant and the kingdom. I can only tentatively launch the idea that divine projects that will endure forever were also decreed in eternity past. However, the fact that covenant and kingdom are so strongly linked with Israel might be an argument *against* this idea (see the next section).

In earlier volumes of the present series, I have dealt extensively with the first two subjects, covenant and kingdom. I have dealt with the third project elsewhere.[33] I therefore limit myself here to a brief survey of the relationships between covenant, kingdom, and church.

In Genesis, the *covenant* principle is manifested for the first time immediately after the flood: "I establish my covenant with you and your offspring after you, . . . that never again shall all flesh be cut off by the waters of the flood, and never again shall there be a flood to destroy the earth" (9:8-17; although some interpret Hos. 6:7 such that there was already a covenant between God and Adam). Scripture knows nothing of such typically Reformed notions as the "covenant of works" and the "covenant of grace."[34]

The *kingdom* is manifested already in Genesis 1, where

---
32. Ouweneel (EDR 10).
33. Ouweneel (EDR 7; EDR 8).
34. On the covenant see extensively, Ouweneel (2016c).

God entrusted the earth to the first human couple: "Let us make man in our image, after our likeness. And let them have *dominion* over the fish of the sea and over the birds of the heavens and over the livestock and over all the earth and over every creeping thing that creeps on the earth. . . . Be fruitful and multiply and fill the earth and *subdue* it, and have *dominion* over the fish of the sea and over the birds of the heavens and over every living thing that moves on the earth." The kingdom of the *last* Adam becomes manifest for the first time in Jacob's blessing (Gen. 49:10): "The scepter shall not depart from Judah, nor the ruler's staff from between his feet, until tribute comes to him [note: until Shiloh comes]; and to him shall be the obedience of the peoples."

The *church* was unknown in the Old Testament: Paul describes "how the mystery was made known to me by revelation . . . the mystery of Christ, which was *not made known* to the sons of men in other generations as it has now been revealed to his holy apostles and prophets by the Spirit. This mystery is that the Gentiles are fellow heirs, members of the same body, and partakers of the promise in Christ Jesus through the gospel" (Eph. 3:3-6; cf. vv. 9-10). And elsewhere he writes of Christ's

> body, that is, the church, of which I became a minister according to the stewardship from God that was given to me for you, to make the word of God fully known, the mystery *hidden* for ages and generations but *now revealed* to his saints. To them God chose to make known how great among the Gentiles are the riches of the glory of this mystery, which is Christ in you, the hope of glory (Col. 1:24-27).

Jesus also spoke of the church as a future reality (Matt. 16:18). Elsewhere I have explained that this was because the existence of the church was to depend on the ascension and glorification of Christ and the outpouring of the Holy Spirit.[35] The church develops within the framework of the kingdom,

---

35. See Ouweneel (EDR 7; 2016c).

which today has a hidden form that was not foreseen by the Old Testament prophets, just as the church was not foreseen by them.[36]

5.7.2 Before and Since the World's Foundation

It may amaze some readers that there is no direct evidence that God's covenant and God's kingdom were part of God's counsel from *before* the foundation of the world, that is, from all eternity. In connection with the kingdom, Jesus quoted a statement from the prophet: "I will open my mouth in parables; I will utter what has been hidden *since* the foundation of the world" (Matt. 13:33; cf. Ps. 78:1–3). Notice the word "since," instead of "before," as in Ephesians 1:4, "[H]e chose us in him *before* the foundation of the world, that we should be holy and blameless before him," and in 3:9–11, Paul speaks of

> the plan of the mystery hidden for ages in God who created all things, so that through the church the manifold wisdom of God might now be made known to the rulers and authorities in the heavenly places. This was according to the *eternal purpose* that he has realized in Christ Jesus our Lord.

The New Testament uses the expression "*before* [Gr. *pro*] the foundation of the world" (John 17:24; Eph. 1:4; 1 Pet. 1:20) — that is, before all ages (1 Cor. 2:7; Jude 25; cf. "before times eternal," 2 Tim. 1:9; Titus 1:2; cf. Rom. 16:25), or from all eternity — and the expression "*from*" or "*since* [Gr. *apo*] the foundation of the world," that is, since the world began, since the beginning of history (Matt. 13:35; 25:34; Luke 11:50; Heb. 4:3; 9:26; Rev. 13:8; 17:8[37]) (cf. §2.1).

Of course, the difference between "before" and "since/from" with respect to covenant, kingdom, and church should not be exaggerated. As to the covenant: the *blood* of the

---

36. See extensively, Ouweneel (2016e).
37. Surprisingly, the ESV has "before" in Rev. 13:8 and "from" in 17:8, whereas in both cases the Greek is *apo* ("from").

covenant is "the precious blood of Christ, like that of a lamb without blemish or spot. He was foreknown *before* the foundation of the world but was made manifest in the last times for the sake of you" (1 Pet. 1:19–20). That is, the plan of redemption was eternally in the mind of God, and this plan is realized within the context of the new covenant, as Jesus himself said at the institution of the Lord's Supper: "This cup that is poured out for you is the new covenant in my blood" (Luke 22:20; cf. 1 Cor. 11:25). As to the kingdom: the "ruler" of Israel is the One "whose goings forth have been from of old, from everlasting" (Mic. 5:2 KJV).

Yet, the church as such is most explicitly the object of God's eternal counsel. In this sense, the church may be called the greatest of the three projects. She was in God's heart from eternity. If the Father loved the Son "before the foundation of the world" (John 17:24), that is, from eternity, we may say that there was eternal love of the Triune God for the church, even though she did not yet exist. In time and history, the church was manifested as the *last* of the three projects; in God's eternal counsel, the church was the *first* of the three projects. (It goes without saying that I am not referring here to institutions and denominations, but to the "body of Christ," which we encounter in many institutions and denominations but which does not coincide with any of them.)

When it comes to eternity *future*, we find that all three projects will endure eternally: the covenant is an eternal covenant (Gen. 17:7, 13, 19; 1 Chron. 16:17; Ps. 105:10; Isa. 24:5; 55:3; 61:8; Jer. 32:40; 50:5; Ezek. 16:60; 37:26; Heb. 13:20; cf. Gen. 9:16; 2 Sam. 23:5), the kingdom is an eternal kingdom (Ps. 145:13; Dan. 2:44; 4:3, 34; 7:14, 27; 2 Pet. 1:11), and of course, the church is also intended for eternity (see, e.g., Eph. 3:21). This is why Israel, the earthly people of God, does not belong to his eternal projects: I know of no biblical evidence that Israel as such will still constitute a separate entity on the new earth. The everlasting character of covenant and kingdom does refer to eternity future, but perhaps *not* to eternity past. However, the church is eternal with respect to both eternity past and eternity future. She was present in God's counsel from eternity, she came into existence on the Day of Pentecost (Acts 2), and she will endure forever.

5.7.3 Connections

The three projects are clearly interconnected. As far as the *covenant* and the *kingdom* are concerned, we could say that the realization of the new covenant is God's program for the kingdom in the present dispensation. The *full* realization, as described in Jeremiah 31, coincides with the parousia of the Messiah, the establishment of the Messianic kingdom, and the restoration of the twelve tribes of Israel.

As far as the *kingdom* and the *church* are concerned: seen from God's perspective, the church as the body of Christ is the true core of the kingdom in the present dispensation — the holy gathering of true Christian believers (Belgic Confession, Art. 27) — whereas the kingdom in its present form is a broader notion: it contains all Christian *confessors*, whether true believers or hypocrites (wheat and weeds, good and bad fishes, wise and foolish virgins, etc.). In a still broader sense, the kingdom encompasses the entire world as the domain of God's rule and the sphere of the Holy Spirit's operation, both in the present age and in the coming age.

As far as the *covenant* and the *church* are concerned, strictly speaking the new covenant is made not with the church as such — as a body gathered from all nations in the world — but with the twelve tribes of Israel (Jer. 31:31; Heb. 8:8). However, the covenant's range is very broad: all those who since Calvary are cleansed by the blood of the new covenant, that is, the church, have a share in the blessings of the new covenant. In other words, they have been brought within the blessed "domain" of Israel's new covenant. The blood is the blood of the covenant, but it is said to the Lamb: "[Y]ou were slain, and by your blood you ransomed people for God from every tribe and language and people and nation" (Rev. 5:9).

5.8 General Principles
5.8.1 God's Counsel and Ways

All three projects revolve around these two principles being discussed throughout the present book: on the one hand, divine sovereign election and grace; on the other hand, human responsibility and freedom. This matter is connected with two core matters that have repeatedly surfaced in our discussions. First, there is the *counsel* of God, which will be ultimately realized, whatever people and demons may undertake. It involves both God's sovereignty and God's grace: God saved us "because of his own purpose and grace, which he gave us in Christ Jesus before the ages began" (2 Tim. 1:9). Because of God's counsel, there *will* be an eternal covenant, an eternal kingdom, and an eternal church (i.e., enduring eternally), in spite of all covenantal disloyalty, all insubordination in the kingdom, and all infidelity in the church.

Second, there are the *ways* of God, the (in our eyes often tortuous) paths along which God realizes his counsel within redemptive history. These ways are *not* part of his eternal counsel because they depend partially on the (often foolish and wicked) choices that people make according to their own responsibility and freedom. Indeed, no matter how many covenants have been broken by people, God has established, and will definitively establish, the new covenant. No matter how many weeds, leaven, bad fishes, unfaithful servants, and foolish virgins there may have been in the kingdom, God will realize the Messianic kingdom in power and glory, together with the wheat, the good dough, the good fishes, the faithful servants, and the wise virgins (to allude to only a few kingdom parables).[38] No matter how many false church members there may have been, and how weak the church may have been at times, church history will end with a pure bride of Christ (cf. Eph. 5:25–32).

It is incorrect to suggest that all these unfaithful elements

---

38. Ouweneel (2016e, chapters 3–4).

within the covenants, the kingdom, and the church were, and are, part of God's *counsel*. There is no biblical basis for this claim. On the contrary, such elements are stumbling blocks, which obstruct the *ways* of God and threaten to prevent the realization of God's eternal counsel. As a consequence, God often must (at least from our perspective) take a detour to reach his goal. God realizes his counsel *together with* the righteous, the faithful, and the wise, and *in spite* of the unrighteous, the unfaithful, and the foolish. The latter can be a burden, and they often force God to choose a different way to reach his purpose.

Let us not be disturbed by the word "force": it is God himself who has *sovereignly* chosen to make himself to some extent dependent on the often foolish and wicked deeds of people. He has chosen a tortuous path that "forces" him to change his direction once in a while. However, no actions of evil people can ever affect God's counsel as such: he realizes it, no matter what counter-actions people may take. Correspondingly, his ways may vary tremendously, but his fixed counsel cannot be changed and will reach its fulfillment.

Here is a brief summary of differences between God's counsel (here in the sense of God's eternal counsel) and God's ways:

God's counsel	*God's ways*
eternal	temporal
unchangeable	changeable
not depending on human choices	depending on human choices
not influenced by Satan	influenced by Satan
involves God's decretive will	involve both God's decretive *and* desiring will
involves God's sovereignty	involve both God's sovereignty and indulgence
involves God's eternal goal	involve means for reaching God's eternal goal

Of course, the correspondences are equally important:

both God's counsel and God's ways involve all his attributes, such as his love, his holiness, his righteousness, his omnipotence, his sovereignty. God's counsel and God's ways have the same purpose: reaching the glorious goal as established once and for all in his glorious counsel.

> All the kings of the earth shall give you thanks, O Lord, for they have heard the words of your mouth, and they shall sing of the ways of the Lord, for great is the glory of the Lord. For though the Lord is high, he regards the lowly, but the haughty he knows from afar (Ps. 138:5).

5.8.2 Christ the Center

It is of essential importance to see that Jesus Christ is the heart and center of all three projects. As to the *covenant*: in him, all the promises of God are Yes and Amen (cf. 2 Cor. 1:20). Christ is the guarantee, mediator, and executor of the new covenant (1 Tim. 2:5; Heb. 6:17; 7:22; 8:6; 9:15-17; 12:24). This covenant is founded upon the blood of his self-sacrifice (Matt. 26:28; Mark 14:24; Luke 22:20; 1 Cor. 11:25; Heb. 9:7, 12-15, 18-28; 12:24; 13:20). This does not hold for the new covenant only; in fact, none of the many Old Testament covenants can be viewed apart from Christ. For instance, the Noahic covenant was closely linked with Noah's burnt offering (Gen. 8:20), which points to Christ's true offering.

As to the *kingdom*: it is God's kingdom, but Christ is its anointed King (the name "Christ," *christos*, means "anointed"). The prophetic books of the Old Testament contain many references to him (Isa. 9:6-7; 32:1; Ezek. 34:23-24; 37:24-25; Mic. 5:2-5; Zech. 9:9-10, to mention a few). The Gospel of Matthew in particular is permeated with Jesus' kingship. In contrast with the Roman emperor, and all the Greek and Roman gods, Paul preached "another king, Jesus" (Acts 17:7; cf. 20:25). And John predicts "the kingdom of our Lord and of his Christ" (Rev. 11:15), "the kingdom of our God and the authority of his Christ" (12:10).

As to the *church:* Jesus Christ is its head: "Christ is the head of the church, his body, and is himself its Savior" (Eph. 5:23; cf. 1:22–23; 4:15; 5:23, 25; Col. 1:18; 2:19). He is also the Bridegroom of the church, which is his bride. Paul wrote to the Corinthian Christians: "I betrothed you to one husband, to present you as a pure virgin to Christ" (2 Cor. 11:2). And to the Ephesian Christians he wrote:

> Husbands, love your wives, as Christ loved the church and gave himself up for her, that he might sanctify her, having cleansed her by the washing of water with the word, so that he might present the church to himself in splendor, without spot or wrinkle or any such thing, that she might be holy and without blemish. . . . [Christ] nourishes and cherishes . . . the church, because we are members of his body. "Therefore a man shall leave his father and mother and hold fast to his wife, and the two shall become one flesh." [Gen. 2:24] This mystery is profound, and I am saying that it refers to Christ and the church (Eph. 5:25–32).

John speaks of "the marriage of the Lamb, and his Bride has made herself ready" (Rev. 19:7). "Come, I will show you the Bride, the wife of the Lamb" (21:9; cf. v. 2; 22:17).

In §2.4.2 I entered briefly into the complicated subject of common grace. We have seen how hyper-Calvinism tends to separate common grace from the person and work of Jesus Christ. We have also seen why this is invalid. All God's decrees and all God's ways are strictly Christocentric. This was so before the Fall and after the Fall, before the patriarchs and after them, before the Torah and after it. It is true for God's specific projects and for his universal providence. It is true for Israel in the Old Testament and the church in the New Testament, but also for God's universal rule over the nations. It is true for the old creation and for the new creation.

5.8.3 Comments

It is wise not to confuse the three projects, for instance, by calling Christ the "King of the church"; this is a confusion of two different metaphors. Church and kingdom are not identical. Yet, the expression "King of the church" is quite common among Christians. Where the Belgic Confession wishes to prove that the church has existed from the beginning, it uses this strange argument (Art. 27): "This church has existed from the beginning of the world and will last until the end, as appears from the fact that Christ is eternal King who cannot be without subjects." In my view, this is a *non sequitur*. Here is another example, of many: Reformed theologian David J. Engelsma writes: "Christ is king of the church. He rules the church by His Word. His Word is law for the church. He exercises His kingship through a body of elders, whom He calls into holy office. These men are rulers in the church. They administer the Word of the king."[39]

Regarding the central position of Christ, Frederick Grant wrote that, in a sense, many theological systems made the first man, Adam, God's central thought instead of the second Man, the last Adam. In effect, Christ was needed "only" to restore the first creation, and to take back what Adam should have obtained or retained.[40] This is invalid. It is not the restoration of (former) humanity, or the pre-Fall world, that is the great goal of all God's counsel, but "bringing the firstborn into the world" (Heb. 1:6). Not even the reconciliation of humanity by the atonement for its sins is God's greatest aim, but "his purpose, which he set forth in Christ as a plan for the fullness of time, to unite all things in him, things in heaven and things on earth" (Eph. 1:9-10). Even individually, forgiveness of sins is not a *goal* but a *means*: ". . . Christ in you, the hope of glory. Him we proclaim, warning everyone and teaching everyone with all wisdom, that we may present everyone mature in Christ" (Col. 1:27-28); ". . . until Christ is formed in you" (Gal. 4:19).

This centrality of Christ is very far-reaching. The *covenant* is not simply for God's people; it is primarily intended for

---

39. Engelsma (n.d., from chapter 6: "The Church as Kingdom").
40. Grant (1956, 13).

the glorification of Christ: "... the God of peace who brought again from the dead our Lord Jesus, the great shepherd of the sheep, by the blood of the eternal covenant" (Heb. 13:20). The *kingdom* is not simply to benefit God's people; it is primarily intended to extol the glory and majesty of Christ. He *is* the kingdom in his own person (cf. Luke 17:21, "the kingdom of God is in the midst of you"). And where we expect Paul to speak of the *church*, he sometimes says "Christ": "For just as the [human physical] body is one and has many members, and all the members of the body, though many, are one body, so it is with Christ," not the body of Christ, but *Christ*, that is: head and body in one. In Ephesians 3:3-9, the mystery is the church, but in Colossians 1:27 precisely the same mystery is described as "Christ in you"; it is the "mystery of Christ" (4:3; cf. 2:2).

After having spoken of covenant, kingdom, and church, we realize that ultimately there is only one project of God, to which all these three projects refer and in which they all culminate: the glory of God, who will be glorified in and through Christ, the One who will be the center of the new creation. Christ is the content, and in some sense even the embodiment, of God's counsel. And all the ways through which this counsel of God is realized run through Christ.

> [T]o the only God, our Savior, through Jesus Christ our Lord, be glory, majesty, dominion, and authority, before all time and now and forever. Amen (Jude 1:25).

> Now may the God of peace who brought again from the dead our Lord Jesus, the great shepherd of the sheep, by the blood of the eternal covenant, equip you with everything good that you may do his will, working in us that which is pleasing in his sight, through Jesus Christ, to whom be glory forever and ever. Amen (Heb. 13:20-21).

Chapter 6
God's Sovereignty, (Im)mutability, (Im)passibility, and (In)temporality

> *Every good gift and every perfect gift is from above,*
> *coming down from the Father of lights*
> *with whom there is no variation*
> *or shadow due to change.*
> James 1:19

> *In all their affliction he was afflicted,*
> *and the angel of his presence saved them;*
> *in his love and in his pity he redeemed them;*
> *he lifted them up and carried them all the days of old.*
> Isaiah 63:9

> *L*ORD*, you have been our dwelling place*
> *in all generations.*
> *Before the mountains were brought forth,*
> *or ever you had formed the earth and the world,*
> *from everlasting to everlasting you are God.*
> Psalm 90:1–2

Summary: *It is hard to grasp God's counsel without some understanding of his being. God is sovereign, but that does not exclude the* *possibility that he has sovereignly decided to involve people in his ways with the world. This implies that when speaking of the will of God, we must realize what aspect of his will is in view. This entire subject is permeated with ancient and medieval ideas about God's being, which makes the discussion quite cumbersome. God is unchangeable in his being, and thus in his counsel – but he is changeable in the ways in which he is involved with the world; he can even change his mind, which earlier theologians considered unthinkable. They also thought that God is not capable of suffering (this is his impassibility), whereas the Bible often refers to his (deep) emotions, including grief. Finally, this chapter deals with God's eternity: is this a timeless eternity, or is God everlasting (a term that implies some form of time)? This question has consequences for our view of God's counsel and ways.*

6.1 God's Sovereignty
6.1.1 Introduction

IN THIS CHAPTER AND THE NEXT, we will examine somewhat more closely a few of God's attributes that are of essential importance for understanding God's counsel and God's being.[1] I believe we cannot begin to understand God's counsel if we do not grasp to some extent what Scripture tells us about these attributes of God. Especially (real or supposed) divine attributes like sovereignty, omniscience, (im)mutability, (im)passibility, omnipotence, and eternity/temporality are involved.

Let us first consider God's absolute, sovereign power over all of created reality: "He is wise in heart and mighty in strength – who has hardened himself against him, and succeeded?" (Job 9:4). "[H]e does according to his will among the host of heaven and among the inhabitants of the earth; and none can stay his hand or say to him, 'What have you done?'" (Dan. 4:35). "Am I not allowed to do what I choose with what belongs to me?" says the master of the vineyard in the parable (Matt. 20:15), thus reflecting God's own feelings. God does with his creation *as pleases him*. This good pleasure of God, his

---

1. Cf. Pinnock (2001, 79–104).

sovereign will, is the foundation of his counsel (Rom. 9:22–23; Eph. 1:5, 9, 11), of his creation (Rev. 4:11), of his rule (Ps. 115:3; Prov. 21:1), of his work of redemption (Matt. 26:42), of acceptance (Rom. 9:15–18), of regeneration (James 1:18), of sanctification (Phil. 2:13; 1 Thess. 4:3), of our sufferings (1 Pet. 3:17), of our life and destination (Acts 18:21; Rom. 5:32; 1 Cor. 4:19; Heb. 6:3; James 4:15), of the gifts in the church (1 Cor. 12:11), and even of the smallest things (Matt. 10:29).

His sovereignty implies that he does not need to give account to anyone: "Why do you contend against him, saying, 'He will answer none of man's words'?" (Job 33:13). People are in his hand like clay in the molder's hand: "[W]ho are you, O man, to answer back to God? Will what is molded say to its molder, 'Why have you made me like this?' Has the potter no right over the clay, to make out of the same lump one vessel for honorable use and another for dishonorable use?" (Rom. 9:20–21; cf. Job 10:9; Isa. 29:16; 30:14; 64:8; Jer. 18:6). People are only instruments in God's hand, tools that cannot withstand their Maker: "Shall the axe boast over him who hews with it, or the saw magnify itself against him who wields it? As if a rod should wield him who lifts it, or as if a staff should lift him who is not wood!" (Isa. 10:15; cf. 45:9). "If one wished to contend with him, one could not answer him once in a thousand times" (Job 9:3). "If he passes through and imprisons and summons the court, who can turn him back?" (Job 11:10).

6.1.2 A Bit of History

Theological reflection upon God's sovereign will has been strongly influenced by ancient thought (Plato, Aristotle, Stoics, Plotinus). This does not mean, contrary to what has been claimed (e.g., by Adolf von Harnack), that the Christian doctrine of God has traditionally been altogether *determined* by Hellenism—nor (contrary to Herman Bavinck) that theology remained entirely free of such influences. The truth presumably lies somewhere in the middle. By the way, those who wish to abolish everything that smacks of Hellenism must abolish theology itself, viewed as a logical-analytical analysis of the Christian *depositum fidei* (the body of Christian beliefs). The origin and development of early Christianity would have been inconceivable without the Hellenistic context in which it took shape. In a positive sense, Wolfhart Pannenberg called the Hellenistic coloring of the biblical doctrine of God the "condition" for its acceptability within the Gentile world of the time.[2] Nevertheless, one may certainly wonder whether in several respects this coloring has gone too far.

This is all the more urgent when we consider the influence of humanism on theological thinking about God's sovereign will; think, for instance, of René Descartes, Georg Hegel, Friedrich Schelling, Arthur Schopenhauer, Eduard von Hartmann. Herman Bavinck argued that the latter three philosophers have been of the greatest significance to theism because they refuted rationalist and idealist pantheism.[3] However, I view such philosophers as dangerous allies for a biblical doctrine of God. For instance, philosophy has sometimes argued that the will is a striving and longing, and thus points to imperfection, dissatisfaction, which cannot be found in God. Thus, this kind of philosophy denied God's will, just as mysticism has often done with its emphasis on God's complacency. Bavinck replied that the will is not only a striving for something that has not yet been reached or obtained, but also an active resting in, and enjoying, that which through this will *has been* attained or obtained.[4] Here we think of the Greek term *autarkēs*, "[being] content," in Philippians 4:11, "Not that I am speaking of being in need, for I have learned in whatever situation I am to be content" —a term that Flavius Josephus applied to God. God is self-contented, self-sufficient, self-satisfied, for he does not need anybody. However, he is free to choose to *want* to have communion with creatures.

---

2. Pannenberg (1991, 1:71–72); cf. Strauss (2007, 183).
3. Bavinck (*RD* 2:231).
4. Ibid.

6.1.3 Concepts and Ideas Again

We should not treat these two different ideas, God's sovereign will and God's autarchy, as concepts with contradictions that must be overcome. Some have argued that God's *propensio in creaturas* ("propensity toward creatures"), as distinct from his *propensio in se ipsium* ("propensity toward himself"), is always for his own name's sake (cf. Prov. 16:4, "The LORD has made everything for its purpose, even the wicked for the day of trouble"). Yet, I believe that every word play designed to reconcile this with God's autarchy is only hubris as long as such notions are treated as concepts instead of ideas.

Many speculations about God's sovereign power and will suffer the same shortcoming. Thus, William of Ockham asserted that God's *potestas absoluta* ("absolute power"), as distinct from his *potestas ordinata* ("ordinary power"), could just as well have demanded an egoistic morality. If this were so, the Decalogue would be merely the product of divine arbitrariness. Creation, incarnation, satisfaction, good and evil, true and untrue — it could all have been different than what it is, if this had pleased God. This cannot be right. First, God's power and will can be understood as ideas only within the context of his entire being, that is, in relationship to his love, his holiness, his righteousness, etc. This excludes arbitrariness. God cannot choose to be, or to become, or to behave like, anything that is contrary to his very love, holiness, etc.

Second, speaking of God's alleged arbitrariness presupposes a *norm* by which we can determine what is and is not arbitrary. However, if we do this, we put God under his own law-order; that is, we place him under the law-boundary that he has instituted between himself and his creation.[5] God's will cannot be subjected to norms; his will is absolute, and does not give account to anyone or anything other than God himself. Even saying, as Bavinck does by quoting Gisbert Voetius: "God himself can never have willed anything

---
5. Kalsbeek (1977, 74); cf. Bavinck (*RD* 2:232–34, 238–40).

unless it is either good in itself or for some other reason,"[6] implies putting God under the law-boundary, as if there is some norm outside God, and independent of God, which determines what God can and cannot want, or what is and is not good. Nothing is good "in itself or for some other reason"; only that is good which is in agreement with the perfect goodness of God's own being: "No one is good except God alone" (Mark 10:18; Luke 18:19). God cannot ever want anything except what is in agreement with his own being. God's deeds are not good because they obey a certain norm defining what is good, but because he himself is good.

6.2 Two Kinds of Will
6.2.1 Decretive and Preceptive

A special difficulty with regard to God's will arises with the existence of evil, and the relationship of God's will to it. Traditionally, theology distinguishes between God's decretive will, which describes what God himself does, and will do (Ps. 115:3; Dan. 4:17, 25, 32, 35; Rom. 9:18–19; Eph. 1:5, 9, 11; Rev. 4:11), and God's preceptive will, which prescribes what people must do (Matt. 7:21; 12:50; John 4:34; 7:17; Rom. 12:2).[7] Sometimes the two look very similar but, strictly speaking, the "your will be done" in Matthew 6:19 belongs to the latter category—because it is people through whom this will must be realized—and the "your will be done" in 26:42 belongs to the former category, for here God's counsel is involved.

We encounter this distinction in many passages. God's will was that Abraham sacrifice his son (preceptive will), but God himself ensured that in the end this did not happen (decretive will) (Gen. 22:2, 12). It was God's will that Pharaoh permit the Israelites to leave (preceptive will), but he hardened Pharaoh's heart, so that the latter did not do it (decretive will) (Exod. 4:21). It was God's will that people not convict

---

6. Voetius, *Selectae disputationes theologicae* I, 387; cited in Bavinck (*RD* 2:239).
7. Bavinck (*RD* 2:243; and elsewhere).

the innocent (preceptive will), but he delivered Jesus to false judges according to his own divine counsel (decretive will) (Acts 2:23; 3:18; 4:28). God does not want sin, yet allows it (Josh. 11:20; 2 Sam. 16:10; Rom. 1:24–26; 2 Thess. 2:11; and many other passages). It is his will that all people be saved (Ezek. 18:23, 32; 33:11; 1 Tim. 2:4; 2 Pet. 3:9), yet "he has mercy on whomever he wills, and he hardens whomever he wills" (Rom. 9:18), and has made "the wicked for the day of trouble" (Prov. 16:4).

In order to explain this difference, theology began to distinguish between two kinds of God's will. On the one hand, Tertullian spoke of a hidden, higher will (i.e., the will of his counsel) and, on the other hand, of a public, lesser will (i.e., the will of his command).[8] Augustine maintained that God often fulfills his good will through the evil will of people.[9] As we have seen (§2.8.2), scholasticism spoke of the *voluntas beneplaciti* ("will of good pleasure"; or *voluntas arcana, decernens, decretiva*, "hidden, decisive, decretive will") and the *voluntas signi* ("will of the sign"; or *voluntas revelata, praecipiens*, "revealed, commanding will"; the *signa*, "signs," are here commandment, exhortation, chastisement, punishment, etc.).[10] This is the irresistible will of God (the will of his immutable counsel, his good pleasure, which will ultimately be realized) and the resistible or desiring will of God, respectively. Many Reformed theologians (e.g., John Calvin, Wolfgang Musculus, Zacharias Ursinus, Amandus Polanus) adopted this view.

6.2.2 A Different Approach

Roman Catholics, Lutherans, and Arminians preferred a distinction between God's *voluntas antecendens* (or *absoluta*, God's "preceding" or "absolute will") and God's *voluntas consequens* (or *conditionata*, "consequential" [following upon (something)] or "conditional will"). That is, the former is the actual

---

8. *De Exhortatione Castitatis* 2–3.
9. *Enchiridion* 101.
10. E.g., Thomas Aquinas, *Summa Theologiae* 1.19.11–12.

will of God, implying that God does not want sin, though he permits it, and that he wants the salvation of all people, and offers it to all. The latter will of God is the will that follows upon the choices of people: if a person has decided for himself what he wants, God agrees with it, and thus saves the believer and condemns the unbeliever. This is not the actual, absolute will of God, but involves God's deed as a *consequence* of a person's deed.

Reformed theologians rejected this distinction. They viewed the *voluntas beneplaciti* as the actual, absolute will of God, which is always realized, entirely independently of what people want or decide. Thus, the salvation or condemnation of people depends exclusively on God's will. The *voluntas beneplaciti* may be distinguished only from his prescribing will in law and gospel, intended as guidelines for human behavior.[11]

Here again, we must reject both approaches. Each combats the other by implicitly—and inadvertently—viewing the other's viewpoint as a conceptual system. From the ideas concerned, properties are derived that do belong to the supposed concepts, but not to these ideas. These properties are then played off against each other such that the opponent's thought system is stamped as internally contradictory. In this way, the system is rejected, and one's own thought system is automatically accepted as the correct one. This fails to recognize that one can treat the other's thought system as a conceptual system only if one is prepared to do the same with one's own thought system. In so doing, one would soon find that, from one's own system too, certain properties can be derived that make the system logically contradictory—as the opponents love to emphasize.

Related to this approach is, for instance, the striking way in which Herman Bavinck defended his Reformed paradigm

---

11. Regarding these two kinds of will, see John Piper in Schreiner and Ware (2000, chapter 5).

against Pelagianism.[12] He did not shrink from asserting that Scripture sometimes says P, but "actually" means non-P. Thus, he claimed that the *voluntas signi* is "actually" not the will of God, for in this will he does not express what *he* will do. This law is not a law for *his* action; it does not prescribe what *God* must do, but only what *people* must do. Therefore, it is "will of God" only "in a metaphorical sense."[13] In this way, Bavinck tells us that God does not *really* want all people to be saved, in spite of 1 Timothy 2:4 and 2 Peter 3:9. This is the consequence of viewing one's own thought system as conceptual, from which contradictions can be derived on the basis of which one may assert that Scripture sometimes means the opposite of what it says. In the approach of Viatorism, this problem does not occur; therefore, in my modest opinion it is closer to Scripture.

6.2.3 The Only Solution

The only solution that I see is that all terms used with regard to God's will are not to be viewed as concepts but as ideas. In this way we can without restriction maintain alongside each other both God's absolute will—in order to guarantee his absolute sovereignty—and God's conditional will, in order to guarantee human responsibility and freedom, that is, the high position of people as God's image-bearers. The reason we can do this is that both ways of speaking are idea-like *approximations* of God's will, which surpass all conceptualization, and thus all logical contradictions that may occur between conceptual systems. In this way we can still speak of God's will in an entirely *rational* way—for our rational knowledge is not at all limited to conceptual knowledge—though in the form of ideas only. Only in this way can we live rationally with apparent contradictions, which would be real contradictions only if we would try to speak of God's will in a conceptual way.

---

12. Bavinck (*RD* 2:244).
13. Ibid.

How easily we can overestimate our theological models in this connection is apparent from Herman Bavinck's claim that "Scripture, though theologically giving prominence to the will of God's good pleasure, by its teaching of the revealed will of God underscores how and in what sense God does not will sin."[14] We respond that Scripture does not "theologically give prominence" to *anything*; it does not supply us, or work with, theological models or theories whatsoever. Our theoretical models, such as the distinction between the *voluntas beneplaciti* and the *voluntas signi*, are always designed by *people*, and imposed upon the biblical data, not the other way round.

Let me point here to the newer twentieth-century views in the philosophy of science: scientific models or theories are in no way derived from the field under investigation. This is because the object of study itself does not contain any theoretical entity, and so a scientific model cannot be taken from the object itself. Scholarly (including theological and philosophical) models and theories are always free, creative designs of the human mind, though, of course, always with the intention of accounting for the data. A scientific theory's *origin*, however, does not lie in the object of study as such, but in the human mind.

No scholarly enterprise needs this insight more urgently than theology, because theologians often behave(d) as if any attack on their theories was an attack on Scripture itself; that is, they viewed their models and Scripture as identical. Just as with all other scientists and scholars, theologians are simply repeating what their object of study, namely, Scripture, is saying. Their theories do not come *from* Scripture, but are designed by theologians for the interpretation *of* Scripture. As perfect as Scripture is, so defective and temporary are its interpretations by theologians, including mine. Many church splits could have been avoided if theologians had modestly recognized the status of their hypotheses, theories, and

---

14. Ibid.

models from the vantage point of the philosophy of science. I have written more extensively elsewhere about the very important subject of the status of theological theories.[15]

6.3 Sovereignty Viewed Differently
6.3.1 "Unworthy" of God?

It may be useful to remember that the term "sovereignty" does not occur in the Bible ("sovereign" does occur in a few translations, but the term is nowhere strictly needed; see chapter 3, note 44). Of course, the notion as such is certainly present in Scripture, but because this notion is nowhere made explicit, the danger is great that theologians fill it in on their own. Thus, it has often been argued that this or that would affect God's sovereignty because it would be "unworthy" of him.[16] For instance, it would be inappropriate — according to William Perkins even "very wicked" (§3.3.1) — to suppose that everything that occurs would *not* have been decreed by God from eternity.

Of course, being "unworthy" of God is a very subjective notion. In my view, it is just as much, or even more, justified to argue that it is "unworthy" of God to create people about whom he has decreed beforehand that they will land in hell; or that it is "unworthy" of God to enter a history whose every detail he himself has already determined, so that there is no room at all for people whom he did create with responsibility, freedom of will, and many options to exercise them.

What view does more justice to God's sovereignty: *either* the view in which all events in the world, including all human actions, have been foreordained in a divine blueprint, which he merely executes, that is, a chess match whose moves are scripted beforehand, moves that he merely executes? *Or* is more justice done to God's sovereignty in the view in which he does not *need* to foreordain all things, or perhaps even fore*know* all things, but in which he trusts his own power and

---
15. Ouweneel (1995a, §1.6; 1997, chapter 6; 2014a; 2014b).
16. So, e.g., Boyd (2000, 14–15, 130–31).

wisdom so much that he is willing to allow people a certain freedom, and yet attains his goals with absolute certainty, that is, by playing a *real* chess match, so to speak?[17]

Consider this comparable metaphor: are we part of a movie that has been recorded beforehand? If so, all our movements have been played out on film long before; there is no longer room for any surprise. *Or* are we part of a theater play, which does follow a certain script, but in which accidents, incidences, spontaneous lines, and the like are still possible? Are we puppets or real people?

Notice the way Clark Pinnock put it.[18] He argued that God knows absolutely everything, including the possible as possible, and the indeterminate as indeterminate. For him, it would be dishonoring God to say that God knew something as determined that was indeterminate. This sounds almost as bad as Perkins' term "wicked," and at any rate as bad as an "insolent sophism," as the Canons of Dordt say (see above). Here, again, someone is telling us, on the basis of his own thought system, what is unworthy of God. Perkins: it cannot be that God did not foreordain everything because this would be unworthy of his sovereignty. Pinnock: it cannot be that God foreknows everything because this would be unworthy of his honor.

In my view, both are mistaken. They speak of God's sovereignty and God's foreknowledge, respectively, as if these were concepts about which properties can be predicated that would dishonor God. As soon as we treat such terms as ideas, we begin to see that God *can* be perfectly sovereign even without having foreordained everything (*contra* decretalism), and that God *can* perfectly foreknow many events that are nonetheless the products of *free* human choices (*contra* Open Theism).

---

17. Ibid., 68.
18. Pinnock (2001, 49).

6.3.2 God's Counsel and Ways

In the distinction between God's counsel and God's ways, God's sovereignty is not at stake at all. The reason is that, apparently, God himself has sovereignly decided to make himself to some extent dependent on the free choices of people. God is "sovereign over his sovereignty,"[19] which means that he himself decides how his sovereignty must be concretely understood. Thus, apparently it was his own sovereign choice to create free beings who would voluntarily follow his will, but who would also be able to oppose his will.

This is an important point. It was God's own sovereign choice to enter history together with humanity, in continual interaction with the latter's choices and decisions. And at the same time, God confirms his sovereignty in that, whatever people may choose or decide, in the end he always attains his own goals. In determining his *counsel* God acts totally alone — but the *ways* through which he realizes his counsel are chosen by him in interaction with the choices and decisions of free people.

Therefore, the assertion of Calvinist R. C. Sproul is not only very one-sided but totally mistaken.[20] He claims that, if God's sovereignty is restricted by man's freedom, then God is not sovereign; man is sovereign. This would be correct only if *against his own will* God's power were restricted by another power, in this case, human freedom — a power that would *prevail* over God's power. Of course, this is not the case at all. Even if God's sovereignty were restricted by man's freedom, his power remains infinitely greater than human power. It is absurd to claim that, if God is not one hundred percent sovereign — in the sense defined by Sproul himself — then automatically man is sovereign. Where is the logic here?

Spoul's fundamental error consists in overlooking the possibility that God, so to speak, *according to his own will*, that

---

19. Pinnock (2001, 92).
20. Sproul (1986, 43).

is, sovereignly, allows his sovereignty to be restricted by human freedom, without making people themselves sovereign in any sense. On the contrary, this human freedom can never interfere with God's *counsel*, but at most only with God's *ways*, and this only to a limited extent.

6.3.3 Open Theism Again

Open Theist Greg Boyd summarizes the Open Theist view in the following way: (a) to a certain extent, the future has been *determined*, and is known to God; (b) to a certain extent, the future is open, yet foreknown to God as definitely P and definitely not Q; (c) to a certain extent, the future is open, and not foreknown to God; he knows this part of the future only as *possibly* P and *possibly* not Q.[21]

Two matters require more clear formulation than what Boyd supplies.

(a) God has partially determined the future in his *counsel*, and this future is foreknown by him. But he does not foreknow all his *ways* through which he will realize his counsel because these ways are partially determined by the choices and decisions of people.

(b) Here is the middle path between (a) and (c): God realizes his own counsel not only through his own actions but also through the actions of particular people; think of what God prophesies about what king Josiah, king Cyrus, and Jesus' persecutors would do (see §4.2.1). Note the careful balance here between God's counsel, as expressed in genuine prophecies, and the human freedom of Josiah, Cyrus, and others.

(c) Part of the future is not only open, but apparently unknown to God, or known to him only as possibilities. According to the manner in which these possibilities are realized—depending on the choices of free people—God responds to them in his *ways*.

Stated in summary form: (a) God foreknows what he will

---

21. Boyd (2000, 15).

do according to his own counsel, (b) he foreknows what certain people will do according to his own counsel, and (c) he does not foreknow the things that he has not decreed and that are done by people according to their God-given freedom.

How should we evaluate these claims? I can fully agree with points (a) and (b); biblical testimony about them is crystal clear. This is one of the central claims of this book. However, point (c) is less self-evident than Boyd and other Open Theists suggest. Does the fact that the future is partially open also mean that God does not entirely foreknow the future? Or can God definitely foreknow future events that he himself has not decreed, that depend on human choices, and of which he is nonetheless aware long before they occur? In chapter 4 we have briefly dealt with these questions, but we must deal with them a bit more extensively.

One thing may be observed immediately: God's omniscience is not at stake, unless this term (which is not in the Bible) is defined *a priori* as necessarily meaning that God foreknows *all* future events. However, in chapter 4 we considered the ample testimony of Scripture suggesting that God does *not* foreknow all things with certainty (see further §7.1). This does not necessarily endanger his omniscience, though. God foreknows all things that *are* foreknowable: he knows all future events that he himself has decreed, and he knows all *possible* events, which he has not decreed but entrusted to human responsibility. He perfectly knows all *possible* choices that people can make, and he also perfectly knows what are the *most likely* choices that people will make. However, one of two claims is made repeatedly. Either human freedom of will makes it possible for God to foreknow what people will choose (the latter is claimed by decretalism). Or human freedom of will makes this impossible, because, given this foreknowledge, all future choices are fixed beforehand, which marks the end of human freedom of will (as Open Theism claims).

Many opponents of Open Theism have launched their attacks on the basis of God's omniscience. Understandably so. Can we really call God omniscient if he does not exactly foreknow all future events? Open Theists assure us, however, that this is not the actual problem.[22] Rather, the greatest question lies in the domain of the future being open or not open: Has all that ever occurs been decreed by God from eternity, or have all things *not* been decreed beforehand? I have indicated why I cannot agree with Open Theists on all points (especially not regarding its view of God's foreknowledge), but as far as *this* question is concerned, I do agree with them: the future has *not* been totally decreed from eternity in the counsel of God. The future is partially open. This is the actual meaning of the unfortunate phrase "Open Theism": it is the theism of the partially open future. The outcome of God's counsel is *not* open; it is divinely certain. But the free human decisions and deeds *are* open, and thus God's ways are open.

6.4 The Classical Idea of God
6.4.1 The Hellenistic Idea of God

The question about the future possibly being partially open has a deeper background. Underlying the view of Augustine and Calvin that the *entire* future has been decreed in God's counsel is an idea of God that in certain respects is more Hellenistic than biblical, as Open Theists emphasize. Huw P. Owen argues that, in the Western world, (classical) theism has a double origin: one is the Bible, the other is Greek philosophy.[23]

Indeed, traditional theism is somewhat affected by Hellenistic views concerning God's immutability (§6.5), impassibility (the incapacity of suffering, insensitivity to feelings and emotions; §6.6), and timelessness (§6.7).[24] Every idea of changes in God's thinking and acting, every idea of a "before

---

22. Ibid., 17.
23. Owen (1971, 1).
24. On the latter point, see Pinnock (2001, 56–60), and references.

and after" in God, every idea of free people who could oppose God's counsel, was viewed as an attack on his perfection. If, for instance, God could suffer and have passions, this would mean—according to this idea of God—that he could be influenced by creatures, and thus to some extent could become dependent on them. To the church fathers and scholastic thinkers, such an idea of God seemed totally inappropriate and inconceivable.[25]

This static idea of God fits perfectly with the ancient idea in which Being is higher than Becoming, immutability higher than mutability, timelessness higher than time. It fits with the ancient, particularly Platonic and Stoic, view of *anangkē*, the fate that rules even the lives of the gods, and of *autarkeia* or *autarchia*, autarchy, the unshakable mind, which remains strong whatever the gods or fate may dispense to people.[26] Ignatius touched upon this problem, writing to Polycarp about God "who is above all time, eternal and invisible, yet who became visible for our sakes; impalpable and impassible, yet who became passible on our account."[27] Origen believed that God's perfection excludes all passions, especially his wrath. Because of this idea that God, according to his being, cannot suffer, in the sixth century the *theopaschitic* conflict arose: if God cannot suffer, and Jesus is truly God, then how could Jesus suffer on the cross?[28]

6.4.2 God's Emotions

The views mentioned are not in line with the Bible. Scripture is full of examples of God's emotions. The following emotions have been mentioned by various psychologists; I illustrate them with a few biblical examples.[29]

---

25. Ibid., 115–16.
26. Ibid., 6–7, 20, 27, 56; on the influence of Hellenism on the Christian idea of God, see extensively Hatch (1891); Wolfson (1970); Blumenthal and Markus (1981); Finan and Twomey (1992); Watson (1996).
27. Ignatius (1885, 153).
28. Cf. Ouweneel (EDR 2:318–19).
29. See, e.g., http://changingminds.org/explanations/emotions/basic%20emo-

Anger, rage, fury: "Now leave me alone so that my anger may burn against them and that I may destroy them" (Exod. 32:10). "God remembered Babylon the Great and gave her the cup filled with the wine of the fury of his wrath" (Rev. 16:19).

Contempt, disgust, derision: "He who sits in the heavens laughs; the LORD holds them in derision." (Ps. 2:4). "I hate, I despise your feasts, and I take no delight in your solemn assemblies" (Amos 5:21).

Desire: "I desire steadfast love and not sacrifice, the knowledge of God rather than burnt offerings" (Hos. 6:6).

Disappointment: "I thought you would call me, 'My Father,' and would not turn from following me. Surely, as a treacherous wife leaves her husband, so have you been treacherous to me, O house of Israel" (Jer. 3:19-20).

Distress: "In all their distress he too was distressed. . . . In his love and mercy he redeemed them" (Isa. 63:9).

Envy, jealousy: "[T]he LORD your God in your midst is a jealous God" (Deut. 6:15).

Expectancy: "What more could have been done to My vineyard that I have not done in it? Why then, when I expected [it] to bring forth [good] grapes, did it bring forth wild grapes?" (Isa. 5:4 NKJV).

Fear: "I feared provocation by the enemy" (Deut. 32:27).

Grief, sadness, sorrow: "And they put away the strange gods from among them and served the LORD; and His soul was *grieved* for the misery of Israel" (Judg. 10:16 KJV). "How often they rebelled against him in the wilderness and grieved him in the desert!" (Ps. 78:40).

Happiness: "As a man is happy with his new wife, so your God will be happy with you" (Isa. 62:5 ERV). Please note that "blessed" in 1 Timothy 1:11 ("the blessed God") is *makarios* ("happy, blissful"), not the common word for "blessed," *eulogētos*.

---

tions.htm.

Hatred: "The boastful shall not stand before your eyes; you hate all evildoers" (Ps. 5:5). "I have had enough of burnt offerings of rams and the fat of well-fed beasts; I do not delight in the blood of bulls, or of lambs, or of goats. When you come to appear before me, . . . incense is an abomination to me. New moon and Sabbath and the calling of convocations—I cannot endure iniquity and solemn assembly. Your new moons and your appointed feasts my soul hates; they have become a burden to me; I am weary of bearing them" (Isa. 1:11–14). "I abhor the pride of Jacob and hate his strongholds, and I will deliver up the city and all that is in it" (Amos 6:8).

Joy: God "will rejoice over you with gladness; he will quiet you by his love; he will exult over you with loud singing" (Zeph. 3:17).

Love: "[T]he Lord loves you" (Deut. 7:8). "God so loved the world . . ." (John 3:16).

Pleasure: "[I]t has pleased the Lord to make you a people for himself" (1 Sam. 12:22); "the Lord takes pleasure in those who fear him" (Ps. 147:11).

Regret: "[T]he Lord regretted that he had made man on the earth, and it grieved him to his heart" (Gen. 6:6).

Wonder: God "saw that there was no man, and wondered that there was no one to intercede" (Isa. 59:16).

In addition, God can apparently change his mind ("Then the Lord relented and did not bring on his people the disaster he had threatened," Exod. 32:14); God "relented and did not bring on them the destruction he had threatened," Jonah 3:10); so it appears that there is "before and after" in his thinking. We will see ample evidence of this.[30]

6.4.3 The Bible versus Hellenism

How is it possible that we can so easily see all those times Scripture speaks of God's emotions, whereas Christians in earlier ages were not able to see them at all? They were, and

---

30. Also cf. Ouweneel (EDR 3:§3.2.2).

we are, all children of our time. It is not only our theological paradigm in the stricter sense that determines what we are able and unable to see, but it is also the general mindset of the era in which we live. We already saw a few examples of this. We understand that many Christians were too unaware of the biblical facts about God as long as ancient thought still had such a great impact on their thinking. For centuries, in Antiquity (Augustine), in the Middle Ages (Anselm of Canterbury), but also in Protestant scholasticism (Theodore Beza and others), people have tried to intertwine the Hellenistic-decretalistic idea and the biblical idea of God, or to read the Hellenistic idea of God into the Bible.

Today we should know better. Abraham Heschel rightly remarked that the God of the (ancient) philosophers is unfamiliar with, and indifferent toward, humanity. This God thinks but does not speak. He is aware of himself but oblivious toward humanity. In contrast with this, the God of Israel is a God who loves, a God who is known to people, and a God who cares about people.[31] Donald Bloesch wrote that it can be convincingly demonstrated that the history of Christian thought exhibits the unmistakable imprint of a biblical-classical synthesis, in which the ontological categories of Greco-Roman philosophy have been merged with the personal-dramatic categories of biblical faith.[32]

Whereas the Hellenistic idea of God speaks of God's *aseitas* (his "being in himself"), and of his simplicity, immutability, and impassibility, the biblical idea of God presents us with a very different picture, a God who expresses love, patience, wisdom, mercy, even regret, disappointment, sadness, anger, wrath.[33] Today, some traditional theologians are willing to acknowledge feelings and emotions in God. However, apparently they realize insufficiently that, if the notion of God's impassibility must be abandoned, this has consequences for

---

31. Heschel (1955, 224).
32. Bloesch (1995, 205).
33. See the highly interesting comparison by Barrett (1962).

the Hellenistic views of God's immutability and timelessness, and ultimately for the Hellenistic views of God's sovereignty and omnipotence. Fortunately, we observe a certain openness to such newer insights in some traditional theological circles.

However, someone like Wolfhart Pannenberg seems to lag behind here. He wrote extensively about the Greek contrast of time and eternity that has permeated Christian thought,[34] and ended his review with these words:

> In distinction from creatures, who as finite beings are subject to the march of time, the eternal God does not have ahead of him any future that is different from his present. For this reason, that which has been is still present to him. God is eternal because he has no future outside himself. His future is that of himself and of all that is distinct from him.[35]

This is true only insofar as there is no past, present, and future in God's *being*. It leaves out of consideration, however, that God has connected himself with his own creation and traverses a history together with it (see §6.7). He is not elevated above that history but *shares* in it. To *this* extent we can even speak of a "history of God," as Karen Armstrong does.[36]

6.5 God's (Im)mutability
6.5.1 Scholasticism and Its Opponents

In physics, we realize today that the constancy of movement is a condition for ascertaining a change; that is, change can be established only on the basis of constancy. Therefore, there can be no polar contrast between constancy and change, as ancient philosophy claimed by placing the constant Being of a thing dialectically over against its changing appearance. On the contrary, an inseparable connection exists between constancy and change, and thus between a supposed (constant) essence and (variable) attributes.

---

34. Pannenberg (1991, 1:401–410).
35. Ibid., 410.
36. Armstrong (2004).

Connected with this, the theological doctrine of God made a dangerous distinction, if not a contrast, between God's (immutable) "being" and his (mutable) "appearance." This led directly to the scholastic distinction between God's incommunicable and communicable attributes, and to the corresponding distinction between the incomprehensibility and knowability of God. Elsewhere, I have sharply criticized this distinction, if not separation, between God's "being" and his "appearance."[37]

We can speak of God's immutability safely only if we sever this characteristic entirely from Greek-scholastic substantialism with its idea of God as the unmoved Mover, the first and uncaused Cause.[38] There *is* no constant *substantia*, which would be opposed to changeable *accidentia*. To be sure, God's identity is constant: "You will change them like a robe, and they will pass away, but you are the same, and your years have no end" (Ps. 102:26-27); "I the LORD do not change" (Mal. 3:6); with the "Father of lights" "there is no variation or shadow due to change" (James 1:17). However, God's relenting, his responsiveness to prayer, his changing his mind (see extensively chapter 8) are just as true as his constancy, his counsel, and his prophetic promises. Christian philosopher Nicholas Wolterstorff therefore declares outright that the theological tradition of God's ontological immutability has no explicit biblical foundation.[39]

Of course, we should not succumb to the reverse tendency, especially as a consequence of Georg Hegel's dialectical philosophy, namely, to emphasize the mutability of and changes in God. Thus, Bram van de Beek described God as fickle and capricious,[40] and Hendrikus Berkhof spoke of

---

37. See Ouweneel (EDR 2:293–96).
38. Prominent in Thomism, but also in a Reformed theologian like Franciscus Junius; see Van Genderen and Velema (2008, 176); cf. Barth (1936, II/1:491–522); Pannenberg (1971, 201–233); Wentsel (1987, 408–13).
39. N. Wolterstorff in Orlebeke and Smedes (1975, 202).
40. Van de Beek (1984, 252–66).

God's "Changeable Faithfulness,"[41] which can be just as imbalanced as the traditional emphasis on God's immutability. Yet, we must appreciate Berkhof's protest against the latter: in the traditional view, God "begins to resemble the enourmous sheet of ice which according to Ezekiel he surely was not (1:22)."[42] In a similar way, Adrio König emphasizes that there is no arbitrariness in God, but that he, as it were, is "immutable" (i.e., faithful and consistent) in his "mutability."[43]

6.5.2 Breakthrough

During the nineteenth century, the greatest breakthrough in thinking about God's immutability came with the study by Isaak Dorner.[44] He connected God's immutability with his love and its immutable ethical goal in contrast with a free and mutable humanity. In the line of Dorner, Karl Barth developed his view of God's *Beständigkeit* ("constancy") as a loving-in-freedom and living—pure immutability is death.[45] Barth emphasized the changes in God's attitudes and works, which, in his view, do not touch upon God's essential immutability. After Barth, it was precisely this point that was criticized, especially in process theology (§3.6.2), which views God as essentially involved in an "unpredictable process of becoming."[46]

Hendrikus Berkhof, who described this development, concluded: "It would also be blasphemous to say that, together with us, he would be controlled by this history. In that process he is what we are not: 'the Rock whose work is perfect' [Deut. 32:4]. But he is not that is a distant and stark eternity, but as our covenant partner on the way through time with all

---

41. Berkhof (1986, 147–54); adopted by Pinnock (2001, 85); cf. Sanders (1998, 184-88).
42. Berkhof (1986, 149–50).
43. König (2006, 322–23).
44. Dorner (1883).
45. Barth (1936, II/1:491–522).
46. Whitehead (1969); Hartshorne (1964); Cobb (1966).

its fluctuations and surprises."⁴⁷ I think here also of the work of Eberhard Jüngel with the subtitle: *God's being is in becoming*, in which he says: "It is not about a 'God who becomes.' God's being is not identified with God's becoming; rather, God's being is ontologically localized."⁴⁸ I understand this to be saying: do not touch God's being — but do not underestimate his becoming, either.

Berkhof rightly warned against the Scylla of Hegel's mutable, becoming God and the Charybdis of Aristotle's *primum movens omnino non motum* ("first mover, [itself] entirely unmoved"). The difference between God and humanity, and within God himself, cannot be captured with terms like "being" and "becoming." On the one hand, there is ontic constancy in human beings themselves in the sense that, if we could not recognize certain *constant* characteristics in people, we would never be able to recognize them as specimens of the species *Homo sapiens*. On the other hand, there is also "becoming" (change) in God; we will see that, at many places, he is described as One *becoming* angry (his anger was "kindled," Exod. 4:14; Num. 11:1, 33; 12:9; 22:22; 25:3; 32:10, 13; etc.) and whose anger is soothed; and particularly, the eternal, divine Logos *became* flesh, God *became* Man (John 1:14; cf. vv. 1-3, 18).⁴⁹ In every case we are dealing with God becoming something that he was not before.

As Clark Pinnock put it, we could say in God's case that *who God is* does not change, but *what God experiences* does; God's nature does not change, but his workings and relationships are dynamic. God's character is stable, but God is not static when it comes to relating with his creation. God is *unchangeable in changeable ways*, that is, unchangeable in his being, but always changing in his love relationships.⁵⁰

---

47. Berkhof (1986, 152).
48. Jüngel (1976, vii).
49. Cf. Ott (1974, 26).
50. Pinnock (2001, 85–86).

6.5.3 The Name YHWH

The description of being and becoming is of Greek-scholastic origin and to be rejected. It gives a misleading, imbalanced picture, both in its scholastic emphasis on God's being and its relativistic emphasis on the "becoming" God.[51] There is much "becoming" within eternity, and much "being" within time. And this is no problem as long as we realize that these terms must never be interpreted in a conceptual way.

How theologians have dealt with the name YHWH is illustrative. God says, "I am who I am" (Hebrew *ehyeh asher ehyeh*, from *h-y-h*, "to be," Exod. 3:14), which the Septuagint renders as "I am the being One" (Gr. *egō eimi ho ōn*). Hence, the name is explained in terms that are Greek-scholastic, using the Latin phrase *summum esse*, the "highest being." Augustine interpreted it as if God is immutable Being itself. Jan van Genderen has rightly criticized this;[52] however, he does injustice to Willem Gispen, who indeed renders God's name (YHWH, which is thought to come from *h-y-h* as well) as the "Constant One," but did not understand by this a metaphysical Being but a reference to God's "guiding providence and expressions of His faithfulness to the covenant made with Abraham. They also brought to mind the promises made to the patriarchs. He was who He was, both for those forefathers and for Israel; He was 'from generation to generation,' never changing."[53]

Indeed, the name YHWH involves not the constancy of an absolute being in any metaphysical sense, but covenantal loyalty, as is apparent in God's own use of the name: "The LORD, the LORD [YHWH, YHWH], a God merciful and gracious, slow to anger, and abounding in steadfast love and faithfulness, keeping steadfast love for thousands, forgiving iniquity and transgression and sin" (Exod. 34:6–7). "I am who I am" thus turns out to mean: "I remain the same, always faithful to my promises," and also, "I will also be there for you and with

---

51. Cf. Brunner (1946, 289–90).
52. Van Genderen and Velema (2008, 136–37).
53. Gispen (1982, 56).

you" (cf. Exod. 3:7–9, and Martin Buber's translation: *Ich bin da*, "I am there," I am present).

I agree with Jan van Genderen[54] that this is a more satisfactory translation than that of Karl Barth and Emil Brunner,[55] who believed that God both reveals and hides himself in this name. "I am who I am" is then: "I am he whose actual name no one pronounces [or, repeats; German *nachspricht*]" (Barth), the "undefinable, unnameable One" (Brunner). An excellent extensive study is the one by Reformed theologian Benne Holwerda,[56] who concludes that the name YHWH "speaks of God's works in history" (264) and explains the "I am who I am" as: "I will be active; I will show you the present realization of my promises that I made to the fathers. . . . I bring about what I say and do what I promise" (242). See, for instance, this promise: "And I will vindicate the holiness of my great name, which has been profaned among the nations, and which you have profaned among them. And the nations will know that I am the LORD, . . . when through you I vindicate my holiness before their eyes" (Ezek. 36:23), namely, through your redemption.

6.6 Impassibility
6.6.1 God's Emotions

More than a century ago, Andrew M. Fairbairn wrote that theology contains no idea more erroneous than that of the impassibility of God.[57] Today, fortunately, most theologians follow him in this, but some still defend the old doctrine.[58] Given the many clear statements of Scripture about God's feelings and emotions, anger, wrath, joy, sadness, relief, disappointment (see §6.4.2), it is hard to understand that the doctrine

---

54. Van Genderen and Velema (2008, 136–37); cf. Pinnock (2001, 116–17).
55. Barth (1936, I/1:365, 369–70); Brunner (1946, 125); also cf. Thielicke (1977, 109–11); Berkhof (1986, 115–17).
56. Holwerda (1971, 200–65); also cf. extensively, Wentsel (1987, 258–98, especially 263–67).
57. Fairbairn (1893, 483).
58. E.g., Weinandy (2000).

of God's impassibility could arise in the first place, and that it has been defended for so long. The reason is simple: God's eternal being, his constancy and immutability, understood in the Hellenistic sense, made it difficult for early theologians to imagine that God could suffer genuine inner grief, for instance. They rejected this in spite of such a clear statement as this: "[T]he LORD regretted that he had made man on the earth, and it grieved him *to his heart*" (Gen. 6:6). "And they put away the strange gods from among them and served the LORD; and His soul was *grieved* for the misery of Israel" (Judg. 10:16 KJV; cf. Isa. 1:14). If God's *heart* or *soul* can be affected like this, who are we to say that God's being is impassible?

Here is an example of God's sadness: "In all their afflictions he was afflicted" (Isa. 63:9). A beautiful example of his joy is this: "The LORD your God is in your midst, a mighty one who will save; he will rejoice over you with gladness; he will quiet you by his love [KJV: he will rest in his love]; he will exult over you with loud singing" (Zeph. 3:17). Imagine: a God who rejoices, exults, and sings (or even "dances," TLV)! (Compare Jesus: "full of joy through the Holy Spirit," Luke 10:21 NIV). Perhaps this is the most remarkable point: how could we imagine a God who loves, yes, who *is* love (1 John 4:8, 16), but who would not know the emotions that are inherent to, and inseparable from, genuine love? How could a God who knows no joy and sadness, no disappointment and relief, no indignation and jealousy, possibly be *love*? Moreover, emotions imply mutability, as David Pawson argues: the Bible ascribes intense emotions to God, and it is characteristic of emotions that they change. If our emotions were always the same, neither we nor God would know any emotions at all.[59] We need think only of Hosea 1–3, where Hosea's emotions toward Gomer are paralleled by God's emotions toward Israel.

In 1978, Rabbi Harold Kushner published his book, *When Bad Things Happen to Good People*. In this book he wrote:

---

59. Pawson (2005, 192).

Christianity introduced the world to the idea of a God who suffers, alongside the image of a God who creates and commands. Postbiblical Judaism also occasionally spoke of a God who suffers, a God who is made homeless and goes into exile along with His exiled people, a God who weeps when He sees what some of His children are doing to others of His children. I don't know what it means for God to suffer. I don't believe that God is a person like me, with real eyes and real tear ducts to cry, and real nerve endings to feel pain. But I would like to think that the anguish I feel when I read of the sufferings of innocent people reflects God's anguish and God's compassion, even if His way of feeling pain is different from ours. I would like to think that He is the source of my being able to feel sympathy and outrage, and that He and I are on the same side when we stand with the victim against those who would hurt him.[60]

In recent times, several books have appeared that try to describe God's being "moved," with a playful allusion to the Aristotelian notion of God as the "unmoved mover." Of course, "unmoved" here means: "moved by nothing/no one else," in which "movement" contains everything that involves growth, change, development, history. Clark Pinnock alludes to this idea in his *Most Moved Mover*,[61] and Henk Medema in his *God: bewegend, bewogen* ("God: Moving, Moved").[62] Jan van Eck used a similar allusion, reminiscent of Galileo's *Eppur' si muove*, "Yet it [i.e., the earth] moves," now applied to God.[63] God is here the One who can be "moved," that is, touched in his emotions. (Note that the words "motion" and "emotion" come from Latin *movere*, "to move.")

6.6.2 Criticism

Huw P. Owen called the doctrine of God's impassibility the

---

60. Kushner (1981, 85).
61. Pinnock (2001).
62. Medema (2007).
63. Van Eck (1997).

most dubious aspect of classical theism,[64] and Clark Pinnock expressed his astonishment that, in earlier times, impassibility could ever have become an orthodox belief. He said that, here perhaps more than anywhere else, we encounter the bankruptcy of traditional (read: scholastic) theology. Divine suffering lies at the heart of Christian faith. Divine pathos experienced in sharing in our world is the very expression of the divine nature.[65]

Pinnock pointed to these beautiful words by Dutch Catholic priest and theologian Henri Nouwen:

> On two occasions, Jesus invited his closest friends (Peter, James and John) to take part in his most intimate prayer. The first time he took them to the summit of Mount Tabor,[66] where they saw his face shining as the sun, and his clothes white as light (Matt. 17:2). The second time he took them to the Garden of Gethsemane, and there they saw his face in anguish, and his sweat falling to the ground like large drops of blood (Luke 22:44). The prayers of the heart take us both to Tabor and to Gethsemane. When we have seen God in the glory, we will also see God in the misery, and when we have felt the ugliness of God's humiliation, we will also experience the beauty of the glorification.[67]

Now we must choose our words here with care. Elsewhere,[68] I have questioned the expression of Luther, adopted by Jürgen Moltmann: the "crucified God."[69] Jesus is God—but seeing Jesus suffer in Gethsemane is not the same as seeing *God* in misery. Therefore, Hendrikus Berkhof rightly said that we must

> be careful with speaking of the *sufferings of God*, as many do

---

64. Owen (1971, 24).
65. Pinnock (2001, 89–90).
66. Whether it really was the Tabor is not relevant here; others have thought of different mountains.
67. Nouwen (1999, 120).
68. Ouweneel (EDR 2:115, 318–19).
69. Moltmann (1993).

since K[azoh] Kitamori, *Theology of the Pain of God*. . . .[70] Then one points to the suffering of Jesus. However, it is not God who was crucified, who died, and who was raised. Otherwise not only theologically but also christologically we end up on a wrong track. . . . In the suffering of Jesus, God is no powerless victim (Rom 8:32), but the one who suffers along with. This is another form of suffering, but not a lesser suffering.[71]

Thus, Berkhof maintains the notion of the suffering God, as long as this is not identified with the suffering Jesus. We should never separate the two natures of Christ, the divine and the human natures, but we should not intermingle them either. For instance, it was according to his *divine* nature that Jesus accepted worship (Matt. 14:33; 28:9, 17) and forgave sins (Mark 2:7). But it was according to his *human* nature that Jesus was crucified and died—God cannot die (cf. 1 Tim. 6:16).[72] Yet, in my view, it is inadequate to say that God (only) suffered (was compassionate) *with* Jesus. We encounter this idea already with Bernard of Clairvaux in his Commentary on the Song of Solomon: *Impassibilis est Deus, sed non incompassibilis*, "God cannot suffer, but he can 'suffer *with*.'"[73] No passion (in the ancient meaning of the word: suffering), but certainly compassion. However, a God who is furious, offended, or grieved, a God who knows intense disgust, disappointment, distress, sorrow, even hatred—that is much more than a God who can express only compassion (can "suffer with" people).

This is similar to the mutability of God: just as God is immutable in his being (including his *counsel*), but mutable in his *ways*, so the passibility of God does not touch his being, as if it would ever be possible that, for instance, God would be so desperate, so "beside himself," that he could be "at a loss,"

---

70. Kitamori (2005).
71. Berkhof (1986, 147).
72. To be precise: it was the dead *Man* Jesus who was raised by God (e.g., Rom. 4:24–25; 6:4), but he *rose* from the dead in his own *divine* nature (e.g., Acts 10:41; 1 Thess. 4:14); see Ouweneel (EDR 2:§8.5.2).
73. Quoted in Ratzinger (2008, 87).

that is, would not know what to do anymore.[74] He is never "at wits' end" because, no matter how grieved, disappointed, offended, disgusted, or angry he may be, his *counsel* stands clearly before him; he merely adapts his *ways* as needed to realize his counsel. God may *suffer* due to the fact that he must adapt his ways, but he can never suffer due to the obstruction of his counsel, for such an obstruction is fundamentally impossible.

6.6.3 Anthropopathisms

Even in the twentieth century, some authors liked to point to "unfounded, primitive *anthropopathisms*," that is, expressions adopted from human sensitive (emotional) life and applied to God, especially in the biblical speaking about God's wrath. Emil Brunner replied to this in a challenging way that those who have difficulty with such expressions do not know the *holy* God and the *Lord* God of the Bible.[75] Precisely because God is holy and righteous, we cannot imagine that he would *not* be deeply indignant about sin—and we cannot imagine indignation without anger, grief, disgust, that is, without emotion.

At the same time, we must underscore God's holiness because his emotions are always pure, whereas the expression *by us* of some of the emotions ascribed to God is scarcely conceivable without sin. Yet, the same emotions are involved.

(a) *Fear*. I know of only one passage that speaks of God's fear (see §6.4.2): God feared the provocation by the enemy if he would punish his people too harshly (Deut. 32:26–27); but, of course, this is sinless fear. Human fear, however, is often sinful; as Saul said, "I have sinned . . . because I feared the people" (1 Sam. 15:24).

(b) *Anger*. The Bible often speaks of the (spotless) anger (wrath, fury) of God, but warns *us*: "In your anger do not sin" (Eph. 4:26 NIV; cf. Ps. 4:4).

---

74. Pinnock (2001, 91–92).
75. Brunner (1946, 167–68), *contra* J. A. L. Wegscheider.

(c) *Jealousy, envy.* What in God is a holy jealousy (Heb. *qin'ah*) (e.g., Num. 25:11; Deut. 29:20; Zech. 1:14; 8:2; etc.) can very easily be, or become, sinful in people (cf. Prov. 6:34; 27:4; Eccl. 4:4). In the New Testament, jealousy (Gr. *zēlos*) and envy (*phthonos*) are called works of the flesh (Gal. 5:19-21), but, remarkably enough, the same words are used for God's (sinless) jealousy (*zēlos*: 1 Cor. 10:22; 2 Cor. 11:2; *phthonos*: James 4:5).

(d) *Regret, relenting.* This is ascribed to God several times (ESV: "regret": Gen. 6:6; 1 Sam. 15:11, 35; "relent": Exod. 32:14; 2 Sam. 24:16; Ps. 106:45; Jer. 18:8; 26:13; etc.). But the same Hebrew word (*n-h-m*) can be used to describe repentance over sin: "no man relents of his evil, saying 'What have I done?'" (Jer. 8:6).

(e) *Hatred.* Several times God expresses his sinless hatred toward evil (e.g., Ps. 26:5; 31:6; 101:3). But this hatred can be a great moral danger for people: "You shall not hate your brother in your heart . . . lest you incur sin because of him" (Lev. 19:17).

In summary, we have at least a twofold difficulty in understanding God's feelings and emotions: first, they are entirely pure and holy, stainless, whereas in people they are very often mingled with sin. And second, they essentially surpass our creaturely emotionality, even if we can speak of them only in creaturely terms. In other words, we can form ideas of God's emotions, but we cannot conceptualize them. *Our* emotions are unthinkable without the activities of our autonomous nervous system and certain brain lobes (the limbic system). God's emotions are not based upon such physiological activities. Nonetheless, we can have no idea of God's anger, joy, or hatred without any knowledge of human anger, joy, or hatred. God's having created us in his image and after his likeness implies, among many other things, that our emotions are a reflection of his emotions.

The so-called *pathos* ("grief, suffering") of God has received special attention particularly through the work by Rabbi

Abraham Heschel.[76] He called the preaching of the prophets "pathetic theology," in contrast with the early Christian view of God's *apatheia*, a view adopted from Plato and the Stoics: God cannot suffer.[77] If this means that God is free, basically independent of people and human influence, we can agree with this to some extent. But the Greek view of the apathetic God also implied the notion that God would be insensitive to, and unconcerned with, human affairs, and would not need partners. As a contrast, Israel's prophets did not preach some unmoved, unconcerned, neutral God, but One who is emotionally intimately involved and concerned with his people. God is the God who has chosen freely and sovereignly to be intensely moved with, and concerned with, his people. God's grief, and even regret, with regard to his people can in no way ever affect his sovereignty.

6.7 Temporality
6.7.1 God Beyond Time?

The questions concerning God's (im)mutability and (im)passibility are directly related to the question whether God is outside or above time (is timeless) or in some way, in his own manner, is within time, that is, participates in time as we know it. We might even ask whether such a thing as time exists in the first place. If by this we mean physical time, which is closely linked with matter, then God can never have been drawn within this physical time. He transcends all matter created by him, including time as linked with it (see further in §7.4). However, it does not necessarily follow that God is timeless. The Bible speaks of God in temporal terms, but these terms must not be understood in a physical way, but in a pistical way, that is, as belonging to the dimension of faith.[78]

These questions are closely related to the way we view

---
76. Heschel (1962) (orig. German ed.: 1936).
77. Cf. Küng (1987, 518–25); Moltmann (1993, 267–70); König (1982, 96–102).
78. Cf. on the modal diversity within time e.g. Van Woudenberg (2004, chapter 5).

the correlation between election and history. Those who embed election in a timeless eternity, preceding all history, will no longer be able to understand its possible relationship with history.[79] In this case, a correlation between election and foreseen faith is indeed inconceivable *a priori*, not only because of a mistaken view of God's sovereignty but especially because of a mistaken view of God's eternality (understood as timelessness).

The idea of God's timelessness stems from Plato, and unfortunately early Christians elevated it to one of the attributes of the God of the Bible. As a consequence of various philosophical speculations, God necessarily had to exist outside of time. We cannot form an image of how we must understand this notion, but of course that is hardly a prerequisite for the correctness of a theological theory. However, far more important is that from the Bible we get a very different picture.

Let us direct attention immediately to Revelation 10:6, which has often been taken as evidence for the notion of (future) timelessness: "[T]ime shall be no longer" (DRA). Matthew Henry explains, "Very soon, as to us, time will be no more."[80] And the Pulpit Commentary: "The advent of this [seventh] woe is, therefore, simultaneous with the end of *chronos*, or 'time,' by which we signify that definite period, cut out of eternity, as it were, which is coeval with the existence of the world, and ceases with its destruction."[81] This is all utterly mistaken. Most modern translations give us the proper sense of the passage: "The time is up" (CEB; cf. MSG); "there will/would be no more delay" (CJB, ESV, GNT, NIV); "there will be delay no longer" (ASV, NASB, NKJV). In the middle of the argument of Revelation 10, a notice about the end of physical time would be nonsensical. Modern translations give us a far more obvious interpretation: not (much) *chronos* is left between the

---

79. Cf. Pannenberg (1991, 3:450–53), with references to Friedrich Schleiermacher and Karl Barth.
80. Henry (n.d., ad loc.).
81. Spence-Jones, (1909a, ad loc.).

moment of Revelation 10:6 and the *eschaton* at hand.

Scripture never speaks of time in any abstract physical sense, and even less of timelessness. The same is true for 2 Corinthians 4:18, where "temporal/temporary" (Gr. *proskairos*) stands in contrast to "eternal" (*aiōnios*), however, not as "temporal" is contrasted to "timeless" but as "transient" (ESV) contrasts to "everlasting," that is, as "limited in time" in contrast to "of endless duration."

6.7.2 "Entirely Human"

Herman Bavinck denied that something like *praescientia* ("foreknowledge") could exist in God because there is no *differentia temporis* ("time difference") with him.[82] The question arises how Bavinck, who is here repeating the church fathers, can say this so assuredly with the Bible in hand. Scripture does not speak explicitly about God and time, or about time as such, but it does speak of "before" and "after" with God. The Bible speaks of God's "*fore*knowledge," "*pre*destination," his "preparing *beforehand*," his counsel from "*before* the foundation of the world," etc. (John 17:5, 24; Rom. 8:29–30; 9:23; Eph. 1:4–5, 11; 1 Pet. 1:2, 20). Some assert that such statements cannot be *actually* true because God is beyond time. Our reply is: God is beyond *physical* time, but (a) as I said, he is not beyond time in the pistical sense (i.e., in the dimension of faith), and (b) it is always possible that he enters physical time and participates in it.

Bavinck referred to a distinction within God's omniscience between *praescientia* ("foreknowledge" in the past or the present with respect to the future), *scientia visionis* (the "knowledge" of "seeing" in the present), and *reminiscentia* (in the present or the future with regard to the past). He objected to this distinction with the argument that this is "a human conception through and through."[83] This is perfectly correct. But Bavinck overlooks two things: (a) his own view of God's

---

82. Bavinck (*RD* 2:196–97).
83. Bavinck (*RD* 2:197).

timelessness is entirely and inevitably a human representation as well, and (b) we have no other way of describing God's omniscience than *in human terms*, because we have no other terms. This is no problem at all—Scripture itself repeatedly does so—as long as we do not understand these terms as concepts but as ideas.

Nicholas Wolterstorff plainly said that the Bible authors present God as fundamentally within time.[84] And Clark Pinnock stated that God "is a temporal agent." He is beyond time in the sense that he is beyond finite experience and time-measurement, but he is not beyond "before and after," or beyond the order of events. Scripture presents God as "temporally everlasting," not as "timelessly eternal."[85] It describes God as planning and considering, acting and reacting within the temporal, as One who experiences past, present, and future as consecutive, not as timeless.[86] As David Pawson wrote, God is in time, or rather, time is in God. He is the God who was, and is, and is to come (Rev. 4:8).[87] How can we say that someone who both was and is *and* is the Coming One is totally outside time in any sense of the word?

6.7.3 Evaluation

Classical theism argues that, if God were within time, his present would be limited by the past and the future. However, as much as God is, in a certain sense, changeable—and change suggests (measurement of) time—he must be temporal, and if he is temporal, he is also changeable. God's sovereign decree to enter history together with people as junior partners—"helpers" (Judg. 5:23) and "fellow workers" (1 Cor. 3:9)—implies that, in a certain sense, God is changeable and temporal similar to the way people are.

Here again, one could emphasize that in many ways, of

---

84. In Orlebeke and Smedes (1975, 200).
85. Cf. Strauss (2007, 184–86), who connects these two descriptions with two meanings of "infinite" in mathematics.
86. Pinnock (2001, 96).
87. Pawson (2005, 186), with reference to Cullmann (1962).

course, God is never *exactly* like people. "From everlasting to everlasting [Heb. *mē'olam 'ad-'olam*] you are God" (Ps. 90:2 CJB; cf. 1 Chron. 16:36; 29:10; Neh. 9:5; Ps. 41:13; 103:17; 106:48; Dan. 2:20)—this immediately places him, so to speak, in a different category. Indeed, "everlasting" (going on endlessly *within some form of time*) seems to be a better rendering than "eternal" (if taken in a timeless sense). As Wolfhart Pannenberg put it, "from everlasting to everlasting" actually means: "from the unimaginable past to the remotest future."[88] Hebrew has no other term for eternity than unlimited duration, whether ahead toward the future or back into the past. The Hebrew *'olam*, "age, eternity," always seems to contain this element of time and duration; some striking examples are "at any time" (*'olam*, Lev. 25:32), "the years long ago" (*shenot 'olamim*, Ps. 77:5), and "a long time" (*mē'olam*, Isa. 42:14; 57:11).

By the way, if, in opposition to the classical doctrine, we declare that God "in some sense" is indeed within time, these words "in some sense" must be heavily emphasized. We should not move to the other extreme, as if God were within time *like we are* (see §7.4). The Bible speaks about God with temporal terms in a certain way, but also says, for instance: "[A] thousand years in your sight are but as yesterday when it is past, or as a watch in the night" (Ps.90:4). Wolfhart Pannenberg commented: "Why yesterday? Why not today? We are accustomed to think of duration as present, but yesterday is the time that is complete before us, yet still present and not lost in the past."[89] Peter quotes this verse in order to make clear that the long time that has elapsed between Christ's ascension and return is not experienced by God as long at all: "[D]o not overlook this one fact, beloved, that with the Lord one day is as a thousand years, and a thousand years as one day" (2 Pet. 3:8).

This point is rather important in opposition to Open Theists because they, in my view wrongly, believe that God

---

88. Pannenberg (1991, 1:401).
89. Ibid.

perfectly knows all past events because they *are* past, and therefore fixed, but he does not know all future events because they are future, and therefore not yet fixed. As Duffield and Van Cleave put it: "God in His Foreknowledge looks ahead to events much as we look back upon them. Foreknowledge no more changes the nature of future events than afterknowledge can change a historical fact."[90]

6.7.4 Again: God's Temporality

Maybe the state of affairs just described forms (part of) the background of the so-called prophetic preterite, with which the prophet describes future events in the past, as though he is looking back at them as already accomplished. Thus, the prophet Micaiah says about the future defeat of Israel: "I saw all Israel scattered on the mountains, as sheep that have no shepherd" (1 Kings 22:17). Regarding Enoch we find this prophecy: "Behold, the Lord comes [Gr. ēlthen] with ten thousands of his holy ones, to execute judgment on all," etc. (Jude 14–15, futurist aorist). Normally, we would have expected here a common future tense, "shall come." In Revelation 10:7, "in the days of the trumpet call to be sounded by the seventh angel, the mystery of God would be fulfilled, just as he announced to his servants the prophets," the verbal form "would be fulfilled" (Gr. *etelesthē*) is not a future tense either, but a futurist aorist: "was fulfilled" in the sense of "shall be fulfilled."[91] Jesus, too, sometimes used the past tense when speaking of the future: "I glorified you on earth, having accomplished [*teleiōsas*, aorist participle] the work that you gave me to do," he says in John 17:4, as if he were already living after the work on the cross (cf. 19:30).

Let us return to God's temporality: the situation here is like that of other attributes of God as described in this and the next chapter: in his being and his counsel, God is immutable, *and* in his ways, he is mutable — yet not like us. God is beyond

---

90. Duffield and Van Cleave (1987, 207).
91. Mayor (1979, 271).

suffering *and* able to suffer—yet not like us. God is eternal, *and* since he is "ever-lasting" he knows a certain temporality—yet not like us. We cannot speak of God's changeability, passibility, and temporality other than in human terms, but these have to be understood as ideas, not as concepts.

Let us apply this again to God's temporality somewhat more concretely: of course, we cannot imagine what it means to be God from eternity, and therefore to have already spent an eternity without creation. However, we cannot imagine it otherwise than that God's eternal counsel necessarily implies that God in some way has looked into the future, has looked forward to the foundation as well as the consummation of the world. If the Lamb was "foreknown before the foundation of the world" (1 Pet. 1:19-20), then God must have looked forward to the work of redemption that the Lamb would accomplish. We not only imagine this, but we even say that the biblical speaking about God's "before and after" approximates the truth better than the idea of God's absolute timelessness, God's dwelling in some scholastic *nunc aeternum* ("eternal now"). If God decreed things before the foundation of the world, then his work of creation came *after* his decrees. God did this "first," and "then" he did that.

Apparently, we *cannot* speak of God other than in a temporal way, and the Bible does so, too. Is it not therefore necessary to abandon ideas that may have a venerable philosophical origin, but are foreign to biblical parlance? Is it not necessary as well to interrelate time and eternity as the Bible does? This means *in concreto* that we should disconnect God's counsel from an abstract timeless eternity, and relate it to redemptive *history*, in which foreseen (un)belief must not necessarily be disconnected *a priori* from election and reprobation. This does not automatically entail Arminianism, because it is doubtful that Arminianism has grasped God's temporality any better than traditional scholastic theology. We will return to this.

Chapter 7
God's Omniscience and Omnipotence

O LORD, you have searched me and known me!
You know when I sit down and when I rise up;
    you discern my thoughts from afar.
You search out my path and my lying down
    and are acquainted with all my ways.
Even before a word is on my tongue,
    behold, O LORD, you know it altogether.
                                    Psalm 139:1-4

Great and amazing are your deeds,
    O Lord God the Almighty!
Just and true are your ways,
    O King of the nations!
Who will not fear, O Lord,
    and glorify your name?
For you alone are holy.
All nations will come and worship you,
    for your righteous acts have been revealed.
                                    Revelation 15:3-4

Summary: More attributes of God are discussed in this chapter. Does God's omniscience entail that he foreknows the entire future, or does he partially know only all **possible** events? Is Open Theism right in asserting that an absolute foreknowledge of God puts *an end to human freedom? Or is this mistaken logic? And what about God's omnipotence (as presumably expressed in his name **El Shaddai**)? Does it mean that God can do anything? Scripture speaks of things that God cannot do! He can do what he **wants**, and what corresponds with his own being. He can even choose to be weak. This chapter sets forth some of the many discussions of these subjects throughout church history, especially concerning free will versus the enslaved will. It is interesting to view this debate against the backdrop of newer philosophical and scientific developments. The chapter closes with a discussion of relevant aspects in the book of Job, especially in regard to God's omnipotence.*

7.1 God's Omniscience
7.1.1 Is God Omniscient?

WE CAN SPEAK OF GOD'S KNOWLEDGE only by using terms that relate to our ordinary experience of knowledge, since divine knowledge transcends all human knowledge.[1] "All You know is too great for me. It is too much for me to understand" (Ps. 139:6 NLV). "[M]y thoughts are not your thoughts, neither are your ways my ways. . . . For as the heavens are higher than the earth, so are my ways higher than your ways and my thoughts than your thoughts" (Isa. 55:8-9).

This is an ancient insight. Wolfhart Pannenberg quoted approvingly the statement by philosopher Baruch Spinoza (1632-1677), that speaking of a divine mind is in principle just as metaphorical as, for instance, speaking of God as the "rock" of our salvation (cf. 2 Sam. 22:32) or as the "light" upon our path (cf. Ps. 119:105).[2] We speak of God's mind because how else should we speak of God's thinking, feeling, willing, etc. (which are metaphors as well!)? We can form an *idea* of God's mind, but we cannot conceptualize it. We speak of God's heart (e.g., Gen. 6:6) and God's soul (e.g., Isa. 1:14) because we have no other terms. On the one hand, we believe that, having been created in God's image, our own heart and

---

1. Ouweneel (EDR 3, §§1.2–1.3).
2. Pannenberg (1991, 1:379).

soul are a reflection of God's heart and soul, while on the other hand, we realize that they far surpass us.

With respect to God's knowledge, using terms as if they were concepts easily yields contradictions. For instance, how can God be omniscient, and at the same time *seek* or *obtain* knowledge? (See, e.g., Gen. 18:21; 22:12; Deut. 8:2; 13:3; Judg. 3:4; Ps. 139:23–24; cf. §4.3.3.) Scripture is very clear about the fact that God now and then makes inquiries. He wishes to "get to know" certain things, whereas at the same time he knows everything, and no person can "teach him knowledge" (Isa. 40:13–14). Both sides of the truth have to be accepted, and can be approximated only in creaturely terms, which, if used as concepts, necessarily contradict each other but, if used as ideas, do not necessarily contradict each other.

God's omniscience is described in creaturely terms because we have no other terms at our disposal: "He who planted the ear, does he not hear? He who formed the eye, does he not see? He who disciplines the nations, does he not rebuke? He who teaches man knowledge..." (Ps. 94:9–10). But this knowledge is not simply or exclusively intellectual knowledge; it is what in people would be called existential knowledge. It is perfect knowledge *concerning* creation but also for the *benefit* of creation: "[T]he eyes of the LORD run to and fro throughout the whole earth [this is omniscience], to give strong support to those whose heart is blameless toward him [this is blessing]" (2 Chron. 16:9). "[N]o creature is hidden from his sight, but all are naked and exposed to the eyes of him to whom we must give account" (Heb. 4:13); this is God's omniscience in view of our repentance and conversion. In this context notice Exodus 2:25, "God saw the people of Israel—and God *knew* [NIV, etc.: was concerned about them]." "[Y]ou, you only, know the hearts of all the children of mankind," says Solomon to God (1 Kings 8:39). This is not just informative knowledge, but implies God's great concern and care for his creatures, in love and mercy, and sometimes anger (cf. Ps. 69:5; 139:2; Jer. 17:9–10; 20:12; Ezek. 11:5; Luke 16:15; Acts 1:24; Rom. 8:27;

also see 1 Sam. 23:10–13; Isa. 41:22–23; 42:9; 46:10; Jer. 32:19; Matt. 6:8, 32; 1 Cor. 3:20; 1 John 3:20 for various other aspects of God's omniscience).

Traditional theology distinguishes within God's knowledge the *scientia naturalis* (or *necessaria, simplicis intelligentiae*) and the *scientia libera* (or *contingens, visionis*), that is, self-awareness and world-awareness, respectively.[3] Herman Bavinck rightly objected to a sharp division between the two, but did adopt scholastic expressions like the Platonic idea that God has chosen "[o]ut of the infinite fullness of ideas present in his absolute self-consciousness."[4] Bavinck also maintained the Greek-substantialistic idea that the *cognitio naturalis* (the knowledge that God has of his own nature) cannot be revealed to creatures, and that it relates to the *cognition libera* (God's world-awareness) as archetype to ectype.[5] As stated earlier, if this were so, then we would not at all have a revelation of *God himself*, but only knowledge of the form in which it pleased God to reveal himself to people. However, if we have no true *self*-revelation of God, I feel the essence of Christianity is at stake.

Moreover, as we have seen, Bavinck claimed that there can be no such thing as *praescientia* (foreknowledge) in God because there is no *differentia temporis* (time difference/distinction) in him.[6] Even though Bavinck could appeal to several church fathers, the idea is mistaken (§6.7.2). Here a Hellenistic view of God has replaced the clear testimony of Scripture with regard to God's "*fore*knowledge" (Rom. 8:29), "*predestination*" (Rom. 8:29–30; Eph. 1:5, 11; 1 Pet. 1:2, 20), "preparing *beforehand*" (Rom. 9:23), his acting "*before* the world existed" (John 17:5), or "*before* the foundation of the world" (v. 24; Eph. 1:4; 1 Pet. 1:20). This idea of God implies that God is both omniscient and timeless, and that references to time therefore

---

3. See Bavinck (*RD* 2:195).
4. Ibid.; cf. 204–207.
5. Ibid., 195–96.
6. Ibid., 196–97.

cannot be actually correct. The truth is that temporal references to God are just as Scriptural as references to his not-time-bound omniscience. Here we encounter the bad consequences of a *conceptual* use of creaturely-temporal terms, on the basis of which it is determined what in the Bible can be, or cannot be, actually correct. Here, one's own thought system governs the exegesis of Scripture.

7.1.2 Omniscience and Responsibility

This study assumes that God is omniscient with regard to all things that at this moment exist or occur on earth (see 1 Sam. 23:10-13; 1 Kings 8:39; Ps. 69:5; 94:9-10; 139:2; Isa. 41:22-23; 42:9; 46:10; Jer. 17:9-10; 20:12; 32:19; Ezek. 11:5; Matt. 6:8, 32; Luke 16:15; Acts 1:24; Rom. 8:27; 1 Cor. 3:20; Heb. 4:13; 1 John 3:20 for other aspects of this omniscience). In my view, this is not where the differences between the various schools lie. Rather, the greatest difference is how God's foreknowledge can be reconciled with human freedom and responsibility. Theology has suggested several solutions to this problem.[7]

(a) *Relativizing or minimizing God's foreknowledge*. This approach is encountered with Marcion (second century), and later with the Socinians (sixteenth century). The Open Theists, too, deny that God foreknows all events; he knows only what he himself has decreed as well as all possible and likely events. For this reason, Open Theists have often been classified with the Socinians, which is rather unfair given the enormous differences. The central issue here is whether God can have foreknowledge of human decisions without endangering human freedom. For centuries, the answers have varied widely.

(b) *Distinguishing between God's foreknowledge and God's foreordination (predestination), as in Romans 8:29*. This was the approach of Origen (third century): God fore*knows* all things without necessarily having fore*ordained* these things. Augustine (c. 400) replied that, if God foreknows a certain thing,

---

7. Cf. ibid., 196–203; Weber (1981, 1:438–47).

this thing must necessarily occur; for if it did not occur, God's foreknowledge would be rendered invalid.[8] That is, foreknowledge seems to entail foreordination. But first, to say that things must necessarily occur is not to say that they had been fore*ordained* by God. And second, is this not another example of the confusion of concepts and ideas? In other words, is it certain that what we can predicate from the *concept* of (fore)knowledge can be predicated also from the *idea* of (fore)knowledge? At the same time, we do have good reasons to closely link foreknowledge and foreordination (predestination), as we will see in §11.3.

(c) *God's foreknowledge encompasses and does not nullify human freedom of will*. Augustine claimed that the human will, with its entire nature and all its decisions, is encompassed within and is not nullified by God's foreknowledge. Rather, it is confirmed and maintained by it.[9] This line was generally followed by scholastic theology during the Middle Ages. However, against the backdrop of the strong denial of post-lapsarian human free will, we may wonder what concretely remains here of the human will in relation to divine foreknowledge. As Steven Baugh has remarked, if God has infallible foreknowledge of the free choices of people, then these choices must be certain, not only according to decretalists but also according to Arminians.[10] Even if the latter accept the (libertarian) idea of free will, they must still admit that human choices, as foreknown by God, are rigidly fixed beforehand. The remarkable thing is that Calvinists and Open Theists agree on this point! For the Calvinist, this entails rejecting the notion of free will in the Arminian sense, and for the Open Theist, this entails rejecting the notion of the divine foreknowledge in the Calvinistic sense. Only in the approach of Viatorism, or one like it, is it possible to maintain both God's full foreknowledge and human freedom of will,

---

8. *De libero arbitrio* III.4.
9. Cf. ibid. III.3; *De civitate Dei* V.9.
10. Baugh in Schreiner and Ware (2000, 183).

because if these terms are used as ideas, they do not necessarily logically contradict each other.

(d) *Distinction of a* scientia media *(middle knowledge) between God's* scientia necessaria *(necessary knowledge) and his* scientia libera *(free knowledge)*. This was the view of the Jesuits, especially of Luis de Molina (§4.6.4). It involves God's knowledge of all that is conditional-future; that is, God knows all future possibilities and all that he will do if a certain possibility becomes reality. *If* P occurs, God knows for certain its consequences. However, in this view, God does not, and cannot, always know *if* P will occur. Both the Lutherans and the Arminians sympathized with this solution, but the Reformed firmly stayed with Augustine.

7.1.3 False Contradictions

Herman Bavinck belonged to those who strongly defended the Augustinian approach.[11] Yet I wonder whether both (c) and (d) above suffer the same problem: both views try to press God's foreknowledge and human freedom of will into one *conceptual* framework. This is a mistake; we are dealing here with matters that surpass all conceptualization; that is, they cannot be enclosed in definitions based on logical-analytical distinctions and identifications as we do with respect to immanent matters.[12] Everything that transcends the immanent-modal-functional horizon also necessarily transcends logical conceptualization.

The fact that we can speak only in human terms of divine foreknowledge and human freedom easily leads to the repeated misunderstanding that therefore we could speak of such matters in a conceptual form. However, such speaking necessarily leads to logical contradictions, which are solved by neither view (c) nor (d). View (c) does not sufficiently account for human responsibility, and view (d) does not sufficiently account for divine foreknowledge and predestination. Nor

---
11. Bavinck (*RD* 2:198–203).
12. See Ouweneel (EDR 3, §§1.2–1.3; 2014a; 2014b).

does it help to relativize or minimize God's foreknowledge (solution [a]). As soon as we give up our attempt to combine these notions in one logical-conceptual framework, we are able to do justice both to God's foreknowledge and to human responsibility and freedom of will. This is necessarily done in creaturely terms, which, however, are to be treated as ideas, not concepts. What would be necessarily contradictory on a conceptual level is not contradictory on the level of ideas, because we realize that such an idea-usage of creaturely terms is only a human *approximation* of the truth. Such terms give us an idea of the matter, not an exhaustive description of it, from which we could predicate all kinds of properties as we wish (which subsequently turn out to be contradictory).

In my view, this is the way Scripture itself reveals such truths. Scripture is never concerned about possible *conceptual* contradictions between such truths, but freely reveals both God's foreknowledge and human freedom of will. Only scholastically oriented theologians introduce contradictions because such notions are treated as concepts. They do not hesitate, in order to rescue their conceptual systems, to say that, at many places, the Bible does say P, but actually means non-P. They do so because P cannot be correct under the conditions of their self-constructed conceptual framework. However, this conceptual framework itself is mistaken. Such theologians do not pay attention to what Scripture really says, but impose their thought systems upon Scripture, and thus make it say the opposite of what it actually says. This scholastic approach was traditionally — and today sometimes still is — encountered in the most orthodox circles.

Once we abandon this approach, and begin to approximate divine truth with creaturely terms used as ideas, both decretalism and Arminianism (including Open Theism) are rendered invalid positions. That is, we can maintain both God's foreknowledge of *all* future events (*contra* Open Theism) as well as human responsibility and freedom of will (*contra* decretalism) without any *conceptual* contradictions. It is pure hubris (or perhaps simply thoughtlessness) to assert that we could treat foreknowledge and responsibility as conceptual systems, whose every property could be predicated.

7.2 God's Omnipotence
7.2.1 The Almighty

What must be said, in the context of God's counsel and ways, about his omnipotence partially overlaps with what has been said of his sovereignty (§§6.1–6.3). Traditionally, it has been assumed that God's sovereignty is manifested particularly in what is called his omnipotence. The fact that God is omnipotent (which is the same as almighty[13]) comes to light in all his creational works and in their preservation, in his providence, in the history of the world, in the redemption, and in the consummation.[14]

In the Bible the word "omnipotence" lies embedded in the name "the Almighty" for God: *El Shaddai*. The meaning of this Hebrew expression is unclear; the main certainty we have is that the Septuagint renders it as *pantokratōr*, "almighty" or "all-ruling," a description that is also used for *tsebaot*, "hosts," in the expression YHWH *tsebaot*, "LORD of hosts." In this sense, *pantokratōr* means not so much "almighty" ("all-powerful") but rather "exalted above all powers." The rendering *pantokratōr* has been sanctioned by the New Testament (2 Cor. 6:18; Rev. 1:8; 4:8; 11:17; 15:3; 16:7, 14; 19:6, 15; 21:22); here it refers to the One who possesses all strength (power, might) over all (counter-)powers.

Interestingly, God and the Lamb are sometimes deemed worthy to *receive* power (Rev. 4:11; 5:12; 7:12) or to have *taken* their power (11:17; cf. 12:10). This cannot mean that God receives or takes something (power, might, glory, honor, wealth,

---

13. Such double terms are due to the unique Germanic as well as Romanic origins of modern English: omnipotent/-tence (but also, e.g., power, just(ice) and saint/sanctity) are of Romanic, while might/almighty (but also strong/strength, righteous[ness] and holy/holiness, respectively) are of Germanic origin.
14. See Bavinck (*RD* 2:245–47).

wisdom, blessing) that he did not possess before. Glory and power belong to him by nature (cf. 19:1). In doxologies, such receiving is virtually equivalent to publicly acknowledging (God's power, might, glory, etc.).

Luther followed the rendering of the Vulgate, *omnipotens*, and thus chose the translation *allmächtig* for *El Shaddai* and *pantokratōr*, which was followed by the King James Version (*almighty*, in Rev. 19:6 *omnipotent*) and the Dutch States Translation (*almachtig*). In a sense, these words are somewhat confusing because they might suggest that God can do anything, when in fact this is never its biblical meaning. *El Shaddai* and *pantokratōr* rather mean that God is the One who, in spite of all the vicissitudes of human history and of all the (human and angelic) opposing powers, irresistibly leads history to its final goal, entirely according to his counsel.[15] Nothing can hinder or stop him. Therefore, Emil Brunner wished to remove from the notion of God's omni*potence* every idea of *posse* ("to be able"):[16] the Bible does not teach that God can (is able to) do anything, but that he has power over everything. Linguistically this is a complicated matter, of course, because both omni*potence* and *power* are derived from this very word *posse*. Let us put it this way: the question is not what God is able to do but who is in charge in this world, or who has the last word. God is not able to do everything (see below) but he is able to lead history to the end he has chosen.

Indeed, in the past the idea of *posse* has led to many absurd-speculative questions about what God can and cannot do, such as: Can God wipe out (parts of) the past? Can God make what he does not make? Can God improve what he has made? Can God create a stone so heavy that he cannot lift it?[17] To be sure, Jesus says, "[W]ith God all things are possible" (Matt. 19:26; cf. Luke 1:37; 18:27); but Brunner rightly remarks that this is not a statement saying that God is able to

---

15. See very extensively, Barth (1936, II/1:522–607).
16. Brunner (1946, 265).
17. Aquinas, *Summa Theologiae* 1.25.4; etc.

do everything but that he can do everything *he wants*.[18] There are no restrictions upon realizing what he wishes to do.

7.2.2 Proper Distinctions

We have to make proper distinctions here. On the one hand, God possesses unlimited energy and capacities, and exerts unlimited authority over the universe.[19] Scripture speaks of "the greatness of his might," and says, "he is strong in power" (Isa. 40:26; cf. Eph. 1:19, "the immeasurable greatness of his power"). "Is anything too hard for the LORD?" (Gen. 18:14). "I know that you can do all things, and that no purpose of yours can be thwarted" (Job 42:2). "Nothing is too hard for you. . . . 'Is anything too hard for me?'" (Jer. 32:17, 27; cf. Zech. 8:6). "Our God . . . does all that he pleases" (Ps. 115:3). "My counsel shall stand, and I will accomplish all my purpose" (Isa. 46:10).

On the other hand, there are things that God cannot do because they are contrary to his being: God cannot lie (Num. 23:19; Titus 1:2; Heb. 6:18); he cannot relent in the human sense of the term (Num. 23:19; 1 Sam. 15:29 [cf. vv. 11, 35!]; Rom. 11:29); he cannot deny himself (2 Tim. 2:13); he cannot be tempted with evil (James 1:13). Augustine emphasized that this does not imply any lack of power; on the contrary, it constitutes the very proof of omnipotence, for it would be a *lack* of power if God could err, sin, lie, etc.[20]

This is more important: not only are there things that God cannot do, but in particular there are things that he does not *want* to do, even if he could. This is so, first, because such things are contrary to his nature. But this is so, secondly, because he consciously, *sovereignly*, limits his omnipotence by putting great power and freedom of will into the hands of humanity. We have seen how disputed this matter is today.[21] However, we have to acknowledge what Karl Barth said:

---

18. Brunner (1946, 270).
19. Cf. Bavinck (*RD* 2:245–49).
20. *Sermones* 213–214; *De civitate Dei* V.10.
21. Also see Van Genderen and Velema (2008, 181–83), and especially the extensive study by Van den Brink (1993).

omnipotence is not primarily a physical but a redemptive-historical idea.[22] Thus, God manifests his omnipotence for instance in the very *powerlessness* of Jesus on the cross: he was "crucified in weakness" (2 Cor. 13:4). This was beautifully expressed in the well-known words of Dietrich Bonhoeffer: "God lets himself be pushed out of the world on to the cross. He is weak and powerless in the world, and that is precisely the way, the only way, in which he is with us and helps us."[23]

Hendrikus Berkhof stated that we can speak of God's omnipotence in the eschatological sense only, but we cannot use the term for today.[24] Today, God is defenseless, as we see in the highest possible way on the cross. However, this is not the defenselessness of powerlessness, but precisely of the highest, though non-violent, power. Therefore, Berkhof speaks of *weerloze overmacht*, which is equivalent to "defenseless superior power." One day, this superiority of love will prevail over all resistance, and then reach its omnipotence, as Berkhof puts it. To me, this language is a bit strong; for instance, in my view it goes too far to say that God's omnipotence "suffers" under God-given human freedom, or under human rebellion.

7.2.3 Recent Insights

Reformed theologian Gijsbert van den Brink, in discussing the views of David and Randall Basinger, William E. Mann, Charles Hartshorne, David R. Griffin, and others, rightly maintained that divine omnipotence and human freedom are compatible.[25] The two principles must never be played off against each other, for when that happens, usually human freedom is forced to yield. God's omnipotence is never damaged if we accept human freedom. God does not always *apply* it to rebellious human actions, but his omnipotence irresistibly reaches its goal, in spite of all rebellion. The Babe in the

---

22. Barth (1936, II/2:604–607).
23. Bonhoeffer (1953, 196).
24. Berkhof (1986, 140–47).
25. Van den Brink (1993, §4.2); cf. also Wentsel (1987, 480–84).

manger, as a human being totally dependent on the help of his mother, was at the very same moment the Son of God who "upholds the universe by the word of his power" (Heb. 1:3). Again, the Man who was crucified in weakness was at that very moment the Son of God who "upholds the universe by the word of his power."

God's omnipotence is evident not so much from the fact that he would never have to adapt his *ways*, for he must often do this because of the freedom that he himself sovereignly gave to humanity. His omnipotence is evident rather from the fact that, in spite of all adaptations, he irresistibly realizes his *counsel*. Theo de Boer points here to Spinoza, who ultimately reduced all things to God's absolute *potentia* ("potency, power").[26] De Boer adds that he can understand the objections by the rabbis against Spinoza because the God of the Bible identifies himself with the destiny of a homeless people. This cannot be the attitude of absolute power, whose highest goal is to validate its own existence. This seems to me correct: it is in weakness that God moves through history *with* his people, and does not always apply his omnipotence in favor of Israel and in resistance to Israel's opponents. In all Israel's affliction "he was afflicted" (Isa. 63:9), and I may add, in all their weaknesses he was weak with them, in all their homelessness he was homeless with them. Where they were defeated or oppressed by their enemies, he was defeated and oppressed with them, so to speak.

However, if terms like "power/omnipotence" and "weakness" are understood as concepts, unnecessary contradictions arise, as when De Boer asks "how these two concepts [!] of power [viz. omnipotence versus defenseless dominance] must be combined. I believe they are contradictory."[27] I do not believe so. As Clark Pinnock said, no one except an almighty God could risk creating free creatures, and yet retain the full confidence that his goals would be ultimately

---

26. De Boer (1989, 55).
27. Ibid., 84.

realized. Omnipotence was needed to create human freedom *and* keep it under control. Omnipotence means either all-determining domination (as decretalism believes), or a power that does not monopolize itself but has the courage to delegate power while remaining all-powerful.[28] Given the reality of evil in the world, for which God cannot be made responsible, the latter must indeed be the case: God has delegated power to people, along with the possibility that they could abuse it. God both remains omnipotent and delegates part of his power in the certainty that his own omnipotence will always prevail over this power delegated to people.

The view of the German dogmatician Wolfhart Pannenberg in certain respects belongs to the same category as that of Open Theism. He emphasized the idea that, for the entire future, God in his dealings is not bound to an order of occurrence founded once and for all. We have to do here with the historical character of divine action, with the openness [!] of the future for every historical present. In the contingency [!] of historical events, the freedom of the God acting in history comes to light. This freedom, however, is always the freedom of the Creator, whose dealings work toward the consummation of creation through ways that surpass all human foreseeing.[29] Here, Pannenberg said the same thing I intend to say: God's omnipotence becomes manifest not so much through the immutability of his ways—for these are the very reverse: mutable—but through the immutability and irresistibility of his counsel. His ways may change, and they do, but his counsel has been established once and for all.

7.3 Protestantism versus Humanism
7.3.1 Erasmus and Luther

In his fascinating and controversial book, *The Wreck of Western Culture*, Australian sociologist John Carroll wrote about the devastating influence of humanism on Western civilization.

---

28. Pinnock (2001, 94–96); cf. Boyd (2001, 358–59).
29. Pannenberg (1991, 1:418).

He mentioned various elements that characterize Western culture since the sixteenth century, and thus came to speak of the Protestant Reformation as well.[30] Interestingly, he saw the Reformation primarily as an attack not upon Rome and Catholicism, but upon humanism. To demonstrate this, he analyzed the work that Martin Luther himself considered to be his best book, *De servo arbitrio* (*On the Bondage of the Will*, literally, *On the Enslaved Will*, 1525). This book was directed not against Rome but against the work of Desiderius Erasmus,[31] *De libero arbitrio* (*On Free Will*, 1524). Erasmus was more interested in harmony than in disputes about right doctrine. In his eyes, living humanely as a good Christian was what mattered, not who was right. This is why, only with great effort on the part of the pope and the British king Henry VIII, Erasmus could be induced to debate Luther.

Erasmus stood in the ancient theological tradition. He, too, accepted that most things that occur have been foreordained by God. However, he could not believe that *all* things were predestined by God, for in that case human freedom would not exist. "Indeed God protects the ship, but it is the mariner who steers it into the harbor," was one of the arguments he adduced. He was not asking for much, but only that *some* room be given to human will. In spite of all divine predestination, there must be room for human freedom. What sense does it make to try to live as a good Christian if everything that I do has been decreed by God from eternity?

According to Carroll, it would be too simple to reduce this reasoning entirely to the typical Protestant–*Catholic* conflict about justification: *sola fide*, "by faith alone" versus "by faith plus works." This aspect played some role, but at a deeper level the Protestant Reformation was rather a Protestant–*humanist* conflict. This debate is about people who, as puppets or robots, have been entirely pre-programmed by God from

---

30. Carroll (2007, chapter 3).
31. Often called Erasmus of Rotterdam; but Erasmus was his surname, not his first name.

eternity versus people who, according to God's creational plan, have received their own freedom, responsibility, and capacity of thought, matters unaffected by the Fall. More fundamentally, this conflict is between the pre-modern idea of humanity versus the modern idea of humanity, which arose in a fresh way almost a century later in the debate between Arminians (Remonstrants) and mainstream Calvinists (Contra-Remonstrants).

Luther's great fear was that, if people begin to reason and assume for themselves their own freedom of will, no matter how limited, this would do away with God and Christ. Any emancipation of humanity (its coming of age) lessens the need for the Father. Therefore, Luther fiercely combated not only the notion of free will but also the adequacy of human reason itself. According to Luther, it is reason that puts humanity on the throne, belittles God's authority, and pushes him into the background. Therefore, on several occasions he called reason a "whore."[32] In this way, he placed reason in opposition to faith.

7.3.2 Melanchton and Calvin

At a later stage, Luther himself took a less extreme stand, and Lutheran scholasticism after him even more so — not to mention the eighteenth-century German Enlightenment that was born from the womb of Lutheranism. Already Luther's closest collaborator, and the first Lutheran systematic theologian, Philip Melanchton, explicitly sought a position between Luther and Erasmus, and in doing so shifted more and more in the latter's direction.[33] On the one hand, he clearly claimed room for human free will, while on the other hand, he acknowledged that no one is able to fear or love God except by the power of the Holy Spirit.

Interestingly, when it comes to the question of the human will, the only consistent old school "Lutheran" was John

---

32. Luther (1883, 10 I, 1.326; 18, 164; 24, 182; 51, 126).
33. Cf. Buis (1958, 79–80).

Calvin, who sharpened the problem even further: *people do not possess freedom of will, but are nonetheless responsible.* In later chapters, we will analyze this position extensively.

By the way, we need to be alert here regarding the term humanism, because Calvin himself is considered as one of the most outstanding representatives of French humanism,[34] just as Melanchton was a representative of German humanism. Here, humanism refers specifically to a Renaissance-like revival of ancient philosophy and literature, whereas in Carroll's thinking humanism is a collective term for the modern philosophies in which God, as the central figure in all thinking, has been replaced by modern Man. Melanchton and especially Calvin were humanists in the former sense, but definitely not in the latter sense.

In Calvin's view, God has from eternity foreordained the Fall, from eternity he has predestined the wicked to go to hell — yet it is not God's fault that the wicked land there, but their own fault, because they did not repent and did not cast themselves upon God's mercy. According to Carroll, the key to understanding this lies in the special meaning that Calvin ascribed to conscience.[35] Conscience (I myself would prefer to say: the heart), not reason, if formed by the Holy Spirit, gives access to the highest knowledge, that of God.

Of course, the latter viewpoint does not reduce the paradox at all. With Calvin's position, the repentant person is saved one hundred percent by the grace of God; he contributes nothing, for faith is a "gift of God" (Eph. 2:8). Conversely, the wicked person is lost one hundred percent by his own fault. This subject runs like a thread throughout the entire *Institutes of the Christian Religion*, whether Calvin dealt with God's providence, with election and reprobation, with justification, and so many other relevant subjects. He wrestled with these topics, he devoted endless discourses to the matter, attacked opponents on his left and right, and repeatedly maintained

---
34. See, e.g., Breen (1968).
35. See especially Calvin, *Institutes* 3.19.15; 4.10.5.

the horrendous paradox. The genial Calvin saw right through the paradoxical character of the matter, acknowledged it — but could not escape from it. He remained a captive of his own system of thought.

7.3.3 Later Development

John Carroll asserted that the history of the next five hundred years proved Luther to be right, and thus Calvin too, and Erasmus to be wrong.[36] But the matter is not that simple. Calvin was the man of an extreme viewpoint, which, in its severity, is not maintained today anymore even by the majority of his followers. It lives on today, pursued in its harshest consequences, only in what we call hyper-Calvinism (ultra-Reformed thinking). This is a *harsh* religion: it can create endless doubts and darkness in its adherents, who wrestle constantly with whether they belong to the elect or the reprobate, which can lead to great mental distress. At the same time, it is an *easy* religion: everything has been neatly decreed in God's eternal counsel, the elect are saved forever, the reprobate are lost forever. This is just as unshakably true as God's decree that the earth revolve on its axis once every twenty-four hours.

This decretalism was no new discovery, and certainly not a biblical one. In essence, it was based on the neo-Platonic and Stoic idea of God, which also influenced Augustine, who in combating Pelagius was more and more captivated by it. Carroll even argued that it entailed a re-introduction from Greek antiquity of what some call "tragedy": humanity is, against will and reason, the toy of what the Greeks called *anangkē*, the Romans spoke of *fortuna* or *fatum*, and Calvin called it God's sovereign will.[37] As Carroll explains, Calvin himself fiercely opposed such an association,[38] but this is understandable precisely because the correspondence between these notions is so striking. Religiously, the three terms are very different;

---

36. Carroll (2007, 63).
37. Ibid., 77–78.
38. Calvin, *Institutes* 1.16.8.

existentially, they amount to very much the same thing: there exists a power beyond you that you cannot control, and to which you have been totally delivered.

Indeed, this entire matter is not of a biblical or theological nature at all, but a matter of cultural history and cultural philosophy. Not that Luther and Calvin turned out to be right (*contra* Carroll), but they represented a pre-modern view of God (*theologia* in its ancient philosophical meaning) and anthropology. Erasmus, as an early representative of modern thinking, adopted a much more difficult position because he tried to maintain both God's sovereignty and human freedom of will. In essence, this was the path followed by later Lutherans, Anabaptists, Arminians, and even many moderate Calvinists, and still later, many Evangelicals. This is not at all because they discovered some better exegesis of Scripture. No, the central issue is that for several centuries now, the great majority of Christians can no longer live with the *theologia* and anthropology of pre-modern times. And *at that point*, they become convinced that their insights do far more justice to the biblical data than the pre-modern view does.

Viatorism, too, still follows the agenda set by Erasmus: how can God's sovereignty be harmonized with human freedom of will, in such a way that neither the one nor the other conviction is swept under the rug? Pre-modern decretalism can no longer be the solution—if it ever *was* a workable solution—and it is dubious whether its counter-force, Open Theism, is the proper solution, and if it is, to what extent.

7.4 Modern Science
7.4.1 Erasmus and Descartes

In my view, a factor vitally important for our discussion is the rise of modern science in the seventeenth and eighteenth centuries. What seemed to be a purely theological issue—especially the relationship between God's sovereign counsel and human freedom—turned out to be a largely philosophical matter, since the sixteenth century was still heavily influenced by the ancient and scholastic views of God and anthropology. Philosophy was always interrelated with developments in the natural sciences. This justifies our brief detour into science, the relevance of which will soon become clear. Science influenced theology, just as theology influenced the rise of modern science.

No one less than — in some respects clearly pre-modern — Calvin exerted great influence on the development of modern science through his emphasis on the immutable law of God. The new natural science can be described as the search for the laws that God had instituted for cosmic reality; Calvin was one of those responsible for the emphasis on the law-principle.[39] As long as nature was viewed as capricious, no true science could ever arise. Only when nature was acknowledged as entirely subject to all-encompassing laws could modern science begin its highly successful and triumphant course.

This new science was thoroughly mechanistic: reality was viewed as a large mechanism or machine, which, to be sure, is continually maintained by God, yet governed by rigid laws, instituted by God in the beginning.[40] The great danger that thinkers in the sixteenth and seventeenth centuries saw emerging is that this mechanicism, so successful in science, would ultimately seek to get humanity within its grasp, and would reduce people to machines, to robots. Early mechanicists argued that living beings must also be understood as mechanisms. Here, the French philosopher René Descartes (d. 1650) must be mentioned, who wished to explain strictly mechanistically not only inanimate things but also plants and animals, as well as the human body. The only exception he made was the human mind, which he dualistically separated from the material body, and to which he assigned tremendous freedom.

The English philosopher Thomas Hobbes (d. 1679) did not

---

39. See, e.g., Hooykaas (1972); Van Riessen (1980); Stafleu (1987); Pearcey and Thaxton (1994).
40. Ouweneel (2000b, §10.4.2).

make this exception; he argued the human mind away, and thus showed himself to be a consistent materialist. Descartes was aware of the enormous danger in this view: if the mind is argued away, people are indeed nothing more than robots, puppets, machines. Therefore he introduced his dualism of the *res extensa*, the "extended thing" (i.e., matter, living bodies), as opposed to the *res cogitans*, the "thinking thing" (the human mind). In opposition to the strictly mechanistic realm of things, of matter, which is governed entirely by the strict and rigid laws of science, he posited the realm of the mind, the human personality possessing an absolutely free will.

It is remarkable that Descartes, who is called the father of modern philosophy, is here in line with Erasmus (d. 1536), who lived a century before him. In essence, they dealt with the same question. Erasmus asked, Against the backdrop of an all-foreordaining God, how can there remain any trace of human freedom? Descartes asked, Against the backdrop of the all-dominating natural laws (instituted by the Creator!), how can there remain any trace of human freedom? The correspondences are striking: natural laws are nothing but a particular expression of divine foreordination. On this point, Descartes, living so long after Erasmus, dared to express himself much more strongly than the latter; as Carroll says, there was no longer need for Erasmus' weak defense of free will. Descartes posited the unlimited free will as a fact, something that people possess *ad infinitum*. It is the tool of reason: people can do whatever reason gives them to do. If governed by reason, they can make no mistakes.[41]

Descartes still tried to keep the two—fixed nature and human freedom—together. On the one hand, there is the realm of the fixed laws, to which Calvin, and after him the mechanicist scientists each in their own way, gave particular form. On the other hand, there is the realm of reason, which assumed for itself unlimited power, and ultimately, in the French

---

41. Carroll (2007, 155).

Enlightenment (Denis Diderot, Voltaire), came to swallow up all of life.

7.4.2 Science and Decretalism

I will not pursue these lines any further at this point,[42] but only refer to the peculiar intermediate position of Erasmus, and later of Descartes. And I refer to the foundations of modern science, on which precisely Protestantism has exerted such a strong influence. Especially the work of Isaac Newton (d. 1727) clearly demonstrates this because he showed that one and the same divine-mathematical order rules both the celestial bodies and the earthly phenomena. If there is one God who has designed the cosmos in all its variety, there must also be one divine order that is valid for all created phenomena, no matter how different they are.

It is all the more striking that ours is a time when not only the ancient worldview but also the Newtonian worldview have in principle become obsolete (Newtonianism is at best a good approximation for that segment of created reality in which we happen to live). One and the same decretalism governs both (hyper-)Calvinism and this Newtonian worldview. The basic refutation of this worldview by the theory of relativity and by quantum mechanics is therefore of great consequence: it may signal the end of *all* forms of decretalism, including the remains of decretalism within theology.

Decretalism is not biblical; it was read into the Bible under the influence of the worldview of antiquity and scholasticism. If theologians manage to free themselves from these bonds they may begin to read the Bible through different glasses, ones that are more appropriate to Scripture as such. I am convinced that in this way they will do more justice to the Bible. As a bonus, they will develop a view that is more in agreement with the way science and philosophy view the cosmos and humanity in our times. In opposition to the very static worldview, which governed both scholastic philosophy

---

42. See more extensively, Ouweneel (2000b, chapters 10–11).

and decretalist theology, we are today dealing both with immensely more dynamic natural sciences and with a similar kind of dynamic applied to various types of theology.[43] The Newtonian view of a world that functions entirely in a decretalist way has been replaced by quantum mechanics, which contains an important non-decretal element. The ancient idea that, in principle, science could predict every future physical event has been totally rejected; I need refer only to the "uncertainty principle" of Werner Heisenberg (d. 1976) and modern chaos theory. According to today's physical worldview, the world is largely indeterminate and unpredictable.

Here is one example: prior to measuring, we can indicate for a quantum particle what *possible* behaviors it may exhibit but not what its precise behavior will be. We can also statistically indicate how a large number of quantum particles will behave, but not how one particle will behave. At the quantum level, reality is exactly what Open Theism, from its own point to view, says about reality: partially determined, and partially open. In other words, also at the quantum level, we encounter within reality a fascinating interaction between fixity and freedom. Not all physicists agree, but most of them believe that the uncertainty principle shows that causal decretalism is untenable, and along with it, traditional rationalism in science has become untenable as well.[44]

7.4.3 Ancient versus Modern Philosophy

Please note, I am not at all asserting that modern science has to prescribe to theologians how they must think. Decretalism is wrong on *theological* grounds, whatever developments in science may occur. My point is rather that, today, it is easier for us to recognize the large extent to which earlier theological views of God, cosmos, and humanity were influenced by (neo)Platonic, Aristotelian, and Stoic views that, especially through Augustine and later through scholasticism, have

---

43. Cf. Boyd (2000, 107–111).
44. Ouweneel (2000b, 338).

entered Western Christianity. Even during the period of the founding of modern, mechanistic and decretalistic science (seventeenth century), these ideas could be easily defended. Today, the scientific paradigm has changed to such extent that it should be less difficult to give up decretalism in theology as well.

Those who claim that decretalism is found in the Bible are mistaken. It is not there. It was put into theological thinking under purely pagan influences. It is time to eliminate these influences. I am convinced that we encounter in the Bible a very different pattern — which happens to agree far more with our modern view of cosmos and humanity than did the previous view.

Some may argue that Open Theism and similar new approaches to Scripture have been inspired by modern science and philosophy, and therefore must be rejected. This is a shallow argument. Such people do not realize that their own view was inspired many centuries ago by pagan Greek thinking. Neither ancient nor medieval, neither modern nor post-modern philosophy should govern theologians. At the same time, we must realize that theologians, like all other scholars, are always children of their time. We cannot *help* being influenced, consciously or unconsciously, by the prevailing ideas and views of our own part of the world and our own cultural era. However, this does not change the fact that those committed to decretalism, Open Theism, Viatorism, and any other position, should endeavor with all their strength to let exegetical and theological arguments ultimately decide. Decretalism is wrong for *theological* reasons; but in order to understand how it could nonetheless arise, it is important to understand the philosophical and cultural context of its rise.

7.4.4 The View of Time

Another topic requires us to take modern science into account, and that is our modern view of time. In general, theologians (and historians as well) work with the idea of a linear, one-dimensional time-axis, running from minus- to plus-infinite. They do so particularly because the idea of a timeless eternity is now largely outdated. Along this axis, we can, within time, look backward and forward, something possible only for those located on this time-axis. In this view, looking back means seeing along the time-axis how certain events have occurred in the past; and looking forward means a corresponding seeing along the time-axis how certain events will occur in the future.

In certain respects, modern physicists look at time in quite a different way. They view time and matter as rigidly interconnected; Albert Einstein (d. 1955) thought of time as the fourth dimension of cosmic reality (in addition to the common three spatial dimensions). This implies, among many things, that physical time began at the moment the universe (at least as we know it today) originated. In fact, the thought that time began with creation goes back to Augustine, but modern physicists add many considerations to this about which Augustine could not have the faintest idea. Thus, it is assumed that not only matter but also time disappear into a "black hole" in the universe; this means there could be places in the universe where there is no time. Einstein's theory of relativity implies that, if a person travels through the universe at the speed of light, he will return to earth in a different time. Even at velocities way below the speed of light, as in the case of satellites, this effect occurs, though the difference can be measured in milliseconds only. Time is neither a matter-independent idea nor a static idea.

It would be worthwhile to thoroughly consider the theological consequences of this view of time. On the one hand, we saw (§6.7) that the contrast between time and a timeless eternity cannot be exegetically and theologically defended. On the other hand, we must not enclose the eternal God within physical time. Whereas we, people, are bound to the time-axis, we might imagine that God has many possibilities to enter the time-axis. To him, foreknowledge is therefore not necessarily a looking forward along the time-axis but, from a position outside our physical time-axis, a looking *at* the time-axis. This does not necessarily mean that God is timeless, but it does mean he is not bound to cosmic, *physical* time, as we are. Earlier in this book and elsewhere, I have tried to address this problem by introducing the notion of "pistical time."[45]

7.5 God's Omnipotence in Job
7.5.1 God versus Job's Friends

Speaking of chaos theory, I find it fascinating to see how various recent theologians have tried to deduce from Job 38–41 that, according to God, too, the cosmos is partially chaotic. Of course, this is not meant in the mathematical-physical sense, but in the pistical sense: chaos is the disorder, the disharmony, which reigns where the dark powers rule and where God supposedly has little control. We refer here to the famous "answer to Job," about which there has been so much debate because people wondered time and again in what *way* God answered Job here, and what *attributes* of God are at stake here.[46] People have thought especially of God's omnipotence here—or even his supposed lack of omnipotence to a certain extent.

It is quite understandable that those who read the book of Job intently for the first time, and then in the end arrive at the "answer" of the Lord, cannot suppress disappointment. Is this all? Sure, God gives a mighty description of creation. First of inanimate nature (38:4–38): the earth, the sea, dawn, the deep, light and darkness, the weather, and the stars. Second of the animal world (38:39–39:30): the lion, the raven, the mountain goat, the wild donkey, the wild ox, the ostrich, the horse, the hawk, the eagle. This is all very interesting, but is this what Job asked for? To put it more strongly, since his

---

45. See Ouweneel (2014a; 2014b).
46. Ouweneel (2000a, §6.2.1); a famous, and yet infamous, specimen of such treatises on God's "answer to Job" is Jung (2010).

friends did their utmost to give their lengthy replies—which were very unhelpful to Job— is Job not entitled to finally hear *God's* reply? These extensive descriptions of nature—is this what he really needs? Is this what he was waiting for?

Jewish author Margarete Susman (d. 1966) tried to give an explanation of the "fundamental difference between the truths of the friends and the truth that Job is striving for."[47] This difference comes to light in the fact that Job, "whose friends felt called to give him a clear answer, does not receive an answer from God." How could the friends think they would be able to give Job what God himself does not give him, neither at the beginning, nor at the end of the story? This is because the friends have God in their pocket, whereas Job has lost God: "[B]ut they have him as a firm possession, as a general knowing; they do not know him as Job does, who, in his very anguish to lose him, in the panic of the mystery pouncing upon him, shouts out his desperate questions to God himself," says Susman.

7.5.2 God's Answer to Job

Now we might argue that, in the end, Job definitely does receive his answer. He had challenged God to confirm Job's innocence and uprightness, and this is what God does in Job 42:7-8, "My anger burns against you [i.e., Eliphaz] and against your two friends, for you have not spoken of me what is right, as my servant Job has. . . . For you have not spoken of me what is right, as my servant Job has." That is, God judges the friends wrong, and Job right. This is quite satisfactory to Job. However, before it came this far, God had a score to settle with Job himself as well. He, and we, should understand that God is not on our level, where we can challenge him, can even blame him, can even doubt his righteousness: "Will you even put me in the wrong? Will you condemn me that you may be in the right?" God asks (40:8). Do you know whom you are talking to, Job? Who is he, and who are you? Creation in its

---

47. Susman (1996, 45–46).

majesty towers high above Job—how much more the Creator.

Job has to be put in his place because he "darkens counsel," that is, discredits God's world rule, and this "by words without knowledge" (38:2). With every manifestation of his omnipotence within the cosmos, God exposes humanity in its powerlessness. But not only this: God humiliates Job but he does not belittle him. He leaves him his dignity; more strongly: he comforts him. At the end of "God's answer," Job still does not have the reply to all his questions; but there is peace in his soul. All his life he had *served* God; now he can also *rest* in God. Precisely in this profound but magnificent way, Job arrives at his spiritual triumph—not only through the restoration of his body, but especially through the restoration of his soul (Ps. 23:3, "He restores my soul").

Susman explains that the Lord's "answer" does not contain specific answers, cast in words and sentences, to Job's specific questions. God is not explaining that he is definitely righteous, that he is definitely concerned with the deeds of the wicked, that he definitely cares about Job and other righteous people, etc. Something else happens: God reveals *himself*, he presents *himself* in the justice of his world rule. God does not *give* an answer; God *is* the answer. If there is anything to give, God gives himself to Job. No logical answers satisfy Job, that is, give him satisfaction, peace, rest; rather God's self-manifestation, God's giving-himself-away satisfies him. People like Job's friends would have been happy with the logical answers; Job finds his happiness in God himself—not in *theology* but in *Theos*. Unquestionably, in this way both the logical and the existential questions will remain; people will have to wrestle with them all their lives. But the questions have become subordinate to the One who is their answer.

This thought that God himself is the answer to Job has been expressed, for instance, by the Swiss Protestant theologian Leonhard Ragaz (d. 1945). He says of God's answer that it is powerful, both smashing and elevating, and, as far as it goes, possessing eternal validity: it is God himself. This means that God does not involve himself in arguments for and against his dominion, but shows *himself*. His answer consists in the manifestation of his greatness in strong language and creative acts. This, and not the arguments of God's defenders (Job's friends), leads Job to become silent before God and to ask his forgiveness. He has no gross sins to confess, but he confesses, as it were, his utter sinfulness. This is true humility. Job has not received answers to the riddles that had tortured him for so long, but he has received a glimpse of God himself.[48]

7.5.3 God's Counter-Questions

If there were any questions to ask, it is God who comes to Job with his counter-questions. These are rhetorical questions; Job does not need to answer them—but they remain hanging in the air. You cannot get around them. The questions themselves suffice to bring Job to self-reflection. Job, you asked me so many things, now I want to ask *you* a couple of questions (38:3–4): "Dress for action like a man; I will question you, and you make it known to me. Where were you when I laid the foundation of the earth?" To every person who, in his distress, ever asked God, "Where were you when I needed you?" comes this counter-question: "Where were you when I laid the foundation of the earth?" Viewed superficially this might look like a platitude, but that is not at all the case. If you have no idea, Job, about how to lay the foundations of a planet, why do you want to cross-examine me about my rule over the earth, or my rule over your life? Are such things not beyond your understanding? How does one explain color television to someone born blind? How does one explain calculus to an infant?

I think that it is in this light that we should view Job 41:11: "Who has first given to me, that I should repay him?"—a question that Paul quotes in Romans 11:35 at the end of his comments on the sufferings and restoration of Israel. No human

---
48. In Glatzer (1969, 129–31); cf. also Ragaz (1949, 257).

and no nation can register any claim against God. He has not the slightest duty toward any people, except the self-imposed duties that flow from his promises, and more generally from his own being. And this being is Love. But this obligation arises from God's side; *we* cannot register any claims. The same God who was asking here, "Where were you?" (Job 38:4), had once asked Adam, "Where are you?" (Gen. 3:9). This was not a reproach, but rather the beginning invitation of his love.[49] Because Christ, when forsaken by God on the cross, asked *him*, so to speak, "Where are you?" (cf. Ps. 22:1; Matt. 27:46), no believer need ever ask this question again. Even if we do not experience his presence, by faith we know it is there. Even if we do not understand God's deeds, we may rest in his love.

"Where were you when I laid the foundation of the earth?" The LORD answers this question in Job 38:21, "You know [it], for you were born then [i.e., when the earth was created], and the number of your days is great!" This sounds sarcastic, but there is more to it than that. In order to fathom God's wisdom, one must be as old as, or older than, the world itself — yes, one must be Wisdom itself. As Proverbs 8 tells us: "The LORD possessed me at the beginning of his work, the first of his acts of old. Ages ago I was set up, at the first, before the beginning of the earth. When there were no depths I was brought forth. . . . When he established the heavens, I was there . . ., then I was beside him, like a master workman, and I was daily his delight, rejoicing before him always, rejoicing in his inhabited world and delighting in the children of man" (vv. 22-31).

Christ, the power of God and the wisdom of God (1 Cor. 1:24), was "in the bosom of the Father" (John 1:18), the One through whom God made the world and upholds it (John 1:3; Col. 1:16-17; Heb. 1:2-3). Christ is the only One who can give an affirmative answer to all the questions of Job 38! Of course, he is still hidden here, but he has since been revealed to *believers*. Therefore, living on the other side of the cross and

---

49. Ouweneel (EDR 3, chapter 10).

having the Holy Spirit dwelling in them, believers can see beyond what Job could see: "'For who has understood the mind of the Lord so as to instruct him?' But we have the mind of Christ" (1 Cor. 2:16, with reference to Isa. 40:13). Those who have the mind of Christ may see things through the eyes of Christ, learn to weigh them as Christ would, by the power of the Holy Spirit. This is not theological knowledge as such, or logical-theoretical scholarship, but the existential knowledge of the heart. It is the enlightened eyes of the heart that matter (Eph. 1:17), and moreover, it is the knowledge of spiritual experience: among those who possess the Spirit of Christ the "Jobs," those who have been sitting *in* the ashes (Job 2:8), will have made more progress than the "friends," those who have only been sitting *around* the ashes.

7.6 Other Aspects of Job
7.6.1 Behemoth and Leviathan

An important part of God's reply consists of his description of *Behemoth* (Job 40:15-24) and *Leviathan* (41:1-34). That consists of forty-four verses! I do not wish to expend my energy trying to show that these cannot be the hippopotamus (as say the CEV, TLB, NLV, OJB) and the crocodile (TLB, NLV), respectively. Behemoth "makes his tail stiff like a cedar," and is "the first [i.e., greatest, but perhaps also the first in time; see below] of the ways of God" (40:17, 19) — this suffices as testimony against the hippopotamus, for it is not old enough, and its tail is inconspicuous. And Leviathan is presented here as far more inaccessible and invincible than the crocodile is. Take, for instance, Job 16:9: in antiquity, the crocodile was definitely caught and sold. And consider 41:25 (if we translate here, which seems to me correct: "He looks down on the proudest of creatures"): Can the crocodile *look down* on other, proud animals?

We will not understand Behemoth and Leviathan unless we grasp their spiritual meaning, and the same verse 25 may help us here. The MEV and NRS contain the word "gods" here as a rendering of Hebrew *gaboah*: "When it raises up himself even the gods [lit., the exalted ones] are afraid." What creatures are these that even scare the "exalted ones" away? Indeed, the ancient rabbis agreed that these are not common animals but special creatures.[50] Some thought that they were created to serve as food for the righteous in the world to come![51] I am more sympathetic toward the conviction of a contemporaneous Jewish woman: "God also boasts in the hazardless, pre-demonic power of the horrible monsters thrown by him in the sea [i.e., Leviathan] and on the land [i.e., Behemoth], monsters that are cosmically so much more powerful than people. In them lives creational power in its nakedness, unclothed with mind and will; in them rules an earnestness of a different, darker nature."[52]

Behemoth and Leviathan are primordial powers of evil, each ruling over its own domain: land and water. These powers, too, have been created by God, although, of course, he did not create them as *evil* powers—they *became* evil powers. I assume that the introductory words (Job 40:10-14) are very important because they seem to indicate beforehand the purpose God's description of Behemoth and Leviathan will serve. Let Job adorn himself "with majesty and dignity": "Pour out the overflowings of your anger, and look on everyone who is proud and abase him. Look on everyone who is proud and bring him low and tread down the wicked where they stand. Hide them all in the dust together; bind their faces in the world below. Then will I also acknowledge to you that your own right hand can save you." Is Job capable of defeating the demonic powers that rise up against the LORD (and against him, Job)? If this is so, God will praise him. But Job is not capable; only God is, and he *will* subdue them. Upon this follows the description of these demonic powers.

The Hebrew *behemoth* literally means "beasts," here with

---

50. See especially *BabT*: Baba Bathra 74a–75a.
51. Reichert (1985, 211).
52. Susman (1996, 138).

a singular meaning: "beastly beast, beast of beasts, beast *par excellence*"; the monster is mentioned only here. *Leviathan* presumably means "tortuous" (from Heb. *l-v-h*, "to wind," to turn") in the sense of a dragon-like sea monster (cf. Isa. 27:1, "Leviathan the twisting [Heb. *'aqallaton*] serpent"). God speaks in the book of Job about the greatest powers that a person can encounter in his life, and over which he has no control at all. On the contrary, he may know or feel himself to be held captive in their demonic grip: "Can one take him [i.e., Behemoth] by his eyes, or pierce his nose with a snare?" (40:24). "Lay your hands on him [i.e., Leviathan]; remember the battle — you will not do it again! Behold, the hope of a man [i.e., to master the monster] is false; he [i.e., the man] is laid low even at the sight of him [i.e., the monster]" (41:8-9). However, God has created these powers, too, and has control over them. If people cannot compete with these powers, even less can they compete with God (Job 41:10): "No one is so fierce that he dares to stir *him* [i.e., Leviathan] up. Who then is he who can stand before *me*?" says God.

7.6.2 Chaos in Job?

On the basis of Job 38–41, several recent theologians believe that, according to God, too, the cosmos is partially chaotic.[53] The idea is that these chapters do not — in the Calvinist sense — wish to make clear to us that God does what he can, and can do what he wants, and that he is fully entitled to this. Rather, according to these newer theologians, God seems to point out that our view of the cosmos is so limited that we are simply unable to understand why things happen as they do. We have no *over*view, we do not see the big picture. The mysteries about the cosmos that Job 38–41 identify involve not the mysteries in God's own character — "he does as pleases him" — but the unintelligibility of this world. It is an

---

53. Keel (1978); Lindström (1983, 154–57); Day (1985, 62–87); Gibson (1988, 416–17); Good (1990, 348); Mettinger (1992); Fretheim (1999, 87–89); Boyd (2001, 215–26) (the latter put me on the track of this interpretation).

ambiguous cosmos, experiencing much disorder within its order, a disorder that undermines this order.

We may think here also of the Greek term *mataiotēs*:[54] the "vanity, futility, frustration, confusion, uselessness, emptiness" to which the creation, as well as the human mind (Eph. 1:17) and speech (2 Pet. 2:18), was subjected as a consequence of the Fall (Rom. 8:20). To a large extent, cosmic reality is a-logical, or even illogical, irrational, not because God made it this way but as a consequence of the Fall, that is, of the powers of chaos. It is basically identical with *hebel*, a key word in Ecclesiastes: "vapor, mist, mere breath," and hence "vanity, futility," anything that is fleeting or elusive or pointless (see the note on Eccl. 1:2 ESV).

In the argument of Job 38–41, Behemoth and Leviathan occupy a strikingly large place, not so much to impress Job with some of God's mightiest creational works but rather to show what powers are at work in this cosmos apart from God. In the Middle East, these monsters were widely known as chaos monsters of cosmic scope, the powers of darkness.[55] Edmond Jacob wrote that God wanted to show Job how hard it is to rule a world with such extraordinary and mysterious creatures that are not afraid of anything, and against which he must constantly wage war. Job must draw the conclusion that God is not unrighteous because of his lack of care toward him since he, God himself, is combating evil at a much higher level.[56] Job is dealing with heavy losses, disease, his wife, his friends—God has to deal with Behemoth and Leviathan.

Fredrik Lindström introduces the chaos-idea into his argument by asserting that YHWH in fact admits to Job that there are parts of the creation that are indeed chaotic, and this would give us insight for understanding the world in which

---

54. *TDNT* 4:523; *NIDNTT* 1:552; cf. *mataiotēs mataiotētōn*, "vanity of vanities," in Eccl. 1:2; 12:8 (Septuagint) and *mataios*, "futile, worthless" (1 Cor. 3:20; Titus 3:9; James 1:26).
55. See Ouweneel (2016b).
56. Jacob (1958, 171).

evil exists independently of God. This evil does not come directly from God, as Job thinks, nor can it be fitted into a world order in which it is ultimately the consequence of wrong human behavior, as Job's friends claim; it occupies some mysterious place of its own.[57] Such a view does *not* necessarily suggest a dualistic explanation,[58] as if good and evil are more or less equal powers, independent of each other, and standing in opposition to each other. However, it does suggest an interpretation in which powers created by God have made themselves more or less independent of him, and are in continual conflict with him. Within the paradigm of decretalism, such a view is unthinkable, but within the paradigms of Open Theism or Viatorism, it is definitely biblical.

As John Gibson puts it, Job must realize that God is on his side and on the side of suffering and protesting humanity, but also that God himself must wage a war and must subjugate a ferocious and merciless enemy before he can deal with human grievances and heal human wounds.[59] And Greg Boyd says that Job is ignorant of the complexity of and the battle within creation, and his arrogance and that of his friends led them to the mistaken conclusion that all misery could be reduced to human sin (the friends' conclusion) or to God (Job's conclusion). Such logic inevitably leads to the conclusion either that people suffer because God punishes them (as Job's friends assert), or that God rules the cosmos in an arbitrary way (as Job himself in fact suggested).[60]

Of course, the last word has not been written about this newer interpretation of the book of Job. The debate will continue, because this is not so much an exegetical matter, but a theological one: what is the origin of misery in our lives? (See further in chapter 9.) At a minimum, it seems to me that the newer explanation is more acceptable than earlier

---

57. Lindström (1983, 154).
58. See Ouweneel (EDR 3, §12.4.2).
59. Gibson (1988, 417).
60. Boyd (2001, 226).

explanations, according to which Job 38–41 would teach that people simply must shut their mouths and submit to the inscrutable sovereignty of God. If this conclusion is correct, these chapters offer remarkable support for a view of redemptive history that is consistent with not only Open Theism but also Viatorism.

Chapter 8
The Meaning of Prayer

And the prayer of faith will save the one who is sick,
   and the Lord will raise him up. . . .
The prayer of a righteous person
   has great power as it is working.
Elijah was a man with a nature like ours,
   and he prayed fervently that it might not rain,
   and for three years and six months it did not rain on the earth.
Then he prayed again,
   and heaven gave rain,
   and the earth bore its fruit.
James 5:15–18

Summary: The subject of prayer is an important part of a study of God's counsel because it raises the question whether prayer can cause God to "change his mind." Apparently it can; we see numerous examples of this in Scripture. Decretalism has a hard job explaining away all these cases. Human prayers and divine answers are not both foreordained because then we could never say that these answers are a consequence of and response to these prayers. Sometimes God refuses to answer; sometimes he would love to answer, but there are no prayers; sometimes he is "persuaded" by fervent prayers to do something else than he had announced. All such cases make it hard to maintain a decretalist approach. To be sure, prayers can never change God's eternal counsel; but they can definitely change God's ways with the world.

8.1 The Power of Prayer
8.1.1 Does Praying Help?

OF ALL THE SUBJECTS THAT demonstrate how the differences between the approaches of decretalism, Open Theism, and Viatorism are of great *practical* significance, scarcely any are more important than those involving the meaning of prayer (this chapter) and of evil and suffering in the world (next chapter). Consistent Calvinism believes that all things were both foreknown and foreordained by God from eternity. One question arising in this context touches on the meaning of prayer. Why would the Israelites call for help against the Egyptians (Exod. 14:10, 15), or the Amalekites (17:8-14), or the Ammonites (Judg. 10:15), or the Philistines (1 Sam. 7:8-9), if each time their salvation had been certain from eternity? Why would Abraham (Gen. 15:2-3), and later Isaac and Rebekah (25:21), pray for a son if this had been decreed by God from eternity? Sure, they had God's promise; why not wait until the appointed time came when God would fulfill his promise? Hannah had no such promise; why pray for children if whether she would have children had already been decided from eternity?

This is the central question: On the basis of decretalism, is it possible to believe that God answers prayers, that is, grants people what they ask him? The Bible often uses the terms "answering," or "hearing/listening" in the sense of "answering" (i.e., doing or granting what was asked): "God listened to Leah, and she conceived and bore Jacob a fifth son. . . . Then God remembered Rachel, and God listened to her and opened her womb" (Gen. 30:17, 22). "[T]he LORD listened to me that time also," that is, by answering my prayers (Deut. 9:19; 10:10). "There has been no day like it before or since, when the LORD heeded [lit., heard] the voice of a man, for the LORD fought for Israel" (Josh. 10:14). We will "cry out to you in our affliction, and you will hear and save" (2 Chron. 20:9). "And the Lord heard Hezekiah and healed the people" (30:20). "When he calls to me, I will answer him; I will be with him in trouble; I will rescue him and honor him" (Ps. 91:15). "Do not be afraid, Zechariah, for your prayer has been heard, and your wife Elizabeth will bear you a son" (Luke 1:13). "In a favorable time I listened to you, and in a day of salvation I have helped you" (2 Cor. 6:2). "Jesus offered up prayers [to God], . . . and he was heard because of his reverence" (Heb. 5:7).

In all these cases, "hearing" or "listening" or "answering" implies doing or giving what the praying person has asked.[1] Can one who holds to a decretalist position really express it in this way? What God was going to do or to give had been decreed from eternity; prayers cannot add anything to this! Of course, decretalists recognize that God sometimes does what people have asked him. But does he do so *because* people have asked him? From the decretalist perspective, one should apparently say: whether we beseech God to grant P or do not ask anything at all, if he wants to do so—that is, if it is part of his eternal decree—then he will indeed grant P, and if he does not want to do so, he will not grant P, whether we entreat him or not. After Hezekiah's prayer, God extended his life (2 Kings 20:1-7)—but on the decretalist standpoint we should say that God had intended to do so anyway. The Lord granted Paul, in spite of his prayer, no deliverance from his thorn in the flesh (2 Cor. 12:1-7)—but from the decretalist viewpoint we should say that basically this prayer was irrelevant to the outcome. It may have been useful for Paul's mood but not for the Lord's answer: from eternity God intended to refuse him this deliverance.

8.1.2 Why Then Pray?

Why then pray? This is what many will ask. Here are some

---

1. The Greek has special words to express this (*akouō* > *epakouō*, *eisakouō*), like German (*hören* > *erhören*) and Dutch (*horen* > *verhoren*).

decretalist answers that are often given.

(a) We pray simply because God commanded us to pray (cf. Matt. 5:44; 6:6; 7:7; 9:38; 24:20; 26:4; 1 Thess. 5:17, 25; 2 Thess. 3:1; Heb. 13:18; James 5:16; Jude 1:20; etc.).
(b) We pray because it is an expression of our dependence upon God.
(c) We pray because, to be sure, prayer does not change God, but at least it changes us.
(d) We pray because both our prayers and God's answers have been decreed from eternity.

Of course, we agree wholeheartedly with (a) and (b), and with the second part of (c); but are (d) and the first part of (c) correct as well? Look especially at (d): Christians are supposed to pray because both their prayers (P) and God's answers (A) have all been decreed in God's eternal counsel (C). A person prays for X, and God grants him X; God "answers" his prayer, we would think (and indeed this is what the Bible says numerous times). But no, decretalists would say that both the prayer and the answer and X itself were decreed from eternity. In the strict sense of the word, the answer is not an "answer" at all. God may have listened to the prayer, but his listening did not at all influence his actions. According to decretalists, the causal relationship is not this (as one might think):

$$P \longrightarrow A \longrightarrow X$$

but this:

$$C \begin{matrix} \diagup & \!\!\!\!\!\! \text{—— P} \\ < & \!\!\!\!\!\! \text{—— A} \\ \diagdown & \!\!\!\!\!\! \text{—— X} \end{matrix}$$

I have a serious question for decretalists at this point: What Christian could *live* with the idea that his supplications

The Meaning of Prayer

accomplish nothing but are just part of God's eternal counsel? If I had to believe this, my prayers would be utterly formal. I would see no reason why I should *entreat, plead, beseech*. What difference would such insistence make? Or would I beseech, not because I believe this will have some effect, but only because I was decreed to do so? Am I merely acting out an elaborate play whose script has been written in eternity past? Jairus *implored* Jesus to come and heal his daughter (Luke 8:41). Jesus came and raised the girl from the dead (vv. 54–55). Decretalists tell us that Jesus would have come and raised the girl anyway; or rather, both Jairus' act of imploring and Jesus' act of healing were part of God's counsel. But is this the way any unbiased person would read the text? Does the Bible anywhere give us this view of prayer?

Decretalists read these things *into* the text because of their Greek-scholastic thought system. Nowhere does the Bible tell us that our prayers and God's answers have all been decreed by God from eternity, but quite the contrary. Such a doctrine renders irrelevant all beseeching, all imploring, all begging, all insistence, all spontaneity. Jews and Christians who are not plagued by such a theory pray with a view to receiving something from God. They pray because they firmly believe that prayer *helps*, that it can truly accomplish something with God. This is indeed what we read hundreds of times in the Bible: people entreat God, he listens to their prayers, and gives them what they have asked.

From a strictly decretalist position, prayer can never *accomplish* anything, since what God will do has been decreed from eternity; as a matter of principle, his actions can never be a *result* of the prayer. Even if the prayer was decreed as well, God's answer cannot be a result of the prayer; both the prayer and its answer can be the result only of God's eternal counsel. How differently James speaks, who says, "The prayer of a righteous person is powerful and effective" (5:16 NIV). No, says the decretalist (if he is honest and consistent), prayer *as such*—even if it comes from the holiest believer—in itself has no power at all, and can accomplish nothing because what God will do has already been decreed beforehand.

8.1.3 Conditions for Answered Prayers

In past decades I have often experienced that, in surroundings where Calvinists were in the majority, group prayer and extended prayer meetings were simply among "things that are not done." At annual thanksgiving services, things went the same way: the pastor said a long prayer during the service, and that was it. If anyone wished to organize a home prayer meeting for some urgent need, the response was often: Why? The pastor prays for that need on the Lord's Day; that should suffice. If, during consistory meetings, one of the members prays to God, that should suffice. Some even cite a Bible verse against group prayer: "[W]hen you pray, do not heap up empty phrases as the Gentiles do, for they think that they will be heard for their many words" (Matt. 6:7). As if one could put the repetitive prayers of pagans on the same level as the supplications of the saints! Among Calvinists in the Netherlands, prayer practices have definitely improved. However, as long as people do not really believe that prayer can *accomplish* something with God (something that otherwise would not have occurred), there will never be much enthusiasm for imploring God. Prayer is a holy and solemn Christian duty — but in practice prayer is often not much more than that.

Scripture speaks very differently: "Be *constant* in prayer" (Rom. 12:12); ". . . praying at all times in the Spirit, with all prayer and supplication. To that end keep alert with all perseverance, making supplication for all the saints" (Eph. 6:18). "Continue steadfastly in prayer" (Col. 4:2); "pray without ceasing" (1 Thess. 5:17), that is, under all circumstances, at every occasion. Jesus presents to us the faith of the poor widow as an example: "[W]ill not God give justice to his elect, who cry to him day and night? Will he delay long over them? I tell you, he will give justice to them speedily. Nevertheless, when the Son of Man comes, will he find faith on earth?" (Luke

18:7-8). Actually, it does not say "find faith," but "find *the* faith," here with the sense of a demonstrative pronoun:[2] "*that* faith," namely, the faith of that widow as well as of God's elect, who cry to him day and night *because they believe that their prayers can occasion God's changing his mind.*

What else could possibly be the meaning of imploring and entreating, and even *striving* in prayers? "I appeal to you, brothers, . . . to *strive* together with me in your prayers to God on my behalf, that I may be delivered from the unbelievers in Judea, and that my service for Jerusalem may be acceptable to the saints, so that by God's will I may come to you with joy and be refreshed in your company" (Rom. 15:30-32). "Epaphras, . . . greets you, always *struggling* on your behalf in his prayers, that you may stand mature and fully assured in all the will of God" (Col. 4:12). Notice the word "that": striving in order that I may be delivered; struggling in order that you may stand mature. This is not the language of someone who believes that all the outcomes have been decreed from eternity; this is the language of someone who believes that prayer as such can *bring about* something with God. *Pray so that* a certain outcome is obtained — because if you do not pray there will be no "so that."

If both our prayers and their *seeming* outcomes have been foreordained by God, how could there ever be such a thing as praying wrongly? This is exactly what James seems to intend: "You ask and do not receive, because you ask wrongly, to spend it on your passions" (James 4:3). Would decretalists say that these wrong prayers were also decreed by God? How can God's answer to prayer depend on the spiritual attitude of the praying person if both the prayer and the answer have been foreordained from eternity? "We know that God does not listen to sinners, but if anyone is a worshiper of God and does his will, God listens to him" (John 9:31). "If I had cherished iniquity in my heart, the Lord would not have listened"

---

2. Cf. Liefeld (1984, 1000): "wait with patient trust."

(Ps. 66:18; cf. 145:18-19; 34:15-16; 1 Pet. 3:10-12). "The LORD is far from the wicked, but he hears the prayer of the righteous" (Prov. 15:29). Such passages demonstrate beyond doubt that God's answer is not (only) a matter of God's counsel but (also) of the praying person's responsibility: if he prays rightly he may expect God's positive response, if he prays wrongly he may not. Therefore Paul says, "I desire then that in every place the men should pray, lifting holy hands without anger or quarreling" (1 Tim. 2:8).

8.1.4 No Resignation But Perseverance

In the Bible, people do not pray in a lifeless, perfunctory manner, as if they are delivering a petition to some earthly government official. If things are right, they pray in *faith*, with no doubting (James 1:6). As Jesus said, "Truly, I say to you, whoever says to this mountain, 'Be taken up and thrown into the sea,' and does not doubt in his heart, but *believes that what he says will come to pass*, it will be done for him" (Mark 11:23). They *implore* the Lord because they have great expectation of such an outcome. Moses *pleaded* with the LORD (Deut. 3:23). Ezra says, "[W]e fasted and *implored* our God for this, and he listened to our entreaty" (8:23). David did the same ("To you, O LORD, I cry, and to the Lord I plead for mercy," Ps. 30:8; cf. 142:1), as well as Jeremiah (42:9) and Daniel (9:18). Job was urged by his friends to do so: "If you will seek God and plead with the Almighty for mercy, if you are pure and upright, surely then he will rouse himself for you and restore your rightful habitation" (8:5-6).

We also read of supplications addressed to Jesus, as in Matthew, for example: a centurion "appealed" to him (8:5), the demons "begged" him (v. 31), he himself commanded, "[P]ray earnestly to the Lord" (9:38), people "implored" him (14:36). Why appeal to him, beg him, implore him, unless one believes that he—at least sometimes—*answers* supplications, that is, grants what people ask him? Apart from decretalists, this is what every seriously entreating person believes: prayer

The Meaning of Prayer

can change things. The moment he becomes convinced that both his supplications and God's answers were all foreordained, he can no longer earnestly beg. He can only *pretend* that he is begging, just as an actor does when playing a role in a theater production whose script was written long ago.

I suppose that, in cases of distress, there are only a few decretalists who can *live* consistently as decretalists. Such persons do exist, champions of surrender, of idle resignation, if not fatalism. They say with Job (1:21): "The LORD gave, and the LORD has taken away; blessed be the name of the LORD" — forgetting that some time later this same Job cursed the day of his birth (3:1), and began arguing with God (7:20-21; etc.). In spite of, or perhaps because of, his disputing, God said of Job that he (Job) had spoken of him (God) what was right (42:6, 8). Apparently, God felt he was being taken more seriously by Job, who argued with him, than by his friends with their idle resignation and the poor theology.[3]

But no, the diehard decretalists say, "It is God's will," and that's it. No wonder: *everything* is God's will. When they are sick, they do pray (but then especially "your will be done"), while they also make use of medicine (for the Bible allows that). But when the doctors can do nothing for them anymore, some of them have firmly declined the anointing of the sick, for this would mean going against God's will; it would be "tempting" God. With indignation they point to — usually misunderstood — healing ministers who believe they can "claim," or even "demand," something from God. But God himself said, "Open your mouth wide, and I will fill it" (Ps. 81:10), which in the rhymed version (Dutch) is even stronger: "Open your mouth, boldly demand from me on behalf of my covenant. All that you are lacking, I will give you, if you beg me for it, mildly and abundantly." Notice not only the "demanding" (Dutch *eisen*) here but also the condition: I give you *if* you beg (*smeken*) me for it. How wonderfully these

---

3. Cf. Hartley (1988, 539).

(Reformed) poets of 1773 soar above some of the decretalists that we know today!

In our own day, the ministry of healing usually takes a position between decretalism ("it is God's will that I am and stay sick") and charismatism ("all disease comes from the devil," and "God wants me to be healed; if this does not happen, it is my fault"). In the former case, the cause of the illness lies in God's counsel, in the latter case, the cause lies in the power of evil, whether the devil or one's own sin, or both. Greg Boyd criticized those who think that they can reduce everything either to God or to human sin. Such a simplistic logic inevitably leads to the conclusion either that people suffer because God punishes them (Job's friends), or that God governs the cosmos in an arbitrary way (Job himself).[4]

8.2 Can Prayer Change God's Ways?
8.2.1 Are Prayers Effective?

In chapter 6, we reflected on the (im)mutability of God. What does this mean with respect to prayer? Can prayer cause God to change his mind, or not? This important question must now be discussed.

So far in this book, we have often distinguished between God's counsel and God's ways. As to the latter, in this and the next chapter, several important aspects of God's *ways* come to the fore, namely, the role of prayer and the concomitant view of the mutability of God and the place of *suffering* in the world in relation to the counsel and the ways of God. As far as prayer is concerned, Viatorism firmly believes that not a single prayer can ever change God's *counsel*, which is fixed and determined forever. For instance, it is no use praying that God will bring judgment upon the entire Christian world because we know that, in the end, he will save his true church. And it is no use praying that God will save all humanity because we already know that the wicked will perish. However, prayer can definitely greatly influence the *ways* of God, that

---
4. Boyd (2001, 226).

is, the manner in which God realizes his counsel.

On this important point, Open Theism and Viatorism agree, namely, in their emphasis on the concrete value of prayer, that prayer brings about something in the heavenly places. Those who believe that prayer can cause God to change his mind apparently are confident that the future is to some extent open, and that God can be persuaded to do something that he otherwise might not have done. According to theologians sympathetic to Open Theism and Viatorism, this is not only possible, but it has happened legions of times. Walter Wink goes so far as to say that history belongs to—i.e., is (partly) determined by—the intercessors.[5] Dutch evangelist Anne van der Bijl, better known in the Anglo-Saxon world as Brother Andrew, published a book entitled *And God Changed His Mind*, about divine action resulting from the prayers of the saints.[6] For consistent Calvinists, this is inconceivable. But they might reconsider if they would accept the distinction between God's ways and God's counsel.

This is all the more interesting in light of Terry Johnson's surprising observation that no Christian tradition devotes as much attention to prayer as the Reformed tradition. He added that one could say, with only mild exaggeration, that the Reformed have invented the prayer for repentance and renewal.[7] The term "invented" seems to me quite appropriate, for Christ and the apostles know nothing of a prayer for repentance; they know only of appealing to humanity to repent. No person in the Bible ever prayed *for* repentance, but many did pray as an expression *of* repentance. Psalm 51 is the well-known example here, which does contain a prayer for renewal: "Create in me a clean heart, O God, and renew a right [or, steadfast] spirit within me" (v. 10).

The *only* (seeming) example of a prayer for conversion that is usually quoted is this: "[T]urn thou me, and I shall be

---

5. Wink (1992, chapter 16).
6. Brother Andrew (1999).
7. Johnson (2006, 128).

turned" (Jer. 31:18 KJV), with this variety: "Turn thou us unto thee, O LORD, and we shall be turned" (Lam. 5:21). However, this prayer essentially means: "bring me back" (as many translations have it), namely, from the Babylonian exile, and restore us to our former circumstances (see on this verse more extensively §13.8.1). For the rest, believers do not pray for repentance and conversion, whereas they *do* repent and they *do* turn back to the Lord (by the power of the Holy Spirit). The biblical command is "repent, repent!" never: "pray for repentance!"

Why does a Calvinist pray, then, according to Johnson? For two reasons: because prayer changes the believer, and prayer changes the world. This is certainly true—but the idea that prayer might also change *God*, or at least God's *ways*, apparently does not occur to Johnson. It seems that his decretalist prejudices render this idea inconceivable to him. But what do we (Calvinists included) pray? We pray, "Lord, please, do this." Does such a prayer change us? Quite likely; it helps us to develop our sense of dependence on God, and to expect our blessings from him. Does it change the world? Perhaps. But do we not pray primarily because we believe that it may change *God's ways*? Do we not pray because we hope, or even firmly believe, that he will do something that he otherwise might not have done? If we believe that God would have done it anyway, why ask for it? If we believe that he does what pleases him, totally irrespective of our prayers, why pray? We pray because we believe that prayers have *effect*. I repeat: "The prayer of a righteous person is powerful and effective" (James 5:16 NIV; HCSB: "The urgent request of a righteous person is very powerful in its effect"). Strict decretalism and faith in the effectiveness of prayer are mutually exclusive.

8.2.2 God Persuaded by Prayer

The fact that God answers prayer implies that prayer can persuade him to do something other than he had originally announced. God first suggested that he would destroy Sodom and Gomorrah. But after Abraham's supplications he promised that, if there were only ten righteous persons in these cities, he would not do so (Gen. 18:20-33). Through the prophet Isaiah, God told king Hezekiah plainly: "[Y]ou shall die." Period. But after the king's earnest supplications, "I have heard your prayer; I have seen your tears. Behold, I will add fifteen years to your life" (2 Kings 20:5). This can be read in one way only: *because* of your prayer, I will lengthen your life. As Greg Boyd asked, how could God really have changed his mind in answer to a prayer if both the prayer and the answer had been in his mind from eternity? How could the text say that God *added* fifteen years to his life if from eternity it had been certain to God that Hezekiah would live these additional fifteen years?[8] Either the Bible does not speak the truth, or there is something wrong with decretalism.

Of course, the adherents of Open Theism or Viatorism do not believe that God changes his mind as easily as many fallible, capricious people do as a result of their changed moods, insights, or circumstances: "[T]he Glory of Israel [i.e., God] will not lie or have regret, for he is not a man, that he should have regret" (1 Sam. 15:29). God's mutability is different from ours (see §6.5). Yet, a number of times we find this pattern in the Bible: Gods *says* he will do P → people beg him to do Q → God does Q (see further in §8.3).

There is an interesting word in Hebrew, *'-t-r*, "to pray," which in the niphal means something close to "be persuaded by prayer" (older Dutch translations have here a unique expression: *zich laten verbidden*, allow oneself to be entreated). Notice the italics indicating this verbal form: "And Isaac prayed [Heb. *vayye'tar*] to the LORD for his wife, because she was barren. And the Lord *granted his prayer* [*vayyi'ater lo*; KJ21: was entreated by him], and Rebekah his wife conceived" (Gen. 25:21). "God *responded to the plea* [one word: *vayyi'atēr*; KJ21: was entreated] for the land" (2 Sam. 24:25). "[T]hey

---

8. Boyd (2000, 7).

cried out to God in the battle, and he *granted their urgent plea* [*vena'tor lahem*] because they trusted in him" (1 Chron. 5:20).

Of king Manasseh we read: "And when he was in distress, he entreated the favor of the LORD his God and humbled himself greatly before the God of his fathers. He prayed to him, and God was *moved by his entreaty* [*vayyi'ater lo*] and heard his plea and brought him again to Jerusalem into his kingdom. Then Manasseh knew that the LORD was God. . . . And his prayer, and how God *was moved by his entreaty* [*vehē'ater*], . . . they are written in the Chronicles of the Seers" (2 Chron. 33:12-13, 19). Ezra says (8:23), "So we fasted and implored our God for this, and he *listened to our entreaty* [*vayyi'atēr lanoe*; KJ21: was entreated by us; HCSB: granted our request]." And Isaiah says (19:22), "[T]hey will return to the LORD, and he *will listen to their pleas for mercy* [*vene'tar lahem*; KJ21: shall be entreated by them; JUB: shall grant them clemency] and heal them."

Notice how difficult it is to render this one verbal form, and the great variety of renderings: to grant one's prayer/plea/entreaty, to respond/listen to one's prayer/plea/entreaty, to be moved by one's prayer/plea/entreaty. A person asks God for something, God is truly moved by this prayer, and decides to grant the person what he has asked. Of course, the element of persuasion is more clear in one case than another. Isaac and Rebekah received their answer to prayer only after twenty years of marriage, and therefore after many years of prayer. In other cases, God granted Israel or individuals their prayers although they had not deserved this. This means that, in this "granting someone's prayer," there is an element of special mercy and favor. In the case of Isaac and Rebekah, one might argue that God wanted to give them a son anyway because he had promised this (Gen. 21:12). But in all the other cases, there is no evidence at all that God ever intended to give them what they prayed for.

8.2.3 God Answers Prayer

In addition to the remarkable expression just considered — respond to/listen to/be moved by/grant one's plea — there are more common words that mean "to answer," "to hear" with the connotation "to grant," such as *'-n-h* (e.g., 1 Kings 8:36; Ps. 3:4; 4:1; 34:4; Isa. 30:19; 41:17; 49:8; Hos. 2:21-22; 14:8; Zech. 10:6; 13:9) and *sh-m-'* (e.g., Gen. 17:20; 30:6, 22; Deut. 1:45; Josh. 10:14; Judg. 13:9; 2 Sam. 22:36; 2 Chron. 30:20; Job 22:27; Isa. 65:24). Though not as powerful in content, these terms, too, indicate that God acts not only on the basis of his own personal, sovereign will, but also on the basis of the praying person's entreaty. Thus for instance: "[As to] the priests and the Levites . . . their voice was heard [NET: the LORD responded favorably], and their prayer came to his holy habitation in heaven" (2 Chron. 30:27). Here the word "hearing" means, as the NET puts it: the LORD responded favorably to their (praying) voice, that is, gave or allowed them what they had asked; he granted them their pleas.

We never read that God says something like this: You requested Q, but know that the reason that I give you Q is not because you asked for it but only because I intended to give you Q anyway. *Sometimes* this may certainly be the case (why not?), but there is no biblical basis for asserting that such is *always* the case. On the contrary, God blessed Ishmael *because* Abraham had asked for that (Gen. 17:20). The sun stood still at Gibeon and the moon in the Valley of Aijalon *because* Joshua had asked for that (Josh. 10:12-14). The man of God visited Manoah and his wife a second time *because* they had asked for that (Judg. 13:8-9). The Lord healed the people *because* Hezekiah had asked for that (2 Chron. 30:20).

One of the clearest examples is what God granted the young king Solomon in answer to his prayer:

> *Because* you have asked this [viz., wisdom], and have not asked for yourself long life or riches or the life of your enemies, but have asked for yourself understanding to discern what is right,

> behold, I now do according to your word. Behold, I give you a wise and discerning mind, so that none like you has been before you and none like you shall arise after you. I give you also what you have not asked, both riches and honor, so that no other king shall compare with you, all your days (1 Kings 3:11-13).

We cannot argue that God actually meant the opposite, namely, that he had decreed from eternity to give all these things to Solomon. Someone's thought system may prescribe such reasoning, but the text says: *because* you asked wisdom, I give you wisdom indeed but also riches and honor (and a long life, v. 14). The only possible escape seems to be that both the prayer and its answer had been foreordained by God. But first, how then can anyone be praised for a good prayer; and second, how can God say "because"? If the prayer and its answer were both foreordained, then, strictly speaking, God gave Solomon wisdom because of his counsel, *not* because Solomon had asked for it.

Sometimes, for reasons that we usually do not fathom, people must pray long and fervently before God answers: "And the people of Israel said to the LORD, 'We have sinned; do to us whatever seems good to you. Only please deliver us this day.' So they put away the foreign gods from among them and served the LORD, and he became impatient over the misery of Israel" (Judg. 10:15-16). For the last phrase compare the AMP: "He could bear the misery of Israel no longer" (cf. the CEB, CEV: "could no longer stand to see Israel suffer"; etc.). To use another biblical expression: God's "bowels" (more correct than "heart") were "troubled" for Israel (Jer. 31:20 KJV, etc.) *as a consequence of their entreaties.*

Hannah prayed so long and intensely for a son that Eli finally told her, "Go in peace, and the God of Israel grant your petition that you have made to him" (1 Sam. 1:10-17); a year later Hannah received a son, called Samuel. The child's name probably means "God hears," or "God has heard"; it was a constant reminder of the fact that he was God's answer to his mother's entreaty.

In the parable of the persistent widow (Luke 18:1-8), Jesus teaches that persistent prayer bears fruit, even if it may take a while: "And will not God give justice to his elect, who cry to him day and night? Will he delay long over them? I tell you, he will give justice to them speedily" (vv. 7-8). The aim of the parable is therefore that Jesus' disciples "ought always to pray and not lose heart" (v. 1). The reason is that God answers the persistent prayer. It would be unfair to make such a promise if in fact the prayer and its answer have been foreordained.

Sometimes God even answers *wrong* prayers: the Israelites "ate and were well filled, for he *gave them what they craved*. But before they had satisfied their craving, while the food was still in their mouths, the anger of God rose against them" (Ps. 78:29-31; cf. Num. 11:31-34; see §8.6.3). Would anyone venture to say that not only God's chastising answer but also the wrong prayer had been decreed from eternity? And if the wrong prayer was *not* foreordained, how could God's answer have been decreed, which is explicitly presented here as a consequence of their ungodly prayer?

8.3 God's Change After a "Definitive" Statement
8.3.1 Moses

In all the examples mentioned so far, prayer turned out to be useful because prayer appealed to God's heart. Supplications "trouble" his "bowels," that is, they stir his mercy. Of course, not *all* prayers do this. We must fulfill certain conditions: we must pray with our heart (Ps. 62:8; Jer. 29:12-13; Lam. 2:19; Hos. 7:14), pray according to his will (1 John 5:14-15; cf. Mark 14:36), and as New Testament believers: pray in the name of Jesus (John 14:13-14; 15:16; 16:23-24), pray in unity (Matt. 18:19-20), pray persistently (Luke 11:5-13; 18:1-8). However, this does not mean that God positively answers only those prayers that he had planned to grant anyway. Remember: there is a wrong way of praying (James 4:3; cf. Ps. 78:29-31); God answers, not because he has decreed to do so, but because his children ask in the right way.

This is particularly evident in those cases in which God firmly announces what he will do—and then, after the entreaties from his people, does something other than he had originally announced. For instance, after the sin with the golden calf, the LORD told Moses, "I have seen this people, and behold, it is a stiff-necked people. Now therefore let me alone, that my wrath may burn hot against them and I may consume them, in order that I may make a great nation of you" (Exod. 32:9-10; cf. Deut. 9:13-14, 18-20, 25-29). This statement cannot be misunderstood; there is no trace in the text of divine pretending. Walter Kaiser suggested otherwise by claiming this statement was God's test for Moses: he commits himself to people whom he himself has prepared to do certain things.[9] Thus, a decretalist view of God is read into the text. In a comparable passage (Num. 14:11-12), Ronald Allen takes God's fury much more seriously.[10] For indeed, God is furious. The "let me alone" in Exodus 32:10 suggests that Moses must not get in God's way during the execution of the sentence. Interestingly, the (Reformed) Annotation to the States Translation (Statenvertaling) says about this "let me alone": "And hinder me not by thy intercession, for the prayer of the faithful prevaileth much with God, Jam. 5.16."[11]

However, Moses jumps in between God and the people, so to speak, with two ironclad arguments. First, with respect to the Gentile nations, God simply could not afford to destroy his own people whom all the Gentiles knew he had led out of Egypt to take to Canaan. Second, God had *promised* to the fathers that he would bring the people into the promised land (vv. 11-13). Then we hear these moving words: "And the LORD relented from the disaster that he had spoken of bringing on his people" (v. 14). Listen to all the translations that say here, "[T]he LORD *changed his mind*" (AMP, CEB, CJB, EXB, GNV,

---

9. Kaiser (1990, 479).
10. Allen (1990, 817–18).
11. Haak (1657, ad loc.).

NASB, NRSV, etc.)! No doubt there is a very human component in this description that Moses had caused the LORD to "change his mind." However, this does not give us the right to move to the other extreme, and to suggest that God is only pretending to change his mind.

The second example describes a virtually identical situation. The people have sinned by giving credence to the words of the ten unfaithful spies, and God announces the apparently unconditional judgment: "How long will this people despise me? And how long will they not believe in me, in spite of all the signs that I have done among them? I will strike them with the pestilence and disinherit them, and I will make of you a nation greater and mightier than they" (Num. 14:11-12). Again, Moses makes a passionate plea, with similar arguments as before (vv. 13-19), and God answers, "I have pardoned, according to your word [Heb. *kidebareka*]" (v. 20); somewhat more freely: "as you requested/asked" (CEB, CJB, ERV, etc.). Here again, God's forgiveness is, as he says explicitly, the direct consequence of Moses' intercession. The decretalist position requires one to argue that this cannot be literally true: God did not pardon "according to" Moses' plea but because he had decreed so from eternity. God expresses himself here inadequately; decretalists pretend they know better. Even if both Moses' plea and God's response had been foreordained, it is still incorrect to say that God pardoned "according to" Moses' plea (i.e., as Moses requested).

By the way, the reverse also occurs with Moses, namely, no positive response by God: after he has protested for some time against being sent by God, the LORD changes his plan, and sends Aaron with Moses to be his spokesman (Exod. 4:10-17). Here again, it turns out that God can "change his mind," and do so as a response to Moses' (negative) plea, but different from what Moses had imagined. The similarity is this: in both cases, in answer to Moses' plea, God changes the *way* through which he realizes his immutable *counsel*.

We are also impressed by those cases in which after powerful intercession God suspends a judgment that had just begun. Thus it happened that, when as a punishment God sent the "fire of the LORD" into the camp, Moses began to intercede: "Then the people cried out to Moses, and Moses prayed to the LORD, and the fire died down" (Num. 11:1-2). On another occasion, God sent a plague among the people by which many were killed. At Moses' command, Aaron took a censer with incense, and with the censer he moved among the people as though in a silent entreaty. As a consequence, a separation was made between those who were killed and those who were spared (16:46-48).

8.3.2 Jonah

Another remarkable example is found in the history of Jonah. Through him, God had clearly announced to the Ninevites: "Yet forty days, and Nineveh shall be overthrown!" (Jonah 3:4). It is hardly appropriate to turn this into a conditional announcement of judgment, if the text does not do so. On the contrary, the judgment was so certain that even a date could be attached to it: it will come after exactly forty days (and the next day Jonah could say, "Thirty-nine days to go"). Of course, one could argue: why else would God send Jonah to the Ninevites except to implicitly call them to repentance? In itself this is true. But it does not explain the language of the text concerning God's relenting. When the Ninevites repented massively and radically, and called "out mightily to God" (v. 8), we again hear this remarkable saying: "When God saw what they did, how they turned from their evil way, God relented of the disaster that he had said he would do to them, and he did not do it" (v. 10).

Again, many translations render "God relented" as "God changed his mind," like the GNT: "God saw what they did; he saw that they had given up their wicked behavior. So he changed his mind and did not punish them as he had said he would." This gives us quite a different picture than that of God just putting the Ninevites to the test as if he wanted to save the city anyway if only the people would repent. If Jonah's message was nothing but an implicit appeal to repentance, there is no plausible explanation for God *relenting* ("changing his mind") because, in that case, his "mind" had all the time been turned toward saving the Ninevites.

It is remarkable to see that apparently the Ninevites were no decretalists or fatalists, filled with idle resignation. On the contrary. No matter how firm and definitive the judgment seemed to be, even in terms of its precise date, they nevertheless reckoned with the possibility that God could be persuaded: "Who knows? God may turn and relent and turn from his fierce anger, so that we may not perish" (v. 9). In other words, although they were pagans, they had some awareness of the God of gods—just as the mariners in chapter 1:14-16—and believed in the power and the meaning of prayer, more than some Christians seem to do.

It is the grumbling Jonah who reluctantly shows that God's "capacity to be persuaded" is a characteristic of his being: "I knew that you are a gracious God and merciful, slow to anger and abounding in steadfast love, and relenting from disaster" (4:2). Concerning this, Henry Ellison says that, when God does not do what he had said he would do, we finite people can only say that he changed his mind or felt sorry, even though we, with Jonah (4:2), would acknowledge that he had already intended or desired this all the time.[12] This seems correct as long as we keep in mind the essential difference between a God desiring a certain outcome, and a God decreeing that outcome. God's relenting fits with his desiring, not with his supposed decreeing.

This point must be very clear. Jonah knew God, and we may assume that he constantly foresaw the *possibility* that God would finally show mercy to the Ninevites. It was even likely that a merciful God would allow himself to be persuaded by

---

12. Ellison (1985, 383–84).

the pleas of the Ninevites. But this does not imply that God had *foreordained* both the announcement of judgment and the conversion of the Ninevites as well as the cancelling of the judgment. On the contrary. This conclusion reads into the text something it does not say. By referring to "finite people," Ellison seems to suggest that *behind* what "finite people" can see there is something hidden that in fact makes the text say the opposite of what it actually says. But no, perhaps the "finite people" are right after all in taking the text at face value: God *said* he would do P, but then he changed his mind, and did non-P because the people entreated him.

8.4 Other Examples
8.4.1 Kings David, Solomon, Rehoboam

As the plague approached Jerusalem in punishment for his sin (2 Sam. 24:17–25), king David pleaded with the Lord: "Then David spoke to the LORD when he saw the angel who was striking the people, and said, 'Behold, I have sinned, and I have done wickedly. But these sheep, what have they done? Please let your hand be against me and against my father's house.'" This caused God to stop the plague and deliver the city. The version of Chronicles states, "And God sent the angel to Jerusalem *to destroy it*, but as he was about to destroy it, the LORD saw, and he *relented* from the calamity. And he said to the angel who was working destruction, 'It is enough; now stay your hand'" (1 Chron. 21:15). After taking a second look, God changed his mind (as many translations have it). Do we really have to believe here, in an attempt to rescue our own dogma, that God had *all along* intended to spare the city? If this is so, Scripture is simply not telling us the truth: in this case, the angel did *not* go to Jerusalem "to destroy it," and God did not "relent" (in any sense of this word) after David's confession.[13]

The truth that the text suggests instead is the general pattern that we find in similar situations: human sin is followed

---

13. Boyd (2000, 81–82).

by the firm announcement of divine judgment, which occasions repentance and supplication, in response to which God "changes his mind" and does not execute the judgment he had announced earlier.

As a general principle, God told king Solomon: "I have heard your prayer and have chosen this place for myself as a house of sacrifice. When I shut up the heavens so that there is no rain, or command the locust to devour the land, or send pestilence among my people, if my people who are called by my name *humble themselves, and pray and seek my face* and turn from their wicked ways, then I will hear from heaven and will forgive their sin and heal their land" (2 Chron. 7:12-14). The same was true for king David, when the plague was approaching Jerusalem (2 Sam. 24:17-25), and for king Ahab, after God had pronounced judgment upon him (1 Kings 21:27-29). The prophet Amos, too, managed to bring about deliverance of the people by his entreaties to God (Amos 7:1-6).

During the rule of king Rehoboam, Pharaoh Shishak came up against Israel but, after Rehoboam and the leaders of Israel had humbled themselves before God, God's wrath turned away, "so as not to make a complete destruction" (2 Chron. 12:1-12). In all these cases there is a clear causal relationship: sin → the announcement of judgment → repentance and supplication → God "changes his mind," and stops/diminishes/interrupts the judgment that he had announced earlier.

The opposite causal relationship exists as well. We read concerning the priest Eli: "Therefore the Lord, the God of Israel, declares: 'I promised that your house and the house of your father should go in and out before me forever,' *but now* [i.e., after the sins of your sons] the Lord declares: 'Far be it from me, for those who honor me I will honor, and those who despise me shall be lightly esteemed. Behold, the days are coming when I will cut off your strength and the strength of your father's house, so that there will not be an old man in your house" (1 Sam. 2:30-31). Apparently, God had made favorable promises to the house of Eli (in spite of its having descended from Aaron's youngest son Ithamar[14]), but because it despised God's sacrifices God "changed his mind," and eventually brought this house to an end. (This took a while, though: the last high priest from the house of Eli was his great-great-grandson Abiathar, who deserted Solomon and was replaced by Zadok, from the house of Aaron's son Eleazar; 1 Kings 2:27.)

8.4.2 King Hezekiah

About king Hezekiah we read at a much later point in time, "Did he not fear the LORD and entreat the favor of the LORD, and did not the LORD relent of the disaster that he had pronounced against them [i.e., Israel]?" (Jer. 26:19), namely, by granting them deliverance against Assyria. Judgment was approaching, the king humbled himself and pleaded with the LORD, and God "changed his mind," and withheld the judgment from him.

Another important moment in Hezekiah's life is relevant here (2 Kings 20:1-6; cf. Isa. 38:1-6). This event seems to illustrate — as decretalists would like to suggest — that God sometimes makes firm statements only to test a person. Through the prophet Isaiah, God told the king, "Set your house in order, for you shall die, you shall not recover" (2 Kings 20:1). Notice the emphasis in these words: not only "you shall die," but also the additional "you shall not recover." It is difficult to uncover some surreptitious condition here. Nevertheless, Hezekiah immediately addressed an intense and emotional supplication to God: "Then Hezekiah turned his face to the wall and prayed to the LORD, saying, 'Now, O LORD, please remember how I have walked before you in faithfulness and with a whole heart, and have done what is good in your sight.' And Hezekiah wept bitterly" (vv. 2–3). This plea was successful, for God let him know almost immediately: "I have heard

---

14. Eli's great-grandson Ahimelech (Exod. 6:23; 1 Sam. 14:3; 22:9, 11, 20) is said to belong to the "sons of Ithamar" (1 Sam. 24:1–3).

your prayer; I have seen your tears. Behold, I will heal you. On the third day you shall go up to the house of the Lord, and I will add fifteen years to your life" (vv. 5-6). Here again, the causal relationship cannot be denied: *because of* Hezekiah's prayer and tears God *added* to his life fifteen years.

By the way, it is remarkable that the first thing Calvin noticed on Hezekiah's part was—in a typically Calvinistic way, as we would say today—resignation:[15] supposedly, Hezekiah considered resignation to be his first duty. He showed this resignation immediately by turning his face away from Isaiah, and to the wall. Only a genuine "resignation theologian" could spot resignation here. Personally, I see no resignation at all, but rather an active wrestling with God in order to make him change his mind.

Commentator John Oswalt said,

> It is evident that Hezekiah knew something of God's character that Moses also knew (Exod. 32:7-14): God is always ready to be entreated. He is unchanging in his intention to bless his creatures and is willing to change his word if people turn to him in intensity of faith (Jon. 4:2). This does not mean that matters will always turn out as *we* wish. But it does mean that prayer can change the course of events, and that failure to pray is not necessarily a sign of submission to God's intractable will. Rather, it may be a sign of apathy and unwillingness to wrestle with God (note Jacob's refusal to let go of the man with whom he wrestled, Gen. 32:26).[16]

It is beautiful to see how Oswalt offers here an original thought about God's immutability: "He is unchanging in his intention to bless his creatures"—and, to this end, he is prepared to renounce earlier statements. In other words, God is willing to change his mind because of his unchangeable love.

We should realize here that whatever interpretation we prefer does not make the context any easier. The text seems

---

15. Calvin (1999a, ad loc.).
16. Oswalt (1986, 675).

to suggest that it was God's decision to save the people of Judah from the Assyrians, but that he apparently would rather do this through Hezekiah's son, Manasseh. However, after the king's entreaty God changed his mind: "I will add fifteen years to your life. I will deliver you and this city out of the hand of the king of Assyria, and I will defend this city for my own sake and for my servant David's sake" (v. 6). Apparently, it was his new plan that Hezekiah would be the one who would be delivered by God from the Assyrians. So, if Hezekiah had died (in 2 Kings 20), what would have become of the house of David, and of Israel as a whole? The program and the person of God were at stake, and Hezekiah believed that in some way his involvement in this was vital.[17] Did he perhaps realize what kind of wicked king his son Manasseh was going to be (2 Kings 21)? Was his prayer in fact: LORD, deliver my people through me, not through my son? Maybe—but this is half of the story. If Hezekiah had indeed died at this moment, he would not have had to undergo the humiliating experience of 2 Kings 20:12-19, when he vainly displayed his treasury to Babylon's envoys, and had to learn how God would punish this: with the people's exile to this very same Babylon.

The story reminds us of the fact that sometimes "we do not know what to pray for as we ought" (Rom. 8:26). What would have been the course of Judah's history if Hezekiah had died before 2 Kings 20:12? And how was this history affected by the LORD adding fifteen years to his life? What would have been the better choice? Fortunately, we do not really need to know that. We boldly pray to God whatever prayer we think best ("in everything . . . let your requests be made known to God," Phil. 4:6). And at the same time, we are convinced that, though the Lord may change his ways, he will always reach his decreed goal: "[W]e know that for those who love God all things work together for good, for those who are called according to his purpose" (Rom. 8:29).

---

17. So Patterson and Austel (1988, 272); cf. Alexander (1980, 77); Bultema (1981, 347).

8.4.3 Not Granting One's Prayer

Of course, there are also cases in which God does *not* grant what the praying believer has requested. After God had said that he regretted having made Saul king, we read: "And Samuel was angry [other translations: sad, moved, upset], and he cried to the LORD all night" (1 Sam. 15:11)—apparently without any result. Perhaps we may say that in this case not just God's ways but God's counsel were at stake. Appointing the house of David had been in his mind all along. Saul was allowed to rule first—a king after the people's heart—before God appointed David, the man after *his* heart (1 Sam. 13:14; Acts 13:22).

Of Bathsheba's child we read, "And the LORD afflicted the child . . . and he became sick. David therefore sought God on behalf of the child. And David fasted and went in and lay all night on the ground. And the elders of his house stood beside him, to raise him from the ground, but he would not, nor did he eat food with them. On the seventh day the child died" (2 Sam. 12:15-18). Here, another aspect seems to be at stake: after Nathan's tale (following upon David's sin with Bathsheba), David had exclaimed: "[T]he man who has done this [i.e., steal the poor man's lamb] deserves to die, and he shall restore the lamb fourfold" (2 Sam. 12:5-6). Indeed, David paid for his crime fourfold by losing four sons during his lifetime: Bathsheba's child, Amnon (2 Sam. 13), Absalom (2 Sam. 18), and Adonijah (1 Kings 2).

Paul was afflicted by a thorn in the flesh (whatever this may mean; there are dozens of explanations[18]), and said of it, "Three times I pleaded with the Lord about this, that it should leave me. But he said to me, 'My grace is sufficient for you, for my power is made perfect in weakness'" (2 Cor. 12:8-9). Paul had to learn the lesson that we have God's "treasure in jars of clay, to show that the surpassing power belongs to God and not to us" (4:7). He could say, "I can do all things" —

---

18. See Ouweneel (2004, 200–203).

but he knew through experience that this was possible only "through him who strengthens me" (Phil. 4:13). Apparently, Paul's prayer was a "wrong" prayer: he had to learn that, the more we become aware of our own weakness (and to this end sometimes "thorns" are needed), the more the Lord can do in and through us (cf. 1 Cor. 2:3–5).

Here are a few other examples, in which God expresses his determined plan with the implication that no supplication will change his mind. God said to the prophet Jeremiah, "Though Moses and Samuel stood before me [in order to intercede], yet my heart would not turn toward this people" (Jer. 15:1). He said to the prophet Ezekiel, "I am the LORD. I have spoken; it [i.e., judgment] shall come to pass; I will do it. I will not go back; I will not spare; I will not relent; according to your ways and your deeds you will be judged" (Ezek. 24:14). And to Zechariah he said, "As I purposed to bring disaster to you when your fathers provoked me to wrath, and I did not relent..." (Zech. 8:14).

In all these cases, entreaties did not have the desired result (God did not relent). But, within the framework of my argument, this is not the real point. What I am arguing is this: both Samuel and David as well as Paul were thoroughly convinced that praying is meaningful, and that an ardent, persistent prayer could cause God to change his mind. When God did reject Saul, when Bathsheba's child did die, and when the thorn in the flesh remained, all three men understood that, in these cases, God did, or would, *not* change his mind. However, this did not at all change the fact that their faith in the power of prayer was justified. The cases mentioned do not demonstrate that God *cannot* change his mind, but that God did not *want* to change his mind.[19]

8.5 God Loves to Act Upon Prayer
8.5.1 "Pray, and You Will Receive"
God loves to bless his people, but he loves in particular to

---
19. Boyd (2000, 79–80).

bless them in answer to their own prayers. As we read in an old German hymn by Paul Gerhardt (*Befiel du deine Wege*): *Es muß erbäten seyn* ("It must be received through prayer"). Elijah had received from God the promise that, if the people would repent, he would grant them rain again (1 Kings 18:1). Yet, after the conversion of the people, Elijah had to pray for rain no fewer than seven times (vv. 42-45). Another example: the LORD told Israel, "This also I will let the house of Israel ask me to do for them: to increase their people like a flock." That is, he will bring about this blessing, but only in answer to Israel's own supplications. In Daniel 9, God gives Daniel an answer after the latter's penance and entreaty. In Mark 10:51 (cf. 6:5-6), Jesus first asks the blind man: "What do you want me to do for you?" And the blind man said to him, "Rabbi, let me recover my sight."[20]

There is no biblical basis for asserting that, in all these cases, God would have granted these blessings anyway, even if his people had not prayed for them. Only on the basis of certain dogmatic prejudices can one claim that sun and moon would have stood still anyway, even if Joshua had not asked for it, or that Joshua's prayer and God's answer were both part of God's eternal decree (Josh. 10:12-14). Only on the basis of certain prejudices can one claim that Hezekiah would have been healed anyway, even if he had not asked for it, or that Hezekiah's prayer and God's answer were both part of God's eternal decree (2 Kings 20:1-6; Isa. 38:5-9). Only on the basis of certain prejudices can one claim that God would have spared the Ninevites anyway, even if they had not called upon God, or that the Ninevites' prayer and God's answer were both part of God's eternal decree (Jonah 3:5-9). *Scripture knows nothing of divinely decreed human prayers.*

First, if the dogmatic prejudices alluded to were correct, in all these cases God's response would not literally be an answer to prayer at all; instead, prayer and response would

---

20. See Ouweneel (2004, 25, 33).

both be part of God's eternal decree. Second, in some cases Scripture tells us explicitly that certain things would *not* have happened if people had not asked for it, or that certain things *would* have happened if people had not prayed against it. Some striking examples are: "You do not have, because you do not ask. You ask and do not receive, because you ask wrongly" (James 4:2–3). James points out here a direct causal relationship between praying and receiving, just as Jesus does: "Ask, and it will be given to you; seek, and you will find; knock, and it will be opened to you. For everyone who asks receives, and the one who seeks finds, and to the one who knocks it will be opened" (Matt. 7:7–8; cf. Luke 11:9–10). Peter would not have walked on the water if he had not asked for it (Matt. 14:28–29). "The effective prayer of a righteous person has great power" (James 5:16 note).

8.5.2 Other Examples

Note the following biblical statements as well: "Delight yourself in the LORD, and he will give you the desires of your heart" (Ps. 37:4). "[I]f two of you agree on earth about anything they ask, it will be done for them by my Father in heaven" (Matt. 18:19). "And whatever you ask in prayer, you will receive, if you have faith" (21:22). "[W]hoever says to this mountain, 'Be taken up and thrown into the sea,' and does not doubt in his heart, but believes that what he says will come to pass, it will be done for him. Therefore I tell you, whatever you ask in prayer, believe that you have received it, and it will be yours" (Mark 11:23–24). "If any of you lacks wisdom, let him ask God, who gives generously to all without reproach, and it will be given him" (James 1:5).

John's writings are especially important: "Whatever you ask in my name, this I will do, that the Father may be glorified in the Son. If you ask me anything in my name, I will do it" (John 14:13–14). "If you abide in me, and my words abide in you, ask whatever you wish, and it will be done for you. . . . I chose you and appointed you that you should go and bear fruit and that your fruit should abide, so that whatever you ask the Father in my name, he may give it to you" (15:7, 16). "[W]hatever you ask of the Father in my name, he will give it to you. Until now you have asked nothing in my name. Ask, and you will receive, that your joy may be full" (16:23-24). "Beloved, if our heart does not condemn us, we have confidence before God; and whatever we ask we receive from him, because we keep his commandments and do what pleases him" (1 John 3:21-22). "And this is the confidence that we have toward him, that if we ask anything according to his will he hears us. And if we know that he hears us in whatever we ask, we know that we have the requests that we have asked of him" (5:14-15).

Jesus said several times that it was the *faith* of a person through which forgiveness (Luke 7:50) or healing was granted to him or her (Matt. 9:22, 29; 15:28; Mark 5:34; 10:52; Luke 8:48; 17:19). It is not the mercy or the sovereign will of God, or of Christ, which in such cases is mentioned as the effective cause of the forgiveness or the healing, although God, of course, is always involved. Rather, it is the confident faith of the person that is underscored. This is quite striking, especially when the *measure* of a person's faith is mentioned: "According to [the measure of] your faith be it done to you" (Matt. 9:29). "O woman, great is your faith! Be it done for you as you desire" (15:28).

Conversely, there are those striking cases in which God, or Jesus, can do little or nothing because there is no faith: Jesus "did not do many mighty works there, because of their unbelief" (Matt. 13:58), or even stronger: "[H]e *could* do no mighty work there, except that he laid his hands on a few sick people and healed them. And he marveled because of their unbelief" (Mark 6:5-6). In other cases, God cannot do anything because nobody asks for it: "He saw that there was no man, and wondered that there was no one to intercede" (Isa. 59:16). If all events that ever occur have been decreed by God from eternity, were Israel's unbelief and this lack of intercessors also decreed by God? But how then could God genuinely "marvel" and "wonder" about things he has decreed himself? And how is it conceivable that Jesus, or God, *cannot* do a thing that he *wants* to do, and is even sad about it? For a decretalist, this must be as astonishing as Luke 13:34, "How often *would* I have gathered your children together as a hen gathers her brood under her wings, and you were not *willing*!" That is, *I* did want your blessing, but *you* do not want such blessing, and therefore it does not happen.

8.5.3   Ezekiel 22

For our purpose, one of the most remarkable passages is undoubtedly Ezekiel 20:30-31, where the LORD says, "And I sought for a man among them who should build up the wall and stand in the breach before me for the land, that I should not destroy it, but I found none. Therefore I have poured out my indignation upon them. I have consumed them with the fire of my wrath. I have returned their way upon their heads." Here we read explicitly that, if only there had been an intercessor for Israel, God would have spared the land. He even *sought* for such an intercessor. But unfortunately, there was none. If there is no prayer, there can be no answer to prayer.

The suggestion coming to us from this passage is that God wants to say: since I could not find an intercessor, I was forced to carry out the judgment I had announced. I had no way out. There was no Abraham (Gen. 18), no Moses (Exod. 32), nor a Daniel (Dan. 9), who stood in the breach, so that God could have turned away, or could have terminated, his judgment. I know no passage in the Bible that declares more clearly than Ezekiel 22 this important truth: the future has not been entirely decreed, for God has made it partially dependent on intercessors. To be sure, these can never change God's *counsel*. But they can definitely change the *ways* through which he realizes his counsel. Apparently, it is possible that God sometimes wishes that things would follow course P, whereas in reality they follow course Q, as a consequence of the prayers of people, *or* of the absence of prayers.[21]

Some people have expressed the opinion that this passage is in conflict with Ezekiel 14:12–20, where it is said that even a man like Noah, Daniel, or Job by his personal righteousness would not be able to save the people. However, in Ezekiel 22 the point is not the personal righteousness of the intercessor but his intercession as such. As Ralph Alexander suggests, in chapter 20 Ezekiel wanted to say "that there was no person to take the lead and lead the nation into confession and a resulting righteous life among the people that would turn away God's wrath."[22]

To a certain extent, the expression "standing in the breach" could be taken literally. That is, God sought a man who, with his own body, could close the breach in the wall, and could stop the enemy. Therefore, Arie Noordtzij thinks in our passage of a "savior" rather than an "advocate."[23] Ultimately, Christ is the Man who "stood in the breach" for his people, and thus saved them from God's judgment. In this, he was not only Savior but also Advocate: "Father, forgive them, for they know not what they do" (Luke 23:34). Sometimes the savior and the advocate are distinct: "And the anger of the LORD was kindled against Israel, and he gave them continually into the hand of Hazael king of Syria and into the hand of Ben-hadad the son of Hazael. Then Jehoahaz sought the favor of the LORD, and the LORD listened to him, for he saw the oppression of Israel, how the king of Syria oppressed them. (Therefore the LORD gave Israel a savior, so that they escaped from the hand of the Syrians, and the people of Israel lived in their homes as formerly" (2 Kings 13:3–5).

In the Bible, the mediator can be both savior and advocate. The notion of a mediator as such already presupposes, as (Reformed) Mart-Jan Paul and others rightly indicate, "that God's plan is changeable (Gen. 6:6; Jon. 3:10). This seems to be

---

21. Cf. Boyd (2001, 107).
22. Alexander (1986, 850).
23. Noordtzij (1932, 245).

in conflict with the dogma of God's immutability. In the end, this contrast is a false contrast. God is unchangeable in the sense that he never lies (1 Sam. 15:29), but he does respond to prayer.... On the one hand, God oversees the course of history, and on the other hand, he allows himself be persuaded by those who seek him with an upright heart."[24] Personally, I would locate God's unchangeability (immutability) in the fact that he never acts contrary to his own immutable being—but for the rest Paul and others are perfectly right: God responds to prayer, and allows himself to be persuaded, especially by the prayers of intercessors.

8.6 Special Circumstances
8.6.1 Worship: Old Testament

In German, the word for "to pray" is *beten*, and "to worship" is *anbeten*, and in Dutch these words are *bidden* and *aanbidden*, respectively. In the English language, there is no such word pair. In Hebrew, there is bit of such a connection. One of the words for "to pray" is *'atar* (see §8.2.2), which in Zephaniah 3:10 is often rendered as "worshiper" (some translations: "suppliant"). The deeper connection between praying and worshiping is this: worshipers receive divine answers: "The one who offers thanksgiving [or, praise] as his sacrifice glorifies me; to one who orders his way rightly I will show the salvation of God!" (Ps. 50:23). Notice the poetic parallelism here: the one who offers praise (the worshiper) is the one who honors God and walks the right way, so that God will show him his (God's) salvation.

The significance of this becomes apparent in our spiritual warfare (see the next chapter). Worship, and more broadly, prayer, involve *power* in battle. The Hebrew *'oz*, "strength, power," is found, for instance, in this appeal: "Ascribe ... to the LORD glory and strength" (Ps. 29:1; 96:7; cf. 68:34). The Septuagint renders *'oz* here not as "strength" (e.g., *ischus*, *kratos*) but as "honor" (*timē*) or "glory" (*doxa*). Thus, Psalm 8:2

---

24. Paul et al. (2004, 887).

says, "Out of the mouth of babies and infants, you have established strength ['*oz*] because of your foes, to still the enemy and the avenger," where "strength" is quite appropriate because the text refers to enemies, and thus to warfare. However, the Septuagint says (and it is rendered this way in Matt. 21:16b), "Out of the mouth of infants and nursing babies you have prepared *praise* [Gr. *ainon*]." Apparently, the Septuagint sees a link between praise and strength in battle. Compare here Revelation 1:6, 4:11, 5:12, and 7:12, where words such as *kratos*, *dynamis*, and *ischus* (meaning "strength, power") are sung unto God and/or the Lamb as signs of worship.

Similarly, Psalm 149:5-7 says, "Let the godly exult in glory; let them sing for joy on their beds. Let the *high praises* of God be in their throats and two-edged *swords* in their hands, to execute vengeance on the nations and punishments on the peoples." Praise and battle go hand in hand here. Worship was the actual weapon by which the walls of Jericho were caused to collapse:

> And at the seventh time, when the priests had blown the trumpets, Joshua said to the people, "Shout, for the LORD has given you the city. And the city and all that is within it shall be devoted to the LORD for destruction. . . ." So the people shouted, and the trumpets were blown. As soon as the people heard the sound of the trumpet, the people shouted a great shout, and the wall fell down flat, so that the people went up into the city, every man straight before him, and they captured the city (Josh. 6:16-20).

Here the shouting was not a sign of thankfulness *because* the walls had fallen but, conversely, the walls collapsed, so to speak, *as a consequence of* the shouting.

In the battle of king Jehoshaphat against the Moabites and the Ammonites, there were three consecutive stages in the people's praise (2 Chron. 20): during the preparation for the battle (vv. 18-19), at the moment of the battle (vv. 21-22), and out of thankfulness after the victory (vv. 26-28). By pure praise, in the "heavenly places" a great victory on the enemies was brought about. The middle of the three was the decisive praise:

> And when he [i.e., Jehoshaphat] had taken counsel with the people, he appointed those who were to sing to the LORD and praise him in holy attire, as they went before the army, and say, "Give thanks to the LORD, for his steadfast love endures forever." And when they began to sing and praise, the LORD set an ambush against the men of Ammon, Moab, and Mount Seir, who had come against Judah, so that they were routed (vv. 21-22).

Compare here Isaiah 30:31-32: "The Assyrians will be terror-stricken at the voice of the LORD, when he strikes with his rod. And every stroke of the appointed staff that the LORD lays on them will be to the *sound of tambourines and lyres*. Battling with brandished arm, he will fight with them."

8.6.2 Worship: New Testament

In a sense, we find the same principle of the significance of praise and worship for spiritual warfare in the New Testament: "[I]f all prophesy, and an unbeliever or outsider enters, he is convicted by all, he is called to account by all, the secrets of his heart are disclosed, and so, falling on his face, he will worship God and declare that God is really among you" (1 Cor. 14:24-25). Here, a spiritual victory is gained through all prophesying, which I understand to refer to either singing God's praises in worship or in other ways magnifying God in ecstasy. Compare the original meaning of Hebrew "prophesying": ". . . a group of prophets coming down from the high place with harp, tambourine, flute, and lyre before them, prophesying [NABRE, VOICE: in prophetic ecstasy]" (1 Sam. 10:5); "when they saw the company of the prophets prophesying [ISV: in prophetic ecstasy], . . . the Spirit of God came upon the messengers of Saul, and they also prophesied [ISV: in prophetic ecstasy]" (19:20).

Also compare here David's singers and musicians: "David

and the chiefs of the service also set apart for the service the sons of Asaph, and of Heman, and of Jeduthun, who prophesied with lyres, with harps, and with cymbals" (1 Chron. 25:1). "To prophesy" may be taken here as "to praise" (CEV, etc.) *or* as "to speak God's Word" (NLV).

Such a remarkable effect as described in 1 Corinthians 14:24-25 occurred during the stay of Paul and Silas in the prison of Philippi: "About midnight Paul and Silas were praying and singing hymns to God, and the prisoners were listening to them, and suddenly there was a great earthquake, so that the foundations of the prison were shaken. And immediately all the doors were opened, and everyone's bonds were unfastened," without any of the prisoners escaping (Acts 16:25-28). There seems to be a causal relationship between Paul's and Silas' worshiping and the earthquake. This physical effect reminds us of Acts 4:31, "And when they [i.e., the early Christians in Jerusalem] had prayed, the place in which they were gathered together was shaken, and they were all filled with the Holy Spirit."

Prayer and praise really do have an effect in the heavenly places (cf. Deut. 26:15; 1 Kings 8:30-49 [8x "then hear in heaven"]; 2 Chron. 30:27; Ps. 68:5) — and sometimes also on earth in the spiritual warfare that believes must wage.

8.6.3 "Stop Praying!"

Prayer is tremendously important. It is not just a duty, an act of obedience, but it can really make a difference. It plays a vital role in the *ways* of God, as Viatorism emphasizes. Prayer cannot change God's counsel; for instance, it is no use praying that God will make sure that Satan will ultimately be saved (cf. Matt. 25:41). But prayer can influence God's ways. God can change his ways because of (good, but often wrong) choices by people, but also because of their prayers. Scripture is very clear about the fact that, because of his people's prayers, God changes his ways sometimes such that otherwise, without those prayers, some events would not have happened.

However, it is also important to realize that sometimes prayer is *not* appropriate or no longer appropriate, especially in three cases. First, we sometimes pray in the wrong way (cf. James 4:3), as we ought to know very well, so we should immediately stop doing so. Second, we should no longer pray if it is clear that we ourselves should become active. Third, it is no use praying if a matter is well-determined with God and can no longer be changed (please note, I am still speaking of his ways, not his counsel). Let me give some examples of all three cases.

First, there is the warning example of the Israelites, who commanded Moses, and thus the LORD, in a threatening way to bring them meat (Num. 11:1–15). Psalm 78 described what then happened: God "rained meat on them like dust, winged birds like the sand of the seas. . . And they ate and were well filled, for *he gave them what they craved*. But before they had satisfied their craving, while the food was still in their mouths, the anger of God rose against them, and he killed the strongest of them and laid low the young men of Israel" (vv. 27–31; cf. §8.2.3). Here, a rebellious prayer aroused God's wrath: he gave them what they had asked for, but in such a way that he caused them to bear the consequences of their sinful prayer. We cannot ask God *anything* as though he must give us whatever we claim from him. *Sinful* prayers can be answered by God in a disastrous way, which actually has the character of a judgment.

An example of the second case that I mentioned, namely, in which people themselves must take action, is found at the Red Sea: "The LORD said to Moses, 'Why do you cry to me? Tell the people of Israel to go forward. Lift up your staff, and stretch out your hand over the sea and divide it, that the people of Israel may go through the sea on dry ground'" (Exod. 14:15–16). The reason why Moses must stop crying to God is that he himself must *do* something. Asking God to do something for a person may return as a boomerang on this person's own head: he himself is the instrument through whom

God wants to work (cf. Jesus' feeding the five thousand: "[T]he disciples came to him and said, 'This is a desolate place, and the day is now over; send the crowds away to go into the villages and buy food for themselves.' But Jesus said, 'They need not go away; *you* give them something to eat'" Matt. 14:15–16).

This is a general principle: I cannot pray for the salvation of my relative or neighbor if I myself am not willing to become a witness to that person. This being God's instrument suggests that, if another person had prayed this prayer, *that* person would have been chosen as God's instrument. This is not the eternal election of God's *counsel* but an election within time, as part of God's *ways*. A striking example is Esther, to whom Mordecai says, "[I]f *you* keep silent at this time, relief and deliverance will rise for the Jews from *another place* [i.e., God and/or another human instrument], but you and your father's house will perish. And who knows whether you have not come to the kingdom for such a time as this?" (Esther 4:14).

Moses must stop crying to the LORD, and take action by splitting the Red Sea with his staff. In a similar way, Joshua, too, receives the command to stop praying and allow himself to be used as a tool in God's hand: "The LORD said to Joshua, 'Get up! Why have you fallen on your face? Israel has sinned; they have transgressed my covenant that I commanded them; they have taken some of the devoted things; they have stolen and lied and put them among their own belongings'" (Josh. 7:10–11). Here again, we find the explicit command to stop praying, and to begin acting. Here again, it is the praying person himself who becomes the instrument in God's hand, in this case to track down the malefactor who had brought a curse on Israel, and to execute God's judgment upon him.

8.6.4 God Refuses to Listen

A poignant example of the third case (it is no use praying if a matter is well-determined with God and can no longer be changed) is found in Jeremiah 7:16, "As for you, do not pray for this people, or lift up a cry or prayer for them, and do not intercede with me, for I will not hear you" (cf. almost the same words in 11:14; also cf. 14:11) — followed by an enumeration of Israel's sins. Here prayer is no longer appropriate because God has definitively decided to bring judgment upon the people: "[T]hus says the LORD, 'The whole land shall be a desolation; yet I will not make a full end. For this the earth shall mourn, and the heavens above be dark; for I have spoken; I have purposed; I have not relented, nor will I turn back'" (4:27-28).

In Jeremiah 15:1, the Lord says, "Though Moses and Samuel stood before me, yet my heart would not turn toward this people. Send them out of my sight, and let them go!" These words are similar to those of Ezekiel 14:13-14, "Son of man, when a land sins against me by acting faithlessly, and I stretch out my hand against it and break its supply of bread and send famine upon it, and cut off from it man and beast, even if these three men, Noah, Daniel, and Job, were in it, they would deliver but their own lives by their righteousness, declares the LORD God."

Another example of this third case is that of Paul: "So to keep me from becoming conceited because of the surpassing greatness of the revelations, a thorn was given me in the flesh [see §8.4.3], a messenger of Satan to harass me, to keep me from becoming conceited. Three times I pleaded with the Lord about this, that it should leave me. But he said to me, 'My grace is sufficient for you, for my power is made perfect in weakness'" (2 Cor. 12:7-9a). Apparently, in this case, too, not only the counsel but also the ways of the Lord were unchangeable. The Lord explained to Paul the purpose of this thorn, after which Paul says, "Therefore I will boast all the more gladly of my weaknesses, so that the power of Christ may rest upon me" (v. 9b).

This threefold prayer of Paul is comparable to the threefold prayer of Jesus in Gethsemane: "And going a little farther he fell on his face and prayed, saying, 'My Father, if it be possible, let this cup pass from me; nevertheless, not as I will, but as you will.' . . . Again, for the second time, he went away and prayed, 'My Father, if this cannot pass unless I drink it, your will be done' . . . he went away and prayed for the third time, saying the same words again" (Matt. 26:39, 42, 44). Of course, Jesus knew all along the *counsel* of God with respect to him (cf. Acts 2:23), but he could nevertheless pray concerning the *ways* of the Father to reach his goal. God's counsel is unchangeable but his ways are changeable. Here, too, however, it turned out that the way that the Father wanted to go with him was different from what Jesus asked. One could say that the Father did not grant him what he had prayed; one could also say that the Father did grant him what he had prayed, for the Father's will was done.

8.7 The Ministry of Healing[25]
8.7.1 The Role of Prayer

As far as the role of prayer is concerned, we find quite a peculiar situation in the ministry of healing that Jesus granted his followers. He told his twelve disciples, "Heal the sick, raise the dead, cleanse lepers" (Matt. 10:8), and to the seventy(-two) (that is, not only to the twelve apostles!) he said, "Whenever you enter a town . . . [h]eal the sick in it and say to them, 'The kingdom of God has come near to you'" (Luke 10:8-9). This imperative "heal!" is encountered as an indicative in Mark 6:13, "And they cast out many demons and anointed with oil many who were sick and *healed* them." Similarly, it is stated as a fact in 16:17-18, "And these signs will accompany those who believe: . . . they will lay their hands on the sick, and they will recover."

This is quite peculiar. After the anointing of the sick or the laying on of hands on the sick, the healing follows without any mentioning of prayer. Jesus himself is the great example.

---
25. See extensively, Ouweneel (2004).

When or where did Jesus ever pray for the sick? Where did he tell his followers that they had to do so? When did the apostles ever do so? Just as Jesus often did (Mark 1:41; 2:11; 3:5; 5:41; 7:34), they simply spoke the word of power: "In the name of Jesus Christ of Nazareth, rise up and walk!" (Acts 3:6). "Aeneas, Jesus Christ heals you; rise and make your bed" (9:34). "Tabitha, arise" (v. 40). "Stand upright on your feet" (14:10). "I command you [i.e., an evil spirit] in the name of Jesus Christ to come out of her" (16:18).

At most one could point to John 11:41–42, where Jesus was at the tomb of Lazarus: "Jesus lifted up his eyes and said, 'Father, I thank you that you have heard me. I knew that you always hear me, but I said this on account of the people standing around, that they may believe that you sent me.'" This is not a prayer for the raising of Lazarus, though, but only an expression of his dependence, and this not primarily for himself but for the crowd (cf. Mark 6:34, "When he went ashore he saw a great crowd, and he had compassion on them, because they were like sheep without a shepherd," in comparison with v. 41, Jesus "looked up to heaven").

Prayer is mentioned only twice in connection with the ministry of healing, but in both cases, this is only the introduction to the actual ministry. The one case is this: "Paul visited him [i.e., the father of Publius] and prayed, and putting his hands on him healed him" (Acts 28:8b). Notice here again the active "healed him" (Gr. *iasato*), not: "prayed for his healing." Paul was not just a passive intercessor here; he was taking action, though with dependence on the Lord, as was expressed by his act of praying.

The other case is the well-known James 5:14–15, "Is anyone among you sick? Let him call for the elders of the church, and let them pray over him, anointing him with oil in the name of the Lord. And the prayer of faith will save the one who is sick, and the Lord will raise him up." Here again, the prayer is not the main element of the ministry (in spite of v. 16), but the sacramental anointing with oil. And notice here again the active Greek verb *sōsei*, "will save" (here with the sense of: "will heal"). Also in this case, there is no question of any prayer *for* healing, but of anointing and prayer that together *bring about* the healing. There is a great difference between a prayer *for* healing and a prayer that *heals*. In the former case, the praying person is passive; in the second case he is active, although, naturally, in cooperation with the Lord: apparently, the phrase "the *prayer* saves the sick" is just as true as — or even the equivalent of — "the *Lord* raises up the sick."

8.7.2 The Underlying Conflict

Behind this passive or active approach, respectively, we encounter at the deepest level the entire conflict between a strong emphasis, on the one hand, on God's sovereign will and, on the other hand, on human responsibility. Based on the former position, people argue: if God wishes to heal, he will do this anyway, whether we ask for it or not, and if he does not so wish, he will not do it, no matter how fervently we ask for it. Based on the latter position, people argue: listen to the Lord's command: *we* must heal the sick! Of course, we do so with dependence on his authority and in the power of the Holy Spirit, yet *we* must take action.

Where the emphasis lies one-sidedly on divine sovereignty, the tenor of the prayers will be: "[Y]our will be done" (Matt. 6:10; cf. 26:42). In this kind of ministry of healing I have never seen much fruit. The praying persons do not fulfill their responsibility; if healing doesn't happen, then apparently "it was not the will of the Lord." Those who underscore human responsibility in this matter listen to the Lord who once said, "*You* give them something to eat" (Matt. 14:16). Of course, the disciples could give to the crowds only what the Lord had first given to them (v. 19). But this changed neither Jesus' command nor the disciples' responsibility. Similarly, he says, "Heal the sick." What we can give is what we ourselves first received from the Lord; this is what we actively pass on, as Peter said to the paralytic: "I have no silver and gold, but what I *do have* I give to you. In the name of Jesus Christ of Nazareth, rise up and walk!" (Acts 3:6). Also notice verse 16 (CJB): "[I]t is through putting trust in his name that his name has given strength to this man whom you see and know." That is, the Lord did it, but through *our faith* (trust, confidence) in his name.

The former approach says to the Lord, "If you *will* [i.e., *want*], you can make me clean" (Mark 1:40), or, "[I]f you *can* do anything, have compassion on us and help us" (9:22). In the latter approach, the emphasis is on the Lord's response: "'If you can'! All things are possible for one who believes" (v. 23). Here it is not only "all things are possible *with God*" (10:27), but also: all things are possible with those who live by their confidence in God. It is as if the Lord here, too, says, Stop praying, and begin taking action; that is, Use the authority that I have given you (and in principle all other believers), and heal the sick.

In the former approach, supposedly all things, including all diseases, have been decreed from eternity in God's counsel. People pray for the sick, sometimes for years, but they see no result. They pray: ". . . if your counsel allows it" (at least in Dutch: *als het in uw raad kan bestaan*, that is, if the healing was included in your counsel from eternity) — but illness is not at all a matter of God's eternal counsel. Many people suffer illness as a consequence of their medically or spiritually wrong lifestyle. Both sickness and healing are aspects of God's *ways* with people. In these ways, healing is not only a matter of God's sovereign will but also of the responsibility of God's "junior partners," involving both the sick themselves and the ministers of healing, as well as the entire environment of the sick.

Chapter 9
The Problem of Suffering

[L]et us run with endurance
 the race that is set before us,
 looking to Jesus,
the founder and perfecter of our faith,
 who for the joy that was set before him
endured the cross, despising the shame,
 and is seated at the right hand of the throne
  of God.
Hebrews 12:1–2

Beloved, do not be surprised at the fiery trial
 when it comes upon you to test you,
 as though something strange were happening
 to you.
But rejoice insofar as you share Christ's sufferings,
 that you may also rejoice and be glad
 when his glory is revealed.
1 Peter 4:12–13

Summary: *A consideration of suffering cannot be omitted from any discussion of God's counsel and God's ways. Is all suffering God's "will" (i.e., foreordained by him)? Are not people, as well as the dark powers, often directly responsible for much suffering? Have the deeds of these people and powers been foreordained by God? And* *how does human suffering relate to God's omnipotence? How can God be both almighty and loving, given the great amount of human misery? How can God be "fighting" evil if he foreordained it himself, and is almighty? And if **we** fight evil, are we then fighting the One who foreordained it? How does suffering fit into the ways of God through which he attains the goals of his counsel? Are they just a nuisance, or do they play their own vital role in these ways? In what way are human sufferings a divine "test," and what light does the book of Job cast on this subject? And what is the relationship between God and Satan in the sufferings that are part of God's ways with the world?*

9.1 The Decretalist's Answer to Suffering
9.1.1 "It Is God's Will"

MANY ASPECTS OF THE COUNSEL of God and of the relationship between divine sovereignty and human responsibility will be discussed in chapters 10–14 (on the doctrine of predestination). At this point, we must pay some attention to the question of suffering in the world, since it relates directly to the relationship just mentioned.[1]

Because of deep-rooted human sinfulness, which is directed especially against fellow people, there is incalculable suffering in the world. However, this is not the only cause of suffering; much suffering in the world is caused not by sinful behavior but, for instance, by diseases, famines, and natural catastrophes. Those who view God through a decretalist lens seem unable to escape the consequence that this God is responsible for all that suffering: he is the direct cause of these diseases, famines, etc. If even the sinful behavior of people was foreordained by God, then God is in fact the ultimate cause of all human suffering, either through human sins or through natural catastrophes.

A striking example of such a consistent decretalist approach was Reformed theologian and philosopher Gordon

---

1. See also Ouweneel (2004, §3.4; 2005, chapter 11). A classic on this topic is still Lewis (2014).

Clark (d. 1985). He emphatically stated that, if a man gets drunk and shoots his family, it was the will of God that he would do so. He added that it might seem strange that God would decree an immoral deed, but the Bible shows that he did so.[2] This is decretalism to the core: in the end there is only one cause, direct or indirect, of all events that occur: God. He not only caused all events, he even decreed them from before the foundation of the world, from all eternity.

At first glance, the Heidelberg Catechism seems to move in the same direction by speaking of the "almighty, every-where-present power of God (Acts 17:25-26), whereby, as it were by His hand, He still upholds heaven and earth with all creatures (Heb. 1:3), and so governs them that herbs and grass, rain *and drought*, fruitful *and barren* years, meat and drink (Jer. 5:24), health *and sickness* (John 9:3), riches *and poverty* (Prov. 22:2), indeed, all things come not by chance, but by His fatherly hand."[3] Only two options are mentioned here: things come to us either by chance, or by God's fatherly hand. Left unmentioned are two other possibilities: things are caused by people or by the dark powers. It is either fate or God — *tertium non datur* (no third possibility is given).

9.1.2 Consolation of the Sick

Quite peculiar is the *Sieckentroost* ("Consolation of the Sick") by Reformed pastor Cornelis van Hille in the Netherlands (1571), which can still be found in many Dutch church Bibles.[4] The full title of this pamphlet is: "Consolation of the Sick, Which Is an Instruction in the Right Faith, in the Way of Salvation, in Order to Die Pliantly." Notice especially these last words: the aim of the booklet is to help people "to die pliantly." The words "sickness," "illness," or "disease" do not occur any further in the text, nor does the word "healing." It is

---

2. Clark (1961, 221–22).
3. Dennison (*RCET* 4:776; italics added); Heidelberg Catechism, Q&A 27; see Ouweneel (2016a).
4. Republished by Van Hille (n.d.).

assumed to be self-evident that the patient's illness will end in death, and the author endeavors to help him find the way of salvation before it is forever too late. The argument is this: one day we all have to die, and the moment when this will happen has been decreed by God (remarkably, Van Hille himself died when he was only about thirty-nine). Since, because of sin, earthly life is miserable, people can do no better than to yearn for death—but then a death in Christ, the Redeemer. Therefore, the patient must yearn to receive forgiveness and redemption. In this case, death will no longer be an abomination but the entrance to heavenly blessedness.

Van Hille describes extensively that here on earth the believer has been destined to share the sufferings of Christ. Without exception, the Bible passages that he quotes to demonstrate this refer to persecutions and tribulations because of faith. Without the slightest theological justification, the author implicitly applies these same passages to illnesses and diseases.[5] In the latter, the sufferer must fight against the devil's temptations, he must be watchful, and he must live by his saving faith. In the end, these sufferings lead to death, but this death takes the believer into the glory, and ultimately to resurrection. So there is nothing to worry about: the best thing that can happen to the sick believer is that he will die to be with the Lord.

A strange argument. The *only* consolation offered here is that if the sick person believes in Christ, he may know that he will go to heaven when he dies. Suffering is part of life as God has arranged it, but that does not matter, for death ushers the patient immediately into eternal blessedness. Not a word about the sacrament of anointing the sick (James 5:14-16), or about possible healing, either natural or supernatural healing, and even less about longing for being healed. Healing is entirely beyond the author's scope. If the sick person is healed, he should almost regret it, for it means that his entrance into

---

5. On the fundamental difference between suffering in the form of disease and suffering in the form of persecution, see Ouweneel (2004, 101–103).

glory is delayed.

Here, we recognize decretalism again, if not fatalism (a word coming from Latin *fatum*, "fate, destiny"). Sickness and other sufferings are means in God's hand to bring the believer to himself in the glory. As long as the sick person comes to faith, everything is all right. He is like clay in the potter's hands. No striving for healing, no fighting against the illness — that would almost be like fighting against God. Isn't it all part of God's plan? The day of one's death has been determined by the Lord from eternity![6] If the person is healed, this is simply part of God's plan as well: apparently, the day of his blessed passing away has not yet arrived. Resignation is the message, with regard to both the illness and its healing. All those sufferings are part of life; already now, you may rejoice in your blissful death. Submit to God's counsel.

9.1.3 Who Is Responsible?

The decretalistic view of things has far-reaching consequences. The Heidelberg Catechism and the *Sieckentroost* originated in the sixteenth century. Would their authors, if they had been alive in our day, have written just as straightforwardly that the Holocaust came upon the Jews "by God's fatherly hand"? Would this not engender serious doubt about God's love and goodness? Moreover, if anyone dares to say such a thing, he must also hint at what could have been the possible "divine goal" of the Holocaust. To be sure, without the Holocaust presumably there would have been no revival of the Jewish identity and no state of Israel. But could God not have reached these valuable goals without the horrible sacrifice of six million innocent victims?[7] And a serious ancillary question that always arises in this context is: How can we maintain the responsibility of the Nazis if everything they did had been foreordained by God from eternity?

With the approach of Viatorism, criminals are held fully

---

6. See §3.2.1 for a more biblical view of a person's "decreed" lifetime.
7. On this see extensively, Ouweneel (2000a).

responsible, their crimes are in no sense part of God's counsel, and we do not need to look for some sense or meaning for these crimes in the ways of God, in order to vindicate God. Sometimes we simply must say with the "master of the house": "An enemy has done this" (Matt. 13:28) — that is, not the master of the house has done it, and even less God.[8] We cannot even say that the master of the house had *allowed* it. Similarly, we must sometimes say that not God but *Satan* has done this or that: "[W]e wanted to come to you — I, Paul, again and again — but *Satan* hindered us" (1 Thess. 2:18), that is, not God. One may add that God permitted it — although the text does not say so — as long as we keep in mind that in this case Satan was the primary agent.

Atrocities are not consequences of God's will; nor were they planned by God. They are consequences of the freedom of will that God has granted his creatures, both people and the spiritual powers. Such crimes belong to the profoundly dark elements of history. On the one hand, God has sovereignly made this freedom of will possible. But on the other hand, in his ways with the world, he is also fighting against the powers of evil — both in the heavenly places and on earth — in order to ultimately and omnipotently realize his glorious *counsel*, in spite of all human sins, and to a certain extent, even *through* all these sins. He is not responsible for these crimes, and he did not foreordain them; but he can use them if and when they occur.

9.2 Omnipotence versus Love
9.2.1 Four Options

Since the earliest days of Christianity, thinkers have pondered the question of *theodicy* (from Gr. *theos*, "God," and *dikē*, "justice"), the "vindication" or "justification of God," that is, the attempt to exculpate a God who is supposed to be both almighty and loving, and thus both able and willing to destroy evil, and yet tolerates evil. Many have undertaken more or

---

8. See extensively, Boyd (2001, chapter 10).

less successful attempts to design such a theodicy, but these have yielded a dilemma that has been beautifully formulated by the French-Dutch Huguenot Pierre Bayle (1647–1706).[9] This dilemma contains the following elements:

(a) Either God is indeed almighty but not loving, for he is able but apparently unwilling to destroy evil. Genuine adherents of this view are hard to find, because even the most outspoken decretalist will never deny the love of God, which is referred to so many times in the Bible.

(b) Or God is loving but not almighty, for he is willing but apparently unable to destroy evil.[10] This view has been defended by Rabbi Harold Kushner (§6.6.1).

(c) Or God is neither loving nor almighty, which means that he cannot actually be called God at all. This view is equivalent to that of atheism.

Yet a fourth possibility is conceivable:

(d) The denial of evil, and thus of the entire problem.[11]

Such a dilemma as posited by Bayle may sound reasonable, but it is based on an over-simplification of the matter. For instance, we must first arrive at a proper definition of "almighty" ("omnipotence," see §7.2). Apparently, Bayle uses the traditional, that is, decretalistic idea of "omnipotence." This is similar to the idea of "sovereignty": God's omnipotence does not mean that God himself has foreordained every event that ever occurs, because this would in effect nullify human responsibility and freedom of will. God has sovereignly chosen to create people who can make their own decisions. Of course, there are many events that are directly brought about by God. And of course, people can make decisions only within the boundaries that God has established for them. But minimally we must say that much evil occurs by people's own free will, without God bearing any responsibility for it.

---

9. Bayle (1995); see Erickson (1998, chapter 20).
10. So Brightman (1940); also see Kushner (1981).
11. So, e.g., the Christian Science movement; cf. Erickson (1998, 445–46).

9.2.2 God Fights Evil

Here we must go one step further. Not only is God not responsible for human misdemeanors, but, as Pinnock wrote, rapes and murders are tragedies that make God cry. He abhors them. God certainly did not send them, and thus he can be "a very present help in trouble" (Ps. 46:1).[12] That is, God does not necessarily first send us trouble in order to subsequently be with us in the trouble. It is similar in Psalm 23:4, "Even though I walk through the valley of the shadow of death, I will fear no evil, for you are with me." The verse is not saying that God causes people to walk through the valley of the shadow of death, but *if* people walk there, God is with them. And Isaiah 43:2 says, "When you pass through the waters, I will be with you; and through the rivers, they shall not overwhelm you; when you walk through fire you shall not be burned, and the flame shall not consume you." The verse is not saying that God causes people to pass through waters or fire—although this is not excluded (cf. Ps. 42:7b)—but that *in* the waters and the fire he is with them.

Troubles (the valley of death, breakers and waves, fire) can come from very different sources: human, demonic, natural; but *in* these troubles believers can always count on God. It was not God but Nebuchadnezzar who had the friends of Daniel thrown into the fiery furnace—but in the fire the Son of God was with them (Dan. 3:25 KJV, etc.). Storms on the Sea of Tiberias are very common and natural—but when a storm struck the boat of the disciples, Jesus was with them in the boat (Mark 4:35-41). Jesus even "rebuked" the wind and the waters, a term often used with respect to demons (4:35, 41; 9:42). It suggests that demonic powers had caused the storm, not God. However, whether the causes are human, demonic, or natural, God (Jesus) is with his people in their troublesome circumstances.

In the summary of Clark Pinnock: God created people

---

12. Pinnock (2001, 47).

in order to develop loving relationships with them. This demanded giving genuine freedom to his creatures, who are not robots, and who, in this way only, are capable of voluntary love.[13] Therefore, Greg Boyd extensively defended the following theses: (a) love must be founded on free choice (enforced love or puppet love is no love), and (b) love entails risks.[14] It is true: freedom implies the risk that love is not requited. God built into the creation the possibility of moral evils and certain natural catastrophes of a seemingly irreparable and demonic nature. However, God does not abandon his world but in Christ promises victory over the powers of darkness.

In such a theodicy, God's omnipotence is guaranteed, for only an almighty God can choose to allow people a certain freedom of will. God's love is guaranteed as well, for without granting people a certain freedom, God's love could not be answered by voluntary love. So rather than human sufferings constituting an argument against God's omnipotence and love, they all fit together within one overarching plan: God's omnipotence is *able* to overcome evil, and God's love *desires* to overcome evil; the only point that has to be added is that it *takes time* to attain this goal, as we will see.

9.2.3 Fighting *and* Permitting Evil

Passages like Isaiah 45:7 ("I create calamity") and Amos 3:6 ("Does disaster come to a city, unless the LORD has done it?") do not mean that *all* catastrophes worldwide are caused by God. Many disasters are the consequences of certain natural laws, but also of human failure, negligence, and sometimes even wicked intentions.

Therefore, it is *not* true that all sufferings befall people directly from God (although they always occur under his permission). The point is that God's omnipotence is not exhibited in all suffering coming from him but rather in his powerful *warfare against* sufferings, though in his manner and *with his*

---

13. Ibid., 131–32.
14. Boyd (2001, especially chapters 2–3).

speed. Every time Jesus healed a sick person, delivered a possessed person, or raised a dead person, he gave a preview of the full salvation that one day will arrive. During the almost two thousand years since his life on earth until today, his followers have experienced thousands of such signs of God's kingdom. God is moving toward the Messianic kingdom, when "no inhabitant will say, 'I am sick'" (Isa. 33:24).

Moreover, it is conceivable that, although an all-good God cannot want evil—as such evil can never be part of his *counsel*—he can certainly make use of this evil as part of his *ways* (cf. Rom. 8:28, "for those who love God all things work together for good"). Thus, it is conceivable that a greater good (a "better world") is attained by tolerating evil to a certain extent and only for a given time; that is, without allowing through his *ways* a certain measure of evil, the realization of his *counsel* is not possible. For instance, people might never truly know righteousness and holiness without having experienced their share of *un*righteousness and *un*holiness. Please notice that before the Fall, Adam and Eve were innocent—but not only did they not yet know evil, they also did not yet know good, either; it was by eating from the tree of the knowledge of good and evil that they began to learn both.

It is also conceivable that what seems to be evil in fact is necessarily part of a greater totality that is good. Or it is conceivable that somehow it conflicts with God's being to eliminate a certain evil, or to eliminate it too soon. For all these options, arguments can be adduced, which we cannot discuss here without moving too far into the arena of the philosophy of religion.

9.3 Divine Arbitrariness?
9.3.1 "Who Can Resist His Will?"

Like the previous "counter-proof," the moral "counter-proof" by the atheist Bertrand Russell (1872–1970), in my view, is based upon an oversimplification of the matter, too.[15]

---

15. See Russell (1970).

Russell's argument is more or less as follows. If the moral law has been instituted by an almighty God, then it is by definition arbitrary, for it could just as well have been a different law, as William of Ockham (c. 1330) believed. In this case, God is not essentially good. If the moral law has not been instituted by God, then it must be a kind of eternal law, as Gottfried W. Leibnitz (c. 1700) believed. In this case, God himself is subject to it, and therefore he cannot be the highest authority. However, a being that is not essentially good or not the highest authority is not worthy to be called God.

The biblical answer to this argument is that the moral law has definitely been instituted by God but is not at all arbitrary. Even an almighty God cannot do just anything, for he cannot act contrary to his own being (see §7.2.2). Therefore, he cannot *want* anything that is contrary to his own being. The moral law is not arbitrary, but issues from God's own moral character. A human being who has been created in the image of God is not allowed to lie, to steal, or to murder, not because God happens to have forbidden this (as if he arbitrarily could have decided otherwise), nor because God *could* not have done otherwise because he was bound to some eternal law, but because lying, stealing, and murdering are contrary to God's holy and righteous being; "no one is good except God alone" (Mark 10:18).

The reproach that there would be arbitrariness in God, especially in the doctrine of election (see chapters 10–14), goes far back in history; we find it in some measure with John Duns Scotus (d. 1308), and especially with William of Ockham (d. 1347).[16] It is related to the reproach referred to in Romans 9:19, "You will say to me then, 'Why does he still find fault? For who can resist his will?'," and verse 20b, "Will what is molded say to its molder, 'Why have you made me like this?'" Paul replies to this by referring not to the unsearchable and unwavering nature of God's counsel, but to the mercy

---

16. See extensively, Berkouwer (1960, chapter 3).

that God shows to all penitent sinners (vv. 23-29).

9.3.2 "Prepared for Destruction/Glory"

We must now pay attention to the following statement: "For he says to Moses, 'I will have mercy on whom I have mercy, and I will have compassion on whom I have compassion.' [Exod. 33:19b] So then it depends not on human will or exertion, but on God, who has mercy" (Rom. 9:15-16). This is not an indication of arbitrariness, either (cf. previous section), but expresses the same thought: on the one hand, mercy and compassion presuppose sin and repentance; on the other hand, hardening presupposes the impenitent nature of people pursuing their own righteousness and rejecting that of God (vv. 30-31; 10:3) (see further §14.3).[17]

Here there is no question at all of some sovereign mercy and hardening *from eternity*. On the contrary, with believers we first encounter sin and repentance, followed by God's mercy. With unbelievers we first encounter their explicit choice for their own righteousness, and against God's righteousness, followed by the hardening of their hearts by God. Why would Paul say that God "has endured with much patience vessels of wrath" (9:22) if these vessels already from eternity had been predestined to destruction in God's own, one-sided, sovereign decree? (Notice the remarkable difference between the passive "prepared for destruction" in v. 22, and the active "which he has prepared beforehand for glory" in v. 23. This passage will play an important role in the following chapters.)

The reproach that there would be arbitrariness in God always tells us more about the person uttering it than about God himself. Gerrit Berkouwer does not hesitate to say that the reproach of arbitrariness with respect to God flows from an evil source.[18] The notion of arbitrariness often contains the reproach that God would be *exlex* (standing outside the

---

17. Ibid., 66–67, 72–73, 77, 124–25.
18. Ibid., 75, 79.

law, being beyond the law; cf. again William of Ockham). In reality, this reproach tacitly presupposes that God would be under a law, for without certain norms, no behavior can be marked as arbitrary: "Only men can act arbitrarily and they do so when their actions do not conform to the norms which God has established for them."[19]

Calvin therefore wrote: "[I]f you proceed further to ask why he so willed, you are seeking something greater and higher than God's will [i.e., a norm or law according to which this will can be judged], which cannot be."[20] In summary, *Deus legibus solutus est, sed non exlex*: God is exalted beyond the laws that he has instituted himself, but he is not lawless, in the sense of arbitrary. Before Calvin, Augustine and Thomas Aquinas had expressed this point that there is indeed logic (*ratio*) in God's will but his will has no reason (*causa*) outside himself.[21]

The *potentia absoluta* ("absolute power") that the nominalists posited in God implies pure arbitrariness, pure power without any content, which is nothing and can become everything.[22] This creates a false image of God. His omnipotence is intrinsically bound to his moral being, his virtues, his consistency. Therefore, nothing in him can be arbitrary. God can do anything except cease to be what he is, that is, act against his own nature.

9.3.3 Priest or Physician?

Equally oversimplified is, in my view, the dilemma posed by the existentialist Albert Camus (1913–1960) in his novel *The Plague* (originally entitled *La Peste* [1947]). The rat-caused bubonic plauge that he describes occasioned the dilemma about how to respond. Should one, for humanitarian reasons, fight alongside the doctor against the plague, or should one, for

---

19. Kalsbeek (1977, 74).
20. Calvin, *Institutes* 3.23.2; cf. Berkouwer (1960, 57–60).
21. Cf. Bavinck (*RD* 2:240).
22. Cf. Weber (1981, 1:403–408, 440–47; especially on Calvin: 448–49).

theistic reasons, maintain along with the priest that fighting against the plague is fighting against God? The conclusion seems to be that people are either humanitarian, and thus cannot be theists, or they are theists, and thus cannot be humanitarian. However, the decisive question is whether the priest was right, that is, whether God was the direct cause of the plague. The answer is: No; usually, such rat infestations result from human ignorance and negligence. Blame belongs not to God, but to people.

A similar discussion arose when in 1953 the southwestern part of the Netherlands was inundated by the sea, which led to 1,836 casualties. Several hyper-Calvinists declared that this was a punishment from God for the many sins of the Dutch. I do not deny these many sins, but the logic is a little awkward.

(a) This logic is that of Job's friends: any calamity must necessarily be a punishment for some wrongdoing. (I heard a well-known hyper-Calvinist preacher[23] say: The German invasion of the Netherlands in 1940 was a punishment upon the Dutch; the flight of the Germans in 1945 was a punishment upon the Germans.)

(b) If the inundations were a punishment from God, how can it be explained that they hit an area where remarkably many hyper-Calvinists were living? Should the sea not rather have flooded the northwestern part of the country, where many godless people were living? (It was similar with the Holocaust: if it was God's punishment for the sins of Israel, why were almost all the pious Jews of Poland murdered, and none of the secularized Jews of North America?)

(c) If the inundations were sent by God, how could people justifiably fight the calamity with every possible effort? Was this not fighting against God (the Camus dilemma)? It is the same with disease: if all diseases are sent by God, as a test or as a punishment, with what right do believers go to the doctor to fight them? People may find Bible verses for this (e.g., Matt.

---

23. Rev. Everard du Marchie van Voorthuysen (1901–1986).

9:12) but that does not explain the riddle: if calamities come from God, with what right do we fight them?

(d) Instead of saying that the inundations were sent by God, we must say that they were rather the consequence of human failure: the Dutch seawalls and river dikes turned out to be far too weak. Today the chance that such a calamity could happen again is a hundred times smaller.

As to point (c), the atheist Henry John McCloskey has formulated the Camus dilemma as follows: if we must not fight against suffering, then the moral law is wrong, for it says that we must fight against evil.[24] However, if conversely we must fight against suffering, then theism is wrong. This is because God's existence is acceptable only if suffering is the condition for a greater good. Therefore, we must not fight against it, else we eliminate this condition for this greater good, and thus this greater good cannot be reached. McCloskey concludes: since the moral law is right, theism must be wrong.

Again, this is a view of the matter that is far too simplistic. Of course, it is very conceivable, and even plausible, that at many places and times God himself fights against evil, and also expects us to do so, all the while knowing very well that evil as such, in the broad sense, is a condition for a greater good, namely, the perfect world to which God is en route. This is the world that is the object of God's counsel. It will be a world without evil. However, it might be that, along the ways leading to the realization of this world, evil is unavoidable. We find that God either fights this evil, or uses it in service to his ways with the world, or both.

9.4 God or People?
9.4.1 God's Part

Behind the question just dealt with, we encounter once again the general problem of *theodicy*: what is the relationship between God and suffering in this world? Is it certain *a priori* that, because of his intrinsic goodness, an all-good God ought

---

24. McCloskey (1964).

to destroy all evil right way? I have indicated before that it is not unthinkable *a priori* that the best conceivable world—that is, the world that constitutes the object of God's *counsel*—can be attained only through *ways* that presuppose evil; or that evil, or what seems to be evil, is in fact a necessary part of a greater totality, which is good; or that it is contrary to God's being to destroy evil too soon. It is not inconceivable or unacceptable *a priori* that God temporarily tolerates evil if, through this way, in the end a greater good is attained.

I state this while at the same time emphasizing that God can never, in any way, be made *responsible* for this evil. That is, he is never the direct *cause* of any evil, unless one wishes to call any punishment sent by God "evil." This is the problem in Isaiah 45:7, where God is said to "create calamity [Heb. *ra'*]," or, as many translations say, "create evil" (cf. Amos 3:6 DRA, "Shall there be evil in a city, which the Lord hath not done?"[25]). The sense is rather judgment sent by God in the form of "mischief, disaster, calamity."

If evil ends up being included in God's *ways*, and if this evil ultimately yields a greater good, this does not mean that this evil originally *came* from God, or that it is part of his *counsel*. Evil comes from free but sinful people, and also from the dark powers behind humanity, which are *opposed* to God.

Opponents of Christianity have always attempted to sharpen the problem of evil by presenting it as "innocent" evil. It is the "poor fellow" who suffers, whereas, according to the persiflage given of Christianity, God passively watches him, without concern or interest. This is a bizarre argument. Non-Christians like to emphasize the freedom and autonomy of people over against the (supposed) deity. They wish to manage their own affairs, without having some God putting

---

25. John Gill (1746, ad loc.): ". . . unless the words should be rendered, as they may be, 'shall there be evil in a city, and shall not the Lord do' or 'work'? Shall sin be committed in a city, all sorts of sin, in the most bold and extravagant manner, and will not the Lord do something to show his resentment of it?"

spokes in their wheels. However, as soon as people must suffer — often as a result of their own or other people's faults — they hasten to blame the (supposed) deity for it. People are praised when things go well; God is blamed when things go wrong. This argument will not work. Atheists cannot have it both ways: either they maintain human autonomy, and then can never blame God; or they blame God, but then must confess human dependence on him.

9.4.2 The Human Part

Indeed, the reality is that, in the great majority of the cases of suffering, human responsibility plays a certain, often very great role. It is not God but people who bring war, violence, pain, sadness, accidents, and sometimes even diseases upon other people. It is people who make themselves responsible for floods by inadequate dikes. It is people's fault that an equally heavy earthquake causes only limited damage in wealthy California, but huge damage in a poor third-world country. It is people who, by economic or agricultural mismanagement as well as the selfish refusal to help the poor, allow famines to occur. And so we could go on. It is strictly monistic decretalism that blames all catastrophes, including those that can be attributed to human failure, on God because these disasters had supposedly been decreed by him from eternity.

However, over against Arminians, Molinists, Open Theists, and Viatorists, the non-Christian cannot have it both ways: both positing human autonomy and blaming God for all human misery (see the end of the previous section). Even though these Christians differ among themselves on important points, they all consistently uphold both God's sovereignty and human responsibility toward God, including human responsibility for suffering that people bring upon each other.

In addition, we ask non-Christians: How could we ever determine something to be evil or unjust without accepting some moral law? Such a law serves as a standard to establish certain conditions in this world as good or bad, righteous or unrighteous. This is possible only if such a law not only exists but transcends this world. Therefore, the Christian will always maintain that the atheist is inconsistent: he necessarily assumes some rational, transcendent, moral law, he judges the God of the theists by this same law, and then wants to tell us that a rational, transcendent, moral law-*giver* (read: God) does not exist. Thus, the burden of proof rests on the atheist to make this inconsistency plausible. Usually, he chooses to simply deny the moral law, but as a consequence he gets entangled in other inconsistencies as mentioned above.[26]

9.5 Suffering as a Facet of God's Ways
9.5.1 A Means to a Goal?

But can the theist make the idea plausible that God does not *decree* suffering (as the hyper-Calvinist wants to have it), but that he does permit it in his ways with the world; that suffering is a necessary route to the realization of his counsel, namely, attaining a better world; and that this route is the best, or even the only way to this higher goal?[27]

Let us begin with the argument of R. C. Sproul. He argued that God's decree to permit sin to enter the world was a good decree. It does not mean that our sin as such is something good, but only that God's permission that we sin — which is evil — was something good. God's permission of evil is good, but the evil that he permits is still evil.[28] Why was this decree good? God foreknew that he would set in motion a plan of redemption for his fallen creation that would contain a perfect manifestation of his righteousness and a perfect expression of his love and mercy.

In itself this is not very plausible. Why is it good that God decreed the Fall and had a plan of redemption ready? Would it not have been better if God had not decreed the Fall, so that

---

26. See Ouweneel (2005, §10.3.2).
27. On this matter see extensively, Geisler (1974: especially chapter 16); cf. Geisler and Corduan (1988).
28. Sproul (1986, 31–32).

a plan of redemption was not needed at all? However, if the Fall was not based upon a decision of God but upon a decision of the first people—foreseen by God—then it is wonderful that God had a plan of redemption ready.

But apart from this, in principle the possibility remains that permitting *evil* is indeed good if in this way something better is attained than otherwise would have been possible. God is a perfectly good and perfectly wise God. The world's creation by this God was not necessary. But if he decrees to create a world, even a world with moral beings, it must be the best possible world that can be produced. A perfectly good and wise God can do nothing less. In other words, everything that is less than such a world is a blow for theism. But it is altogether plausible that the best possible moral world presupposes a historical process leading to this perfect world. In such a world people will be absolutely morally free, but will never do evil. The route to this world is a route by which people are absolutely free but unfortunately have chosen evil.

It is also plausible that the process through which this perfect moral world is attained must contain enough evil to teach people how to discern between good and evil, to learn to avoid evil, and pursue what is good. It is far more difficult to see how a perfect moral world could ever be attained without this evil. In fact, we believe that no world more adequately satisfies the conditions for attaining a better world than the present world. The all-good and all-wise God is the best guarantee that the present world will ultimately be transformed into the perfect world. At the beginning of human history, we find *a tree of the knowledge of good and evil* (Gen. 2:9, 17), as a signpost pointing forward. At the end of this history, we see the *tree of life* (Rev. 2:7; 22:2, 14, 19) as the ultimate goal—a tree that we see at the beginning of human history only as a promise.[29]

This is more or less, in brief, the argument of many

---

29. See Ouweneel (EDR 3:§§9.1–9.2).

Christians concerning suffering: it is an inevitable part of God's *ways* for the realization of his *counsel*. The objections to it are obvious.

* The *atheist* may deny any sense and meaning in the cosmos, but he himself cannot live with such a view. Every human lives *as if* what he says and does is to a certain extent meaningful, even if this meaning extends no further than his own selfish interests. Why would atheists so eagerly defend their position if, by their own definition, the whole debate is meaningless?

* The *hyper-Calvinist* denies human free will, but has chosen this view by his own free will because it does not follow from the biblical data. In a sense his view is easy: it has no room for free people, and everything has been eternally foreordained by God.

* Both the traditional *Arminian* and the *Open Theist* also have an easy view: here, everything depends on the free choices that free people make, so that God cannot be blamed. It is just as one-sided as hyper-Calvinism.

* The *Viatorist* chooses the most difficult way, for he seeks to maintain the absolute sovereignty of God and of his eternal decree, as well as God's foreknowledge of all future events (without having *decreed* them all), as well as human freedom and responsibility.

9.5.2 Testing the Best[30]

What is the best possible world to which God is en route in history? How can one determine what is the best world, that is, the world that in his history is actually emerging? In order to turn out to be really the best, it must undergo the most severe tests. Nowhere do we see this in a more remarkable and touching manner in history than in God's ways with Israel from the beginning. All four "elements" of the ancient worldview were applied in this testing:

---

30. See Ouweneel (2000a, §3.2.2).

The Problem of Suffering

* testing through *earth* (one method of torture was to bury Jews alive);
* testing through *fire* (from the fiery furnace in Babylon [Dan. 3] to the cremation ovens in the Nazi destruction camps);
* testing through *air* (the gas chambers);
* testing through *water* (already in Egypt infant Israelite boys were drowned).

This was—through Satan—God's way with Job, who is one of the most remarkable types of Israel:[31]

* he himself says that soon the *earth* will cover him (7:21);
* the "*fire* of God" consumed his sheep and servants (1:16);
* a heavy storm (*air*) destroyed the house in which his children were gathered, and killed them (1:18-19);
* a "flood of *water*" covered him (22:11); just like Jonah, as a type parallel with Job, he could say, "[Y]ou cast me into the deep, into the heart of the seas, and the flood surrounded me; all your waves and your billows passed over me" (Jonah 2:3).

Nowhere do we see more clearly than in Job what testing the *best* involves. This test is necessarily the *worst* test. This, too, is the core of anti-Semitism: hatred and envy against the best of God. If the true Israel is the best that world history has known, then the test of Israel is the worst that world history has ever seen. God triumphs over Satan because, by his own grace, the best that he has produced is sustained under the worst circumstances.

This is manifested in the highest manner in Christ, who is the true Israel. He is also in the midst of Israel itself the best that this nation has ever seen. Therefore, it was his test that really was the worst:

* he descended in the "lower parts of the *earth*" (Eph. 4:9 NKJV);
* the *fire* of God's wrath was burning in his bones (cf. Ps.

---

31. Ouweneel (2000a, chapter 1).

102:3);

* the storm (*air*) of God's judgment raged over him (cf. Ps. 83:13-15);

* the *water* of God's "breakers and waves," the "deep waters" and the "flood" overwhelmed him (Ps. 42:7; 69:2).

9.5.3 Christ in the Psalms

Jesus' sufferings as *atoning* sufferings, the sufferings that, at the cross, blotted out sins under the judging hand of God, were unique. However, in all his sufferings that he underwent at the hands of *people*, Christ made himself perfectly one with the true Israel. Just about all psalms from which parts are quoted in the New Testament, and which are applied to him, deal with the sufferings of the true *Israel*. This is true for Psalms 69 and 102, but also for Psalms of suffering like 22, 41-44, 88, and others. He is with his people in the *water* and in the *fire* (Isa. 43:2), he is with them in the *storm* (Mark 4:35-41), with them he allows his life to be "crushed to the *ground*" (Ps. 143:3; cf. 17:11).

The idea of Christ as the true Israel is very helpful,[32] for it provides great clarity to many of the Psalms that speak of both Christ and the true Israel in an inextricable way. The "true Israel" is what is sometimes called the "remnant" of Israel (e.g., Isa. 10:19-21; 11:11, 16; 37:31-32; 46:3). It is basically the same as the "Israel of God" in Galatians 6:16. A similar parallelism is found in the book of Job, who is a type of both (the true) Israel and Christ; in the book of Jonah, who is an identical type; and in Isaiah 42-53, where the servant of YHWH is both Israel (Isa. 49:3) and Christ (cf., e.g., Isa. 53:7-8 with Acts 8:32-35). In the book of Lamentations, the first person singular speaker is sometimes the prophet, but at other places we see how the voice of the true Israel and that of the Messiah merge.[33]

---

32. This idea is found often in the works of the Dutch theologian and cultural philosopher, Frank de Graaff (1918–1993).
33. This can be seen in ancient Christian liturgy: on Holy Saturday, Lam. 1:12 (*O vos omnes qui transitis per viam*) is sung and applied to the suffering Christ,

The Problem of Suffering

In the Psalms, therefore, we find a deep moral connection between Christ and the remnant of Israel. This connection is manifested in a beautiful way in Jesus' Beatitudes. In them, he describes the moral characteristics of his true disciples, who represent the true Israel, the "Israel of God"; but at a deeper level these are the moral characteristics of Christ himself: *he* was meek, *he* hungered and thirsted for righteousness, *he* was merciful, *he* was pure in heart, *he* was a peacemaker, *he* was persecuted for righteousness' sake, *he* was reviled and falsely accused.

This sheds light on the sufferings of both Christ and the remnant of Israel.[34] Throughout the centuries and until the end of history, the faithful endure many trials and sufferings before they will enter the Messianic kingdom. "[W]e suffer with him in order that we may also be glorified with him" (Rom. 8:17). "[I]f we endure, we will also reign with him" (2 Tim. 2:12). "[R]ejoice insofar as you share Christ's sufferings, that you may also rejoice and be glad when his glory is revealed" (1 Pet. 4:13). In grace, Christ walked this very route ahead of his faithful ones: we are "looking to Jesus, the founder and perfecter of our faith, who for the joy that was set before him endured the cross, despising the shame, and is seated at the right hand of the throne of God" (Heb. 12:2). Christ was afflicted with all the afflictions that faithful Jews had to undergo from the Gentiles (cf. Isa. 63:9). Suffering from the unbelief and the wickedness of the unfaithful majority of Israel and of the oppressing nations, Christ in the Spirit made himself one with all the miseries that true Israel would have to endure.

I repeat: these are not the atoning sufferings that Christ had to undergo; in these, he was entirely alone ("no man can ransom another," Ps. 49:7). I am referring to the sufferings that any soul faithful to God and his Torah must endure in

---

whereas in Lam. 1 it is the complaint of "Zion," the remnant of Israel.
34. See J. N. Darby on many Psalms in his *Synopsis of the Books of the Bible* (www.sacred-texts.com/bib/cmt/darby/).

a wicked and miserable world. Especially in many Psalms, these sufferings and their accompanying feelings are expressed perfectly.[35]

9.5.4 The Three Tests

Just as in the Garden of Eden, Adam was put to the test and failed, it was inevitable that Christ was put to the test as well, if God wanted to prevail over Satan. This was indeed what happened. Adam was tested under the most ideal circumstances, in a wonderful garden; Christ was tested after he had stayed forty days in the wilderness and was hungry. The temptations to which the first Adam and the last Adam were subjected are very similar.[36] These are mentioned in 1 John 2:16, "... all that is in the world—the desires of the flesh and the desires of the eyes and pride of life." As to the first Adam (Gen. 3:6):

* *The desires of the flesh*: "the tree was good for food."

* *The desires of the eyes*: "the tree was a delight to the eyes."

* *The pride of life*: "the tree was to be desired to make one wise."

As to the last Adam (Luke 4:1-13):

* *The desires of the flesh*: "command this stone to become bread."

* *The desires of the eyes*: "the devil took him up and showed him all the kingdoms of the world ... and said to him, ... 'I give it to whom I will.'"

* *The pride of life*: "If you are the Son of God, throw yourself down from here, for it is written, 'He will command his angels concerning you, to guard you.'"

Just like Christ, who is the true Israel, Israel has to be put to the test as well; by and large, Israel failed as the first Adam had failed. However, the Spirit of God making himself one

---

35. See also J. N. Darby, *The Sufferings of Christ* (1858), now part of *CW* (7:139–237; for a summary, see http://www.mybrethren.org/doctrine/framsuff.htm).
36. Ouweneel (EDR 3, §10.1.2).

with the faithful remnant of Israel made it prevail during the temptations. This we see represented in the sufferings of Job:

* All that was *desirable* to the *flesh* and to the *eyes* was, with the LORD's permission, taken away from Job by Satan, including Job's health (Job 1–2);

* And all the *pride of life* that might be present in him was broken down until he repented in dust and ashes (42:6).

But he remained faithful to the LORD, who testified of him that he had spoken of the LORD what was right, in contrast with his friends (v. 7). It was the same with Israel throughout the centuries:

* Israel's *desires of the flesh* were contained in the promised land, a land "flowing with milk and honey" (Exod. 3:8, 17; etc.), which they had to give up when they went into exile (cf. Jer. 32:21–24; Ezek. 20:6, 15 within the context of the full chapter).

* *The desires of the eyes*: God commanded Ezekiel to tell Israel, "Behold, I will profane my sanctuary, the pride of your power, the delight of your eyes, and the yearning of your soul, and your sons and your daughters whom you left behind shall fall by the sword" (Ezek. 24:21).

* *The pride of life*: each pogrom against Israel involved breakdown, humiliation, destruction. All that was desirable to the flesh and to the eyes was, under the Lord's allowance, taken away from Israel by Satan, with the help of the Gentiles. And nowhere was Israel undressed and robbed more severely, even of its last bit of dignity, nowhere humiliated and destroyed in a more radical, undignified, and massive way, than in the Holocaust.

9.6 Again: the Book of Job
9.6.1 The Meaning of Job

An *atheist* will not find any meaning or purpose in a history like that of Job. He might agree with many of the "whys" in Job, Psalms, Ecclesiastes, and the Prophets, without at the same time clinging to God as the godly believers in the Old Testament did. His "whys" are detached, even scornful; those of the godly were despondent, yet confident.

A *hyper-Calvinist* does not know how to handle the very frank way in which Job argues with God[37] because he believes that Job ought to have accepted his sufferings with compliance and resignation. This is because all that happened to Job had supposedly been foreordained by God from eternity. Such defeatism is quite similar to those who argue that no one can escape his ill fate (although decretalists fiercely resist such a comparison).

The traditional *Arminian* as well as the *Open Theist* also follow an easy path: here, everything depends on the free choices that people like Job and his friends make, and God cannot be blamed (although in Job 1–2 it was God who took the initiative for his "wager" with Satan). For those thinking along the lines of Harold Kushner (§6.6.1) it is easy too: God watched Job, and felt very sorry for him, but could not do very much for him.

What determined the course of the book of Job? Certainly not Satan; after chapter 2, we do not hear about him again. He was at best a bit player on the scene. Moreover, Job could not have been aware of what happened in heaven in Job 1–2. He does not care: ". . . the LORD has taken away" (1:21). "Shall we accept good from God, and not trouble?" (2:10 NIV).

Was it God, then? It says that the LORD "restored the fortunes of Job" (42:10). Does this mean that the entire course of the book was nothing but the carrying out of a schedule that had been foreordained by God? What difference did all the words of Job and his friends make? If they all had spoken very differently, would it have changed anything in the course of the story? Or was all that Job and his friends said foreordained by God as well? But if so, how could God praise Job and blame his friends (42:7–8) if they merely played their

---

37. Ouweneel (2000a, chapter 5).

prescribed roles?

So what determined the course of the book of Job? Job himself, with or without his friends? But it was God who "restored the fortunes of Job"; was this God's sovereign and foreordained action, or was it because of Job's faithfulness? Or was Job's faithfulness equally foreordained by God? Time and again, it is this burning question with which we are confronted: How can we maintain both God's absolute sovereignty and full human freedom and responsibility? Viatorism tries to avoid the one-sidednesses of the previously mentioned schools.

9.6.2 Consolation

What consolation can one offer to a sick or dying person if one is an atheist, or a hyper-Calvinist, or an Arminian? The consistent atheist has little answer to offer to the suffering person's question about the meaning or the goal of his suffering, or the perspective beyond these sufferings. The consistent hyper-Calvinist basically has a fatalistic message, which differs only in degree from the Islamic *Insh'Allah*, "if God wills," and acquiesce in this! This type of consolation is, in my view, very similar to that of Job's friends. The consistent Arminian can do nothing else than put all the blame for the illness on the devil, or on the poor sick person himself.[38]

However, someone committed to Viatorism may endeavor to maintain the balance between divine sovereignty and human responsibility, but in the end, he too has to bow his head. All theistic reasonings about suffering as the divine way to a better world will not help a person one bit when he or she is standing at the deathbed of a loved one.[39] This is one of the things that make reading and pondering Job such a moving experience. In Job, we do not find a treatise in the field of the philosophy of religion on the "problem of suffering," but rather a literary portrait of this suffering man Job, to

---
38. Cf. Ouweneel (2004, 87–91).
39. Plantinga (1974, 63–64).

whom all the theories of his friends do not apply.[40]

Another point that makes Job one of the greatest literary works on the sufferings of humanity consists of these two aspects. On the one hand, Job does not curse God (*contra* atheism), which even his own wife had recommended (Job 2:9). On the other hand, Job does not sink down in a defeatist, apathetic resignation (*contra* decretalism). Rather, he wrestles with God, as other great men of God have done as well: Abraham (Gen. 18:22-32), Jacob (32:22-31),[41] Moses (Exod. 32:7-14), Jeremiah (Jer. 20:7-18).[42]

To me, one of the most touching statements in Job is spoken by Job himself: "Though he slay me, I will hope in him" (Job 13:15). I know there are other translations possible (ESV note: "Behold, he will slay me; I have no hope"), but I prefer the former rendering. Job is saying, Whatever God does to me will not shatter my confidence in him. I do not understand him, but I trust him.[43] This is perhaps the greatest statement a believer can make in his sufferings. Theological and philosophical theories about the meaning of suffering may be useful to a certain extent. But they are of limited help to the sufferer: it is his confidence in a God whom he does not understand that will help him through.

9.6.3 The Sufferer and His God

This is the moment to explain a little further why human sufferings ought to be a much larger problem to the atheist than to the Christian, both intellectually and existentially. Even though the Christian very often does not understand the meaning of *these* or *those* specific sufferings—this is why he wrestles with his God—he does understand that sufferings and death have a divine purpose, are part of the greater and

---

40. See extensively, Ouweneel (2000a).
41. Assuming that Jacob's opponent is not a dark angel; see Ouweneel (2016b).
42. See Ouweneel (2005, §10.2.1); cf. extensively, Laytner (2005).
43. The Lutheran nun Mother Basilea Schlink (d. 2001), co-founder of the Evangelical Sisterhood of Mary (Darmstadt, Germany), prayed every day: "My Father, I do not understand you, but I trust your love"; see Schlink (2010).

wider ways of God, and that, by divine justice, their meaning will ultimately be explained *on the basis of both the sufferings and the victory of Christ.*

To the atheist, however, sufferings, have no meaning or goal—or perhaps only as a part of the evolutionistic "struggle for life" and the "survival of the fittest" (a term coined by English philosopher Herbert Spencer, d. 1903). But how could anyone consistently believe such things, and at the same time keep believing in humaneness, in the meaning of love and self-sacrifice, in the notion of meaning and purpose in human existence? The most consistent atheists do not believe in the latter either—but what a miserable life this is, both intellectually and existentially.

Believers not only know God—in the sense of having (theological) knowledge of him—they not only have a relationship with him, but they sometimes *wrestle* with him. This is because, although they may have nice theories about suffering, and over against atheism they may find them very plausible, nevertheless these theories offer no help when such Christians speak with a mother who has just lost her child. However, there is something that surpasses all their theories: *confidence* in God, being convinced of his love, even though God might appear to be on the wrong side. They are persuaded that the wide perspective of life in Christ grants meaning and purpose, and they are convinced that their own sufferings somehow fit with this life, even if at this moment they cannot see how.

Such believers remind us of Job. Thank God, usually they do not curse God, often they do not fall in idle resignation, but they cry to him, they argue with him, they wrestle with him, sometimes they accuse him—and then throw themselves into his arms again. As the Message says:

> God is educating you; that's why you must never drop out. He's treating you as dear children. This trouble you're in isn't punishment; it's training, the normal experience of children.

Only irresponsible parents leave children to fend for themselves. Would you prefer an irresponsible God? We respect our own parents for training and not spoiling us, so why not embrace God's training so we can truly *live*? While we were children, our parents did what *seemed* best to them. But God is doing what *is* best for us, training us to live God's holy best. At the time, discipline isn't much fun. It always feels like it's going against the grain. Later, of course, it pays off handsomely, for it's the well-trained who find themselves mature in their relationship with God (Heb. 12:7-11).

Very often, believers do not understand the ways of God. They have no answers to all their questions, they wrestle with those (almost?) irresolvable questions. This is why they can pursue allegiance to so many different schools of thought: Open Theism, (hyper-)Calvinism, Arminianism, Molinism, even Viatorism. They are wrestling with the *experiences* of suffering, which is appropriate for *theologians* to do. But if suffering draws near, they wrestle with the *God* who is in their suffering and this is appropriate for *believers*.

9.7 God and Satan
9.7.1 The Will of God[44]

A biblical figure who was an adherent of unbiblical decretalism was the sinful priest Eli, who responded to the announcement of the divine judgment upon him by saying: "It is the LORD. Let him do what seems good to him" (1 Sam. 3:18). He believed that it was appropriate for him to acquiesce to God's judgment. Instead, Eli should have repented, he ought to have called his sons to order, and to have cried to God for mercy. Resignation is passive, if not apathetic; it simply *complies* with God's will instead of actively *accomplishing* God's will.[45]

The petition, "[H]allowed be your name, your kingdom come, *your will be done*" (Matt. 6:9-10), expresses not a general, noncommittal desire, but means primarily: may your

---

44. See Ouweneel (2004, §3.4.2).
45. Cf. Ouweneel (2004, §3.3).

name be hallowed *through and by me*, may your kingdom be realized ever further *in my life through and by me*, may your will be done *through my words and deeds*.

Similarly, Jesus' prayer in Gethsemane, "[N]ot my will, but yours, be done" (Luke 22:42), did not contain any resignation. As in the Lord's Prayer, it was not Jesus' intention to submit to God's will with acquiescence, but to actively *accomplish* God's will. His prayer was not characterized by resignation but by resolution, not by passive submission but by obedience (cf. Heb. 5:8). Even less was his prayer one of decretalism: how could he ask whether there was a "way out" if his pathway had been foreordained in God's decree from eternity (cf. §8.6.4)? The statement by Paul's friends, "Let the will of the Lord be done" (Acts 21:14), does not necessarily point to resignation either, but rather to the desire that Paul would accomplish the will of the Lord.

If believers do pray God for healing or deliverance, they often do so with a repeated "if it is your will" (assuming that this is not simply a phrase of awe or of habit). As if God would not *love* to be persuaded by people (§8.2)! In this way, they appear simply to be imitating the leper: "Sir, if you want to, you can make me clean" (Matt. 8:2 GNT) — but if they would allow the story to have more impact on them, they would have heard the Lord's answer all along: "I do want to. . . . Be clean" (v. 3).

9.7.2 The Boy with the Unclean Spirit

Let me illustrate this important point a little more fully in relation to the ministry of healing. Duffield and Van Cleave rightly wrote, in opposition to decretalism, that the leper's theology when he came to Jesus is the current theology of many Christians today. By closing the prayer of healing with the words, "if you want to, Lord," we cast all responsibility upon God. Thus, we make God responsible for the illness, for in fact we are saying that God would be able to heal if he only wanted to. This is not biblical, said the authors. The Lord places the responsibility on the one who seeks the healing. The father who took his son to Jesus, just after the transfiguration on the mount, cried out: "[I]f you can do anything, have compassion on us and help us" (Mark 9:22). By saying, "If you can do anything," the father put the responsibility on the Lord, but the latter immediately put the responsibility back on the father: "'If you can'! All things are possible for one who believes" (v. 23).[46]

In my view, this is a proper presentation of things. People lay the responsibility for the affliction of their fellow human on the Lord, whereas the Lord lays the responsibility on these people themselves. As Jesus said at one occasion to his disciples: "They need not go away; *you* give them something to eat" (Matt. 14:16). The father of the boy with the unclean spirit suggested that the boy's being healed or not depended on (the power of) the Lord. However, the healing did not depend primarily on the Lord at all, but on the father's faith, who therefore responded with: "I believe; help my unbelief!" (v. 24). And the disciples who had not been able to heal the boy were blamed in this way: "O *faithless* generation, how long am I to be with you? How long am I to bear with you?" (v. 19).

Kenneth MacKenzie has written important things about decretalists who associate "God's will" so easily with the sufferings in this world. He said that their fear of his will is so great that they train themselves to be prepared, when this will hits them, to view it like a pest that occasionally plagues the country. They associate God's will with infirmaries, almshouses, loss, casualties, funerals, and open graves. For such people God is always clothed in black. Such a view of God's will creates ailing Christians, weak faith, joylessness, and lack of victory. MacKenzie asked whether, when we pray "Your will be done," we are always aware of the meaning of these words. God's will is not merely to mete out punishment and

---

46. Duffield and Van Cleave (1987, 373).

to ensure that, sooner or later, we get what we deserve. How we have distorted the Father's favor into a miserable complex of ideas! His will is a blessed companion, illuminating our path, rejoicing our mind, filling our lives with joy, and rendering our deeds fruitful.[47]

9.7.3 Again: Resignation

In chapters 10–14, we will see that the decretalist doctrine of providence (especially the doctrine of resignation) is closely related to hyper-Calvinism, or at least with the doctrine of double predestination. Here, the sinner's will and responsibility have been *de facto* switched off, and people can only wait with acquiescence for God's sovereign intervention. The people who pray, "Lord, heal me if it is your will," are often the same ones who pray, "Lord, save me if it is your will." In both cases, people are supposed to wait passively and patiently. In such circles, faith is never an active deed of people but a passively received gift of God. It is purely by the grace of God that, with such a one-sided, that is, unbiblical view, any people are saved at all (from eternal or temporal death).

The well-known Chinese evangelist—certainly not a Pentecostal or a Charismatic—Watchman Nee said that God often desires to heal his children but he is forced to let their sickness continue because of their unbelief and lack of prayer for healing (cf. Mark 6:5). If God's saints agree with sickness, or even welcome it, as if it would deliver them from the world and would make them holier, then God cannot do anything else than give them what they expect from him. God often deals with his children according to what they are able to receive (cf. Matt. 8:13).[48]

The report of the Dutch Reformed Church in the Netherlands, written concerning the Pentecostal movement, says, in a lovely anti-decretalist way, about the false resignation in illness:

---

47. MacKenzie (n.d., 32–33); quoted in Duffield and Van Cleave (1987, 374).
48. Nee (2002, 734).

> We may be dealing with a disobedient resistance against what begins to become clearly God's will, but we may also be dealing with a very healthy resistance against what one cannot accept as coming from God, because in Jesus Christ one has come to know God as being himself the great Warrior against sickness and death. And similarly, when one sometimes encounters at the bedside a remarkable "patience," which, as two drops of water, resembles the surrender of faith, we again will have to fathom seriously the deepest motives of this patience; it might be a camouflage of an unhealthy apathy, or fear, or flight into illness, in fact a form of unbelief, of ignoring God's intentions and possibilities.[49]

In this quotation, the report uses the word "accept" in a negative sense: in general, we should say that the believer cannot "accept" the illness. Bernard Martin used the word in another, rather positive sense, but the result amounts to the same: "Accepting one's illness is . . . staring it right in the face, and acknowledging its existence. Not in order to subsequently submit to it in a wrong way, by resignation, but to be thoroughly aware of the need to fight against it, and of the value of the necessary help."[50]

The ministry of healing constitutes a concrete illustration of what we have seen in the previous chapter regarding the value, significance, and effectiveness of prayer. The stronger one's hyper-Calvinist position, the less one will expect from the ministry of healing, or rather, one will reject the ministry of healing altogether. The farther people are removed from this position, the greater their expectations for the effectiveness of the ministry of healing, because they have become familiar with the notion of a God who loves to be persuaded by prayer. Thus, the debate around the counsel of God has not only theological meaning but also tremendous pastoral consequences. In the next chapters, this should become even

---

49. Hervormde Raad (1960, 97).
50. Martin (1955, 103).

more clear.

9.8 The Role of Satan
9.8.1 Satan or God's Spirit?

At the conclusion of this chapter, a few words must be added concerning the role of Satan. In the decretalist model, in which everything is viewed as foreordained by God, also the devil, even though he has his own will, cannot do anything other than that to which God has predestined him. In the approaches of Arminianism, Open Theism, and Viatorism, God has sovereignly given leeway to the devil, just as he has to humanity. As a consequence, Satan plays his own active role in world events. God has sovereignly allowed him to put a spoke in God's wheels from time to time. Mind you, this refers only to the ways of God, never to his counsel. This is another point in which we see how important it is to distinguish between God's counsel and God's ways.

A remarkable example of this is found in Daniel 10. In response to the prophet's prayer, God immediately sends him an angel with his reply. However, in the spiritual world this angel is prevented by the dark powers from coming to Daniel during no fewer than three weeks. Apparently this is possible: an evil power attempts with all its might to frustrate God's will, and manages to do so for three weeks.[51]

We have seen that God sometimes wants something, yet it does not happen because certain people do not want it (e.g., Luke 13:34). This is not an attack on God's sovereignty, for God himself sovereignly gave people this room to maneuver. He did the same with Satan. Thus, it is possible that the devil time and again disturbs the ways of God. There is not the slightest biblical basis for claiming that all these devilish disturbances have been foreordained by God. A remarkable example is found in the parable of the wheat and the weeds (Matt. 13:24–30). When the servants of the master of the house ask him how the weeds grew up among the wheat, he

---
51. Wink (1992, 310).

answers, "An enemy has done this" (v. 28). In the interpretation of this parable, Jesus makes clear that this enemy is the devil (v. 39). In no way can the parable be interpreted such that the reply actually means that the master of the house has permitted, or even decreed, that the enemy would do this. This would go entirely against the tenor of Jesus' story.

If everything the devil does would have been foreordained by God there could be no question at all of a genuine spiritual battle—and such a battle definitely exists.[52] People, but especially the spiritual powers of darkness, have their assigned leeway for opposing God's work. The believer who discerns the spirits (cf. 1 Cor. 12:10 NKJV) knows where and when this is the case. We may sometimes wonder what hindered us from reaching a certain goal, but Luke knew it for sure: the apostles "went through the region of Phrygia and Galatia, having been forbidden by the *Holy Spirit* to speak the word in Asia. And when they had come up to Mysia, they attempted to go into Bithynia, but the *Spirit of Jesus* did not allow them" (Acts 16:7). Luke said so with the same certainly as the apostle Paul, who tells us on another occasion: "[W]e wanted to come to you—I, Paul, again and again—but *Satan* hindered us" (1 Thess. 2:18). God's men and women often are aware of what is going on behind the scenes. (In other cases, Paul expresses himself in a more neutral way: "This is the reason why I have so often been hindered from coming to you," Rom. 15:22; cf. 1:13).

9.8.2 The Superior Master

In §4.6.2 I used the image of a chess grandmaster. We could also use the image of a mighty, invincible warrior, who fights against much weaker opponents. It is unmistakably true that these opponents determine to a large extent the behavior of the great warrior: whether and how he must evade or attack, where and when and how he himself must inflict blows, etc. Many opponents might certainly "keep him busy" for some time. But there can be no doubt as to who will gain the

---

52. Cf. Wink (1992, 308–17); Boyd (1997, 9–22); Pinnock (2001, 135–36).

victory: the great warrior always wins. It is equally certain that people, and especially the dark powers, who fiercely oppose God's work in the end will utterly fail. I emphasize again that God's counsel is certain, but the ways to its realization depend to a considerable extent on the actions of people and spiritual powers.

Many have wondered why Satan is and always remains so active even though he knows the outcome. He knows the Bible (cf. Luke 4:10-11)! Thus, he also knows that his time is limited (Rev. 10:6), and that his end will come soon (12:7-9; 20:1-3, 7-10). So why does he continue to do evil? The answer, it seems to me, is that Satan cannot do otherwise than to act in an evil way; he is the "evil one" (Matt. 13:19, 38; John 17:15; Eph. 6:6; 2 Thess. 3:3; 1 John 2:13-14; 3:12; 5:18-19). He can do nothing other than act according to his nature.

Especially Greg Boyd has ardently defended the position that it is most meaningful and supplies the best insight if we view history not as a script or blueprint written by God from eternity and neatly worked out in the course of time, but as a genuine spiritual warfare with genuine actors.[53] In this war, God allows his opponents room to maneuver, which means that not all events have been predetermined, but God must constantly respond to the moves of his opponents. The outcome may be sure, but this does not change the fact that this warfare is very realistic. Boyd believes that this approach does the most justice to Scripture, to history, and to the being of God. He therefore speaks of a "trinitarian warfare theodicy."[54] To my mind, his view is also quite useful for a fresh look at the New Testament doctrine of the kingdom of God.[55]

9.8.3 Sickening Spirits

If many Christians, who accept all the misery in their lives

---

53. Boyd (1997 [title: "God at War"; 2001, 13–16: *blueprint worldview* vs. *warfare worldview*]).
54. See the subtitle of Boyd (2001).
55. See especially Boyd (1997, chapters 6–8).

from God's "fatherly hand" (Heidelberg Catechism, Lord's Day 10), were more conscious of this spiritual battle, they would respond differently to their misery, and pray differently. The poor woman who was bent over (Luke 13:11-17) was not supposed to accept her ailment from God's hand, for the text clearly says she had a "disabling spirit" (other translations: "spirit of infirmity"; CEV: "crippled by an evil spirit"), and that she was "bound by Satan" (vv. 11, 16).[56]

In decretalism, the ministry of healing is a humble prayer for God's will. In the Bible, however, this ministry is often an outright *battle* against the powers, in which not only the will of God, but also the commitments of the sick person himself (Matt. 9:22, 28-29; Mark 10:52; Luke 17:19; Acts 14:9-10), of the accompanying people (Matt. 8:10, 13; 9:2; 15:21-28; Mark 5:36; 7:32; 9:23-24), the environment (Mark 6:5-6, 40; 7:33; 8:23), and especially of the minister of healing (Acts 3:16; James 5:15) play a decisive role.

When in Mark 9 we read that Jesus' disciples could not deliver the boy from his evil spirit, Jesus did not respond: "Then apparently it was not God's will" — but he told them: "O faithless generation, how long am I to be with you? How long am I to bear with you?" (Mark 9:19). Notice also how Jesus addressed this evil spirit: "You mute and deaf spirit ..." (v. 25), that is apparently, an evil spirit that makes its victim mute and deaf (cf. v. 17). I am certainly not saying that *all* diseases are caused by evil spirits, as many Pentecostals and Charismatics do. But some phrases in the book of Acts are quite remarkable: Jesus "went about doing good and *healing* all who were oppressed by the devil" (10:38). "God was doing extraordinary miracles by the hands of Paul, so that even handkerchiefs or aprons that had touched his skin were carried away to the sick, and their *diseases* left them and the *evil spirits* came out of them" (19:11-12). Such passages suggest that there might be more connections between diseases and

---

56. On this case and on powers of illness in general, see Ouweneel (2004, chapter 6).

the spiritual world than some of us presume.

Finally, I refer to cases in which Satan does his own evil work but God explicitly permits him to do so. Perhaps the best known case is Job 1–2, where Satan, with God's permission, takes everything away from Job, eventually even his health. It is difficult to say here who made Job sick: Satan, who was the primary agent, or God, who permitted it? It is similar in the history of David, where we find a remarkable discrepancy between 2 Samuel 24:1 ("[T]he anger of the LORD was kindled against Israel, and he incited David against them, saying, 'Go, number Israel and Judah'") and 1 Chronicles 21:1 ("Then Satan stood against Israel and incited David to number Israel"). Satan is the one inciting, but God in some way is at work in the background.

Thus it is also in 2 Corinthians 12:7, where Paul is harassed by a "messenger [or, angel] of Satan," but apparently with the permission of the Lord (vv. 8–9). If Christians would be less committed to decretalism and more to Viatorism, they would pay more attention to the power that Satan has, and to the spiritual battle in which they find themselves.[57] Such a battle is not an opportunity for acquiescing but for gaining spiritual victory.

---

57. See extensively, Ouweneel (1998).

Chapter 10
Introduction to Predestination

> [T]hose whom he foreknew he also predestined
>   to be conformed to the image of his Son,
>   in order that he might be the firstborn among
>   many brothers.
> And those whom he predestined he also called,
>   and those whom he called he also justified,
>   and those whom he justified he also glorified.
> Romans 8:29–30

Summary: *There is an eternal and a temporary election, as well as a corporate and an individual election. Election is particularistic, not universalistic. Election is both conditional and unconditional: the Arminian and the (hyper-)Calvinist positions should not be played off against each other. Both viewpoints are strongly supported by Scripture. Viatorism points out that their mutual exclusivity is due to the ancient confusion of concepts and ideas, and to people's preconceived (logical) ideas about sovereignty and responsibility ("it is inconceivable that . . ."). The parable of the prodigal son is used as an illustration. The biblical terminology for election, predestination, foreordination, and purpose is analyzed and summarized. They clearly point to several categories of election, which are often confused. Finally, attention is paid to the phrase "book of life" and its meanings.*

10.1 Introductory Questions
10.1.1 Five Questions

IN OUR MORE GENERAL TREATISE on the counsel of God (chapters 2–9), implicitly or explicitly several questions surrounding predestination have arisen, such as the following (in which I place in italics the position of Viatorism):[1]

(a) Are certain people chosen (elected) for an earthly service, or for eternal salvation, or *for both*? We will see that especially Calvinists have wrongly used certain Bible passages that refer to an election for an earthly position or service in their argument for election unto eternal salvation.

(b) Is election corporate (Israel, the church; thus many non-Calvinist theologians), individual (believers, servants of God), or *both*?

(c) Seen from God's viewpoint, is election a conditional and passive matter (i.e., [partly] based on foreseen faith), or an unconditional and active matter (i.e., based exclusively upon God's sovereign will)? In other words, is it based on divine foreknowledge only, or on divine foreordination (including foreknowledge)? The former is Arminian, the latter is (hyper)Calvinist. Or is this a *false dilemma*?

(d) Does predestination *include only election from eternity*, or also reprobation from eternity? The former is the view of some moderate Calvinists today, the latter is (hyper-)Calvinistic or (ultra-)Reformed (one could also say: classically Reformed!).

(e) Is election unto eternal salvation universalistic (i.e., intended for all people, although effective only in those who believe), or *particularistic* (i.e., referring to certain people only)? The latter is the view of Calvinists but also of many Evangelicals. The former may mean that all people indeed will share in this salvation (Karl Barth, universalism), or that salvation is offered to all people but is not accepted by all (many Evangelicals).

---

1. Cf. Demarest (1997, 97–118).

Introduction to Predestination

These and other questions must be dealt with in this and the following chapters.

10.1.2 Five Options

With respect to identifying the relationship between the sovereign God and a fallen world, there are in principle four options, according to R. C. Sproul; I add one option (number 2) and elaborate on all the options in my own way.[2]

(1) God could decide to offer the opportunity to be saved to *no* people at all. (If humanity chose to fall into rebellion against God, it will have to bear the full consequences of that.)

(2) God could decide to offer the opportunity to be saved to *some* people. (Although all fallen people deserve eternal destruction, God chose to offer a way out to some of them.)

(3) God could decide to offer the opportunity to be saved to *all* people. (All did fall into sin, but all are allowed to repent and return to God in order to receive redemption.)

(4) God could intervene, and assure salvation to *some* people. (Although all fallen people deserve eternal destruction, God chose to save some of them.)

(5) God could intervene, and assure salvation to *all* people. (All did fall into sin, but ultimately all are redeemed by God.)

All Christians will immediately dismiss the first option. Apart from adherents of universalism ("ultimately all people will be saved"), many Christians will also dismiss the fifth option.

Some hyper-Calvinists have opted for the second possibility: they argued that, if God elected only part of humanity, it can only be to this part that he offers with sincere intention the opportunity to be saved. In the Netherlands, there was even a church split on this point within the Netherlands Reformed Congregations (1953). Cornelis Steenblok (d. 1966) defended the stricter viewpoint, whereas the more moderate party maintained that God's offer of salvation is seriously

---

2. Sproul (1986, 33).

presented to all people. (The Netherlands Reformed Congregations in North America belong to the more moderate party.)

Most Calvinists will in principle accept the third option, but they will hasten to add that, without God's gracious and sovereign intervention, no people would be either willing or able to accept God's offer because of their corrupted will. Therefore, they will feel more at home with the fourth option because here the initiative remains with God, and salvation is assured only to some (the elect), not to all.

Arminians and Open Theists would hesitate to accept the fourth option because the emphasis would then lie too strongly on God's gracious intervention, and too weakly on human responsibility and freedom of will. They would therefore prefer the third option in such a way that it depends on a human choice, made in freedom, whether some will indeed accept the opportunity to be saved. (Of course, in such a choice the indispensible help of God is not excluded at all.)

10.1.3 A Heated Debate

Here we have the essence of the debate set out in all its sharpness. Arminians believe that all people *ought to* accept God's salvation and, no matter how corrupt they are, in principle *can* accept it. If Calvinists would argue that no person by himself is able to come to faith, Arminians might answer that God makes available to all people the power to accept the gospel. Calvinists agree that all people *ought to* accept God's salvation, but by nature do not *want* to do so because their will is corrupted; God's gracious intervention is required to bend this will toward him.

Arminians ask, But if this salvation depends on God's sovereign interaction only, why does God not graciously intervene in the lives of *all* people? Where is God's righteousness, or his love, if he intervenes in the lives of only *some* people, namely, his elect? Calvinists reply to this that, if all fallen people were to be eternally lost, they have only themselves to blame for this. The fact that God nonetheless desires to show mercy to *some*, so that not *all* will perish, is the very demonstration of his love. The question *why* God has elected only a limited number is not answered in the Bible. But we do know that all the wicked are eternally lost by their own fault, and that God is not obliged to save even one single person. Where this is the case, it is not clear why God would be unrighteous if he saves only some, and not all. That is the view of Calvinism.

Of course, this does not answer some burning questions: (a) Did God indeed decree the Fall? How can we demonstrate this from the Bible? (b) If God decreed the Fall (not just foreknew it!), how can Adam and Eve still be held responsible for their fall? (c) If the Fall was indeed decreed, so that *all* have become sinners, why was not the salvation of *all* people decreed as well?

Calvinists in turn also have a few burning questions for the Arminians: How can a person, who is "prone by nature to hate God and [my] neighbor"[3] (cf. Luke 19:14; John 3:20; 7:7; 15:18, 23–25; Titus 3:3), ever begin to repent and to love God by his own free will? If Arminians say that this occurs with the help of God, the question forcefully comes back to them: Why then does God not grant this help to *all* people? If he *offers* this help to all people, but not all people accept it, then in the end it is still people's own choice that is decisive. And the Calvinist will repeat: How can a wicked person, with a corrupted will and a heart full of hatred toward God, ever *want* to be saved? In other words, how can people ever *make* the good choice?

Arminians will answer with this counter-question: How can the Bible speak so often of the urgent, yes, imploring appeal of God toward people, and even of God's sadness when people do not accept his offer of salvation (see §13.5)? How could this be true if God knows very well that people are not *able* to accept salvation unless he himself first changes their

---

3. Heidelberg Catechism, Lord's Day 2, Q&A 5; cf. Dennison (*RCET* 4:771).

hearts, as Calvinists would have us believe? How can Jesus complain that he *wanted* to save the people of Jerusalem but that *they* did not want his salvation (Luke 13:34)? God *appeals* to the human will: "If anyone's *will* is to do God's will, he will know whether the teaching is from God or whether I am speaking on my own authority" (John 7:17). "All who are thirsty may come; they can have the water of life as a free gift *if they want it*" (Rev. 22:17 ERV).

10.2 The Conflict
10.2.1 The Two Sides

Here we have arrived at the core of the problem. The central question is this: Why are some saved, and others lost? The Arminian will answer: Because some people accept the offered salvation, and others do not. It is people's own fault if they refuse to accept God's salvation that is offered to them. The (hyper-)Calvinist will answer: Because some have been elected by God for this salvation, and others have not. It is time that we place alongside (or, over against) these two answers the reply of Viatorism: The fact that some are saved, and others are lost, is one hundred percent due to people's own responsibility, and one hundred percent due to God's sovereign decree. From a superficial standpoint, this might sound unsatisfying, and even impossible, because supposedly the Arminian and the (hyper-)Calvinist standpoints are logically contradictory. The answer of Viatorism to this, as I see it, is twofold.

(a) Saying that some are saved and others are lost due entirely to their own responsibility is *just as biblical* as saying that it is due entirely based upon God's sovereign decree. We will have to leave these two biblical lines entirely intact, the one alongside the other, like the two rails of a train track.

(b) Arminianism and (hyper-)Calvinism are logically contradictory only if the terms involved (election, reprobation) are treated as concepts, not as ideas, as in statements like this one: if a person was not elected from eternity, it is logical that he was reprobate from eternity. (This apart from the presence of another fallacy here: non-elect is not necessarily identical with reprobate.)

Only some self-made logic, which wishes to rescue at all costs the inner coherence of one's own thought system and treats the terms involved as concepts, not as ideas, feels forced to choose either the Arminian or the (hyper-)Calvinist position, and to argue the other away.

Fortunately, today we encounter many moderate Cavinists. Thus, the guidelines of the Dutch Reformed Church in the Netherlands rightly state: "[A] dogmatic reflection and consideration of this mystery [of election] is allowed and needed, but on the condition that at the same time the relativity of the truth of our human reflection is realized. Human logic does not coincide with the divine Logos."[4] This is a wise word. However, a bit later we read, "The church expects of her theologians that they attempt to reflect further about this contradiction [viz., God's work versus human work]; she must call a halt to everyone who wants to weaken or remove [this contradiction]."[5] My comment is that this contradiction arises only if the matters involved are conceptualized.

As I see it, Arminians, including Open Theists, ignore the *biblical* fact that the salvation of some wicked people is not based on their own merit but is founded in an eternal, sovereign, gracious decree of election. Decretalists, including hyper-Calvinists, ignore the *biblical* fact that the salvation of some wicked people involves not only God's work but also their own action. To Arminians we say: If God would not graciously and sovereignly intervene, no person would or could be saved. To hyper-Calvinists we say: If a person does not repent and accept the gospel, as he is obliged to do, he cannot and will not be saved. To both we say that salvation is one hundred percent a work of God's sovereign grace, *and* one hundred percent the work of human responsibility and

---

4. Hervormde Kerk (1962, 10).
5. Ibid., 19.

freedom. No person should try to play off the one side against the other side of the matter, as, in my view, both Arminians and hyper-Calvinists do.

10.2.2 The Proof Texts

Of course, both positions have had their powerful defenders. It is therefore naïve to think that these positions could be refuted by a simple appeal to certain Bible verses. Nevertheless, it has been tried many times.

Against Arminians the following texts have been adduced: "All that the Father gives me will come to me.... No one can come to me unless the Father who sent me draws him" (John 6:37a, 44a). However, over against this, verse 37b sounds very "Arminian": "[W]hoever comes to me [without any exception!] I will never cast out." (Hyper-)Calvinists may reply: But only those will actually come who have been "given" or "drawn" by the Father (vv. 37a, 44a). Arminians may reply: If all may come, then all are in principle given or drawn by the Father.

Against Arminians one could also adduce this verse: "[B]y grace you have been saved through faith. And this is not your own doing; it is the gift of God" (Eph. 2:8). However, in support of Arminians, we note that (a) it is not clear whether the word "it" indeed refers back to "faith" (opinions are divided), and (b) the verse does not say that this gift is intended only for some (cf. Eccl. 3:13, "[E]veryone should eat and drink and take pleasure in all his toil — this is God's gift to man," that is, to *all* people).

Against (hyper-)Calvinists this passage has been adduced: "How often would I have gathered your children together as a hen gathers her brood under her wings, and you were not willing!" (Luke 13:34b). However, (hyper-)Calvinists will argue that this is only the desiring (preceptive) will of the Lord (cf. 1 Tim. 2:4; 2 Pet. 3:9); no one can resist his absolute, decretive will. Or this passage: "[W]e know, brothers loved by God, that he has chosen you, because ... you *received* [many translate: *accepted*] the word" (1 Thess. 1:4-6). Apparently, only those who have accepted the gospel have been elected. However, (hyper-)Calvinists will reply: (a) this "because" does not mean that believers were elected *because* they accepted the gospel, but only that they accepted because they were elected. (b) The complete verse 5 says, ". . . because our gospel came to you not only in word, but also in power and in the Holy Spirit and with full conviction," which implies that these believers could never have accepted the gospel without this power of the Holy Spirit.

The debate surrounding predestination is a remarkable example of a very complex theological subject, which cannot be resolved with a direct appeal to a select group of Bible verses. Thus, one could argue that Arminians cannot circumvent this "clear" statement: "[N]o one *seeks* for God" (Rom. 3:11; cf. Ps. 14:2; 53:2) — for how can they maintain that repentance is people's free choice if *no one* seeks for God? However, one could just as easily argue that (hyper)Calvinists do not know what to do with this "clear" statement: God "made from one man every nation of mankind to live on all the face of the earth . . . that they should *seek* God, and perhaps feel their way toward him and find him" (Acts 17:26-27) — for how can they take such an appeal seriously if no person by himself is able and willing to seek God? God even entreats his people: "*Seek* the LORD while he may be found" (Isa. 55:6; cf. Amos 5:4-6, 14; 8:12).

The evasion of R. C. Sproul that this concerns only Israel[6] is mistaken, (a) because of Acts 17:26-27, just quoted (which addresses all humanity), and (b) because no one could seriously believe that here God is addressing only people who already know him. (This is different in, e.g., Ps. 32:6, "Therefore let everyone who is godly offer prayer to you at a time when you may be found.")

---

6. Sproul (1986, 110).

10.2.3 The Response of Viatorism

Viatorism can do justice to *both* sides. Salvation is equally the consequence of God's sovereign intervention and of the free choice of the human will. Viatorism does justice both to the fact that no one can be saved without the operation of the Holy Spirit, and to the fact that God entreats people to accept his salvation but that some do not receive it because they do not want to. Only Viatorism claims that an eternal decree of election does not necessarily imply an eternal decree of reprobation, as consistent Calvinists want to have it. Only Viatorism claims that God's foreknowledge does not exclude the human freedom of will, as Open Theists want to have it.

Only Viatorism insists that we no longer need to choose between one or the other answer to questions such as: Do people believe because they were predestined for this, or were people predestined for salvation because God foresaw that they would believe? Or, what came first: regeneration or repentance? (Or, was Noah righteous because he had found favor in God's eyes, or had he found favor in God's eyes because he was righteous? Gen. 6:8-9.) To both questions (hyper-)Calvinists will reply: the former; and Arminians: the latter. Viatorism replies: both are causally and temporally true; they are the two sides of the same coin. All these points and many more will be explained in this and subsequent chapters.

People have sometimes used the following metaphor: God's sovereignty and human freedom are like parallel lines, which meet in eternity. This is a wonderful mental picture, although, of course, such a metaphor has little persuasive power. However, it is very telling that such a rectilineal (!) thinker as R. C. Sproul ridicules this metaphor by stressing that parallel lines never *can* meet; this would be a flagrant contradiction.[7] With such cheap shots, *every* metaphor can be destroyed. But with the help of Albert Einstein we have come to realize, however, that if our universe is curved in the fourth

---

7. Ibid., 39–40.

dimension, perfectly parallel lines do indeed meet. (Or, in a simpler example, the meridians on our globe are perfectly parallel, yet meet at the North and South Poles.)

This Einsteinian discovery makes the metaphor all the more beautiful: the parallel lines of God's sovereignty and human freedom will never meet in our three-dimensional world, but in *God's* world they apparently do. That is more satisfactory than Sproul's "solution," in which one of the two lines is—not formally, but at least *de facto*—simply obliterated with the eraser of his logic.

10.3 Predestination and God's Counsel
10.3.1 Election

Gerrit Berkouwer writes:

> Indeed, we can say that especially two dogmas of the Church have constantly borne the brunt of attack from those on the outside. These are *divine election* and *original sin*. Apart from the other ciricism levelled, it has always seemed to some that these two teachings especially demonstrate, with a unique cogency, the irrationality of Christian faith. *Both* of these doctrines have been called harsh and entirely arbitrary.[8]

About the doctrine of original sin I have written elsewhere;[9] the doctrine of divine election is our focus here. It is highly important; people have sometimes called it *cor ecclesiae*, "the heart of the church,"[10] and the underlying problem of God's sovereignty versus human responsibility belongs to the heart of Scripture as well.[11] Although eternal divine election comes to light clearly in the New Testament for the first time, the notion of election occurs in the Old Testament as well. Already

---

8. Berkouwer (1971, 424; the final italics was present in the Dutch original, but omitted from the published English translation).
9. Ouweneel (EDR 3, chapter 12).
10. Cf. Vermeulen (1986) on the election doctrine of Barth (1936, II/2:3: "The doctrine of election is the sum of the Gospel . . ."), but the term is older; cf. Berkouwer (1960, 51).
11. Cf. Ouweneel (EDR 3, §§3.3.2, 13.2.6, and 14.4.3).

here, there is a tension between God choosing people, and people choosing God. Thus, on the one hand we read, "Blessed is the one you [i.e., God] *choose* and bring near, to dwell in your courts" (Ps. 65:4); on the other hand, the believer says, "I have *chosen* the way of faithfulness" (Ps. 119:30; cf. v. 173; Josh. 24:15, "choose this day whom you will serve"). Or on the one hand we read, "[T]he LORD will have compassion on Jacob and will again *choose* Israel" (Isa. 14:1), and on the other hand there are those "who keep my Sabbaths, who *choose* the things that please me and hold fast my covenant" (56:4).

The subject of the predestination of people is a part of the broader subject of the counsel of God. Therefore, many of our considerations expressed in previous chapters will return here, but then within the specific context of election and reprobation. One of the central questions discussed earlier in §2.1 was this: Is everything that ever happened, happens, and will happen included in the counsel of God? Does this also mean that everything that happens was *wanted* by God, and if so, in what sense? Does this mean that there are things that God does not want in themselves, such as sins, but which he, from eternity, does want in another sense, namely, insofar as they serve his eternal purposes?

With regard to predestination this, among other things, implies the following questions: If everything that ever happens is included in God's counsel, does this mean that the eternal destination of every human is included in this same counsel? Conversely, if there are doubts concerning whether everything is included in God's counsel, is it not equally doubtful whether God has decreed from eternity the destiny of every human? If everything that happens was decreed by God, does this imply that from eternity God also wanted the eternal destruction of unbelievers? What higher purpose is served in this way? If this purpose is God's glorification, and if God has decreed everything that happens, why did he not rather decree that all people would ultimately believe in him? Is he not glorified more by the salvation of *all* people than by the salvation of only some, and the destruction of the others?

10.3.2 Responsibility

How does all this relate to human responsibility and freedom of will? First, did Adam and Eve have a free will before the Fall? How can this be maintained if the Fall as such was decreed by God from eternity? If God wanted them to fall—because the Fall would help realize his purposes—what role did their own will play?

And what about *since* the Fall? If since the Fall people have no free will, how is it possible that they make free decisions every day of their lives?[12] One may even *freely* choose the view that maintains the notion of the free will (Arminianism), or *freely* choose the view that rejects the notion of the free will ([hyper-]Calvinism). Or, if the entire notion of a free will is only an illusion, how can people ever be held accountable for their actions?

To what extent are people responsible for their conversion—or their permanent inconvertibility, for that matter—if these matters, too, have been decreed by God from eternity? But the opposite question is also appropriate: If a person's conversion or his permanent inconvertibility is entirely a matter of his free choice and responsibility, to what extent is this influenced by God's assistance? How can this human responsibility be reconciled with God's sovereignty?

Given the free choice and responsibility of people, *can* there be genuine election and predestination from before the foundation of the world? If these terms must be maintained—and they must, for they are *biblical* terms—does this mean that God elected certain people entirely according to his own will and choice, *or* because he foresaw that these people would come to faith in him? Or something in between? Or something of both? Or nothing of both?

Is it an illusion that we will ever be able to reconcile divine

---
12. See ibid., §14.4.3.

sovereignty and human responsibility, or divine predestination and human freedom? Or must we follow (hyper)Calvinists and downplay human freedom? Or must we instead follow Arminians, including Open Theists, and downplay God's sovereignty and foreknowledge? Or will we simply have to live with this tension, accept that it cannot be resolved, and try to be happy with this situation?

10.3.3 The Prodigal Son

Let me give a biblical example that helps us to practically illustrate the problems mentioned, namely, the so-called parable of the prodigal son (Luke 15:11–32).[13] Here, God is depicted as a father who longs for a genuine, loving fellowship with *both* his sons. If we cast the parable as a story about divine salvation, then we see that one son leaves the Father, while the other one stays with him. One son squanders the wealth of the Father, but repents and comes back to the Father, who graciously accepts him. The other son is decent and neat, but no more than that. He stayed with the Father, but never had a real relationship with him. With the youngest son, the genuine, loving fellowship is formed for which the Father has longed so much, but not with the eldest son.

If we apply this parable to reality, some questions that arise and that have enormous consequences for our view of divine sovereignty and human responsibility are the following.

(a) Was the eldest son *predestined* from eternity to remain outside, and the youngest son to fall within, this fellowship? If so, how can the Father long so intensely for fellowship with the eldest son as well, if he himself has rejected him from eternity?

(b) Conversely, to what extent is this fellowship purely the free choice of these sons? Or are they not free, but just products of their circumstances?

---

13. Cf. Pinnock (2001, 3–4, 81, 96).

(c) Does the Father extort love from his sons, or are the sons perfectly free to choose to love the Father or not?

(d) Was the detour of sin necessary to bring the youngest son to this genuine fellowship, or could this also have been reached without it?

(e) Did the Father *foreordain* the ways of his sons, or did he grant a certain amount of freedom to his sons, and did he voluntarily accept the risk that his sons would go their own ways?

(f) Did the Father *foreknow* what his two sons would choose, or did he have to wait and see what they would do? At the end of the parable, it is not even said whether the eldest son will yet enter the house, or not! The future of the eldest son is open, as Open Theists would say.

Of course, we cannot base our entire theology on a parable, and of course, the best comparison fails at certain points, so we must be careful with our conclusions. But at least we could say that it will hardly do to make a parable say the opposite of what it actually says. This is a parable about *voluntary* love, about a Father who assumes risks by granting his sons free options, about a God who does not determine and control all things, but longs for genuine, voluntary love and fellowship with his creatures, and implores them to enter into this relationship with him. He is presented here as a God who does not force his sons to *stay* home, or to *come* home, but awaits his sons with open arms. He waits for both the eldest and the youngest sons, who at a given moment are both outside and must decide whether they wish to come in. The question whether they indeed will come in does not depend on the Father's mercy only but also on the sons' willingness.

10.4 Doxology
10.4.1 Doxological Context

The questions mentioned are extraordinarily tricky, and have led to numerous controversies, and even church splits. All the more remarkable, then, that in the New Testament the topic of election never arises in contexts of controversy but rather of doxology:

> Blessed be the God and Father of our Lord Jesus Christ, who has blessed us in Christ with every spiritual blessing in the heavenly places, even as he *chose* us in him before the foundation of the world, that we should be holy and blameless before him. In love he *predestined* us for adoption as sons through Jesus Christ, according to the *purpose* of his will, to the praise of his glorious grace, with which he has blessed us in the Beloved (Eph. 1:3-6).

Whereas the subject of predestination has brought many to a state of great uncertainty, or of fear, or of apathetic resignation, we find it in the New Testament in a jubilating context:

> For those whom he foreknew he also predestined to be conformed to the image of his Son, in order that he might be the firstborn among many brothers. And those whom he predestined he also called, and those whom he called he also justified, and those whom he justified he also glorified. What then shall we say to these things? If God is for us, who can be against us? ... Who shall separate us from the love of Christ? (Rom. 8:29-31, 35).

Paul's treatise of election in Romans 9-11 ends with this doxology in 11:33-36:

> Oh, the depth of the riches and wisdom and knowledge of God! How unsearchable are his judgments and how inscrutable his ways! 'For who has known the mind of the Lord, or who has been his counselor?' [Isa. 40:13] 'Or who has given a gift to him that he might be repaid?' [Job 41:2] For from him and through him and to him are all things. To him be glory forever. Amen.

Peter's first letter begins as follows:

> To those who are elect exiles of the Dispersion ... according to the *foreknowledge* of God the Father, in the sanctification of the Spirit, for obedience to Jesus Christ and for sprinkling with his blood: May grace and peace be multiplied to you. Blessed

be the God and Father of our Lord Jesus Christ! According to his great mercy, he has caused us to be born again to a living hope through the resurrection of Jesus Christ from the dead, . . . (1 Pet. 1:1–3).

10.4.2 Doxological Goal

Moreover, election occurs *with a view to* glorifying God. That is, from eternity, God had elected for himself "a chosen race, a royal priesthood, a holy nation, a people for his own possession, that you may proclaim the excellencies of him who called you out of darkness into his marvelous light" (1 Pet. 2:9).

This verse is an allusion to several Old Testament passages, where the expressions mentioned are applied to Israel (Exod. 19:5; Deut. 7:6; 14:2; 26:18). It is remarkable that, in the course of history, especially before the foundation of the state of Israel, the nation was known as the people of the "Jews." The word "Jew" comes from the Hebrew *Yehudi* (Gr. *Ioudaios*), which means "descendant of Judah [Heb. *Yehudah*]." (Judah was only one of the twelve tribes, but gradually *all* the Israelites were referred to as "Jews"; cf. Est. 3:6, 13) The name Judah means something like "praise"; compare what we read about his mother: "And she conceived again and bore a son, and said, 'This time I will praise [*y-d-h*] the Lord.' Therefore she called his name Judah" (Gen. 29:35). The people of Israel are a people *chosen* by God to be a constant praise to him; the same holds for the *chosen* church of God.

Paul says of the saints, "To them God *chose* to make known how great among the Gentiles are the riches of the glory of this mystery, which is Christ in you, the hope of glory" (Col. 1:27). That is, they are the public display of divine and eternal glory. "[T]hrough the church the manifold wisdom of God [is] now made known to the rulers and authorities in the heavenly places. This was according to the *eternal purpose* that he has realized in Christ Jesus our Lord" (Eph. 3:10–11).

In these chapters, we will try to rise above uncertainty, idle resignation, and controversy in order to echo these doxological tones. The doctrine of predestination should not be threatening, but should bring consolation and joy. It should turn us into true worshippers of God. As Herman Bavinck put it: "But to believe in and to confess election is to recognize even the most unworthy and degraded human being as a creature of God and an object of his eternal love. The purpose of election is not — as it is so often proclaimed — to [reject] the many but to invite all to participate in the riches of God's grace in Christ."[14]

10.5 Essential Aspects
10.5.1 Two Questions

Reformed pastor Henry Kersten summarized the controversy just mentioned in the following way: "One of the two must be true: either God's decree determines the condemnation and salvation of His creatures, or they depend on the creature himself. As we saw in the previous chapter, the latter of these alternatives violates the Essence of God."[15] Is it really that simple? I could immediately add two other options: (c) eternal blessedness has been determined by God's decree, but damnation depends on the creature; (d) damnation and blessedness have been determined by God's decree and they depend on the creature. Which of these four options "attack God in his being"? Who decides that? By what criteria? Is the slightest involvement of creatures already an attack on God's sovereignty? What if God himself has *sovereignly* decided to *actively involve* creatures?

In my view, Kersten is a typical example of someone who has not even *fathomed*, much less solved, the underlying problems. Therefore, to get a clearer picture of the controversy, let

---

14. Bavinck (*RD* 2:402; although the published English translation renders "om velen af te stoten" as "to turn off the many," our translation of the Dutch verb *afstoten* seems preferable); cf. Demarest (1997, 138–39).
15. Kersten (1980, 1:119).

me ask six questions that in my view are essential, in which my points (c) and (d) are addressed. These questions are not intended to be suggestive, as if they would necessarily *a priori* disclose my own views.

(1) Why could we not equally well view it as an attack on God's being if we suppose that, even before he had created any human, he intended to create millions of people with no other goal than to deliver them to eternal damnation? Please note, God supposedly did primarily do this, on the basis not of these people's (wrong) choices and actions as such, but of his own, free, sovereign decision. If (hyper-)Calvinists wish to defend God's sovereignty in this way, what answer do they have to those critics who object that these (hyper-)Calvinists thus attack God's *righteousness*? The various parties in this conflict sometimes blame the other party for shortchanging the honor of God's being. This is not only meaningless but also arrogant: people thereby pretend to fathom God's being so well that they know precisely what things shortchange this being, and what things do not.

(2) Why could it not be the case that eternal damnation and blessedness are perfectly determined *both* by God's decree *and* depend on human responsibility and free choices? Logically, this might seem impossible. However, many logical objections evaporate as soon as we begin to see that election, predestination, and reprobation must be treated not as concepts but as ideas.[16] I repeat, this is not a flight into mysticism and irrationalism; we can speak about ideas in an entirely rational way.

10.5.2 Four More Questions

(3) In the latter case (see question [2]), why could eternal election unto eternal salvation not be *both* a matter of God's own free, sovereign choice *and* of foreseen faith? This too might sound like an "insolent sophism,"[17] but this might be so

---

16. See Ouweneel (EDR 3, §§1.2–1.3).
17. Cf. the Canons of Dordt, Conclusion.

only in the ears of those who treat election and predestination as concepts. Where this happens, theologians always feel compelled to make a logical choice. Either they choose human responsibility — understandably so, for there are many Bible verses pointing in this direction — and argue away all the verses that stress God's sovereign decree (Pelagianism, Arminianism, Open Theism). Or they choose election as an act of God's sovereign will — understandably so, for there are many Bible verses pointing in this direction — and argue away all the verses that stress human responsibility ([hyper-]Calvinism).

Perhaps this is a good time to speak about my continual hesitation about whether I should write Calvinism or hyper-Calvinism. As to the former, Wolfhart Pannenberg, when dealing with Calvin's personal view, rightly spoke of "the logical pressure of the thought of an election and predestination that rests solely on the eternal will of God."[18] And Otto Weber said (in my view equally rightly), "However, Calvin's doctrine of predestination, although it certainly did not arise out of speculation and he did warn much against theological construction, still did not by any means elude it."[19] Thus, in a certain sense, the thesis could be defended that hyper-Calvinism is closest to Calvin's own view. It is therefore a reason for joy and thankfulness that present-day moderate Calvinists on essential points have *moved away* from Calvin's personal view. And understandably so: for almost five centuries we have had time to evaluate Calvin's thoughts, and it would be strange if we had not made some progress (see §1.3.2 above).

(4) If we use terms like "election" and "predestination" strictly as ideas, and not as concepts, why could it not be the case that there *is* an eternal predestination to salvation (a thing mentioned many times in Scripture) but not an eternal predestination to damnation (a thing never mentioned in Scripture)? In other words, if we treat the terms concerned as

---

18. Pannenberg (1991, 3:446).
19. Weber (1983, 2:426).

ideas, an eternal decree of reprobation does not necessarily follow from an eternal decree of election, such as might be the case if we treated these terms as concepts.

(5) Just as, in the heat of the debate, divine sovereignty and human responsibility are unduly severed, could it not be that similarly, eternity and history, or God's counsel and God's ways, are unduly severed? Is it really so self-evident that God's election and predestination belong to (timeless, a-historical!) eternity, and human choices to time and history? Wolfhart Pannenberg disapprovingly wrote about viewing election in a way that "makes the divine decision timeless, in abstraction from the concerte historicity of the divine acts of election as the Bible bears witness to them," and in a way that "restricts the purpose of election to participation in future salvation in disjunction from any historical function of the elect."[20]

(6) How can we be so sure that predestination applies to each human being individually? Why could it not be a corporate notion, for instance, in the sense that there is a church elected from eternity? It is precisely with regard to the one church of God that Paul writes about God's "eternal purpose" (Eph. 3:10–11). Similarly, Peter says about believers collectively that they are a "chosen *race*" (1 Pet. 2:9). God took from the Gentiles a *people*, not just individual believers (Acts 15:14). Christ purified for himself a "*people* for his own possession" (Titus 2:14; cf. Exod. 19:5; Deut. 7:6; 14:2; 26:18). The idea would then be that every believer receives a share in this race or people, without the necessity of assuming that from eternity it has been decreed which persons will have a share in this elected church (cf. §11.9.3). Pannenberg wrote disapprovingly about a view of election that "detaches individuals as the objects of election from all relations to society."[21]

---

20. Pannenberg (1991, 3:442).
21. Ibid.

10.6 Three Theses
10.6.1 First Thesis

Let me supplement my previous considerations with three theses, which reflect my own position.

First, Scripture *never* speaks either implicitly or explicitly of an eternal decree of reprobation, nor does such a decree logically follow from any biblical statement. Therefore, we can only conclude that it is a purely human invention. Scripture teaches nowhere that the eternal destiny of *every* human being has been decreed by God from eternity. It is not even necessarily logical: excluding some people from certain blessings is something very different from foreordaining them for eternal damnation.

It is a bit like telling a limited number of youngsters in the classroom that they have been chosen to visit the king's palace. It is obvious that the other members of the class are excluded from this privilege. But it would be weird to conclude that therefore these excluded youngsters are automatically condemned to go to prison. There are more places than the palace or prison. The comparison would fail only if, in eternity future, there would be nothing but heaven and hell. But first, this presupposes the Fall; without the Fall, it might have been conceivable that some were elected for eternal blessedness in the "heavenly places" (Eph. 1:3-5; 2:4-7), but would have continued living on the earth. Second, some have made a distinction between living on the new earth (Rev. 21:1-4) and dwelling in the Father's house (John 14:1-4). (This is only understandable for those who make a distinction between the members of the New Testament church and all other believers.[22])

For further arguments and biblical evidence, see chapter 14 below.

---

22. See Ouweneel (EDR 7, chapters 2–3; 2016c, chapters 6–7).

10.6.2 Second Thesis

Scripture never stressed God's gracious and sovereign blessings at the expense of people's own will and responsibility, both before and after the Fall. In no biblical passage are people ever treated as "stocks and blocks" (to quote an expression from the Canons of Dordt[23]), that is, as completely passive recipients of God's blessings; they are for those who *want* them (Luke 13:34; John 7:17; Rev. 22:17).

To be sure, there is no question here of any form of real *synergy* (cooperation), in this case a synergy between God and humanity, as if the two could be thought to be working together on more or less equal footing (see §5.4.3). That is, taking into account human responsibility may never occur at the expense of honoring God's sovereignty and of grounding election in the unmerited and undeserved grace of God.

Berkouwer wrote extensively about the notion of synergism and the refutation of it,[24] for instance, by insisting that Scripture knows nothing of the idea of *complementing*, in the sense that the human side would complement the divine side.[25] He pointed to Philippians 2:12-13, "[W]ork out your own salvation with fear and trembling, for it is God who works in you, both to will and to work for his good pleasure." Here, the human side ("work out your own salvation") is *based upon* the divine side (note the "for" at the beginning of v. 13).[26]

---

23. "But as man by the fall did not cease to be a creature endowed with understanding and will, nor did sin which pervaded the whole race of mankind deprive him of the human nature, but brought upon him depravity and spiritual death; so also this grace of regeneration *does not treat men as senseless stocks and blocks, nor take away their will and its properties*, or do violence thereto; but it spiritually quickens, heals, corrects, and at the same time sweetly and powerfully bends it [i.e., this will], that where carnal rebellion and resistance formerly prevailed, a ready and sincere spiritual obedience begins to reign; in which the true and spiritual restoration and freedom of our will consist. . . ." (Canons of Dordt III/IV.16; italics added; Dennison [2008, 4:139]).
24. Berkouwer (1960, chapter 2).
25. Berkouwer (1960, 44).
26. Berkouwer (1960, 45); cf. Calvin, *Institutes* 2.5.11.

The Lutheran *Torgisches Buch* ("Book of Torgau")[27] of 1576 denies that God and people cooperate "like two horses together draw a cart." Conversely, Berkouwer rightly said, "In the light of the gospel it is foolish to let man's acts and decision shrink to *nothingness* in a system of monergism"[28] (the opposite of synergism). Without detracting at all from God's sovereign grace, the doctrine of election must leave room, no matter how small, for human responsibility and freedom of will. It might be an exaggeration, when the elephant and the mouse clomped across a wooden bridge, for the mouse to say, "Listen to the noise we are making!" Yet, the mouse's steps definitely contributed to the noise.

10.6.3 Third Thesis

The doctrine of the unilateral emphasis on God's sovereignty in predestination (at the expense of human responsibility) and of eternal reprobation is rooted strictly in human logic, based upon erroneously treating terms like election and predestination as concepts from which various properties are predicated without any warrant from Scripture. Therefore, Reformed theologian Lubbert van der Zanden rightly wrote, "We can apply neither our notion of time nor our logic to God's eternal decree."[29]

Let me provide three remarkable examples of this error, one of which combats the error, and two that support it. First, concerning John Calvin, the report of the Synod of the Dutch Reformed Church in the Netherlands wrote disapprovingly about him, "Logic as well drives Calvin to seek the actual basis of reprobation in God's eternal decree because, in his view, election and reprobation logically presuppose each other."[30]

The second example is from Louis Berkhof, who *supported* this kind of logic: "The doctrine of reprobation naturally fol-

---

27. Not the *Formula Concordiae*, as Berkouwer erroneously states.
28. Berkouwer (1960, 50; italics in the Dutch original, but omitted from the published English translation; cf. 51–52).
29. Van der Zanden (1949, 45).
30. Hervormde Kerk (1962, 35).

lows from the logic [!] of the situation. The decree of election inevitably implies the decree of reprobation. If the all-wise God, possessed of infinite knowledge, has eternally purposed to save some, then He *ipso facto* also purposed not to save others. If He has chosen or elected some, then He has by that very fact also rejected others."[31] Speaking of logic: notice how, in Berkhof's argument, "not saving" smoothly slips into "rejecting," which is not logical at all (see the example given in §10.6.1).

The third example is Lewis Sperry Chafer: "Election and retribution are counterparts of each other. There can be no election of some that does not imply the rejection of others."[32] A bit later he wrote, "It is impossible actively to choose some from a company and not, at the same time and by the same process, actively reject the remainder."[33] Here we find the same problem as with Berkhof: exempting certain people from certain blessings does not automatically mean eternal damnation.

Herman Ridderbos insists that such arguments

> place Paul's pronouncements concerning the church as foreknown by God and elect in Christ under *another point of view* than that of Paul himself and thus abstract and extrapolate them from the context of the Pauline doctrine of salvation, an extrapolation that easily leads to conclusions Paul himself does not draw and which are entirely in conflict with the tenor of his preaching.[34]

In my view, the Reformed Ridderbos speaks here more wisely than the dispensationalist Chafer! I will try to elucidate this point below.

The Reformed Jan van Genderen wrote, "It is not clear to

---

31. Berkhof (1996, 117–18).
32. Chafer (*ST* 1:244).
33. Chafer (*ST* 1:247).
34. Ridderbos (1975, 350; italics in the Dutch original, but omitted from the published English translation).

all believers how important the doctrine of [election] really is. The Reformed are more aware of this than others."[35] I would rather say that Reformed theologians have elaborated the subject more than others, and therefore have also made more mistakes in connection with this matter than others. We will have to investigate whether this claim can be supported. At any rate, even if it were for this reason alone, Evangelicals living among Reformed and Presbyterian Christians will be obliged to pay attention to this subject. The great nineteenth-century pioneer John N. Darby set the example: "I believe that predestination to life is the eternal purpose of God, by which, before the foundations of the world were laid, He firmly decreed, by His counsel secret to us, to deliver from curse and destruction those whom He had chosen in Christ out of the human race, *and to bring them, through Christ, as vessels made to honour, to eternal salvation.*"[36]

10.7 Terminology
10.7.1 Basics

"Predestination" (Latin *praedestinatio*[37]) means "destining beforehand," which the New Testament states as having occurred before the foundation of the world (Eph. 1:4; Rev. 13:8; cf. John 17:24; 1 Pet. 1:20). In the (hyper-)Calvinist view, it includes both the eternal election (*electio*) of those saved (*electi*, "elect [or chosen] ones") and the eternal rejection (*reiectio*) or reprobation (*reprobatio*) of the wicked ones (*reprobi*, "rejected ones"). Calvin has defined predestination as "God's eternal decree, by which he determined with himself what he willed to become of each man. For all are not created in equal condition; rather, eternal life is forordained for some, eternal

---

35. Van Genderen and Velema (2008, 201; throughout this section, the English translators incorrectly and inconsistently render "verkiezing" as "predestination").
36. Darby (*CW* 3:3).
37. I mention the Latin terms as well because of their role in the history of theology, and because they are often similar to the corresponding English terms.

damnation for others."[38]

Calvinists sometimes speak of a "double predestination" (*gemina praedestinatio*); that is, they believe in a predestination of some to eternal blessedness as well as a predestination of others to eternal damnation. They also speak of a decree of election and a decree of reprobation. Calvin himself called the latter as "[God's] just and irreprehensible but incomprehensible judgment,"[39] and even said, *Decretum quidem horribile, fateor* ("The decree is dreadful indeed, I confess").[40]

One could defend the position that (a) the doctrine of double predestination as well as (b) the doctrine that the relationship between God and humanity is fundamentally covenantal are the two distinguishing features of Calvinism; they share all other doctrines with other orthodox Christians. If I may add a personal note here: in a certain sense, I sympathize with both dogmas, but in the strict sense I can accept neither one.[41] That is to say, I believe in an eternal decree of election, but not in an eternal decree of reprobation; and I believe that especially the father–child relationship between God and the believer can in no way be viewed as covenantal. So, strictly speaking, I cannot be called a Calvinist, although in principle I accept all of the so-called "Five Points of Calvinism" (TULIP; see §12.3),[42] and even though I have published a congenial work on the Heidelberg Catechism.[43]

We must notice here that the phrase "double predestination" does not necessarily mean that election and reprobation are strictly parallel, an observation that many authors have emphasized.[44] Thus, the Canons of Dordt (Conclusion) *deny*

---

38. Calvin, *Institutes* 3.21.5; on Calvin's view, see extensively, Klooster (1977).
39. Calvin, *Institutes* 3.21.7.
40. Calvin, *Institutes* 3.23.7; on the Augustinianism in Calvin's view, see Hughes (1989, 152–58).
41. See extensively, Ouweneel (EDR 7–10).
42. A North American Reformed scholar once called me the "most Reformed non-Reformed person" he knew.
43. Ouweneel (2016a).
44. See, e.g., Bavinck (*RD* 2:395–99); Barth (1936, II/2:16–17, 18, 133–35, 174–

that "in the same manner in which the election is the fountain and cause of faith and good works, reprobation is the cause of unbelief and impiety." Such criticism of the supposed parallelism is theologically very important, as we will see. But at this point I would ask: Does this criticism perhaps mean that Calvinists, as the Reformed dogmatician Gerrit Berkouwer put it, make "a last-minute retreat from the 'consequences' of [their] own doctrine of election"?[45]

The term "predestination" has been adopted from the Vulgate, where we encounter the Latin word *praedestinare* in several passages. It is the translation of the Greek *prohorizō*, derived from *pro*, "prae-, before," and *horizō*, "to destine, to ordain." We disregard here Acts 4:27-28 and 1 Corinthians 2:7-8, because these passages deal with the predestination of Jesus, and we limit our attention to those passages that refer to people who from eternity have been destined for a certain purpose. There are only four of them, in only two Bible chapters.

* "[T]hose whom he foreknew he also predestined [Gr. *prohōrisen*, Lat. *praedestinavit*] to be conformed to the image of his Son, in order that he might be the firstborn among many brothers . . . those whom he predestined [same Gr. and Lat. words] he also called" (Rom. 8:29-30).

* God "predestined [Gr. *prohōrisas*, Lat. *praedestinavit*] us for adoption as sons through Jesus Christ, according to the purpose of his will. . . . In him we have obtained an inheritance, having been predestined [Gr. *prohoristhentes*, Lat. *praedestinati*] according to the purpose of him who works all things according to the counsel of his will" (Eph. 1:5, 11).

10.7.2 Choosing, Election

In addition to the previous terms, the New Testament contains a number of terms, the great majority of which may be

---

75); Dijk (1952, 141–43); Althaus (1952, 2:436); Berkouwer (1960, 175–79).
45. Berkouwer (1960, 179; internal punctuation is present in the Dutch original, but omitted from the published English translation).

viewed more or less as synonyms, referring to human beings (excluding the "elect angels" of 1 Tim. 5:21).

* *To choose, to elect* (Gr. *eklegomai*, Lat. *eligo*; see the next term):[46] "[M]any are called, but few are chosen" (Matt. 22:14); "for the sake of the elect those days [of tribulation] will be cut short . . . false christs and false prophets will arise and perform great signs and wonders, so as to lead astray, if possible, even the elect . . . he will send out his angels with a loud trumpet call, and they will gather his elect from the four winds, from one end of heaven to the other" (24:22, 24, 31).

"This is my Son, my Chosen One; listen to him!" (Luke 9:35). "[W]ill not God give justice to his elect, who cry to him day and night?" (18:7). "He saved others; let him save himself, if he is the Christ of God, his Chosen One!" (23:35).

"Did I not choose you, the Twelve? And yet one of you [i.e., Judas] is a devil" (John 6:70). "I am not speaking of all of you; I know whom I have chosen. But the Scripture will be fulfilled, 'He who ate my bread [i.e., Judas] has lifted his heel against me'" (13:18). "You did not choose me, but I chose you and appointed you that you should go and bear fruit . . . because you are not of the world, but I chose you out of the world, therefore the world hates you" (15:16, 19).

Jesus "had given commands through the Holy Spirit to the apostles whom he had chosen" (Acts 1:2). "And they prayed and said, 'You, Lord, who know the hearts of all, show which one of these two you have chosen to take the place in this ministry and apostleship from which Judas turned aside'" (vv. 24-25). "Brothers, you know that in the early days God made a choice among you, that by my [i.e., Peter's] mouth the Gentiles should hear the word of the gospel and believe" (15:7).

"Who shall bring any charge against God's elect?" (Rom. 8:33). "Greet Rufus, chosen in the Lord" (16:13). "God chose

---

46. We should not make a distinction between "choose" (of Germanic origin) and "elect" (of Latin origin); in the present context, they mean the same.

what is foolish in the world to shame the wise; God chose what is weak in the world to shame the strong; God chose what is low and despised in the world, even things that are not, to bring to nothing things that are" (1 Cor. 1:27-28). "[H]e chose us in him before the foundation of the world, that we should be holy and blameless before him" (Eph. 1:4). "Put on then, as God's chosen ones, holy and beloved, compassionate hearts," etc. (Col. 3:12). "[W]e know, brothers loved by God, that he has chosen you" (1 Thess. 1:4). "I endure everything for the sake of the elect, that they also may obtain the salvation that is in Christ Jesus with eternal glory" (2 Tim. 2:10). "Paul, a servant of God and an apostle of Jesus Christ, for the sake of the faith of God's elect and their knowledge of the truth, which accords with godliness" (Titus 1:1).

"[H]as not God chosen those who are poor in the world to be rich in faith and heirs of the kingdom, which he has promised to those who love him?" (James 2:5).

"To those who are elect exiles of the Dispersion . . . according to the foreknowledge of God the Father" (1 Pet. 1:1-2). "As you come to him, a living stone rejected by men but in the sight of God chosen and precious. . . . 'Behold, I am laying in Zion a stone, a cornerstone chosen and precious'" (2:4, 6). "[Y]ou are a chosen race, a royal priesthood, a holy nation" (v. 9). "She who is at Babylon, who is likewise chosen, sends you greetings" (5:13).

"The elder to the elect lady and her children, whom I love in truth and her children. . . . The children of your elect sister greet you" (2 John 1:1, 13).

The devilish armies "will make war on the Lamb, . . . and those with him are called and chosen and faithful" (Rev. 17:14).

* *Election* (Gr. *eklogē*, Lat. *electio*, see the previous word pair): Paul "is a chosen instrument [lit., instrument of election; cf. DRA] of mine" (Acts 9:15); ". . . in order that God's purpose of election might continue" (Rom. 9:11). "So too at the present time there is a remnant, chosen by grace [lit., a remnant according to the election of grace; NKJV] .... What then? Israel failed to obtain what it was seeking. The elect [lit., election] obtained it, but the rest were hardened ... as regards election, they are beloved for the sake of their forefathers" (11:5, 7, 28). "Therefore, brothers, be all the more diligent to confirm your calling and election" (2 Pet. 1:10).

* *To choose, elect* (Gr. *hairetizō* resp. *haireō*, Lat. *eligo*): "Behold, my servant whom I have chosen, my beloved with whom my soul is well pleased" (Matt. 12:18). "God chose you as the first fruits to be saved" (2 Thess. 2:13).

10.7.3 Other Terms

* *To appoint*: God "may send the Christ appointed [Gr. *procheirizō*,[47] Lat. *praedicare*] for you" (Acts 3:20). "[W]hen the Gentiles heard this [i.e., the gospel], they began rejoicing and glorifying the word of the Lord, and as many as were appointed [Gr. *tassō*, Lat. *praeordino*] to eternal life believed" (13:48). "The God of our fathers appointed [Gr. *procheirizō*, Lat. *praeordino*] you [i.e., Paul] to know his will" (22:14). "I have appeared to you for this purpose, to appoint [Gr. *procheirizō*, Lat. *constituo*] you as a servant" (26:16).

* *To destine*: "[Y]ou yourselves know that we are destined [Gr. *keimai*,[48] Lat. *pono*] for this [i.e., afflictions]" (1 Thess. 3:3). "God has not destined [Gr. *tithēmi*, Lat. *pono*] us for wrath, but to obtain salvation through our Lord Jesus Christ" (5:9). "They stumble because they disobey the word, as they were destined [Gr. *tithēmi*, Lat. *pono*] to do" (1 Pet. 2:8).

* *To prepare beforehand*: "... vessels of mercy, which he has prepared beforehand [one word: Gr. *prohetoimazō*, Lat. *praeparo*] for glory" (Rom. 9:23; cf. Eph. 2:10, which deals with good works).

* *To write beforehand*: "[C]ertain men, long ago having been

---

[47]. The Greek verb *procheirizō* contains the word *cheir*, "hand," suggesting here: "to take into one's hand."
[48]. Lit., "to lie," hence "to set," hence "to appoint, destine."

written beforehand [one Gr. word: *prographō*, Lat. *praescribere*] to this judgment..." (Jude 1:4 YLT).

* *Purpose* (Gr. *prothesis* [from *protithēmi*, cf. *tithēmi* above; Lat. *propositum* [from *propono*; cf. *pono* above]): "...those who are called according to his purpose" (Rom. 8:28; see above: 9:11; Eph. 1:11). "[T]hrough the church the manifold wisdom of God [is] made known to the rulers and authorities in the heavenly places. This was according to the eternal purpose that he has realized in Christ Jesus our Lord" (Eph. 3:10-11). God "who saved us and called us to a holy calling, not because of our works but because of his own purpose and grace, which he gave us in Christ Jesus before the ages began [lit., before times eternal]" (2 Tim. 1:9).

* Also, some unspecific expressions seem to imply election, such as: "I have many in this city who are my people" (Acts 18:10); at that moment, many of these "people of God" at Corinth still had to come to faith.[49]

10.8 Categories
10.8.1 Chosen for the Earth and for Heaven

In the Bible passages quoted in §10.7 we can easily distinguish a number of different categories. First, not all implied decrees of God are necessarily eternal. This is true, for instance, for the afflictions mentioned in 1 Thessalonians 3:3, which, in my view, belong to the ways of God rather than to the counsel of God. This is also true for a calling to an *earthly* ministry, which does not necessarily go back to an eternal decree. Examples are the calling of the twelve (!) apostles (including Judas; John 6:70; 13:18; 15:16, 19; Acts 1:2), especially Peter (Acts 15:7). Afterward, it included Matthias (Acts 1:24-25); still later Paul is called a chosen instrument (9:15; 26:16). The latter does not differ very much from what he said of himself: "called to be an apostle" (Rom. 1:1; 1 Cor. 1:1).

Similarly, in the Old Testament, Aaron and his house were chosen for the priesthood (Deut. 18:5; 21:5; Ps. 105:26), and

---
49. Demarest (1997, 127).

David and his house were chosen for kingship (2 Chron. 6:6; Ps. 89:19). Also, Moses with his special calling and ministry (and also a type of Christ) is called a "chosen one" (Ps. 106:23).

In the Old Testament, Israel is called a "chosen people" (Deut. 7:6-7; 14:2; 1 Kings 3:8; Ps. 33:12; 105:43; Isa. 43:20; 65:22; cf. 1 Pet. 2:9) or "chosen nation" (cf. Ps. 106:5) (more generally: Deut. 4:37; 10:15; 1 Chron. 16:13; Isa. 49:7). However, this was the election of one nation above all other nations of the earth. Reformed authors such as Henry Kersten, Jan Gerrit Woelderink, Johan Heyns, and Jan van Genderen write as if such Old Testament elections are of the same order as the eternal election of all believers.[50] Other authors do make a distinction.[51] Rightly so, for Israel's being chosen (elect) does not tell us anything about individual Israelites being elected, or not, for eternal blessedness. Only the remnant of Israel (Isa. 10:20-22; 28:5) contains the true elect (65:9, 14-15, 22). This is, so to speak, an "election within the election." This is clearly implied in Romans 11:7, which makes, within the chosen people of Israel, a distinction between the elect (i.e., eternally saved) and the rest, which is hardened (and eternally lost).[52] (Keep in mind that the terms "chosen" and "elect" come from the same Greek verb.)

It is the same with the *chosen* twelve, of whom eleven were chosen (elect) for eternal salvation as well, and one was eternally lost (John 6:70). Calvin rightly said that, in the case of the twelve disciples, we are not dealing with the *communis electio piorum* ("ordinary election of the godly") but with an *electio particularis* ("special election") of the disciples, even if this cannot be entirely severed from eternal election.[53]

In 2 Kings 23:27, God speaks of the threat that he would

---

50. Kersten (1980, 1:131–32); Woelderink (1951, 43–50); Heyns (1988, 82, 88); Van Genderen and Velema (2008, 210–11; however, see also 217–18).
51. E.g., Berkhof (1996, 114); Hervormde Kerk (1962, 14–15); Wentsel (1982, 167–68); Demarest (1997, 119–21); König (2006, 431–32).
52. So, e.g., Jewett (1985, 43); Hughes (1989, 163); Demarest (1997, 137); cf. also Roos (2001, 57) with reference to Calvin.
53. Calvin, *Comm. on John*, ad loc.; cf. Demarest (1997, 118–19).

cast off the city that he had chosen, Jerusalem (cf. 1 Kings 8:44, 48; 11:32; 14:21; 2 Chron. 6:34, 38; 12:13). Again, we see here that it is possible to have been chosen (elected) by God, and yet be rejected. This is because this is an election within time, for a time, and for this earth; not a rejection for eternity, not even necessarily decreed in eternity. On the new earth, old Jerusalem no longer exists, but only the new Jerusalem, the bride of the Lamb.

10.8.2 Christ the Chosen One

Jesus Christ, too, is sometimes called the Chosen One: "Behold, my servant whom I have chosen [Gr. *hēretisa*], my beloved with whom my soul is well pleased" (Matt. 12:18 [Isa. 42:1]; cf. Isa. 43:10, "my servant whom I have chosen," referring to Israel). "This is my Son, my Chosen One [Gr. *eklelegmenos*; Byzantine Text: my beloved Son; so, e.g., NKJV]; listen to him!" (Luke 9:35). "He saved others; let him save himself, if he is the Christ of God, his Chosen One!" (*eklektos*, 23:35). In such passages, the phrase "Chosen One" could almost be viewed as a title of the Messiah. Not only Moses (Ps. 106:23) but also David, both types of the Messiah, are called the "chosen one" in Psalm 89:3, 19 (Septuagint: *eklektos*).

"As you come to him [i.e., Christ], a living stone rejected by men but in the sight of God chosen and precious, you yourselves like living stones are being built up as a spiritual house, to be a holy priesthood, to offer spiritual sacrifices acceptable to God through Jesus Christ . . . 'Behold, I am laying in Zion a stone, a cornerstone chosen and precious'" (1 Pet. 2:4, 6 [Isa. 28:16], *eklektos*). The link with the priesthood reminds us of Aaron and his priestly house: in addition to Moses as the "chosen" prophet, and David as the "chosen" king, Aaron as the "chosen" priest is a type of Christ (§10.8.1).

The election of Christ has more to do with his offices (King, Priest, Prophet) than with eternal blessedness. In this case, this is self-evident: Jesus was predestined to bring salvation, not to be saved (although he was "saved" from death,

Heb. 5:7). Yet, this *is* a predestination from eternity: Christ is the "lamb without blemish or spot . . . [he was] foreknown before the foundation of the world but was made manifest in the last times for the sake of you" (1 Pet. 1:19–20). Just as the elect have been "foreknown" (Rom. 8:29; 1 Pet. 1:2), the Chosen One was "delivered up according to the definite plan and foreknowledge of God" (Acts 2:23).

10.8.3 Temporary Election and Rejection

As far as rejection (reprobation) is concerned, we must be careful not to draw hasty conclusions (cf. §10.8.1). For instance, Esau was rejected as what we might call the "vessel of promise," and Jacob was chosen instead as the spiritual heir of Abraham and Isaac (Rom. 9:10–12). Saul was rejected as king of Israel (1 Sam. 15:23), and David was chosen instead. Judah was threatened with rejection just as the ten tribes had been rejected: "I will remove Judah also out of my sight, as I have removed Israel, and I will cast off this city that I have chosen, Jerusalem, and the house of which I said, 'My name shall be there'" (2 Kings 23:27, see §10.8.1). None of these examples as such tell us anything about the eternal blessedness or damnation of the persons concerned.

I repeat: a chosen Israel can be threatened with rejection. Compare what God said about many among the *chosen* nation: "[T]he LORD rejected all the descendants of Israel and afflicted them and gave them into the hand of plunderers, until he had cast them out of his sight" (2 Kings 17:20; Rom. 15).[54] Just as the term "chosen" does not necessarily mean chosen for eternity, the term "rejected" does not necessarily mean rejected for eternity: after a certain time, God may have mercy again toward those whom he had rejected and given into the hand of oppressors, that is, save them from these oppressors and restore them in their own land.

Sometimes "choosing" means merely "accepting again" after such a temporary rejection: "My cities shall again

---

54. König (2006, 431–33).

overflow with prosperity, and the Lord will again comfort Zion and again choose Jerusalem" (Zech. 1:17). These examples of temporary election (e.g., of Jerusalem), temporary rejection, and renewed election are striking examples of election and rejection sometimes *being simply aspects of God's ways, not of his counsel.*

Sometimes, the phrase "being rejected" has simply the weak meaning of "not being chosen," as in the case of Samuel considering the sons of Jesse:

> [T]he LORD said to Samuel, 'Do not look on his [i.e., Eliab's] appearance or on the height of his stature, because I have rejected him. For the LORD sees not as man sees: man looks on the outward appearance, but the LORD looks on the heart.' Then Jesse called Abinadab and made him pass before Samuel. And he said, 'Neither has the LORD chosen this one,' . . ." (1 Sam. 16:7-8).

It seems to me that this principle is true when it comes to eternal election: the fact that God elected some implies that he left the others out—if you like: rejected them, put them aside—but it does *not* necessarily imply that from eternity they have been foreordained for eternal damnation. Not being destined for (a certain) blessing does not automatically mean being destined for curse.

10.8.4 Chosen Unbelievers

If there is such a thing as a temporary election, an election only for rendering a specific service on this earth, it is understandable that some of these elected servants may turn out to be unbelievers. King Saul is a clear example of this. In the enumeration given in §10.5, there are several passages that speak of election as referring to unbelievers (see more in §14.2):

(a) 1 Thessalonians 5:9 seems to imply that there are those "destined for wrath." Later, we will see that this does not necessarily imply a reprobation from eternity (§§11.7.2, 14.2.2).

(b) There are unbelievers who have been "destined" to stumble over Jesus who is the Stone of stumbling (1 Pet. 2:8;

see §14.2.2).

(c) Jude 4 speaks of "certain people" who were "long ago designated" (KJV: "of old ordained") for God's condemnation. "Long ago" (or "of old") does not necessarily imply a reprobation from eternity. Rather, it seems to refer to prophecy, such as the one by Enoch mentioned in verses 14–15 (see §14.2.3).

(d) In John 6:70, Judas is one of the "chosen ones," although it is said of him that in fact, he is a "son of destruction" (17:12). Here again, he was prophesied about beforehand (". . . that the Scripture might be fulfilled").

Such verses suffice to make clear that not all election is necessarily election based on an eternal decree and destined for eternal blessedness, just as not all rejection is necessarily rejection based on an eternal decree and destined for eternal damnation. Judas belonged to those who had been chosen to be the twelve disciples of Jesus on earth, but this had little to do with whether he would be eternally saved or lost. In fact, John 17:12 applies to him the word "lost."

10.8.5 A Special Category

Several New Testament passages deserve some special attention.

* "[M]any are called, but few are *chosen*" (Matt. 22:14; the Byzantine Text contains this phrase in 20:16 as well); in §11.1 I will return to this interesting contrast between "called" and "chosen."

* "[W]hen Rebekah had conceived children by one man, our forefather Isaac, though they were not yet born and had done nothing either good or bad — in order that God's *purpose of election* might continue, not because of works but because of him who calls — she was told, 'The older will serve the younger.' As it is written, 'Jacob I loved, but Esau I hated'" (Rom. 9:10–13; see §14.3 for our discussion of this oft-misunderstood passage).

* "As regards the gospel, they [i.e., the Israelities] are

enemies for your [i.e., believers from the Gentiles] sake. But as regards election, they are beloved for the sake of their forefathers" (Rom. 11:28; on the election of Israel, see §10.6.1).

* "Greet Rufus, chosen [Gr. *eklekton*, Lat. *electum*] in the Lord" (Rom. 16:13), which presumably means an "excellent" or "eminent" person (cf. the way we speak of "choice quality").[55]

* In Ephesians 3:10-11, the church is presented as the object of God's "eternal purpose." This verse deals with God's counsel with respect to the church as a totality (cf. v. 9 with Col. 1:26) rather than with the eternal predestination of individual believers (although, of course, the two cannot be separated).[56]

10.8.6 Eternal Election

In my view, the following Bible passages clearly refer to the eternal election of believers, that is, their eternal predestination for heavenly blessedness. I distinguish two categories.

(a) *General references to (certain groups of) believers*, which, in my view, do not allow specific dogmatic conclusions: Matthew 24:22, 24 ("the elect"), 31 ("his elect"); Luke 18:7 ("his elect"); 1 Corinthians 1:27-28 ("God chose what is foolish/weak/low and despised in the world"); Colossians 3:12 ("God's chosen ones"); 2 Timothy 2:10 ("the elect"); 1 Peter 2:9 ("you are a chosen race"); 5:13 ("She . . . who is likewise chosen [one word: *syneklektē*]," viz., Peter's wife or some local church);[57] 2 John 1:1, 13 ("the elect lady [*eklektē kyria*] . . . your elect sister," i.e., individual believing women [*eklektē* can mean "eminent'; see §10.6.5] or local churches);[58] Revelation 17:14 ("called and chosen and faithful").

(b) *Dogmatically important* are the following passages: Acts

---

55. Ridderbos (1959, 346); Denney (1979, 720); Morris (1988, 231).
56. On the special position of the church in God's counsel, see Ouweneel (EDR 7).
57. See Davids (1990, 201–202).
58. See Lalleman (2005, 36–38).

13:48 ("as many as were appointed to eternal life believed"); Rom. 8:28-30, 33 (quoted before); 9:23 ("... in order to make known the riches of his glory for vessels of mercy, which he has prepared beforehand for glory"); 11:5, 7 ("a remnant, chosen by grace ... the elect obtained it"); Eph. 1:4-5, 11 (quoted before); 1 Thess 1:4 ("we know, brothers, loved by God, that he has chosen you"); 5:9 ("God has not destined us for wrath, but to obtain salvation through our Lord Jesus Christ"); 2 Tim. 1:9 (God "called us to a holy calling, ... because of his own purpose and grace, which he gave us in Christ Jesus before the ages began"); Titus 1:1 ("... for the sake of the faith of God's elect and their knowledge of the truth, which accords with godliness"); James 2:5 ("has not God chosen those who are poor in the world to be rich in faith and heirs of the kingdom?"); 1 Peter 1:1-2 ("To those who are elect exiles ... according to the foreknowledge of God the Father"); 2 Peter 1:10 ("be ... diligent to confirm your calling and election").

All these passages will be discussed throughout the remainder of this book.

10.9 The Book of Life
10.9.1 The Old Testament

In a discussion of biblical terminology concerning election and predestination, we should not overlook the interesting phrase "book of life" (Heb. *sefer chayyim*, Gr. *biblos/biblion [tēs] zōēs*, Lat. *liber vitae*). The use of this phrase in the Bible is certainly not uniform. In Exodus 32:32, Moses prays after Israel's sin with the golden calf: "But now, if you will forgive their sin—but if not, please blot me out of your book that you have written." The Lord replies however: "Whoever has sinned against me, I will blot out of my book" (v. 33). This can hardly refer to the register of the eternally elect because, as Jan Gerrit Woelderink argued, in this register no person can ever be added, and no person can ever be blotted out of it.[59]

---
59. Woelderink (1951, 63–65); cf. Berkouwer (1960, 110–15); Venema (1992, 157–59).

We encounter a similar problem in Psalm 69:28, where it is said of the wicked, "Let them be blotted out of the book of the living; let them not be enrolled among the righteous." This again seems to be the book of all the living rather than the book of all the righteous. If this is correct, being blotted out of this book implies physical death (cf. also Ps. 109:13, "May his posterity be cut off; may his name be blotted out in the second generation!").[60]

In Isaiah 4:3, the nuance is a bit different: "And he who is left in Zion and remains in Jerusalem will be called holy, everyone who has been recorded for life in Jerusalem." Apparently, this means: recorded in order to receive life, that is, to remain alive at the coming judgment. Something similar we seem to find in Daniel 12:1, "[A]t that time your people shall be delivered, everyone whose name shall be found written in the book."

Some expositors want to see in such passages references to an eternal election, based solely on God's sovereign decision.[61] However, Psalm 69:28 speaks of the "righteous," and this term implies people's own choices and responsibility. Even more clear is Malachi 3:16, "The LORD paid attention and heard them, and a book of remembrance was written before him of those who feared the LORD and esteemed his name." Apparently, being written in God's "book of remembrance" is not (only) a matter of sovereign divine election but (also) of the godliness of the people concerned.[62]

This "book" must be distinguished from the "book" in which God writes beforehand the vicissitudes of a person: "Your eyes saw my unformed substance; in your book were written, every one of them, the days that were formed for me, when as yet there was none of them" (Ps. 139:16). It must also be distinguished from the book in which God afterwards records these vicissitudes: "You have kept count of my toss-

---

60. Ridderbos (1958, 214).
61. E.g., Young (1965, ad loc.).
62. Oswalt (1986, 147).

ings; put my tears in your bottle. Are they not in your book?" (Ps. 56:8).[63] Perhaps the idea of such "books" was inspired by the genealogies, national registers, and family lists known in Israel (Ezra 2:2–62; 4:15; Neh. 7:5–64; 12:22–23; Esther 6:1; Jer. 22:30; Ezek. 13:9; cf. Ps. 87:6).

10.9.2 Judaism

Judaism gave rise to the idea of two books, in which all the words and deeds of the righteous and the wicked, respectively, are recorded.[64] Thus, Wisdom 4:20 says of the wicked (DRA): "They shall come with fear at the thought of their sins, and their iniquities shall stand against them to convict them" (Ps. 149:9, "the judgment written"). Gabriel is viewed as the principal recording angel; he is identified with the "man clothed in linen, who had the writing case at his waist" in Ezekiel 9:3–4. In 2 Enoch (or Slavonic Enoch) 22:11 and 23:2, Pravuil is called God's scribe and recordkeeper.[65]

In connection with the judgment seat of God, we read in Daniel 7:10, "[T]he court sat in judgment, and the books were opened"; and Revelation 20:12, "I saw the dead, great and small, standing before the throne, and books were opened. Then another book was opened, which is the book of life. And the dead were judged by what was written in the books, according to what they had done."

As far as the righteous are concerned, we may think of Nehemiah 13:14, "Remember me, O my God, concerning this, and do not wipe out my good deeds that I have done for the house of my God and for his service."

The rabbis tell us about angels writing down the good things that God's people do (a thought adopted subsequently by Roman Catholics and Muslims). Thus, the Talmud speaks of Metatron (one of the highest angels in Judaism), whom

---

63. Cf. *TDNT* 1:619–20, which does not distinguish between the two.
64. Gen. R. 81 (on Gen. 35:1); Lev. R. 26 (on Lev. 21:1); 1 Enoch 47:3; 108:3; Jubil. 19:9; 30:19–23; 36:10; Ta'anit 11a; cf. Van Gemeren (1996, 4:446–47).
65. http://www.sacred-texts.com/bib/fbe/fbe129.htm.

God gave "permission . . . to sit and write down the merits of Israel."[66] Metatron needed the permission to "sit down" because normally angels stand in the presence of God.

The Jewish Qumram community knew the idea of a heavenly book with the names of the righteous: "God has with him in heaven the book with the names of his own, in which he has laid down his covenant of peace with them."[67] God's people contain "everyone that has been recorded in the book of life."[68]

I may add that Islamic tradition speaks of the two angels Raqib and Atid, who are believed to sit on a person's shoulders, and to record all his deeds, thoughts, and feelings in a book, with which the person will be confronted on the Day of Judgment. This notion seems to have been derived directly from Judaism, for the school of Rabbi Shila taught, "The two ministering angels who accompany every man testify against him, as it is said, 'For He will give His angels charge over thee' [Ps 91:11]. . . . [The Rabbis] said: When a man departs to his eternal home all his deeds are enumerated before him and he is told, Such and such a thing have you done, in such and such a place on that particular day. . . ."[69]

Roman Catholic popular faith, too, is acquainted with the "recording angel," the angel who writes down the good and bad deeds of people in the book of life. The American priest John P. Donelan wrote in the nineteenth century about the weeping mourner at the grave of a beloved: "[T]he recording angel dips his pen in the falling tear, and with it writes the pardon of the dead!"[70]

---

66. *BabT*: Hagigah 15a.
67. 1QM 12, 3.
68. 4Q504 6, 14.
69. *BabT*: Ta'anith 11a.
70. https://books.google.nl/books?id=-4LOAAAAMAAJ&pg=PA735&lp-g=PA735&dq=%22recording+angel%22+catholic&source=bl&ots=ea2D-vklKAp&sig=I0MVMqHddNJ1EA2H9gyVUcv76b4&hl=nl&sa=X&redir_esc=y#v=onepage&q=%22recording%20angel%22%20catholic&f=false

10.9.3 The New Testament

In the New Testament, the wicked are identical with those "whose names have not been written in the book of life from the foundation of the world" (Rev. 17:8; cf. 20:12), which is "the book of the Lamb who was slain" (13:8). It reminds us of Jude 4 (YLT), "[C]ertain men, long ago having been written beforehand [one Gr. word: *prographō*] to this judgment. . . ." The reverse is said of the righteous; they are "those who are written in the Lamb's book of life" (21:27).

Apparently alluding to Exodus 32:32-33 and Psalm 69:28, Revelation 3:5 says, "The one who conquers will be clothed thus in white garments, and I will never blot his name out of the book of life." Paul speaks of his "fellow workers, whose names are in the book of life" (Phil. 3:5). Probably the "book of life" in the latter two cases is the book of the righteous because the texts refer to those who in the world count little but are highly regarded by God.

Finally, I point here to what Jesus said to his disciples: "[D]o not rejoice in this, that the spirits are subject to you, but rejoice that your names are written in heaven" (Luke 10:20). It is more important to be loved by God and to have been accepted by him than to be feared in the demonic world. Hebrews 12:23 speaks of "the assembly of the firstborn who are enrolled [Gr. *apographō*] in heaven." Here again, it seems to be a reference to a token of dignity.

Ben Wentsel discussed the book of life within the framework of election, and said of it: "The book is the symbol of the firmness of God's choice."[71] However, it is questionable whether it is God's choice that is in the forefront. No Bible text connects being written in this book explicitly and one-sidedly with God's sovereign, elective grace. On the contrary, in various passages this being written in the book of life is emphatically associated with the dedication and righteousness of the people involved.

---

71. Wentsel (1982, 171).

Chapter 11
Predestination in the New Testament

Blessed be the God and Father of our Lord Jesus Christ,
  who has blessed us in Christ
  with every spiritual blessing in the heavenly places,
  even as he chose us in him before the foundation of the world,
  that we should be holy and blameless before him.
In love he predestined us for adoption as sons through Jesus Christ,
  according to the purpose of his will,
  to the praise of his glorious grace,
  with which he has blessed us in the Beloved...
In him we have obtained an inheritance,
  having been predestined according to the purpose of him
  who works all things according to the counsel of his will.

Ephesians 1:3–6, 11

Summary: *Who are "the elect" in the Gospels, and especially in John? What is eternal election and what temporal election? How does divine election relate to human responsibility? Are "foreknowledge" and "predestination" the same? And how does divine election relate to the problem of sin? Are being "prepared for glory" and being "prepared for destruction" on the same level? Are believers elected to receive back what Adam lost, or does it involve more? Who is the first beneficiary of predestination: the believer or God? What precisely have we been predestined for? What precisely does it mean that election is "in Christ"? What are the "good works" prepared beforehand? How can one **know** one has been elected? How do election and calling relate? How are the divine and the human sides of the topic balanced in the Book of Acts? How can one "confirm" one's election? In this chapter these many questions receive, understandably, only tentative answers.*

11.1 The Synoptic Gospels
11.1.1 The "Elect"

ON THE WHOLE, THE SYNOPTIC GOSPELS supply us with less material for a biblical doctrine of predestination than the Gospel of John. In the Olivet Discourse, Jesus speaks three times of the "elect" (sing. Gr. *eklektos*):

> And if those days [of great tribulation] had not been cut short, no human being would be saved. But for the sake of the elect those days will be cut short.... For false christs and false prophets will arise and perform great signs and wonders, so as to lead astray, if possible, even the elect.... And he will send out his angels with a loud trumpet call, and they will gather his elect from the four winds, from one end of heaven to the other (Matt. 24:22, 24, 31; cf. Mark 13:20, 22, 27).

In this passage, the term "elect" clearly stands for those who belong to the new people of God, that is, all those who have accepted the "gospel of the kingdom" (Matt. 24:14), that is, have become disciples (followers) and subjects of the King (v. 13). It is fascinating to see here how the relationship between divine predestination—or election—and human responsibility is underscored: it is a matter of "enduring to the end" (v. 13), of "staying awake" (v. 42), and of "being ready" (v. 44). Of course, these statements must be balanced by the verses telling us that safely reaching the final goal also depends on divine preservation (vv. 22, 24).

We find a similar situation in Luke 18:7, "And will not God give justice to his elect, who cry to him day and night? Will he delay long over them?" The elect suffer great difficulties in their circumstances on earth, just like the widow in the parable. It is therefore their responsibility to "cry" to God as much as they can ("day and night"). On the divine side, precisely because they are God's elect, there can be no doubt that he cares for them, and answers them in their distress, so that they will safely reach the final goal of their earthly journey.

11.1.2 "Few Are Chosen"

Jesus' most conspicuous, and often hotly debated, statement concerning election is this: "[M]any are called, but few are chosen" (Matt. 22:14; the Byzantine Text contains this phrase also in 20:16; see, e.g., the NKJV). This is the closing statement of the parable of the wedding feast, and can be related to the previous parables as well: those of the two sons and of the tenants (21:28–44). The "called ones" are those who have received a command (21:28–30, 33b) or an invitation (22:4, 9). The "elect" are those who have responded to the command or the invitation in the proper way. These are the obedient son (21:29, 31), the new tenants to whom the vineyard is entrusted (v. 41), and those who not only accept the invitation but also the wedding garment (22:10–11).[1] Those who were called but apparently not elect are the disobedient son (21:30), the unrighteous tenants (vv. 34–41), and those who originally had been invited (22:4–6), but also the man who was present at the

---

1. Grosheide (1954, 331); Schlatter (1961, 328); Ridderbos (1987, 407); Carson (1984, 457).

wedding but had no wedding garment (vv. 11-23).²

Please note that in none of these cases is it primarily God's sovereign choice that comes to the fore, but rather human choices made according to people's own responsibility: the choice to be an obedient or a disobedient son, the choice to be a faithful or an unfaithful tenant, the choice to accept or reject the invitation to the wedding, the choice to accept or reject the wedding garment. We would therefore betray the text if, because of our dogmatic prejudices, we would think that people in these parables simply respond on the basis of an *a priori* divine elective decision. The good ones do not act in a good way because they had been elected but because they themselves decided to make good choices. God can in no way be made responsible for these choices.

The guidelines of the Dutch Reformed Church in the Netherlands express the matter very carefully: "One who is obedient to the calling turns out to be, and is called here, 'elect,' because in him God's graciously elective acting is realized. The text therefore wishes to say that our election, which came as an invitation to us, occurs only when the confirmation of faith and obedience is awakened in the person" (cf. 1 Thess. 1:4-6).³

11.1.3 Who Are the Chosen?

The parable language should caution us against drawing conclusions from Matthew 22:14 that are too dogmatic, certainly as far as the number of the elect is concerned ("few are chosen"). It is striking that, when someone asked Jesus, "Lord, will those who are saved be few?" he gives an indirect answer: "Strive to enter through the narrow door. For many, I tell you, will seek to enter and will not be able" (Luke 13:23-24). That is, it is up to you and many others whether there will be few saved, or many saved.

Lubbert van der Zanden believes that these "few" refer

---

2. See Ouweneel (2016e, §§4.1-4.2).
3. Hervormde Kerk (1962, 31).

especially to the small number of Israelites who would accept Jesus.[4] However, in the parable the invited persons (Matt. 22:3-8) refer to Israel, the majority of whom rejected Jesus' invitation and whose city was burned (v. 7; Jerusalem, AD 70). After this, the invitation came to "as many as you find" (v. 9), that is, the Gentiles. Thus, the entire world population is invited; therefore, the called ones are "many." But only a part of them accepts the invitation, and receives the wedding garment; these are the elect. Notice here how divine election and human responsibility go hand in hand: God's people have been chosen to receive the wedding garment, but if a person refuses this garment, it is his own fault that he will be lost (v. 13, "Bind him hand and foot and cast him into the outer darkness. In that place there will be weeping and gnashing of teeth").

Wolfhart Pannenberg introduces another accent: he believes that this "statement ascribed to Jesus" ("many are called, but few are chosen") involves a contrast that was common in Jewish apocalyptic literature (cf. 4 Ezra 8:3).[5] It is a warning against an all too certain confidence in Israel's corporate election. Israel is a "called" nation, but not all Israelites have been "elected" for eternal blessedness (see again Rom. 11:7, only a few from the "chosen" nation share in the eternal election). This is correct, at least if the parable is referring especially to Israel. However, the parable also points to Gentiles who were "called" but apparently not "chosen," such as the man without the wedding garment. Therefore, it is probably better to think more generally of all those who have been "called," both from Israel and from the Gentiles, whereas the "chosen" ones constitute only a limited part of these "called" ones. They form the New Testament people of God, which includes a small number of Israelites and a large number of Gentiles. Their being "chosen" goes back to God's sovereign

---

4. Van der Zanden (1949, 86); some have referred in this context to Jer. 3:14, "one from a city and two from a family."
5. Pannenberg (1991, 3:439n6).

choice but depends just as much on the choice made by these people themselves.

Of course, "few" and "many" are relative concepts. In Noah's ark there were "a few, that is, eight persons" (1 Pet. 3:20). But when a couple has eight children, this is "many." "Few are chosen" but, viewed from a different angle, they are many: the Son of Man gave "his life as a ransom for many" (Matt. 20:28); the "blood of the covenant . . . is poured out for many for the forgiveness of sins" (Matt. 26:28). "[B]y the one man's obedience [i.e., Christ] the many will be made righteous" (Rom. 5:19b).

11.2 John's Gospel
11.2.1 Given by the Father

In the Gospel of John, we find some quite remarkable statements of Jesus that, though lacking the Greek term *prohorizō* (Lat. *praedestino*), clearly refer to predestination.[6] Let me give some striking examples. "[A]s the Father raises the dead and gives them life, so also the Son gives life to whom *he will*" (5:21), that is, on the basis not of the choices of the people involved but of the good pleasure of the Son himself. "All that the Father gives me will come to me, and whoever comes to me I will never cast out. . . . No one can come to me unless the Father who sent me draws him. And I will raise him up on the last day. . . . This is why I told you that no one can come to me unless it is granted him by the Father" (6:37, 44, 65). Those are saved who have been "given" by the Father to the Son, or have been "drawn" by the Father, or to whom the Father "grants" to come to the Son.

Perhaps some other passages refer to the eternal predestination as well. "Whoever is of God hears the words of God. The reason why you do not hear them is that you are not of God" (8:47). But perhaps the meaning is simpler. Jesus may be saying here: I can see that there is no work of God going on

---

6. See extensively, R. W. Yarbrough in Schreiner and Ware (2000, chapter 2), although he "sees" election far more often in John than I do.

in your souls; there is no divine "sounding board" within you all for the words of God that I am preaching to you. Nowhere in John, certainly not in a chapter like John 8, which appeals so strongly to the conscience, may we may exclude human responsibility. Jesus does not say in resignation: You are not predestined, therefore you all cannot hear me, but rather: You have no relationship with God at all, no matter how committed you are to your Jewish traditions. If you *had* such a relationship, my words would reverberate in your souls.

"[Y]ou do not believe because you are not among my sheep" (10:26). In this verse, Jesus is not saying: You do not belong to my sheep because you do not believe, but: you do not believe because you do not belong to my sheep. In itself, this does not necessarily point to a great difference in content and meaning. The meaning might be similar to what I suggested for John 8:47, that is: You do not believe because you have no relationship with God. Yet, these verses might point to a certain predestination, especially because of verse 29: "My Father, who has given them to me, is greater than all."[7] This is the same "giving" as in 6:37 (see above), and also in John 17: ". . . since you have given him authority over all flesh, to give eternal life to all whom you have given him. . . . I have manifested your name to the people whom you *gave* me out of the world. Yours they were, and you *gave* them to me. . . . I am not praying for the world but for those whom you *have given* me, for they are yours. . . . Father, I desire that they also, whom you have given me, may be with me where I am" (vv. 2, 6, 9, 24). See 18:9 as well: "Of those whom you gave me I have lost not one."

11.2.2 Temporary Election

A little different is John 6:70, where Jesus says, "Did I not *choose* you, the Twelve? And yet one of you is a devil." As the implicit reference to Judas makes clear, this verse refers to a certain temporary calling on earth for a particular service

---

7. Demarest (1997, 126–27).

rather than to eternal predestination for heavenly blessedness. It seems to be similar in 15:16, 19, although eternal predestination seems to be included as well: "You did not *choose* me, but I chose you and appointed you that you should go and bear fruit and that your fruit should abide, so that whatever you ask the Father in my name, he may give it to you. ... If you were of the world, the world would love you as its own; but because you are not of the world, but I *chose* you out of the world, therefore the world hates you."

Interestingly, in John 13:18 Jesus makes a distinction between Judas and the other disciples: "I am not speaking of all of you; I know whom I have chosen." Here, being chosen apparently has a more limited sense than in 6:70. That is, Judas was chosen to be one of the followers of Jesus here on earth, but apparently he had no part in eternal election. This distinction is the more remarkable because of what we read in Mark 6: Jesus "called the twelve and began to send them out two by two, and gave them authority over the unclean spirits. ... So they went out and proclaimed that people should repent. And they cast out many demons and anointed with oil many who were sick and healed them" (vv. 7, 12-13). Apparently, Judas, as part of "the twelve," had also gone out, had proclaimed the gospel, had cast out demons, and had healed the sick! Of course, he had gone out with a companion, and perhaps the power of God flowed through this other disciple. Yet, the passage may illustrate that Judas' earthly and temporary "chosenness" was not meaningless. (By the way, people other than Jesus' disciples were active in casting out demons as well; Matt. 7:22; 12:27; Mark 9:38; Acts 19:13-16.)

11.2.3 Election and Responsibility

In John's Gospel, human responsibility is never played off against divine election; on the contrary, it is fully maintained, as in 7:17, "If anyone's *will* is to do God's will, he will know whether the teaching is from God or whether I am speaking on my own authority." Also notice the term "accepting" [Gr.

lambanō]:⁸ "[T]o all who did accept him and believe in him he gave the right to become children of God" (1:12 NCV). "Whoever accepts what he says has given proof that God speaks the truth" (3:33 ERV). "Those who reject me and don't accept what I say have a judge—the word which I have spoken will judge them on the Last Day" (12:48 CJB). "I gave them the words you gave me and they accepted them" (17:8 NIV).

Of course, such accepting cannot be severed from God's gracious work in human hearts: "A person cannot receive [or, accept] even one thing unless it is given him from heaven" (3:27). However, this does not change the fact that the receiving/accepting is a responsible human action. It is God who gives, but people must stretch out their hands to receive his gifts; the gift is not forced upon them (cf. Eccl. 3:13).

Another notable thing in John is the universality of God's offer of salvation (see extensively chapter 13 below): "[W]hoever believes in him may have eternal life. For God so loved the *world*, that he gave his only Son, that *whoever* believes in him should not perish but have eternal life. . . . *Whoever* believes in him is not condemned, . . ." (3:15-16, 18). "[W]hoever drinks of the water that I will give him will never be thirsty again" (4:14). "[W]hoever hears my word and believes him who sent me has eternal life" (5:24). "[W]hoever comes to me shall not hunger, and whoever believes in me shall never thirst. . . . [T]his is the will of my Father, that *everyone* who looks on the Son and believes in him should have eternal life, . . ." (6:35, 40). "I am the resurrection and the life. *Whoever* believes in me, though he die, yet shall he live, everyone who lives and believes in me shall never die" (11:25-26). "And I, when I am lifted up from the earth, will draw *all* people to myself. . . . I have come into the world as light, so that *whoever* believes in me may not remain in darkness" (12:32, 46).

Notice especially John 6:37, "*All* that the Father gives me

---

8. Many translations have "to receive" in the passages quoted, but this may be too easily understood as a passive term (which it is not). "To accept" involves more human activity; see further in §13.9.3.

will come to me, and *whoever* comes to me I will never cast out." On the one hand, we find here the side of God's sovereign grace: those who come to Jesus are those whom the Father has given him (cf. v. 44, "No one can come to me unless the Father . . . draws him"). On the other hand, there is the universality of God's offer of salvation: no one shall ever knock on Jesus' door in vain. We have to realize, however, that such passages can never ultimately decide between Arminianism/Open Theism and decretalism (although this has been often attempted).

(a) Arminians will always argue that those whom the Father "draws" and "gives" to Jesus are those in whom he observes a repentant heart and the desire to come to Jesus. Thus, Greg Boyd argued that the Father draws, or does not draw, people *in response to* their hearts.[9] Joseph Ratzinger (pope Benedict XVI) also wondered whether John 6 has anything to do with election. Is the point of the passage not rather that the Father draws a person if, and only if, this person fulfills certain conditions?[10]

(b) Decretalists will always argue that those who come to Jesus, and whom he does not cast out, are those who had first been chosen sovereignly by the Father.

An example of this twofold approach is John 12:32 ("And I, when I am lifted up from the earth, will draw *all* people to myself"). Arminians will emphasize the apparent fact that salvation is offered to *all* people. Decretalists will point to the fact that "drawing" (Gr. *helkuō*) here is the same word as in 6:44 ("No one can come to me unless the Father . . . draws him"). Therefore, Robert Yarbrough wishes to read here: "I will draw *all elect* people to myself."[11] There is the tension: are *all* drawn, or are only the elect drawn? Or, are all invited, but the invitation becomes effective only in the elect? Or is this reading too much into the text?

---

9. Boyd (2001, 411–12).
10. Ratzinger (2008, 341–42).
11. Yarbrough in Schreiner and Ware (2000, 52).

We will have to live with the tension. Nonetheless, I would suggest that, in John's Gospel, divine sovereignty and human responsibility are always in perfect balance. Salvation depends harmoniously on both, even if it seems impossible to logically account for this.[12]

11.3 Romans 8
11.3.1 Foreknowing and Foreordaining

Romans 8:28-30, 33 says,

> [W]e know that for those who love God all things work together for good, for those who are called according to his purpose [Gr. *prothesis*, Lat. *propositum*].[13] For those whom he foreknew [Gr. *proegnō*, Lat. *praescivit*] he also predestined [Gr. *prohōrisen*, Lat. *praedestinavit*] to be conformed to the image of his Son, in order that he might be the firstborn among many brothers. And those whom he predestined [Gr. *prohōrisen*, Lat. *praedestinavi*] he also called, and those whom he called he also justified, and those whom he justified he also glorified. . . . Who shall bring any charge against God's elect [Gr. *eklektōn*, Lat. *electos*]?

One reason why the passage is important for our purpose is the apparent distinction made between "foreknown" and "predestined" ("fore" and "pre" are the same: Gr. *pro*, Lat. *prae*). Divine foreordination is more than just foreknowledge, the latter perhaps not meaning anything more than knowing which persons will accept the gospel, and which wont (as Arminians may argue). Foreordination is truly a *destining* (or ordaining, or electing, or preparing, or appointing) before the foundation of the world, that is, from eternity; it is a sovereign act of God.

This does not mean, by the way, that "foreknown" involves only a matter-of-fact knowing; it certainly involves a relationship as well, as in Romans 11:2, "God has not rejected

---

12. Cf. G. R. Osborne in Pinnock (1989, 245, 258), but also the discussion of the subject by Yarbrough in Schreiner and Ware (2000, 56–60).
13. See chapter 10, note 37 above.

his people whom he foreknew." It is like the Hebrew *y-d-'*, "to know," which often involves relationship, even intimacy (Gen. 4:1; 18:19; Exod. 2:25; Deut. 7:6–8; Amos 3:2; cf. *ginōskō* in Matt. 1:25). *Proginōskō* "assumes the aspect of a personal relationship with a group of people which originates in God himself."[14] Romans 8:29 makes a distinction between "foreknowledge" and "predestination," but the difference is smaller than people might think.[15] We see this clearly in 1 Peter 1:20: the Lamb being "foreknown" (Gr. *proegnōsmenou*, Lat. *praecogniti*) before the foundation of the world hardly differs here from being "predestined."[16]

In Acts 2:23 again, the Greek word *prognōsis* (Lat. *praescientia*) involves more "predestination" than just "being aware of beforehand." This is supported by the parallelism with the "will" (Gr. *boulē*) of God. In Acts 26:5, the verb *proginōskō* (Lat. *praescio*) means "to know for a long time (or, from the beginning)," and in 2 Peter 3:17 it means "to know beforehand," which seems to be a bit more matter-of-factly: "being aware of beforehand."

In summary, perhaps we could paraphrase Romans 8:29–30 this way: those people whom he had in view beforehand for the purpose of entering into a relationship with them were at the same moment foreordained by him to resemble the image of his Son, or to be called, justified, and glorified (which amounts to the same thing). If we compare this with 1 Corinthians 2:7, we may conclude that *believers* have been predestined to glory, and God's *wisdom* has been predestined for the glory of the believers.

11.3.2 Predestination and Sin

Romans 8 is important in the debate about infra- and supra-

---

14. *NIDNTT* 1:692–93; cf. Fernhout (1921, 27); Murray (1968, 316–18); Denney (1979, 652); Boyd (2001, 117–18).
15. See, e.g., Demarest (1997, 128). Duffield and Van Cleave (1987, 207–208) are among those who exploit the supposed distinction in favor of the Arminian view.
16. *NIDNTT* 1:693.

lapsarianism, that is, whether predestination presupposes the Fall (see §14.6). Please notice that, in our passage, the problem of sin is not at all in the picture. The subject here is not that a person is elected to be delivered from sin and Satan, or is predestined to go to heaven, but that he is chosen to be conformed to the image of God's Son. Even prelapsarian Adam and Eve, created in the image of God, cannot properly be called holy and righteous, but only innocent.[17] Just like us, they would have needed to be elected from eternity to be conformed to the Son's image (cf. 1 John 3:2, "[W]e know that when he appears we shall be like him"). This conformity implies sharing in the Son's eternal glory and holiness (Luke 1:75; Eph. 1:4; 4:24).

This is an essential point to understand. By nature, no human being, fallen or not, is conformed to the image of God's Son; one has to be predestined for it. Prelapsarian Adam and Eve were destined to have an endless life on earth, and to receive all the blessings that this earth could offer. *Nothing more.* They had no promise of any heavenly glory, of any eternal dwelling with the Father and the Son in the Father's house (John 17:1-3), of "eternal life" in the sense of John 17:3 (intimacy with the Father and the Son). They did not even *know* the Father and the Son. Even without the Fall, people would have needed to be eternally predestined for this Trinitarian glory and fellowship. Now that the Fall has intervened, people first need forgiveness of sins and deliverance from sin, Satan, and death. The same Son to whose image believers are conformed has also become the Lamb who takes away their sins. But this is hardly the subject of election and predestination as the New Testament describes them; this subject rather involves everything that elected people receive *beyond* this forgiveness and deliverance.

In salvation, God would conceivably have granted believers nothing more than what Adam had lost, so that they

---

17. See Ouweneel (EDR 3, §§8.4.1, 9.2.3; 2016a, 17).

would live forever on earth, enjoying the earthly blessings—and they would also risk falling into sin again. It ruins the entire biblical idea of election if we see redemption as basically little more than the restoration of the earthly Paradise of Genesis 2. Predestination involves not what Adam lost, but what he never possessed. It involves the Trinitarian blessings that infinitely surpass Adam's strictly earthly blessings. Of course, after the Fall, receiving the blessings for which one has been predestined must be preceded by forgiveness and redemption—but predestination as such surpasses this.

In the New Testament, election and predestination are rarely associated explicitly with the solution to the problem of sin. Perhaps these statement by Paul come closest: "God chose you as the firstfruits to be saved" (2 Thess. 2:13), and: "I endure everything for the sake of the elect, that they also may obtain the salvation that is in Christ Jesus with eternal glory" (2 Tim. 2:10). However, in these two verses, salvation is broader than redeeming people from sin and Satan; it is linked with eternal glory (cf., e.g., Rom. 8:23; 13:11; Phil. 1:19). Election and predestination involve positive goals and heavenly blessings that *as such* do not necessarily presuppose sin and redemption. This is clear from the fact that prelapsarian Adam did not possess these heavenly blessings, either; he was *not* "blessed with every spiritual blessing in the heavenly places" (Eph. 1:3), so he could not lose these blessings. Election refers to blessings that *Adam never had, and thus could never lose*.

Election and predestination refer primarily not to redemption but to Christ and to what believers possess in him: chosen in Christ before the foundation of the world to be holy and blameless before God in love (Eph. 1:4); endowed with the "new man," who in accordance with God's own being has been created in true righteousness and holiness (4:24 NKJV). This is not the *restoration* of an image that Adam had supposedly lost, but the origin of a new creation such as had never existed before. Adam was innocent, but he could have no idea of what holiness and righteousness were. The forbidden tree was the tree of the knowledge of not only evil but of good and evil, and Adam had not yet eaten of it. He did not know what evil was, but neither did he know what good was. He was in the image of God, but nothing more than a germ of this could be seen in him before the Fall. He did not resemble God any more than a newborn baby boy resembles his father. It is none other than the "new man" who has been endowed with God's own holiness and righteousness, and who must be clothed with these characteristics: the elect of God, the holy and beloved ones, must "put on" the moral features of Christ (Col. 3:12–13). Be what you are!

11.3.3 Destined for Righteousness and Glory

The word "predestined," that is, destined beforehand, refers in Romans 8:30 at least to something before a person's conversion, for one is first destined before one is called, justified, and glorified, that is, before one's destiny is fulfilled. From other passages we know that this predestination occurred before the foundation of the world (Eph. 1:4), that is, from eternity (cf. 3:11). Before a person is called, he has been destined from eternity to that for which he is called.

Before a person is justified (declared righteous) he has been destined from eternity to be endowed with the righteousness of God in Christ (cf. 2 Cor. 5:21), or endowed with the new self, which resembles God in holiness and righteousness (Eph. 4:24). Scripture does not give the slightest hint that such things could have been said about prelapsarian Adam.

Before a person is glorified he has been destined from eternity to be endowed with this glory, which is the glory of Christ himself: "The glory that you have given me I have given to them" (John 17:22). "[W]e all, with unveiled face, beholding the glory of the Lord, are being transformed into the same image from one degree of glory to another" (2 Cor. 3:18). Christ "will transform our lowly body to be like his glorious body" (Phil. 3:21). "When Christ who is your life appears, then you also will appear with him in glory" (Col. 3:4). One day, Jesus will come "to be glorified in his saints" (2 Thess. 1:10). The elect will "obtain the salvation that is in Christ Jesus with eternal glory" (2 Tim. 2:10). "[W]hat we will be has not yet appeared; but we know that when he appears we shall be like him, because we shall see him as he is" (1 John 3:2). Again, Scripture does not give the slightest hint that such glories belonged to prelapsarian Adam.

Apparently, the text does not make any distinction between predestination and election: the predestined of Romans 8:29 are the elect of 8:33. The term "election" involves being chosen from a larger company of people; the term "predestination" means that these chosen ones have been destined for a purpose, namely, to be called, justified, and glorified.

11.4 Other Passages in Romans
11.4.1 Twice "Prepared"

In Romans 9:22-23 Paul says, "God, desiring to show his wrath and to make known his power, has endured with much patience vessels of wrath prepared for destruction, in order to make known the riches of his glory for vessels of mercy, which he has prepared beforehand for glory." People are viewed here as instruments [Gr. sing. *skeuē*, Lat. *vas*, "vessel") that are destined to demonstrate God's wrath and God's mercy, respectively.

In doing so, Paul makes a remarkable distinction. Of the "vessels of mercy" he tells us that God beforehand had prepared them for glory, but he does not say this of the "vessels of wrath"; here, he uses the more vague expression "prepared for destruction." Very notably, the "beforehand" (Gr. *pro*) is lacking here; thus, Paul does not speak of a being prepared from eternity for destruction. For those who believe in an eternal decree of reprobation this is regrettable; how easily Paul could have said here that God had "prepared" the wicked "beforehand for destruction." Thus, we would have had the two eternal decrees neatly presented to us, one alongside the other, in perfect symmetry. However, Paul did not do so. To me, the most obvious reason is that Paul did believe in an eternal predestination unto glory, but not in an eternal predestination unto destruction.

The distinction goes even further; not only is the *pro* lacking with respect to the wicked but there is no subject of the sentence, either. Calvin does suggest that, also in the case of the wicked, God is the subject of their preparation for destruction,[18] but the text does not say so. If Paul really had intended this, why would he not have used the same expression twice?[19] But no, he seems to purposely avoid saying that God has prepared the wicked for destruction. No wonder, 2 Peter 2:1 tells us explicitly that the wicked bring "swift destruction" upon *themselves*. In other words, the fact that some people attain heavenly glory is a wonder of God's sovereign grace; the fact that some other people end in eternal destruction is their own fault.[20] The truth is that it was not God who predestined them from eternity unto destruction, but the wicked, through their stubbornness, which prevents them from surrendering to God, destine *themselves* unto destruction.

Moreover, even if we would take God as subject—it is he who prepares the wicked for destruction—this does not necessarily imply that we are dealing with an eternal decree here; as the report of the Dutch Reformed Church in the Netherlands states, "The expression used [in v. 22], 'prepared for destruction,' does . . . not refer to an eternal decree either. 'Prepared' means here in a general sense 'ready,' 'ripe' (see Luke 6:40, where we find the same word in the Greek), in the sense of: ripe through their own sin and rebellion."[21] We find a similar situation in Matthew 25: in verse 34 it is *God* who has prepared a kingdom for the righteous, but in verse 42, the

---

18. Calvin (1999b, ad loc.).
19. Cf. Greijdanus (1933, ad loc.); Morris (1988, ad loc.); *contra* Kersten (1980, 1:119–20, 124–25, 137, 141), who does not respect the difference at all.
20. Demarest (1997, 136–37).
21. Hervormde Kerk (1962, 32–33).

"eternal fire" is said to have been prepared for the devil and his angels. That is, it is *not* said that hell has been prepared from eternity for the wicked. The fact they nonetheless end up there is due entirely to their own sins.

Although Herman Bavinck clings to the notion of an eternal decree of reprobation, he does make this distinction: "There is a distinction, after all, between the decree of reprobation and reprobation itself. The former, namely, the decree, has its ultimate ground in the will of God alone, but the act of reprobation itself takes account of sin."[22] As we will see (§14.6), this is typically infralapsarian. The important point in Bavinck's remark is that he recognizes that the ultimate destruction of the wicked is not just rooted in a divine decree but is due to the wicked's own wickedness. It is not only a matter of divine sovereignty but also of human responsibility.

11.4.2 The Election of Grace

There are more passages in Romans 9 that are quite important for our discussion, but they will have to wait until §14.3. Rather, I wish at this point to discuss Romans 11:5-7, "So too at the present time there is a remnant, chosen by grace.... Israel failed to obtain what it was seeking. The elect obtained it, but the rest were hardened."

Here again, we must conclude that nothing in the text suggests that this is an election and reprobation that exclusively depends on God's sovereign will, leaving out human responsibility. In my view, Paul's presentation of things is rather that the entire chosen people of Israel has failed in its calling, and has made itself guilty toward God, but that God nonetheless wished to save some Israelites, and left the others in their own destruction, hardening their hearts (cf. v. 25, "a partial hardening has come upon Israel, until the fullness of the Gentiles has come in"). People are not hardened because they were eternally reprobated to be hardened, but because they made

---

22. Bavinck (*RD* 2:396).

themselves guilty and persevered in their guilt (see §4.7.2).[23]

Please note the literal translation of verse 5: "remnant according to the election of grace" ([N]KJV, etc.). God's eternal election is rooted not only in God's sovereignty but also in his grace and love (cf. Deut. 4:37; 7:8; 23:5; Luke 2:14; Eph. 1:4–5; 2 Tim. 1:9). Therefore, Jan van Genderen says, "The confession that God has chosen us in Christ from before the foundation of the world is the confession of God's eternal love."[24] It is quite remarkable (and regrettable) that, in all discussions with Calvinists about election and predestination, the term "sovereignty" plays such a major role, and the terms "grace" and "love" play such a minor role.[25] Paul writes about God "who saved us and called us to a holy calling, not because of our works but because of his own *purpose and grace*,[26] which he gave us in Christ Jesus before the ages began [lit., before times eternal]" (2 Tim. 1:9).

Grace does *not* necessarily presuppose sin and the need of redemption.[27] Grace is God's favor toward humanity in a very general sense. Every blessing that God grants humanity, either before or after the Fall, is a token of his grace and favor because people do not deserve any of these blessings—not only because they are sinners but because they are creatures. Finding favor in the eyes of the Lord, or of any earthly king (e.g., Gen. 18:3; 19:19; 30:27; 39:4; 47:29; etc.), does not necessarily presuppose sin at all; it only means receiving without any merit. Everything that God has prepared for believers from eternity and that belongs to his counsel, of election and predestination, is nothing but undeserved grace. In other words, the fact that grace is involved in election and predestination is not an argument against a supralapsarian approach: they do not necessarily presuppose the Fall and sin.

---

23. Cf. Berkouwer (1960, 244–53).
24. Van Genderen and Velema (2008, 226).
25. Cf. Woelderink (1951, 67).
26. Perhaps a hendiadys: his own gracious purpose.
27. See Ouweneel (2016c, §3.6.1).

11.5 Ephesians 1
11.5.1 Elected for Heavenly Blessing

Some of the most important statements about election are found in Ephesians 1:3-5, 11:

> Blessed be the God and Father of our Lord Jesus Christ, who has blessed us in Christ with every spiritual blessing in the heavenly places, even as he chose us in him before the foundation of the world, that we should be holy and blameless before him. In love he predestined [or, before him in love, having predestined] us for adoption as sons through Jesus Christ, according to the purpose of his will. . . . In him we have obtained an inheritance, having been predestined according to the purpose of him who works all things according to the counsel of his will.

Here again, we note that election and predestination are not at all viewed primarily in relation to the problem of sin. This reality surfaces first in verses 6-7, where Paul speaks of "the Beloved [in whom] we have redemption through his blood, the forgiveness of our trespasses, according to the riches of his grace." His starting point is that God has blessed his people with heavenly blessing. Here he is not promising that one day they will be allowed into heaven, but he views them as blessed with heavenly blessing *already now*. All the blessings mentioned here are already our present possession, except for the actual inheritance (v. 14). This "already now" is also implied in 2:6, where Paul says that God "raised us up with him [i.e., Christ] and *seated us* with him in the heavenly places in Christ Jesus." That is, Christ is sitting in the heavenly places (1:20), and in him we are *already* sitting there as well.

This is such an extraordinary statement that regrettably has been weakened in some translations: "given us a position in heaven with him" (GW, NOG); "gave us a place to sit with him in heaven" (WE). This is missing the point. Ephesians 1 tells us that the very One who by God was "raised from the dead and seated at his right hand in the heavenly places, far above all rule and authority and power and dominion, and above every name that is named," was given by God "as head over all things to the church, which is his body, the fullness of him who fills all in all" (vv. 20-23). Paul emphasizes so strongly the unity of this head and this body that whatever the head possesses, the body possesses, and wherever the head is, there is the body. If the head is at God's right hand, then "in him" the body is there as well.

11.5.2 Comparison with Adam

Adam never possessed such a position "in Christ" in the heavenly places, and he therefore could not lose it, either. We have no biblical basis for claiming that he was predestined for such a position. It is believers in the New Testament church who have been predestined for it.[28] The individual election of Ephesians 1:3-5 is indissolubly connected with the corporate election of the (New Testament) church in 3:8-12. This church is characterized by being unified with the glorified Man at God's right hand (1:20-23), which is the dwelling-place of the Holy Spirit (2:20-22). *This* is what divine election in the New Testament sense involves.

By God's grace, even Abraham, Moses, and David were not only redeemed from sin, but they received so much more than Adam had lost through the Fall: justification by faith, new life, peace with God, holiness, and righteousness. But about none of them are we told that they had been predestined to be conformed to the image of God's Son, and to be seated in him in the heavenly places, or even to be temples of the Holy Spirit, both individually and collectively (cf. 1 Cor. 3:16; 6:19; Eph. 2:20-23). The fact that David could pray, "[T]ake not your Holy Spirit from me" (Ps. 51:11), showed that he did not yet know the truth of John 14:16-17, "the Father . . . will give you another Helper, *to be with you forever*, even the Spirit of truth." Even John the Baptist, the "friend" of the "bridegroom" (John 3:29), who died before

---

28. On the differences in position and blessings between Old and New Testament believers, see extensively, Ouweneel (2016c, chapter 7).

Easter, did not belong to the post-Pentecost "bride," the body of Christ (cf. Matt. 11:11, "[T]he one who is least in the kingdom of heaven is greater than John the Baptist").

If election and predestination primarily implied being redeemed *from* evil, there would be no essential difference between Old Testament and New Testament believers. Both groups have been redeemed by the very same blood of the Lamb, both groups have been justified by faith, and have new life through regeneration. However, this is not what election primarily refers to. It implies being destined *for* the unique New Testament blessings: (a) elected to be "holy and blameless before him [i.e., God] in love" (v. 4 note), which amounts to being "conformed to the image of God's Son" (Rom. 8:29); (b) predestined for adoption as sons (Eph. 1:5); and (c) predestined for heirship (receiving the inheritance). Please note again that Abraham, Moses, and David did not possess any of these blessings, nor did prelapsarian Adam and Eve:

(a) Adam and Eve were innocent but capable of falling; however, being "holy and blameless in love" implies conformity to the image of Christ, who cannot fall. The "first man" could fall, and he did; the "new man" — which is Christ manifested in believers (Col. 3:9-11) — will not fall, and *cannot* fall. Adam and Eve had been created in the image of God, but it was only in Christ that the *full* image of God has become manifest (cf. 2 Cor. 4:4; Col. 1:15): light (holy and blameless; cf. 1 John 1:5) and love (cf. 1 John 4:8, 16).

(b) Being predestined for adoption as sons is being predestined to be sons of God — not in the creaturely sense, as Adam was (Luke 3:38), but in the way Christ was: God sent his Son in order that his redeemed could become *sons* of God (Gal. 4:4-5, "God sent forth his Son, . . . so that we might receive adoption as sons"). Therefore, this predestination was "through [Gr. *dia*] Jesus Christ." Adam could never say, "Abba! Father!" (Rom. 8:15; Gal. 4:6), as Jesus said it (Mark 14:36), for believers have become sons like he was Son from eternity. God is their

Father, not only because he is their Creator (as the Israelites could say, e.g., Deut. 32:6; Isa. 64:8; Mal. 2:10) but because the eternal Son of the eternal Father has become their life (1 John 5:12).

(c) Being predestined to be heirs[29] means not only, as in Adam's case, ruling over the earth, but ruling *with Christ*— collectively as his bride or wife—over "all things: things in heaven and things on earth" (Eph. 1:10-11), namely, one day in the renewed creation (1 Cor. 6:2; 2 Tim. 2:12; Rev. 5:10; 20:4, 6). It is a "sharing in the inheritance of the saints in light" (Col. 1:12). It is "an inheritance that is imperishable, undefiled, and unfading, kept in heaven for" believers (1 Pet. 1:4). Which of these statements could possibly have been applied to prelapsarian Adam?

11.5.3 Predestination Is for God

Predestination was not intended primarily as a blessing for *us*, but as a benefit for God himself. Some translations say that God predestined us "to" or "unto himself" ([N]KJV, ASV, DRA, GNV, NASB, etc.; Gr. *eis auton*); other translations have strangely left these words out. The expression "unto himself" has been explained in slightly different ways, but I favor the interpretation that God wanted to have sons and daughters who would be a joy to *his* heart, who would be for his honor and satisfaction. The New Testament believers are "[children] in whom he delights" (Prov. 3:12 NLT; cf. 29:17; Heb. 12:6). In this respect, too, they have been conformed to the image of Christ: "This is my beloved Son, in whom I am well pleased" (Matt. 3:17; 17:5; cf. 12:18).

This being a pleasure for God's heart has a very practical aspect as well: "[A]ll who are *led* by the Spirit of God are sons of God" (Rom. 8:14); it does not just say, all those who *possess* the Spirit, although in itself this would have been correct. True

---

29. Here I am ignoring the other possible but less likely translation: "in whom also were made a heritage" (ASV, etc.); cf. Grosheide (1960, 22–23); Wood (1978, 26, 28); Salmond (1979, 263–64).

sonship must be realized practically by learning (through the Spirit) to live like sons of God: "Therefore 'go out from their midst, and be separate from them,' says the Lord, 'and touch no unclean thing; then I will welcome you, and I will be a father to you, and you shall be sons and daughters to me,' says the Lord Almighty" (2 Cor. 6:17–18). Separation from evil is a condition for realizing our sonship practically.

"[T]he one who conquers will have this heritage, and I will be his God and he will be my son" (Rev. 21:7). In all these cases, it is not redemption, being redeemed from sin, that comes to the fore, but the position of redeemed people before God in Christ, and what they mean for the heart of God, not only positionally but also practically. In a similar way, Paul speaks of the relationship between Christ and his church: "... so that he [i.e., Christ] might present the church *to himself* [Gr. *heautōi*] in splendor, without spot or wrinkle or any such thing, that she might be holy and without blemish" (Eph. 5:27).

Thus, the letter to the Ephesians speaks of what true sons and daughters are to the heart of God, and what the true (bridal) church is to the heart of Christ. Too often, the sinner stands at the center of gospel preaching, as if all that matters are his needs instead of God's desires. But no, it is "the gospel of the glory of the blessed [or: blissful; it is Gr. *makarios*, not *eulogētos*] God" (1 Tim. 1:11). We might say that the gospel is about *God's* blessedness, not primarily *our* blessedness. In colloquial English: the gospel is about God having been made happy with children, and Christ having been made happy with a bride.

11.5.4 Purpose and Will

Ephesians 1 is one of the Bible passages in which God's sovereignty in election and predestination comes to light most clearly. The predestination for adoption as sons is "according to the *purpose* of his *will*" (v. 5). He has made "known to us the mystery of his will, according to his purpose, which he set forth in Christ" (v. 9). Our predestination for the inheritance is "according to the *purpose* of him who works all things according to the counsel of his *will*" (v. 11). Not any human (foreseen) will determined the election of people, but God's own sovereign purpose and will.

God's sovereignty is also underscored by means of the term "grace": ". . . to the praise of his glorious grace, with which he has blessed us in the Beloved. In him we have redemption through his blood, the forgiveness of our trespasses, according to the riches of his grace, which he lavished upon us" (vv. 6–8). It reminds us of the verse quoted earlier: Paul writes about God's "own *purpose and grace,* which he gave us in Christ Jesus before times eternal" (2 Tim. 1:9). As we have seen, this is not primarily God's grace for sinners (although this may be included) but grace (favor) in the sense of blessings granted apart from creatures being able to claim them on the basis of supposed merit.

The ultimate goal of election and predestination is clearly manifested here as well: our predestination is "to the praise of his glorious grace, with which he has blessed us in the Beloved" (v. 6; not just "in Christ," but in God's "beloved Son," Matt. 3:17; 17:5, in this quality: the "Son of his love," Col. 1:13). Our predestination for the inheritance is "to the praise of his glory" (v. 12); and at the end of the passage it says again, ". . . to the praise of his glory" (v. 14). Not only our blessing but also, or in particular, God's glory is in view (cf. again 2 Tim. 1:9). Just as he made us sons "for himself" (v. 5), election in the end is for the praise of his glory. The primary "beneficiary" of divine election and predestination is not primarily people but far more God himself.

11.6 Other Aspects
11.6.1 "In Christ"

Much attention has been paid to the expression "in Christ," or "in him," in Ephesians 1:3-4, 6-7, 10-11 and 13. What is the purport of this expression?[30] I mention no fewer than seven

---
30. See Van der Zanden (1949, chapter 1), and extensively, Berkouwer (1960,

interpretations.

(a) Christ is the *executor* of God's counsel. This description has rightly been called far too meager. God's counsel is not only "through [Gr. *dia*] Christ," as if he were merely the means, but "in [Gr. *en*] him," which is more than an *en instrumentalis*. The election is not only realized through (the work of) Christ but the election *itself* is "in him"; he is its *foundation*. However, this word "foundation" can again be understood in various ways.

(b) Election is motivated by the (foreseen) work of Christ: Jesus Christ, as *causa salutis* ("cause of salvation"), would, through his work, supposedly have moved the Father to assume a conciliatory attitude toward humanity. Elsewhere I have extensively refuted the notion of an *Umstimmung* in God: a "change of mind" in him, from a hostile to a conciliatory attitude toward humanity, thanks to Christ's mediatorship.[31]

(c) The Arminians argued that without faith no person is "in Christ," so that election in Christ would mean the election of those who beforehand had been recognized as believers.[32] Francis Gomarus refuted this effectively.[33] Paul does not say that the elect have been elected as being already in Christ; on the contrary, their election rests in Christ, and not in themselves or in their foreseen faith. In other words, they have not been elected because they were in Christ (on the basis of their foreseen faith) but *in order that* they would be in him.

(d) The Canons of Dordt (I.7) explain being "in Christ" such that God made Christ "from eternity . . . Mediator and Head of the elect and [thus] the foundation of salvation." This ties in with what Paul says, ". . . Christ Jesus, whom God put forward as a propitiation by his blood, to be received by faith" (Rom. 3:23–24). And Peter speaks of Christ as "a lamb

---

134–37), and the references there.
31. Ouweneel (EDR 5, §§10.2–10.3).
32. So Arminius (Verboom (2005, 38, 70); also see Duffield and Van Cleave (1987, 207–208).
33. Gomarus, *Opera Omnia* (1644, 2:60).

without blemish or spot . . . foreknown before the foundation of the world" (1 Pet. 1:19–20). Similarly, Bruce Demarest speaks of Christ as the "sphere" of election.[34]

(e) John Calvin gave this beautiful description: "[S]ince among all the offspring of Adam, the Heavenly Father found nothing worthy of his election, he turned his eyes upon his Anointed, to choose from that body as members those whom he was to take into the fellowship of life." [35] Here, election is based upon the *excellency* of Christ. Ephesians 1:6 expresses this in the most touching way: believers are blessed with grace "in" him who is called the Father's "Beloved" (cf. "the Son of his love," Col. 1:13 ASV, NKJV, etc.). Their election is not only *per* (Lat. "through") but also *propter Christum* ("on account of Christ").[36]

(f) The election "in Christ" of believers is related to the election of Christ himself; as Bavinck says,

> Hence, both Christ and the church are included in the decree of predestination. . . . Christ was also preordained and together with the church was the object of God's election. . . . In this sense, then, the election of Christ logically precedes our own. But no matter how this logical order was construed, all Reformed theologians agreed that Christ together with his church, that is, the mystical Christ [i.e., Christ as one with his mystical body], was the real object of election.[37]

Indeed, Christ is called several times the Chosen One (Luke 9:35; 23:35; cf. 1 Pet. 1:20; Isa. 42:1 and typologically Ps. 89:19).

(g) In opposition to this view of Christ as (co-)*object* of election, we find Karl Barth's view of Christ as *subject* of election.[38] He based this on John 13:18, "I know whom I have chosen," and 15:16, 19, "I chose you." No doubt God the Son

---

34. Demarest (1997, 133).
35. Calvin, *Institutes* 3.22.1.
36. Bavinck (*RD* 2:401).
37. Ibid., 2;402–404.
38. Barth (1936, II/2, 111–113; see on Barth's view of the election Sharp [1990]).

took part in the work of election, in which the entire Trinity was involved; but it is questionable whether this is the real point of being "in Christ." It is "the God and Father of our Lord Jesus Christ" who chose (elected) "in Christ" (Eph. 1:3-4); this picture is quite different from that of the Son (Christ) choosing (electing).

My own preference lies with interpretation (d), in combination with (e) and (f).

11.6.2 Ephesians 2:10

Finally, I draw the reader's attention to Paul's remarkable words in Ephesians 2:10, where he says that believers are God's "workmanship, created in Christ Jesus for good works, which God prepared beforehand, that we should walk in them." When he says "created," Paul is apparently thinking of the "new creation" (v. 15; 2 Cor. 5:17; Gal. 6:15) or the "new self" (KJV: "new man") "created after the likeness of God in true righteousness and holiness" (Eph. 4:24; cf. Col. 3:9-10).

The verse has given rise to much speculation, caused partially by the Greek construction: *ergois agathois hois* instead of *ergois agathois ha*. Desiderius Erasmus preferred to translate the *hois* literally: believers "*for whom* God has prepared beforehand," and Martin Luther offered this rendering: the works "*for which* God has prepared us beforehand."[39]

Another question involves the meaning of "beforehand" in this verse. Grosheide thought the "preparing beforehand" refers "to the redeeming work of Christ. That is what God has prepared, one could say, in eternity, so that believers would enjoy it, cf. 1:4."[40] F. F. Bruce connected the word "beforehand" to the law and Jesus' teaching,[41] that is, not to works that would have been prepared already before the foundation

---

39. Quoted in Salmond (1979, 290), who himself represents the widely accepted view that Greek *hois* must be read here as *ha* (thus also the Syrian and Gothic translations, the Vulgate, and many exegetes). Grosheide (1960, 41n20) has his doubts.
40. Grosheide (1960, 40-41).
41. Bruce (1984, 291).

of the world.

Here the good works are seen as the *goal* for which believers have been created, but also as being part of God's eternal plan.[42] Marvin Vincent explained this to mean that God pre-arranged for us a sphere of moral action to walk in.[43] Such a general description prevents viewing the good works prepared beforehand as a specific program for every individual Christian's life, which has to be carried out step by step. Thus, William Kelly, too, spoke more generally of

> a new character, heavenly and of grace, which was in God's mind and all determined about us before the scene existed into which we are now brought. The same God that had a purpose of saving us and blessing us with Christ before the world was made, had in a certain line of walk [in mind], a special course of action, in which He expected the recipients of such favour to walk.[44]

Such an approach to the text is important for preventing room any longer for believers' own personal options and responsibilities.

11.7 Thessalonians and Timothy
11.7.1 Knowing One's Election

Paul writes, "[W]e know, brothers loved by God, that he has chosen you [lit., knowing . . . your election], because our gospel came to you not only in word, but also in power and in the Holy Spirit and with full conviction. You know what kind of men we proved to be among you for your sake. And you became imitators of us and of the Lord, for you received the word in much affliction, with the joy of the Holy Spirit" (1 Thess. 1:4–6).

Paul makes the remarkable statement here that he *knows* believers in Thessalonica share in God's election. Many

---

42. Salmond (1979, 290); Wood (1978, 36).
43. Vincent (1887, 3:377).
44. Kelly (*BT* 4:281).

Christians, ranging from Roman Catholics to hyper-Calvinists, believe that people on earth in fact can seldom be certain of their salvation, and thus can never be certain of their election. Or at least they may have grave doubts about their *own* election. Was Paul here, as an inspired apostle, allowed to look into God's books? No, he validates his "knowing" with a "because": he knows about the election of these believers, on the one hand, because he has confidence in the power of the Holy Spirit in the message that he has preached, and on the other hand, because he trusts the result of it: the Thessalonian believers had "received" ("accepted," Gr. *dexamenoi*) the message in spite of the affliction, and the validity of this "accepting" came to light in their "joy of the Holy Spirit." The Spirit first manifested himself in the preaching, second in the fact that some accepted the preaching, and third in the lives of those who had accepted the preaching.[45]

According to the general testimony of Scripture, this is the only way to find out whether one has been elected: by accepting the gospel. As Reformed dogmatician Jan van Genderen put it: "Only coming in response to the invitation or calling is proof of election."[46] Here we may mention the metaphor that has often been used: the gospel is like a gate on which is written: "Come to me, all who labor and are heavy laden, and I will give you rest" (Matt. 11:28). After having entered through the gate, one finds written on the inside: "Chosen before the foundation of the world" (cf. Eph. 1:4).[47] Indeed, I think that no person ever received the conviction of having been elected unless they first humbled themselves before God and threw themselves into the arms of God's grace.

We must emphasize here that, to unbelievers, Scripture never speaks about having been elected or not, but rather about repentance and conversion. With God, election comes first, but people become aware of election only after having

---

45. Cf. Woelderink (1951, 51).
46. Cf. Van Genderen and Velema (2008, 212).
47. See, e.g., Lightner (1991, 147); Duffield and Van Cleave (1987, 207–208).

come to God. As Hendrikus Berkhof put it: "Election is the first word in God's activity and the last in the confession of believers."[48] God says, "Fear not, for I have redeemed you; I have called you by name, you are mine" (Isa. 43:1), but he says it only to those who have first humbled themselves: "I dwell . . . with him who is of a contrite and lowly spirit, to revive the spirit of the lowly, and to revive the heart of the contrite" (57:15).

Klaas van der Zwaag approvingly quoted the Puritan Walter Marshall (d. 1680): "Marshall says that we cannot have certain knowledge of our election for eternal life before we believe."[49] He further referred to John Calvin, William à Brakel (the Second Reformation, the Netherlands), and Thomas Boston (Scottish Presbyterianism),[50] who have written in the same vein. Van der Zwaag therefore rejected all "elective fatalism,"[51] that is, all fatalistic waiting for the certainly of election, whereas instead of this, people must do nothing other than repent and put their confidence in God's promises made to all those who humble themselves before him.

Surely, the emphasis in 1 Thessalonians 1 is also on the work of the Holy Spirit; we know that conversion and regeneration are counterparts,[52] and that a person is not born again in his own strength but "of water and the Spirit."[53] However, our chapter also shows the side of human responsibility: the Thessalonians had "accepted" or "received" the gospel. This cannot be done without the power of the Spirit (cf. John 3:27, "A person cannot receive even one thing unless it is given him from heaven"). But this does not change the fact that the "accepting" was *their* act: *they* had to stretch out their hands. This aspect is often underscored: ". . . if you are willing to

---

48. Berkhof (1986, 483).
49. Van der Zwaag (2003, 123).
50. Ibid., 122–24.
51. Ibid., 125–28.
52. See extensively, Ouweneel (EDR 6).
53. Ouweneel (EDR 1, §8.2.1).

accept it . . ." (Matt. 11:14); "receiving" is coupled to "believing" (John 1:11-12; 17:8); if people refuse to "receive" they are threatened with judgment (12:48; cf. 2 Thess. 2:10); people must make sure they accept the "right" gospel (2 Cor. 11:4; cf. 1 Thess. 2:13; see further Mark 4:16; John 3:33; Acts 2:41; 8:14; 11:1; 1 Cor. 15:1; 1 Tim. 1:15; 4:9).

We could put it as follows: the gracious work of the Holy Spirit is a necessary condition for our salvation. But is it also a *sufficient* condition, in this sense: does the Spirit accomplish it, totally independent of what people want and do themselves? If we would assert this, we would nullify human responsibility: "All who are thirsty may come; they can have the water of life as a free gift *if they want it*" (Rev. 22:17 ERV). Because of this very freedom, the Spirit can be *quenched*, says the same letter (1 Thess. 5:19), and elsewhere: the Spirit may be *grieved* (Isa. 63:10; Eph. 4:30) and *resisted* (Acts 7:51).

11.7.2 Other Passages in 1 Thessalonians

In 1 Thessalonians 5:9 we read, "God has not destined [Gr. *etheto*, from *tithēmi*] us for wrath, but to obtain salvation through our Lord Jesus Christ." In fact, this is not a clear proof text with respect to election because the key words "elect" and "predestine" do not occur here. Being "destined" is just as timeless as the being "made" in Proverbs 16:4, "The LORD has made everything for its purpose, even the wicked for the day of trouble." Neither passage can therefore serve as a proof of a decree of reprobation. Even if 1 Thessalonians 5:9 would imply that there are other people who *are* "destined for wrath" (cf. 1:10; 2:16; 1 Pet. 2:8), this does not demonstrate that before the foundation of the world those people were destined for judgment. One could just as well conclude that people who manifest themselves as wicked, and persevere in their wickedness, are *then and therefore* destined for judgment (see further §§14.1-14.4).

Reference is being made here to being destined to obtain salvation, as in 2 Timothy 2:10, where Paul says, "I endure everything for the sake of the elect, that they also may obtain the salvation that is in Christ Jesus with eternal glory." "Salvation" (Gr. *sōtēria*) here is not only deliverance from sin, Satan, and death, but represents positively the fullness of blessing that God has prepared for his elect: every spiritual blessing in the heavenly places (Eph. 1:3). Therefore, in German and Dutch the Greek word *sōtēria* is often rendered as *Heil/heil*, related to English *hail* (old English), *heal(th)*, and *whole*. This term has a much fuller meaning than just deliverance; it refers to a state of well-being, comparable to the Hebrew *shalom* and the English *bliss*. In our verse this is hinted at by linking the term "salvation" with "eternal glory."

Here I would also refer to Paul's statement that believers are "destined" (Gr. *keimetha*, from *keimai*) for afflictions (1 Thess. 3:3; cf. 2 Tim. 3:12). This destining occurs *within time*, as an aspect of God's ways with believers. Such passages smoothly fit into the view that not all destining is from eternity, and that not all destining is part of God's counsel. In his *ways* with his children, God may temporarily destine them for afflictions, but this does not at all affect his *counsel*, that is, believers having been destined for eternal glory before the foundation of the world. This is similar to the fact that believers may be destined or chosen for particular ministries and services within history (John 13:18; 15:16, 19; Acts 1:2, 24–25; 9:15; 15:7; 26:16; see §10.8.1). It may even turn out that some of these chosen people are not genuine believers at all (cf. John 6:70), which underscores the fact that not all destining or choosing is from eternity and for eternity.

11.7.3 2 Thessalonians 2:13

Paul says, "[W]e ought always to give thanks to God for you, brothers beloved by the Lord, because God chose you as the firstfruits [Gr. *aparchēn*] to be saved, through sanctification by the Spirit and belief in the truth" (2 Thess. 2:13). Instead of "firstfruits" (*aparchēn*), the KJV and others have "from the beginning" (reflecting the *ap' archēs* of the Byzantine Text).

The Annotators of the Dutch States Translation (the equivalent of the King James Version) say about this,

> Namely, [from the beginning] of the world, as Mic. 5:1; 1 John 1:1. That is, from eternity, or before the foundation of the world (Eph. 1.4), although some others understand it from the beginning when the Gospel was published unto them, when God by his Spirit chose or separated them out of the corrupt heap of people; as the word *choose* or *select* is also taken elsewhere (see John 15.16; 1 Cor. 1.27), but the first exposition seems as fit to agree with the following verse, seeing the choosing whereof Paul here speaks goes before calling, as is to be seen also Rom. 8.29, 30 and chap. 9.23,24, but the actual choosing out of the corrupt heap of men, which is done in time, follows after calling, seeing that separation is brought to pass by the calling of the Gospel.

First, the Annotators prefer the doubtful reading of the Byzantine Text (rendered as "from the beginning"). Second, they do not distinguish between "*before* the foundation of the world" (John 17:24; Eph. 1:4; 1 Pet. 1:20; see §5.7.2) and "*from* [or *since*] the foundation of the world," that is, since the world began (Matt. 13:35; 25:34; Luke 11:50; Heb. 4:3; 9:26; Rev. 13:8; 17:8; see §2.1.2).[54] Third, the Annotators point to a possible alternative interpretation, namely, that of an "actual election," directly connected with the calling of the person in time, as, for instance, in 1 Corinthians 1:27 (where, by the way, the Annotators view the "election" as "eternal election"). An "actual election" is not an election from eternity but one that is within time, an election that occurs when a person comes to faith and is "elected" (taken out, separated) from the mass of unbelievers.

Reformed theologian Jan Gerrit Woelderink praised the Annotators because "they are still aware of a direct election

---

54. Some translations do not honor this distinction when they render the Gr. *apo katabolēs* in some of the latter verses as "before," as if the text said *pro katabolēs* (cf. §2.1.2 above).

.... Among us [i.e., Reformed Christians], this view of election has been almost entirely lost, and everywhere where election is mentioned the church thinks of election from eternity."[55] In other words, it may be that, in a number of Bible passages where election is mentioned, far more often the "actual" (temporal) election (i.e., the one that coincides with one's being called) is intended.

11.7.4 2 Timothy

In 2 Timothy 1:9-10, Paul says that God

> saved us and called us to [or, with] a holy calling, not because of our works but because of his own purpose and grace, which he gave us in Christ Jesus before the ages began [lit., before times eternal], and which now has been manifested through the appearing of our Savior Christ Jesus, who abolished death and brought life and immortality to light through the gospel.

God's saving call, leading to regeneration and conversion, is rooted not in any human merit, but exclusively in his own purpose and grace. "Purpose" (Gr. *prothesis*, from *protithēmi* plus accusative, "to set forth," "to put forward as," "to appoint as," "to present as"; see Rom. 3:25) is an important technical term in connection with election: believers have been "called according to God's purpose" (Rom. 8:28); the "purpose of God" is "according to election" (9:11 NKJV); "predestined according to the purpose of him . . ." (Eph. 1:11); ". . . so that through the church the manifold wisdom of God might now be made known to the rulers and authorities in the heavenly places. This was according to the eternal purpose that he has realized in Christ Jesus our Lord" (3:10-11).

There is a correspondence between the latter passage and 2 Timothy 1:9: election and predestination are "in Christ Jesus," that is, obtain their foundation in his person and his work (cf. §11.6.1). Paul speaks of "eternal life, which God, who never lies, promised before the ages began [lit., before times

---

55. Woelderink (1951, 51).

eternal]." If the promise was made in eternity past, *to whom* was it made? It was made to benefit prospective believers, but that is not the same as asking to whom the promise was made. It seems to me that the answer can only be: to Christ. This is not a divine promise given in time, somewhere in the Old Testament, but a promise given before the foundation of the world. Therefore, it cannot have been a promise to people, and not to angels either; instead, it was a promise within the Triune God: an eternal promise by the Father to the Son.

John says, "If what you heard from the beginning abides in you, then you too will abide in the Son and in the Father. And this is the promise that he made to us—eternal life" (1 John 2:24-25). Notice the remarkable "he" in verse 25, which seems to refer back to both the Father and the Son in verse 24. It is, as it were, a promise between the Father and the Son, made in eternity, to grant eternal life to those who one day would become believers. In 2 Timothy 1:10 it is a promise of life as well: "the promise of the life that is in Christ Jesus" (v. 1). Before the foundation of the world, eternal life has been promised in Christ to the elect; they were "appointed to eternal life" (Acts 13:48). From eternity, they are the people whom the Father has given from the world to the Son (John 6:37; 10:29; 17:2, 6, 9, 24).

We are dealing here with the important Trinitarian character of election.[56] God chooses, undertakes his purpose, grants from eternity promises, "in Christ"; the Father gives the elect to his Son. And believers are elect "according to the foreknowledge of God the Father, in the sanctification of the Spirit" (1 Pet. 1:2). The Holy Spirit is the One who, within time, calls and regenerates those who were elected from eternity (John 3:5).

11.8 The Book of Acts
11.8.1 The Divine Side

In Acts 13:48, we read concerning Paul's visit to Antioch in

---
56. Cf. Heyns (1988, 79–80).

Pisidia: "[W]hen the Gentiles heard this [i.e., the gospel], they began rejoicing and glorifying the word of the Lord, and as many as were appointed [Gr. *tetagmenoi*, from *tassō*] to eternal life believed." F. F. Bruce rejects attempts to understand this to mean: "as many as were disposed to eternal life."[57] It is possible, however, to translate: "as many as had set themselves to eternal life" (cf. "set themselves" in 1 Cor. 16:15 ASV, etc.).[58] The guidelines of the Dutch Reformed Church in the Netherlands understand "appointed" to mean "ordered, ordained" (*geordend*):"It belongs to God's order, ordination, appointment, that 'all' these, that is, the Gentiles just mentioned, are called to salvation."[59]

F. F. Bruce emphasizes that *tassō* in Koine Greek means "to enroll"; in our verse this would mean to be enrolled in the book of life. He does not mention that this book sometimes rather seems to be the book of all the living (Exod. 32:32-33; Ps. 69:28), and that this book does not always necessarily mean a being enrolled for eternal life from eternity (see §10.9). Moreover, if the book of life were indeed the record of the elect, no one could ever be added to it, and no one could ever be blotted out from it.[60] However, Bruce's point remains strong: Acts 13:48 probably speaks of a being enrolled for eternal life already before one's conversion. Compare "recorded for life" (Isa. 4:3), the "book of remembrance . . . of those who feared the LORD" (Mal. 3:16); "your names are written in heaven" (Luke 10:20); ". . . whose names are in the book of life" (Phil. 4:3); "the firstborn who are enrolled in heaven" (Heb. 12:23); "I will never blot his name out of the book of life" (Rev. 3:5); ". . . everyone whose name has not been written before [read: from] the foundation of the world in the book of life of the Lamb who was slain" (13:8); "those who are written in the

---

57. Bruce (1988, 267–68).
58. Knowling (1979, 300); *contra* Van Genderen and Velema (2008, 212).
59. Hervormde Kerk (1962, 31).
60. Woelderink (1951, 63–65); cf. Berkouwer (1960, 110–15); Venema (1992, 157–59).

Lamb's book of life" (21:27).[61]

Thus, the text seems to suggest that only those people come to faith who have been predestined for this by God. Yet, this text, if properly viewed in its context, can hardly function as an argument for the decretalist view. Verse 46 speaks of Jews who judged themselves "unworthy of eternal life," that is, rendered a judgment demonstrating that they were unworthy of eternal life. They were not unworthy because they happened to fall outside the decree of election, but *because of their behavior*. This corresponds to what Jesus said in the parable: "The wedding feast is ready, but those invited were not worthy" (Matt. 22:8), and elsewhere: "[T]hose who are considered worthy to attain to that age and to the resurrection from the dead . . ." (Luke 20:35).

11.8.2 The Human Side

The last point in the previous section underscores the importance of human responsibility. The text does not suggest that the one person *in himself* is more worthy of eternal life than another person, for all people are sinners by nature. The point is rather that those who "thrust" the gospel "aside" (see Acts 13:46 again) *in this way* show themselves to be unworthy, and those who accept it in faith *in this way* show themselves to be worthy. Worthiness here is a matter not of being good versus being bad, but of being penitent and believing versus being impenitent and unbelieving. However, if this is so, we must conclude that eternal salvation is a matter not only of divine predestination but just as much of human acceptance of the gospel. A person is worthy of the gospel not by having been elected but by accepting it in a spirit of repentance and faith. Therefore, Greg Boyd argues that Acts 13:48 does not speak of *eternal* destiny at all, and that here being destined is based much more on the willingness of the hearts of these believers under the preparatory working of God's Spirit.[62]

---

61. On Jewish ideas concerning predestination, see also Strack (1986, 2:726).
62. Boyd (2001, 412).

This suggestion seems to be supported by what we read five verses later, in Acts 14:1, "Now at Iconium they [i.e., the apostles] entered together into the Jewish synagogue and spoke in such a way that a great number of both Jews and Greeks believed." Here, salvation is described as depending not on divine predestination but on the persuasive strength of the apostles: they spoke "in such a way that" (Gr. *houtōs hōste*) many believed. If salvation depends on divine predestination alone, why would persuasion be needed? However, apparently it *is* needed: Paul "reasoned in the synagogue every Sabbath, and tried to persuade Jews and Greeks" (18:4; cf. 17:4). He "persuaded" the people "about the kingdom of God" (19:8). He writes, "Therefore, knowing the fear of the Lord, we persuade others" (2 Cor. 5:11).

In summary: Acts 13:46–14:1 strongly suggests that salvation of people depends both on divine predestination (from eternity or in time) and on human acceptance or rejection of the gospel, in connection with the persuasion of the preacher. People accept the gospel through the work of the Holy Spirit in their hearts (see §11.8.3) — that is the divine side. They accept the gospel through the persuasive force of gospel preachers — that is the human side.

People accept the gospel because they were elected for it — that is the divine side. People accept the gospel because they ardently desire to escape eternal judgment and attain divine glory — that is the human side.

11.8.3 Other Passages

Luke tells us: "One who heard us was a woman named Lydia, from the city of Thyatira, a seller of purple goods, who was a worshiper of God. The Lord opened her heart to pay attention to what was said by Paul" (Acts 16:14).

Such passages can hardly be used as evidence for either the (hyper-)Calvinist or the Arminian view. The reason is that the text does not tell us why the Lord opened Lydia's heart so that she believed. Was it because she had been elected from eternity (as Calvinists might argue)? Or did the Lord open her heart because he foresaw that she would believe, or even because he saw at that moment the longings of her heart (as Arminians might argue)? The text does not tell us. We must say, however, that the Lord opening Lydia's heart did not exclude her own responsibility. She expressed this herself, after her conversion, by telling Paul and his companions, "If you have judged me to be faithful to the Lord, come to my house and stay" (v. 15).

Similarly, the fact that Satan had filled Ananias' heart "to lie to the Holy Spirit" did not at all diminish Ananias' own responsibility. Ananias was not predestined to be filled with Satan in this way; it was his own fault. Therefore, he had to die (Acts 5:1-6). *He* had opened his heart to Satan, just as Lydia opened her heart to the Lord. It is just as true to say that the Lord opened Lydia's heart (the divine side) as to say that Lydia opened her heart to the Lord (the human side).

It is similar in Acts 18:10, where the Lord tells Paul in a vision at Corinth: "I have many in this city who are my people." Here again, the verse as such does not give us a clue whether God was speaking here about people whom he had elected from eternity (as Calvinists might argue), or whether he saw beforehand that many people in Corinth would accept the gospel and come to him (as Arminians might argue). In my view, such passages rather suggest a balance of the two aspects: it is Lydia's and these Corinthians' own step of faith that matters — but such a step can never be isolated from God's gracious operation in the hearts of the people concerned: "[W]ork out your own salvation with fear and trembling, *for* it is God who works in you, both to will and to work for his good pleasure" (Phil. 2:12-13). That is, exercise your responsibility — but realize that it is God who gives you the strength to do that.

11.9 Other Letters
11.9.1 James

Just as Paul does in Romans 8:20 and Ephesians 1:4-5, so James links election not so much with deliverance from sin but rather with the fullness of blessing that God has to offer: "[H]as not God chosen those who are poor in the world to be rich in faith and heirs of the kingdom, which he has promised to those who love him?" (James 2:5). Here faith is not primarily something negative — in the sense of faith that saves us *from* something — but positive: "the faith in our Lord Jesus Christ, the Lord of glory" (v. 1).[63] Unfortunately, the faith of some Christians, even today, entails little more than "fleeing from the wrath to come" (Luke 3:7; cf. 1 Thess. 1:10).

True faith directs itself to the glory and wisdom of God in Christ, a wisdom that again is from before the foundation of the world: "[W]e impart a secret and hidden wisdom of God, which God decreed before the ages for our glory. None of the rulers of this age understood this, for if they had, they would not have crucified the *Lord of glory*" (1 Cor. 2:7-8). God has elected his own for this true faith, which rises beyond the problem of sin — no matter how important that problem is — and directs itself to, and surrenders to, the "Lord of glory."

11.9.2 1 Peter 1:1-2

Peter writes to "those who are elect exiles of the Dispersion in Pontus, Galatia, Cappadocia, Asia, and Bithynia, according to the foreknowledge of God the Father, in the sanctification of the Spirit, for obedience to Jesus Christ and for sprinkling with his blood" (1 Pet. 1:1-2).

This passage illustrates again that foreknowledge sometimes can hardly be distinguished from predestination (cf. vv. 19-20, "the lamb foreknown," and see §11.3.1). Therefore, the ERV and other translations render the term "foreknowledge" as follows: "God planned long ago to *choose* you." Indeed, the text does not refer to some passive foreknowledge,

---

63. Ouweneel (1981, 37).

an awareness that God would have with regard to some or all things, but to knowing his elect beforehand, a knowledge that implies concern, love, intimacy, even before humanity was created. 1 Peter 1:1-2 may be viewed as one of the most remarkable examples in the New Testament indicating that, seen from God's perspective, salvation is not based upon the longings of people reaching out to a distant God. Rather, it is based upon the decree of God who—from eternity, that is, long before the creation of the world—approaches people in love and reaches out to them.[64] God's grace was granted to people in eternity before they actually existed (2 Tim. 1:9).

The most notable parallel is Romans 11:2, "God has not rejected his people whom he foreknew." The Greek word for foreknowledge in 1 Peter 1:2 is *prognōsis*, from which the English word "prognosis" was derived. It is derived from the verb *proginōskō*, which word is used in Romans 11:2. The people whom God foreknew are the people with whom he had had an intimate relationship for so many centuries. How deep this goes is strikingly seen in Exodus 2:25 (DRA), God "looked upon the children of Israel, and he knew them," that is, "took notice of them" (NASB, etc.), and even "was concerned about them" (NIV, etc.), or "cared about them" (NLV) (cf. 3:7, "I know their sufferings"). The deepest source of election is God's heart, from which he reaches out to people in love. On the one hand, he is full of mercy toward totally corrupted people, that is, in order to remove all the negatives that affect their relationship with him. On the other hand, more positively, he reaches out to people to exalt them to the highest glory.

11.9.3 2 Peter 1:10

I find this statement by Peter fascinating: "Therefore, brothers, be all the more diligent to confirm your calling and election, for if you practice these qualities you will never fall" (2 Pet. 1:10). The verb "to confirm" (Gr. *bebaiō*) has a legal meaning: *bebaiōsis* is the legal certificate that a buyer receives

---

64. Davids (1990, 48); Blum (1981, 270–71).

from a seller (to which he can appeal if a third party would claim ownership of the goods that he bought), or the legal ratification of a will (cf. Phil. 1:7; Heb. 6:16).[65] This means that Peter challenges his readers here to show a "certificate of," or to "ratify," their "calling and election," to give evidence thereof.

This probably refers especially to the fruits that are enumerated in verses 5-7: faith, virtue (Gr. *aretē*, i.e., divine strength and excellence), knowledge (in the existential sense), self-control, steadfastness, godliness, brotherly affection (Gr. *philadelphia*), and love (*agapē*); taken together these are identical with the fruit (sing.) of the Holy Spirit (Gal. 5:22). It is walking "in a manner worthy of the calling to which you have been called" (Eph. 4:1), or "worthy of the gospel of Christ" (Phil. 1:27), or "in a manner worthy of the Lord" (Col. 1:10), or "in a manner worthy of God, who calls you into his own kingdom and glory" (1 Thess. 2:12).[66] Those who do not give, or no longer give, such "certificates," such demonstrations of their election, no matter how strongly they confess that they are Christians, are merely showing that they have never been genuinely called and elected. The "ratification" is lacking. If there are no fruits, then apparently there never was a seed.

It is not easy to demonstrate from the New Testament that election is strictly individual. No wonder such individuality has been denied by some. For instance, Reformed dogmatician Adrio König writes, "Therefore, it is not elect persons who come to faith, it is sinners who come to faith, and thus become part of the elect, the church."[67] Some have argued that, in 1 Peter 1:1 and 2 Peter 1:10, election is meant in the corporate sense because "calling" and "election" are governed by one article in the Greek (*tēn klēsin kai eklogēn*; the Granville Sharp Rule), while "calling" can indeed have a corporate meaning (cf. Matt. 22:14). But why should "calling" in 1 Peter 1:15; 2:9, 21; 3:9; 5:10 and 2 Peter 1:3 be taken in the

---

65. See Strachan (1979, 128); *TDNT* 1:600–603; *NIDNTT* 1:658–60.
66. *Contra* Heyns (1988, 86), who wishes to read in this verse a call *to* faith.
67. König (2006, 433; cf. 430, 434).

corporate sense (cf. Rom. 8:29-30)? Is not every human called to salvation individually?

To be sure, believers are sometimes addressed corporately as "elect," especially in an expression such as "you are a chosen race" (1 Pet. 2:9; cf. Mark 13:20, 22; Eph. 1:4-5; Col. 3:12; 1 Thess. 1:4; 1 Pet. 1:2; Rev. 17:14).[68] Paul Jewett points out that the election of Abraham and Sarah was individual as well as corporate, the latter with respect to their progeny;[69] they were personally chosen, and they were ancestors of a chosen people. In the New Testament, the *church* is this "chosen race," the object of God's "eternal purpose that he has realized in Christ Jesus our Lord" (Eph. 3:10-11).[70] However, election also definitely has an individual meaning, for it is the distinct names of believers that are inscribed in God's book (cf. Luke 10:20; Phil. 4:3; 2 Tim. 2:19; Heb. 12:23; 2 John 1:1, 13; Rev. 3:5; 13:8).[71] The New Testament mentions several individual elect persons (if "elect" is used here in the sense we are describing), such as Rufus (Rom. 16:13), the "lady" of 2 John 1:1, and her "elect sister" (v. 13).

11.9.4 Summary

Let us summarize what we have found, and supply some additional information. Here are seven entities and (groups of) people (not counting the "elect angels," 1 Tim. 5:21) that from eternity have been prepared, promised, appointed, foreknown, or predestined.

(1) *The Lamb of God,* "foreknown" before the foundation of the world (1 Pet. 1:20). According to God's foreknowledge he was delivered up to the cross and to death, without this fact taking away anything from his enemies' responsibility: he was "delivered up according to the definite plan and foreknowledge of God, . . . crucified and killed by the hands of

---

68. Cf. Heidelberg Catechism, Q&A 54; Bavinck (*RD* 2:390); Heyns (1988, 85).
69. Jewett (1985, 118; cf. 47: salvation is both corporate and individual).
70. See extensively, Ouweneel (EDR 7).
71. Jewett (1985, 48).

lawless men" (Acts 2:23; cf. 4:27-28). Also note the remarkable connection between "before the foundation of the world" and "the book of life of the Lamb who was slain" (Rev. 13:8).[72]

(2) *God's wisdom*, "which God decreed before the ages for our glory" (1 Cor. 2:7; cf. the wisdom in Prov. 8:22-31).

(3) *God's grace*, "which he gave us in Christ Jesus before the ages began" (2 Tim. 1:9); this is God's "favor," a collective expression for all his promised blessings.

(4) *Eternal life*, "which God, who never lies, promised before the ages began" (Titus 1:2; cf. 1 John 2:25); that is, eternal knowledge of (fellowship with) the Triune God (John 17:3; 1 John 1:1-4; 5:20).

(5) *Good works*, "which God prepared beforehand [i.e., from eternity?], that we should walk in them" (Eph. 2:10).

(6) *Believers* have from eternity been foreknown and predestined and elected for (again seven points):

* eternal life (Acts 13:48; see point 4);

* eternal salvation (1 Thess. 5:9; 2 Tim. 1:9; 2:10);

* conformity to the image of God's Son (Rom. 8:29; cf. John 17:22; Phil. 3:21; 1 John 3:2);

* being holy and blameless in love (Eph. 1:4; cf. 4:24; Col. 3:12);

* adoption as children of God (Eph. 1:5; cf. Rom. 8:15; Gal. 4:5-6);

* being heirs of God, that is, the kingdom of God (Eph. 1:11; James 2:5);

* glory (Rom. 8:30; 9:23; cf. 1 Cor. 2:7).

(7) *The church*, "according to the eternal purpose that he has realized in Christ Jesus our Lord," has been destined for this aim that, through her, "the manifold wisdom of God might now be made known to the rulers and authorities in

---

72. Cf. the ESV ("written before the foundation of the world in the book of life of the Lamb who was slain") versus the NKJV ("written in the Book of Life of the Lamb slain from the foundation of the world").

the heavenly places" (Eph. 3:10-11).

Chapter 12
The Battle Over Predestination

What do you have that you did not receive?
If then you received it,
  why do you boast
  as if you did not receive it?
                    1 Corinthians 4:7

Summary: *The battle over predestination began with Pelagius and Augustine; the latter was the first to defend an eternal decree of reprobation. It played a great role in Calvin's thinking, but little in the Calvinistic creeds, except the Canons of Dordt. In the Five Points of Calvinism (TULIP), there is little to object to, except for the constant danger of underrating human responsibility. During the early seventeenth century, the battle became fierce in the Dutch conflict between Arminians (Remonstrants) and Gomarists (Contra-Remonstrants). In this chapter, the Remonstrance as well as the Canons of Dordt are analyzed with respect to election and reprobation. Apart from so much that is highly valuable in the Canons, one gets the impression that, due to the conflict, the Contra-Remonstrants fell into a reactionary position. In later generations, more moderate Calvinists softened the harsh elements in the Canons, whereas hyper-Calvinists strengthened these elements.*

12.1 Augustine
12.1.1 The Earlier and the Later Augustine

THE EARLY CHURCH FATHERS expressed themselves hardly at all on the subject of predestination, and instead emphasized human responsibility and free will.[1] They did so particularly in their battle against Gnosticism, which taught that human nature had been created so evil that people were not free to choose the good. Thus, the germ of the Arminian view is encountered at an early stage, namely, with Clement of Alexandria and Origen, and with the later representatives of both the Alexandrian and the Antiochian schools. They did put more emphasis on original sin, including the corruption of the will, and on the dominant role of God's grace in redemption. Their anthropocentric view is found also with the early Latin fathers (Tertullian, Cyprian, Hilary, Ambrose), even though the emphasis came to be placed increasingly on God's grace.

The problems that occupy us in these chapters all received their shape during these first four centuries: the relationships between the free and the bound will (the will in bondage), between an optimistic and a pessimistic view of humanity, between grace and works, between divine sovereignty and human responsibility.[2]

Originally, Augustine held to a form of synergism as well. Thus, in his early period he taught that God had predestined no one except those whom he foreknew would believe and respond to his call.[3] Afterward he said of this period that he had not yet very carefully studied or examined the nature of the election of grace about which the apostle speaks.[4] This was the period when, especially on the basis of 1 Corinthians 4:7 (cited above at the head of this chapter), he had moved from the generally accepted synergism to a strict monergism:

---

1. See Buis (1958, 6–9); Weber (1983, 2:422–23, 426); Pannenberg (1991, 3:440–42); Brümmer (2005, 126–31).
2. Oorthuys (1931, 9–56); Ditmanson (1977, 51–53).
3. *Expositio quarumdam propositionum ex Epistola ad Romanos* 55; cf. 61.
4. *De praedestinatione sanctorum* 3.7.

redemption is not based on a cooperation between God's grace and the human free will, but is exclusively the work of God's grace.

Augustine's new insights came to expression in many of his later writings.[5] Compared with what he had written earlier, his thesis was now: the elect have not been elected because they believe, but *in order that* they would believe. Especially by the teaching of Pelagius he was stimulated to reconsider the problem of election and reprobation.[6] Pelagius denied original sin and preached free will, through which people, by their own strength, could choose for or against God. On the basis of his foreknowledge of people's choices, God predestines some to blessedness, and others to damnation. Thus, people themselves determine their destiny entirely by their own choices.

Pelagius appeared to have been driven by *respect* for people as noble and free creatures of God. Many have wondered, however, whether in reality it is not cruel to put people at the mercy of their own (supposed) freedom, choices, and will. As Herman Bavinck put it: "[I]f Pelagius's doctrine were the standard, and the virtuous were chosen because of their virtue, and Pharisees because of their righteousness, wretched publicans would be shut out [Luke 18:9–14]. Pelaginaism has no pity."[7]

Later *semi*-Pelagians, who teach a kind of "half Pelagianism," made more room for God's grace by emphasizing synergy (cooperation) between divine grace and human responsibility. Forms of semi-Pelagianism can be found in many theological movements: Roman Catholic, Lutheran, and Evangelical. People have diligently searched for a

---

5. E.g., *De praedestinatione sanctorum* ("On the Predestination of the Saints"), *De correptione et gratia* ("On Rebuke and Grace"), and *De perfectione iustitiae hominis* ("Human Perfection in Righteousness").
6. See the review by Erickson (1998, 921–24; for the subsequent history: 924–27).
7. Bavinck (*RD* 2:402).

middle path between strict Augustinianism/Calvinism and Pelagianism. In the Middle Ages, we find great thinkers on this middle path, such as Anselm of Canterbury (d. 1109). In his work *On Free Will* (*De libero arbitrio*), he distinguished between true freedom and what he called the faculty of the will. Fallen humanity has retained this faculty but does no longer possess the true freedom. In his work *On the Harmony of the Foreknowledge, the Predestination, and the Grace of God with the Free Will* (*De concordia praescientiae et praedestinationis et gratiae Dei cum libero arbitrio*), he sought to be as fair as possible to the Augustinian position.

12.1.2 An Eternal Decree of Reprobation?

Resuming our discussion of Augustine, we note with fascination how he wrestled in his day with the issue of an eternal decree of reprobation.[8] Originally, Augustine argued — in my view, rightly so — that the election of some from eternity does not entail the damnation of others from eternity. All people share in the consequences of the Fall, and thus lie in misery and corruption. Nonetheless, God in his grace decreed to save some of them. According to the earlier Augustine, the others were not the object of an eternal decree of God; this means that from eternity God had not actively decreed them to destruction; they were simply non-elect.

His opponents did not accept this view. Trapped by their logic, they argued that an eternal, sovereign decree of election had to have a counterpart in an eternal, sovereign decree of reprobation. Augustine was certainly receptive to this argument, and his successors, especially Gottschalk of Orbais (d. 867?), Gregory of Rimini (d. 1358), and John Calvin (d. 1564) even more so. This matter also had direct consequences for the doctrine of atonement: if some people have been rejected from eternity, it was impossible to assume that

---

8. See especially his *De Civitate Dei* ("On the City of God"), his *De praedestinatione sanctorum* ("On the Predestination of the Saints"), and his *De dono perseverantiae* ("On the Gift of Perseverance").

Christ had blotted out their sins—otherwise, how could they be condemned for these same sins? Apparently, a limited election also implied a limited atonement.[9]

12.2 Creeds
12.2.1 The Belgic Confession

With Martin Luther we see initially, in his *The Bondage of the Will* (*De servo arbitrio*, 1525, against Erasmus), a one-sided emphasis on God's sovereignty, but afterward this view retreated into the background of his thinking. With Calvin the reverse occurred: whereas, in the 1536 edition of his *Institutes of the Christian Religion* (*Institutio Christianae Religionis*) and his Catechism of Geneva (1542), he scarcely referred to it, in the 1559 edition of the *Institutes*, predestination was raised often in a rather polemical way.

The *Heidelberg Catechism* hardly touches upon election. Q&A 52 speaks of "all His [i.e., Christ's] chosen ones," and Q&A 54 refers to Christ gathering, defending, and preserving "for Himself unto everlasting life a chosen communion."

The *Belgic Confession* (Art. 16) deals with the subject somewhat more extensively: "We believe that, all the posterity of Adam being thus fallen into perdition and ruin by the sin of our first parents, God then did manifest Himself such as He is; that is to say, merciful and just: **merciful**, since He delivers and preserves from this perdition all whom He in His eternal and unchangeable counsel of mere goodness has elected in Christ Jesus our Lord, without any respect to their works; **just**, in leaving others in the fall and perdition wherein they have involved themselves."[10]

Remarkably enough, there is no mention of an eternal decree of reprobation here.[11] On the contrary, here reprobation is based not upon an eternal divine decree but

---
9. See McGrath (2016, 403–404); see extensively, Ouweneel (EDR 5).
10. Dennison (*RCET* 4:433); see the historical review in Berkhof (1986, 454–56).
11. Cf. Hervormde Kerk (1962, 36).

exclusively upon the guilt of the wicked themselves. Toward the elect, God's attitude is active: he delivers and preserves them "from this perdition," but toward the reprobate his attitude is passive: "leaving others in the fall and perdition wherein they have involved themselves." In fact, here the Belgic Confession follows a (seeming) inconsistency that, in my view, is inherent to Scripture itself, and which we also find in the Canons of Dordt: if people are saved this is purely and solely God's grace — if people are lost this is purely and solely their own fault. As Gerrit van Itterzon put it: "It is clear that in the relationship between the two statements of faith the logic is lost, but both are experienced and acknowledged as perfectly true."[12] This approach of the Belgic Confession and the Canons of Dordt is infralapsarian, as we will see later (§14.6).

12.2.2 Righteousness and Mercy

It seems that the Belgic Confession is seeking to escape the apparent inconsistency by linking election and reprobation rather artificially to two different attributes of God: election to his mercy, and reprobation to his righteousness. Of course, this is not very satisfactory. Elsewhere, I have tried to show that salvation is just as much an act of God's righteousness as an act of his mercy.[13] This does not mean that we are allowed to view righteousness and mercy as synonyms here,[14] for this can never be the case. Rather it means that, in salvation, God is both righteous and merciful.

Conversely, in several of his writings C. S. Lewis has pointed out that even in reprobation we may find something of — not God's mercy but at least — God's benevolence.[15] Lewis saw hell as evidence of God's respect for his own creature. If a person has said all his life, "My will be done," then at the

---

12. Van Itterzon (1975, 142); see Van der Zwaag (2003, 137–45) for similar statements by R. Baxter, J. Bunyan, A. de Reuver, H. F. Kohlbrugge, C. A. van der Sluys, J. G. Feenstra, S. Rutherford, and others.
13. See Ouweneel (2016d).
14. Cf. Bavinck (*RD* 2:252).
15. See, e.g., Lewis (2014).

end of his life God responds, "Your will be done," and brings that person to a place where for eternity he will be bothered by God no longer. Therefore, as Lewis has expressed it, the door to hell is locked only from the inside. It is horrible to have to stay in hell, but for the wicked, heaven is even more horrible, because there everything exists for the honor of God and his name is forever glorified.

12.2.3 An Insoluble Problem

In the Belgic Confession (§12.2.1), Guido de Brès chose an unobjectionable formulation. He merely alluded to the theological problem but did not (try to) solve it. The year it was written, 1561, was too early for a solution. Moreover, a church confession is not an academic treatise. Only after the confict between Jacob Arminius and Francis Gomarus had erupted in 1604 — which later became the conflict between the Remonstrants and the Contra-Remonstrants — was the Protestant church in the Netherlands forced to consider the problem far more thoroughly. The result of these considerations was not an academic treatise but a confessional and pastoral piece of work: the Canons of Dordt (see §§12.6 and 12.7). The name "Dordt" is a shortened form of Dordrecht, the Dutch city where the well-known national and international Synod of Dordt was held (1618-1619) (see the Preface of this book).

We will see, incidentally, that the Canons of Dordt did not go far beyond the Belgic Confession. The Canons (I.6) use the same verb "to leave": ". . . He leaves the non-elect in His just judgment to their own wickedness and obduracy." And just as in the Belgic Confession, election is linked with God's grace, and reprobation with God's righteousness. The Canons also teach that reprobation is *because of* guilt — but at the same time they base reprobation on an eternal decree of God. We will return to this.

The Belgic Confession and the Canons of Dordt are not examples of unsatisfactory solutions of a theological problem. First, solving theological problems can never be the intention of non-academic ecclesiastical confessions. Second, perhaps they are instead illustrations of the impossibility of finding such an academic solution. No document, from any theological or ecclesiastical conviction, has fared any better than the Canons. Therefore, the battle in the Netherlands over this insoluble problem is regrettable, since it has led to several church splits, in other countries as well, which continue to our own day. Later in this chapter, we must investigate this matter further; but first we will try to get a clearer picture of the Reformed view.

12.3 TULIP
12.3.1 Total Depravity

Calvin devoted little attention to the doctrine of predestination,[16] and dealt with it only after he had treated the subject of grace. His successor, however, Theodore Beza (1519-1605), made this doctrine—viewed in a strictly supralapsarian way (see §14.6)—along with limited atonement, the cornerstone of his theology.[17] Largely through Beza, Calvinism developed into a theological system with five main principles, identified with the acronym TULIP (hinting at the Netherlands because of the Synod of Dordt?).[18] Let me explain the Five Points,[19] with some brief comments.

The first point is *Total depravity*, that is, the entire corruption of the "old self," the human being in his natural state of sinner.[20] This means that people have been corrupted in every respect by sin; they have a sinful nature. It does not mean that they are as sinful as possible; sinners with knowledge of the master's will are going to receive a "severe beating," whereas sinners without knowledge of the master's will are going to receive a "light beating" (Luke 12:47-48). There are both

---

16. Calvin, *Institutes* 3.21–24; on this, see Klooster (1977); Graafland (1987, 5–46).
17. On Beza, see Graafland (1987, 47–70); cf. Van der Zwaag (2003, 130–31).
18. See, e.g., Palmer (1996); Ryken (2003); König (2006, 422–26).
19. See Ouweneel (2016c).
20. Cf. Ouweneel (EDR 3, chapters 11–14).

decent sinners and serious criminals. But because of their sinful nature, all of them are sinners, and as such make themselves worthy of eternal condemnation. In the words of R. C. Sproul: No matter how much each of us has sinned, we could imagine more wicked sins than what we may have done. Even Adolf Hitler refrained from killing his own mother[21] (as did the emperor Nero).

Comments: I suppose that all Evangelical theologians will entirely agree with this point, although some might prefer the term *radical* depravity (depraved in the *radix* ["root"] of one's being). Many, however, will argue that this does not necessarily mean that a person is unable to come to faith. Most Arminians acknowledge that people need God's gracious help to believe (cf., e.g., Matt. 16:17; John 6:44-45; 15:16), but they insist that the decision must proceed primarily from the person, if human responsibility is to mean anything. Greg Boyd claimed that people are not free or morally responsible with regard to things that they cannot change.[22]

We must maintain, however, that the doctrine of total depravity in no way nullifies human responsibility, as some might fear. To be sure, people cannot change their own moral corruption, yet they are fully responsible for its manifestations. John Darby therefore rightly denied that personal inability excuses personal responsibility: one who has borrowed a sum of money, and wastes it, so that he is unable to repay it, nonetheless remains responsible for the repayment.[23] Herman Ridderbos argued that "where freedom has been lost and has become spiritual impotence and blindness, the responsibility of man as the creature of God is nevertheless not taken away or abrogated. God maintains his right as Creator even where man has been sold and blinded under the power of sin."[24]

---

21. Sproul (1986, 103–104).
22. Boyd (2001, 133).
23. Darby (n.d.-a, 501).
24. Ridderbos (1975, 354).

12.3.2 Unconditional Election

The second of the Five Points of Calvinism is *Unconditional election*, that is, an election not rooted in any human merit (works, qualities, fruits), nor in any foreseen, or unforeseen, faith surrender of people, but in the sovereign will of God alone. In predestination, there is no contribution from the human side; everything originates and proceeds from the divine side. This does not necessarily nullify human responsibility; it says something only about God's absolutely one-sided and eternal initiative.

Comments: Many Evangelical theologians approach this subject from the Arminian angle, or they teach, as does Viatorism, that election is indeed rooted in God's sovereign, gracious, redemptive will, but one should not leave people's foreseen faith out of consideration. Apart from Open Theists, many theologians believe that God *foreknows* whether people will believe. It is hard to maintain both that God knew whether people would believe, and that this knowledge did not play any role in his decree of election. On the other hand, many theologians realize that faith itself is a gift of God (cf. Eph. 2:8), so that all of salvation begins and ends with the sovereign and gracious God.

We will always have to live with this tension. Election is indeed unconditional, but salvation is not: there is no salvation without repentance, faith, and perseverance. Think of the "ifs" in statements like these: "[I]*f* you confess with your mouth that Jesus is Lord and believe in your heart that God raised him from the dead, you will be saved" (Rom. 10:9). "[Y]ou are being saved, *if* you hold fast to the word I preached to you" (1 Cor. 15:2). "And you . . . he has now reconciled . . . *if* indeed you continue in the faith, stable and steadfast" (Col. 1:21–23). "[W]e are his house *if* indeed we hold fast our confidence and our boasting in our hope . . . we have come to share in Christ, *if* indeed we hold our original confidence firm to the end" (Heb. 3:6, 14). These are powerful appeals to human responsibility.

In fact, unconditional election is nothing but another formulation of the truth that salvation is entirely of grace, not of works, not even the "work" of faith. And if salvation is nonetheless conditional, then the conditions involved, too, can be fulfilled only by God's sovereign grace and the working of the Holy Spirit. The two sides always exist: on the one hand, election is *unconditional*, but if people do not repent and believe they cannot, and will not, receive the blessings promised in the decree of election. On the other hand, salvation is *conditional*, but how could anyone fulfill the conditions without God's gracious work in the soul?

12.3.3 Limited Atonement

The third of the Five Points of Calvinism is *Limited atonement*, that is, an atonement destined for only part of humanity; in other words, Christ died for the elect only.

Comments: In fact, the matter is a little more complicated because at least four positions are possible with respect to the scope of Christ's sacrificial death.[25]

(a) *Limited substitution, limited atonement:* Christ died for the elect alone, and blotted out only their sins (the traditional Calvinist position).

(b) *Universal substitution, limited atonement:* Christ died for all people (2 Cor. 5:14–15, "one has died for all"; Heb. 2:9, Christ tasted "death for everyone"), so that the gospel can be freely and seriously offered to all people (cf. Matt. 11:28; John 1:29; 3:16; 4:42; Rom. 3:23–24; 5:18; 2 Cor. 5:19; 1 Tim. 2:3–4; Titus 2:11; 2 Pet. 3:9; 1 John 2:2; 4:14). But Christ actually blotted out the sins of believers alone (Amyraldism or sublapsarianism; see further in §14.6.1). This is the view that I have defended elsewhere.[26]

(c) *Universal substitution, universal atonement, limited*

---

25. See Ouweneel (EDR 5, §§12.1–12.2).
26. Ouweneel (EDR 5, §12.1.2).

application: Christ blotted out the sins of all people, but only those who believe actually share in this atonement (general atonement). The insurmountable difficulty of this view is that, if Christ blotted out all sins, it is hard to see how God could still condemn any person for his sins. Some respond that only because of their unbelief are such persons condemned. However, they overlook the fact that unbelief is also a sin, and thus one of the sins that Christ has supposedly blotted out.

(d) *Universal substitution, universal atonement, universal application:* Christ blotted out the sins of all people so that ultimately all people will be saved (universalism). Defenders of this view, first, perniciously confuse the *offer* of salvation (to all people) with the effectuation of salvation (in believers only) and, second, dismiss all the passages pointing to eternal damnation (e.g., Matt. 18:8; 25:41, 46; 2 Thess. 1:9; Heb. 6:2; Jude 1:6–7; Rev. 14:11; 19:3; 20:10).

12.3.4 Irresistible Grace

The fourth of the Five Points of Calvinism is *Irresistible grace,* that is, God's grace saves all the elect without anyone being able of resisting (refusing, declining) this grace. The sinner is overcome, overwhelmed, by God's grace.

Comments: This point does not mean that God forces some people to believe, and prevents other people from believing. It is always people who must make the step of faith, and in a sense, this is valuable in God's eyes only if this step is taken voluntarily. People are urged, persuaded, but not coerced.

Another observation is that, in some sense, grace *can* be resisted.[27] People can resist the Holy Spirit (Acts 7:51), they can resist what God has appointed (Rom. 13:2), they can outrage the Spirit of grace (Heb. 10:29), they may fail to obtain the grace of God (12:15), they may refuse "him who is speaking" (v. 25). It is not enough to claim that God's external call may be resisted but not his internal call, because the passages just referred to also include Christians who resist the Lord.

---

27. Sproul (1986, 120–22).

Many believers, too, neglect or ignore some of God's demonstrations of grace.

Instead, the core of this fourth point is that, if God has a person in view whom he wishes to save, his grace overwhelms such a person, as happened to Saul of Tarsus on the Damascus road.[28] This claim can be maintained if its counterpart is maintained as well: people's own responsibility and freedom of will. By the way, many Arminians do accept that God's saving grace in conversion is indispensible. They, too, know very well that salvation is of grace, not of works, not even the "work" of faith. However, because they emphasize human responsibility, they also point to examples of those who did resist the grace of God, such as the Pharisees and the scribes (Matt. 23:13; Luke 7:30), the people of Jerusalem (Matt. 23:37; Luke 13:34; 19:41-42), and the Israelites in general (Acts 7:51; Rom. 10:21 [Isa. 65:1-3]).

12.3.5 Perseverance of the Saints

The fifth of the Five Points of Calvinism is the *Perseverance of the saints*, that is, no genuine elect person can ever fall away from faith and lose his/her salvation. By God's grace, they will persevere in their faith until the end of their earthly existence.

Comments: Here again, opinions vary; some theologians (Roman Catholics, Lutherans, Arminians, some Evangelicals) teach that believers can, others (Calvinists, some Evangelicals) that believers cannot, fall away from faith.[29] Both parties quote many Bible passages in defense of their position: the former have their proof texts (e.g., 1 Sam. 10:6, 9 vs. 16:14; 28:16; Matt. 10:22; John 15:6; Rom. 11:20-21; 14:15; 1 Cor. 5:11; 8:11; 9:27; 10:12; 15:1-2; 2 Cor. 5:2-3; 13:5; Col. 1:22-23; 2 Thess. 2:3; 1 Tim. 4:1; Heb. 3:6, 12-14; 4:1, 11; 6:4-6; 10:26-29, 35-36; 12:25; 1 Pet. 5:8; 2 Pet. 2:20-21; 3:17; 1 John 2:24), as do the latter (e.g., Ps. 138:8; Isa. 54:10; Luke 8:15; 21:19; 22:32; John 5:24;

---

28. Apparently, this is not properly distingsuihed by König (2006, 425).
29. See extensively, Ouweneel (EDR 6, §§6.3–6.4).

6:39; 10:28-29; 14:16; 17:15, 24; Rom. 2:6-7; 8:35, 38-39; 9:11; 11:29; 15:5; Phil. 1:6; 1 Tim. 4:16; Heb. 7:25; 10:36; 12:1; James 1:4; 5:11; 1 Pet. 1:4-5; 5:10).

There seems to be a parallel with the relationship between divine sovereignty and human responsibility; the two do not share a common denominator. Similarly, no matter how paradoxical it may sound, here we have two other positions that do not share a common denominator, and seem to be mutually exclusive: Christians can fall away versus Christians cannot fall away. Many have endeavored to disprove the arguments of the other party, but others have argued that they believe a middle way is possible.[30] I believe the latter is hardly possible if the problem is formulated more sharply: Can a *truly regenerate person* fall away? If the problem is stated this way, I side with the Reformed position: truly regenerate persons can never undo the genuine divine life that is in them.

However, from a pastoral point of view I emphasize that Christian *confessors* may certainly fall way. Therefore, if such confessors live in gross sins, they must never acquiesce to the idea that the saints will persevere. Holy Christians do not fall away, but unholy "Christians" certainly do fall away (cf. Acts 8:15-23; 1 Tim. 1:20; 2 Tim. 2:17). Let me put it this way: before someone's conversion, I am a Remonstrant to him, so to speak: I urge him to make the *good choice* of coming to Christ. Afterward I am a Contra-Remonstrant to him: I explain to him that his rebirth and conversion and faith were all due to God's grace. Similarly, to Christians living in gross sin I am a Remonstrant by telling them that the road on which they are walking ends in eternal damnation. To others, however, I speak as a Contra-Remonstrant, expressing my conviction that, if these Christians are truly regenerate, the Lord will certainly bring them back from their evil path.

12.3.6 Additional Comments

James White was dissatisfied with these Five Points. He

---

30. Just two examples: Marshall (1969) and König (2006, 475).

believed that in the present time, especially in opposition to Open Theism, we need a sixth point: *Sovereignty of God*.[31] The acronym then simply becomes TULIPS. White believes that God's sovereignty is being heavily attacked nowadays, but it would be fair if he had written: the Augustinian-Calvinist view of God's sovereignty. This is not necessarily the same. White defines God's sovereignty in such a way that God can do as he pleases, without obtaining permission from anyone, including human beings.[32] This term "permission" is a persiflage: who would really believe that God would need permission for anything? From what kind of authority would his permission come?

The heart of the dispute is really this: Did God decree beforehand everything that occurs? *Or* did he *sovereignly* decide to allow people a certain measure of freedom, so that his ways are partially influenced by human actions? To be sure, God's counsel cannot possibly be affected from the outside, but his ways are definitely to some extent influenced by what people do and say, while nonetheless it is certain *a priori* that his counsel will ultimately be realized. To me, it is impossible to see how the latter view concerning God could constitute an attack upon his sovereignty.

Notably, Jacob Arminius was a full-fledged Calvinist with respect to the first (§12.3.1) and the fifth points (§12.3.5). No wonder: these are not the points where we encounter the greatest differences of opinion. The most important ones are *unconditional* election (§12.3.2) and *irresistible* grace (§12.3.4), because in both points the emphasis is placed one-sidedly on the work of God, while human responsibility seems to be neglected.

At the same time, it is true that, in these Five Points, there can be great harmony between Calvinists and Evangelicals. Therefore, the opinion of Roger Forster and David Pawson, that present-day Evangelical thinking must be freed from

---
31. White (2000, 41).
32. Ibid.

Five Points Calvinism, seems quite an exaggeration.³³ They seemed to receive support from James Packer, who wrote that the Five Points are inseparable, and that we cannot reject one of them without rejecting them all.³⁴ This, too, is an exaggeration. I myself agree with the Points 1, 4, and 5 as long as they do not *de facto* exclude human responsbibility. I agree with Point 2 as long as not only God's sovereign choice but also foreseen human choices are taken into account. And I agree with Point 3 insofar as Christ indeed bore the sins of only believers, though he can be said to have "died for everyone."

The School of Saumur (Amyraldism; see §§12.3.3 and 14.6.1) is generally considered a strand of Calvinism, although holding to what is called Four Point Calvinism; Amyraldus took issue with Point 3, as I do today. Thus, the men of Saumur and I are proof that Packer's claim is mistaken, as is Forster's and Pawson's claim. One can disagree with some elements of TULIP without disrupting the others. Pawson is not a very reliable witness anyway, as is evident from his simplistic claim that Augustine thoroughly departed from the early church and the New Testament when he transposed Christian theology from a Hebrew into a Greek framework.³⁵ This is historically absurd.

12.4 The Remonstrance
12.4.1 Introduction

At the beginning of the seventeenth century, a religious war raged in the Netherlands, namely, the infamous battle between Remonstrants and Contra-Remonstrants. The former were also called Arminians, after Jacob Arminius (1560-1609).³⁶ The latter are sometimes referred to as Gomarists, after Francis Gomarus³⁷ (1563-1641), although it must be

---
33. In Pawson (2005, 10).
34. Packer (1991, 169).
35. Pawson (2005, 145).
36. On his doctrine, see extensively, Graafland (1987, chapter 2).
37. Arminius is the Latinized version of Harmen[szoon], "son of Harmen/Herman [= man of the army]." Gomarus is the Latinized version of Gomae-

remembered that the Contra-Remonstrants, who were certainly the authors of the Canons of Dordt, generally held a more moderate position than Gomarus did. For instance, the latter was a supralapsarian, whereas the Canons present the more moderate infralapsarian position (see §14.6).

In several disputations (academic debates) from about 1600, the theological differences between the Leyden theology professors Arminius and Gomarus on the subject of predestination became more clear. In 1609, the conflict reached a tragic nadir; in the same year, Arminius passed away at 49 years old. A year later, his intellectual sympathizers, under the guidance of Johannes Uytenbogaert (1557–1644), summarized his views in the famous *Remonstrance*.[38]

Without describing the entire battle, I will deal only with the two principal positions in this conflict: the *Remonstrance* (1610) versus the *Canons of Dordt*, formulated by the Synod of Dordt (1618-1619) and directed explicitly against the *Remonstrance*.

Please note that this was not a purely Dutch conflict, although it started at Leyden. During the Synod of Dordt many foreign delegates participated, who were rather evenly divided among the two groups. Thus, the Lutherans followed Philip Melanchthon, who had spoken of three causes of conversion: the Word, the Holy Spirit, and the human will.[39] Internationally, the Lutherans fully backed the Arminians, which the latter deeply appreciated.[40] In the present Protestant Church in the Netherlands, in which Lutherans and Calvinists work together in a more or less fraternal manner, this seems no longer to be an issue. In 2004, this new denomination accepted both the Canons of Dordt and the Leuenberg Agreement (adopted

---

r[szoon], "son of Gothmar [= famous through battle]." I have always found the bellicose names Herman and Gothmar ominous.

38. For the text of the articles that follow, see Dennison (*RCET* 4:41–44).
39. *Loci communes* (1535).
40. Bavinck (*RD* 2:355–58); extensively, Loosjes (1926); cf. Berkouwer (1960, 32–34).

in 1973 by major European Lutheran and Reformed churches) as guidelines of faith, in spite of the contradictions between the two documents (see §14.1.1).

In the *Remonstrance*, first, five views are rejected, and then five theses are affirmed; these are "The Five Articles of Remonstrance."[41] The rejected positions are (cf. §12.3): (1 and 2) supra- and infralapsarianism, (3) limited atonement (Christ died for the elect alone), (4) irresistible grace (a point that, according to the Remonstrants, nullifies human responsibility), and (5) the perseverance of the saints, that is, true believers cannot lose their salvation (which, according to the Remonstrants, implies a license to sin).

12.4.2 The First Article

Article 1: "God, by an eternal and unchangeable decree in His Son, Christ Jesus, before laying the foundation of the world, determined, out of the human race fallen in sin, to save those in Christ, on account of Christ, and through Christ, who through the grace of the Holy Spirit, would believe on His same Son, and who would persevere in that very faith and obedience of faith, through the same grace without ceasing to the end; but on the other hand, to leave the obstinate and unbelieving under sin and wrath, and condemn them as alienated from Christ, according to the word of the gospel: 'He that believes in the Son has eternal life; but he that does not obey the Son will not see life, but the wrath of God remains on him' (John 3:36). To which other expressions of Scripture correspond."

Comments: In my view, the first article contains nothing erroneous; it is only incomplete. It is correct that God has elected from eternity those who would believe in Christ. However, the article suggests — although it does not explicitly say — that

---

41. The text of these articles is found in Dennison (*RCET* 4:42–44); an alternate translation is available at http://www.esvbible.org/resources/creeds-and-catechisms/article-the-five-arminian-articles-1610/#1121; on the contents and evaluation of the Remonstrance, see Verboom (2005, 111–23).

God elected them *because* they would believe in Christ. As such, this thought is contradicted by no Bible passage at all; yet, one could ask a few questions here: (a) Is it *supported* by any Bible passage? (b) What is there for God to *choose* or to *destine* if this "choice" is entirely determined by the foreseen choices of people themselves? (c) If God chooses or rejects people on the basis of their foreseen faith or unbelief, respectively, how can this election be believed to be based upon his sovereign grace?[42]

We will see that, *if* it is true at all that believers have been elected because they would believe (so the Remonstrants), on the basis of good biblical arguments it is equally true that they are going to believe because they have been elected (so the Contra-Remonstrants). The sad thing about the entire seventeenth-century conflict was perhaps that both parties believed that, logically speaking, only one of these two statements could be true, and that according to scholastic tradition and the rules of rationalism, both were fully convinced that they could not live with the paradox implying that *both* statements might be true at the same time. I have noted the cause of this unnecessary conflict earlier: the terms involved are treated as concepts, not as ideas, so that unnecessary logical contradictions arise.

12.4.3 The Second Article

Article 2: "Accordingly Jesus Christ, Savior of the world, has died for each and every man, and through His death on the cross has merited reconciliation and forgiveness of sins for all; nevertheless so that no one in fact becomes a partaker of this forgiveness except believers, and that also according to the words of the gospel of John: 'For God so loved the world that He gave His only begotten Son, that whoever believes in Him, should not perish, but have eternal life' (3:16). And in the first

---

42. Cf. Wentsel (1982, 161: "This doctrine of God's sovereignty opposes that of prae-scientia (foreknowledge) or prae-visio (the foreseeing), according to which God chooses people on the basis of foreseen, ascertained faith."

epistle of John: 'He is the propitiation for our sins, and not for ours only, but also for the sins of the whole world' (2:2)."

Comments: The first part of this article agrees with Hebrews 2:9, "by the grace of God" Jesus has tasted "death for everyone" (ESV, etc.), or "for all [humanity]" (CJB) (Gr. *hyper pantos*); the Vulgate has the plural: *pro omnibus*, "for all [people]." The next part of the article must be read carefully: it does not say that Christ has actually blotted out the sins of all people—which would be incorrect (see §12.3.3)—but the intention is apparently that his atoning sacrifice is *sufficient* for all people, so that whoever believes may indeed receive forgiveness of sins.

This is exactly what is then qoted from 1 John 2:2, "He is the propitiation... for [the sins of] the whole world" (Gr. *peri holou tou kosmou*). The (Contra-Remonstrant) Annotators of the Dutch States Translation (1637) interpret the latter phrase as follows: "That is, [the sins] of all men in the whole world out of all Nations, who shall yet believe in him, Job 11.52; Rev. 5.9." This is a remarkable example of eisegesis (reading into the text). Less far-fetched is the claim of Klaas Fernhout that the term "world" here refers not to all people, head by head, but to the human race as a whole, with no distinction between Jews and Gentiles.[43] The text obviously means that Christ's atoning sacrifice is available for all humanity (§§13.1-13.3). This is acknowledged even by hyper-Calvinist Henry Kersten.[44]

12.4.4 The Third Article

Article 3: "Man has no saving faith of himself, nor from the strength of his own free will, since in the state of apostasy and sin he is not able to think, will, or do anything good (what indeed is truly good, such as saving faith is in the first place); but it is necessary that he be regenerated and also renewed by God, in Christ, through His Holy Spirit in his intellect, affec-

---

43. Fernhout (1921, 33–34).
44. Kersten (1980, 1:142).

tions, or will, and all his powers, that he may rightly understand, ponder, will, and also accomplish the true good as it is written: 'Without me you are able to do nothing' (John 15:5)."

Comments: The natural person (1 Cor. 2:14) is unable to do any good, at least if his deeds are measured according to God's norms, because even his noblest deeds are not done explicitly or implicitly for the honor of God (cf. Isa. 64:6, "all our *righteous* deeds are like a polluted garment"). The natural person is unable to accomplish even this one thing: to come to saving faith. Therefore, on the basis of Ephesians 2:8 Arminius emphasized that faith is a "gift of God."[45] Thus, he clearly rejected the Pelagian position linking repentance one-sidedly with a human decision of the will. The Remonstrance says that regeneration through the Holy Spirit, and renewal of the understanding, inclination, and will, are needed in order that people may rightly understand, think, will, and perform what is truly good, according to the Word of Christ. It is difficult to see how the Contra-Remonstrants could object to this.

12.4.5 The Fourth Article

Article 4: "This grace is the beginning, the increase, and completion of every good thing; to be sure even that the regenerate person himself is not even able to think, will, or accomplish good, nor resist any temptation to evil apart from or preceding that prevenient, moving, accompanying, and cooperating grace, so that all good works and actions which are able to be conceived must be ascribed to the grace of God in Christ. As for the rest, what pertains to the manner of operation of this grace—that it is not irresistible, since indeed it is written about many that 'they resisted the Holy Spirit,' Acts 7:[51] and several other places."

Comments: People can live and persevere only by God's grace. However, confessing Christians may also fail to obtain (GNV: fall away from; NIV: fall short of) the grace of God (Heb. 12:15), and what will happen then? This is similar to what

---
45. E.g., in his Disputation of 1604; see Verboom (2005, 38).

we found with the first article: it is not what it says that gives us trouble, but what it does not say, or what it seems to suggest. Thus, the article leaves open the question whether truly regenerate people can fall away from grace, and thus can be eternally condemned (see §12.3.5). Those truly regenerated have been overwhelmed by the grace of God; they cannot resist it. False "Christians" can resist the grace of God, and sooner or later invariably do so.

12.4.6 The Fifth Article

Article 5: "Those who are ingrafted into Christ by true faith and as a consequence have been made participants of His life-giving Spirit, have been abundantly equipped by this power, by which they are able to fight against Satan, sin, the world, and their flesh, and therefore also obtain the victory over them; nevertheless always (because we wish to be careful) assisted in every temptation by the help of the grace of the Holy Spirit; and Jesus Christ Himself, through His Spirit, holds out His hand, and (if only they are prepared to fight themselves, and beseech His help, and do not desert Him themselves), secures and confirms them, so that they are seduced by no deceit or power of Satan, nor are able to be ripped out of the hands of Christ, according to the word of Christ: 'No one takes my sheep out of my hand' (John 10:28). As for the rest, whether they themselves are not able through carelessness την αρχην της υποστασεως χριστου καταλειπειν (to abandon the beginning of their subjection to Christ), and embracing again this present world, to forsake the holy doctrine once delivered to them, to let a good conscience slip away, and to despise grace; must be more accurately sought from the sacred Scripture before we are able to teach others with πληροφορια (full persuasion) of our minds."

Comments: Again, I can agree wholeheartedly with the first part of the article: in the Holy Spirit, the believer finds abundant strength to gain victories in his spiritual warfare. The second part is striking, because the Remonstrants do not dare to speak here with any certainty; they desire more investigation of Scripture. Is this a token of modesty (over against the firm statements of the Gomarists), or of weakness? Do professors and doctors of theology first need more theological "field work" on such vital matters? I would prefer the notion of modesty here because we are still overwhelmed, even four hundred years later, by the powerful biblical arguments that are supplied by both parties (see §12.3.5). Orthodox Protestantism is as divided as ever over these matters.

There is no doubt that "Christians" can fall in love with "this present world" (2 Tim. 4:10), can depart from "the faith that was once for all delivered to the saints" (Jude 3), can reject "a good conscience," and thus can make "shipwreck of their faith" (1 Tim. 1:19), can "fall away from grace" (Gal. 5:4; cf. Heb. 10:29; 12:15, 28), etc. However, the essential question remains whether any such statement is valid not only for unconverted (pseudo-)Christians, but also for true (regenerate) Christians.[46]

12.5 The Antithesis
12.5.1 The First Three Contrasts

The first response to the Remonstrance of the Arminians came from theologian, astronomist, cartographer, and geographer Petrus Plancius (1552–1622) and his fellow intellectuals (1610).[47] His response need not occupy our attention, because its significance was subsequently far surpassed by that of the Canons of Dordt (1618–1619).

It may be useful at this point to itemize the contrasts between the teaching of Francis Gomarus (abbr.: G), the teaching of Jacob Arminius and of the Remonstrance as based upon it (abbr.: R), and the Canons of Dordt (abbr.: D). I summarize the enumeration by Willem Verboom,[48] and add to it the teachings of D, and of Viatorism (V). In the first three of

---

46. See again Ouweneel (EDR 6, §§6.3–6.4).
47. See extensively, Verboom (2005, 135–57).
48. Verboom (2005, 61–62; cf. 106–108).

the seven contrasts (§12.5.1), D stands in opposition to R, but also to G; in the last four (§12.5.2), G and D stand together in opposition to R.

(1) *Predestination:*
   * *G:* symmetrical double predestination (i.e., election and reprobation are perfect mirror images of one another);
   * *R:* only eternal (conditional) election;
   * *D:* assymmetrical double predestination;
   * *V:* only eternal (unconditional) election.

N.B. The Roman Catholic and Arminian views are symmetrical, too, because election and reprobation are based on "double foreknowledge."[49]

(2) *Supra-/infralapsarianism:*
   * *G:* supralapsarian;
   * *R:* rejects both supra- and infralapsarianism;
   * *D:* infralapsarian;
   * *V:* supralapsarian with respect to election, infralapsarian with respect to reprobation.

(3) *Reprobation:*
   * *G:* reprobation is based upon God's sovereign will only;
   * *R:* reprobation is based upon human guilt (foreseen or not) and unbelief (foreseen or not);
   * *D:* reprobation is based upon God's eternal sovereign will, but also upon foreseen human guilt and unbelief.
   * *V:* the same as R.

12.5.2 The Last Four Contrasts

(4) *Conditional/unconditional election:*
   * *G and D:* unconditional election, that is, based entirely and exclusively upon God's eternal sovereign grace;
   * *R:* conditional election, that is, based not only upon

---

49. Demarest (1997, 138).

God's eternal sovereign grace but also on foreseen faith;
* V: unconditional election, yet not to be separated from foreseen faith.

(5) *Corruption of the Human Will:*
* G and D: the human will is entirely and thoroughly corrupt, and thus not free, without this fact excluding human responsibility.
* R: the human will is indeed corrupt, yet free to choose for (with God's help) or against God;
* V: seeks the harmony of both views.

(6) *Perseverance:*
* G and D: the regenerate person cannot fall away from grace, that is, cannot lose his salvation;
* R: the regenerate person can fall away from grace, and thus lose his salvation;
* V: the same as G and D.

(7) *Limited/unlimited atonement:*
* G and D: Christ died for the elect alone, so that only they receive eternal salvation;
* R: Christ died for all people, but only those who come to faith, and persevere in it, will share in salvation;
* V: Christ died for all people, but bore the sins of the elect only.

These last four points show that D to some extent is Gomarist, but in the first three points mentioned (§12.5.1) D takes a more moderate position. This concerns infra- versus supralapsarianism (see §14.6) and the supposed decree of reprobation (see §§14.1–14.4).

12.6 The Canons of Dordt
12.6.1 Introduction
The definitive answer to the teaching of the Remonstrants was ultimately given in the Canons of Dordt, written and

adopted by the Synod of Dordt (1618-1619).[50] The entire gospel is discussed, especially subjects such as faith, justification, regeneration, and the perseverance of the saints. I have discussed most of these subjects elsewhere;[51] at this point, we will focus on the first chapter of the Canons: "Divine election and reprobation."[52]

There is very much that is good and beautiful in the Canons; the ecclesiastical and pastoral elements clearly overshadow the scholastic-intellectual aspects, as is suitable for an ecclesiastical confession.[53] It is a document that all Evangelicals should examine, especially those theologians among them who, with some pride, call themselves "Arminians," and often seem to have little knowledge of the arguments that were adduced by both parties in the conflict.

Chapter 1 of the Canons begins with eighteen articles (§12.6), followed by nine objections to the teachings of the Arminians (§12.7). Next, the Five Points of the Remonstrance are discussed one by one. In my view, the most controversial of the eighteen articles are the following ones (see the next sections).

12.6.2 Head I, Article 6

"That some receive the gift of faith from God, and others do not receive it, proceeds from God's eternal decree. *For known unto God are all his works from the beginning of the world* (Acts 15:18, A.V.). *Who worketh all things after the counsel of his will* (Eph. 1:11). According to which decree He graciously softens the hearts of the elect, however obstinate, and inclines them to believe; while He leaves the non-elect in His just judgment to their own wickedness and obduracy. And herein is especially displayed the profound, the merciful, and at the same time

---

50. See on this extensively, Graafland (1987, chapter 3 and §5.1); Verboom (2005, 208–54).
51. Ouweneel (EDR 3, 5, and 6; 2016d).
52. Verboom (2005, 211–25).
53. Woelderink (1951, 23): the Canons are much less scholastic than Gomarus and Arminius *both* were.

the righteous discrimination between men equally involved in ruin; or that decree of election and reprobation, revealed in the Word of God, which, though men of perverse, impure, and unstable minds wrest it to their own destruction, yet to holy and pious souls affords unspeakable consolation."[54]

Comments: Very little in this article is objectionable, except perhaps the fact that it speaks of the "decree of election and reprobation," thus suggesting that reprobation is as much from eternity as is election. However, none of the Bible verses mentioned, or any other Bible passages, suggest reprobation from eternity. Interestingly, in the next lines the notion of reprobation from eternity is softened along the well-known infralapsarian way: the non-chosen are rejected, not primarily because of some sovereign decree of God but because of "their own wickedness and obduracy"! It is even called "righteous" that God "leaves" such people in their wicked state. In other words, the Canons claim not that people are wicked because they are reprobate, but that they are reprobate because they are wicked. The Canons do not reject the notion of an eternal decree of reprobation, but do soften its harshness: the wicked are lost, not because they were destined from eternity for damnation, but because they are wicked.

But then, why not apply this, with even more force, to the elect as well? The Bible is just as clear about an eternal decree of election. But if people's own wickedness is introduced in order to explain their eternal damnation, why not bring in the faith of the elect as well? In other words, if God rejects certain people on the basis of both an eternal decree *and* their own wickedness—without people seeing a contradiction between these two grounds—why could it not be that God saves certain people on the basis both of an eternal, sovereign decree *and* their own faith?

In this article of the Canons, reprobation is viewed as a logical consequence of the fact of election. That is, those who

---

54. Dennison (*RCET* 4:121).

are not elected are apparently rejected by God—as if "not elected" is logically necessarily identical with "reprobate." Reformed theologian Willem Verboom says, "We may wonder whether this view is not more the consequence of a rational, causal way of reasoning than of a repeating what the Word says."[55] I would go one step further: it is not even logical. The denial of A does not yield B, but yields non-A, unless it can be demonstrated that B equals non-A.

12.6.3 Head I, Article 7

"Election is the unchangeable purpose of God, whereby, before the foundation of the world, He has out of mere grace, according to the sovereign good pleasure of His own will, chosen from the whole human race, which had fallen through their own fault from their primitive state of rectitude into sin and destruction, a certain number of persons to redemption in Christ, whom He from eternity appointed the Mediator and Head of the elect and the foundation of salvation. This elect number, though by nature neither better nor more deserving than others, but with them involved in one common misery, God has decreed to give to Christ to be saved by Him, and effectually to call and draw them to His communion by His Word and Spirit; to bestow upon them true faith, justification, and sanctification; and having powerfully preserved them in the fellowship of His Son, finally to glorify them for the demonstration of His mercy, and for the praise of the riches of His glorious grace; as it is written: *Even as he chose us in him before the foundation of the world, that we should be holy and without blemish before him in love: having foreordained us unto adoption as sons through Jesus Christ unto himself, according to the good pleasure of his will, to the praise of the glory of his grace, which he freely bestowed on us in the Beloved* (Eph. 1:4, 5, 6). And elsewhere: *Whom he foreordained, them he also called: and whom he called, them he also justified: and whom he justified, them he also*

---

55. Verboom (2005, 214).

glorified (Rom. 8:30)."[56]

Comments: Many Evangelicals will fully agree, perhaps with two qualifications, though. First, this eternal, sovereign, gracious decree of God was made entirely by himself, without any human influence—yet cannot be separated from repentance and faith, since God foreknew that in due time the elect would repent and believe (see the next two articles). Either people believe because, and only because, they have been elected for this, in which case human freedom and responsibility vanish. Or their foreseen faith functions somehow in the decree of election.

Second, the text of this article implicitly indicates the tremendous difference with the decree of reprobation. The decree of election was made in eternity, that is, before the creation and Fall of the first people. However, if one wishes to speak of a "decree of reprobation" at all (see I.15 below), then such a decree was made *in time*: God rejects unbelievers because they manifest themselves as sinners and because they are unwilling to repent and come to faith, and die in their wickednesses (see the previous article, and see more extensively our chapter 14 below).

12.6.4 Head I, Article 9

"This election was not founded upon foreseen faith and the obedience of faith, holiness, or any other good quality or disposition in man, as the prerequisite, cause, or condition on which it depended; but men are chosen to faith and to the obedience of faith, holiness, etc. Therefore, election is the fountain of every saving good, from which proceed faith, holiness, and the other gifts of salvation, and finally eternal life itself, as its fruits and effects, according to the testimony of the apostle: *He hath chosen us* (not because we were, but) *that we should be holy, and without blemish before him in love* (Eph. 1:4)."[57]

---

56. Dennison (*RCET* 4:122).
57. Ibid., 4:123.

Comments: According to the Canons of Dordt, election is based not on foreseen faith (*praevisa fide*) but on the sovereign will of God. This view goes back to Calvin, who argued: if God chose us *in order that* we would be holy (Eph. 1:4), this means he did not choose us *because* he foresaw that we would be holy.[58] The Remonstrant has an easy answer to this argument: indeed, God chose us *in order that* we would be holy, but he did so on the basis not of foreseen holiness but of foreseen *faith*, which, thanks to God's election, would *lead* to holiness.

According to the Canons, election is not "founded upon foreseen faith" (Latin *ex praevisa fide*; Dutch **uit** *het voorgezien geloof*), but "unto faith" (Latin *ad fidem*, Dutch **tot** *het geloof*). That is, faith is not the basis of election, but election is the basis of faith; you are not chosen because you believe, but you believe because you are chosen. This is an interesting thesis, but in no way can it be demonstrated from Scripture. I would venture to say that the very idea—"I believe because I was chosen"—is foreign to the explicit statements as well as the spirit of Scripture. Therefore, Adrio König, a dogmatician in a traditionally Calvinist church (the Dutch Reformed Church of South Africa) says unreservedly, God "chooses those who believe in Jesus, and he rejects those who reject Jesus. . . . He does not choose you because you believe, as if this makes you better than others, but because he has decreed to choose those who believe"—which is a purely Arminian point of view.[59]

As I said, such a view cannot be proven, but neither can it be refuted. Those wishing to do justice to both God's sovereignty and human responsibility may claim with equal validity that election is based either on God's free, sovereign will or on foreseen faith. Please note that the latter claim does not necessarily turn faith into something meritorious, *nor* does it detract at all from God's sovereign grace. Even the Lutheran dogmatician Johann Gerhard (1582-1637), who held to a more Remonstrant view, maintained that faith is never the merito-

---

58. See extensively, Calvin, *Institutes* 3.22–23.
59. König (2006, 434–35).

rious cause (*causa meritoria*) of election, or salvation, nor the effectuating cause of election (*efficiens electionis*).[60]

Of course, none of the arguments being used on both sides can remove the tension. Hence, the repeated question rightly posed by Gerrit Berkouwer, for instance, in this form: "For is it possible that this [notion of synergy], unavoidable in connection with man's cooperation, still leave room for a full recognition of God's sovereigh grace?"[61] Time and again, such a question calls forth the counter-question: Can the notion of sovereign grace still leave room for the radical acknowledgement of human responsibility and freedom? In this conflict, our reason (*ratio*) should not try to force us either to the former view (Contra-Remonstrants), or to the latter view (Remonstrants). Here again, both parties are arranging these two elements in opposition against each other by treating them as concepts instead of ideas.[62]

12.6.5 Head I, Article 15

"What peculiarly tends to illustrate and recommend to us the eternal and unmerited grace of election is the express testimony of sacred Scripture that not all, but some only, are elected, while others are passed by in the eternal decree; whom God, out of His sovereign, most just, irreprehensible, and unchangeable good pleasure, has decreed to leave in the common misery into which they have wilfully plunged themselves, and not to bestow upon them saving faith and the grace of conversion; but, permitting them in His just judgment to follow their own ways, at last, for the declaration of His justice, to condemn and punish them forever, not only on account of their unbelief, but also for all their other sins. And this is the decree of reprobation, which by no means makes God the Author of sin (the very thought of which is blasphemy), but declares Him to be an awful, irreprehensible, and

---

60. *Loci Theologici* II, 89.
61. Berkouwer (1960, 42).
62. See Ouweneel (EDR 3, §§1.2–1.3).

righteous Judge and Avenger thereof."[63]

Comments: Here we can clearly see that the Contra-Remonstrant position tends to one-sidedness just as much as the Remonstrant position. However, there is a distinction. According to the Canons, election is not rooted in foreseen faith; but do they view reprobation as similarly separated from foreseen unbelief? We considered this question earlier in §12.6.2; here we see that, in an infralapsarian way (see §14.6), reprobation is a divine decision to "leave" the wicked "in the common misery into which they have wilfully plunged *themselves*."

We have to read carefully here: the Canons claim that God decreed reprobation from eternity, but the wicked plunge themselves into misery *within time*. Does this not suggest that the decree of reprobation is based both on God's free, sovereign will and also on foreseen unbelief? If this is admitted, then the next question is obvious: Could it not be equally true that the decree of election is based not only on God's free, sovereign will but also on foreseen faith? If the Canons do not consider the former statement (about reprobation) to infringe upon God's sovereignty, why would the latter statement (about election) be seen to infringe on divine sovereignty?

Speaking of this article, Reformed theologian Willem Verboom attempted, on the one hand, to maintain the eternal nature of the decree of reprobation, and on the other hand, to place the decree of reprobation logically after the guilt and unbelief of humanity: "God's election means that God's choice always precedes our choice. Of God's reprobation it must be said that God's choice comes *after* our choice."[64] So far so good. But then we read the following surprising sentences: "God has decreed this from eternity. God can put up with people's own hardening for a long time, but there is a limit. When this limit is reached, God responds with reprobation. This is his eternal decree." But then, *what* exactly does this eternal decree entail? That God indeed has reprobated a

---

63. Dennison (*RCET* 4:124–25).
64. Verboom (2005, 221).

number of people specifically destined for this? *Or* does it entail only that God, in a very general way, rejects people who reject him? Does Verboom think that he is speaking here in the spirit of the Canons, or is he giving us a very new, unique interpretation of the "eternal decree of reprobation"?

12.7 Antithetical
12.7.1 The Fifth Objection

Among the Rejection of Errors that the Canons of Dordt formulate against the Remonstrants, the most relevant in my view are the Fifth and the Eighth. Let us look at the former first.

Paragraph 5 rejects the ideas of those "[w]ho teach: That the incomplete and non-decisive election of particular persons to salvation occurred because of a foreseen faith, conversion, holiness, godliness, which either began or continued for some time; but that the complete and decisive election occurred because of foreseen perseverance unto the end in faith, conversion, holiness, and godliness; . . . and that therefore faith, the obedience of faith, holiness, godliness, and perseverance are not fruits of the unchangeable election unto glory, but are conditions which, being required beforehand, were foreseen as being met by those who will be fully elected, and are causes without which the unchangeable election to glory does not occur."[65] (Against this the Canons adduce John 15:16; Acts 13:48; Rom. 9:11-12; 11:6; Eph. 1:4; and 1 John 4:10.)

Comments: The Arminians made a distinction between an "incomplete and conditional" election, based on foreseen faith, and a "complete and nonconditional" election, based on a person's foreseen perseverance until the end. The Canons reject this unbiblical distinction because it presupposes that those truly regenerated could fall away (cf. §12.3.5).

For the rest, here again we encounter the false dilemma: Is predestination rooted in God's free, sovereign will, or in foreseen human faith or unbelief? As long as people feel

---
65. Dennison (*RCET* 4:128).

compelled by their logic to choose, we will have Gomarists and Arminians, Contra-Remonstrants and Remonstrants around. As soon as we distinguish between concepts and ideas, as Viatorism does, room is created for considering the possibility that both positions are simultaneously true.

12.7.2 The Eighth Objection

Paragraph 8 rejects the ideas of those "[w]ho teach: That God, simply by virtue of His righteous will, did not decide either to leave anyone in the fall of Adam and in the common state of sin and condemnation, or to pass anyone by in the communication of grace which is necessary for faith and conversion."[66] (Against this the Canons adduce Matt. 11:25-26; 13:11; and Rom. 9:18.)

Comments: If we take this objection literally, we have no choice but to side with the Arminians, for it is true and biblical: God leaves no one in the state of sin "simply by virtue of His righteous will." On the contrary, it is his explicitly revealed will to save sinners (1 Tim. 2:4; 2 Pet. 3:9). The "vessels of wrath" prepare *themselves* for destruction (cf. Rom. 9:22): there are "false teachers . . . bringing upon themselves swift destruction" (2 Pet. 2:1). They suffer damnation, not because of some decree of reprobation, but because of their wickedness. No person is ever condemned for any other reason than "according to his works" (Rev. 20:13 NKJV, etc.; cf. 2:23; Rom. 2:6; 2 Cor. 5:10; 11:15; 2 Tim. 4:14).

Of course, these things are not necessarily denied by Contra-Remonstrants. However, to this biblical basis they add a non-biblical basis for the eternal condemnation of the wicked: the supposed eternal decree of reprobation. If they would abandon this notion—as several Reformed scholars have done[67]—the pieces of the puzzle would fit together much better.

---

66. Ibid., 4:129.
67. Thus, e.g., Jan Hoek in Hoek and Ouweneel (2011).

12.7.3 In Retrospect

We have to emphasize again that, if God has decreed in his grace to redeem some of those who had fallen into sin, this does not mean that the others automatically fall under a decree of reprobation. Let me give a brief survey of some of the arguments.

First, such logical arguments always fall into the snare of dealing with terms such as election, predestination, and reprobation as concepts (about which a number of properties can be predicated), and not as ideas (about which only those properties can be predicated for which we have explicit evidence in Scripture).

Second, that some persons are the objects of an eternal decree of election does not logically require that non-elect persons fall under some *eternal decree* of reprobation. It could very well be that God has made an eternal decree regarding some people, namely, to bless them in a special way, and simply has not made an eternal decree regarding the others, such that these on their own fall prey to their own sins. They are destined to damnation, not on the basis of an *eternal* decree but on the basis of a divine decree made *within time*, effectuated *after* these sinners have manifested their sinfulness and stubbornness (impenitence, inconvertibility) (see §§14.1-14.4). We ought, then, to view reprobation in a strictly infralapsarian way, as do the Canons of Dordt.

Third, conversely, Scripture speaks of election in a supralapsarian way; that is, election is not so much about forgiveness of sins and about redemption from death and hell, but rather about holiness, righteousness, glory, and blessedness. The New Testament decree of election is about *blessings that Adam never possessed, and thus never lost*. Although it is dangerous to speculate, we get the impression that, even without the Fall, humanity would have lived forever in the enjoyment of earthly blessings, but some would have been elected unto heavenly blessedness. If this argument is tenable, it shows most powerfully that election as such does not necessarily or logically require a corresponding eternal decree of reprobation.

Here again we see the bad effects of a constricting thought system, according to which Calvinists feel forced to bring everything that ever existed or ever occurred under an eternal decree of God in some way or another. As soon as one is freed from such coercion, which is not rooted in Scripture at all, one will no longer have any difficulty letting go of the unblical idea of an eternal decree of reprobation.

Looking back at the Canons of Dordt, which in many respects is such a beautiful document, I regret that the doctrine of reprobation has received such a prominent place. Hermann Kohlbrugge opined that the Synod of Dordt was lured into a snare by the Remonstrants by placing in the foreground not justification but election.[68] As a consequence, the Canons have become the least favorite among the Three Forms of Unity. One reason is that the confession focuses upon only one part of the doctrine of salvation, which thereby receives far too much importance and one-sided attention. Another reason is that the Canons are undeniably polemical, with all the reactionary dangers accompanying that feature.

I hasten to add that the Canons nonetheless give an impression of balance and even-temperedness. The Canons are scarcely as grim and dogged as Francis Gomarus was to Jacob Arminius, and scarcely as inclined to extremism. Perhaps due to the Synod's president, Johannes Bogerman (1576-1637), the Canons are far less scholastic than the arguments of both Gomarus and Arminius.[69] Here, the term "scholastic" means finding its strength in "irrefutable syllogistic arguments." In the battle between these two "fighting roosters," the Canons of Dordt have found a benevolent middle position, partially because of its infralapsarian approach with respect to

---

68. Kohlbrugge in his 1835 letter to H. van Heumen (www.derokendevlaswiek.nl).
69. See on this Verboom (2005, especially 26, 29, 35, 39).

reprobation.

One can only regret that the Arminians could not agree with it. However, there were two valid reasons for this. First, at crucial points the Canons evidently follow more the line of Gomarus than that of Arminius. Second, the Arminians' disagreement was caused partially by the fact that they had already been sent away from the Synod before the Canons were published. They were no longer taken seriously as discussion partners. After the Synod of Dordt (1619), all the pastors who sympathized with the Remonstrance were deposed; many of them went into exile, voluntarily or under pressure.

12.8 Further Developments
12.8.1 Contra-Remonstrants

In the previous section, I spoke of a "constricting thought system" — a snare that threatens every theological thought system, by the way. In the conflict between Remonstrants and Contra-Remonstrants, both parties seemed driven to formulate a one-sided, and thus unhealthy, logical argument.

The *Remonstrants* argued: it would be unrighteous if some people would be saved and others condemned solely on the basis of a sovereign decree of God. Moreover, it is a belittling of people as God's highest creatures, endowed with responsibility and freedom. *Therefore*, election is apparently based upon foreseen faith. Thus, for instance, Henry Thiessen, who called election a sovereign act of the gracious God, namely, that in Jesus Christ he chose all those people to be saved whom he foreknew would accept him.[70] This is the "prevision" (*praevisio*) or "prescience" (*praescientia*), that is, from eternity foreseeing or foreknowing what people would eventually do: believe or not believe.

This notion clearly offers a solution for the problem why God chooses one person but not another. However, this solution generates new questions: If predestination is based upon foreseeing, how can we still speak of destining? What is left

---
70. Thiessen (1948, 344).

for God to destine if people destine for themselves by believing or not?[71] Such questions do not really constitute a refutation; it is always conceivable to maintain the term "destination" even if God's decree is based upon human foreseen faith or unbelief (as long as the terms involved are taken as ideas, not as concepts). Yet, some of the power of the term "(pre)destination" seems to be lost.

The *Contra-Remonstrants* argued: it would be an attack upon God's sovereignty if the eternal salvation of people depended on their own choice (and this apart from the fact that natural persons by themselves are not at all *able* to make good, God-honoring choices). *Therefore,* a person's eternal election as well as his conversion within time are based exclusively on God's free, sovereign will. This will is a will preceding faith (*voluntas antecedens*), whereas the Remonstrants assumed in God a will following upon (or resulting from) a person's foreseen faith (*voluntas consequens*). Insofar as the latter did speak of a will preceding faith (*voluntas antecedens*), this will is of a universal nature: God has decreed from eternity that all those who will believe will be saved.[72]

In my view, the Contra-Remonstrant arguments were partially the product of a reactionary theology. If Arminian opposition had not arisen at such an early stage, Calvinist theology might have developed in a more balanced way. Instead, the Remonstrants endangered God's freedom, and the Contra-Remonstrants endangered human freedom. We cannot assert that the former is more serious than the latter because it concerns God. The reason is that, if it is God himself who endowed people with responsibility and freedom, people affect God's honor just the same if they belittle human freedom.

12.8.2 Moderate Calvinism

In practice and over time, Contra-Remonstrants learned to express themselves in a more nuanced way, especially by

---

71. Cf. Calvin, *Institutes* 1.18.1.
72. Berkouwer (1960, 34–35).

maintaining the doctrine of predestination while simultaneously strongly emphasizing human responsibility. A notable example is Reformed dogmatician Johan Heyns, writing entirely within the Dordt tradition when he states: "Is there a reprobation in Christ as there is an election in Christ? He who thinks this way about election and reprobation in terms of the duality of a logical side and a reverse side becomes guilty of the error of conclusivism, and ends with a kind of symmetrical theology that can never be biblically warranted. Reprobation is not God's second decree that supplements, rounds off, and completes his first one (about election)."[73] For this reason, Heyns rejected the phrase "double predestination" (*gemina praedestinatio*; cf. §§14.1–14.4 below).

As to "side" and "reverse side," reprobation has been called the "reverse side" and the "shadow" of election, like the two sides of a coin.[74] In opposition to this, Reformed dogmatician Willie Jonker rightly spoke of the asymmetry of election and reprobation.[75] And Reformed theologian Lubbert van der Zanden emphasized: "Scripture does not contain a double predestination in the sense of a juxtaposition of election and reprobation."[76] As far as conclusivism is concerned, I refer to Reformed theologian Jan Gerrit Woelderink: "[T]he exposition of this doctrine [of the election from eternity] is necessarily linked to thought constructions that have been derived not from Scripture but from the conclusion-drawing intellect."[77]

Gerrit Berkouwer commented about how to reconcile the cause of sin and unbelief with predestination: "The [logical] imbalance in the *causa*-concept which we observe in Calvin and in the Canons [of Dordt] is, on the level of human insight,

---

73. Heyns (1988, 89).
74. Fernhout (1921, 55).
75. Jonker (1988, 136–41).
76. Van der Zanden (1949, 70); cf. Dijk (1924, 391); Weber (1983, 2:426, 471–74).
77. Woelderink (1951, 29).

a proof of the inexplicability of sin and unbelief. We prefer this imbalance rather than any synthesis [whether that of determinism or that of the position of praescientia]."[78]

Returning to Heyns for a moment: whatever (hyper-)Calvinists may object, he stated very clearly: "An election to unbelief, and thus to sin and eternal damnation, would make God responsible for sin, whereas this would remove the guilt from humanity.... Therefore, we will have to say: as election precedes faith, and thus is the cause of faith..., reprobation follows upon unbelief."[79] A little later he said, "Therefore, in reprobation the sin of the unbelieving person is causally included and taken into account."[80] But if Heyns reached this point, why did he not take the final step, and conclude, as a perfect parallel of the previous sentence, that in election the faith of the believing person is "causally included and taken into account"?

A little later, Heyns said,

> By not accepting Christ, [unbelievers] confirm God's eternal decree: in Christ there is salvation, but outside Christ damnation. Thus, they reject God's election in Christ. However, this does not give us the right to say: in this way they have chosen God's reprobation outside Christ. Their reprobation is God's decree as a seal upon, and confirmation of, the ultimate consequence of human deeds within the room that God in his counsel has allowed them.... Thus, election remains pure grace in Christ to the sinner, and reprobation remains pure guilt of the sinner. ... The deed of God's reprobation is, as a reactive deed, a holy divine response to human guilt.... Whereas election is a cause of faith, reprobation is not a cause of unbelief. Only within this asymmetric structure can the true biblical contents of election

---

78. Berkouwer (1960, 181; the published English translation of the words supplied above in brackets mistakenly reads: "... from the point of view of the *praescientia* of determinism."); also cf. Hervormde Kerk (1962, 19).
79. Heyns (1988, 90).
80. Ibid.

and reprobation be determined.[81]

Here, too, Heyns weakens his own clear argument somewhat by saying: "An eternal reprobation? As decree of the eternal God, yes!" Heyns does not need such a sophism for his argument. But aside from this, these insights of Heyns, which, in my view, have transcended the Canons of Dordt, constitute an enormous step forward. Another South African Reformed theologian, Adrio König, has leveled sharp criticism against what he calls Calvin's "all-arranging doctrine" (the teaching that all things have been arranged from eternity by God).[82] Other Reformed theologians don't go as far, but the prudence of a question like that of Reformed dogmatician Jan van Genderen is praiseworthy: "Does the New Testament teach that both election and reprobation are from eternity? A number of texts appear to point in this diretion (1 Peter 2:8; Rev. 13:8; 17:8)."[83] A bit later we read, "There is an election from eternity, but it is nowhere placed side by side with reprobation from eternity. There is a Book of Life, but we do not read of a book of death."[84] This is even more beautiful!

12.8.3 Gravamina

In addition to the writings of theologians, the *gravamina* (grievances, complaints) that were presented between 1953 and 1977 in Calvinist churches were very promising. They addressed especially the doctrine of the eternal reprobation. I mention the complaints of Abraham Duetz, from the Dutch Reformed Church in the Neterlands, Bastiaan J. Brouwer, from the (Kuyperian) Reformed Churches in the Netherlands, and Harry R. Boer, from the Christian Reformed Churches in North America.[85] In each instance, we encounter a healthy intuition that — often inadvertently, it seems — reduces a certain

---

81. Ibid., 91–92.
82. König (2006, 478–83).
83. Van Genderen and Velema (2008, 218).
84. Van Genderen and Velema (2008, 231).
85. See the enumeration in Wentsel (1982, 181–82); Van Genderen and Velema (2008, 232–33).

harshness from Contra-Remonstrantism. Thus, Reformed dogmatician Gordon Spykman makes election and rejection (stealthily?) partially dependent of the human side: "'Obey Me!' said God—his Word of election. 'For otherwise!' said God in one breath—his Word of reprobation."[86]

Note as well the way Hendrikus Berkhof placed the entire subject of election within the framework of the covenant:

> [T]he confession of election is rooted in a covenant fellowship which is not comprehensively characterized by the word 'election.' For the word only states what God does. It expresses his unilateral initiative by which he makes specific people and groups the objects of his grace and calling. . . . In the covenant, however, man is given a subjective standing. The covenant also involves man in his responsibility, his guilt, his conversion, his obedience. All that is not contained in the word 'election.'. . . Lifting the word out of the covenant context from which it arises causes accidents, as is abundantly proven in church history. . . . [As a consequence,] *either* we have to believe in a god who is arbitrary and fickle [hyper-Calvinism], *or* in a god who is powerless and thus totally dependent on the intitative of man himself [Arminianism].[87]

In other words, Berkhof did not want to be forced to choose between God as subject or people as subject, but chose instead "the uniqueness of the biblical-covenantal (inter-subjective) speaking,"[88] where here the term "inter-subjective" means: between God as a covenantal subject and humanity as a covenantal subject. Therefore, he did not endeavor to resolve the dilemmas posed in the sixteenth and seventeenth centuries, but argued "that we will be better able to see their insolvability from different thought frameworks."

As we review the history of the predestination doctrine, we can understand the concluding judgment of Reformed

---

86. Spykman (1992, 509–10).
87. Berkhof (1986, 483–84).
88. Berkhof (1986, 485).

theologian Cornelis Graafland. Regarding the imbalance brought to this doctrine already with Calvin, he states: "It was not a listening to Scripture but the theological polemics with spiritual opponents that has brought Calvin to this view."[89] The same was true already in the battle between Pelagius and Augustine, and even more so in the conflict between the Remonstrants and the Contra-Remonstrants: "How else would [the latter conflict's] history perhaps have developed if the Dordt fathers had not fallen into this snare but, in line with the Reformation, had continued orienting themselves to the justification of the sinner by faith in Christ"[90] (cf. Kohlbrugge in §12.7.3).

12.9 Hyper-Calvinism
12.9.1 The Path of Subjectivism

In contrast to moderate Calvinists, hyper-Calvinists succeeded in making the reactionary theological position of the Canons still more imbalanced. Whereas Willem Teelinck (1579–1629) and Gisbert Voetius (1589–1676) had assigned a wise and modest place to the election doctrine, especially the Scottisch-Dutch Reformed theologian Alexander Comrie (1706–1774) assigned to this doctrine a far too exalted position, and thereby distorted it still further. The ultra-Reformed, constituting what is called the "experiential" or "experimental" wing of Reformed churches (the *bevindelijk gereformeerden*, those Reformed people who strongly emphasize the experiential-emotional side of the life of faith, and the inner voice of God through his Word and Spirit) have consistently followed Comrie.[91]

The Canons of Dordt themselves are partially responsible for this development, by pointing, for the assurance of election, not only to Christ but also to this (I.12): the elect "attain the assurance of this their eternal and unchangeable election

---

89. Graafland (1987, 594).
90. Ibid.
91. Van der Zwaag (2003) has devoted significant attention to the role of Comrie.

... by observing in themselves with a spiritual joy and holy pleasure the infallible fruits of election pointed out in the Word of God—such as, a true faith in Christ, filial fear, a godly sorrow for sin, a hungering and thirsting after righteousness, ..."[92]

Although in itself this statement is perfectly correct, when it was overemphasized by subsequent hyper-Calvinists, it led to unhealthy spiritual introspection. Therefore, we can understand the guidelines of the Dutch Reformed Church in the Netherlands: "[C]hurch history after [the Synod of] Dordt has shown that in this way the path to passivity, self-contemplation, and fatalism has been opened, on which innumerable people have wandered, disregarding the only gate to election, namely, faith in the Christ presented to them through preaching."[93]

We must add that Arminianism also risks catapulting the Christian into uncertainty by making salvation strictly dependent on the person's own choices as well as their perseverance.[94] Hyper-Calvinists may ask: "How can I know I have been eternally elected?" Arminians may ask: "How can I know I will persevere until the end?" In both cases, salvation can remain a doubtful thing until your last breath. Thus, both hyper-Calvinism and Arminianism have led people down a path of uncertainty and subjectivism, though in different ways.

Despite hyper-Calvinist denials,[95] the doctrine of election has received a genuinely determinist character (see chapter 3). Gerrit Berkouwer complained that in this view, "the consolation of election gives way to a powerless submission which [structurally] cannot be distinguished from submission to destiny and fate, ..."[96] Sadly, this is very true. Many

---

92. Dennison (*RCET* 4:124).
93. Hervormde Kerk (1962, 40).
94. Verboom (2005, 219).
95. See, e.g., Kersten (1980, 1:117).
96. Berkouwer (1960, 12–13; the word within brackets was present in the Dutch

pray daily for a "new heart" — but where do we find such a prayer in Scripture? (see §8.2.1) — and although they "use the means," as the Canons put it (I.16; III/IV.17: the Word, the sacraments, discipline), they believe they can do no more than wait with acquiescence and resignation, whereas the Bible emphatically says, "Believe in the Lord Jesus, and you will be saved" (Acts 16:31).

12.9.2 Deviation from the Canons of Dordt

How far hyper-Calvinism has deviated from the Canons of Dordt may be evident from a review, first, of Article I.16: there need be no fear of the doctrine of reprobation on the part of those "who, though they seriously desire to be turned to God, to please Him only, and to be delivered from the body of death [Rom. 7:24], cannot yet reach that measure of holiness and faith to which they aspire; since a merciful God has promised that He will not quench the smoking flax, nor break the bruised reed [Isa. 42:3]. . . ."[97]

Wonderful words! But what happens when, in ultra-Reformed circles, such a wavering believer does indeed begin to grow in his personal confidence and assurance of salvation? Well-meaning people will warn him to beware of going to hell with a "stolen Jesus" or an "imaginary heaven," that is, to beware of deceiving himself (see §14.8.1). The basic error of such well-meaning people is that they begin with what is *for God* the starting point (viz., election) but *for us* the end point. As Johan Heyns put it: "We begin with the believing acceptance of the offer of grace in Jesus Christ, and from there conclude that we are elect. For human thought, election is not a beginning but an end [a word play: *begin-sel* and *eind-sel*]."[98]

My second example comes from Article I.17 in the Canons: "Since we are to judge of the will of God from His Word,

---

original, but omitted from the published English translation); cf. Bavinck (*RD* 2:240); Weber (1981, 1:507–11).
97. Dennison (*RCET* 4:125).
98. Heyns (1988, 87).

which testifies that the children of believers are holy, not by nature, but in virtue of the covenant of grace, in which they together with the parents are comprehended, godly parents ought not to doubt the election and salvation of their children whom it pleases God to call out of this life in their infancy (Gen. 17:7; Acts 2:39; 1 Cor. 7:14)."[99] Aside from whether the argument of the Canons at this point is fully biblical with respect to the covenant,[100] hyper-Calvinism has drifted very far from Article 17. People in those circles assume that children of believers who die in infancy are likely lost because, in their view, the number of the elect is very small.

Their favorite Bible passages include: "I will take you, one from a city and two from a family" (Jer. 3:14, which refers, however, to Israel's return to Zion), and especially this one: "Enter by the narrow gate ... the gate is narrow and the way is hard that leads to life, and those who find it are few" (Matt. 7:13-14), and: "On that day many will say to me, 'Lord, Lord, did we not prophesy in your name, and cast out demons in your name, and do many mighty works in your name?' And then will I declare to them, 'I never knew you; depart from me, you workers of lawlessness'" (vv. 22-23), and: "[M]any are called, but few are chosen" (22:14; cf. §11.1).

12.9.3 Harshness

Augustine concluded that "far more persons are left under the punishment than are delivered from it."[101] In opposition to this, Reformed theologian Benjamin Warfield remarkably stated that the number of those ultimately lost will be very small compared with the entire number of those saved.[102]

There is a gaping chasm between these two standpoints ("few saved – many saved") that seems too large to bridge. This chasm is much narrower, however, between the adher-

---

99. Dennison (*RCET* 4:125).
100. See extensively, Ouweneel (2016c).
101. *De Civitate Dei* 21.12.
102. Warfield (1952, 350).

ents of the second view ("many saved") and a number of other views. For example, think of (a) those Calvinists who do not wish to emphasize predestination at the expense of human responsibility; or (b) those post-millennialists (such as Warfield) who believe that an enormous number of people will come to faith in the end times; or (c) those inclusivists who believe that, even among those who have never heard the gospel, many will be saved on the basis of Christ's atoning sacrifice, and through the work of the Holy Spirit (cf., e.g., Acts 10:35, "in every nation anyone who fears him and does what is right is acceptable to him");[103] or (d) those who believe that all little children who die young—including children who were aborted—will be saved.[104]

The well-known Evangelical Anglican John Stott trusted that the majority of the human race would be saved, and he had a firm biblical basis for this view.[105] I have heard other Evangelicals observe: Those who know God can believe nothing else but that God's harvest will be much larger than Satan's.

On the one hand, in opposition to Remonstrants, Viatorism maintains that salvation is one hundred percent a matter of God's grace and free, sovereign will. A person is saved by grace, but even this faith is a gift of God; it is all grace (Eph. 2:8). On the other hand, in opposition to hyper-Calvinists, Viatorism maintains that salvation is one hundred percent a matter of human responsibility, which is manifested in repentance and faith. A person is lost, not because God happens to have decreed so, but because he is a sinner, and rebelliously perseveres in his sinfulness and inconvertibility. The latter point is indeed acknowledged by hyper-Calvinists, but then with the conviction that God *wanted* the Fall and the sins of the reprobate.[106]

---

103. See Ouweneel (EDR 5, chapter 13).
104. See Ouweneel (EDR 6, §2.6.1).
105. Edwards and Stott (1988, 327).
106. E.g., Kersten (1980, 1:126–27).

Herman Bavinck insisted that Pelagianism "has no pity" (see §12.1.1). But in the same breath he implicitly criticized the harshness of hyper-Calvinists, which drives so many people to fear that they are reprobate. He wrote: "No one has *a right* to believe that he or she is a reprobate, for everyone is sincerely and urgently called to believe in Christ with a view to salvation. No one *can* actually believe it, for one's own life and all that makes it enjoyable is proof that God takes no delight in his death. No one *really* believes it, for that would be hell on earth."[107] The latter point seems inaccurate, for there are such people whose life on earth is a hell because of an imbalanced doctrine of predestination. But for the rest, however, Bavinck clearly depicts and condemns the consequences of hyper-Calvinism. The guidelines of the Dutch Reformed Church in the Netherlands rightly say about the question: Have I been elected?: "As a theoretical consequence of an election doctrine, this question does not occur in the Bible."[108]

In this context, indeed, it is a relief to read these balanced guidelines: "Never may the doctrine of election be presented in such a way that it would detract from God's worldwide grace and from human responsibility. The way of thinking in the seventeenth century was such that people found it much harder to confess the apparently contradictory realities of God's sovereignty and human responsibility without the one diminishing the other."[109] The guidelines rightly argue that this is exactly what we should seek to do today: live with both realities, without being concerned about the paradox. God has loved the whole world, he wants all people to be saved, he offers this salvation to all people, and he does not want anyone to be lost. It is people's own firm responsibility to seize this salvation—but if they do so, they will realize afterward that at that very same time the wonderful, electing grace of God was at work in them. We can be satisfied with nothing less

---

107. Bavinck (*RD* 2:402).
108. Hervormde Kerk (1962, 10).
109. Hervormde Kerk (1962, 43).

than this.

Chapter 13
The Universal Offer of Grace

One act of righteousness
  *leads to justification and life for **all** men.*
                              Romans 5:18

*God our Savior, who desires **all** people to be saved*
  and to come to the knowledge of the truth.
For there is one God,
  and there is one mediator between God and men,
    the man Christ Jesus,
    *who gave himself as a ransom for **all**.*
                              1 Timothy 2:3-6

For the grace of God has appeared,
  *bringing salvation for **all** people.*
                              Titus 2:11

Summary: *Some ideas that should trouble (hyper-)Calvinists include the notions that salvation is sincerely offered to **all** people, and that it is up to them whether they accept it or not. God even **wants** all people to be saved—but many people do **not** want to be saved. Christ's sacrifice is sufficient for all: everyone can be saved if he or she only believes. God is imploring, begging, people to accept the gospel. To put it more strongly: God is commanding people to* *receive Christ; this is not a matter of taste. Those who do accept the gospel have been compelled by God but not forced. With respect to the direction of his sinful heart, the natural person does not have a free will; but with respect to the creational structuredness of reality, he does. God appeals to this human will all the time. But some ideas that should trouble Arminians include the notion that Christ bore the sins of believers only, but not of all people. God addresses human responsibility but simultaneously makes clear that people cannot come to him except by his power.*

13.1 Freedom
13.1.1 In Brief: the Issue Again

BOTH THE DIMENSION OF God's eternal, sovereign decree and the dimension of human responsibility and free will are equally important. Repentance is *entirely* a matter of God's sovereign grace — but it is also *entirely* a matter of human responsibility, without the one aspect diminishing the importance of the other. Only old-fashioned scholastic conclusivists are unable to live with the tension between these two dimensions, and will therefore invariably try to sweep one of them under the rug.

Which dimension gets chosen for this treatment is determined largely by one's theological tradition. Traditional Calvinists will confess human responsibility with the mouth, but will never allow it to affect the absolute priority of God's eternal decree. Traditional Arminians in the broad sense (Roman Catholics, Lutherans, Remonstrants, many Evangelicals) will confess God's eternal decree with the mouth, but will never allow it to affect the absolute priority of human *freedom*. In a sense, this issue is about freedom — either God's freedom to elect and to reprobate whomsoever he chooses, or human freedom to choose for or against God.

This is the tragic aspect of the issue, because no Christian in his right mind would ever wish to belittle *God's* freedom, God's eternal decree, in short: God's sovereignty. But no contemporary Christian would ever wish to belittle *human* freedom either. I say "contemporary" because in earlier centuries the lives of by far the majority of people were planned from the outset: the small area where one would live, the work one would perform (farmer, baker, blacksmith), the partner one would marry (a girl from the village), the church, society, and country one belonged to. *People had very few choices*; everything in life was decreed from Above, that is, by the circumstances in which one was born and which God had arranged. In those days it was not very difficult to believe that even your eternal destiny was decreed from Above, and that you had no influence upon it.

Today it is very different. People make choices all the time: where to live (perhaps on the other side of the globe), what study to undertake, what job to choose, what partner to marry (perhaps from the other side of the globe), what denomination to choose, etc. We are no longer living in the seventeenth century. We may choose to be generous and benevolent (or not), to be active members of the communities to which we belong (or not so active), to be socially and politically engaged (or not), etc. So we have a hard time believing that there is one choice we are unable to make: to choose whether we want to serve Jesus Christ. This has at least one consequence: more and more Reformed theologians emphasize human freedom and responsibility to such an extent that they can no longer be considered to be in complete harmony with the Canons of Dordt. We have met several of these theologians, especially those who no longer believe in an eternal decree of reprobation.

13.1.2 Human Choice

In this chapter I wish to underscore the subject of human responsibility and freedom by dealing with three claims, based upon Scripture.

(a) Christ came into this world not just for the elect but for *all* people (§13.2). If there were not only an eternal decree of election but also an eternal decree of reprobation, then when Christ came into the world it was certain who would listen to him and begin to follow him, and who would not. What possible business could Christ have had with the reprobate? To increase their culpability by his preaching? But that would have been cruel, because their refusal to listen to him would have been determined from eternity. In other words, what is the meaning of the fact that Christ genuinely and sincerely came for all people in the world?

(b) This issue is deeper, however: through Christ, and later through Christ's apostles and evangelists, God addressed, and addresses, *all* people genuinely and sincerely, inviting them, urging them, entreating them, beseeching them (never forcing them), often with a deeply moved and moving attitude (§13.5). But why is this so? How can God sincerely, movingly entreat people to come to him if he himself had decreed from eternity to leave them in the misery of their sins?

(c) The importance of this dimension of human freedom and responsibility is evident from the fact that God *commands* people to repent, to come, to believe, and to return to him (§13.7). Commanding is not forcing. After an earthquake, people are commanded not to loot, but they are not locked in their houses to prevent them from looting. They can choose whether to follow the command. But if they choose to loot, and are caught, then force is used: they are handcuffed and thrown into prison. God never forces people, not even the elect: he invites them, and commands them. But it is one's choice whether to follow the command. We hasten to add that choosing to do so occurs by God's gracious working in one's heart, but let us not say this too quickly. Let us first stress human responsibility: people receive salvation because they *want* it, that is, because they *choose* to receive it in faith.

13.2 Christ Came for All
13.2.1 Salvation Offered to All
Let us begin with the first claim. All Bible passages that point to the universality of the offer of salvation can be found in Desiderius Erasmus' work *On the Freedom of the Will* (*De libero*

arbitrio). However, as the German Reformed dogmatician Otto Weber wrote, "[B]oth Luther and Calvin devoted great efforts to disprove the scriptural argumentation which challenged their position. Augustine had taken the same approach. But all of their counter-arguments did not silence the opposition, which appealed to Scripture."[1] This is absolutely true. Every theologian should be alarmed if he discovers that he is trying, like a ventriloquist, to make clear Bible passages say something other than — or even the opposite of — what they do say, to rescue his own intellectual paradigm.

Thankfully, Reformed dogmatician Herman Bavinck powerfully defended the doctrine of the universal offer of grace,[2] using eight arguments that I will formulate in my own words in this chapter. In his view, there was no contradiction between this universal offer of grace and the doctrine of predestination. Bavinck had Scripture on his side here (see our discussion in §11.2 of the Gospel of John). There are many passages showing that the offer of God's salvation comes to *all* people, and in this way he is drawing *all* people; Jesus said, "I, when I am lifted up from the earth, will draw all people to myself" (John 12:32). Scripture makes it very clear why some do not come: because they do not *want* to. Scripture never says that they did not come because they had not been elected.

Jesus said, "Come to me, *all* [i.e., believers and unbelievers, Jews and Gentiles] you who are weary and burdened, and I will give you rest" (Matt. 11:28 NIV). Compare this with the words of the prophet, "Come, *everyone* who thirsts, come to the waters" (Isa. 55:1), which is first said to Israel, but then eventually includes all the Gentiles as well (Isa. 56). Who would have the courage to limit this "all" and "everyone," or to assert that the Lord did not *mean* this cordial invitation (for instance, because most of his addressees had been reprobated from eternity)? Some have tried to rescue their intellectual paradigm by claiming that such statements are valid for those

---

1. Weber (1983, 2:432–33).
2. Bavinck (*RD* 4:35–40).

only who, by a one-sided, sovereign initiative of God, have first been *made* weary, burdened, and thirsty. No Bible passage suggests anything of the kind. Here again, one's theological theory is dominating sound and straightforward exegesis.

Speaking of thirst, "Let the one who is thirsty, come. Let the one who wants to drink of the water of life, drink it. It is a free gift" (Rev. 22:17b NIV). The water of life is for everyone; one need only *want* it. Every thirsty person may come to Jesus and drink, so that "rivers of living water" will flow out of his inner parts (John 7:37-38). Sure, it is God who works the willing in a person (Phil. 2:13); everyone who has wanted and accepted the gospel will afterward testify to God's saving grace. But who would dare say that God works this willing only in those whom he has predestined for this, entirely apart from a person's own will and responsibility? Does such a person will by God's instigation only, apart from his own will? Such willing is no willing at all; it describes only programmed robots.

13.2.2 All and Many

Paul can say, "[T]he gospel . . . is the power of God for salvation to everyone who believes, to the Jew first and also to the Greek" (Rom. 1:16; cf. 10:4, 11, 13), and, "*[A]ll* have sinned and fall short of the glory of God, and are justified by his grace as a gift, through the redemption that is in Christ Jesus" (3:23-24). This does not mean that all sinners are actually redeemed, for not all come to faith (vv. 22, 25-31). But it does mean that the group to whom salvation is offered is as large as the group that has sinned, that is, all people. Thus, this is an important verse because the word "all" cannot be limited here in any way: salvation comes to all who have sinned, that is, to all humanity.

It is worthwhile to pay attention here to the alternate reading in Romans 3:22. The ESV and many modern translations read: "for [Gr. *eis*] all who believe," but the KJV and other older translations read: "unto [*eis*] all and upon [*epi*] all them that believe." This could be explained as follows: salvation comes (is offered) to all people, but only becomes the possession of those who believe.[3]

A similar distinction is found in Romans 5:18–19, "[A]s one trespass led to condemnation for all men, so one act of righteousness leads to justification and life for all men. For as by the one man's [i.e., Adam's] disobedience the many were made sinners, so by the one man's [i.e., Christ's] obedience the many will be made righteous." Notice that the phrases "all men" (v. 18) and "the many" (v. 19) each appear twice. Verse 18 deals again with the group under God's condemnation, namely, "all people," and this group is just as large as the group to whom salvation is offered. Just as in 3:23–24, this is irrefutable evidence that salvation comes to all people, not only to all *elect* people, as Reformed expositors have often claimed.[4]

However, as certainly as salvation is offered to all people, just as certainly it becomes the actual possession only of a group identified as "the many," namely, the many who belong to Christ. Verse 18 refers twice to the *same* group: "all people," but verse 19 refers to two *different* groups, two human families: those of Adam and of Christ, respectively. The former are and remain sinners, the latter, though born as sinners, become righteous because salvation not only came to them, but they also accepted it in faith.[5] Verse 18 involves the identity of those to whom the offer of salvation comes; these belong to "all people." Verse 19 involves the identity of those who actually receive salvation; these belong to "the many," that is, those who belong to Christ by faith.

Something similar is found in Romans 10:11–13, "[T]he Scripture says, 'Everyone who believes in him will not be put to shame [Isa. 28:16].' For there is no distinction between Jew and Greek; for the same Lord is Lord of all, bestowing his riches on all who call on him. For 'everyone who calls on the

---

3. See, e.g., Kelly (*BT* 6:376); Grant (1901, 204).
4. Hughes (1989, 174).
5. Kelly (*BT* 7:185–86); Grant (1901, 223).

name of the Lord will be saved [Joel 2:32].'" There is no exception: each and every Jew or Gentile who appeals to him for salvation will receive it.

13.2.3 God's Will: Salvation for All

We encounter the same universality of the offer of salvation in this statement: "God our Savior, who desires *all people* to be saved and to come to the knowledge of the truth. . . . Christ Jesus, who gave himself as a ransom for *all*" (1 Tim. 2:3-4, 6), and its counterpart: "The Lord is not slow to fulfill his promise [of coming again] as some count slowness, but is patient toward you, not wishing that any should perish, but that *all* should reach repentance" (2 Pet. 3:9; cf. Ezek. 33:11, "I have no pleasure in the death of the wicked, but that the wicked turn from his way and live"). I already mentioned several attempts to explain these passages in terms of the classical predestination paradigm. But time and again we see how hard it is to reconcile the doctrine of eternal reprobation with the biblical fact that God wants all to be saved, and wants none to perish.

The guidelines of the Dutch Reformed Church in the Netherlands state in this connection, "Afterward, dogmatics began to use both expressions [the counsel of God, the good pleasure of God] as if they referred to both a reprobation and an election from eternity. That usage of terms, however, is unscriptural. Both expressions describe entirely unambiguously God's will to salvation."[6]

Elsewhere, Paul argues: "[T]he grace of God has appeared, bringing salvation for *all* people, training us to renounce ungodliness and worldly passions, and to live self-controlled, upright, and godly lives in the present age" (Titus 2:11-12). The Reformed Annotators of the Dutch States Translation (1637) explained the phrase "all people" to mean "all kinds of people, men, women, aged, youth, free and bondmen, as follows from what preceded." This sounds rather weak, but it does not necessarily exclude any people. In this way, the

---

6. Hervormde Kerk (1962, 29–30).

difference is clear between those to whom salvation comes—"all people"—and those who effectively share in salvation: it is offered to "all," but it trains "us."

Thus, we also read in Romans 11:32, "God has consigned *all* to disobedience, that he may have mercy on *all*." The latter "all" must be identical with the former "all," that is, salvation is offered to *all* the disobedient (sinners). Hebrews 2:9 says of Jesus that through "the suffering of death . . . by the grace of God he [would] taste death for *everyone* [Gr. *huper pantos*, Lat. *pro omnibus*, "for all (people)"]."

13.3 Evaluation
13.3.1 Sufficient and Efficient

In none of the Bible passages mentioned so far is it necessary to assume a universal atonement ("Christ bore the sins of all people"), or a universal salvation ("in the end all people will be saved") (§12.3.3). It is equally important to see what these passages do say: salvation is sincerely and seriously offered to all people without any exception, not just to the elect. Christ's sacrificial death was powerful and sufficient to bring salvation to all people—if all people would only believe, which they don't. This offer of salvation is seriously meant (see below), for God sincerely desires *all* people to be saved.

Willem Verboom summarized the difference between Remonstrants and Contra-Remonstrants on this point in the following way: the former teach that Christ died for all people, but only those who believingly accept this death share in the results of this sacrificial death. The latter teach that Christ's sacrifice is sufficient for all humanity, but only the elect share in its results.[7] The two positions seem very similar, yet the difference is essential. The consequence of the former view is that, if nobody would come to faith, Christ would have died in vain. The latter view implies that there most certainly will be people who will share in the results of Christ's sacrificial death, for these are those who from eternity have been elected

---
7. Verboom (2005, 230).

for it.[8]

Christ's sacrifice is sufficient (Latin *sufficiens*) for all people, but becomes effective (Latin *efficax*) only in the elect. In what does this sufficiency consist? The Canons of Dordt deny that Christ died for all people; in what sense, then, is Christ's sacrifice sufficient for all people? Remonstrants go to the other extreme: Christ bore the sins of all people; one needs only to believe this. But how can God ever condemn sinners for sins that Christ has already borne at the cross? Viatorism chooses the middle position: as Scripture clearly says, Christ died for all people, so that salvation can be sincerely offered to all people. But his death becomes effective only for those who believe; Christ bore the sins only of true believers.

Let me add, for the sake of completion, that the phrase "all (people)" does not mean "all humanity" in *every* Bible verse. In the expression "he died for all" (2 Cor. 5:15) we must perhaps (but not necessarily) assume that "all" here means all believers, for the text continues as follows: ". . . [so] that those who live might no longer live for themselves but for him who for their sake died and was raised." In Romans 3:23–24, "[A]ll have sinned and fall short of the glory of God, and are justified by his grace as a gift, through the redemption that is in Christ Jesus," the first clause refers to all humanity, and the next clause refers to all believers.

13.3.2 "The World"

Other passages refer not to "all people" but to "the world," which means the human world, that is, humanity: "God so loved the world, that he gave his only Son, that whoever believes in him should not perish but have eternal life" (John 3:16). "[I]n Christ God was reconciling the world to himself, not counting their trespasses against them, and entrusting to us the message of reconciliation" (2 Cor. 5:19). God's love was toward the entire world population, therefore the "message

---

8. Regarding the discussion of the former claim in the Canons of Dordt, cf. Verboom (2005, 231).

of reconciliation" can be freely preached to all people; but in Christ's days, this love became effective only in those who came to faith. I repeat: Christ's atoning death is sufficient for all people, but effective only for his own.

Under other circumstances, the Greek phrase ēn katallassōn, "he was reconciling" (v. 19), could be translated as "he reconciled," as the GNT and Phillips in fact do, but here this does not seem advisable. If indeed the entire world, that is, all humanity, *has been* reconciled to God, why is God still making the appeal through his servants: "*Be* reconciled to God" (v. 20)?[9] In Christ, God *was* reconciling the world to himself, and through his servants he still *is* reconciling the world to himself in the sense that he still extends his reconciling hand to humanity: "Be reconciled to me!" However, the entire world is never reconciled; that is, "all *things*" (the entire cosmos) will indeed be reconciled to God (Col. 1:20; cf. John 1:29), but not all *people*. Even all the elect have not yet been reconciled; each of them shares effectively in this reconciliation only at the moment he or she comes to faith.

Notice here Romans 11:15, where Paul speaks of the "reconciliation of the world" (Gr. *katallagē kosmos*), which, on the one hand, is the reconciliation that is offered *to* all humanity (here, cosmos is not "all things" but "all people," as in John 3:16) and, on the other hand, the reconciliation of all those of this world who have come to faith.

John says that Christ "is the propitiation for our sins, and not for ours only but also for the sins of the whole world" (1 John 2:2). It is disputable whether we should translate the Greek phrase *peri holou tou kosmou* as: "for the whole world" (ASV, NKJV, WEB, etc.), or "for [the sins of] the whole world" (KJV, ESV, NIV, etc.). Universalists abuse the verse to argue that all humanity will ultimately be saved, which neither this text nor any other passage says. Hyper-Calvinists in turn abuse the verse by limiting the expression to the "world of the elect."[10]

---
9. Grant (1956, 154).
10. Kersten (1980, 1:134–35).

However, the "whole world" is more than the elect only. The elect in this verse are identified with the words "our" and "ours," so "the world" must be a wider concept: it is all humanity.[11]

Again, Viatorism follows the middle path: God has made Christ's propitiatory work available to all humanity, that is, it is sufficient to save all people. However, it becomes effective only in those who believe. Notice that it is "our sins" *and* "[the sins of] the whole world." So again, the world cannot be the world of the elect; it is here the reverse: "the world" includes all the "others," in addition to "us" (believers). Christ is the propitiation for *our* sins, but his propitiatory sacrifice is available also for all other (not-yet-believing) people in the world. Whether they in faith *accept* Christ and his atoning work is another matter.

If the "whole world" would mean the "world of the elect" here, how do hyper-Calvinists escape the force of their argument when the same apostle tells us: "We know that we are from God, and the whole world lies in the power of the evil one" (1 John 5:19)?[12] Is this also the "world of the elect"? Of course not. In the two passages the "whole world" has precisely the same referent: the "world" of *un*believers in contrast to "we" and "us." Thus, some hyper-Calvinists make the text say the very opposite of what it means. Notice that *nowhere* in the New Testament does the "(whole) world" refer to the "world" of the elect (see, e.g., Rom. 1:8; 3:19; Col. 1:6; Rev. 3:10; 12:9; 16:14).

Other passages discuss the personal offer of salvation, but in a way that presupposes the universal offer of grace. Take, for example, the jailer at Philippi, who asked Paul and Silas, "Sirs, what must I do to be saved?" They replied, "Believe in the Lord Jesus, and you will be saved, you and your household" (Acts 16:30–31). How would this answer have been meaningful unless Paul and Silas knew for sure that they

---

11. Grant (1956, 179–80; cf. 190–91).
12. Grant (1956, 188).

could tell *this* man what they told *all* people?[13] If you believe, we guarantee you that you will be saved—and this without limiting notes such as: But of course you *cannot* believe yourself; you will have to wait until God converts you, or until God grants you faith, or until God reveals to you that you have been elected. Or begin to pray for a new heart, and perhaps God will answer your prayer someday. Or place yourself under "the means of grace," that is, come to church regularly, listen to the preaching, read your Bible, pray every day, and *perhaps*, someday God will have mercy on you. Such limitations to the offer of salvation are *never* made in the entire New Testament; they are the inventions of hyper-Calvinist theologians. Instead, we hear this: Believe, and you will be saved.

13.4 No Equal Opportunities
13.4.1 The Reach of the Gospel

Of course, the fact that salvation has come to all people does not mean that all people receive equal *opportunities*. All of the approaches we have studied—Arminianism, Open Theism, as well as Viatorism—acknowledge that God did not reveal himself to Hammurabi in the same way he did to Moses; that he gave blessings to Israel that he did not give to Persia; that he did not appear to Paul in the same way he did to Pilate.[14] In the first period after Acts 2, the Middle East and Europe were evangelized on a large scale, but the rest of Africa and Asia only centuries later. As Paul says, "How then will they call on him in whom they have not believed? And how are they to believe in him of whom they have never heard? And how are they to hear without someone preaching?" (Rom. 10:14).

With respect to the ways of God and the universality of God's offer of salvation, we must admit that some people receive greater opportunity to know the gospel than others. On the one hand, this is a *privilege*: those who are allowed to hear

---

13. Cf. Hughes (1989, 167).
14. Sproul (1986, 37).

the gospel gladly and thankfully accept this as a gift from God. On the other hand, this is a *responsibility*:

> [T]hat servant who knew his master's will but did not get ready or act according to his will, will receive a severe beating. But the one who did not know, and did what deserved a beating, will receive a light beating. Everyone to whom much was given, of him much will be required, and from him to whom they entrusted much, they will demand the more (Luke 12:47-48).

We may tell every person that salvation is intended for him or her, but in reality this declaration *is* not spoken to every person. This may induce us to announce the gospel with even greater zeal to even more people, near and far away (cf. Rom. 10:4). But even then, we will not be able to offer equal opportunities to all people, in part because of the great differences in political and religious freedom in various countries. To be sure, through modern radio and the Internet the gospel can reach virtually *all* countries of the world, in languages that can be understood by virtually *all* people — but not all people have access to radio or the Internet. And if they do, who helps them understand what they are hearing or reading (cf. Acts 8:30)?

To some hyper-Calvinists we must declare that God offers salvation in a serious and sincere way to *all* people. To some Arminians we must declare that, in reality, God in his providence does not offer salvation in equal measure to all people.

13.4.2 Limited Atonement Again

Let me return for a moment to the expression "limited atonement" (see §12.3.3). No matter how we take this, it is a confusing expression. If people mean by it that only a part of humanity through faith shares in the atonement that Christ has brought about, we have no difficulty with it. However, in this case, the expression is not typically Calvinistic at all. *All* Christians subscribe to it, except universalists, who believe that all people will ultimately be saved. However, if people mean by the expression that the atonement was *intended* for only a part of humanity—that is, that Christ died for the elect only—then we must protest against it. Such an idea conflicts with the clearest testimony of Scripture.

In my view, the basis of this misunderstanding involves a failure to distinguish clearly between what theologians have properly learned to distinguish as *satisfaction* and *substitution*.[15] The satisfaction that Christ gave to God through his work of atonement is sufficient for *all* people, without exception. This work of satisfaction is so great and vast that whoever wants to come may receive a share in it by faith. But the substitution is only for those who actually accept in faith the atoning sacrifice of Christ. Christ died *for* (the benefit of) all, but he died *instead of* (i.e., vicariously, as a substitute for) believers only. The former is objective: all are invited, and all may come; the latter is subjective: only believers (or if you like: the elect) receive a share in it. This is why it is false to claim that Christ died for the elect only (traditional Calvinists); it is a distortion of satisfaction. It is also false to say that Christ bore the sins of all people (Arminians); it is a distortion of substitution. This is what I have tried to demonstrate from Scripture: Christ died for all, but he bore the sins of believers only.

The doctrine of limited atonement is a striking example of how human dogmas sometimes come to dominate the clearest statements of Scripture. This is one of the consequences of a predestination doctrine that has gone too far. And Arminianism, as a typical example of reactionary theology, has not fared much better.

13.5 God's Pressing Appeal
13.5.1 God's Will—the Human Will

In the New Testament, we not only find a universal offer of salvation, but this offer is often linked with a very urgent, pressing, and moving appeal by God. This is so strong that it

---
15. See extensively, Ouweneel (EDR 5, chapter 9).

is entirely against the spirit of Scripture to believe that, at one and the same time, God would urge people to receive salvation while in reality having made it impossible *that* they will do so. This supposed impossibility involves the fact that he has decreed from eternity whom he will save and whom he will not, or has decreed that people can accept the gospel only if he works this in them himself.

Such a one-sided approach comes close to attacking God's integrity. In other words, nothing is a stronger counter-argument against hyper-Calvinism than this pressing, moving, and loving appeal to *all* people to come to salvation: "Come, *everyone* who thirsts, come to the waters" (Isa. 55:1). "Come to me, *all* who labor and are heavy laden, and I will give you rest" (Matt. 11:28).

Look at this moving passage again: "O Jerusalem, Jerusalem, the one who kills the prophets and stones those who are sent to her! How often I wanted to gather your children together, as a hen gathers her chicks under [her] wings, but you were not *willing*!" (Matt. 23:37; Luke 13:34 NKJV). Earlier I distinguished between the resistible will of God—which we find in this verse—and the irresistible will of God, which will be carried out under all circumstances (§2.8.2). Viatorism emphasizes that the former will always involve God's *ways*, and the latter, God's *counsel*.

We must be careful here not to assign to God—inadvertently and unconsciously, I suppose—a form of hypocrisy. On the one hand, God *wants* to save all people (1 Tim. 2:4; 2 Pet. 3:9), he pleads with them to accept his gospel of reconciliation (2 Cor. 5:20), he has spread out his arms to them (Isa. 65:2), he weeps over them (cf. Luke 19:41–42). On the other hand, according to the most extreme form of the classic predestination doctrine, God has already decreed from eternity, entirely by his own initiative and not because of foreseen unbelief and wickedness, that a (large) part of humanity will not want to receive salvation, will not be *able* to receive it, and so *will* never receive it.

Why would God weep over people who are completely *unable* to believe in Christ because this same God has decreed *from* eternity to reject them *for* eternity? What hyper-Calvinist can explain this riddle to the rest of humanity? If the Bible clearly said such a thing, we would have to bow under such an incomprehensible mystery. But the Bible does not contain any eternal decree of reprobation, in either the supralapsarian or the infralapsarian sense of the expression. It is an invention of purely human conclusivism.

13.5.2 Examples

Let me give some examples to illustrate the pressing, even pleading character of God's appeal to people. In Isaiah 50:2 we find these moving words: "Why, when I came, was there no man; why, when I called, was there no one to answer? Is my hand shortened, that it cannot redeem? Or have I no power to deliver?" And in chapter 55: "Why do you spend your money for that which is not bread, and your labor for that which does not satisfy? Listen diligently to me, and eat what is good, and delight yourselves in rich food. Incline your ear, and come to me; hear, that your soul may live" (vv. 2-3).

In Isaiah 65:1-3 (cf. Rom. 10:21) God says, "I was ready to be sought by those who did not ask for me; I was ready to be found by those who did not seek me. I said, 'Here I am, here I am,' to a nation that was not called by my name. I spread out my hands all the day to a rebellious people, who walk in a way that is not good, following their own devices; a people who provoke me to my face continually, sacrificing in gardens and making offerings on bricks."

What a moving picture: God addressing his people with entreaties and stretching out his arms to them, but the majority of Israel does not want to return to him. How can God so ardently plead with people whom he himself had already rejected from eternity? We find this picture several times in Jeremiah: "What wrong did your fathers find in me that they went far from me, and went after worthlessness, and became worthless? . . . [F]or my people have committed two evils: they have forsaken me, the fountain of living waters, and hewed out cisterns for themselves, broken cisterns that can hold no water. . . . Your evil will chastise you, and your apostasy will reprove you. Know and see that it is evil and bitter for you to forsake the LORD your God; the fear of me is not in you" (2:5, 13, 19).

"Return, faithless Israel, . . . I will not look on you in anger, for I am merciful, . . . I will not be angry forever. Only acknowledge your guilt, that you rebelled against the LORD your God and scattered your favors among foreigners under every green tree, and that you have not obeyed my voice. . . . Return, O faithless sons; I will heal your faithlessness" (3:12-13, 22).

13.5.3 The Pleading God

Even more striking is 2 Corinthians 5:20 (NKJV), "Now then, we are ambassadors for Christ, as though God were pleading through us: we implore [you] on Christ's behalf, be reconciled to God." There are two noteworthy verbs here: "to plead" (Gr. *parakaleō*, Lat. *exhorto*; usually: "to exhort, to admonish") and "to implore" (Gr. *deomai*, Lat. *obsecro*; usually: "to pray"). Both God and his servants are appealing (pleading, imploring, begging, beseeching, entreating) here: "It is like God is calling to people through us. We speak for Christ when we beg you to be at peace with God" (ERV). It is God himself who is pleading through his gospel preachers.

This is a very general entreaty, for evangelists address all people in the world. That is, God pleads with *all people* to be reconciled to him. This is not a purely formal message, for instance, to make sure that the reprobate will have no excuse. On the contrary, it is a very emotional, pervasive, and urgent appeal on his behalf. Behind this, we find God's intense desire that all people will find his salvation. For I repeat: God "is patient toward you, not wishing that any should perish, but that all should reach repentance" (2 Pet. 3:9).

God's ambassadors represent Christ who died, arose, and ascended to glory, who uses his servants to announce God's saving grace. Notice the "as though" (NKJV), as if Paul hesitates to speak too absolutely about a God pleading through his servants. Yet he ventures to say that God's servants beseech people on behalf of, or instead of, Christ himself: Be reconciled to God.[16]

It is not people who have to beg God for grace, as if God had to be persuaded. It is *not* true that above the reprobate — or above all people, for that matter — there would be a "heaven of bronze" (cf. Deut. 28:23), that people would have to beg God for a new heart, that they would have to storm heaven continually (cf. Job 21:15b VOICE, "What can we *possibly* gain by asking favors of Him? *Isn't He generous enough already?*"). On the contrary, it is God himself who "did not spare his own Son but gave him up for us *all*" (Rom. 8:32). The sacrifice of his Son is so great, so precious, so vast, that because of it God can freely entreat all people to be reconciled to him. He pleads with them because it would be awful if the glory of this atoning work would not come to benefit all people. This means that no person will perish because he happens to fall under some decree of reprobation. No, God wants to save all, but not all *are* saved because they do not *want* to be saved. As Jesus said, I wanted, but you did not want (Matt. 23:37; Luke 13:34). "*All* who are thirsty may come; they can have the water of life as a free gift if they *want* it" (Rev. 22:17b ERV) — and those who do not want it shall perish in eternal thirst. "If anyone's *will* is to do God's will, he will know whether the teaching is from God or whether I am speaking on my own authority" (John 7:17) — and those who do not have this will shall perish in eternal ignorance.

---

16. Kelly (n.d., 118).

13.6 God's Sincerity
13.6.1 No Noncommittal Offer

It is quite necessary to clearly emphasize that a well-meant offer of grace to all people (§13.1) is *not* a plea for Arminianism. God's offer is not noncommittal, as if God would implore people to accept his offer such that this acceptance in the end would depend entirely on the initiative and the benevolence of the people to whom the offer comes.[17] The universal offer of grace may never be played off against the sovereignty of God's election. On the one hand, this does not change whatsoever the pressing and entreating character of God's appeal to humanity, as we will see in a moment. On the other hand, the well-meant offer of grace does not contradict the realities either that the offer of grace is universal, or that election is particular.[18]

This we maintain over against, for instance, Karl Barth, who claimed that, in some sense, all people have been elected (chosen) by God.[19] The notion of an election of all humanity is foreign to Scripture. Even where an entire nation, Israel, turns out to have been chosen (elected), this is not an automatic election unto eternal blessedness but only unto a privileged position on earth. Such a claim does not deny that this particular election of Israel as a nation aimed at being a blessing for all peoples and generations on the earth (Gen. 12:3; 18:18; 22:18; 26:4; 28:14; etc.). When it comes to the eternal election for heavenly blessedness, *within* the chosen people of Israel, as we have seen, are not only those chosen for eternal blessedness but also those hardened unto perdition (Rom. 11:7). Quite a few New Testament statements are based upon this distinction between the elect and the non-elect (Matt. 22:14; 24:22, 24, 31; Luke 18:7; John 13:18; 1 Cor. 1:27-28; James 2:5; 1 Pet. 2:8-9).

However, just as the universal offer of salvation does not

---

17. Van der Zanden (1949, 86–94; 27–28, 237–38).
18. Cf. Pannenberg (1991, 3:493).
19. See on this Berkouwer (1956, chapters 4 and 10; 1960, 229–30).

affect the particularity of election, so too the particularity of election should not affect the universality of the offer of salvation. Viatorism acknowledges that Christ bore the sins only of those who believe (substitution). But it also acknowledges that Christ died for all people (satisfaction). In this respect, Viatorism agrees with the Canons of Dordt on one important point: Christ's sacrifice and the offer of grace are universal in scope, whereas election and the efficacy of atonement are particular.

13.6.2 The Well-Meant Offer

In 1953, a split occurred within the Reformed Congregations in the Netherlands (the second largest Reformed denomination outside the Dutch Reformed Church). People wondered whether God's "offer of grace" was extended ("well-meant") to all people, that is, also to the reprobate, or only to the elect. Cornelis Steenblok taught the latter;[20] in the United States, Herman Hoeksema (at first Christian Reformed, later Protestant Reformed) taught the same.[21] Henry Kersten, founder and principal leader of the Reformed Congregations (*Gereformeerde Gemeenten*), who passed away in 1948, had taught God's "well-meant offer of grace" to all people.[22]

After the split, the congregations led by Steenblok became known as the "Reformed Congregations in the Netherlands," and the congregations following Kersten were known as the "Reformed Congregations in the Netherlands and North America" (later the addition "in the Netherlands and North America" was dropped; the congregations in North America are called the Netherlands Reformed Congregations).

The former party argued that God cannot extend a well-meant offer of salvation to people whom he himself has rejected *a priori*. Given the force of its own logic, this party was right. The latter party argued that this well-meant offer of

---

20. Steenblok (1978).
21. See De Jong (1954); Graafland (1987, §6.3).
22. Kersten (1980, 1:141).

salvation is clearly taught in Scripture; this party was right, too. This is the consequence of conclusivism: two parties begin with the same errors, and allow (supposedly) logical arguments to overrule Scripture. As Paul Jewett put it, more than any other theological topic, the matter of individual election has led more people to read Scripture through their filter (instead of listening to Scripture say things they might be afraid to hear).[23]

Later spokesmen from both parties have tried to soften the problem by making various distinctions, such as the distinction between God's external call and internal call. Thus, L. M. P. ("Bert") Scholten (member of the Steenblok party) wrote,

> In the external call, the command "repent" does come to all. But the appeal to come to Christ does not come to all. First, through preaching the law, room must be made in the heart of the elect sinner for the evangelical grace. Therefore, there can be no question of a general offer to all and to everyone to whom the preaching is done.[24]

So the command "repent!" is something else than "come to Christ!"? (Cf. Acts 2:38; 3:19-20; 5:31; 8:22; 9:35; 11:18, 21; 17:30-31; 20:21; 26:18.) And where do we read in Scripture that the law must first be preached to the sinner?

The Canons of Dordt do not distinguish between an external and an internal call, and speak unreservedly of God's well-meant offer of grace (III/IV.8): "As many as are called by the gospel are unfeignedly called. For God has most earnestly and truly declared in His Word what is acceptable to Him, namely, that those who are called should come unto Him. He also seriously promises rest of soul and eternal life to all who come to Him and believe."[25] The approach of Scholten is not biblical, but scholastic speculation; it only increases the number of sophistries in hyper-Calvinism. As someone who

---

23. Jewett (1985, 67).
24. Scholten in Mallan and Scholten (n.d., 191).
25. Dennison (*RCET* 4:136); cf. Verboom (2005, 236).

is almost a Calvinist, I am closer to the spirit and tenor of the Canons of Dordt than are these hyper-Calvinists.

13.7 The Command to Repent
13.7.1 Compelled or Coerced?

That God beseeches people while respecting their freedom and responsibility is clear when we see that he does not force people to repent against their will. Representatives of the traditional doctrine of election, beginning with Augustine and the Reformers,[26] have strongly denied that this doctrine is identical with decretalism, for if that were so, repentance and faith would be superfluous, or would be entirely God's unilateral work. However, the latter is precisely what hyper-Calvinists do teach, which is why the terms "determinism" and "decretalism" fit their view.

Repentance and faith cannot be God's exclusive and unilateral work because God never forces the sinner to repent and believe. The latter may be overwhelmed by the knowledge of his sins and by the greatness of the gospel (cf. §12.3.4), but he is not forced like a robot is programmed. To be sure, God does not leave people a free choice; on the contrary, he *commands* them to repent and to accept the gospel in faith. But this is something very different from forcing.

Notice the statement in Luke 14:23 (in the parable of the great banquet), "Go out to the highways and hedges and *compel* [or, *urge*] people to come in, that my house may be filled." People are compelled, urged, to come in, but the verb "drag" (MESSAGE) goes too far. They are persuaded, not coerced. This is what God does: he urges the sinner, persuades him (Acts 17:4; 18:4; 19:8; 26:28; 2 Cor. 5:11). The difference is this: in the case of persuasion, human will, feeling, and intellect are involved (enlightened by the Holy Spirit); in the case of coercion, they are not. A robot does not have to want, to feel, or to think when it is programmed to do a certain thing. It is true, faith is a gift of God (Eph. 2:8). Food and drink are

---
26. Cf. §11.7.1 and see Kersten (1980, 1:117); Hughes (1989, 163).

also gifts of God (Eccl. 3:13; 5:18), but this does not mean that God forces them down our throats. We accept them gratefully from his hand, but we ourselves must chew and swallow.

People are not puppets that must be programmed for repentance. Reformed dogmatician Gerrit Berkouwer admits that election in the traditional sense "seems to clash with the digmity of man and to make man hardly more than a pawn in the divine decision."[27] Precisely; God regards his creature so highly that he will never bypass a person's will, thought, and feelings. Also in salvation, God respects the people's humanity. By nature, people are wicked sinners; but they are never nothings:

> But as man by the fall did not cease to be a creature endowed with understanding and will, nor did sin which pervaded the whole race of mankind deprive him of the human nature, but brought upon him depravity and spiritual death; so also this grace of regeneration does not treat men as senseless stocks and blocks, nor take away their will and its properties, or do violence thereto; but it spiritually quickens, heals, corrects, and at the same time sweetly and powerfully bends it, that where carnal rebellion and resistance formerly prevailed, a ready and sincere spiritual obedience begins to reign; in which the true and spiritual restoration and freedom of our will consist (Canons of Dordt III/IV.16).[28]

13.7.2 Examples

In addition to making an entreaty, God has also given a command: "The times of ignorance God overlooked, but now he *commands* [Gr. *parangellei*] all people everywhere to repent" (Acts 17:30). This is why Scripture speaks of the "obedience of faith" (Gr. *hypakoē pisteōs*, Rom. 1:5; 16:26), that is, obedience to the command to believe. Thus, "to believe" has as its counterpart "to disobey": "Whoever believes in the Son has

---

27. Berkouwer (1960, 8).
28. Dennison (*RCET* 4:139).

eternal life; whoever does not obey [Gr. *apeithōn*] the Son shall not see life, but the wrath of God remains on him" (John 3:36). "[W]hen some were becoming hardened and disobedient [Gr. *ēpeithoun*], speaking evil of the Way before the people, he withdrew from them" (Acts 19:9 NASB). Unbelievers are "those who are self-seeking and do not obey [Gr. *apeithousi*] the truth, but obey [Gr. *peithomenois*] unrighteousness" (Rom. 2:8); they are "sons of disobedience" (Gr. *huioi tēs apeitheias*; Eph. 2:2; 5:6; Col. 3:6; cf. Titus 1:16; 3:3; 1 Pet. 2:7–8).

The command to repent comes with a warning about what will happen if a person does *not* repent: "No, I tell you; but unless you repent, you will all likewise perish" (Luke 13:3, 5). "Remember therefore from where you have fallen; repent, and do the works you did at first. If not, I will come to you and remove your lampstand from its place, unless you repent" (Rev. 2:5). It would be unjust if God gave people a command that they, by God's own decree, were unable to obey, and then would punish them for their disobedience. It is remarkable that hyper-Calvinists so often emphasize God's *sovereignty*, but do not seem to realize that their arguments cast suspicion on God's *righteousness*. A God who pleads to certain people to repent, but has decided beforehand that these people *will* not repent—what kind of God is that?

It does not help to argue here that people's incapacity and unwillingness are not God's fault but are a consequence of the Fall. Indeed, in a *moderate* version of the predestination doctrine, the Fall is not included in the eternal counsel of God (at least not as an active decree), and reprobation is based upon foreseen unbelief, *or* is decreed only *after* people have manifested themselves in unrepentant wickedness. But in the *consistent* (classic) predestination doctrine, the Fall, too, is included in God's counsel, and eternal reprobation rests not in (foreseen) human wickedness as such but in a sovereign decision of God. No room remains for any human freedom.

The emphasis upon human responsibility and freedom of

will, however, does not mean that everything is now up to the person. If God gives people a command, he also provides the strength to follow this command. Thus, people must be *willing* to obey the command, but only by the power of God are they truly *willing* and *able* to obey: "[W]ork out your own salvation with fear and trembling, for it is God who works in you, both to will and to work for his good pleasure" (Phil. 2:12-13).

A beautiful illustration of the two-sidedness of this matter is the man who had been an invalid for thirty-eight years. Jesus told him, "Get up, take up your bed, and walk" (John 5:8). The man could have answered: "I am not *able* to do that; otherwise, I would not have been lying here all these years!"[29] Instead, he obeyed the command; and as he stood, he experienced the Lord's healing power, through which he could stand on his legs. The man could not wait until he felt this power coming, because then it would not have been an act of faith (cf. Acts 14:8-10). No, he had to stand in faith. Conversely, he did not have to stand before the Lord's power came, for he would not have been able to do that. (Hyper-)Calvinism might argue that he first had to wait for God's power before he could stand. Arminianism might argue that he first had to begin to stand, and then God would come with his power. Viatorism argues that the man's faith and Jesus' power were perfectly synchronous.

13.8 The Ability to Repent
13.8.1 "Convert me"

Hyper-Calvinists often argue: Preaching the gospel is of no avail to me, for though I do hear the call to repent, I am *unable* to repent; God must bring this about in me. Often such people appeal to Jeremiah 31:18 (KJV), "[T]urn thou me, and I shall be turned" (Heb. *hashibēni w'ashubah*; also see Lam. 5:21). Compare other translations: "[B]ring me back [to the land of Israel; WJO] that I may be restored" (ESV), but also: "[C]onvert me, and

---

29. See Ouweneel (2004, 267).

I shall be converted" (DRA, GNT). Or they quote this verse, taken in a typological sense: "Draw me, we will run after thee" (Song 1:4 KJV; cf., e.g., NIV: "Take me away with you—let us hurry!"). Such an appeal to Scripture is a half-truth.

Why not quote a verse like this: "O people of Israel, return [Heb. *shubu*] to the LORD, the God of Abraham, Isaac, and Israel, that he may turn again [Heb. *w'yashob*] to the remnant of you" (2 Chron. 30:6). Here, the same verb is used (Heb. *shub*), but the picture is the perfect opposite: the conversion (return) to God was the *condition* for the return of God to the people. They had to take the initiative, *then* God would redeem them. The prodigal son must arise and go to his father, otherwise the father will be unable to embrace him (Luke 15:18–20). The son must make the first step, not the father. Hyper-Calvinists love to quote Jeremiah 31 and Lamentations 5, Arminians love to quote 2 Chronicles 30 and Luke 15. Every theologian runs the risk of quoting only a selected number of Bible verses to support his own thought system.

God never encourages us to pray for conversion or for a new heart. Sure, the "new heart" is a biblical notion; God promises his people: "I will give you a new heart, and a new spirit I will put within you. And I will remove the heart of stone from your flesh and give you a heart of flesh" (Ezek. 36:26; cf. 11:19). But notice Ezekiel 18:31, "Cast away from you all the transgressions that you have committed, and *make yourselves a new heart* and a new spirit! Why will you die, O house of Israel?" This is the opposite of praying for a new heart: *make yourself* a new heart! How? By repenting and turning to God. This is God's sequence: a person must repent and believe, otherwise God cannot bless him or her. Repent, *then* God can give you a new heart. This is exactly the same as saying: Repent, and thus *make yourself* a new heart. You do it, for *you* must repent. But also: *God* does it, he is the One who gives penitent people a new heart.

The same is true of forgiveness. A person must confess his

sins, *then* God will forgive him his sins (Ps. 32:5; Prov. 28:13; 1 John 1:9). Of course, believers sometimes say: "Forgive me/us!" (Exod. 34:9; Num. 14:19; 1 Kings 8:34, 36, 39, 50; Ps. 25:11, 18; Dan. 9:19; Hos. 14:2; Amos 7:2; so also Matt. 6:12) — but confession of sins is always entailed, either implicitly or explicitly. The *person* must repent and confess his sins. Then God performs his action: he grants forgiveness, a new heart, eternal blessing. God does not repent for this person, or confess his sins for him. This is what the *person* must do, and then God does what *he* alone can do. Conversion is part of human responsibility, renewal is God's work.

13.8.2 Balanced Emphases

However, putting all the emphasis on human responsibility is just as wrong as putting all the emphasis on divine sovereignty. Those who repent and believe, realize afterward that these were completely and exclusively by God's power and grace. Therefore Jesus says, "No one can come to me unless the Father . . . draws him" (John 6:44), and: "[A]part from me you can do nothing" (15:5b). Thus, Paul says too, "[N]o one can say 'Jesus is Lord' except in the Holy Spirit" (1 Cor. 12:3b). Therefore, *no* person left to himself will ever seek after God (Ps. 14:2-3; 53:3-4; Rom. 3:11-12); as God says, "I was ready to be sought by those who *did not ask* for me; I was ready to be found by those who *did not seek* me" (Isa. 65:1).[30]

Grace has been called "prevenient" (Latin *praeveniens*, "coming before");[31] grace precedes conversion, in eternity as well: God "saved us and called us . . . because of his own purpose and grace, which he gave us in Christ Jesus before the ages began" (2 Tim. 1:9). However, this does not at all deny that conversion is and remains the full responsibility of people. *They* must repent and believe — this is an unshakable truth. But this is possible only in *God's* strength, that is, in the power of the Holy Spirit — this, too, is an unshakable truth.

---

30. Cf. Berkouwer (1960, 30).
31. See, e.g., Demarest (1997, 83–84).

Jesus told the man with the withered hand (Matt. 12:13), "Stretch out your hand." The man could not first wait until he would feel the healing power. No, he simply had to obey—then he *would* feel the healing power at the same moment: "And the man stretched it out, and it was restored, healthy like the other." He did not first feel the healing power (*contra* hyper-Calvinists); instead, he had to obey the command. If he had not done this, his hand would not have healed, and this would have been entirely his own fault. However, it is equally true that he could stretch out his hand only by the power of God (*contra* many Arminians). Thus, such healings were one hundred percent the work of God's power—but also one hundred percent the responsibility of the obeying person.

It is no different with conversion. No one must, or needs to, wait until he or she experiences the power of God. Many are waiting for this, sometimes for decades, until they are set free (if this happens at all). But this is not the path that God points out in his Word. The person must simply do what God commands him to do: confess his sins to God, trust the promises of God's Word, and in faith grab hold of the only sacrifice that can save him: the vicarious atoning work of Jesus Christ. People must simply obey the command to repent and to believe, and God will do the rest. Only *afterward* will they realize that it was only by God's strength that they were able to do all this.

13.8.3 The "Order of Salvation"

The examples mentioned in §13.7 illustrate how speculations about the "order of salvation" are really confusing and misleading. This order involves questions like: What happens first, conversion (faith) or regeneration? In other words, are the Arminians right who claim that it all starts with conversion, or are the (hyper-)Calvinists right who claim that it all starts with regeneration? This question is just as senseless as asking: What came first, the obedience to the command to arise (Matt. 9:6; Mark 5:41; Luke 7:14; John 5:8; Acts 3:6; 9:34,

40; 14:10) and to stretch out the hand (Luke 6:10), *or* the healing that the Lord granted to the body? Viatorism emphasizes that the work of divine grace and the work of human obedience are two sides of the same coin; those who insist that one precedes the other, emphasize divine sovereignty at the expense of human responsibility (Calvinists) — or the reverse (Arminians).

"[W]ork out [Gr. *katergazesthe*] your own salvation with fear and trembling" (Phil. 2:12) — this is the one side of the coin. "[F]or it is God who works [*energōn*] in you, both to will [Gr. *thelein*] and to work [Gr. *energein*] for his good pleasure" (v. 13) — this is the other side. Notice how the Greek root *erg-* is used here both for God and for people: the person must "work out," but it is God who "works" the "working" in him. Yet, it is not a genuine syn-*erg*-y because the strongest emphasis is clearly on God, as the "for" indicates: a person *can* "work out" his salvation *for* it is God who "works" this "working" in him. And because it is all God's work, the believer can "work out" his salvation only "with fear and trembling" with regard to himself.[32]

However, this does not diminish the force of the imperative: "[W]ork out your own salvation." This is not only "[W]ork with fear and trembling to discover what it really means to be saved" (CEV), but also: "Keep on working . . . to complete your salvation" (GNT).[33] (Salvation is viewed here as a matter that will be completed in the future only; cf. Matt. 10:22; Acts 15:11; Rom. 5:9–10; 13:11; 1 Cor. 3:15; 5:5; 15:2; Phil. 1:19, 28; 2 Tim. 2:10; 3:15; Heb. 7:25; 9:28; 1 Pet. 1:5,9; 2:2; 4:18.) Live as if your ultimate salvation depends one hundred percent on your own efforts; but realize at the same time that it depends one hundred percent on God's power. Reformed theologian Hendrik Matter says of it, believers

---

32. Müller (1984, 92).
33. Matter (1965, 61); elsewhere in the New Testament, *katergazomai* means "to bring about," "to raise," "to accomplish," "to prepare," "to carry out."

must bring it about entirely. A superhuman task. But *if* they give themselves obediently to this task, they will experience that their work is the work of Another. If, in this "great seriousness" [i.e., with fear and trembling], they strive to enter [Luke 13:24], as if everything still depended on them, they will discover, to their consolation, that everything depends on God: . . . .[34]

It is understandable that Paul Jewett speaks here of a "kerygmatic universality" and a "didactic particularity."[35] In our preaching (Gr. *kerygma*) we necessarily act "universalistically," which is not intended figuratively, since salvation really is intended for all people. However, in our doctrine (Gr. *didachē*) we preserve the particularism of election: not all people have been elected. Seen from the viewpoint of preaching, salvation is for all people; seen from the viewpoint of election, salvation is for some people. Preaching is *a priori*: it precedes the human decision (conversion). But the doctrine of election is *a posteriori*: it follows upon conversion in the sense that we may testify to all who are converted that they have been elected from eternity.[36]

13.9 Again: Structure and Direction
13.9.1 The Image of God

In §4.1, we discussed the distinction between structure and direction,[37] and claimed that sin did not affect the creational structures as such. Sin cannot alter God's law, and structures are basically structural *laws* that things, plants, animals, and people must obey. God's law is his will for creation; neither Satan, nor sinful people can affect this will. But sin did affect the direction, that is, human functioning *under* this law, in a sinful, apostate, idolatrous directedness away from God. I am returning to this distinction, in order to emphasize again that, also after the Fall, people have retained their responsibility

---

34. Ibid., 62.
35. Jewett (1985, 129–31).
36. Demarest (1997, 142).
37. See Ouweneel (EDR 3, §14.2; and most volumes in the present series).

and freedom.

Reformed philosopher Herman Dooyeweerd has strongly emphasized the radicality of the Fall, and argued: "[A]part from the law, which commands the good, there could be no sin."[38] Sin parasitizes on the law, that is, it presupposes the law because it involves disobedience to, and rebellion against, the law. But it cannot affect the law as such; if it could, Satan and sin would be more powerful than God himself. At the Fall, the structural laws were retained. Apples are still apples, lions are still lions, people are still people. Therefore, we say that what has been affected is not the *structure* of our reason (our intelligence) but the *function* of our reason. After the Fall, we are still moderately or very intelligent; but fallen people abuse their intellect in rebellion against God.

The same is true for the will: after the Fall, we can still make decisions of the will, for in the creaturely-structural sense our will has not been affected. What has been affected is the *direction* of our will: it is sinful, apostate, idolatrous, and directed away from God. Fallen people are rebels.[39] With respect to their *ontic structure*, people are just as much divine image-bearers as before the Fall. With respect to the *direction* of their hearts, these reflections of God are terribly and unrecognizably distorted. The heart has been corrupted by sin (e.g., Jer. 17:9; Matt. 15:19; Rom. 1:21, 24; Eph. 4:18). Out of this heart spring the "issues of life" (Prov. 4:23 NKJV), including all that goes on in our intellect, our will, our feelings. If the heart (the root, the source) is corrupt, then so is everything that flows from it.

It is remarkable that Philip Hughes connected this image of God with the responsibility that people have retained after the Fall.[40] He argued that people cannot escape their own nature; they cannot blot out the divine image with which their being is stamped. In spite of the unbeliever's self-orientation

---

38. Dooyeweerd (1963, 36).
39. See Ouweneel (EDR 3, §13.1.5).
40. Hughes (1989, 168).

and hardness of heart, in spite of his determination to suppress the truth about God and thus about himself, his very rebellion and desire to escape this truth about his divinely given creatureliness indicates that he knows the truth (cf. Rom. 1:18).

13.9.2 Greatness and Wretchedness

The intellect and the will of fallen people are radically directed away from God, and only God's Spirit can alter this direction. But this does not change the fact that this same Spirit appeals to this same intellect and will, as well as to the responsibility that people possess because of the *greatness* of this intellect and will. This greatness also comes to light in the fact that fallen people still have functioning consciences, to which an appeal can be made (cf. Rom. 2:15; 9:1). Those who view people as completely passive in receiving God's grace ignore the image of God in fallen people, ignore the greatness of their intellects, their wills, their consciences, their responsibilities. To be sure, human thinking and willing are *radically* oriented away from God (*direction*); but a person is still able to do excellent thinking, willing, feeling, and still has a functioning conscience (*structure*).

Therefore, the Holy Spirit appeals to this thinking. "'Come now, let us reason [or, dispute; ERV, etc.: discuss; LEB, etc.: argue] together,' says the LORD: 'though your sins are like scarlet, they shall be as white as snow; though they are red like crimson, they shall become like wool'" (Isa. 1:18). God calls upon transgressors: "Remember!" (Deut. 9:7; Isa. 44:21), "Consider!" (Hag. 1:5, 7; 2:15, 18); also "See!" (in the sense of "remember, consider"; Exod. 16:29). Think, people, consider where you came from, where and what you are, and where you are heading; come to yourself.

Quite important here is Romans 1: fallen people "who by their unrighteousness suppress [KJV, etc.: hold] the truth. For what can be known about God is plain to them, because God has shown it to them" (vv. 18–19). Yes, fallen people know

God, even though "they did not honor him as God or give thanks to him, but they became futile in their thinking, and their foolish hearts were darkened" (v. 21). Structurally, they remain the image of God; as a result, they are not only able to think and to know in general, but they *know the truth* and they *know God*. As to their anthropological structure, this is their *greatness* — but as to their heart's orientation, it is their *wretchedness* that they suppress this truth in unrighteousness.

This greatness as well as this wretchedness have been superbly underscored by the French Catholic philosopher Blaise Pascal (d. 1662) in his famous *Pensées*; he spoke of *grandeur* ("grandness") and *misère* ("misery"), respectively.[41]

* "The greatness of man is great in that he knows himself to be miserable. A tree does not know itself to be miserable. It is then being miserable to know oneself to be miserable; but it is also being great to know that one is miserable. All these same miseries prove man's greatness. They are the miseries of a great lord, of a deposed king" (nos. 397–398).

* "The greatness of man is so evident, that it is even proved by his wretchedness. For what in animals is nature we call in man wretchedness; by which we recognize that, his nature being now like that of animals, he has fallen from a better nature which once was his" (no. 409).

* "Wretchedness being deduced from greatness, and greatness from wretchedness, some have inferred man's wretchedness all the more because they have taken his greatness as a proof of it, and others have inferred his greatness with all the more force, because they have inferred it from his very wretchedness. All that the one party has been able to say in proof of his greatness has only served as an argument of his wretchedness to the others, because the greater our fall, the more wretched we are, and *vice versa*" (no. 416).

* "The greatness and the wretchedness of man are so evident that the true religion must necessarily teach us both that

---

41. Pascal (1958, esp. nos. 397–98, 409, 416, 430).

there is in man some great source of greatness, and a great source of wretchedness. It must then give us a reason for these astonishing contradictions" (no. 430).

As to structure, the intellect of people is great; it may even be superb. As to direction, it is wretched: their "foolish hearts are darkened." Because of the latter, they depend entirely on God's grace; because of the former, they are fully responsible for their behavior, attitude, and knowledge. Therefore, Emil Brunner could write: "Even as a sinner man can only be understood in the light of the original Image of God, namely, as one who is living in opposition to it."[42]

13.9.3 The Role of the Human Will

According to the New Testament, the human will plays a major role in conversion; in the light of what was just said this should be fully understandable. As to structure, the will in fallen people is free; they are still fully able to make thousands of free choices in their lives. As to direction, their will is *not* free: "[W]e all conversed in time past, in the desires of our flesh, fulfilling the *will* of the flesh and of our thoughts, and were by nature children of wrath, even as the rest" (Eph. 2:2 DRA).

By the way, when we speak here structurally with respect to free will, this is not the way Arminius meant it. He wrongly based the idea that in their conversion people would exercise free will upon the view that Romans 7:7-26 is speaking about the unregenerate person.[43] This cannot be correct: no unregenerate person "hates" sin (cf. v. 15), no unregenerate person can distinguish between his self and indwelling sin (v. 17, "now it is no longer I [i.e., the new self] who do it, but sin that dwells within me"; cf. v. 20), and no unregenerate person can truly say that he has the desire to do what is right (v. 18), at least not according to God's standards. The will being discussed in Romans 7:7-26 is the *renewed* will of the

---

42. Brunner (1937, 105).
43. See Verboom (2005, 24–27).

regenerate person.

The role of the *structurally* free will of the natural person cannot be dismissed by a one-sided emphasis on God's sovereign grace. Think again of Jesus' touching words: *I* wanted, but you did not want (Matt. 23:37; Luke 13:34), and this other statement: "If anyone's *will* is to do God's will, he will know whether the teaching is from God or whether I am speaking on my own authority" (John 7:17). In other words, if this person does *not* want, he will not know. The one receives, the other does not, depending on whether they *want* to receive or not. "Come, whoever is thirsty; accept the water of life as a gift, whoever *wants* it" (Rev. 22:17 GNT). And if this person does not want, then let him not do it. God does not force anyone. Apparently, he belongs to those who "reject the purpose of God for themselves" (Luke 7:30).

In the Bible, some things become reality only if a person accepts them, and not (only) because God has decreed so. Thus, Jesus said of John the Baptist: "[I]f you are willing to accept it, he is Elijah who is to come" (Matt. 11:14), with the implication: if you are not *willing to accept* it, then he is not Elijah (cf. John's outright denial in John 1:21, "[T]hey asked him, 'What then? Are you Elijah?' He said, 'I am not.' 'Are you the Prophet?' And he answered, 'No'"). In other words, if the people had wanted it, John would have been the fulfillment of Malachi 4:5–6. But they did *not* want it, so John was not the (definitive) fulfillment of this prophecy; Malachi's word still stands (cf. Rev. 11:3–12).

Sometimes, even the verb "to accept" (namely, the gospel) used in gospel preaching seems to be suspect in certain hyper-Calvinist circles. It's no use pointing to John 1:11–12 ("his own people did not accept [Gr. *parelabon*, Lat. *receperunt*] him. But some people did accept [Gr. *elabon*, Lat. *acceperunt*][44] him. They believed in him, and he gave them the right to become children of God," ERV, etc.), or to 1 Thessalonians 1:6 ("you

---

44. On the possible (but not likely) difference in meaning between *parelabon* (v. 11) and *elabon* (v. 12), see Morris (1971, 97n70).

accepted [Gr. *dexamenoi*, Lat. *excipientes*] the word," DARBY, MOUNCE, etc.; cf. 2:13; 2 Thess. 2:10). I have heard some hyper-Calvinists argue that we should not translate the Greek verb *lambanō* as "to accept" (which sounds too active) but as "to receive" (which sounds more passive). But the KJV often rendered the Greek verb *lambanō* in a very active way, namely, as "to take" (Matt. 13:31, 33; 25:1, 3; 26:26; 27:30; John 12:3; Acts 9:25; 16:3; 27:35; Rev. 5:8; etc.). The gospel freely offers you salvation: *take it* in faith, for it is yours! There is nothing Arminian in such a rendering—unless the Bible itself is Arminian. Evangelical Christians, who try to take human responsibility seriously, are sometimes offended when they are labeled as Arminians. This is a label they themselves do not accept, one that is unfair.

13.9.4 Contemporary Arminianism

Today, the situation is far more complicated because many Arminians differ widely from their seventeenth-century spiritual ancestors. In addition to "Arminians of the heart" (evangelical, pietistic), there are "Arminians of the head" (deists, liberals). Jan Gerrit Woelderink said of the latter movement that later, Remonstrantism

> was rampant in a different form. It no longer spoke about an election based upon a foreseen faith, but . . . it gave back to people their dignity, especially by overestimating their rational capacities. Here, Remonstrantism found a point of contact with Contra-Remonstrantism, and could help prepare the church for the acceptance of rationalism and the so-called Enlightenment, and also laid the foundation for the Neo-Protestantism of the nineteenth century.[45]

As far as the former movement is concerned, these people wish to take seriously the biblical speaking of God's urgent appeal to humanity to accept his offer, and his sadness about those who do not accept it.

---

45. Woelderink (1951, 26–27).

According to hyper-Calvinists, people supposedly *cannot* accept anything; it must be given to them by God. Those who believe they can accept (that is, illegitimately take) Jesus for themselves supposedly run the risk of going to hell with a "stolen" Jesus and some "imaginary salvation" (cf. §14.8.1). Apparently, such people overlook the New Testament passages that speak of "receiving" or "accepting" the gospel in faith (e.g., Matt. 10:40; John 3:33; 13:20; 17:8), or they twist such verses to fit them into their paradigm.

Let me add two notes for the sake of completeness. First, of course, there is certainly a wrong "receiving" or "accepting." The parable of the sower says: "[T]hese are the ones sown on rocky ground: the ones who, when they hear the word, immediately receive [Gr. *lambanousin*, Lat. *accipiunt*] it with joy. And they have no root in themselves, but endure for a while; then, when tribulation or persecution arises on account of the word, immediately they fall away" (Mark 4:16–17). But this is no reason to suspect all manner of "receiving."

Second, hyper-Calvinists like to point to John 3:27, "A person cannot receive [Gr. *lambanein*, Lat. *accipere*] even one thing unless it is given him from heaven." Now, to begin with, it is doubtful that this verse is speaking about people who, by faith, can receive salvation only as a gift of God. Rather, the text is speaking about John the Baptist and Jesus himself, who preached only what God had entrusted to them.[46] However, as a general application the words do not yield any problem in the light of everything we have discussed. On the one hand, there is the *act* of the person: he accepts the gospel in faith. On the other hand, there is the *power* of God: no person can accept the gospel, or come to faith, other than by God's working. Never may these two sides be played off against each other, nor may the one be overemphasized at the expense of the other. This has simply been the error of (hyper-)Calvinism on the one hand, and Arminianism on the other.

---

46. Ibid., 39–40.

A really harmonious approach, as Viatorism endeavors to provide, means that not only God's sovereign grace but also human responsibility are each given full consideration. As a result, the person who does not accept the gospel is fully culpable: "The one who rejects me and does not receive [Gr. *lambanôn*, Lat. *accipit*] my words has a judge; the word that I have spoken will judge him on the last day" (John 12:48). And: "*[Y]ou were not willing!* Behold, your house is forsaken. And I tell you, you will not see me until you say, 'Blessed is he who comes in the name of the Lord!'" (Luke 13:34–35).

Chapter 14
Predestination: Remaining Topics

> *Oh, the depth of the riches and wisdom and knowledge of God!*
> *How unsearchable are his judgments and how inscrutable his ways!*
> *"For who has known the mind of the Lord, or who has been his counselor?"*
> *"Or who has given a gift to him that he might be repaid?"*
> *For from him and through him and to him are all things.*
> *To him be glory forever. Amen.*
> Romans 11:33–36

Summary: *One of the most contested features of the doctrine of election, from Augustine to Karl Barth, has always been the supposed eternal decree of reprobation. The tension surrounding this feature is present within the Canons of Dordt. Bible passages thought to support this notion are investigated, especially Romans 9. The discussion has been further complicated by the conflict between supra- and infralapsarians. This conflict did not arise from an analysis of Scripture but from scholastic conclusivism. Today, many Protestant theologians seek to rise above the battle between Arminianism, supra- and infralapsarian Calvinism, moderate and hyper-Calvinism; some of these theologians call themselves "Calminians," but* *often remain caught in the same type of logic that underlies the entire conflict. The doctrine of election was supposed to be a comfort, not a battlefield.*

14.1 An Eternal Decree of Reprobation?
14.1.1 Contradictory Statements

IN THE PREVIOUS CHAPTERS, we have discussed the (supposed) eternal decree of reprobation several times. We must now delve into it a little further in order to arrive at a more balanced evaluation of the entire subject of predestination.

Henry Kersten described the (supposed) eternal decree of reprobation as "the decree, whereby God from eternity, in His sovereign good pleasure, foreordained in which rational creatures He shall glorify Himself by His avenging justice to their eternal punishment in hell."[1] Louis Berkhof distinguished two elements in the decree of reprobation: (a) *preterition*: the decree to (passively) "pass some men by," wherewith God leaves them in their misery, and (b) *precondemnation*: the decree to (actively) bring eternal condemnation on "those who are passed by for their sins."[2] Often, only the passive element is mentioned, as in the Belgic Confession (Art. 16) and the Canons of Dordt (I.6).

Considering such apodictic formulations, one would not think that the doctrine of reprobation, at least according to Reformed theologian Klaas Dijk, is the "most difficult part" of the doctrine of election.[3] The matter was already hotly debated in the conflict between Augustine and Pelagius. At the beginning of the present century, the subject became topical again during the formation of the Protestant Church in the Netherlands, in which the Dutch Reformed Church, the (Kuyperian) Reformed Churches, and the Dutch Lutherans were united (2004). This new church embraced both the Canons of Dordt and the Leuenberg Agreement (adopted in

---
1. Kersten (1980, 1:136).
2. Berkhof (1996, 116); cf. Kersten (1980, 1:137).
3. Dijk (1924, 368).

1973 by major European Lutheran and Reformed churches) as guidelines for faith, in spite of the evident contradictions between the two documents (see §12.4.1). Thus, the former document claims an eternal divine decree of reprobation, as we have seen, whereas the latter says: "Scripture's testimony to Christ forbids us to suppose that there is an eternal decree of God for the definite condemnation of certain persons or a certain people."[4]

The Protestant Church in the Netherlands can live with this contradiction because its creeds and confessions explicitly function more as guidelines than as binding statements of faith. Reformed theologian Willem Verboom described this contradiction, and how it worked out in the church order of the Protestant Church, which accepts both the Canons of Dordt and the Leuenberg Agreement. Verboom himself is unhappy with this situation, and understandably so. Even if the creeds are only guidelines, it is confusing to have contradictory guidelines.

14.1.2 Tension in the Canons of Dordt

There is also a clear tension within the Canons themselves, as many have pointed out. On the one hand, the Canons speak unmistakably of an eternal decree of reprobation; on the other hand, they very clearly suggest that people are rejected because of their own foreseen guilt (see §12.6). In other words, is the reprobation of the wicked rooted ultimately (a) in an eternal decree that was entirely God's own sovereign choice, or (b) in an eternal decree that was based upon the foreseen guilt of the wicked, or (c) (which the Canons do not mention) in a *temporal* decree, based upon the guilt of the wicked once it became manifested? In the terminology of Viatorism: Is reprobation a matter of God's (eternal) *counsel*, or of God's *ways* (within time)?

Of course, the authors of the Canons were aware of this tension between the first two options, (a) and (b). They

---

4. http://www.ctsfw.net/media/pdfs/drickamertheleuenbergconcord.pdf.

quietly let this paradox stand, apparently because they were convinced that this tension exists within the biblical testimony itself. It seems conceivable to me that they sincerely believed that *both* things might be true at the same time: reprobation is both a matter of God's eternal, sovereign decree and a matter of foreseen guilt and unbelief.

Two notes seem to be appropriate here. First, is it really true that the tension exists within the Bible itself? Where in the Bible do we find an eternal decree of reprobation? And where in the Bible do we find that reprobation is based upon *foreseen* sin, instead of being based on *manifested* sin? In other words, does reprobation precede human rebellion, or does it follow upon it?

Second, if reprobation is both a matter of God's eternal, sovereign decree and of foreseen guilt and unbelief, one can only deeply regret that the Dordt divines did not believe the same with respect to election, namely, that it is both a matter of God's eternal, sovereign decree and a matter of foreseen faith. In fact, they would have come very close to Arminius! It might even have led to a reconciliation of the two parties. In this case, church history would have followed a very different course. This does not mean that I am suggesting a symmetry between election and reprobation. My argument is simply this: with regard to election, Scripture speaks of an eternal divine decree, but with regard to reprobation it does not speak of an eternal divine decree. This implies that election is based upon both God's eternal, sovereign decree as well as upon foreseen faith—but the decree of reprobation occurs *within* time, and is based exclusively upon the *manifested* guilt and unbelief of the wicked.

14.1.3 Eternal Reprobation in the Bible?

Consider Herman Bavinck's assertion: "It is true that Scripture seldom speaks of reprobation as an eternal decree."[5] This is misleading, for Scripture *nowhere* speaks of reprobation as an

---

5. Bavinck (*RD* 2:393).

eternal decree, as we will see. As Reformed theologian Klaas Dijk rightly said, the Bible speaks of reprobation only "as an act of God in time, and an entering of God into our history."[6]

Reformed dogmatician Ben Wentsel claimed that the reprobation doctrine has a certain right to exist because it manifests "that God is omnipotent and sovereign, and that history does not consist of a chain of fatalities or coincidences."[7] My response: this argument is a *non sequitur* (B does not at all follow from A). Presumably, Wentsel meant to say that the only alternative to "a chain of fatalities and hazards" is divine decrees, and if divine, then they are necessarily eternal (which is incorrect), and if election was eternal, then reprobation is too. A fine example of conclusivism (i.e., an accumulation of logical conclusions).

Willem Verboom wrote, "It is very questionable whether the Scriptures speak that directly of an eternal decree of God to reprobate certain people."[8] My response: this is not questionable at all; the Scriptures simply do not teach any eternal decree of reprobation, neither directly nor indirectly.

Klaas Dijk cautioned readers about "how dangerous it is to condemn or to deny the conclusion drawn from the revelation of God's *acts* to his *decrees*."[9] My response: it seems to me that we could argue the opposite with more force. Apparently, Dijk thinks that God's acts must always proceed from divine decrees, and that these decrees are necessarily eternal decrees. This is a striking example of failing to distinguish between God's *counsel* (eternal or temporal, or both) and God's *ways* (which are always within time). In other words, it is *not* true at all that every act of God—and by the way, every human act as well—*must* proceed from an eternal divine decree. On the contrary, Scripture testifies very differently, as we have seen.

---

6. Dijk (1952, 129).
7. Wentsel (1982, 180).
8. Verboom (2005, 222).
9. Dijk (1952, 130).

In the entire election debate this is perhaps one of the most questionable axioms: all God's acts must proceed from eternal decrees. Thus, if God reprobates the wicked, there must be some underlying eternal decree. My response is: God's *counsel* consists of eternal decrees, but his *ways* do not proceed from an eternal decree; they involve many decisions that God apparently has taken within time and history, depending on the actions and words of people.

In principle, I agree with Duffield and Van Cleave, who argued that a decree of reprobation is entirely superfluous, "since all people are sinners, and as such are already on the way to eternal loss."[10] Of course, this argument has relevance only for infralapsarians. Supralapsarians believe that reprobation was eternally decreed independently of the Fall and of human guilt. For them, God's eternal decree did contain the decision that people would fall, but this decision was preceded by the decrees of election and reprobation.

14.2 Relevant Bible Passages
14.2.1 The Wicked Made for the Day of Evil

What are the Bible verses that supposedly teach an eternal decree of reprobation? They are few in number, and in my view, none of them teaches that. Scripture never speaks of being predestined by God for hell, and this from eternity. On the contrary, the "eternal fire" was originally "prepared for the devil and his angels" (Matt. 25:41) from the foundation of the world[11] (not before the foundation of the world; it is fair to presume that hell was prepared for the devil after his fall).

One may ask two questions here. First, if there is indeed such a thing as an eternal decree of reprobation, why does the text not say that the "eternal fire" was "prepared," not only for the devil and his angels, but also for "the wicked"? Second, how does one explain the lack of symmetry between verses 34 and 41? That is, why does verse 41 not speak of "you

---
10. Duffield and Van Cleave (1987, 208).
11. Cf. Woelderink (1951, 72).

cursed from [or even: before] the foundation of the world"?[12]

People often refer to Proverbs 16:4 (NASB), "The LORD has made everything for its own purpose, even the wicked for the day of evil." There are a number of issues to be discussed here. First, we have to assume that the "day of evil" refers to the day of eternal condemnation, which is not self-evident (cf. CEB, "an evil day"; CJB, "day of disaster"; ESV, etc., "day of trouble").

Second, the text does not speak of a judgment executed by God; Matthew Henry's first explanation of the verse is: "God makes use of the wicked to execute righteous vengeance on each other; and he will be glorified by their destruction at last."[13] That is, the text may be referring to what occurs within time, and not at all to what will happen in eternity future.

Third, people assume that, if the Lord makes something for a purpose, this must have been from eternity. Within the given context, it is far more likely that God destines the wicked for doom *after* they have manifested themselves in their wickedness and in their unwillingness to repent.[14] Reformed theologian Willem Gispen said, without even referring to the current Calvinist explanation: "We must not forget that the goal of this proverb is to move the wicked to repentance through fear of the coming judgment."[15] In other words, the verse does not refer to an unchangeable eternal divine judgment, but is rather an appeal to escape from this judgment.

It is in this sense that we apparently must read 1 Samuel 2:25, where it is said that the sons of Eli "would not listen to the voice of their father, for it was the will of the LORD to put them to death." This verse does not suggest that the sons did not listen because of some eternal decree of God, but rather the opposite: God had hardened their hearts because of their

---

12. Demarest (1997, 135–36).
13. Henry (n.d., ad loc.).
14. Cf. Boyd (2001, 407).
15. Gispen (1954, 11).

preceding misbehavior.[16] In the Bible, the decision to punish someone for his sins follows these sins; it never precedes them. At best one could say in a very general sense that, since the Fall, every wicked person should know that eventually he will be punished for his continued rebellion.

14.2.2 Rejected Before or After?

If we find the word "destined" in Scripture, as in Proverbs 16:4 ("Everything the LORD has made has its destiny; and the destiny of the wicked is destruction," GNT), it is irresponsible to think immediately of an eternal decree. Thus, 1 Peter 2:8 says that the wicked "stumble because they disobey the word, as they were destined to do." Why would this verse necessarily involve an eternal, individual reprobation of the wicked? The Christ whom God had sent into the world was destined to be "precious" to believers, and a "stone of stumbling" for unbelievers (vv. 6-8). But this is something very different from establishing beforehand who would be counted believers, and who would be counted unbelievers: "Unbelievers have not been destined to be disobedient to the word; but *if* they disobey, *then* they are destined to the outcome that Christ becomes to them a fall to them instead of a rising [cf. Luke 2:34]."[17]

It is the same in other Bible passages. Esau did not reject God's grace *because* he had been rejected from eternity, but he was rejected *after* he himself had rejected God's grace (Heb. 12:16-17). Pharaoh did not harden his heart *because* God had rejected him, but God rejected him *after* Pharaoh himself had hardened his heart several times (see §6.2.1).[18] Saul did not reject God *because* God had rejected him from eternity, but God rejected him *after* Saul had rejected *him*: "Because you have rejected the word of the LORD, he has also rejected you from being king" (1 Sam. 15:23). In no single biblical example

---

16. Boyd (2001, 401).
17. Hervormde Kerk (1962, 33).
18. Pawson (2005, 191).

does the hardening of someone's heart proceed from some preceding divine rejection of such a person, that is, on the basis of God's sovereign decree rather than on the basis of the person's rebellion.[19]

Israel's disobedience was in some way included in the ways of God (cf. Rom. 11:8, 11, 30–32). However, it was each individual Israelite's personal responsibility whether he belonged to the believing (chosen) or the unbelieving (hardened) part of the people (v. 7) — even though it was equally true that the good choice was evidence of God's grace (v. 5).[20] Therefore, the majority of the Israelites were rejected *after* the word had come to them and they had rejected it (Acts 13:46). Also, some Christian heretics ("men of depraved mind") are "rejected in regard to the faith" (2 Tim. 3:8 NASB) — not because they had been destined for this from eternity but because they did not accept the truth. First there is the sin, then the reprobation; it is never the reverse.

In §11.7.2, I pointed to 1 Thessalonians 5:9, "God has not destined us for wrath, but to obtain salvation through our Lord Jesus Christ." This being "destined for" is just as timeless as in Proverbs 16:4. If the text does not explicitly speak of an *eternal* predestination, we are not allowed to read this into the text because our theological paradigm requires this. Paul's words do not necessarily imply that there are other people who *have* been destined for wrath, and even if some were destined for wrath, the text does not teach that these people had been destined for wrath before the foundation of the world. The disturbing and ever recurring problem here is that some people, when they think of God's acts, (a) feel forced to believe that God's acts must always proceed from some counsel of God, (b) never distinguish this divine counsel from God's ways, and (c) always necessarily think of an *eternal* counsel, as if God could never decree anything in time, as part of his ways with the world. Scripture refers to God's eternal *counsel*,

---

19. Demarest (1997, 135–37).
20. Cf. Hart (1979, 57); Blum (1981, 230).

but also to his ways within time and history, which just as well contain many (temporal) decrees and decisions of God.

14.2.3 Destined "Long Ago"

One Bible verse that seems to teach an eternal decree of reprobation is Jude 4, "[C]ertain people have crept in unnoticed who long ago were designated [lit., written about] for this condemnation, ungodly people" (cf. 2 Pet. 2:3, the wicked's "condemnation from long ago is not idle, and their destruction is not asleep"). The Annotators of the Dutch States Translation (1637) explain the word "written": "Namely by God in the register of the reprobate people"[21] — but Scripture does not know such a record (cf. §10.7). Joseph Mayor sees in this a reference to the book of Enoch (see Jude 14–15), which has announced the judgment upon the wicked.[22] Seakle Greijdanus thinks of 2 Peter 2 and 3, which in his view had been written shortly before.[23] Others think of the Old Testament because of the Old Testament examples that follow Jude 4.[24] At any rate, the text does not speak of an eternal reprobation or an eternal record of the reprobate.

Let us be perfectly clear about the fact that, of course, God does destine certain people to eternal destruction: "[T]he Lord knows how to rescue the godly from trials, and to keep the unrighteous under punishment until the day of judgment. . . . These are waterless springs and mists driven by a storm. For them the gloom of utter darkness has been reserved" (2 Pet. 2:9, 17). However, in all relevant cases the texts refer to wicked people who, if they persevere in their wickedness, are destined by God to hell *because of*, and *after*, their manifested wickedness. Never do the texts refer to a *preceding, eternal* decree of reprobation, which would supposedly exist entirely apart from people's own responsibility.

---

21. Cf. Calvin, commentary ad loc.: "eternal counsel of God."
22. Mayor (1979, 256); Blum (1981, 388–89).
23. Greijdanus (1950, 96).
24. Hervormde kerk (1962, 33).

Those who advocate the notion of an eternal decree of reprobation adduce much more evidence.[25] This concerns Bible passages that refer to a "blinding" or "hardening" that God brings over certain people (John 12:39-40; Rom. 1:28; 9:18; 11:7, 25; 2 Cor. 3:14; 2 Thess. 2:10-12), or that tell us that God hides certain things from unbelievers (Matt. 11:25-26; 13:11-13; John 8:47; 10:26; 2 Cor. 3:14-16). We need not discuss all these passages separately because, in his interpretation, the hyper-Calvinist always makes the same basic mistake. He overlooks the fact that none of these verses speaks of an eternal decree of reprobation. Instead, they show how *within time* God brings hardening and blindness upon the wicked who rebelliously persevere in their wickedness, whether apostate pagans (Rom. 1:28), apostate Jews (11:7, 25), or apostate pseudo-Christians (2 Thess. 2:10-12).[26]

This judgment of hardening is a striking example of what Elihu says:

> God speaks in one way, and in two [or: once, yea twice], though man does not perceive it. In a dream, in a vision of the night, when deep sleep falls on men, while they slumber on their beds, then he opens the ears of men and terrifies them with warnings, that he may turn man aside from his deed and conceal pride from a man; he keeps back his soul from the pit, his life from perishing by the sword (Job 33:14-18).

Once or twice, in this way or that way — "The Lord is not slow to fulfill his promise as some count slowness, but is patient toward you, not wishing that any should perish, but that all should reach repentance" (2 Pet. 3:9). However, the number of times is not infinite, nor is the number of ways. If a person continues stubbornly to rebel against God, God may harden his heart, so that he will no longer be able to repent.

---

25. See, e.g., Kersten (1980, 1:139-43).
26. Contra Dijk (1924, 378) and Kersten (1980, 1:123-26, 139-40), both of whom are commenting on Matt. 11:25-26.

14.3 Romans 9 Again
14.3.1 Mistaken Views

Some people believe they can deduce the most important evidence for an eternal decree of reprobation from Romans 9, especially from verse 13, which is a quotation from Malachi 1:3, "Jacob I loved, but Esau I hated."[27] It is astonishing how often this verse is quoted as proof that God *a priori*, from eternity, loved certain people, and hated other people. Thus, for instance, the Annotators of the Dutch States Translation (1637): ". . . God's eternal and undeserved love towards Jacob, and just hatred against Esau. . . ." In my view, these and many other expositors are making four basic mistakes.

First, there is no basis in this verse for equating love with election, and hatred with reprobation.

Second, according to Hebrew idiom, this loving and hating do not have to be taken in an absolute sense, unlike what we read in Deuteronomy 21:15 (KJV), "two wives, one beloved, and another hated." Many translations soften the expression by substituting "unloved" for "hated" (ESV, NASB, etc.), but in fact the sense is even weaker: the husband "loves one wife more than the other" (cf. CEV, ERV, NET). We find something similar in Luke 14:26, "If anyone . . . does not hate his own father and mother . . ., he cannot be my disciple," where "hate them" means "love them less than me." This is clear from the parallel in Matthew 10:37, "Whoever loves father or mother more than me is not worthy of me."[28]

The third mistake occasions my greatest objection to the current abuse of Romans 9:11–13. Verse 11 refers to the election of Jacob instead of Esau as the one to whom the earthly and national promises concerning future Israel were made (cf. v. 12), and this is something fundamentally different from eternal predestination to heavenly blessedness (§10.8.3). Those who apply Romans 9:11–13 to the latter

---
27. So, e.g., extensively, Dijk (1924, chapter 30).
28. Cf. Hervormde Kerk (1962, 32); Hodge (1972, 310); Hughes (1989, 161–62); Demarest (1997, 123).

kind of predestination apparently hold what has been called the *predestinarian* position,[29] whereas I, with others,[30] hold a *redemptive-historical* view of Romans 9. Think of the Israelites, who were chosen like ancestor Jacob, but this only in the redemptive-historical sense because many in this nation died as wicked persons. Therefore, Paul refers to the chosen ones within Israel, as distinct from the hardened ones within this same chosen nation (Rom. 11:7).

14.3.2 Two Nations
Fourth — and this objection is even more fundamental — the words of Romans 9:13 were not spoken about Jacob and Esau beforehand (in spite of the link with v. 12), but only in Malachi 1:3, which is perhaps some 1,400 years after the two brothers had lived. Neither in Malachi 1, nor in Romans 9, is there any basis in the text to think that loving Jacob and hating Esau occurred before their birth, even in eternity. That God loved the one and hated the other were not *a priori* eternal sovereign divine choices, but choices based upon the godly life of Jacob (in spite of all his failures) and the godless life of Esau. In fact, the statement refers to the entire history of the nations born of them: Israel and Edom. The text's perspective is not that Jacob was godly because God loved him, but that God loved him because he was godly.

It is helpful to quote here at some length the well-known Pulpit Commentary:

> But Malachi is not speaking of the predestination of the one brother and the reprobation of the other; he is contrasting the histories of the two peoples represented by them; as Jerome puts it, "In Jacob vos dilexi [i.e., I have loved you (Israelites)], in Esau Idumæos odio habui [i.e., I have hated the Edomites]."

---

29. So Augustine, Calvin (Bavinck, *RD* 2:346); Greijdanus (1933, ad loc.); De Groot (1952, 27); Van Genderen and Velema (2008, 213); Demarest (1997, 129–30); Schreiner in Schreiner and Ware (2000, chapter 4).
30. Woelderink (1951, 45–46); Berkouwer (1960, 211); Ridderbos (1959, 216); Venema (1965, 111–12; 1992, 49); Pannenberg (1991, 3:442–43).

> Both nations sinned; both are punished; but Israel by God's free mercy was forgiven and restored, while Edom was left in the misery which it had brought upon itself by its own iniquity. Thus is proved God's love for the Israelites . . . . That it is of the two nations that the prophet speaks, rather than of the two brothers, is seen by what follows.[31]

Apart from the emphasis on God's sovereignty at the expense of human responsibility, this author has seen clearly that Malachi 1 and Romans 9 do not refer to the eternal election of Jacob and the eternal reprobation of Esau, but to God's dealings in history with Israel and Edom.

Again, Jacob was not godly because God loved him, but God loved him because he was godly. However, perhaps it is wiser to let the two formulations stand in juxtaposition; that is, perhaps both are correct at the same time. Look at Noah, for instance: did he find favor in the eyes of the LORD because he was righteous (Gen. 6:8-9)? Or was Noah righteous because he had found favor in the eyes of the LORD? Or should we accept both truths—which one might call the Arminian and the Calvinist approaches, respectively—without speculating about the "order of salvation" (§13.8.3)?

14.3.3 Pharaoh's Hardening

Romans 9:14-18, where Paul speaks of the Pharaoh at the time of the Exodus, is no proof either that people's eternal destiny is determined by an *a priori* divine choice. There is no question here of an eternal reprobation of Pharaoh by God, but of a hardening of his heart after Pharaoh had first hardened his own heart (Exod. 7:13-14, 22; 8:15, 19, 32; 9:7, 34-35). Only after this, it was God who hardened Pharaoh's heart as a form of judgment (9:12; 10:1, 20, 27; 11:10; 14:4, 18). To be sure, God had announced beforehand that this would happen (4:21; 7:3); apparently he foresaw Pharaoh's self-hardening. But this is something essentially different from the idea that

---

31. Spence-Jones (1909, 337).

God had *decreed*—even decreed from eternity!—that Pharaoh was to be reprobated.

Thus, this hardening of Pharaoh's heart was indeed a matter of God's sovereign will (Rom. 9:18), but it was just as much a matter of the rebellious Pharaoh's own choice and responsibility. Here we touch upon the core of the text. Paul's intention is not at all to say that God *beforehand*—from eternity—"has mercy on whomever he wills" and "hardens whomever he wills" (v. 18; cf. Exod. 33:19). Instead, he is saying that, after people have lost everything through their sins, God is free to nonetheless save some people and leave others in the misery in which they have brought *themselves*.

God's decree does not come first here, but human guilt. All salvation comes from God, and this from eternity, on the basis of God's sovereign grace. All damnation comes from God, too; however, not as decreed from eternity but within time, due to people's own rebellion (cf. vv. 30–32; 10:3; 11:20).[32] All entreaties, warnings, and offers by God confirm that damnation is due to people's own guilt, not to some eternal decree of God. And a refused grace is still grace to be proclaimed to God's honor.[33]

14.3.4 Two Kinds of Vessels

Exactly the same—people must blame themselves for their damnation—is the case in Romans 9:19–21:

> You will say to me then, "Why does he still find fault? For who can resist his will?" But who are you, O man, to answer back to God? Will what is molded say to its molder, "Why have you made me like this?" Has the potter no right over the clay, to make out of the same lump one vessel for honorable use and another for dishonorable use?

In this passage, the verb "to make" does not refer to creation, as if from eternity God has destined one person for glory and

---

32. Boyd (2001, 359–66, 413–14); cf. Woelderink (1951, 53).
33. Grant (1956, 194).

another for corruption, and *then* created them. Rather, it refers to God's sovereign will over people who have *first* made themselves guilty. God "makes" certain sinners to become vessels for his honor after all (through regeneration and salvation), and he leaves others in the dishonor into which they have brought themselves.

This point is of the greatest significance, clearly illuminated in a comparison with Jeremiah 18, to which Romans 9:21 apparently alludes.[34] See especially verse 4: "[T]he vessel he [i.e., the potter] was making of clay was spoiled in the potter's hand, and he reworked it into another vessel, as it seemed good to the potter to do." This is what had happened to Israel. Sometimes a nation is "spoiled," that is, it has plunged deeply into sin and made itself ripe for judgment. However, if it repents, God will "rework" the clay, and make a new vessel out of that same clay. By the grace of God, a renewed nation is born. This is what God did to Israel through and after the Babylonian exile. In no way can the parable of the potter be (ab)used to support the doctrine of eternal reprobation. The reason is simple: potters do not make pots with the intention of destroying them.[35]

The general conclusion of Herman Ridderbos with regard to Romans 9(–11) is very important:

> The purport of Paul's argument is not to show that all that God does in history has been foreordained from eternity and therefore, so far as his mercy as well as his hardening is concerned, has an irresistible and inevitable issue. Rather, it is his intention to point out in the omnipotence of God's activity the real intention of his purpose. Everything is made subservient to the electing character of God's grace, not based on human merit or strength, and of the calling and formation of his people. ... [O]ne may not identify the omnipotence and sovereignty of God's grace thus upheld on the one hand and of his reprobation

---

34. Boyd (2000, 44, 75–77); Pinnock (2001, 55); Pawson (2005, 190–91).
35. Cranfield (1975, 2:492).

and hardening on the other with irrevocable 'eternal' decrees, in which God would once and forever have predestined the salvation or ruin of man: for God has not only reprobated and hardened Israel in order to display his mercy to the gentiles, but no less to provoke Israel itself to repentance and 'jealousy' (Rom. 11:11-24).[36]

14.4 Historical Aspects of the Reprobation Doctrine
14.4.1 Again John Calvin

In order to do justice to the Augustinian-Calvinist notion of a decree of reprobation, we must carefully notice the distinction between this decree and the decree of election. As Harry Buis has formulated it, God chooses some for salvation, and by not choosing the others for salvation he inescapably chooses to let them go the way they wish to go, which leads to their destruction.[37]

Escaping the force of such an argument is difficult. This is not an endorsement of an active, eternal *decree* to *predestine* the non-elect to eternal destruction, but simply to leave them where their own sins have taken them. This, of course, is a divine decree, but not necessarily an *eternal* decree. In fact, Calvinists and Arminians agree here: the wicked are destined for destruction because of their own guilt. They differ about two things: first, whether this destining was from eternity (yes, say Calvinists; no, say Arminians). Second, they differ about why some people are *saved* at all. The former reply: because God in his mercy predestined them for this. The latter reply: because these people, in contrast with the others, repented and turned to God in faith. Viatorism replies: both answers are perfectly correct, without logically pitting one against the other.

It is fascinating to see that, already with Calvin, we get the impression that, in his view, reprobation is based on foreseen

---

36. Ridderbos (1975, 345-46).
37. Buis (1958, 133).

sin and unbelief.[38] He argued that by nature we are hateful toward God, not on the basis of some cruel decree but because of our own sins:

> If all are drawn from a corrupt mass, no wonder they are subject to condemnation! Let them not accuse God of injustice if they are destined by his eternal judgment to death, to which they feel—whether they will or not—that they are led *by their own nature* of itself. How perverse is their disposition to protest is apparent from the fact that they deliberately suppress the cause of condemnation, which they are compelled to recognize *in themselves*, in order to free themselves by blaming God (ital. added).

He went on to add: "Besides, their perdition depends upon the predestination of God in such a way that the cause and occasion of it are found in themselves."[39]

At other places, however, Calvin does seek the cause of reprobation again exclusively in God's sovereign counsel.[40] The tension in his thinking remains. In some way, he sees eternal reprobation as part of God's sovereign counsel, but this cannot be separated from the cause of reprobation found in humanity itself: sin and unbelief. Calvin may never be accused of defending an eternal decree of reprobation apart from people's guilt, for which they alone are responsible. But neither may he be charged with teaching that the divine and the human *cause* (of the wicked's eternal destruction) are correlative factors, placed in juxtaposition.[41] Calvin is not an "indecretalist," that is, someone who places human responsibility over against, or views it as equivalent with, God's sovereign acting. But neither is he a decretalist, as if he saw sin as a consequence of reprobation in the same way that holiness is

---

38. Calvin, *Institutes* 3.23.3.
39. Ibid., 3.23.8.
40. On this tension see extensively, Jacobs (1937).
41. Berkouwer (1960, 188–89).

a consequence of election.[42]

14.4.2 John Wesley and Karl Barth

With respect to predestination, the great opponent of Calvinism was Arminianism. In the Netherlands, we think of theologians such as Jacob Arminius, Johannes Uytenbogaert, and Simon Episcopius. Internationally, other names draw our attention. As we observe the wide influence of Arminianism within the Evangelical world, the first name that comes up is that of John Wesley (d. 1791) within Methodism; for years, he edited the magazine *The Arminian*. Therefore, during the great revivals in the eighteenth century, the Calvinist George Whitefield (d. 1770) and the Arminian John Wesley had to part ways because of their different views of predestination. Unfortunately, this was a repetition of what had happened at the Synod of Dordt, where the Arminians had been sent away by chairman Johannes Bogerman.

Nevertheless, for half a century now, Calvinist and Arminian Evangelicals in the Anglo-Saxon world have cooperated reasonably well, as is true in the Netherlands as well. To be sure, in recent decades some new troubles have arisen, especially with the rise of Open Theism. Yet, it is promising that some Arminians and Calvinists are prepared to face their own one-sidednesses, and to learn from each other. In my view, both groups would benefit from searching for a middle path like Viatorism; this route would bring them above the conflict by maintaining (a) faith in the individual, eternal, sovereign election of believers, as well as (b) the role of human responsibility (if faith is a matter of both God's sovereign grace and of human freedom, then this is also the case with election), and by clarifying (c) the notion of an "eternal decree of reprobation" (that is, the reprobation of the wicked is a biblical fact but then as an aspect of God's ways within time, not of his eternal counsel), and especially (d) the fundamental distinction between the counsel and the ways of God.

---

42. Jacobs (1937, 156).

I do not believe that Karl Barth found for us the "more excellent way," even though many Reformed theologians were enamored of him.[43] Barth was innovative in calling Jesus both the electing God and the one elected Man, as well as the only real Reprobate. But none of these three identifications is entirely correct; we cannot biblically speak of election in this way. First, it is God who elects — whether we think here of the Triune God or of God the Father makes little difference — namely, *in the Man Christ* (§11.6.1).

Second, Christ is indeed the Chosen One, but individual believers are chosen ones just the same, though chosen in him. We must observe that Christ's election is of the same nature as believers' election, however. He was not chosen to be holy and blameless (Eph. 1:4), but chosen to be the instrument through which people could become holy and blameless: "Christ became a servant . . . in order that the Gentiles might glorify God for his mercy" (Rom. 15:8-9).

Third, Christ is never called the Reprobate; it is an exaggeration to equate his being (temporarily) *forsaken* by God at the cross with an (everlasting) *reprobation*. And even if one says that Jesus at the cross was reprobated on behalf of the elect, this does not change the fact that the lost are reprobate, that is, destined for eternal destruction. As to this latter point: Barth's formulation ultimately comes to mean there can be no reprobation at all. Thus, Barth's predestination doctrine debouches in universalism: in the end, all people will share in God's election. In fact, this means that there is no e-lection (Gr. *ek-logē*, Lat. *e-lectio*, Eng. *choosing from/out of*) at all. If all members are chosen from a certain group, the term "choosing" loses its meaning.

Thus, in Barth's thinking, not much remains of the biblical doctrine of election, nor of human responsibility ("no salva-

---

43. Barth (1936, II/2:3); see Graafland (1987, chapters 7, 9), and the summaries in Berkhof (1996, 111); Woelderink (1951, chapter 6); Wentsel (1982, 192-95); Erickson (1998, 934-36); Heyns (1988, 93-96); Van Genderen and Velema (2008, 222-24); Pannenberg (1991, 3:449); McGrath (2016, 408-409).

tion without repentance and faith"), nor of eternal judgment.

14.5 Two Types of Decrees
14.5.1 Once More: The Canons of Dordt

With respect to the doctrine of election, Evangelicals have contended especially against decretalism or hyper-Calvinism. In this battle, people often failed to realize that the Canons of Dordt took a much more "Evangelical" position than did later hyper-Calvinists. The latter strongly appealed to the Canons because they sought to underscore their link with traditional Reformed thinking. However, this should not obscure the undeniable *gap* between the Canons and hyper-Calvinism. If Evangelicals could keep Arminianism at arms' length and would not identify the Canons with hyper-Calvinism, they could comfortably endorse most of what the Canons teach.

In this context, notice the masterful Conclusion of the Canons, which *denies* that God is the author (cause) of sin and unbelief. It *denies* that election ". . . renders men carnally secure, since they are persuaded by it that nothing can hinder the salvation of the elect, let them live as they please; and, therefore, that they may safely perpetrate every species of the most atrocious crimes; . . . ." It *denies* that ". . . if the reprobate should even perform truly all the works of the saints, their obedience would not in the least contribute to their salvation; . . . ." It *denies* ". . . that the same doctrine teaches that God, by a mere arbitrary act of his will, without the least respect or view to any sin, has predestinated the greatest part of the world to eternal damnation, and has created them for this very purpose; . . . ." It *denies* ". . . that in the same manner in which the election is the fountain and cause of faith and good works, reprobation is the cause of unbelief and impiety; . . . ."[44]

The Canons of Dordt display great wisdom, not only in the Conclusion but throughout, by dealing prudently with the decree of reprobation. Reprobation is not placed on one line with election. To state it even more strongly, whereas the

---
44. Dennison (*RCET* 4:151–52).

Canons emphasize that election is *not* based upon foreseen faith, one senses that in connection with reprobation foreseen sin and foreseen unbelief *are* taken into consideration. To suggest that reprobation is *based upon* foreseen sin and unbelief would be too strong: "God rejects the person who rejects him, without thereby becoming dependent on the negative decision of the person."[45] Yet, the two are linked in some way: reprobation cannot be viewed apart from foreseen sin and unbelief. As Gerrit Berkouwer said, ". . . Scripture repeatedly speaks of God's rejection as a divine *answer* in history, as a reaction to man's sin and disobedience, not as its *cause*."[46]

Several Bible passages indicate the order of rejection: "Because you [i.e., king Saul] have rejected the word of the Lord, he has also rejected you from being king" (1 Sam. 15:23; cf. v. 26). "Judah did not keep the commandments of the Lord their God, but walked in the customs that Israel had introduced. And the Lord rejected all the descendants of Israel and afflicted them" (2 Kings 17:19-20). "[B]ecause of your hard and impenitent heart you are storing up wrath for yourself on the day of wrath when God's righteous judgment will be revealed" (Rom. 2:5).[47] First, people reject God, then God rejects them; it is never the other way round.

We arrive here at an important (Viatorist) conclusion, which fits within the entire framework of the present book: the election of believers belongs to the eternal counsel of God; the reprobation of unbelievers belongs to the ways of God within history with respect to "those who do not know God and on those who do not obey the gospel of our Lord Jesus" (2 Thess. 1:8). As soon as the fundamental difference between the counsel and the ways of God is taken into account, people will immediately recognize the difference between an eternal decree of election and a non-eternal decree of reprobation.

---

45. Hervormde Kerk (1962, 19).
46. Berkouwer (1960, 188); italics added.
47. See Bavinck (*RD* 2:393-94).

14.5.2 Living with the Tension

Reformed (!) dogmatician Gerrit Berkouwer properly raises the question that has been put to Calvinists repeatedly: Why cling to the notion of an eternal, sovereign divine decree of reprobation?[48] Scripture does not speak of it, and apparently the sovereignty of this supposed decree can hardly be separated from people's own sin and unbelief. So what do we gain with the notion of an eternal, sovereign divine decree of reprobation? In his profound analysis, Berkouwer can do no better than echo this grand statement by Augustine: even what occurs against God's will (*contra voluntatem Dei*) does not occur apart from his will (*praeter voluntatem Dei*).[49] Calvin rightly emphasized that the reprobate have no reason to seek the cause of their perdition anywhere else than in their own guilt, and not in the eternal will of God. And yet, together with Augustine and so many theologians after him, he believed that this destruction of the wicked cannot be separated from God's eternal will.

Perhaps the difficulty is simply that the word "eternal" is inappropriate. The Fall and all its consequences may never be viewed as occurring apart from God's will. But this is God's will within time, God's will manifested in his ways, God's will at the moment sins and mischief occur. As soon as we introduce the word "eternal" and link the Fall with God's will from eternity—God's counsel—we become mired in all the problems that have arisen with the doctrine of election and reprobation. Viatorism identifies the underlying problem as the age-old confusion of God's counsel and God's ways.

Here is the tension once again. On the one hand, who but a consistent decretalist would make God the cause of the wicked's destruction? On the other hand, who would wish to separate any event, including the inconvertibility of the wicked, from God's will? But then, do we mean God's will manifested in his ways? Or must this will be linked to his eternal

---
48. Berkouwer (1960, 184–85).
49. *Enchiridion* 100, quoted in Berkouwer (1960, 193, 201, 203, 276).

counsel? Sin, unbelief, and destruction never find their cause in God, but they do not occur apart from God's will, as if anything could escape God's government. But this government, or providence, pertains to God's ways, not his counsel. Compare the way Berkouwer put it: "Nothing can be made independent of the counsel of God [neither the guilt of the wicked, nor the faith of the converted; WJO]. . . . This counsel overcomes man's sinful acts; and who is able to maintain concepts like *praescientia* and *permissio* at the cross of Christ?"[50] This is fine — but it would have been more consistent with Viatorism if Berkouwer had said "ways" instead of "counsel."

The positive element in Berkouwer's words is this: who would wish to diminish God's sovereignty with notions like human autonomy, synergy between God and humanity, divine permission as distinct from his will, etc.? Such an indecretalism is just as objectionable as the opposite error of decretalism, which, in a very orthodox way, assures us that God is not the author of sin while simultaneously including both the Fall and the corruption of the wicked entirely within the counsel of God. From eternity God has chosen his people; this is his counsel. However, this does not alter the fact that, in his ways with the world, he urgently appeals to all people, he has great sorrow over their sins, he sent his Son into the world to die for all people, and he wholeheartedly desires all people to receive the benefits of this sacrificial death. If nevertheless many refuse this offer, it is their own fault that they will perish, both because of their sins and because of their refusal to accept the gospel. And at the same time, it is true that all the believers may know that God has chosen them in his grace from all eternity.

We can do nothing but live with the tension that inevitably arises if we attempt to understand the connection between God's counsel and human sin. This tension is solved neither by decretalism, nor by indecretalism, nor by trying to

---

50. Berkouwer (1960, 201).

press the two into one logical framework. The tension can be resolved only by prayer and doxology. This is the praise with which New Testament discussions of election often end (see §10.4). The path to resolution is adoration.

14.6 Infra- and Supralapsarianism
14.6.1 Description

After the Arminians had been driven out of the Synod of Dordt, the remaining church leaders soon agreed on the matter of predestination. However, there was still another matter that divided the divines—but they were wise enough to avoid a collision over this subject in order to avert agitating the Protestant world any further. Some of them were infralapsarians, and others were supralapsarians (*infra* = after, *supra* = before, *lapsus* = the Fall).[51] On this question Scripture sheds no direct light, so we are forced to engage in theological speculation here. Indeed, the entire discussion is rich in speculation![52] One can be all the more thankful that the Dordt divines were unwilling to risk another church split over this subject.[53]

The issue involves the order in God's decree concerning the eternal state of human beings.[54] That predestination is eternal, and thus chronologically precedes creation and the Fall, is not the issue; the issue is whether it also logically precedes the Fall. Actually, the issue itself is strange, since, as Jan Gerrit Woelderink observed: "In order to speak of a logical order in God's decrees, one would first have to demonstrate that a logical order may be assumed in God also outside time, and second, one would have to suppose that God's thinking is also subject to the same laws of logic that govern our thinking."[55]

---

51. The Dutch has two terms that only theological connoisseurs understand: *onder-* and *bovenvaldrijvers*.
52. On this see Woelderink (1951, 23–29); Berkouwer (1960, 254–55; all of chapter 8); Hoek (1988, 36); Spykman (1992, 508); McGrath (2016, 406).
53. Cf. Oorthuys (1931, 71–76).
54. Kersten (1980, 1:126).
55. Woelderink (1951, 25).

The heart of the issue is this: In his eternal decree, does God view people as fallen or not? In other words, was it the fallen human being (*homo lapsus*) who — in eternity past, before he actually fell! — was chosen or rejected? Yes, says infralapsarianism. Or was it the unfallen human being (*homo labilis*, the person able to fall but not yet fallen) who was chosen or rejected? Yes, says supralapsarianism. In the latter case, humanity had to fall, or else election and reprobation would make no sense. Creation as well as the Fall are the means that enable the decrees to be carried out. Therefore, supralapsarianism views the Fall as included in the eternal decree, namely such that predestination logically precedes the decree of the Fall. In infralapsarianism, however, God does have foreknowledge of the Fall, and predestination is his response to the Fall, but the Fall as such is not necessarily included in his decree.

With respect to the decree of reprobation, in supralapsarianism this decree rests entirely upon God's sovereign good pleasure; in infralapsarianism, this decree rests also upon the foreseen guilt of humanity (*praevisio peccati*). In other words, election and reprobation are purely and entirely decrees of God's sovereignty (so supralapsarianism), *or* election is a decree of God's mercy, in response to the foreseen Fall, and reprobation is a decree of God's righteousness, in response to foreseen guilt (so infralapsarianism).

The issue becomes more complicated because supra- and infralapsarianism gradually moved toward each other. Infralapsarianism came to view the Fall as included in God's decree after all (apart from foreseen human guilt), while supralapsarianism came to acknowledge that, in the decree of reprobation, God did take sin into account.[56] Millard Erickson mentioned a third option: *sublapsarianism*, that is, the idea of unlimited atonement (God has prepared salvation for all people), and limited application (God has chosen some to receive this salvation).[57]

---

56. Berkhof (1996, 118).
57. Erickson (1998, 931).

As far as I can see, this is no different from Amyraldism, the view of Calvinist Moïse Amyraut (or Moyses Amyraldus, d. 1664), also called the School of Saumur: Christ accomplished atonement for all, but the efficacy of atonement is limited to those who believe, which is the same as those that have been elected. Of course, mainstream Calvinists have eagerly attacked this view with their logic. Thus Benjamin Warfield called it an inconsistent form of Calvinism[58] — as if *any* view of these complicated matters could ever be consistent without dismissing important biblical evidence. R. C. Sproul claimed that anyone who really understands the other Four Points of Calvinism must believe in limited atonement (the Fifth Point) because of what Martin Luther called a "resistless logic."[59] Here we meet scholastic conclusivism again, which (unconsciously) believes that we can treat the terms involved as concepts instead of ideas.

14.6.2 Positions

At times, Augustine seemed to assume a supra-, at other times an infralapsarian, position. Supralapsarianism was defended by Martin Luther, John Calvin, Ulrich Zwingli, and Theodore Beza. During and after the Synod of Dordt, it was defended in the Netherlands by Festus Hommius, Francis Gomarus, Johannes Maccovius, Gisbert Voetius, and others. Beza defended supralapsarianism in his Hungarian Confession (1560): from eternity, God has decreed to create some in order to save them by his mercy, and to create others in order to condemn them by his righteous judgment. To this end, God had to create humanity good, in order to subsequently allow it to fall into sin.

In the time of the Reformation, infralapsarianism was defended by Heinrich Bullinger and others, and during the Synod of Dordt, by Theodore Wallaeus, Johannes Polyander, and Samuel Maresius, as well as the foreign theologians. During

---

58. Warfield (1942).
59. Sproul (2007, 140–42).

the Second Reformation (Nadere Reformatie) in the Netherlands, Alexander Comrie was a supra-, and William à Brakel was an infralapsarian.

In the twentieth century, Klaas Schilder, Henry Kersten, and Cornelis Steenblok were supralapsarians,[60] and Jacob J. van der Schuit, Arnold A. van Ruler, and Willem D. Jonker were infralapsarians.[61] Abraham Kuyper, Herman Bavinck, Karl Barth, and Gerrit Berkouwer criticized both viewpoints, though Kuyper seemed more inclined to supra-, Bavinck and Berkouwer more to infralapsarianism.[62] Kersten and Louis Berkhof argued that the election of angels (cf. 1 Tim. 5:12) can be understood only in the supralapsarian sense, since God did not choose a number out of a mass of fallen angels.[63] They used this as an argument for supralapsarianism with regard to people.

The Synod of Dordt did not want to burn its fingers on this complicated matter.[64] Interestingly, the Arminians suggested that they were combatting only the supra-, not the infralapsarians. However, both supra- and infralapsarians united in the statement that predestination is entirely rooted in God's sovereignty, with which they together opposed the Arminians.[65] At the same time, it is obvious that the tenor of the Belgic Confession (see Art. 16), the Heidelberg Catechism (see Lord's Day 21), and the Canons of Dordt (see I.6, I.7, I.15) is more infra- than supralapsarian. By the way, pure supralapsarianism cannot be found in any Calvinist confession. We do find infralapsarianism, although Reformed theologians never wished to fully exclude supralapsarianism.[66]

---

60. See Schilder (1947); Kersten (1980, 1:126–30); Steenblok (1978).
61. See Van der Schuit (1937); Van Ruler (1978); Jonker (1988).
62. Kuyper (1892, 2:170); Bavinck (*RD* 2:361–68; 382–92); Barth (1936, II/2:127–45); Berkouwer (1960, chapter 8).
63. Kersten (1980, 1:123); Berkhof (1996, 113).
64. See extensively, Berkouwer (1960, 17–22).
65. Dijk (1912, 99–115).
66. Bavinck (*RD* 2:367–68); Dijk (1912, 279).

14.6.3 Differences

In supralapsarianism, all the emphasis is placed on God's sovereignty, who supposedly even decreed the Fall and the sins of all people. To be sure, human responsibility is not denied, for it is emphasized that people perish because of their sins — but these sins are viewed as having been committed according to God's sovereign decree. In this position, the decree of Christ's incarnation logically precedes the decree of the Fall, that is, it does not presuppose the Fall. This means that Christ would have become Man even if the Fall had never occurred (which was impossible because also the Fall was decreed by God). Another feature is that, in supralapsarianism, election and reprobation are viewed as a whole, and as each other's counterpart.

Infralapsarians believe in double predestination as well, but emphasize human responsibility much more strongly, and thus have wrestled more intensely with the relation of the Fall to God's eternal decree. Infralapsarians believe that the decree of Christ's incarnation presupposes the Fall. This means that, if the Fall had not occurred, the Son of God would not have become Man. Another feature is that, in infralapsarianism, election and reprobation are distinguished much more clearly: election is the cause of the faith of those saved, whereas reprobation is not the *cause* but rather the *consequence* of the unbelief of those lost.[67]

At the deepest level, both supra- and infralapsarianism suffer from the same error: the belief that whatever occurs, including the Fall and people's sins, must proceed from God's eternal counsel. While Viatorism claims that God made, and makes, decisions within time involving his *ways* with the world, Calvinism cannot accept this. Any decision of God must necessarily have been made in eternity. Thus, the reprobation of the wicked must also be linked somehow with this eternal counsel of God, so that consistent Calvinists

---

67. Thus also the Canons of Dordt (Conclusion).

necessarily believe in double predestination. They may differ at most about the extent to which God took into consideration the foreseen guilt of the wicked and the foreseen faith of the righteous. Arminians say: both were taken into account. Supralapsarians say: neither of the two was taken into account. Infralapsarians say: God took into account the foreseen guilt of the wicked, but not the foreseen faith of the righteous.

Reformed (!) dogmatician Herman Bavinck saw that both supra- and infralapsarianism erred because "they placed all the things that are antecedent to the ultimate goal [creation, Fall, election, reprobation, conversion, perseverance, etc.; WJO] as means in subordinate relations also to each other. It is true, of course, that the means are all subordinate to the ultimate goal, but they are not for that reason subordinate to each other."[68] In my terms, both supra- and infralapsarianism suffer from the same scholastic conclusivism. In this sense, strictly speaking, both are wrong.

Reformed (!) dogmatician Gerrit Berkouwer spoke of "a subtle controversy, which owes its existence to a trespassing of the boundaries set by revelation," and wondered "whether theology has not become a *gnosis* [knowledge in an elitist, esoteric sense; WJO], which can never become quite transparent to the Church and can never really affect the Church's belief," and "whether we are here really confronted by a dilemma of faith and if we are not obeying the teaching of Scripture if we refuse to make a choice here."[69]

Reformed (!) dogmatician Jan Hoek spoke of "subtle reasonings, which do not really help us any further in understanding the biblical message."[70] Reformed (!) dogmatician Gordon Spykman said that supra- and infralapsarians presented us with "false and cruel dilemmas,"[71] and Alister McGrath (an Anglican, sometimes considered a Calvinist) spoke

---

68. Bavinck (*RD* 2:390).
69. Berkouwer (1960, 254–55).
70. Hoek (1988, 36).
71. Spykman (1992, 508).

of "this extremely pedantic debate, the summit of theological obscurantism."[72]

14.7 Evaluation
14.7.1 Three Theses

In opposition to infra- and especially supralapsarianism, Viatorism posits the following three claims.

(a) The only basis for the idea that everything that happens must somehow be related to the eternal will of God, even if not *decreed* in the eternal counsel of God, is based not on the Bible but on scholastic conclusivism.

(b) It is impossible to establish a logical, to say nothing of a chronological order within God's eternal counsel without humanizing God to a certain extent, that is, talking about him as if he were like us in his thinking and dealing, (cf. Isa. 55:9, "my thoughts are higher than your thoughts").[73]

(c) It is as one-sided to base (supposed) reprobation from eternity exclusively on God's sovereignty (who supposedly even foreordained the Fall) as it is to base it on the foreseen unbelief of the wicked, and thus upon God's righteousness. The former threatens God's righteousness, the latter God's sovereignty. None of the many intermediate solutions has ever sufficed. This was because they always threatened to fall into one of two snares: either a righteous God has decreed the Fall—and thus inevitably bears responsibility for it—or the sovereign God is made dependent on human choices.

The core question is and remains: How are God's eternal sovereign decrees and human sin and guilt related? If advocates of Viatorism were made to choose, they would feel more at home with infra- than with supralapsarianism. But regarding infralapsarianism it would continually insist: *in no way can the Fall, or any human sin as such, be attributed to some eternal decree of God*. They are exclusively the consequence of

---

72. McGrath (2016, 406).
73. Cf. Van der Zanden (1949, 39); Schilder (1947, 1:310); Berkouwer (1960, 266–67).

the responsibility and freedom with which God had endowed humanity. God's permission of the Fall and of individual sins, and God's *responses* to the Fall and these sins, *all involve his ways within time, not his eternal decrees.*

One of the well-known (hyper-)Calvinist sophisms is this: God decreed the Fall (because he decreed everything) but he is not responsible for it. It is people who fell, and they alone are to blame. *They* are culpable, not God. Now who can take such an argument seriously? It reminds me of the man sitting at a boiling lava stream. Without thinking he threw a stick into the stream, and his dog jumped after it right away—and was burned alive. Who was responsible for this tragedy? The dog of course, said the man! It was the dog's own decision to jump after the stick; *I* did not tell him to do this. Now who would accept this man's argument? It was the dog that jumped, but the man who had taught him to jump after sticks he threw was responsible for its death. If (hyper-)Calvinism is right, it was indeed humanity that fell into sin, but it was God who had from eternity decreed that it would do so, and thus was responsible.

14.7.2 Twofold Opposition

In the course of this book, it may have become clear that Viatorism opposes both (hyper)Calvinism and Arminianism.

In opposition to (hyper-)Calvinism, Viatorism maintains that human eternal salvation is rooted one hundred percent in God's eternal sovereign decree and one hundred percent in human responsibility. The inevitable tension between these two aspects cannot be logically resolved. Nor does the emphasis on the second aspect logically and necessarily diminish God's sovereign grace, as Calvinists usually object.

In opposition to (hyper-)Calvinism, Viatorism maintains that Scripture contains no hint of an eternal decree of reprobation. The wicked will perish because of their sins, and it is God's will that this should happen, because this is what God has threatened to do to them since Genesis 2. But this is something very different from an eternal decree of reprobation. In his ways with the wicked he destines them to destruction if they persevere in their wickedness. But this is very different from an eternal counsel.

In opposition to Arminianism (including Open Theism), Viatorism maintains that the eternal salvation of certain people is rooted one hundred percent in human responsibility and one hundred percent in God's eternal sovereign decree. This decree may not be reduced to God's foreknowledge, or the foreseen faith of people, although these elements must not be separated from the decree either. But first and foremost, the decree is rooted in God's own will. The fundamental issue involves the relationship between the divine freedom of will and the human freedom of will.

If Viatorism had to choose—which it need not—it would feel more at home with Contra-Remonstrantism because it is more afraid of denigrating God's sovereign grace than of denigrating the freedom of the (thoroughly sinful) human will. However, Viatorism wishes that Evangelical theology would abandon this kind of false dilemma. Viatorism wishes to live with the paradoxes of God's Word rather than with the results of a rationalistic-scholastic, conclusivist theology. As Philip Hughes has said, the paradoxes of the Christian faith exist because we are confronted with truths that surpass the capacities of our finite understanding. If there were no mystery, we would not be speaking of God's infinite being and the Creator's transcendent ways and goals, but only of human matters. It is possible to solve every paradox of the Christian faith only by putting our weight on one leg of the paradox, neglecting the other leg. But this destroys doctrinal balance by appealing to human reason in an attempt to contain all truth about God and the universe within the boundaries of human insight.[74] Hughes then applied this to the doctrine of election with its two legs of divine sovereignty and human

---

74. Hughes (1989, 178).

responsibility.[75]

14.7.3 "Calminianism"

In addition to thoroughly reconsidering their own positions, it is time for all parties—hyper-Calvinists and Arminians, supra- and infralapsarians—to abandon their false prejudices about each other (cf. §1.7). Thus, Arminians must realize that some Calvinists do question the idea of an eternal decree of reprobation, especially if this decree is viewed as having the same weight and character as the eternal decree of election. Similarly, Calvinists must know that there are certainly Arminians who believe in the radical corruption of the unregenerate, in the absolute necessity of God's saving grace and the working of his Spirit in regeneration, and in the perseverance of the saints.

In this way, Calvinists and Arminians are finding rapprochement, leading some North American theologians to call themselves "Calminians."[76] Of course, the more extreme movements within Calvinism and Arminianism are not amused by this new label. For instance, the staunch Calvinist James White[77] sharply blamed Norman Geisler,[78] who formerly called himself a Calminian, but afterwards presented himself as a moderate Calvinist, whereas in fact he was an Arminian (said White; cf. §1.6.1). Of course, this always happens with such intermediate positions. Pure (hyper-)Calvinists will call Calminians either "crypto-Calvinists," or dismiss them as "crypto-Arminians." Similarly, Arminians will call Calminians either "crypto-Arminians," or dismiss them as "crypto-Calvinists." The same is likely to happen to Viatorism: it will be probably branded as either "crypto-Calvinism" (by staunch Arminians) or as "crypto-Arminianism" (by staunch Calvinists).

---

75. Ibid., 178–80.
76. See, e.g., Olson (1999); Houdmann (n.d., 1).
77. White (2000, passim; also see 13–16 for the sharp preface by Sproul).
78. Geisler (1999).

Calling Viatorism a form of Calminianism would be disappointing. I view the latter term as rather unfortunate because Viatorism is not pursuing a blend of Calvinist and Arminian elements, or a middle position between the two. More precisely and correctly, Viatorism is seeking a *different* way. Calminianism—inadvertently or consciously—still runs the risk of remaining within the framework of rationalist scholasticism, with its tremendous respect for human logic. Its alternative is not a kind of mysticism, or another form of irrationalism, but a view that *surpasses* both rationalism and irrationalism. It transcends the scholastic logic of *both* (hyper)Calvinism and Arminianism, which is characterized especially by the confusion of concepts and ideas.

Viatorism is not a compromise; it is not rooted in a fear of apodictic positions; it is not an intermediate position. It *chooses* to live with the paradoxes of Scripture, being convinced that it is not only impossible but also undesirable to try to squeeze all biblical truths into one logical system. History teaches us that such an attempt is possible only by overemphasizing some aspects of the truth at the expense of other aspects that seem to undermine the former aspects. Scripture teaches unequivocally God's sovereign grace, as well as the eternal election of the saints. It also teaches unequivocally human freedom of will and responsibility. Let both truths stand; do not play them off against each other, or press them into a conclusivist mold. This will be possible only if we no longer confuse concepts and ideas.

Time and again we meet Arminians as well as Calvinists who tell us that they do precisely what I just recommended: preserve the balance between divine sovereignty and human responsibility. If that were so, why do they still call themselves Arminians and Calvinists, respectively? And are they sure that they truly represent the viewpoints of the Remonstrants and Contra-Remonstrants, respectively, of the early seventeenth century? Are they not in fact moderate (or weakened) Arminians and Calvinists, not all that different from

Calminians?

14.8 Election As Threat *and* Comfort
14.8.1 Imaginary Salvation

The saddest development surrounding the doctrine of election occurs where this doctrine has become a dark doctrine full of threats and fearmongering instead of a doctrine of comfort, which in the New Testament leads repeatedly to a doxology (see §10.4). In this atmosphere, we can hear warnings addressed to those who think they are saved: Be careful, for there are those who will say, "Lord, lord, open to us," but to whom Jesus says, "Truly, I say to you, I do not know you" (Matt. 25:11-12; cf. 7:22-23). People who utter such warnings forget that Jesus is saying this to those who do not possess the oil of the Spirit, and therefore were called "foolish" beforehand. The Holy Spirit is the "Spirit of wisdom" (Eph. 1:17); without the Spirit, we necessarily fall into some form of folly.

A well-known warning is this: Be careful that you do not go to hell while believing in an imaginary heaven (Dutch: *ingebeelde hemel*) for yourself. Considering all the weak and wavering Christians who are longing for salvation, one can understand those who have replied that many of these hyper-Calvinists will go to heaven while believing in an imaginary hell (Dutch: *ingebeelde hel*) for themselves. Of course, this is said only of those who have sincerely confessed their sins to God (cf. 1 John 1:9), and who confess Jesus as the only way to salvation (cf. Acts 4:12), but who do not venture to appropriate this salvation for themselves because of the ultra-Reformed predestination preaching to which they are exposed.

Is it possible to go to hell while believing in an imaginary heaven for oneself? Definitely. But this *never* pertains to the anxious who thirst for salvation; on the contrary, it pertains exclusively to self-righteous people, hypocrites, those who are complacent about their good works (cf. Luke 18:9-14). All the warnings of Paul in Romans 9 that one should not too quickly count oneself among the chosen ones are not at all addressed to the vacillating souls being kept in bondage by hyper-Calvinism. They are addressed rather to those who have not accepted Christ; these are they who think they will receive salvation automatically because they belong to the chosen nation of Israel (or some "true church"), or because of their self-righteousness. It is safe to say that in the weakest denomination there will be those who will be saved; and in the "truest" denomination there will be those who will perish.

To hypocrites Paul writes this key statement: "[T]hey are not all Israel, who are of Israel" (v. 6b KJ21), that is, not all those who belong to the chosen people have been chosen for eternity. As we have seen, there is an (eternal) election within the (earthly) election.

14.8.2 Election Within Election

This is clearly seen in the following summary by Paul:

> Even so then, at this present time there is a *remnant* according to the election of grace. And if by grace, then [it is] no longer by works; otherwise grace is no longer grace. But if [it is] of works, it is no longer grace; otherwise work is no longer work. What then? Israel has not obtained what it seeks; but the elect [lit., the election] have obtained it, and the rest were blinded (Rom. 11:5–7 NKJV).

Who is included in this election, that is, this company of elect? These have been neither arbitrarily chosen from Israel by God, nor are they the self-righteous elite of New Testament Israel; instead, they are those Jews who have accepted Christ in faith. Many of the chosen nation have perished, or will perish, because of their wickedness, but the *chosen* ones from the chosen nation will receive it.

As Berkouwer put it: "Election is *not* a threat against faithful listening to God's promise; it is a threat against the faithless claim."[79] That is, divine election is no threat to the

---

79. Berkouwer (1960, 68; italics in the Dutch original, but omitted from the published English translation).

doubtful ones of little faith, but it is a threat to those who believe they can claim salvation purely on the basis of their descent, their position, or their self-righteousness.

Salvation is based upon divine grace and human faith, not upon human works (Rom. 3:27-28; 4:5; 11:6; Gal. 2:16; 3:1-2, 10-11; 2 Tim. 1:9; Titus 3:4-7). Therefore, self-righteous people do not share in it, and the wretched and little ones, who come to cast themselves into the arms of grace, do share in it, even if they themselves hardly dare to believe so. *They are God's chosen.* Consider this somewhat free application of James 2:5, "Listen, my beloved brothers, has not God *chosen* those who are [spiritually] poor in the world to be rich in faith and heirs of the kingdom, which he has promised to those who love him?" They love him, not because they were chosen for this, but they received the promise because they love him; it is "those who love God" who are "those who are called according to his purpose" (Rom. 8:28).

"For thus says the One who is high and lifted up, who inhabits eternity, whose name is Holy: 'I dwell in the high and holy place, and also with him who is of a contrite and lowly spirit, to revive the spirit of the lowly, and to revive the heart of the contrite'" (Isa. 57:15).

14.8.3 The Extremes Meet

The French have a proverb, *Les extrêmes se touchent*, which means something like: "The extremes meet." That is, things that seem to be far apart sometimes exhibit remarkable similarities. For instance, nowhere does the aversion to Roman Catholicism seem greater than in hyper-Calvinism. Yet, we encounter here a remarkable correspondence between them: the great lack of assurance of salvation, which exists in hyper-Calvinism as a result of an extreme doctrine of election, meets its counterpart in the Roman Catholic teaching on election.

As a protest against Protestant teaching, the Council of Trent (1545-1563) spoke explicitly of election as a "mystery," which because of its "hidden" character can never offer any assurance *se omnino esse in numero praedestinatorum* ("that he belongs to those that are destined to be saved"), unless one receives a special revelation (*ex speciali revelatione*) from God.[80] In a more or less analogous way, hyper-Calvinism, too, has often taught that the assurance of election is based on special revelations from, or special experiences with, God. The wavering little souls feel all the more discouraged in their faith by reading extensive conversion stories of "the Lord's people," with great emphasis upon such revelations and experiences, special states of the soul,[81] which they themselves have never experienced. Things have become complicated, as Reformed scientist Johan Blaauwendraad has put it, coming from a hyper-Calvinist background.[82]

How far removed this is from the simplicity and directness of the gospel: "'Sirs, what must I do to be saved?' And they said, 'Believe in the Lord Jesus, and you will be saved, you and your household'" (Acts 16:30-31). "[I]f you confess with your mouth that Jesus is Lord and believe in your heart that God raised him from the dead, you will be saved. For with the heart one believes and is justified, and with the mouth one confesses and is saved" (Rom. 10:9-10). "If we confess our sins, he is faithful and just to forgive us our sins and to cleanse us from all unrighteousness" (1 John 1:9).

John Calvin radically rejected the notion of a special revelation given to the elect. He described those who are sometimes enamored of the thought:

> [W]hat revelation do you have of your election? This thought, if it has impressed itself upon him, either continually strikes him in his misery with harsh torments or utterly overwhelms him. Truly, I should desire no surer argument to confirm how basely persons of this sort imagine predestination than that very

---

80. Denziger (ESD 805); quoted in Berkouwer (1960, 104–105, 107–108; cf. 118–24 about the "hidden God" [Lat. *deus absconditus*]).
81. An extreme example is Moerkerken (1997).
82. Blaauwendraad (1997).

experience, ...[83]

What, asks Calvin, must such people do? Let them not desperately look forward to special revelations and experiences, but "rightly and duly examine it as it is contained in his Word [in order to] reap the inestimable fruit of comfort." In other words, the assurance of election does not lie in special revelations, but in the one revelation of God, that is, in the promises of God as contained in his Word. Calvin adds that our confidence arises from simply looking to Christ, whom he calls "the mirror wherein we must, and without self-deception may, contemplate our own election."[84]

14.8.4 Conclusion

Hyper-Calvinists have often implicitly claimed to know the answer to the question of Luke 13:23, "Lord, will those who are saved be few?" Their answer is Yes, with an appeal to several Bible passages (see §12.9.2). One can imagine how discouraging this is for vexed souls: there is but little chance to belong to these happy few, the truly chosen ones.

However, the question was addressed to Jesus, and his reply was very different: "Strive to enter through the narrow door. For many, I tell you, will seek to enter and will not be able" (v. 24). In other words, he did not enter at all into the actual question that was asked, but cast the one asking the question, yes, all people, back upon—not the counsel of God but—people's own responsibility: Overcome the hindrances that are placed in your way—we would say today: also those hindrances erected by hyper-Calvinism!—and enter through the narrow door. Do not puzzle over the number of elect, but you yourself enter in! This is not merely a kind invitation; no, the Lord urges you to do this as a believing act of obedience.

Election is a tremendous blessing and comfort to believers. However, in order to belong to the company of the elect,

---

83. Calvin, *Institutes* 3.24.4.
84. Calvin, *Institutes* 3.24.4–5; cf. Van der Zwaag (2003, 122).

we are not supposed to wait for special revelations, or to be worried about the number of the elect, but simply come to Christ. The history of post-lapsarian humanity began already in Paradise with the outstretched hand of God, and with his asking each of us: "Where are you?" (Gen. 3:9). The Bible ends with this same outstretched hand: "Let the one who is thirsty come; let the one who desires take the water of life without price" (Rev. 22:17). This water is free; God gives it by pure grace. As a matter of principle, he offers it to all people; in practice it benefits only those who are indeed *thirsty* as well as *willing*.

The Bible begins with a tree of life, from which the first people were driven (Gen. 3:22-24). The Bible ends with people who have a share in the tree of life, in the Paradise of God, and in the holy city (Rev. 2:7; 22:1-5, 19). It is because they wanted to receive such a share, and accepted it in faith. But in the end, it is by God's sovereign, eternal, and infinite grace that some receive it.

"For from him and through him and to him are all things. To him be glory forever. Amen" (Rom. 11:36).

"[T]o him be glory in the church and in Christ Jesus throughout all generations, forever and ever. Amen" (Eph. 3:21).

"[T]o him who is able to keep you from stumbling and to present you blameless before the presence of his glory with great joy, to the only God, our Savior, through Jesus Christ our Lord, be glory, majesty, dominion, and authority, before all time and now and forever. Amen" (Jude 1:24-25).

Bibliography

Aalders, G. C. 1962. *Daniël*. COT. Kampen: Kok.

Alexander, J. A. (1846/47) 1980. *Commentary on the Prophecies of Isaiah*. Grand Rapids, MI: Zondervan.

Alexander, R. H. 1986. *Ezekiel*. EBC 6. Grand Rapids, MI: Zondervan.

Allen, R. B. 1990. *Numbers*. EBC 2. Grand Rapids, MI: Zondervan.

Althaus, P. 1952. *Die christliche Wahrheit: Lehrbuch der Dogmatik*. 3rd ed. 2 vols. Gütersloh: Bertelsmann.

Archer Jr., G. L. 1985. *Daniel*. EBC 7. Grand Rapids, MI: Zondervan.

Armstrong, K. 2004. *A History of God: The 4000-Year Quest of Judaism, Christianity and Islam*. New York: Gramercy Books.

Barrett, W. 1962. *Irrational Man: A Study in Existential Philosophy*. New York: Anchor Books/Doubleday.

Barth, K. 1936-1988: *Church Dogmatics*. Trans. by T. H. L. Parker et al. Vols. I/1–IV/4. Louisville, KY: Westminster John Knox.

Basinger, D. and R. Basinger, eds. 1986. *Predestination and Free Will: Four Views of Divine Sovereignty and Human Freedom*. Downers Grove, IL: InterVarsity Press.

Bavinck, H. 1953. *The Philosophy of Revelation*. Grand Rapids, MI: Eerdmans.

———. 2002–2008. *Reformed Dogmatics.* Edited by John Bolt. Translated by John Vriend. 4 vols. Grand Rapids, MI: Baker Academic.

Bayle, P. (1696, 1740) 1995. *Dictionnaire historique et critique.* Genève: Slatkine.

Beilby, J. K. and P. R. Eddy, eds. 2001. *Divine Foreknowledge: Four Views.* Downers Grove, IL: InterVarsity.

Berkhof, H. 1986. *Christian Faith: An Introduction to the Study of the Faith.* Translated by S. Woudstra. Grand Rapids, MI: Eerdmans.

Berkhof, L. 1996. *Systematic Theology.* New edition. Grand Rapids, MI: Eerdmans.

Berkouwer, G. C. 1952. *The Providence of God.* Translated by L. B. Smedes. Studies in Dogmatics. Grand Rapids, MI: Eerdmans.

———. 1956. *The Triumph of Grace in the Theology of Karl Barth.* Grand Rapids, MI: Eerdmans.

———. 1960. *Divine Election.* Translated by H. Bekker. Studies in Dogmatics. Grand Rapids, MI: Eerdmans.

———. 1971. *Sin.* Translated by P. C. Holtrop. Studies in Dogmatics. Grand Rapids, MI: Eerdmans.

Blaauwendraad, J. 1997. *Het is ingewikkeld geworden: Pleidooi voor gewoon gereformeerd.* Heerenveen: Groen.

Bloesch, D. G. 1995. *God the Almighty: Power, Wisdom, Holiness, Love.* Downers Grove, IL: InterVarsity Press.

Blum, E. A. 1981. *1, 2 Peter, Jude.* EBC 12. Grand Rapids, MI: Zondervan.

Blumenthal, H. J. and R. A. Markus, eds. 1981. *Neo-Platonism and Early Christian Thought.* London: Variorum Publications.

Boettner, L. 1941. *The Reformed Doctrine of Predestination.* Grand Rapids, MI: Eerdmans.

Bonhoeffer, D. 1953. *Letters and Papers from Prison.* Edited by E. Bethge. Translated by R. Fuller. New York: The Macmillan Company.

Bouma, C. 1937. *De brieven van den apostel Paulus aan Timotheüs en Titus.* KV. Kampen: Kok.

Boyd, G. A. 1997. *God at War: The Bible and Spiritual Conflict.* Downers Grove, IL: InterVarsity.

———. 2000. *God of the Possible: A Biblical Introduction to the Open View of God.* Grand Rapids, MI: Baker.

———. 2001. *Satan and the Problem of Evil: Constructing a Trinitarian Warfare Theodicy.* Downers Grove, IL: IVP Academic.

Breen, Q. 1968. *John Calvin: A Study in French Humanism.* Grand Rapids, MI: Eerdmans.

Brightman, E. S. 1940. *A Philosophy of Religion.* Englewood Cliffs, NJ: Prentice-Hall.

Brother Andrew and S. DeVore Williams. 1999. *And God Changed His Mind.* Grand Rapids, MI: Chosen Books.

Bruce, A. B. 1979. *The Synoptic Gospels.* EGT 1. Grand Rapids, MI: Eerdmans.

Bruce, F. F. 1984. *The Epistles to the Colossians, to Philemon, and to the Ephesians.* NICNT. Grand Rapids, MI: Eerdmans.

———. 1988. *The Book of the Acts.* NICNT. Grand Rapids, MI: Eerdmans.

Brümmer, V. 1988. *Over een persoonlijke God gesproken: Studies in de wijsgerige theologie.* Kampen: Kok Agora.

———. 2005. *Ultiem geluk: Een nieuwe kijk op Jezus, verzoening en Drie-eenheid.* Kampen: Kok.

Brunner, E. 1937. *Man in Revolt: A Christian Anthropology.* Philadelphia, PA: Westminster Press.

Brunner, E. 1946. *Die christliche Lehre von Gott: Dogmatik*, Bd. I. Zürich: Zwingli-Verlag.

Buis, H. 1958. *Historic Protestantism and Predestination.* Philadelphia, PA: Presbyterian and Reformed Publishing Company.

Bultema, H. 1981. *Commentary on Isaiah.* Grand Rapids, MI: Kregel.

Calvin, J. 1960. *Institutes of the Christian Religion*. Edited by John T. McNeill. Translated by Ford Lewis Battles. 2 vols. Library of Christian Classics 20–21. Philadelphia: Westminster Press.

———. 1989. *Calvin's Calvinism: Treatises on the Eternal Predestination of God [and] The Secret Providence of God*. Translated by H. Cole. Grand Rapids, MI: Reformed Free Publishing Association.

———. 1999a. *Commentary on Isaiah*. Translated by W. Pringle. Vol. 3. Grand Rapids, MI: Christian Classics Ethereal Library. http://www.ccel.org.

———. 1999b. *Commentary on Romans*. Translated by J. Owen. Grand Rapids, MI: Christian Classics Ethereal Library. http://www.ccel.org.

Carroll, J. [2007]. *De teloorgang van de westerse cultuur: Een andere kijk op 500 jaar humanisme*. Wormer: Inmerc.

Carson, D. A. 1981. *Divine Sovereignty and Human Responsibility: Biblical Themes in Tension*. Atlanta, GA: John Knox.

———. 1984. *Matthew*. EBC 8. Grand Rapids, MI: Zondervan.

Chafer, L. S. 1983. *Systematic Theology*. 15th ed. 8 vols. Dallas, TX: Dallas Seminary Press.

Clark, G. H. 1961. *Religion, Reason, and Revelation*. Philadelphia, PA: Presbyterian and Reformed Publishing Company.

Cobb, J. B. 1966. *A Christian Natural Theology: Based on the Thought of Alfred North Whitehead*. Philadelphia, PA: Westminster Press.

Craig, W. L. 1987. *The Only Wise God: The Compatibility of Divine Foreknowledge and Human Freedom*. Grand Rapids, MI: Baker Book House.

———. 1991. *Divine Foreknowledge and Human Freedom*. New York: E. J. Brill.

Cranfield, C. E. B. 1975. *The Epistle to the Romans*. International Critical Commentary. Edinburgh: Clark.

Cullmann, O. 1962. *Christ and Time: The Primitive Christian Conception of Time and History*. London: SCM.

Darby, J. N. n.d. *The Collected Writings of J. N. Darby*. Kingston-on-Thames: Stow Hill Bible and Tract Depot.

Darby, J. N. n.d.-a. *Letters*, Vol. 2: *1868–1879*. Kingston-on-Thames: Stow Hill Bible and Tract Depot.

Davids, P. H. 1990. *The First Epistle of Peter*. NICNT. Grand Rapids, MI: Eerdmans.

Day, J. 1985. *God's Conflict with the Dragon and the Sea*. Cambridge: Cambridge University Press.

De Boer, Th. 1989. *De God van de filosofen en de God van Pascal: Op het grensgebied van filosofie en theologie*. 's-Gravenhage: Meinema.

De Groot, D. J. 1952. *De wedergeboorte*. Kampen: Kok.

De Jong, A. C. 1954. *The Well-Meant Gospel Offer: The Views of H. Hoeksema and K. Schilder*. Franeker: Wever.

Demarest, B. 1997. *The Cross and Salvation: The Doctrine of Salvation*. Wheaton, IL: Crossway Books.

Denney, J. 1979. *St. Paul's Epistle to the Romans*. EGT 2. Grand Rapids, MI: Eerdmans.

Dennison, J. T., Jr., ed. 2008–2014. *Reformed Confessions of the 16th and 17th Centuries in English Translation*. Grand Rapids, MI: Reformation Heritage Books.

Dijk, K. 1912. *De strijd over Infra- en Supralapsarisme in de Gereformeerde Kerken van Nederland*. Kampen: Kok.

———. 1924. *Om 't eeuwig welbehagen: De leer der praedestinatie*. Amsterdam: De Standaard.

———. 1952. *Van eeuwigheid verkoren: De belijdenis der praedestinatie*. Delft: Meinema.

Ditmanson, H. H. 1977. *Grace in Eperience and Theology*. Minneapolis, MN: Augsburg Publishing House.

Dooyeweerd, H. 1963. *Vernieuwing en bezinning: Om het reformatorisch grondmotief*. 3rd ed. Zutphen: J. B. van den Brink and Co.

Dorner, I. A. 1883. "Über die richtige Fassung des dogmatischen Begriffs der Unveränderlichkeit Gottes." In *Gesammelte Schriften aus dem Gebiet der systematischen Theologie. Exegese und Geschichte.* 188–377. Berlin: Verlag von Wilhelm Hertz.

Duffield, G. P. and N. M. Van Cleave. 1987. *Foundations of Pentecostal Theology.* San Dimas, CA: L.I.F.E. Bible College.

Edwards, D. and J. Stott. 1988. *Evangelical Essentials.* Downers Grove, IL: InterVarsity Press.

Ellison, H. L. 1985. *Jonah.* EBC 7. Grand Rapids, MI: Zondervan.

Engelsma, D. J. n.d. *The Kingdom of God.* http://www.reformedspokane.org/ Doctrine_pages/The%20doctrine%20of%20the%20church/Church%20%26%20Kingdom/Kingdom_of_God_DE/The_Kingdom_of_God1.html.

Epstein, I., ed. 1961. *The Babylonian Talmud.* London: Soncino Press.

Erickson, M. J. 1998. *Christian Theology.* 10th ed. Grand Rapids, MI: Baker Book House.

———. 2003. *What does God Know and When does He Know it? The Current Controversy over Divine Foreknowledge.* Grand Rapids, MI: Zondervan.

Fairbairn, A. M. 1893. *The Place of Christ in Modern Theology.* New York: Charles Scribner's Sons.

Fernhout, K. 1921. *De leer der uitverkiezing.* Amsterdam: W. Kirchner.

Finan, T. and V. Twomey, eds. 1992. *The Relationship Between Neo-Platonism and Christianity.* Dublin: Four Courts Press.

Flint, Th. 1998. *Divine Providence: The Molinist Account.* London: Cornell University Press.

Frame, J. 2001. *No Other God: A Response to Open Theism.* Phillipsburg, NJ: Presbyterian and Reformed Publishing Company.

Fretheim, T. E. 1984. *The Suffering of God: An Old Testament*

Perspective. Minneapolis, MN: Fortress.

———. 1999. "God in the Book of Job." *Currents in Theology and Mission* 26: 82–85.

Geisler, N. L. 1974. *Philosophy of Religion*. Grand Rapids, MI: Zondervan.

———. 1997. *Creating God in the Image of Man? The New "Open" View of God – Neotheism's Dangerous Drift*. Minneapolis, MN: Bethany House.

———. 1999. *Chosen But Free*. Minneapolis, MN: Bethany House.

Geisler, N. L. and W. Corduan. 1988. *Philosophy of Religion*. 2nd ed. Grand Rapids, MI: Baker.

Geisler, N. L. and H. W. House. 2001. *The Battle for God: Responding to the Challenge of Neotheism*. Grand Rapids, MI: Kregel.

Gibson, J. C. L. 1988. "On Evil in the Book of Job." In *Ascribe to the Lord: Biblical and Other Studies in Memory of Peter C. Craigie*, edited by L. Eslinger and G. Taylor, 399–419. Sheffield: Sheffield Academic Press.

Gill, John. 1746–1763. *An Exposition of the Old Testament*. London: n.p.

Gispen, W. H. 1982. *Exodus*. Translated by E. van der Maas. The Bible Student's Commentary. Grand Rapids, MI: Zondervan.

———. 1954. *De Spreuken van Salomo*. Vol. 2. KV. Kampen: Kok.

Glatzer, N. N., ed. 1969. *The Dimensions of Job: A Study and Selected Readings*. New York: Schocken.

Good, E. 1990. *In Turns of Tempest: A Reading of Job*. Stanford, CA: Stanford University Press.

Goslinga, C. J. 1962. *Het tweede boek Samuël*. COT. Kampen: Kok.

———. 1987. *Joshua, Judges, Ruth*. Translated by R. Togtman. Bible Student's Commentary. Grand Rapids, MI: Zondervan.

Graafland, C. 1987. *Van Calvijn tot Barth: Oorsprong en ontwikkeling van de leer der verkiezing in het gereformeerd protestantisme.* 's-Gravenhage: Boekencentrum.

Grant, F. W. 1901. *The Numerical Bible: Acts to II Corinthians.* New York: Loizeaux Brothers.

_____. (1888) 1956. *Atonement in Type, Prophecy and Accomplishment.* 8th ed. New York: Loizeaux Brothers.

Greijdanus, S. 1925. *De brief van den apostel Paulus aan de Epheziërs.* KV. Kampen: Kok.

_____. 1931. *De eerste brief van den apostel Petrus,* en *De tweede brief van den apostel Petrus.* KV. Kampen: Kok.

_____. 1933 (repr. 1983). *De brief van den Apostel Paulus aan de gemeente te Rome.* 2 vols. Kommentaar op het Nieuwe Testament. Amsterdam, Van Bottenburg.

_____. 1950. *De brief van Jakobus. De brief van Judas.* KV. Kampen: Kok.

_____. 1955. *Het evangelie naar Lucas.* Vol. 2. KV. Kampen: Kok.

Grogan, G. W. 1986. *Isaiah.* EBC 6. Grand Rapids, MI: Zondervan.

Grosheide, F. W. 1954. *Het heilig evangelie volgens Mattheüs.* 2nd ed. CNT. Kampen: Kok.

_____. 1960. *De brief van Paulus aan de Efeziërs.* CNT. Kampen: Kok.

Guelzo, A. C. 1989. *Edwards on the Will: A Century of American Theological Debate.* Middletown, CT: Wesleyan University Press.

Haak, T. 1657. *The Dutch Annotations upon the Whole Bible.* Translated by T. Haak. London: H. Hills.

Harrison, R. K. 1969. *Introduction to the Old Testament.* Grand Rapids, MI: Eerdmans.

Hart, J. H. A. 1979. *The First Epistle General of Peter.* EGT 5. Grand Rapids, MI: Eerdmans.

Hartley, J. E. 1988. *The Book of Job*. NICOT. Grand Rapids, MI: Eerdmans.

Hartshorne, C. E. 1964. *The Divine Relativity: A Social Conception of God*. New Haven, CT: Yale University Press.

Hasker, W. 1989. *God, Time, and Knowledge*. London: Cornell University Press.

Hatch, E. 1891. *The Influence of Greek Ideas and Usages Upon the Christian Church*. 3rd ed. Edited by A. M. Fairbairn. London: Williams and Norgate.

Henry, M. n. d. *Matthew Henry's Concise Commentary on the Bible*. Grand Rapids, MI: CCEL.

Hervormde Kerk, Generale Synode van de Nederlandse. 1962. *De uitverkiezing: Richtlijnen voor de behandeling van de leer der uitverkiezing*. 2nd ed. 's-Gravenhage: Boekencentrum.

Hervormde Raad, Generale Synode van de Nederlandse. 1960. *De kerk en de pinkstergroepen*. 's-Gravenhage: Boekencentrum.

Heschel, A. J. 1955, 1962. *The Prophets*. New York: Harper and Row.

Heyns, J. A. 1988. *Dogmatiek*. Pretoria: NG Kerkboekhandel.

Hodge, C. A. (1864) 1972. *A Commentary on Romans*. London: Banner of Truth Trust.

Hoek, J. 1988. *Zonde: Opstand tegen de genade*. Kampen: Kok.

Hoek, J. and W. J. Ouweneel. 2011. *Gereformeerden en evangelischen: Overeenkomsten en verschillen in actueel perspectief*. Heerenveen: Medema.

Hoeksema, H. 1927. *De plaats der verwerping in de verkondiging des Evangelies*. Grand Rapids, MI: Mannenvereenigingen van de eerste Protestantsche Gereformeerde Gemeente.

Holwerda, B. 1971. *Oudtestamentische voordrachten*. Vol. 1. *Historia Revelationis Veteris Testamenti*. Kampen: Van den Berg.

Hooykaas, R. 1972. *Religion and the Rise of Modern Science*. Edinburgh: Scottish Academic Press.

Houdmann, S. M. n.d. "What is Calminianism?" http://www.blogos.org/gotquestions/calminianism.html

Hughes, P. E. 1989. *The True Image: The Origin and Destiny of Man in Christ*. Grand Rapids, MI: Eerdmans.

Ignatius. 1885. *The Epistle of Ignatius to Polycarp*. In *The Apostolic Fathers with Justin Martyr and Irenaeus*, edited by Alexander Roberts et al. Vol. 1: The Ante-Nicene Fathers. Buffalo, NY: Christian Literature Company.

Jacob, E. 1958. *Theology of the Old Testament*. New York: Harper and Row.

Jacobs, P. 1937. *Prädestination und Verantwortlichkeit bei Calvin*. Neukirchen-Vluyn: Neukirchener Verlag.

Jewett, P. K. 1985. *Election and Predestination*. Grand Rapids, MI: Eerdmans.

Johnson, T. L. 2006. *Tijd voor genade*. Barneveld: De Vuurbaak.

Jonker, W. D. 1988. *Uit vrye guns alleen: Oor uitverkiesing en verbond*. Pretoria: NG Kerkboekhandel.

Jung, C. G. (1954) 2010. *Answer to Job*. Princeton, NJ: Princeton University Press.

Jüngel, E. 1976. *The Doctrine of the Trinity: God's Being is in Becoming*. Edinburgh: Scottish Academic Press.

———. 1983. *God as the Mystery of the World*. Grand Rapids, MI: Eerdmans.

———. 2003. "Thesen zum Verhältnis von Existenz, Wesen und Eigenschaften Gottes." In *Ganz werden: Theologische Erörterungen*. Vol. 5. 253–73. Tübingen: Mohr (Siebeck).

Kaiser Jr., W. C. 1990. *Exodus*. EBC 2. Grand Rapids, MI: Zondervan.

Kalsbeek, L. 1975. *Contours of a Christian Philosophy*. Edited by B. and J. Zylstra. Toronto: Wedge.

Keel, O. 1978. *Jahwes Entgegnung an Ijob: Eine Deutung von Ijob 38–41 vor dem Hintergrund der zeitgenössischen Bildkunst*. Forschungen zur Religion und Literatur des Alten und Neuen Testaments 121. Göttingen: Vandenhoeck and

Ruprecht.

Kelly, W., ed. 1856–1920. *Bible Treasury: A Monthly Review of Prophetic and Practical Subjects.* Available at https://bibletruthpublishers.com/bible-treasury/lpvl22465.

———. 1896. *Lectures on the Gospel of Matthew.* London: A. S. Rouse.

———. 1970 (repr. 1870). *Lectures Introductory to the Study of the Pentateuch.* Winschoten: H. L. Heijkoop.

———. n.d. *Notes on the Second Epistle of Paul the Apostle to the Corinthians.* London: G. Morrish.

Kersten, G. H. 1980. *Reformed Dogmatics: A Systematic Treatment of Reformed Doctrine Explained for the Congregations.* Translated by J. R. Beeke and J. C. Westrate. 2 vols. n.p: Netherlands Reformed Book and Publishing Committee (vol. 1), and Grand Rapids, MI: Eerdmans (vol. 2).

Kitamori, K. (1958) 2005. *Theology of the Pain of God.* Eugene, OR: Wipf and Stock

Kittel, G. et al., eds. 1964–1976. *Theological Dictionary of the New Testament.* Translated by G. W. Bromiley. 10 vols. Grand Rapids, MI: Eerdmans.

Klooster, F. H. 1977. *Calvin's Doctrine of Predestination.* 2nd ed. Grand Rapids, MI: Baker Book House.

Knowling, R. J. 1979. *The Acts of the Apostles.* EGT 2. Grand Rapids, MI: Eerdmans.

König, A. 1982. *Here Am I! A Christian Reflection on God.* Grand Rapids, MI: Eerdmans.

———. 2006. *Die Groot Geloofswoordeboek.* Vereeniging: Christelike Uitgewersmaatskappy.

Küng, H. 1987. *The Incarnation of God: An Introduction to Hegel's Theological Thought as Prolegomena to a Future Christology.* New York: Crossroad.

Kushner, H. S. 1981. *When Bad Things Happen to Good People.* New York: Schocken Books.

Kuyper, A. 1892. *E Voto Dordraceno*. 4 vols. Amsterdam: J. A. Wormser.

Lalleman, P. J. 2005. *1, 2 en 3 Johannes: Brieven van een kroongetuige*. CNT. 3rd series. Kampen: Kok.

Laytner, A. 2005. *Arguing with God: A Jewish Tradition*. Northvale, NJ: Jason Aronson.

Leibnitz, G. W. 1890. "Abridgment of the *Theodicy*, 1710." In *Philosophical Works of Leibnitz*. Translated by G. M. Duncan. 194–204. New Haven, CT: Tuttle, Morehouse and Taylor.

Lewis, C. S. 2012. *Mere Christianity*. New York: HarperOne.

⸻. 2014. *The Problem of Pain*. New York: HarperCollins.

Lewis, G. R. and B. A. Demarest. 1996. *Integrative Theology: Historical, Biblical, Systematic, Apologetic, Practical*. Grand Rapids, MI: Zondervan.

Lightner, R. P. 1991. *Sin, the Savior, and Salvation: The Theology of Everlasting Life*. Nashville, TN: Thomas Nelson Publishers.

Lindström, F. 1983. *God and the Origin of Evil: A Contextual Analysis of Alleged Monistic Evidence in the Old Testament*. Lund: Gleerup.

Loosjes, J. 1926. *Luthersen en Remonstranten in den tijd van de Dordtsche Synode*. Martinus Nijhoff.

Luther, Martin. 1883–2009. *Luthers Werke*. Weimarer Ausgabe. Weimar: Böhlau Verlag.

McCloskey, H. J. 1960. "God and Evil." *The Philosophical Quarterly* 39:97–114.

McDowell, J. 1979. *Daniel in the Critics' Den: Historical Evidence for the Authenticity of the Book of Daniel*. San Bernardino, CA: Campus Crusade for Christ International.

McFague, S. 1983. *Metaphorical Theology*. London: SCM Press.

⸻. 1987. *Models of God*. London: SCM Press.

McGrath, A. 2016. *Christian Theology: An Introduction*. 6th ed. Hoboken: Wiley.

MacGregor, K. 2015. *Luis de Molina: The Life and Theology of the*

Founder of Middle Knowledge. Grand Rapids, MI: Zondervan

Mackintosh, C. H. n.d. *Aantekeningen op Deuteronomium.* Winschoten: Uit het Woord der Waarheid.

Maddox, R. L. 1994. *Responsible Grace: John Wesley's Practical Theology.* Nashville, TN: Kingswood Books.

Mallan, F. and L. M. P. Scholten. n.d.. *Uit ons uitgegaan.* Zwijndrecht: Van den Berg.

Marshall, I. H. 1969. *Kept by the Power of God: A Study of Perseverance and Falling Away.* Minneapolis, MN: Bethany Fellowship.

Martin, B. 1955. *De dienst der genezing in de kerk.* Amsterdam: Ten Have.

Matter, H. M. 1965. *De brief aan de Philippenzen en de brief aan Philémon.* COT. Kampen: Kok.

Mayhue, R. L. 2001. "The Impossibility of *God of the Possible.*" *The Master's Seminary Journal* 12.2: 203-220.

Mayor, J. B. 1979. *The General Epistle of Jude.* EGT 5. Grand Rapids, MI: Eerdmans.

Medema, H. P. 2007. *God: bewegend, bewogen: Over prachtige mensen en een machtige God.* Vaassen: Medema.

Mettinger, T. N. D. 1992. "The God of Job: Avenger, Tyrant, or Victor?" in *The Voice from the Whirlwind: Interpreting the Book of Job*, edited by L G. Perdue and W. C. Gilpin, 39–49. Nashville, TN: Abingdon.

Moerkerken, A. 1997. *Bethel en Pniël: Standen in het genadeleven.* Houten: Den Hertog.

———. 2004. *Ons troostboek: Verklaring van de Heidelbergse Catechismus.* Houten: Den Hertog.

Moltmann, J. 1993. *The Crucified God: The Cross of Christ as the Foundation and Criticism of Christian Theology.* Translated by R. A. Wilson and J. Bowden. Minneapolis, MN: Fortress Press.

Morris, L. 1971. *The Gospel According to John.* NICNT. Grand Rapids, MI: Eerdmans.

———. 1988. *The Epistle to the Romans.* Grand Rapids, MI: Eerdmans/Leicester: Inter-Varsity Press.

Muis, J. 2010. "The Truth of Metaphorical God-Talk." *Scottish Journal of Theology* 63.2 (2010): 146–62.

Müller, J. J. (1955) 1984. *The Epistle of Paul to the Philippians.* NICNT. Grand Rapids, MI: Eerdmans.

Murray, J. 1968. *The Epistle to the Romans.* NICNT. Grand Rapids, MI: Eerdmans.

Nee, W. 1968. *Spiritual Man.* Richmond, VA: Christian Fellowship Publishers.

Noordtzij, A. 1932. *De profeet Ezechiël.* KV. Kampen: Kok.

Nouwen, H. 1999. *The Only Necessary Thing: Living a Prayerful Life.* New York: Crossroad.

Olson, R. E. 1999. *The Story of Christian Theology.* Downers Grove, IL: InterVarsity.

Oorthuys, G. 1931. *De leer der praedestinatie.* Wageningen: Veenman.

Orlebeke, C. and L. Smedes, eds. 1975. *God and the Good: Essays in Honor of Henry Stob.* Grand Rapids, MI: Eerdmans.

Oswalt, J. N. 1986. *The Book of Isaiah Chapters 1–39.* NICOT. Grand Rapids, MI: Eerdmans.

Ott, H. 1974. *God.* Edinburgh: St. Andrew Press.

Ouweneel, W. J. 1981. *Glaube und Werke: Eine Auslegung des Jakobusbriefes.* Schwelm: Heijkoop Verlag.

———. 1995a. *Christian Doctrine: I. The External Prolegomena.* Amsterdam: Buijten and Schipperheijn.

———. 1997. *Wijs met de wetenschap: Inleiding tot een christelijke wetenschapsleer.* Leiden: Barnabas.

———. 1998. *Geestelijke strijd.* Geloofsleven. Vol. 4. Medema: Vaassen.

———. 2000a. *Het Jobslijden van Israël: Israëls lijden oplichtend uit het boek Job*. Vaassen: Medema.

———. 2000b. *De zesde kanteling: Christus en 5000 jaar denkgeschiedenis: Religie en metafysica in het jaar 2000*. Metahistorische Trilogie. Vol. 3. Heerenveen: Barnabas.

———. 2004. *Geneest de zieken! Over de bijbelse leer van ziekte, genezing en bevrijding*. 4th ed. Vaassen: Medema.

———. 2005. *De God die is: Waarom ik geen atheïst ben*. Vaassen: Medema.

———. 2007b. *De Christus van God: Ontwerp van een christologie*. EDR 2. Vaassen: Medema.

———. 2008a. *De schepping van God: Ontwerp van een scheppings-, mens- en zondeleer*. EDR 3. Vaassen: Medema.

———. 2008b. *Het plan van God: Ontwerp van een voorbeschikkingsleer*. EDR 4. Vaassen: Medema.

———. 2009a. *Het zoenoffer van God: Ontwerp van een verzoeningsleer*. EDR 5. Vaassen: Medema.

———. 2010. *De Kerk van God (I): Ontwerp van een elementaire ecclesiologie*. EDR 7. Heerenveen: Medema.

———. 2012. *De Toekomst van God: Ontwerp van een eschatologie*. EDR 10. Heerenveen: Medema.

———. 2012. *Het Woord van God: Ontwerp van een openbarings- en schriftleer*. EDR 11. Heerenveen: Medema.

———. 2014a. *Wisdom for Thinkers: An Introduction to Christian Philosophy*. Jordan Station, ON: Paideia Press.

———. 2014b. *What Then Is Theology? An Introduction to Christian Theology*. Jordan Station, ON: Paideia Press.

———. 2016a. *The Heidelberg Diary: Daily Devotions on the Heidelberg Catechism*. Jordan Station, ON: Paideia Press.

———. 2016b. *The Ninth King: The Last of the Celestial Empires, The Triumph of Christ Over the Powers*. Jordan Station, ON: Paideia Press.

———. 2016c. *The Eternal Covenant: An Evangelical Theology of Living With God*. Jordan Station, ON: Paideia Press.

_____. 2016d. *Eternal Righteousness: An Evangelical Theology of Living Before God*. Jordan Station, ON: Paideia Press.

_____. 2016e. *The Eternal Kingdom: An Evangelical Theology of Living Under Christ*. Jordan Station, ON: Paideia Press.

Owen, H. P. 1971. *Concepts of Deity*. New York: Herder and Herder.

Packer, J. I. 1991. *Among God's Giants: Puritan Vision of the Christian Life*. London: Kingsway Communications.

Pailin, D. A. 1986. *Groundworks of Philosophy of Religion*. London: Epworth Press.

Palmer, E. H. 1996. *The Five Points of Calvinism*. Grand Rapids, MI: Baker Books.

Pannenberg, W. 1971. *Basic Questions in Theology: Collected Essays*. Translated by G. H. Kehm. Vol. 2. Philadelpia, PA: Westminster Press.

_____. 1991. *Systematic Theology*. Translated by G. W. Bromiley. 3 vols. Grand Rapids, MI: Eerdmans.

Pascal, B. 1958. *Pascal's Pensées*. New York: E. P. Dutton and Co., Inc. http://www.gutenberg.org/files/18269/18269-h/18269-h.htm.

Patterson, R. D. and H. J. Austel. 1988. *1, 2 Kings*. EBC 4. Grand Rapids, MI: Zondervan.

Paul, M. J., G. Van Den Brink, and J. C. Bette, eds. 2004. *Bijbelcommentaar Genesis/Exodus*. Studiebijbel OT. Veenendaal: Centrum voor Bijbelonderzoek.

Pawson, D. 2005. *Eens gered, altijd gered? De noodzaak van volharding en de zekerheid van het geloof*. Putten: Stg. Opwekking. (English edition: 1996. *Once Saved, Always Saved? A Study in Perseverance and Inheritance*. London: Hodder and Stoughton.)

Pearcey, N. R. and C. B. Thaxton. 1994. *The Soul of Science: Christian Faith and Natural Philosophy*. Wheaton, IL: Crossway Books.

Peterson, M., W. Hasker, B. Reichenbach, and D. Basinger.

2009. *Reason and Religious Belief: An Introduction to the Philosophy of Religion.* 4th ed. New York/Oxford: Oxford University Press.

Pinnock, C. H., ed. 1989. *The Grace of God, the Will of Man: A Case for Arminianism.* Grand Rapids, MI: Zondervan.

———. 2001. *Most Moved Mover: A Theology of God's Openness.* Grand Rapids, MI: Baker.

Pinnock, C. H., R. Rice, J. Sanders, W. Hasker, and D. Basinger, eds. 1994. *The Openness of God: A Biblical Challenge to the Traditional Understanding of God.* Downers Grove, IL: InterVarsity.

Piper, J. 1991. *The Pleasures of God.* Portland, OR: Multnomah.

Plantinga, A. 1974. *God, Freedom, and Evil.* New York: Harper and Row.

Ragaz, L. 1949. *Die Bibel: Eine Deutung.* Vol. 4. Zürich: Diana.

Ratzinger, J. (Benedict XVI). 2008. *Jesus of Nazareth: From the Baptism in the Jordan to the Transfiguration.* Translated by A. J. Walker. San Francisco, CA: Ignatius Press.

Reichert, V. E. 1985. *Job.* The Soncino Books of the Bible. 14 vols. London: Soncino.

Ridderbos, H. 1959. *Aan de Romeinen.* CNT. Kampen: Kok.

———. 1967. *De pastorale brieven.* CNT. Kampen: Kok.

———. 1975. *Paul: An Outline of His Theology.* Translated by J. R. DeWitt. Grand Rapids, MI: Eerdmans.

———. 1987. *Matthew.* Translated by R. Togtman. Bible Student's Commentary. Grand Rapids, MI: Zondervan.

Ridderbos, J. 1958. *De Psalmen.* Vol. 2. *Psalm 42-106.* COT. Kampen: Kok.

Roos, G. 2001. *Méér dan een belofte: Tweeërlei kinderen des verbonds.* Kampen: De Groot Goudriaan.

Russell, B. (1927) 1970. *Why I Am Not a Christian.* London: Unwin Books.

Ryken, P. G. 2003. *What Is a True Calvinist? Basics of the Reformed Faith.* Phillipsburg, NJ: Presbyterian and Reformed

Publishing Company.

Salmond, S. D. F. 1979. *The Epistle to the Ephesians*. EGT 3. Grand Rapids, MI: Eerdmans.

Sanders, J. 1998. *The God Who Risks: A Theology of Providence*. Downers Grove, IL: InterVarsity.

Schilder, K. 1947-1951. *Heidelbergsche Catechismus*. 4 vols. Goes: Oosterbaan and Le Cointre.

Schlatter, A. 1961. *Das Evangelium nach Matthäus*. Stuttgart: Calwer Verlag.

Schlink, B. 2010. *Der niemand traurig sehen kann: Ein Wort des Zuspruchs für jeden Tag des Jahres*. 22nd ed. Darmstadt: Evangelische Marienschwesternschaft.

Schreiner, T. R. and B. A. Ware, eds. 2000. *Still Sovereign: Contemporary Perspectives on Election, Foreknowledge and Grace*. Grand Rapids, MI: Baker Books.

Sharp, D. R. 1990. *The Hermeneutics of Election: The Significance of the Doctrine in Barth's Church Dogmatics*. Lanham, MD: University Press of America.

Spence-Jones, H. D. M., ed. 1909. *Malachi*. The Pulpit Commentary. New York: Funk and Wagnalls Company.

_____. 1909a. *Revelation*. The Pulpit Commentary. New York: Funk and Wagnalls Company.

Sproul, R. C. 1986. *Chosen by God*. Wheaton, IL: Tyndale House Publishers.

_____. 1997. *Willing to Believe: The Controversy over Free Will*. Grand Rapids, MI: Baker.

_____. 2007. *The Truth of the Cross*. Sanford, FL: Reformation Trust.

Spykman, G. J. 1992. *Reformational Theology: A New Paradigm for Doing Dogmatics*. Grand Rapids, MI: Eerdmans.

Stackhouse, J. G., ed. 2000. *Evangelical Futures: A Conversation on Theological Method*. Grand Rapids, MI: Baker.

Stafleu, M. D. 1987. *Theories at Work: On the Structure and Functioning of Theories in Science, in Particular During the Coper-*

nican Revolution. Lanham, MD: University Press of America.

Steenblok, C. 1978. *Om de oude waarheid, of: Het leergeschil aangetoond*. 3rd ed. Gouda: Gereformeerde Pers.

Strachan, R. H. 1979. *The Second Epistle General of Peter*. EGT 5. Grand Rapids, MI: Eerdmans.

Strack, H. L. and P. Billerbeck. (1922-1928) 1986-1997. *Kommentar zum Neuen Testament aus Talmud und Midrasch*. 4 vols. München: Beck.

Strauss, D. F. M. 1973. *Begrip en idee*. Assen: Van Gorcum.

———. 1983. "The Nature of Philosophy." *Journal for Christian Scholarship* 18:40-55.

———. 2009. *Philosophy: Discipline of the Disciplines*. Grand Rapids, MI: Paideia Press.

———. 2010. "'God in Himself' and 'God As Revealed to Us': The Impact of the Substance Concept." *Acta Theologica* 30/1:123-44.

Susman, M. (1946) 1996. *Das Buch Hiob und das Schicksal des jüdischen Volkes*. Frankfurt a.M.: Jüdischer Verlag.

Thielicke, H. 1977. *The Doctrine of God and of Christ*. Vol.2: *The Evangelical Faith*. Translated and edited by G. W. Bromiley. Grand Rapids, MI: Eerdmans.

Thiessen, H. C. 1948. *Introduction to the New Testament*. 4th ed. Grand Rapids, MI: Eerdmans.

———. 1949. *Introductory Lectures in Systematic Theology*. Grand Rapids, MI: Eerdmans.

Troost, A. 2012. *What is Reformational Philosophy? An Introduction to the Cosmonomic Philosophy of Herman Dooyeweerd*. Jordan Station, ON: Paideia Press.

Van De Beek, A. 1984. *Waarom? Over lijden, schuld en God*. Nijkerk: Callenbach.

Van den Brink, G. 1993. *Almighty God: A Study of the Doctrine of Divine Omnipotence*. Kampen: Kok Pharos.

Van der Schuit, J. J. 1937. *De Dordtsche Synode en het supra-lapsarisme*. Dordrecht: Van Brummen.

Van der Zanden, L. 1949. *Praedestinatie: Onze verkiezing in Christus*. Kampen: Kok.

Van der Zwaag, K. 2003. *Afwachten of verwachten? De toe-eigening des heils in historisch en theologisch perspectief*. Heerenveen: Groen.

Van Eck, J. 1997. *En toch beweegt Hij: Over de godsleer in de Nederlandse belijdenisgeschriften*. Franeker: Van Wijnen.

Van Gelderen, C. and W. H. Gispen. 1953. *Het boek Hosea*. COT. Kampen: Kok.

Van Gemeren, W. A., ed. 1996. *The New International Dictionary of Old Testament Theology and Exegesis*. 4 vols. Carlisle: Paternoster.

Van Genderen, J. and W. H. Velema. 2008. *Concise Reformed Dogmatics*. Translated by G. Bilkes and E. M. van der Maas. Phillipsburg, NJ: Presbyterian and Reformed Publishing Company.

Van Herck, W. 1999. *Religie en metafoor: Over het relativisme van het figuurlijke*. Leuven: Peeters.

Van Hille, C. n.d. *De ziekentroost*. Utrecht: De Banier.

Van Itterzon, G. P. 1975. "De Canones van Dordrecht, dogmenhistorisch." *Kerk en Theologie* 26: 138–152.

Van Niftrik, G. C. 1961. *Kleine dogmatiek*. Nijkerk: Callenbach.

Van Riessen, H. 1980. *Wijsbegeerte*. Kampen: Kok.

Van Ruler, A. A. 1978. *Verwachting en voltooiing*. Nijkerk: Callenbach.

Van Til, C. 1955. *The Defense of the Faith*. Philadelphia, PA: Presbyterian and Reformed Publishing Company.

———. 1969. *A Survey of Christian Epistemology*. Vol. 2: *In Defense of the Faith*. n.p.: Den Dulk Christian Foundation.

Van Woudenberg, R. 2004. *Gelovend denken: Inleiding tot een christelijke filosofie*. 2nd ed. Amsterdam: Buijten and Schipperheijn.

Venema, H. 1965. *Uitverkiezen en uitverkiezing in het Nieuwe Testament*. Kampen: Kok.

———. 1992. *Uitverkiezing? Jazeker! Maar hoe?* Kampen: Van den Berg.

Verboom, W. 2005. *De belijdenis van een gebroken kerk: De Dordtse Leerregels, voorgeschiedenis en theologie*. Zoetermeer: Boekencentrum.

Vermeulen, C. 1986. *Cor ecclesiae: Een onderzoek naar de pneumatologische consequenties van Karl Barths verkiezingsleer in het geheel van zijn "Kirchliche Dogmatik."* Utrecht: Proefschrift Rijksuniversiteit.

Vincent, M. *Word Studies in the New Testament*. 1887. Vol. 3. New York: Charles Scribner's Sons.

Vine, W. E. (1940) 1952. *An Expository Dictionary of New Testament Words*. London: Oliphants.

Ware, B. A. 2000. *God's Lesser Glory: The Diminished God of "Open Theism."* Wheaton, IL: Crossway.

Warfield, B. B. 1942. *The Plan of Salvation*. Grand Rapids, MI: Eerdmans.

———. 1952. *Biblical and Theological Studies*. Grand Rapids, MI: Eerdmans.

Watson, G. 1996. *Greek Philosophy and the Christian Notion of God*. Dublin: Columbia Press.

Weber, O. 1981/1983. *Foundations of Dogmatics*. Translated by D. L. Guder. 2 vols. Grand Rapids, MI: Eerdmans.

Weinandy, T. G. 2000. *Does God Suffer?* Notre Dame, IN: Notre Dame University Press.

Wentsel, B. 1982. *De openbaring, het verbond en de apriori's*. Vol. 2: *Dogmatiek*. Kampen: Kok.

———. 1987. *God en mens verzoend: Godsleer, mensleer en zondeleer*. Vol. 3a: *Dogmatiek*. Kampen: Kok.

White, J. 2000. *The Potter's Freedom: A Defense of the Reformation and a Rebuttal of Norman Geisler's "Chosen But Free"*. Amityville, NY: Calvary Press Publications.

White, N. J. D. 1979. *The First and Second Epistles to Timothy.* EGT 4. Grand Rapids, MI: Eerdmans.

Whitehead, A. N. (1929) 1969. *Process and Reality.* New York: Free Press.

Wilson, D., ed. 2001. *Bound Only Once: The Failure of Open Theism.* Moscow, ID: Canon Press.

Wink, W. 1992. *Engaging the Powers.* Minneapolis, MN: Fortress.

Woelderink, J. G. 1951. *De uitverkiezing.* Delft: Van Keulen.

Wood, A. S. 1978. *Ephesians.* EBC 11. Grand Rapids, MI: Zondervan.

Wright, R. K. M. 1996. *No Place for Sovereignty: What's Wrong with Free Will Theism?* Downers Grove, IL: InterVarsity Press.

Young, E. J. 1965. *The Book of Isaiah.* 2 vols. Grand Rapids, MI: Eerdmans.

Scripture Index

OLD TESTAMENT

Genesis
1	207
1:26	10
1:26-28	208
1:28	10
1:31	76
2	436, 590
2:9	357
2:17	357
2:19	149
2:24	215
3:6	362
3:9	288, 599
3:22-24	599
3:24	14
4:1	434
4:7	203
6:5-6	113
6:6	160, 161, 237, 245, 250, 260, 327
6:8	42
6:8-9	195, 388, 572
6:12	14
8:20	214
8:21	64, 138
8:22	64
9:1	10
9:8-17	207
9:16	210
11:5	149
12:3	538
15:2	117
15:2-3	296
17:7	210, 514
17:13	210
17:19	210
17:20	20, 309
18	161, 326
18:3	441
18:14	269
18:16-33	182
18:18	538
18:19	14, 434
18:20-33	307
18:21	149, 161, 261
18:22-32	366
19:19	441
20:6	93
21:12	308
22:1	150
22:2	224
22:12	150, 224, 261
22:18	538
25:21	296, 307
26:4	538
28:14	538
29:35	395
30:6	309
30:17	296
30:22	296, 309
30:27	441
32:22-31	366
32:26	319
35:1	419
37:21-22	94
38:15	22
38:21	22
39:2	94
39:4	441
41:32	52
45:5	86, 90, 94
45:8	94
47:29	441
49:10	208
50:20	86, 90, 94

Exodus
2:25	261, 434, 464
3:7	464
3:7-9	244
3:8	363
3:14	243
3:17	363
3:19	205
3:20	205

4:8-9	147	32:14	160, 237, 250, 312	25:11	250
4:10-15	20			32:10	242
4:10-17	313	32:32	417	32:13	242
4:11	92	32:32-33	97, 421, 459		
4:14	242	32:33	417	**Deuteronomy**	
4:21	173, 205, 224, 572	33	57	1:26	139
		33-34	183	1:34	163
6:23	318	33:3	114	1:45	309
7:3	205, 572	33:5	57, 114	3:23	302
7:4	152	33:13	15	4:21	163
7:13	173	33:19	350, 573	4:37	411, 441
7:13-14	205, 572	34:6	42	6:15	236
7:22	173, 572	34:6-7	243	7:6	395, 399
8:15	205, 572	34:9	546	7:6-7	411
8:19	173, 205, 572			7:6-8	434
8:32	205, 572	**Leviticus**		7:8	237, 441
9:7	205, 572	19:17	250	8:2	149, 261
9:12	173, 205, 572	20:23	161	8:6	14
9:34-35	205, 572	21:1	419	8:10	182
9:35	173	25:32	255	8:20	139
10:1	205, 572	26	204	9:7	551
10:20	173, 205, 572	26:14-16	147	9:13	114
10:27	173, 205, 572	26:16	92	9:13-14	312
11:10	173, 205, 572	26:18	147	9:18-20	312
13:17	146	26:21	147	9:19	163, 296
14:4	173, 205, 572			9:25-29	312
14:8	173, 205	**Numbers**		10:10	296
14:10	296	11:1	163, 242	10:12	14
14:15	296	11:1-2	314	10:15	411
14:15-16	332	11:1-15	332	10:16	114
14:17	173, 205	11:31-34	311	13:3	149, 261
14:18	572	11:33	242	14:2	395, 399, 411
15:26	92	12:9	242	18:5	410
16:4	150	14:11	151	21:5	410
16:28	151	14:11-12	312, 313	21:15	570
16:29	551	14:13-19	313	23:3-6	22
17:8-14	296	14:18	42	23:5	441
18:11	150	14:19	546	26:15	331
19:5	395, 399	14:20	313	26:18	395, 399
21:12-13	91	14:27	151	28-29	204
32	326	14:28-35	21	28:22	92
32:7-14	319, 366	16:46-48	314	28:23	537
32:9-10	312	22:22	242	28:59-61	92
32:10	236, 312	23:19	269	29:20	250
32:11-13	312	25:3	242	29:29	118, 120, 192

Scripture Index

30:1–10	120, 204	15:11	160, 162, 250, 269, 321	2:3	14
30:19–20	137			2:27	318
31:16–17	174	15:23	413, 566, 580	3:8	411
31:27	114	15:24	249	3:11–13	310
32:4	15, 241	15:26	580	3:14	14, 310
32:6	445	15:29	128, 162, 269, 307, 328	8:30–49	331
32:26–27	249			8:34	546
32:27	236	15:35	160, 162, 250, 269	8:36	309, 546
				8:39	261, 263, 546
Joshua		16:7–8	414	8:44	412
2:1	22	16:14	481	8:48	412
6:16–20	329	19:20	330	8:50	546
7:10–11	333	22:9	318	9:4–7	147
10:12–14	309, 323	22:11	318	11:32	412
10:14	296, 309	22:20	318	12:6	63
11:20	225	23:10–12	153	12:9	63
22:5	14	23:10–13	262, 263	12:13–14	63
24:15	137, 190, 390	23:11–12	104	13:2	141, 171
		24:1–3	318	14:21	412
Judges		28:16	481	18:1	323
2:22	14, 149			18:42–45	323
3:4	149, 261	**2 Samuel**		21:27–29	317
5:23	143, 254	2:4	21	22:17	256
10:15	296	2:11	21	22:20	151
10:15–16	310	5:1–5	21		
10:16	161, 236, 245	11:2–5	22	**2 Kings**	
13:8–9	309	12:5–6	321	5:15	150
13:9	309	12:15–18	321	13:3–5	327
17:13	150	13	321	17:19–20	580
		16:10	95, 225	17:20	413
1 Samuel		16:15–17:14	63	20	320
1:10–17	310	17:14	95	20:1	318
2:25	565	18	321	20:1-6	318, 323
2:30	204	22:22	14	20:1-7	297
2:30–31	317	22:32	260	20:2–3	318
3:18	181, 368	22:36	309	20:5	307
7:8–9	296	23:5	210	20:5–6	319
8:7–9	21	24:1	95, 377	20:6	320
10:5	330	24:12–13	157	20:12	320
10:6	481	24:16	160, 250	20:12–19	320
10:9	481	24:17–25	316, 317	21	320
12:22	237	24:25	307	22:13	163
13:14	21, 321			22:17	163
14:3	318	**1 Kings**		23:15–16	171
15	162	2	321	23:27	411, 413

625

1 Chronicles
5:20	308
16:13	411
16:17	210
16:36	255
21:1	95, 377
21:7-13	157
21:15	316
25:1	331
29:10	255

2 Chronicles
6:6	411
6:31	14
6:34	412
6:36	163
6:38	412
7:12-14	317
12:1-12	317
12:13	412
16:9	261
17:6	14
20	329
20:9	297
20:18-19	329
20:21-22	329, 330
20:26-28	329
21:18-19	92
28:9	163
30	545
30:6	545
30:9	42
30:20	297, 309
30:27	309, 331
32:31	93, 150
33:12-13	308
33:19	308
34:21	163
34:25	163

Ezra
2:2-62	419
4:15	419
8:23	302, 308

Nehemiah
7:5-64	419
9:5	255
9:17	42
9:31	42
12:22-23	419
13:14	419

Esther
3:6	395
3:10	21
3:13	395
4:4	21
4:14	333
6:1	419

Job
1	96
1-2	363, 364, 377
1:8-12	96
1:12	94, 182
1:15	96
1:16	359
1:18-19	359
1:21	182, 303, 364
2	96, 364
2:3-6	96
2:4-10	93
2:6	94
2:8	289
2:9	366
2:10	364
3:1	303
5:9	10
5:13	4
7:20-21	303
7:21	359
8:5-6	302
9:3	221
9:4	220
9:10	10
10:9	221
11:7	11
11:7-10	1
11:10	221
11:52	488
13:15	366
14:5	8
15:8	11
15:32	97
16:9	289
21:14	14
21:15	537
22:11	359
22:27	309
23:13-14	53
23:14	8
26:12-14	15
33:13	221
33:14-18	569
34:27	14
38	288
38-41	284, 291, 292, 294
38:2	12, 286
38:3-4	287
38:4	288
38:4-38	284
38:21	288
38:39-39:30	284
40:4	105
40:8	285
40:10-14	290
40:15-24	289
40:17	289
40:19	289
40:24	291
41:1-34	289
41:2	394
41:8-9	291
41:10	291
41:11	11, 287
41:25	289
42	183
42:2	6, 269
42:3	12
42:6	303, 363
42:7	363
42:7-8	285, 364
42:8	303

Reference	Page(s)
42:10	364
Psalms	
2:4	236
2:7	10
3:4	309
4:1	309
4:4	249
5:5	237
8:2	328
14:2	387
14:2–3	546
17:11	360
18:21	14
18:50	21
19:14	93
20:6	150
22	360
22:1	288
23:3	286
23:4	346
25:4	14
25:9	14
25:11	546
25:12	137
25:18	546
26:5	250
29:1	328
30:8	302
31:6	250
31:15	62
31:16	144
32:5	546
32:6	387
32:8	63
33:10–12	89
33:11	5, 6, 12
33:12	411
34:4	309
34:15–16	302
37:4	324
41–44	360
41:9	176
41:13	255
42:7	346, 360
46:1	346
49:7	361
50:23	328
51	305
51:10	305
51:11	443
53:2	387
53:3–4	546
56:8	419
62:8	311
64:2	4
65:4	390
66:18	302
67:2	14
68:5	331
68:34	328
69	360
69:2	360
69:5	261, 263
69:28	97, 418, 421, 459
73:24	5, 63
77:5	255
77:13	14
77:19	14
78	332
78:1–3	209
78:27–31	332
78:29–31	311
78:40	116, 161, 236
78:49	163
78:70–72	21
81:10	303
81:12	94
83:13–15	360
86:11	14
86:15	42
87:6	419
88	360
89:3	412
89:3–4	21
89:19	411, 412, 449
89:19–21	21
90:1–2	219
90:2	255
90:4	255
91:11	420
91:15	297
94:9–10	261, 263
95:10	15, 161
95:10–11	163
96:7	328
101:3	250
102	360
102:3	360
102:23–24	97
102:26–27	240
103:6–7	179
103:7	15, 87
103:8	42
103:17	255
103:19	117
105:10	210
105:24–25	95
105:26	410
105:43	411
106:5	411
106:13	6, 12, 63
106:23	411, 412
106:45	250
106:48	255
107:11	6, 12, 63
109:13	418
111:7–8	8
115:3	8, 221, 224, 269
119:30	390
119:105	260
119:173	390
124:1–3	94
132:11–12	21
135:6	96
138:4–5	15
138:5	214
138:8	481
139:1–4	151, 189, 259
139:2	261, 263
139:4	141, 145
139:6	260

139:16	8, 97, 141, 418	**Song of Solomon**		30:31-32	330
		1:4	545	32:1	214
139:23-24	150, 151, 261			33:24	348
		Isaiah		37:26	9
142:1	302	1:11-14	237	37:31-32	360
143:3	360	1:14	245, 260	38:1	154
145:8	42	1:18	551	38:1-6	318
145:13	210	2:3	14	38:1-8	182
145:17	15, 87	4:3	418, 459	38:5	97, 154
145:18-19	302	5:2	158	38:5-9	323
147:11	237	5:4	158, 236	40:3	14
149:5-7	329	5:19	6, 12	40:13	11, 289, 394
149:9	419	6	151	40:13-14	7, 11, 261
		6:8	151	40:26	269
Proverbs		6:10	95	41:17	309
3:12	445	9:6-7	214	41:22-23	262, 263
4:23	550	10:5	163	42-53	360
6:34	250	10:7-19	163	42:1	412, 449
8	288	10:15	221	42:3	513
8:22	15	10:19-21	360	42:9	262, 263
8:22-31	288, 467	10:20-22	411	42:14	255
15:29	302	10:22-23	52	42:24	14
16:4	95, 105, 121, 223, 225, 454, 565, 566, 567	11:11	360	43:1	453
		11:16	360	43:2	346, 360
		12:1	163	43:10	412
16:9	98	14:1	390	43:20	411
16:33	104	14:24-27	12, 52	44:21	551
19:21	5, 6, 12, 98	14:26	6	44:28	6, 141, 172
20:24	98	18:4	116	45:1	172
21:1	98, 175, 182, 221	18:5	116	45:6-7	99
		19:12	12	45:7	92, 99, 347, 354
22:2	182, 341	19:17	6, 12		
27:4	250	19:22	308	45:9	221
28:13	546	22:11	9	45:13	172
29:17	445	23:9	12	46:3	360
		24:5	210	46:9-10	12
Ecclesiastes		25:1	6	46:9-11	99
1:2	292	27:1	291	46:10	8, 28, 99, 141, 145, 262, 263, 269
3:13	386, 431, 542	28:5	411		
4:4	250	28:16	412, 525		
5:18	542	28:29	6, 11	46:10-11	6
9:1	144	29:16	221	46:11	9
12:8	292	30:14	221	47:6	163
		30:15	139	48:3	8, 99
		30:19	309	48:4	114

48:11	9	3:7	158	31:18	306, 544	
48:14	6	3:12–13	536	31:20	310	
49:3	360	3:14	427, 514	31:31	211	
49:7	411	3:19–20	158, 236	32:17	269	
49:8	8, 309	3:22	536	32:18–19	11	
50:2	535	4:14	151, 153	32:19	262, 263	
53:7–8	360	4:27–28	334	32:21–24	363	
53:10	6, 8, 92	4:28	53	32:27	269	
54:9	163	5:24	182, 341	32:35	159	
54:10	481	7:5–7	147	32:40	210	
55	535	7:16	334	33:3	11	
55:1	523, 534	7:18	161	36:3	146	
55:2–3	535	7:26	114	38:17–18	155	
55:3	210	7:27	152	38:17–21	148	
55:6	387	7:31	159	42:9	302	
55:8–9	15, 87, 260	8:6	250	49:20	6, 12	
55:9	11, 589	10:23	98	50:5	210	
56	523	11:14	334	50:45	6, 12	
56:4	390	13:27	151, 153	51:11	6	
57:11	255	14:11	334	51:12	53	
57:15	453, 596	15:1	322, 334			
57:16–17	163	17:9	550	**Lamentations**		
59:16	237, 325	17:9–10	261, 263	1	361	
61:8	210	18	574	1:12	360	
62:5	236	18:4	574	2:19	311	
63:9	75, 219, 236, 245, 271, 361	18:6	221	3:37–38	99	
		18:7–10	60	3:39	99	
63:10	96, 113, 161, 454	18:8	250	4:11	163	
		19:5	159	5	545	
64:5	163	20:7–18	366	5:21	306, 544	
64:6	138, 489	20:12	261, 263			
64:8	221, 445	21:5	163	**Ezekiel**		
64:9	163	22:4–5	148	1:22	241	
65:1	546	22:30	419	9:3–4	419	
65:1–3	481, 535	23:18	11	11:5	261, 263	
65:2	113, 534	23:20	6, 11	11:19	545	
65:9	411	23:22	155	12:3	146	
65:14–15	411	23:29	131	13:9	419	
65:22	411	26:2–3	146	14:12–20	327	
65:24	309	26:13	250	14:13–14	334	
		26:19	318	16:60	210	
Jeremiah		29:11	6	18:23	225	
2:5	536	29:12–13	311	18:25	14, 15	
2:13	536	30:24	6	18:29	14, 15	
2:19	536	31	211, 545	18:31	545	

18:32	225	9:25–27	178	3:8	314
20	58, 59, 327	9:27	53	3:9	315
20:6	363	10	373	3:10	160, 237, 314, 327
20:8–10	58	11	172		
20:9	9	11:36	53	4:1	154
20:13–14	59	12:1	418	4:2	42, 160, 315, 319
20:15	363				
20:21–22	59	**Hosea**			
20:25	93	1–3	245	**Micah**	
20:30–31	326	2:21–22	309	4:2	14
22	326, 327	5:8	153	4:12	6, 12
24:14	322	6:4	153	5:1	456
24:21	363	6:6	236	5:2	210
33	59, 60, 61	6:7	207	5:2–5	214
33:11	225, 526	7:14	311		
33:13–15	59	8:5	151	**Nahum**	
34:23–24	214	11:8–9	162	1:3	14
36:23	244	14:2	546		
36:26	545	14:8	309	**Habakkuk**	
36:37	323	14:9	14	1:13	26, 99, 116
37:24–25	214				
37:26	210	**Joel**		**Zephaniah**	
		2:13	42	2:1–2	53
Daniel		2:32	526	3:7	159
2	172			3:10	328
2:20	255	**Amos**		3:17	237, 245
2:22	11	3:2	434		
2:44	210	3:6	93, 99, 347, 354	**Haggai**	
3	359			1:5	551
3:25	346	3:7	6, 10	1:7	551
4	174	5:4–6	387	2:15	551
4:3	210	5:14	387	2:18	551
4:17	224	5:21	236		
4:25	224	6:8	237	**Zechariah**	
4:32	224	7:1–6	160, 317	1:2	163
4:34	210	7:2	546	1:12	163
4:35	220, 224	8:12	387	1:14	250
7	172			1:15	163
7:10	419	**Jonah**		1:17	414
7:14	210	1:14–16	315	3:7	14
7:27	210	2:3	359	6:1	98
8	172	2:4	204	8:2	250
9	323, 326	3:2	154	8:6	269
9:18	302	3:4	154, 314	8:14	322
9:19	546	3:5–9	323	9:9–10	214

Scripture Index

10:6	309	9:12	353	15:28	325
13:9	309	9:18–19	190	16:17	477
		9:20–22	190	16:18	208
Malachi		9:22	190, 325, 376	17:2	247
1	571, 572	9:28–29	376	17:5	445, 447
1:3	194, 570, 571	9:29	325	17:12	104
2:9	14	9:38	298, 302	17:22–23	176
2:10	445	10	76	18:8	480
3:6	240	10:8	335	18:19	324
3:16	418, 459	10:22	481, 548	18:19–20	311
4:5–6	554	10:29	75, 221	19:8	94
		10:37	570	19:26	268
NEW TESTAMENT		10:40	556	20:15	220
Matthew		11:11	444	20:16	415, 425
1:1–17	22	11:14	454, 554	20:17–19	176
1:25	434	11:21	104	20:28	23, 66, 428
3:17	445, 447	11:21–23	155	20:30–34	190
4:4	131	11:23	104	21:16	329
5:44	298	11:25–26	53, 502, 569	21:22	324
6:6	298	11:26	53	21:28–30	425
6:7	300	11:28	452, 479, 523, 534	21:28–44	425
6:8	262, 263			21:29	425
6:9–10	368	12:13	547	21:30	425
6:10	337	12:18	409, 412, 445	21:31	425
6:12	546	12:27	430	21:33	425
6:19	224	12:50	224	21:34–41	425
6:32	262, 263	13:11	502	21:37	160
7:1	31, 33	13:11–13	569	21:41	425
7:7	298	13:19	375	22:3–8	427
7:7–8	324	13:24–30	373	22:4	425
7:12	37	13:28	344, 374	22:4–6	425
7:13–14	514	13:31	555	22:7	427
7:21	224	13:33	209, 555	22:8	460
7:22	430	13:35	19, 209, 456	22:9	425, 427
7:22–23	514, 594	13:38	375	22:10–11	425
8:2	369	13:39	374	22:11–23	426
8:2–3	190	13:58	325	22:13	427
8:3	369	14:15–16	333	22:14	407, 415, 425, 426, 465, 514, 538
8:5	302	14:16	337, 370		
8:10	376	14:19	337		
8:13	371, 376	14:28–29	324	23:13	481
8:25	39	14:33	248	23:37	111, 481, 534, 537, 554
8:31	302	14:36	302		
9:2	376	15:19	550	24:13	424, 425
9:6	547	15:21–28	376	24:14	62, 424

24:20	298	5:36	376	**Luke**	
24:22	407, 416, 424, 425, 538	5:41	336, 547	1:13	297
		6	430	1:37	268
24:24	407, 416, 424, 425, 538	6:5	371	1:75	435
		6:5–6	323, 325, 376	1:76	14
24:31	407, 416, 424, 538	6:7	430	2:14	7, 441
		6:12–13	430	2:34	566
24:42	425	6:13	335	2:49	12
24:44	425	6:34	336	3:7	463
25	439	6:40	376	3:38	444
25:1	555	6:41	336	4:1–13	362
25:3	555	7:21–23	138	4:10–11	375
25:11–12	594	7:32	376	4:43	12
25:34	19, 50, 51, 209, 439, 456, 564	7:33	376	6:6-10	191
		7:34	336	6:10	548
		8:23	376	6:40	439
25:41	104, 331, 480, 564	9	376	7:14	547
		9:17	376	7:29–30	13
25:42	439	9:19	370, 376	7:30	96, 481, 554
25:46	480	9:22	338, 370	7:50	190, 325
26:4	298	9:23	338, 370	8:15	481
26:24	76	9:23–24	376	8:41	299
26:26	555	9:24	370	8:48	190, 325
26:28	214, 428	9:25	376	8:54–55	299
26:39	335	9:38	430	9:35	407, 412, 449
26:42	23, 221, 224, 335, 337	9:42	346	10:8–9	335
		10:18	224, 349	10:20	421, 459, 466
26:44	335	10:27	338	10:21	245
27:30	555	10:51	323	11:5–13	311
27:46	288	10:52	190, 325, 376	11:9–10	324
28:9	248	11:23	302	11:50	50, 209, 456
28:17	248	11:23–24	324	12:47–48	476, 532
		12:6	160	13:3	543
Mark		13:7	13	13:5	543
1:40	338	13:10	13	13:11	376
1:41	336	13:20	424, 466	13:11–17	376
2:7	248	13:22	424, 466	13:16	376
2:11	336	13:27	424	13:23	598
3:5	336	13:32	62, 176	13:23–24	426
4:16	454	14:24	214	13:24	549, 598,
4:16–17	556	14:30	177	13:34	96, 108, 111, 135, 139, 326, 373, 384, 386, 401, 481, 534, 537, 554
4:35	346	14:36	311, 444		
4:35–41	346, 360	16:17–18	335		
4:41	346				
5:34	190, 325				

Scripture Index

13:34–35	557	3:16	111, 237, 479, 487, 528, 529	9:32	50
14:23	541			10:26	429, 569
14:26	570	3:18	431	10:28	490
15	545	3:20	383	10:28–29	482
15:11–32	392	3:27	431, 453, 556	10:29	429, 458
15:18–20	545	3:29	443	11:25–26	431
16:15	261, 263	3:33	431, 454, 556	11:41–42	336
17:19	190, 325, 376	3:36	140, 486, 543	12:3	555
17:21	217	4:4	12	12:32	109, 431, 432, 523
18:1	311	4:14	431		
18:1–8	311	4:34	224	12:39–40	569
18:7	407, 416, 425, 538	4:42	479	12:46	431
		5:1–9	191	12:48	431, 454, 557
18:7–8	300, 311	5:8	544, 547	13:11	175
18:9–14	471, 594	5:21	428	13:18	407, 410, 430, 449, 455, 538
18:19	224	5:22	66		
18:27	268	5:22–29	66	13:20	556
18:42	190	5:24	431, 481	13:27	175, 176
19:14	383	5:27	66	14:1–4	400
19:41–42	112, 481, 534	5:30	23	14:2	130
20:35	460	6	432	14:13–14	311, 324
21:6	75	6:7	53	14:16	482
21:19	481	6:35	431	14:16–17	443
22:20	210, 214	6:37	386, 428, 429, 431, 458	15:5	489, 546
22:22	176			15:6	481
22:29	10	6:38	23	15:7	325
22:32	481	6:39	482	15:15	10
22:42	23, 369	6:40	431	15:16	193, 311, 325, 407, 410, 430, 449, 455, 456, 477, 501
22:44	247	6:44	386, 428, 432, 546		
23:34	327				
23:35	407, 412, 449	6:44–45	477		
24:26	12	6:65	428	15:18	383
		6:70	22, 176, 407, 410, 411, 415, 429, 430, 455	15:19	407, 410, 430, 449, 455
John					
1:1–3	242			15:23–25	383
1:3	64, 288	6:70–71	175	16:23–24	311, 325
1:11–12	454, 554	7:7	383	17	429
1:12	431	7:17	139, 224, 384, 401, 430, 537, 554	17:1–3	435
1:14	64, 242			17:1–5	65
1:18	242, 288			17:2	429, 458
1:21	554	7:37–38	524	17:3	435, 467
1:29	479, 529	8	429	17:4	256
3:5	458	8:47	428, 429, 569	17:5	253, 262
3:14	12	9:3	182, 341	17:6	429, 458
3:15–16	431	9:31	301	17:8	431, 454, 556

633

17:9	429, 458	5:1–6	462	16:25–28	331
17:12	22, 175, 415	5:31	540	16:30–31	530, 597
17:14	50	7:51	96, 454, 480,	16:31	513
17:15	375, 482		481, 489	17:4	461, 541
17:22	437, 467	8:14	454	17:7	214
17:24	19, 48, 209,	8:15–23	482	17:25–26	341
	210, 253, 262,	8:22	203, 540	17:25–28	182
	404, 429, 456,	8:30	532	17:26–27	387
	458, 482	8:32–35	360	17:26–28	65
18:4	176	9:15	408, 410, 455	17:30	139, 542
18:9	429	9:25	555	17:30–31	540
19:11	104	9:34	336, 547	18:4	461, 541
19:30	256	9:35	540	18:10	410, 462
		9:40	336, 548	18:21	221
Acts		10:35	515	19:8	461, 541
1:2	407, 410, 455	10:38	376	19:9	543
1:7	11, 62	10:41	248	19:11–12	376
1:24	261, 263	11:1	454	19:13–16	430
1:24–25	407, 410, 455	11:18	540	20:21	540
2	211, 531	11:21	540	20:25	214
2:23	10, 23, 30, 49,	12:23	92	20:27	5, 10
	57, 94, 104,	13:22	21, 321	21:11–12	156
	121, 160, 172,	13:36	5, 10	21:14	156, 369
	176, 225, 335,	13:46	460, 567	21:27–33	156
	413, 434, 467	13:46–14:1	461	22:14	53, 409
2:36	94	13:48	190, 409, 417,	26:5	434
2:38	203, 540		458, 459, 460,	26:16	409, 410, 455
2:39	514		467, 501	26:18	540
2:41	203, 454	14:1	190, 461	26:28	541
3:1–8	191	14:8–10	544	27:12	63
3:6	336, 338, 547	14:9–10	376	27:21	63
3:16	190, 338, 376	14:10	336, 548	27:35	555
3:18	225	14:16	94	28:8	336
3:19	203	14:16–17	64		
3:19–20	540	15:7	54, 407, 410,	**Romans**	
3:20	409		455	1	551
3:21	12	15:11	42, 140, 548	1:1	410
4:12	594	15:14	399	1:5	139, 542
4:24	117	15:18	49, 50, 104,	1:8	530
4:27–28	10, 49, 95,		494	1:13	374
	104, 121, 176,	16:3	555	1:16	524
	406, 467	16:7	374	1:18	551
4:28	5, 30, 172,	16:14	461	1:18–19	551
	225	16:15	462	1:21	138, 550, 552
4:31	331	16:18	336	1:24	94, 95, 550

1:24-26	225	8:20	292, 463		502, 569, 573
1:26	94, 174	8:23	436	9:18-19	224
1:28	94, 569	8:26	320	9:19	349
2:5	580	8:27	261, 263	9:19-21	573
2:6	502	8:28	5, 10, 348,	9:20	349
2:6-7	482		410, 457, 596	9:20-21	221
2:8	140, 543	8:28-30	47, 417, 433	9:21	574
2:14-15	138	8:29	83, 107, 141,	9:22	350, 439, 502
2:15	551		262, 263, 320,	9:22-23	105, 221, 438
3:11	387		413, 434, 438,	9:23	49, 50, 253,
3:11-12	546		444, 456, 467		262, 350, 409,
3:19	530	8:29-30	49, 253, 262,		417, 456, 467
3:22	524		379, 406, 434,	9:23-29	350
3:22-25	125		466	9:24	456
3:23-24	448, 479, 524,	8:29-31	394	9:30-31	350
	525, 528	8:30	437, 456, 467,	9:30-32	573
3:24	42, 140		497	10:3	350, 573
3:25	457	8:32	248, 537	10:4	524, 532
3:25-31	524	8:33	407, 417, 433,	10:9	478
3:27-28	596		438	10:9-10	597
4:4	43	8:35	182, 394, 482	10:11	524
4:5	596	8:38-39	182, 482	10:11-13	525
4:16	42	9	440, 559, 570,	10:13	524
4:24-25	248		571, 572, 594	10:14	531
5:1-2	42	9-11	394, 574	10:16	139
5:3	182	9:1	551	10:21	481, 535
5:9-10	548	9:6	595	11:2	433, 464
5:18	109, 479, 519,	9:10-12	413	11:5	125, 409, 417,
	525	9:10-13	415		441, 567
5:18-19	525	9:10-23	193	11:5-7	440, 595
5:19	428, 525	9:11	5, 10, 49, 104,	11:6	501, 596
5:32	221		117, 193, 194,	11:7	174, 409, 411,
6:4	248		408, 410, 457,		417, 427, 538,
6:17	139		482, 570		567, 569, 571
7:7-26	553	9:11-12	501	11:8	567
7:15	553	9:11-13	570	11:11	567
7:17	553	9:12	570, 571	11:11-24	575
7:18	553	9:13	104, 194, 570,	11:15	94, 529
7:20	553		571	11:20	573
7:24	513	9:14-18	572	11:20-21	481
8	433, 434	9:15	104	11:25	62, 174, 440,
8:7	138	9:15-16	350		569
8:14	445	9:15-18	221	11:25-26	94
8:15	444, 467	9:16	104	11:28	409, 416
8:17	361	9:18	95, 104, 225,	11:29	269, 482

11:30-32	567	6:2	445	5:21	437
11:32	527	6:19	443	6:2	297
11:33	71, 104	7:14	514	6:17-18	446
11:33-35	11	8:11	481	6:18	267
11:33-36	394, 559	9:27	481	11:2	215, 250
11:34	11	10:5	21	11:4	454
11:35	287	10:12	481	11:15	502
11:36	9, 100, 599	10:13	94	12:1-7	297
12:2	224	10:22	250	12:7	377
12:12	300	10:23	138	12:7-9	334
13:2	480	11:23	10	12:8-9	321, 377
13:11	436, 548	11:25	210, 214	12:9	334
14:15	481	12:3	546	13:4	270
14:23	138	12:10	374	13:5	481
15	413	12:11	7, 221		
15:5	482	12:18	7	**Galatians**	
15:8-9	578	13:9	187	2:16	596
15:18	139	13:12	187	3:1-2	596
15:22	374	14:3	202	3:10-11	596
15:30-32	301	14:24-25	330, 331	4:4-5	444
16:13	407, 416, 466	15:1	454	4:5-6	467
16:25	19, 209	15:1-2	481	4:6	444
16:26	542	15:2	478, 548	4:19	216
		15:38	7	5:4	491
1 Corinthians		16:15	459	5:19-21	250
1:1	410			5:22	465
1:24	288	**2 Corinthians**		6:15	450
1:27	456	1:19-20	67	6:16	125, 360
1:27-28	408, 416, 538	1:20	64, 214		
2:3-5	322	3:14	174, 569	**Ephesians**	
2:7	19, 49, 50, 209, 434, 467	3:14-16	569	1	442, 446
		3:18	437	1:3	436, 455
2:7-8	406, 463	4:4	138, 444	1:3-4	447, 450
2:8	156	4:7	321	1:3-5	400, 442, 443
2:14	138, 139, 489	4:18	253	1:3-6	394, 423
2:16	11, 289	5:2-3	481	1:4	19, 29, 48, 50, 51, 52, 57, 68, 209, 262, 404, 408, 435, 436, 437, 444, 450, 452, 456, 467, 496, 497, 498, 501, 578
2:14-16	12	5:10	66, 502		
3:9	143, 254	5:11	190, 461, 541		
3:15	548	5:14-15	479		
3:16	443	5:15	528		
3:20	262, 263, 292	5:17	450		
4:7	469, 470	5:18	100		
4:19	221	5:19	479, 528, 529		
5:5	548	5:20	113, 190, 529, 534, 536	1:4-5	49, 253, 417, 441, 463, 466
5:11	481				

Scripture Index

1:5	6, 53, 221, 224, 262, 406, 444, 446, 447, 467, 496	3:3–9	217		
		3:8–12	443	**Colossians**	
		3:9	50, 416	1:6	530
		3:9–10	207, 208	1:10	465
1:5–6	9, 105	3:9–11	19, 209	1:12	445
1:6	447, 449, 496	3:10–11	49, 395, 399, 410, 416, 457, 466, 468	1:13	447, 449
1:6–7	42, 442, 447			1:15	64, 66, 444
1:6–8	447			1:16	9, 66
1:7	140	3:11	5, 437	1:16–17	288
1:9	6, 49, 53, 221, 224, 446	3:21	210, 599	1:18	64, 66, 215
		4:1	465	1:20	529
1:9–10	7, 216	4:9	359	1:21–23	478
1:10	66, 101	4:15	215	1:22–23	481
1:10–11	445, 447	4:17–18	138	1:24–27	208
1:11	5, 49, 101, 104, 221, 224, 253, 262, 406, 410, 417, 423, 442, 447, 457, 467, 494	4:18	550	1:26	19, 50, 416
		4:24	435, 436, 437, 450, 467	1:27	217, 395
				1:27–28	216
		4:26	249	2:2	217
		4:30	96, 113, 161, 454	2:19	215
				3:4	438
1:12	9, 447	5:6	543	3:6	543
1:13	447	5:23	215	3:9–10	450
1:14	9, 442, 447	5:25	215	3:9–11	444
1:17	289, 292, 594	5:25–32	212, 215	3:12	408, 416, 466, 467
1:17–18	10	5:27	446		
1:19	269	6:6	375	3:12–13	437
1:20	442	6:17	131	3:17	138
1:20–23	443	6:18	300	4:2	300
1:22–23	215			4:3	217
2:2	140, 543, 553	**Philippians**		4:12	301
2:3	139	1:6	482		
2:4–7	400	1:7	465	**1 Thessalonians**	
2:5	140	1:19	436, 548	1	453
2:6	442	1:27	465	1:4	408, 417, 466
2:7	42	1:28	548	1:4–6	387, 426, 451
2:8	42, 125, 140, 195, 275, 386, 478, 489, 515, 541	2:12	548	1:5	387
		2:12–13	401, 462, 544	1:6	554
		2:13	221, 401, 524, 548	1:10	454, 463
				2:12	465
2:10	191, 409, 450, 467	3:5	421	2:13	454, 555
		3:21	437, 467	2:16	454
2:15	450	4:3	459, 466	2:18	344, 374
2:20–22	443	4:6	320	3:3	409, 410, 455
2:20–23	443	4:11	222	4:3	221
3:3–6	208	4:13	322	4:14	248

5:9	409, 414, 417, 454, 467, 567	6:16	248	3:6	478, 481
5:17	298, 300	**2 Timothy**		3:7–10	163
5:18	182	1:1	458	3:8	96
5:19	454	1:9	5, 19, 49, 50, 140, 209, 212, 410, 417, 441, 447, 457, 464, 467, 546, 596	3:10	15
5:25	298			3:12–14	481
				3:14	478
2 Thessalonians				3:15	96
1:8	139, 580			4:1	481
1:9	480	1:9–10	457	4:3	19, 50, 209, 456
1:10	438	1:10	458	4:7	96
2:3	481	2:10	408, 416, 436, 438, 454, 467, 548	4:11	481
2:3–10	174			4:12	131
2:10	454, 555			4:13	261, 263
2:10–12	569	2:12	361, 445	5:7	297, 413
2:11	225	2:13	184, 269	5:8	369
2:11–12	95, 174	2:17	482	6:2	480
2:13	409, 436, 455	2:19	466	6:3	221
3:1	298	3:8	567	6:4–6	481
3:3	375	3:12	455	6:16	465
		3:15	548	6:17	12, 104, 214
		4:10	491	6:18	269
1 Timothy		4:14	502	7:22	214
1:11	236, 446			7:25	482, 548
1:15	454			8:6	214
1:19	491	**Titus**		8:8	211
1:20	482	1:1	408, 417	9:7	214
2	110	1:2	19, 49, 50, 184, 209, 269, 467	9:12–15	214
2:1	109			9:15–17	214
2:1–2	110			9:18–28	214
2:3–4	479, 526	1:16	543	9:26	50, 209, 456
2:3–5	108	2:11	109, 479, 519	9:28	548
2:3–6	519	2:11–12	526	10:26–29	481
2:4	86, 109, 225, 227, 386, 502, 534	2:14	399	10:29	480, 491
		3:3	138, 140, 383, 543	10:35–36	481
2:5	214	3:4–7	596	10:36	482
2:6	526	3:7	140	12:1	482
2:8	302	3:9	292	12:1–2	339
4:1	481			12:2	361
4:9	454	**Hebrews**		12:15	491
4:10	109	1:2	67	12:16–17	566
4:16	482	1:2–3	67, 288	12:25	481
5:12	586	1:3	271, 341	12:28	491
5:21	104, 407, 466	1:6	216	12:6	445
6:15	117	2:9	479, 488, 527	12:7–11	368

12:15	480, 489	1:5	548	2:3	568
12:23	421, 459, 466	1:9	548	2:9	568
12:24	214	1:15	465	2:17	568
12:25	480	1:19–20	29, 210, 257,	2:18	292
13:18	298		413, 449, 463	2:20–21	481
13:20	210, 214, 217	1:20	19, 48, 50,	3	568
13:20–21	217		209, 253, 262,	3:8	255
			404, 434, 449,	3:9	77, 86, 110,
James			456, 466		225, 227, 386,
1:3	182	1:22	140		479, 502, 526,
1:4	482	1:23	131		534, 537, 569
1:5	324	2:2	131, 548	3:12	61
1:6	302	2:4	408, 412	3:17	434, 481
1:17	240	2:6	408, 412		
1:13	91, 104, 269	2:6–8	566	**1 John**	
1:17	104	2:7–8	543	1:1	456
1:18	7, 221	2:8	140, 409, 414,	1:1–4	467
1:19	219		454, 509, 566	1:5	104, 444
1:26	292	2:8–9	538	1:9	546, 594, 597
2:1	463	2:9	395, 399, 408,	2:2	479, 488, 529
2:5	408, 417, 463,		411, 416, 465,	2:13–14	375
	467, 538, 596		466	2:16	362
4:2–3	324	2:21	465	2:18	174
4:3	301, 311, 332	3:1	140	2:22	174
4:5	250	3:9	465	2:24	458, 481
4:15	221	3:10–12	302	2:24–25	458
4:17	139	3:17	221	2:25	458, 467
5:11	482	3:20	428	3:2	435, 438, 467
5:14–15	336	4:2–3	139	3:12	375
5:14–16	342	4:12–13	339	3:20	262, 263
5:15	376	4:13	361	3:21–22	325
5:15–18	295	4:17	140	4:8	245, 444
5:16	298, 299, 306,	4:18	548	4:10	501
	312, 324, 336	5:8	481	4:14	479
		5:10	465, 482	4:16	245, 444
1 Peter		5:13	408, 416	5:12	445
1:1	465			5:14–15	311, 325
1:1–2	408, 417, 463,	**2 Peter**		5:18–19	375
	464	1:3	465	5:19	530
1:1–3	395	1:5–7	465	5:20	467
1:2	140, 253, 262,	1:10	409, 417, 464,		
	413, 458, 464,		465	**2 John**	
	466	1:11	210	1:1	408, 416, 466
1:4	445	2	568	1:13	408, 416, 466
1:4–5	482	2:1	66, 439, 502		

Jude		14:11	480
3	491	15:3	15, 267
4	410, 415, 421, 568	15:3-4	179, 259
		16:7	267
6-7	480	16:14	267, 530
14-15	256, 415, 568	16:19	236
20	298	17:8	19, 52, 209, 421, 456, 509
24-25	599		
25	50, 209, 217	17:14	408, 416, 466
		19:1	268
Revelation		19:3	480
1:5	66	19:6	267, 268
1:6	329	19:7	215
1:8	267	19:15	267
2:5	543	20:1-3	375
2:7	357, 599	20:4	445
2:23	502	20:6	445
3:5	97, 421, 459, 466	20:7-10	375
		20:10	480
3:10	530	20:12	419, 421
4:8	254, 267	20:13	502
4:11	9, 10, 221, 224, 267, 329	21:1-4	400
		21:2	215
5:8	555	21:7	446
5:9	211, 488	21:9	215
5:10	445	21:22	267
5:12	267, 329	21:27	421, 460
6:10	117	22	61
7:12	267, 329	22:1-5	599
10	252	22:2	357
10:6	252, 253, 375	22:12	66
10:7	256	22:14	357
11:3-12	554	22:17	139, 215, 384, 401, 454, 524, 537, 554, 599
11:15	214		
11:17	267		
12:7-9	375		
12:9	530		
12:10	214, 267	22:19	60, 357, 599
13	174	22:21	42
13:8	19, 48, 50, 52, 68, 209, 404, 421, 456, 459, 466, 467, 509		

Subject Index

A
À Brakel, William 453, 586
Aalders, G. C. 172
Aaron 20, 313, 314, 410, 412
Abiathar 318
Abimelech 93
Abinadab 414
Abraham 20, 21, 150, 161, 182, 224, 238, 243, 296, 309, 326, 366, 413, 443, 444, 466, 545
Absalom 321
Adam 28, 74, 75, 78, 83, 84, 103, 104, 105, 106, 108, 114, 115, 117, 207, 208, 216, 288, 348, 362, 383, 391, 424, 435, 436, 437, 438, 443, 444, 445, 449, 473, 502, 503, 525
Adam's Fall 66, 68, 69, 72, 80
Admah 162
Adonijah 321
Aeneas 336
Agabus 156, 157
Ahab 151, 317
Ahasuerus 21
Ahimelech 318
Ahithophel 63, 95
Alexander, J. A. 320
Alexander, Ralph 327
Allen, Ronald 312
Althaus, P. 406
Amalekites 296
Ambrose 470
Ammon 330
Ammonites 296, 329
Amnon 321
Amyraldism 479, 484, 585
Amyraut, Moïse 585
Anabaptists 277
Ananias 462
Ancient philosophy 239, 275
Angels 8, 87, 104, 105, 362, 407, 419, 420, 424, 440, 458, 466, 564, 586
Anointing 303, 335, 336, 337, 342
Anselm of Canterbury 238, 472
Anthropomorphisms 59, 146,

	152, 159, 168		591, 592, 593
Antichrist	174, 175	Arminians	4, 27, 37, 38, 43, 137, 140, 168, 187, 188, 199, 200, 202, 225, 264, 265, 274, 277, 355, 382, 383, 385, 386, 387, 388, 392, 432, 433, 448, 462, 469, 477, 481, 484, 485, 491, 494, 501, 502, 505, 512, 520, 532, 533, 545, 547, 548, 555, 575, 577, 583, 586, 588, 592, 593
Antiquity	238, 276, 280, 289		
Apostasy	119, 136, 139, 140, 159, 160, 488, 536		
Apostles	190, 191, 208, 305, 335, 336, 374, 407, 410, 461, 522		
Aquinas, Thomas	169, 206, 225, 268, 351		
Archer, G. L.	172		
Aristotle	221		
Arminianism	1, 3, 16, 17, 18, 19, 20, 25, 28, 37, 38, 73, 89, 122, 123, 124, 126, 136, 167, 169, 171, 187, 192, 193, 194, 195, 200, 202, 257, 266, 368, 373, 384, 391, 398, 432, 510, 512, 531, 533, 538, 544, 555, 556, 559, 577, 579, 590,	Arminius, Jacob	3, 17, 18, 35, 70, 103, 136, 169, 448, 475, 483, 484, 485, 489, 491, 494, 504, 505, 553, 562, 577
		Armstrong, Karen	153, 239
		Asaph	331
		Asia	374, 463, 531

Assyria	163, 318, 320
Assyrians	320, 330
Atheists	107, 355, 358, 367
Atonement	65, 118, 216, 472, 473, 476, 479, 480, 486, 493, 527, 532, 533, 539, 584, 585
Augustine	29, 35, 44, 55, 69, 70, 74, 87, 109, 115, 136, 169, 225, 234, 238, 243, 263, 264, 265, 269, 276, 281, 283, 351, 469, 470, 472, 484, 511, 514, 523, 541, 559, 560, 571, 581, 585
Augustinianism	56, 405, 472
Augustus	178
Austel, H. J.	320
Austin Bible Church	5
Author of sin	28, 34, 40, 41, 99, 104, 105, 106, 114, 499, 582

Subject Index

B
Babylon 92, 99, 148, 149, 155, 236, 320, 359, 408
Babylonian exile 306, 574
Barrett, W. 238
Barth, Karl 44, 63, 240, 241, 244, 252, 268, 269, 270, 380, 389, 405, 449, 538, 559, 577, 578, 586
Basinger, David 31, 80, 270
Basinger, Randall 80, 270
Bathsheba 22, 321
Baugh, Steven 264
Bavinck, Herman 54, 55, 64, 66, 70, 71, 85, 101, 132, 174, 221, 222, 223, 224, 226, 227, 228, 253, 262, 265, 267, 269, 351, 396, 405, 440, 449, 466, 471, 474, 485, 513, 516, 523, 562, 571, 580, 586, 588

Baxter, R. 474
Bayle, Pierre 345
Beeke, Joel R. 31
Behemoth 289, 290, 291, 292
Beilby, J. K. 80, 171
Belgic Confession 99, 211, 216, 473, 474, 475, 560, 586
Believers 10, 30, 47, 60, 61, 62, 65, 66, 68, 110, 182, 211, 288, 289, 306, 311, 338, 346, 350, 352, 364, 367, 368, 369, 380, 387, 399, 400, 404, 411, 416, 424, 434, 435, 436, 441, 443, 444, 445, 448, 449, 450, 451, 452, 453, 455, 457, 458, 460, 466, 467, 479, 480, 481, 484, 486, 487, 514, 520, 523, 528, 530, 533, 546, 548,

566, 577, 578, 580, 582, 598
Ben-hadad 327
Benedict XVI 432
Berkhof, Hendrikus 104, 142, 143, 240, 241, 242, 244, 247, 248, 270, 453, 473, 510
Berkhof, Louis 69, 73, 105, 106, 121, 169, 402, 403, 411, 560, 578, 584, 586
Berkouwer, Gerrit 18, 57, 72, 73, 84, 85, 100, 101, 111, 112, 118, 119, 187, 188, 192, 195, 349, 350, 351, 389, 401, 402, 406, 417, 441, 447, 459, 485, 499, 506, 507, 508, 512, 538, 542, 546, 571, 576, 580, 581, 582, 583, 586, 588, 589, 595,

643

597
Bernard of Clairvaux
248
Bethsaida 155
Beza, Theodore
238, 476,
585
Biblical evidence
20, 83,
180, 181,
183, 185,
187, 207,
210, 400,
585
Bithynia 374, 463
Bloesch, Donald
238
Blum, E. A.
464, 567,
568
Blumenthal, H. J.
235
Body of Christ
210, 211,
217, 444
Boer, Harry R.
509
Boettner, Loraine
33, 34
Bogerman, Johannes
504, 577
Bonhoeffer, Dietrich
270
Book of life
50, 52, 97,
379, 417,
419, 420,
421, 459,
460, 467,
509
Boston, Thomas
453
Bouma, Cornelis
109

Boyd, Gregory A.
17, 22, 31,
32, 54, 62,
69, 76, 79,
80, 90,
101, 123,
124, 125,
143, 145,
146, 157,
158, 159,
162, 165,
166, 167,
168, 170,
171, 172,
173, 177,
178, 197,
229, 232,
233, 272,
281, 291,
293, 304,
307, 316,
322, 327,
344, 347,
374, 375,
432, 434,
460, 477,
565, 566,
573, 574
Breen, Q. 275
Brightman, E. S.
345
Brother Andrew
305
Brouwer, Bastiaan J.
509
Bruce, A. B.
13
Bruce, F. F. 450, 459
Bullinger, Heinrich
585
Brümmer, V.
130, 470
Brunner, Emil
243, 244,
249, 268,

269, 553
Buis, Harry
39, 40,
274, 470,
575
Bultema, H.
320
Bunyan, J. 474
Byzantine Text
412, 415,
425, 455,
456

C
Caiaphas 23
Calamities 96, 100,
353
Calcidius 17
Calminianism
592, 593
Calminians
559, 592,
594
Calvin, John
16, 44, 55,
69, 70, 71,
72, 76, 78,
82, 103,
104, 118,
119, 122,
154, 225,
234, 274,
275, 276,
277, 278,
279, 319,
351, 401,
402, 404,
405, 411,
439, 449,
453, 472,
473, 476,
498, 506,
507, 511,
523, 568,
571, 575,

Subject Index

Calvinism 576, 581, 585, 597, 598
2, 16, 17, 18, 19, 25, 31, 32, 33, 34, 38, 39, 40, 41, 42, 44, 56, 73, 83, 84, 114, 115, 122, 168, 169, 170, 178, 188, 192, 193, 194, 195, 200, 202, 280, 296, 368, 383, 384, 391, 398, 405, 469, 472, 476, 478, 479, 480, 481, 484, 506, 544, 556, 559, 577, 585, 587, 590, 592, 593

Calvinists 15, 30, 31, 32, 33, 34, 35, 37, 38, 40, 41, 73, 84, 102, 103, 107, 110, 117, 137, 168, 187, 188, 202, 264, 274, 277, 300, 305, 306, 380, 382, 383, 384, 386, 387, 388, 392, 397, 398, 405, 406, 441, 462, 469, 481, 483, 485, 504, 508, 511, 515, 519, 520, 533, 547, 548, 575, 577, 581, 585, 587, 590, 592, 593

Camus, Albert 351, 352, 353
Canaan 20, 312
Canaanites 149
Canons of Dordt 16, 26, 73, 91, 187, 230, 397, 401, 405, 448, 469, 474, 475, 476, 485, 491, 493, 494, 495, 498, 500, 501, 502, 503, 504, 505, 507, 509, 511, 513, 514, 521, 528, 539, 540, 541, 542, 559, 560, 561, 579, 580, 586, 587

Capernaum 155

Cappadocia 463
Carroll, John 272, 273, 275, 276, 277, 279
Carson, D. A. 113, 425
Catastrophes 24, 93, 340, 347, 355
Chafer, Lewis Sperry 68, 79, 101, 403
Chaldeans 148, 155
Chorazin 155
Chosen One 407, 411, 412, 413, 449, 578
Chosen ones 404, 408, 415, 416, 427, 438, 473, 571, 578, 594, 595, 598
Christ Jesus 42, 49, 140, 191, 208, 209, 212, 395, 408, 410, 417, 436, 438, 441, 442, 447, 448, 450, 455, 457, 458, 466, 467, 473, 486, 519, 524, 526, 528, 546, 599

Christian thought
238, 239
Christian world
43, 95, 304
Christians 4, 70, 107,
132, 156,
189, 215,
216, 237,
238, 252,
277, 298,
299, 315,
331, 355,
358, 367,
369, 370,
375, 377,
381, 404,
405, 452,
457, 463,
465, 480,
482, 489,
490, 491,
532, 555,
594
Christianity
31, 122,
132, 222,
246, 262,
282, 344,
354
Church fathers
122, 235,
253, 262,
470
Church history
52, 212,
260, 510,
562
Clark, Gordon
106, 109,
341
Cobb, J. B. 241
Common grace
48, 65, 215
Compatibilism
33, 48, 72

Comrie, Alexander
511, 586
Concepts 33, 34, 35,
36, 37,
107, 114,
126, 127,
129, 130,
131, 145,
179, 183,
184, 185,
186, 223,
226, 227,
230, 254,
257, 261,
264, 266,
271, 379,
384, 385,
397, 398,
399, 402,
428, 487,
499, 502,
503, 506,
582, 585,
593
Conceptual
knowledge
127, 128,
131, 133,
227
Conclusivism
5, 107,
114, 507,
535, 540,
559, 563,
585, 588,
589
Congruism 179, 192,
193, 202
Contra-Remonstrants
274, 469,
475, 484,
485, 487,
489, 499,
502, 505,
506, 511,

527, 593
Conversion
2, 81, 110,
139, 261,
305, 306,
316, 323,
391, 437,
452, 453,
457, 459,
462, 481,
482, 485,
499, 501,
502, 506,
510, 545,
546, 547,
549, 553,
588, 597
Corduan, W.
356
Council of Trent
596
Counsel of God
4, 5, 8, 10,
12, 15, 16,
17, 18, 19,
20, 21, 23,
26, 29, 40,
43, 47, 48,
50, 55, 56,
61, 62, 63,
66, 68, 69,
70, 79, 87,
100, 102,
119, 122,
127, 164,
192, 204,
212, 217,
234, 335,
340, 372,
380, 390,
410, 526,
543, 567,
568, 580,
582, 587,
589, 598

Subject Index

Covenant 10, 44, 147, 180, 207, 209, 210, 211, 212, 214, 216, 217, 241, 243, 303, 333, 390, 420, 428, 510, 514
Covenant of grace 44, 207, 514
Covenant of works 207
Covenants 212, 213, 214
Craig, W. L. 171, 180
Cranfield, C. E. B. 574
Creator 8, 26, 51, 93, 101, 131, 136, 143, 272, 279, 286, 445, 477, 591
Cullmann, O. 254
Cyprian 470
Cyrus 141, 171, 172, 173, 178, 197, 232

D

Damnation 396, 397, 398, 400, 403, 405, 413, 414, 415, 471, 472, 480, 482, 495, 502, 503, 508, 573, 579
Darby, John N. 361, 362, 404, 477
David 10, 21, 22, 67, 93, 95, 141, 147, 150, 153, 154, 157, 158, 170, 171, 302, 316, 317, 320, 321, 322, 330, 377, 411, 412, 413, 443, 444
Davids, P. H. 416, 464
Day, J. 291
Day of Pentecost 203, 211
Day of trouble 121, 223, 225, 454, 565
De Boer, Theo 271
De Brès, Guido 475
De Graaff, Frank 360
De Groot, D. J. 97, 571
De Jong, A. C. 539
De Reuver, A. 474
Decree of election 16, 17, 67, 385, 388, 399, 403, 405, 460, 472, 478, 479, 495, 497, 500, 503, 521, 575, 580, 592
Decree of reprobation 7, 16, 45, 67, 95, 113, 388, 399, 400, 403, 405, 438, 440, 454, 469, 472, 473, 493, 495, 497, 499, 500, 501, 502, 503, 504, 521, 535, 537, 559, 560, 561, 562, 563, 564, 568, 569, 570, 575, 576, 577, 579, 580, 581, 584, 590, 591, 592
Decretalism 25, 27, 28, 30, 39, 54, 55, 58, 72, 73, 74, 75, 81, 82, 86, 89, 90, 91, 96, 112, 113, 115, 122, 123, 126, 135, 136, 141, 148, 155, 167, 169,

172, 179, 180, 181, 183, 184, 185, 187, 188, 189, 190, 194, 195, 198, 200, 203, 230, 233, 266, 272, 276, 277, 280, 281, 282, 293, 295, 296, 304, 306, 307, 341, 343, 355, 366, 368, 369, 376, 377, 432, 541, 579, 582

Decretalist view 59, 68, 159, 312, 460

Decretalists 27, 35, 73, 77, 90, 91, 94, 95, 100, 117, 118, 120, 122, 137, 143, 152, 154, 157, 159, 171, 173, 176, 177, 183, 186, 189, 191, 199, 200, 264, 297, 298, 299, 301, 302, 303, 304, 313, 315, 318, 364, 370, 385, 432

Demarest, Bruce 19, 40, 43, 122, 380, 396, 410, 411, 429, 434, 439, 449, 492, 546, 549, 565, 567, 570, 571

Denney, J. 416, 434

Dennison, J. T. 78, 91, 105, 127, 182, 187, 341, 383, 401, 473, 485, 486, 495, 497, 500, 501, 512, 513, 514, 540, 542, 579

Descartes, René 199, 222, 277, 278, 279, 280

Determinism 72, 73, 195, 508, 541

Devine, A. 204

Diderot, Denis 280

Dijk, Klaas 105, 118, 406, 507, 560, 563, 569, 570, 586

Diseases 92, 338, 340, 342, 352, 355, 376

Ditmanson, H. H. 470

Divine decree 1, 52, 63, 71, 78, 206, 440, 473, 503, 561, 562, 563, 575, 581

Divine election 2, 66, 188, 389, 418, 424, 427, 430, 443, 447, 494, 595

Divine foreknowledge 37, 130, 145, 179, 180, 183, 186, 187, 188, 264, 265, 380

Divine predestination 17, 136, 187, 273, 392, 425, 460, 461

Divine sovereignty 36, 37, 137, 186, 187, 188, 199, 201, 337, 340, 365, 392, 399, 433, 440, 470, 482, 500, 546, 548, 591, 593

Doctrine of election 41, 349, 389, 402,

Subject Index

406, 512, 516, 541, 549, 559, 560, 578, 579, 581, 591, 594, 596
Doctrine of predestination 38, 95, 340, 396, 398, 424, 476, 507, 516, 523
Doctrine of reprobation 402, 504, 513, 560
Dogma 95, 111, 152, 159, 173, 316, 328
Dogmas 102, 168, 389, 405, 533
Donelan, John P. 420
Dooyeweerd, Herman 136, 550
Dorner, Isaak 241
Dordrecht 475
Double predestination 73, 371, 405, 492, 507, 587, 588
Duetz, Abraham 509
Duffield, G. P. 41, 256, 369, 370, 371, 434, 448, 452, 564

Duns Scotus, John 349
Dutch Reformed Church 71, 371, 385, 402, 426, 439, 459, 498, 509, 512, 516, 526, 539, 560
Dutch States Translation 110, 111, 268, 456, 488, 526, 568, 570

E
Eddy, P. R. 80, 171
Edom 194, 571, 572
Edomites 571
Edwards, D. 515
Egypt 20, 52, 58, 59, 90, 91, 92, 146, 205, 312, 359
Egyptians 92, 296
Einstein, Albert 283, 388
Eleazar 318
Eli 181, 204, 310, 317, 318, 368, 565
Eliab 414
Elihu 569
Elijah 295, 323, 554
Eliphaz 97, 285
Elizabeth 297

Ellison, Henry 60, 315, 316
Emotions 113, 138, 161, 162, 163, 220, 234, 235, 237, 238, 244, 245, 246, 249, 250
Enchiridion 29, 74, 225, 581
Engelsma, David J. 216
Enoch 256, 415, 419, 568
Ephraim 153, 162
Episcopius, Simon 577
Erasmus, Desiderius 35, 136, 272, 273, 274, 276, 277, 279, 280, 450, 473, 522
Erickson, Millard 8, 80, 86, 93, 95, 99, 168, 192, 196, 198, 201, 202, 345, 471, 578, 584
Esau 194, 413, 415, 566, 570, 571, 572
Esser, Hans-Helmut 51
Eternal blessedness 3, 342, 396, 400,

405, 411, 412, 413, 415, 427, 538
Eternal counsel
18, 19, 20, 22, 25, 26, 30, 36, 48, 50, 52, 57, 63, 68, 70, 71, 72, 91, 100, 102, 113, 116, 128, 129, 191, 198, 206, 210, 212, 213, 257, 276, 296, 298, 299, 338, 543, 561, 567, 568, 577, 580, 587, 589, 591
Eternal damnation 397, 400, 403, 405, 414, 415, 480, 482, 495, 508, 579
Eternal decree 16, 52, 53, 55, 57, 67, 72, 78, 95, 97, 98, 103, 198, 297, 323, 324, 358, 388, 399, 400, 402, 404, 405, 410, 415, 438, 439, 440, 469, 472, 473, 475, 494, 495, 499, 500, 501, 502, 503, 504, 508, 520, 521, 535, 559, 560, 561, 562, 563, 564, 565, 566, 568, 569, 570, 573, 575, 576, 577, 580, 584, 587, 589, 590, 591, 592
Eternal decrees 47, 48, 54, 55, 438, 563, 564, 575, 590
Eternal destiny 72, 87, 400, 460, 521, 572
Eternal destruction 381, 390, 439, 568, 575, 576, 578
Eternal election 3, 35, 41, 125, 333, 397, 404, 411, 414, 416, 418, 424, 427, 430, 441, 456, 506, 538, 572, 593, 595
Eternal glory 3, 395, 408, 435, 436, 438, 455
Eternal life 49, 65, 66, 119, 190, 404, 409, 417, 429, 431, 435, 453, 457, 458, 459, 460, 467, 486, 487, 497, 528, 540, 543
Eternal perdition 3, 16, 41, 77
Eternal predestination 4, 30, 187, 398, 416, 428, 430, 439, 567, 570
Eternal salvation 16, 380, 397, 404, 411, 460, 467, 493, 506, 590, 591
Eternity future 207, 210, 211, 400, 565
Eternity past 121, 166, 189, 207, 211, 299, 458, 584
Evangelical theologians 31, 477, 478

Subject Index

Evangelicals
   15, 17, 38,
   43, 122,
   277, 380,
   404, 481,
   483, 494,
   497, 515,
   520, 577,
   579
Evans, C. Stephen
   32
Eve   74, 75, 83,
   84, 105,
   108, 114,
   115, 348,
   383, 391,
   435, 444
External call
   193, 480,
   540

F
Fairbairn, Andrew M.
   244
Fatalism   182, 195,
   303, 343,
   453, 512
Feenstra, J. G.
   474
Fernhout, Klaas
   434, 488,
   507
Finan, T.   235
Five Points of
   Calvinism
   405, 469,
   478, 479,
   480, 481
Flint, Th.   156, 171
Foreknowledge of
   God
   1, 10, 22,
   23, 30, 57,
   82, 94,
   121, 135,
   160, 176,
   259, 394,
   408, 413,
   417, 458,
   463, 466
Foreordination
   53, 135,
   168, 187,
   263, 264,
   279, 379,
   380, 433
Foreseen faith
   3, 16, 18,
   28, 126,
   129, 195,
   197, 252,
   380, 397,
   448, 478,
   487, 493,
   497, 498,
   500, 501,
   505, 506,
   555, 562,
   580, 588,
   591
Forster, Roger
   483, 484
Foundation of the
   world
   19, 23, 29,
   48, 49, 50,
   51, 52, 56,
   68, 125,
   209, 210,
   253, 257,
   262, 341,
   391, 394,
   404, 408,
   413, 421,
   423, 433,
   434, 436,
   437, 441,
   442, 449,
   452, 454,
   455, 456,
   458, 459,
   463, 466,
   467, 486,
   496, 564,
   565, 567
Frame, J.   80
Free choices
   23, 25,
   116, 123,
   142, 171,
   172, 178,
   181, 183,
   188, 189,
   197, 200,
   203, 204,
   231, 264,
   358, 364,
   397, 553
Free human choices
   165, 177,
   206, 230
Free will   24, 32, 43,
   81, 124,
   135, 136,
   137, 138,
   140, 144,
   145, 165,
   169, 170,
   186, 200,
   260, 264,
   273, 274,
   279, 345,
   358, 383,
   391, 470,
   471, 472,
   488, 520,
   553, 554
Freedom of will
   1, 22, 25,
   27, 28, 30,
   38, 39, 48,
   82, 166,
   169, 170,
   173, 174,
   183, 185,

188, 229, 233, 264, 265, 266, 269, 274, 275, 277, 344, 345, 347, 382, 388, 391, 402, 481, 591, 593
Fretheim, Terence E. 152, 153, 291
Freud, Sigmund 199

G
Gabriel 419
Gad 157
Galatia 374, 463
Galilee 155
Galileo 246
Garden of Eden 14, 362
Geisler, Norman L. 31, 32, 34, 80, 356, 592
Gentiles 10, 49, 51, 54, 62, 111, 113, 121, 156, 176, 208, 300, 312, 361, 363, 395, 399, 407, 409, 416, 427, 440, 459, 488, 523, 575, 578
Gerhard, Johann 498
Gerhardt, Paul 323

Gethsemane 23, 247, 335, 369
Gibeon 309
Gibson, John 291, 293
Gill, John 119, 150, 354
Gispen, Willem 243, 565
Glatzer, N. N. 287
Glorification 9, 208, 217, 247, 390
God's absolute foreknowledge 145, 183, 201
God's absolute sovereignty 35, 37, 181, 365
God's counsel 1, 2, 5, 9, 10, 11, 12, 13, 15, 17, 18, 19, 21, 22, 23, 24, 26, 28, 29, 30, 35, 36, 40, 48, 51, 54, 60, 63, 67, 68, 69, 74, 78, 80, 87, 89, 90, 91, 96, 100, 101, 110, 111, 121, 122, 148, 165, 167, 180, 192, 198, 203, 204,

205, 206, 207, 209, 211, 212, 213, 214, 216, 217, 219, 220, 224, 231, 232, 234, 235, 257, 267, 295, 299, 302, 304, 305, 321, 326, 331, 333, 335, 338, 339, 343, 344, 349, 353, 354, 373, 375, 389, 390, 399, 416, 448, 455, 483, 534, 543, 563, 564, 581, 582
God's decree 56, 69, 70, 86, 103, 105, 141, 169, 177, 181, 196, 276, 356, 369, 396, 397, 506, 508, 573, 583, 584
God's emotions 235, 237, 244, 245, 250
God's eternal counsel 18, 20, 30, 48, 50, 63, 68, 70, 72,

91, 116, 198, 210, 213, 257, 276, 296, 298, 299, 338, 567, 587, 589

God's foreknowledge
3, 24, 25, 48, 82, 125, 157, 168, 186, 187, 188, 200, 202, 230, 234, 263, 264, 265, 266, 358, 388, 466, 591

God's grace
39, 43, 44, 138, 212, 396, 443, 447, 452, 464, 467, 470, 471, 474, 475, 480, 481, 482, 489, 515, 551, 553, 566, 567, 574

God's impassibility
238, 245, 246

God's kingdom
207, 209, 214, 348

God's knowledge
132, 260, 261, 262, 265

God's omnipotence
80, 81, 143, 184, 188, 260, 267, 268, 270, 271, 272, 284, 340, 345, 347

God's omniscience
39, 80, 81, 135, 143, 144, 145, 146, 152, 233, 234, 253, 254, 259, 260, 261, 262

God's plans
56, 86, 98, 160, 207

God's providence
17, 18, 51, 71, 104, 107, 197, 198, 200, 275

God's purpose
1, 6, 7, 8, 9, 10, 12, 13, 23, 49, 193, 408, 415, 457

God's righteousness
120, 181, 350, 382, 397, 474, 475, 543, 584, 589

God's sovereign decree
206, 254, 384, 398, 567, 587

God's sovereignty
15, 20, 24, 25, 32, 33, 36, 38, 81, 82, 102, 107, 108, 115, 117, 118, 120, 126, 131, 135, 164, 165, 166, 170, 181, 182, 184, 185, 188, 190, 195, 199, 212, 213, 219, 220, 229, 230, 231, 239, 252, 267, 277, 355, 373, 388, 389, 391, 392, 396, 397, 401, 402, 441, 446, 447, 473, 483, 487, 498, 500, 506, 516, 520, 543, 572, 582, 584, 586, 587, 589

God's Spirit
169, 193, 373, 460, 551

God's ways
14, 15, 18, 19, 20, 22, 24, 29, 52, 53, 63, 91, 97, 99, 100, 101, 110, 148, 198, 203, 205, 206,

	213, 214, 215, 231, 232, 234, 296, 304, 305, 306, 321, 331, 333, 338, 339, 340, 354, 356, 358, 373, 399, 414, 455, 534, 561, 563, 567, 577, 581, 582		448, 475, 484, 485, 491, 494, 504, 505, 585	Harrison, R. K.	172
				Hart, J. H. A.	567
				Hartley, J. E.	303
		Gomorrah	182, 307	Hartshorne, Charles	241, 270
		Good, E.	291	Hasker, W.	171
		Goslinga, C. J.	96, 143	Hatch, E.	235
		Gottschalk of Orbais	472	Hauck, Friedrich	51
		Graafland, Cornelis	38, 476, 484, 494, 511, 539, 578	Hazael	327
				Healing	29, 190, 191, 299, 303, 304, 325, 335, 336, 337, 338, 341, 342, 343, 369, 370, 371, 372, 376, 544, 547, 548
God's will	10, 14, 29, 37, 74, 78, 84, 96, 98, 101, 103, 109, 111, 112, 114, 115, 139, 162, 167, 170, 222, 223, 224, 225, 226, 227, 301, 303, 304, 340, 344, 351, 368, 369, 370, 372, 373, 376, 384, 430, 526, 533, 537, 554, 581, 582, 590				
		Grant, Frederick	194, 216, 525, 529, 530, 573		
		Greeks	190, 276, 461		
		Gregory of Rimini	472		
		Greijdanus, Seakle	13, 110, 191, 439, 568, 571		
				Health	182, 341, 363, 377
		Griffin, David R.	270	Heaven	1, 7, 12, 53, 56, 64, 66, 69, 75, 96, 101, 130, 150, 155, 182, 216, 220, 295, 309, 317, 324, 331, 336, 341, 342, 364, 400, 407, 410, 420, 421, 424, 431, 435, 442, 444, 445, 453, 459, 475, 513,
		Grogan, G. W.	172		
		Grosheide, F. W.	23, 425, 445, 450		
		H			
God's wrath	249, 317, 327, 332, 359, 438	Haak, T.	312		
		Hagar	20		
		Haman	21		
		Hammurabi	531		
Gomarists	469, 484, 491, 502	Hannah	296, 310		
		Harnack, Adolf von	221		
Gomarus, Francis	35, 136,				

Subject Index

Heavens 8, 9, 11, 15, 52, 87, 149, 208, 236, 260, 288, 317, 334
Hegel, Georg 222
Heidelberg Catechism 75, 181, 341, 343, 376, 383, 405, 466, 473, 537, 556, 594
Heisenberg, Werner 281
Hellenism 221, 235, 237
Heman 331
Henry VIII 273
Henry, Matthew 98, 119, 252, 565
Herod 23, 48, 92, 95, 121, 122
Hervormde Kerk 26, 72, 385, 402, 411, 426, 439, 459, 473, 508, 512, 516, 526, 566, 568, 570, 580
Hervormde Raad 372
Heschel, Abraham 238, 251
Heyns, Johan 8, 54, 55, 56, 86, 87, 94, 121, 195, 411, 458, 465, 466, 507, 508, 509, 513, 578
Hezekiah 93, 97, 149, 154, 182, 297, 307, 309, 318, 319, 320, 323
Hilary 470
Hitler, Adolf 477
Hobbes, Thomas 278
Hodge, C. A. 570
Hoek, Jan 71, 502, 583, 588
Hoeksema, H. 7, 539
Holiness 30, 39, 108, 120, 130, 181, 214, 223, 244, 249, 267, 348, 435, 436, 437, 443, 450, 497, 498, 501, 503, 513, 576
Holocaust 343, 352, 363
Holwerda, Benne 244
Holy Spirit 4, 10, 11, 36, 113, 156, 161, 208, 245, 274, 275, 289, 306, 331, 337, 374, 387, 388, 407, 443, 451, 452, 453, 454, 458, 461, 462, 465, 479, 480, 485, 486, 488, 489, 490, 515, 541, 546, 551, 594
Hommius, Festus 585
Hooykaas, R. 278
Houdmann, S. M. 592
House, H. W. 80
Hughes, Philip 76, 78, 104, 106, 154, 165, 405, 411, 525, 531, 541, 550, 570, 591
Human choices 21, 47, 63, 157, 165, 177, 181, 185, 188, 198, 203, 206, 213, 230, 233, 264, 399, 426, 484, 589
Human deeds 54, 89, 114, 173, 181, 185,

508
Human freedom
3, 16, 24,
30, 33, 36,
37, 39, 48,
89, 102,
116, 123,
126, 127,
128, 130,
142, 145,
169, 174,
183, 186,
187, 188,
192, 196,
198, 199,
201, 231,
232, 233,
260, 263,
264, 265,
266, 270,
272, 273,
277, 279,
358, 365,
388, 389,
392, 497,
506, 520,
521, 522,
543, 577,
591, 593
Human heart
129, 136,
137, 138,
175
Human history
56, 90,
153, 268,
357
Human mind
199, 228,
278, 279,
292
Human nature
44, 177,
248, 401,
470, 542

Human responsibility
16, 25, 35,
37, 72, 73,
81, 82,
105, 109,
114, 117,
118, 128,
130, 137,
139, 140,
169, 170,
173, 179,
180, 183,
185, 188,
190, 192,
195, 196,
197, 198,
201, 205,
206, 212,
227, 233,
265, 266,
337, 340,
345, 355,
365, 382,
385, 389,
391, 392,
397, 398,
399, 401,
402, 424,
425, 427,
429, 430,
433, 440,
453, 454,
460, 469,
470, 471,
477, 478,
479, 481,
482, 483,
486, 493,
498, 499,
507, 515,
516, 520,
521, 522,
543, 546,
548, 555,
557, 572,

576, 577,
578, 587,
590, 591,
593
Human sins
100, 205,
340, 344
Human will
37, 136,
138, 139,
140, 264,
273, 274,
350, 384,
388, 485,
493, 520,
533, 541,
553, 591
Humanism
222, 272,
273, 275
Hushai   63
Hyper-Calvinism
16, 42,
136, 163,
199, 202,
206, 215,
276, 358,
371, 398,
510, 511,
512, 513,
514, 516,
534, 540,
559, 579,
595, 596,
597, 598
Hyper-Calvinists
15, 73,
110, 112,
114, 139,
140, 199,
352, 381,
385, 386,
452, 469,
511, 512,
515, 516,

Subject Index

I

Iconium 190, 461
Idolatry 31, 174
Ignatius 235
Incarnation
    67, 223, 587
Infralapsarianism
    66, 122, 486, 492, 584, 585, 586, 587, 588, 589
Infralapsarians
    559, 564, 583, 586, 587, 588, 592
Institutes of the Christian Religion
    69, 76, 104, 119, 275, 276, 351, 401, 405, 449, 473, 476, 498, 506, 576, 598
Internal call
    193, 480, 540
Irrationalism
    397, 593
Irresistible grace
    480, 483, 486
Isaac 20, 296, 529, 530, 532, 541, 543, 544, 545, 547, 555, 556, 579, 592, 594, 598
Iscariot, Simon 175
Ishmael 20, 309
Israel 6, 8, 20, 21, 49, 52, 58, 59, 87, 92, 93, 94, 95, 99, 100, 113, 114, 120, 121, 125, 139, 146, 147, 149, 152, 153, 155, 158, 159, 160, 161, 162, 170, 172, 173, 174, 175, 179, 183, 194, 204, 205, 207, 210, 211, 215, 236, 238, 243, 245, 256, 261, 271, 287, 296, 307, 308, 310, 317, 318, 320, 323, 326, 327, 332, 333, 343, 352, 358, 359, 360, 361, 362, 363, 377, 380, 390, 395, 409, 411, 412, 413, 307, 308, 413, 415, 545
Israelites 113, 224, 296, 311, 332, 395, 411, 427, 440, 445, 481, 567, 571, 572
Ithamar 318

J

Jacob 194, 237, 296, 366, 390, 413, 415, 570, 571, 572
Jacob, Edmond 292
Jacobs, P. 576, 577
Jairus 190, 299
Jeduthun 331
Jehoahaz 327
Jehoram 92
Jehoshaphat 329, 330
Jericho 329
Jerome 571
Jerusalem 108, 112, 135, 139, 151, 156, 178, 301, 308, 316, 317, 331, 384, 412, 413, 414, 418, 427, 416, 419, 420, 427, 440, 464, 523, 531, 535, 536, 538, 544, 545, 570, 571, 572, 574, 575, 580, 595

Jesus Christ 481, 534, 9, 10, 44, 49, 63, 67, 125, 214, 215, 217, 336, 338, 372, 394, 395, 406, 408, 409, 412, 417, 423, 442, 444, 448, 450, 454, 463, 487, 490, 496, 505, 513, 521, 547, 567, 599

Jewett, Paul 411, 466, 540, 549

Jews 21, 43, 111, 156, 176, 190, 299, 333, 343, 352, 359, 361, 395, 460, 461, 488, 523, 569, 595

John the Baptist 13, 443, 444, 554, 556

Johnson, Terry 305, 306

Jonker, Willem D. 507, 586

Joseph 90, 91, 94

Josephus, Flavius 222

Joshua 149, 309, 323, 329, 333

Josiah 141, 171, 172, 173, 178, 197, 232

Judah 95, 146, 153, 208, 320, 330, 377, 395, 413, 580

Judaism 246, 419, 420

Judas 22, 53, 175, 176, 407, 410, 415, 429, 430

Judea 301

Jüngel, Eberhard 130, 242

Junior partners 25, 120, 135, 143, 166, 254, 338

Junius, Franciscus 240

Justification 109, 125, 273, 275, 342, 344, 443, 494, 496, 504, 511, 519, 525

K

Kaiser, Walter 312

Kalsbeek, L. 184, 223, 351

Keel, O. 291

Keilah 153, 154

Kelly, William 51, 120, 194, 451, 525, 537

Kersten, Henry 37, 38, 65, 72, 102, 103, 105, 109, 110, 111, 114, 186, 396, 411, 439, 488, 512, 515, 529, 539, 541, 560, 569, 583, 586

Kitamori, K. 248

Kingdom of God 12, 42, 50, 51, 217, 335, 375, 461, 467

Klooster, F. H. 405, 476

Knowling, R. J. 459

Kohlbrugge, Hermann 474, 504, 511

König, Adrio 75, 152, 241, 251, 411, 413, 465, 476, 481, 482, 498, 509

Krauth, Charles 73

Küng, H. 251

Kushner, Harold 245, 246, 345, 364

Subject Index

Kuyper, Abraham 586

L
Lalleman, P. J. 416
Lamb 29, 50, 52, 68, 210, 211, 215, 237, 257, 267, 321, 329, 408, 412, 413, 421, 434, 435, 444, 448, 459, 460, 463, 466, 467
Last Day 428, 431, 557
Laytner, A. 182, 366
Lazarus 336
Leah 296
Leibnitz, Gottfried 197, 349
Leuenberg Agreement 485, 560, 561
Leviathan 289, 290, 291, 292
Lewis, C. S. 124, 340, 474, 475
Lewis, G. R. 19, 122
Leyden 3, 485
Liberals 43, 555
Liefeld, W. 301
Lightner, R. P. 452
Limited Atonement 473, 476, 479, 486, 532, 533, 585

Lindström, Fredrik 90, 291, 292, 293
Loosjes, J. 485
Logic 39, 40, 78, 82, 107, 117, 118, 120, 130, 180, 181, 183, 184, 185, 231, 260, 293, 304, 351, 352, 385, 389, 402, 403, 472, 474, 502, 539, 560, 583, 585, 593
Luther, Martin 35, 44, 69, 136, 247, 268, 272, 273, 274, 276, 277, 450, 473, 523, 585
Lutherans 225, 265, 277, 481, 485, 520, 560
Lydia 461, 462

M
Maccovius, Johannes 102, 103, 585
MacGregor, K. 156, 171
MacKenzie, Kenneth 370, 371
Mackintosh, C. H. 120
Maddox, R. L. 39
Mallan, F. 540
Manasseh 308, 320
Mann, William E. 270
Manoah 309
Marcion 263
Maresius, Samuel 102, 103, 585
Markus, R. A. 235
Marshall, I. H. 482
Marshall, Walter 453
Martin, Bernard 372
Matter, Hendrik 548
Matthias 410
Mayhue, Richard L. 31
Mayor, Joseph 256, 568
McCloskey, Henry J. 353
McDowell, J. 172
McFague, S. 130
McGrath, Alister 473, 578, 583, 589
Medema, Henk 246
Melanchton, Philip 274, 275
Meroz 143
Messiah 10, 12, 67, 172, 204, 211, 360, 412
Messianic kingdom 211, 212,

348, 361
Metaphors 127, 130, 131, 152, 159, 216, 260
Metatron 419, 420
Mettinger, T. N. D. 291
Middle Ages 238, 264, 472
Middle East 292, 531
Middle knowledge 156, 169, 170, 265
Moab 330
Moabites 329
Moderate Calvinism 32, 84, 506
Modern science 277, 278, 280, 281, 282
Moerkerken, Aart 105, 597
Molina, Luis de 156, 169, 265
Molinism 156, 169, 170, 179, 202, 368
Molinists 170, 355
Moltmann, Jürgen 247, 251
Moral responsibility 26, 34, 72
Mordecai 21, 333
Morris, L. 416, 439, 554
Moses 12, 15, 20, 57, 67, 87, 139, 147, 149, 179, 183, 302, 311, 312, 313, 314, 319, 322, 326, 332, 333, 334, 350, 366, 411, 412, 417, 443, 444, 531
Mount Seir 330
Mount Tabor 247
Muis, J. 130
Müller, J. J. 548
Murray, J. 434
Musculus, Wolfgang 225
Mysia 374
Mysticism 36, 129, 131, 133, 222, 397, 593

N
Nathan 321
Nations 12, 13, 15, 52, 58, 64, 89, 99, 100, 149, 163, 172, 179, 211, 215, 244, 259, 261, 312, 329, 361, 411, 488, 571, 572
Nazareth 336, 338
Nazis 343
Nebuchadnezzar 174, 175, 346
Nee, Watchman 371
Nero 477
Netherlands 3, 30, 71, 199, 300, 341, 352, 371, 381, 382, 385, 402, 426, 439, 453, 459, 475, 476, 484, 485, 509, 512, 516, 526, 539, 560, 561, 577, 585, 586
Netherlands Reformed Congregations 381, 382, 539
New Testament 1, 4, 21, 63, 89, 96, 100, 125, 209, 215, 250, 267, 311, 330, 360, 375, 389, 393, 394, 400, 404, 406, 415, 421, 423, 427, 435, 436, 443, 444, 445, 464, 465, 466, 484, 503, 509, 530, 531, 533, 538, 548, 553, 556, 583, 594, 595

Subject Index

Newton, Isaac 280
Nile 147
Nineveh 154, 160, 204, 314
Ninevites 154, 314, 315, 316, 323
Noah 195, 327, 334, 388, 572
Noordtzij, Arie 327
North America 31, 352, 382, 509, 539
Nouwen, Henri 247

O

Old Testament 14, 20, 42, 55, 152, 182, 208, 209, 214, 215, 328, 364, 389, 395, 410, 411, 417, 444, 458, 568
Olson, R. E. 592
Oorthuys, Gerardus 107, 470, 583
Open Theism 1, 2, 16, 17, 19, 20, 24, 25, 28, 30, 31, 32, 34, 38, 54, 80, 81, 82, 84, 89, 90, 123, 126, 127, 135, 136, 140, 142, 144, 148, 155, 157, 158, 167, 168, 169, 170, 171, 172, 177, 178, 179, 180, 181, 183, 184, 185, 186, 187, 188, 189, 190, 192, 194, 200, 201, 202, 203, 206, 230, 232, 233, 234, 259, 266, 272, 277, 281, 282, 293, 294, 296, 305, 307, 368, 373, 398, 432, 483, 531, 577, 591
Open Theists 27, 30, 31, 32, 34, 35, 37, 38, 39, 40, 117, 137, 140, 142, 143, 144, 145, 147, 152, 154, 157, 168, 171, 172, 173, 174, 176, 178, 186, 187, 189, 191, 202, 233, 234, 255, 263, 264, 355, 382, 385, 388, 392, 393, 478
Origen 235, 263, 470
Orlebeke, C. 240, 254
Osborne, G. R. 433
Oswalt, John 172, 319, 418
Ott, H. 242
Owen, Huw P. 234, 246, 247

P

Packer, James 484
Pagans 94, 300, 315, 569
Pailin, D. A. 130
Palmer, E. H. 476
Pannenberg, Wolfhart 222, 239, 240, 252, 255, 260, 272, 398, 399, 427, 470, 538, 571, 578
Pantheism 122, 222
Paradise 105, 436, 599
Pascal, Blaise 552

Patterson, R. D. 320
Paul 10, 11, 42, 49, 82, 94, 101, 108, 110, 113, 125, 156, 190, 193, 194, 208, 209, 214, 215, 217, 287, 297, 302, 321, 322, 323, 331, 334, 336, 344, 349, 350, 369, 374, 376, 377, 395, 399, 403, 408, 409, 410, 421, 436, 438, 439, 441, 442, 443, 446, 447, 448, 450, 451, 452, 454, 455, 456, 457, 461, 462, 463, 524, 526, 529, 530, 531, 537, 546, 571, 572, 594, 595
Paul, Mart-Jan 327, 328
Pawson, David 158, 159, 165, 166, 245, 254, 483, 484, 566, 574
Pearcey, N. R. 278
Pelagianism 73, 169, 171, 227, 398, 471, 472, 516
Pelagians 37, 43
Pelagius 35, 136, 276, 469, 471, 511, 560
People of Israel 20, 87, 173, 179, 205, 207, 261, 310, 327, 332, 395, 411, 440, 538, 545
Perkins, William 38, 103, 107, 122, 229, 230
Perseverance of the Saints 481, 486, 494, 592
Peter 54, 94, 110, 176, 177, 178, 180, 203, 247, 255, 324, 338, 399, 410, 448, 463, 464, 465
Peterson, M. 130
Pharaoh 152, 173, 174, 205, 224, 317, 566, 572, 573
Pharisees 13, 471, 481
Philippi 331, 530
Philistines 146, 296
Philosophers 222, 238
Philosophy 222, 228, 229, 234, 238, 239, 240, 275, 277, 278, 279, 280, 281, 282, 348, 365
Pilate, Pontius 23, 48, 95, 121, 122, 178, 531
Pinnock, Clark H. 24, 31, 32, 33, 34, 39, 80, 99, 123, 146, 157, 159, 161, 165, 166, 189, 190, 191, 220, 230, 231, 234, 241, 242, 244, 246, 247, 249, 254, 271, 272, 346, 374, 392, 433, 574
Piper, John S. 31, 33, 226
Plan of redemption 51, 210, 356, 357
Plancius, Petrus 491

Subject Index

Plantinga, A. 171, 365
Plato 221, 251, 252
Plotinus 221
Polanus, Amandus 225
Polyander, Johannes 585
Polycarp 235
Pravuil 419
Prayer 23, 40, 151, 189, 240, 247, 295, 296, 297, 298, 299, 300, 301, 302, 304, 305, 306, 307, 308, 309, 310, 311, 312, 315, 317, 319, 320, 321, 322, 323, 324, 326, 328, 331, 332, 333, 334, 335, 336, 337, 369, 371, 372, 373, 376, 387, 513, 531, 583
Prayers 54, 143, 247, 295, 296, 297, 298, 299, 300, 301, 304, 305, 306, 308, 311, 323, 326, 327, 328, 331, 332, 337
Predestination 4, 17, 18, 25, 27, 28, 29, 30, 38, 39, 41, 48, 53, 73, 82, 95, 96, 104, 123, 125, 126, 127, 128, 136, 141, 187, 192, 195, 201, 206, 253, 262, 263, 264, 265, 273, 340, 371, 379, 380, 387, 389, 390, 391, 392, 394, 396, 397, 398, 399, 402, 404, 405, 406, 413, 416, 417, 423, 424, 425, 428, 429, 430, 434, 435, 436, 437, 438, 439, 441, 442, 444, 445, 446, 447, 449, 457, 460, 461, 463, 469, 470, 471, 472, 473, 476, 478, 485, 492, 501, 503, 505, 507, 510, 515, 516, 523, 526, 533, 534, 543, 559, 560, 567, 570, 571, 576, 577, 578, 583, 584, 586, 587, 588, 594, 597
Process Theology 19, 25, 122, 123, 241
Procrustean logic 117, 120, 181
Prodigal son 379, 392, 545
Prophecies 20, 171, 173, 202, 203, 204, 205, 206, 232
Prophecy 10, 60, 154, 156, 172, 202, 203, 204, 205, 206, 256, 415, 554
Prophets 6, 10, 12, 37, 50, 96, 99, 135, 139, 155, 208, 209, 251, 256, 330, 363, 407, 424, 534

Protestant Church
475, 485,
560, 561
Protestantism
32, 272,
280, 491,
555
Publius 336
Purpose of God
5, 6, 8, 10,
13, 66,
404, 457,
496, 554

Q
Quantum mechanics
280, 281
Qumram 420

R
Rabbi Akiba
145
Rabbi Shila
420
Rabbis 119, 271,
290, 419,
420
Rachel 296
Ragaz, Leonhard
286, 287
Rahab 15, 22
Ramoth-gilead
151
Rational knowledge
128, 131,
132, 133,
227
Rationalism
131, 281,
487, 555,
593
Ratzinger, Joseph
248, 432
Rebekah 296, 307,
308, 415

Red Sea 332, 333
Redemption
1, 21, 27,
29, 30, 39,
42, 51, 64,
65, 66, 67,
110, 130,
140, 161,
210, 221,
244, 257,
267, 342,
356, 357,
381, 436,
441, 442,
446, 447,
470, 471,
496, 503,
524, 528
Redemptive history
15, 19,
212, 257,
294
Reformation
273, 453,
511, 585,
586
Reformed Christians
4, 457
Reformed churches
486, 509,
511, 560,
561
Reformed theologians
30, 32, 71,
225, 226,
404, 449,
509, 521,
578, 586
Reformers 69, 122,
541
Rehoboam 316, 317
Reichert, V. E.
290
Remonstrance
469, 484,

485, 486,
489, 491,
494, 505
Remonstrants
274, 469,
475, 484,
486, 487,
490, 493,
499, 501,
502, 504,
505, 506,
511, 515,
520, 527,
528, 593
Repentance
13, 86,
110, 112,
139, 162,
250, 261,
305, 306,
314, 315,
317, 350,
387, 388,
452, 460,
478, 489,
497, 515,
520, 526,
537, 541,
542, 565,
569, 575,
579
Reprobation
7, 16, 18,
36, 41, 45,
55, 56, 67,
68, 73, 78,
95, 113,
257, 275,
380, 384,
388, 390,
397, 399,
400, 402,
403, 404,
405, 406,
413, 414,

Subject Index

415, 438, 440, 454, 469, 471, 472, 473, 474, 475, 492, 493, 494, 495, 497, 499, 500, 501, 502, 503, 504, 505, 507, 508, 509, 510, 513, 521, 526, 535, 537, 543, 559, 560, 561, 562, 563, 564, 566, 567, 568, 569, 570, 571, 572, 574, 575, 576, 577, 578, 579, 580, 581, 584, 587, 588, 589, 590, 591, 592

Resignation 181, 182, 302, 303, 315, 319, 343, 364, 366, 367, 368, 369, 371, 372, 394, 396, 429, 513

Ridderbos, Herman 109, 403, 416, 425, 477, 571, 574, 575

Ridderbos, J. 418
Robots 2, 124, 166, 273, 278, 279, 347, 524
Roman Catholics 43, 225, 419, 452, 481, 520
Romans 156, 276
Roos, G. 411
Rufus 407, 416, 466
Russell, Bertrand 348
Ruth 22
Rutherford, S. 474
Ryken, P. G. 476

S
Sabeans 96
Salmond, S. D. F. 445, 450, 451
Salvation 13, 16, 23, 39, 40, 41, 42, 43, 44, 64, 65, 66, 68, 78, 85, 86, 108, 109, 110, 111, 112, 113, 123, 127, 193, 226, 260, 296, 297, 328, 333, 341, 342, 348, 380, 381, 382, 383, 384, 385, 388, 390, 391, 392, 396, 397, 398, 399, 401, 403, 404, 408, 409, 411, 412, 417, 431, 432, 433, 435, 436, 438, 448, 452, 454, 455, 459, 460, 461, 462, 464, 466, 467, 474, 478, 479, 480, 481, 486, 493, 496, 497, 499, 501, 504, 506, 508, 512, 513, 514, 515, 516, 519, 522, 523, 524, 525, 526, 527, 528, 530, 531, 532, 533, 534, 536, 538, 539, 540, 542, 544, 547, 548, 549, 555, 556, 567, 572, 573, 574, 575, 579, 584, 590, 591, 594, 595, 596

Samaria 12, 151

Samuel 310, 321, 322, 334, 414
Sanders, John E. 31, 39, 80, 165, 241
Sarah 93, 466
Satan 74, 75, 78, 83, 84, 94, 95, 96, 175, 213, 331, 334, 340, 344, 359, 362, 363, 364, 368, 373, 374, 375, 376, 377, 435, 436, 455, 462, 490, 549, 550
Saul 21, 153, 154, 160, 162, 249, 321, 322, 330, 413, 414, 566, 580
Saul of Tarsus 481
Schelling, Friedrich 222
Schilder, Klaas 54, 56, 586, 589
Schlatter, A. 425
Schleiermacher, Friedrich 252
Schlink, Basilea 366
Scholastic theology 247, 257, 264
Scholasticism 225, 238, 239, 274, 280, 281, 593
Scholten, L. M. P. 540
School of Saumur 484, 585
Schopenhauer, Arthur 222
Schreiner, T. R. 80, 90, 226, 264, 428, 432, 433, 571
Sea of Tiberias 346
Second Helvetic Confession 78
Second Reformation 453, 586
Semi-Pelagianism 471
Semi-Pelagians 43, 471
Septuagint 243, 267, 292, 328, 329, 412
Sharp, D. R. 449
Shimei 95
Shishak 317
Sickness 92, 93, 182, 338, 341, 343, 371, 372
Sidon 155
Sieckentroost 341, 343
Silas 331, 530
Smedes, L. 240, 254
Socinians 263

Sodom 155, 161, 182, 306
Solomon 147, 248, 261, 309, 310, 316, 317, 318
Son of God 66, 67, 111, 271, 346, 362, 587
Son of Man 12, 23, 66, 146, 176, 300, 334, 428
Sovereign will of God 27, 325, 478, 498
Sovereignty of God 3, 18, 31, 34, 81, 194, 294, 358, 483
Spence-Jones, H. D. 252, 572
Spencer, Herbert 367
Spinoza, Baruch 260, 271
Spiritual warfare 328, 330, 331, 375, 490
Sproul, Robert C. 31, 33, 34, 41, 84, 106, 107, 122, 231, 356, 381, 387, 388, 477, 480, 531, 585, 592

Subject Index

Spykman, Gordon 510, 583, 588
Stackhouse, John G. 38
Stafleu, M. D. 278
Statenvertaling 110, 312
Steenblok, Cornelis 381, 539, 540, 586
Stoics 221, 251
Stott, John 515
Strachan, R. H. 465
Strack, H. L. 460
Strauss, D. F. M. 127, 132, 222, 254
Sublapsarianism 479, 584
Suffering 75, 77, 118, 220, 234, 247, 248, 250, 257, 293, 296, 304, 339, 340, 342, 347, 353, 355, 356, 358, 360, 361, 365, 366, 367, 368, 527
Sufferings 221, 246, 247, 287, 339, 340, 342, 343, 347, 360, 361, 362, 363, 364, 365, 366, 367, 370, 464
Supralapsarianism 66, 67, 493, 583, 584, 585, 586, 587, 589
Supralapsarians 67, 564, 583, 586, 588
Suprarational knowledge 129, 131, 133
Supreme Being 199, 200
Susman, Margarete 285, 286, 290
Synergism 43, 44, 195, 401, 402, 470
Synod of Dordt 102, 103, 475, 476, 485, 494, 504, 505, 512, 577, 583, 585, 586
Syria 327
Syrians 327

T
Tabitha 336
Talmud 67, 419
Tamar 22
Teelinck, Willem 511
Tertullian 225, 470
Thaxton, C. B. 278

The Bondage of the Will 273, 473
Theodicy 197, 344, 345, 347, 353, 375
Thielicke, H. 244
Thiessen, Henry 125, 505
Thomism 31, 169, 202, 240
Thyatira 461
Torah 13, 67, 119, 120, 215, 361
Total Depravity 43, 44, 476, 477
Traditional theology 32, 80, 165, 262
Tree of life 14, 60, 357, 599
Troost, A. 127
TULIP 405, 469, 476, 484
Twomey, V. 235
Tyre 155, 157

U
Unbelievers 66, 301, 350, 390, 414, 452, 456, 497, 508, 523, 530, 543, 566, 569, 580
Unconditional Election 478, 479, 483, 492, 493

Universal atonement 65, 479, 480, 527
Universalism 44, 380, 381, 480, 578
Universalists 529, 532
Ursinus, Zacharias 225
Uytenbogaert, Johannes 485, 577

V
Valley of Aijalon 309
Van Cleave, N. M. 41, 256, 369, 370, 371, 434, 448, 452, 564
Van de Beek, Bram 240
Van den Brink, Gijsbert 269, 270
Van der Bijl, Anne 305
Van der Schuit, Jacob 586
Van der Sluys, C. A. 474
Van der Zanden, Lubbert 402, 426, 427, 447, 507, 538, 589
Van der Zwaag, Klaas 453, 474, 476, 511, 598
Van Eck, Jan 246
Van Genderen, Jan 56, 79, 240, 243, 244, 269, 403, 404, 411, 441, 452, 459, 509, 571, 578
Van Herck, W. 130
Van Heumen, H. 504
Van Hille, Cornelis 341, 342
Van Itterzon, Gerrit 474
Van Niftrik, G. C. 40
Van Riessen, H. 278
Van Ruler, Arnold A. 586
Van Til, Cornelius 131, 132
Van Woudenberg, R. 251
Velema, Willem 56, 78, 79, 240, 243, 244, 269, 404, 411, 441, 452, 459, 509, 571, 578
Venema, Henk 31, 56, 57, 71, 72, 99, 101, 144, 160, 162, 163, 164, 173, 194, 417, 459, 571
Verboom, Willem 18, 70, 103, 448, 486, 489, 491, 494, 496, 500, 501, 504, 512, 527, 528, 540, 553, 561, 563
Vermeulen, C. 389
Viatoric theology 25, 29
Viatorism 1, 17, 18, 20, 25, 27, 30, 48, 56, 82, 83, 123, 136, 140, 168, 179, 180, 188, 191, 192, 198, 202, 203, 204, 206, 227, 264, 277, 282, 293, 294, 296, 304, 305, 307, 331, 343, 365, 368, 373, 377, 379, 380, 384, 388, 478, 491, 502, 515, 528, 530, 531, 534, 539, 544, 548, 557, 561, 575,

Subject Index

577, 581, 582, 587, 589, 590, 591, 592, 593
Vincent, Marvin 451
Vine, William 51
Voetius, Gisbert 223, 224, 511, 585
Voltaire 280
Vulgate 268, 406, 450, 488

W

Wallaeus, Theodore 585
Ware, B. A. 38, 80, 90, 226, 264, 428, 432, 433, 571
Warfield, Benjamin 192, 193, 201, 202, 514, 515, 585
Watson, G. 235
Ways of God 15, 17, 18, 19, 20, 21, 22, 23, 25, 27, 29, 30, 42, 48, 55, 100, 119, 167, 205, 207, 212, 213, 289, 304, 331, 340, 344, 367, 368, 373, 410, 531, 567, 577, 580
Weber, Otto 142, 263, 351, 398, 470, 507, 513, 523
Wegscheider, J. A. L. 249
Weinandy, T. G. 244
Wentsel, Ben 240, 244, 270, 411, 421, 487, 509, 563, 578
Wesley, John 39, 577
Wesleyans 43
Westminster Confession 104, 127
Westminster Shorter Catechism 68, 70
White, James R. 31, 32, 33, 482, 483, 592
White, Newport 110
Whitefield, George 577
Whitehead, A. N. 241
Will of God 27, 71, 75, 78, 85, 86, 87, 104, 109, 111, 112, 164, 191, 193, 220, 225, 226, 227, 228, 301, 325, 341, 376, 398, 440, 478, 498, 513, 534, 581, 589
William of Ockham 223, 349, 351
Wilson, D. 80
Wink, Walter 305, 373, 374
Woelderink, Jan Gerrit 31, 72, 73, 411, 417, 441, 452, 456, 457, 459, 494, 507, 555, 564, 571, 573, 578, 583
Wolterstorff, Nicholas 240, 254
Wood, A. S. 445, 451
Word of God 78, 129, 131, 208, 495, 512
World history 38, 55, 116, 198, 359
Wright, Robert K. McGregor 165

Y

Yarbrough, Robert 428, 432, 433

YHWH	117, 243, 244, 267, 292, 360
Young, E. J.	418

Z

Zadok	318
Zeboiim	162
Zedekiah	148, 155
Zion	361, 408, 412, 414, 418, 514
Zwingli, Ulrich	585

www.ingramcontent.com/pod-product-compliance
Lightning Source LLC
Chambersburg PA
CBHW070241010526
44107CB00041B/1482/J